ETHICS: An Examination of Contemporary Moral Problems

Gerald Runkle
Southern Illinois University at Edwardsville

Holt, Rinehart and Winston

New York Chicago San Francisco Philadelphia
Montreal Toronto London Sydney
Tokyo Mexico City Rio de Janeiro Madrid

To my parents:

Alberta Lee Abbett Runkle
Frank Irvin Runkle

Library of Congress Cataloging in Publication Data

Runkle, Gerald.
Ethics : an examination of contemporary moral problems.

Includes bibliographies and index.
1. Ethics. 2. Social ethics. I. Title.
BJ1012.R83 170 81-6902
ISBN 0-03-058318-7 AACR2

Address correspondence to:
383 Madison Avenue
New York, N.Y. 10017

Printed in the United States of America
Published simultaneously in Canada
6 7 8 9 10 059 10 9 8 7 6 5 4

CBS COLLEGE PUBLISHING
Holt, Rinehart and Winston
The Dryden Press
Saunders College Publishing

CONTENTS

PREFACE

This book is designed as a text for use in college courses that deal with ethics. Students who use this text are not expected to have a background in philosophy. If, however, they have done previous work in philosophy, it is unlikely that any significant amount of duplication will occur. This book is thus suitable for nonmajors in philosophy as well as for specialists. It would serve students at all undergraduate levels, although the sophomore and junior years seem best: many freshmen perhaps lack sufficient maturity, and most seniors are involved in advanced work in their specialty.

The subject of ethics is approached from both an individual point of view and a social point of view. That is, both these questions are raised: What ought *I* to do? What ought *society* to do? The problem of extramarital sex, for example, would seem to be a personal one, while the problem of distributive justice would seem to be a social one. Yet there are important relations between the personal and social approaches, and each conditions the other. The social consequences of a viewpoint on extramarital sex must be considered; and a viewpoint on distributive justice has consequences for the individual who holds it.

The title contains the words *ethics* and *moral.* Although *ethics* and *morals* have very similar meanings, they have different connotations. The first suggests a theoretical slant, while the second (perhaps because of its derivation from *mores*) has a more practical connotation. For this reason philosophy courses are entitled "Ethics," while acceptable social behavior falls in the area of morals. The lexicographer H. W. Fowler offers this statement to indicate the difference: "His ethics may be sound, but his morals are abandoned." Since we are concerned in this book both with sound philosophical principles and their application to practical problems of human conduct, we are dealing with both ethics and morals.

What about the expressions *ethical problems* and *moral problems?* The former often denotes theoretical problems encountered in determining sound principles of human conduct, while the latter denotes practical problems of applying them to actual social conditions. This book will be concerned with both, although the latter receives the greater emphasis. Because the distinction between *ethical* and *moral* is somewhat arbitrary and artificial, we will in the text use the two words in a way that is virtually interchangeable. As Fowler observes, "It is in the nature of things that the dividing line between adjectives should be less clear than with the nouns."*

This brings us to the organization of the book. The theoretical element is contained in the first and last chapters. The first chapter presents straightforward

*H. W. Fowler, *A Dictionary of Modern English Usage,* 2nd ed. (New York: Oxford University Press, 1965), pp. 170–171.

expositions of important ethical theories. It provides the student with principles and vocabulary which will be useful later. Presumably, the student will also make some judgments about the relative truth or adequacy of the various theories. The last chapter returns to the theoretical concern present in the first. Now, however, ethics is considered within the context of epistemology, psychology, and metaphysics.

The heart of the book consists of the seven chapters in between. It is here that the "examination of contemporary moral problems" takes place. As the table of contents indicates, three specific problems are examined in each of seven general areas: sex, life and death, business, education, justice, liberty, and war and peace. There are thus twenty-one specific moral problems. For each problem two conflicting points of view are presented. The student is encouraged to decide which point of view has a greater claim for acceptance. To assist the student, concluding summaries, discussion questions, and bibliographies are provided for each problem.

The twenty-one essays utilize both ethical theory and factual material. It is believed that a responsible approach to contemporary issues requires both philosophical understanding and a grasp of the relevant scientific and historical "realities." Some of the latter, of course, will have to be updated by the teacher and the students, but this should pose no insuperable problem.

I should like to take this opportunity to thank many people who have been of assistance in the conception and execution of this book: First of all, my students in traditional ethics courses who have sought to direct discussion to concrete issues of contemporary life. Second, Russ Boersma, sales representative for Holt, Rinehart and Winston, who served as a catalyst in my reflections on alternative approaches to ethics texts. Third, David P. Boynton, philosophy editor of Holt, Rinehart and Winston, who was consistently supportive and encouraging. Fourth, my colleague Ronald G. Glossop, who shared with me some of his insights into the field of ethics. Fifth, Donald Thompson, expert librarian, who helped me locate and utilize many resources of Lovejoy Library. Sixth, my chairperson, Thomas Paxson, and dean, Carol Keene, who provided me with every help within their power for completing this project. Seventh, the officials of Southern Illinois University at Edwardsville who provided me with an early sabbatical leave in the winter of 1981. Eighth, Karen West, typist, whose work was accurate and conscientious.

Finally, I should like to thank the authors whom I have quoted in the text and the companies that have published their work.

Gerald Runkle

Chapter 1

ETHICS

Before we examine concrete issues in moral judgment, we should look briefly at some of the important ethical theories that have been set forth in Western history.

An ethical theory seeks to provide criteria that distinguish between actions that are right and actions that are wrong. An ethical theory presents and defends norms with which actions, if they are to be moral, must be in accordance. Some theories are based on a conception of value: Certain things are *good,* and rightness consists of promoting these goods. Some are based on a conception of what is *right,* and goodness is the mark of the person who is inspired by a sense of duty. Some theories emphasize the nature of the agent; others emphasize the consequences of his or her actions. Some are based on religious beliefs; others are set forth as theories possessing no basis but reason itself.

What all ethical theories have in common, however, is this: They offer us guidance when we are in a quandary and want to know where our moral duty lies. We may oppose (or support) abortion, for example, only when we see that our position is based upon a reason, an ethical principle, a theory of ethics. That we happen to be *disposed* against (or in favor of) abortion is not in itself an adequate warrant for our conviction that it is wrong (or right). Facts are useful, but the *is* cannot itself yield the *ought.* Solution to contemporary problems of *what should be done* by the individual or the state requires an ethical framework.

There are at least three difficulties in this view. The first is that these ethical theories we are about to examine, being all different, often yield different "solutions" to the same problem. Which one do we appeal to? The answer, of course, is that we appeal to the one we think is most likely to be true. That John Stuart Mill was convinced that his theory is correct for all ethical decisions does not mean that we have to be similarly convinced. Each person must adopt his or her own ethical standard, and it is not an easy matter to select in the light of our best thought those principles upon which we can conscientiously act. Unless we do so, however, we are destined to act in an unprincipled way, a way that, according to many philosophers, is the very abdication of moral responsibility.

This is not to say that we must become a partisan of *one* of the major theories and cast aside as worthless all the others. It is quite possible that a major theory is deficient in some respect and can be improved by taking on some of the insights of another theory. An ethics of love, for example, might be supplemented by a theory of justice for those cases in which not everyone can be the object of loving action. That one must be consistent in one's ethical attitudes does not rule out a possible union of Aristotle's humanism and John Dewey's concern with consequences. It is also possible for one to refrain from accepting a general theory but feel that philosophizing on a particular case will yield a defensible conclusion nonetheless.

This suggests the second problem. How do we know whether ethical judgments are true? How do we choose from among competing theories or positions? Is it not perhaps the case that ethical utterances are *neither* true nor false but devoid of cognitive significance? And even if they are not, is one free to act on the basis of one's convictions? Or is one's conduct determined by natural law? Perhaps people are necessarily egoists, and any talk of duties to others is a case of requiring the impossible.

A third difficulty is that theoretical solutions for some contemporary problems are not easily seen to be implicit in the theories themselves. What did Mill know about nuclear warfare? What did Plato know about genetic engineering? In some cases solutions are implicit and can be brought out. In other cases it would seem that the theory provides us with no guidance at all. But choices have to be made We have to decide whether sending food to Cambodia is right or wrong, whether we are obligated to serve in the armed services, whether firefighters have the right to strike. Where an established theory fails to provide guidance, we have to provide a theory of our own. This can supplement an old theory or function as one in its own right. When we have to take a stand on an issue, we must use true principles from the past or look to something else.

Many ethical issues are inescapable. We must act one way or another—as agents or as participants in a democracy—and it is not a matter of indifference which way we incline. If we have any sexual drive at all, we must get clear in our own minds whether or not nonmarital sex is moral. If we are to vote intelligently, we must decide whether to support a candidate who favors forced busing or one who is opposed to it. The thought of philosophers who have tried to present a comprehensive view of the good life, as well as the arguments of thoughtful individuals who have pondered the particular issue from an ethical point of view, may be helpful in reaching a conclusion, but we must finally reach our own decision on the basis of our own thought. We have a better chance of being correct when we are acquainted with the great traditions in ethics, as well as the facts of, and opinions on, the particular issue.

This chapter is on the great traditions in ethics. The next seven chapters are on contemporary problems. In these seven chapters a reasoned argument will be presented on each side of a particular issue (twenty-one in all). Each of these arguments will present some of the relevant facts of the problematic situation, appeal to traditional theories (when possible), and utilize more specific ethical arguments directly related to the issue at hand. The last chapter will discuss the validity of ethical judgment. To deal with this crucial question *last* may seem unreasonable. But it is thought better to examine the nature of ethical reasoning after having had some experience of it (in others and ourselves) than to try to decide the issue in advance.

In this chapter we will discuss ethical theories under four main headings: theories of self-realization, religious theories, consequentialist theories, and deontological theories. This classification is not perfect, for there is no consistent principle of division. Still, it provides general categories into which most ethical theories can be placed. Also, there may be some overlapping. A theory that describes an ideal condition of the human person will not be oblivious to the consequences of human behavior on others. A theory that emphasizes religious faith may be concerned with self-realization as well as with moral duty. Most major ethical viewpoints have a tendency to reach beyond the rather arbitrary boundaries that classifiers fix for them. Nevertheless, while recognizing that self-realization, consequences, rightness, and God are fundamental ethical concerns that often are dealt with by the same ethical theory, we will approach the various ethical theories, in the first instance, on the basis of which of the four seems to be the most central concern of their proponents.

THEORIES OF SELF-REALIZATION

The philosophers discussed in this section are concerned with the state or condition of the human person. A good person is one who exhibits a certain state of being. Actions both foster this state and follow from it, but the aim of life is to achieve a quality of selfhood that can be called virtuous, admirable, or worthy. The human being has a potential for several kinds of character. Each of these philosophers chooses one and tells us that our duty is to achieve it. *What kind of person should I seek to become?*

Plato

The Greek philosopher Plato (427–347 B.C.) argues that anything is good to the degree that it performs its *function.* A pruning knife is good if it trims branches neatly and expeditiously. It has a sharp blade and a long handle, which contribute toward its proper use. Given its nature, we can expect no greater performance than that it function well in pruning trees. Some pruning knives will do the job better than others. Although we were not so obviously manufactured for a certain task, we, too, have a function based upon our human nature. What is that nature?

The human soul, according to Plato, has three parts or elements. Each expresses itself as a desire for a certain object. The first element is *appetite:* we seek food, drink, sex, and a great many other things having to do with our physical being. The second element is *spirit:* we seek honor, fame, competition, excitement. The third element is *reason:* we seek knowledge. That the human soul has these different parts is indicated by the fact that inner struggle often occurs. Shall I drink the beer or stay in training for the big game on Saturday? Shall I travel with the team or stay at home and study?

Plato believes that these three parts of the individual correspond to the three classes in a society: those who get and spend (workers); those who fight in defense of their country (soldiers); and those who pursue knowledge (philosophers). The good (or just) state is thus an analogy for the good (or just) person. The just state is one in which philosophers rule. They take thought "not for some particular interest, but for the best possible conduct of the state as a whole in its internal and external relations."[1] They are endowed with reason and have been trained to put it to use in practical matters and theoretical speculation. The soldiers are directed by the rulers for the preservation of the state. They are devoted to this end and stand firm against domestic and foreign enemies. The workers perform the material tasks of society, providing its food, clothing, shelter, and trade—all under the direction of the rulers and the control of the soldiers.

We find the four cardinal virtues present in the good state. *Temperance* is found when all classes willingly accept control from above and work together in an orderly way; *courage,* when the soldiers (and rulers, who once were soldiers) know what to fight for and seek honor in doing so; *wisdom,* when the rulers know best what serves the whole. The fourth great virtue, *justice,* is present to the degree that each class is kept in its place under the enlightened leadership of the philosophers. Each part in the state does that for which it is best fitted. From disparate parts, harmony results.

In the individual, too, harmony will be the result when his or her parts function together under the leadership of reason. One will be *temperate* when one's appetites are controlled by one's higher nature. One will be *courageous* when one aspires to great deeds under the guidance of reason. One will be *wise* when one knows how to control oneself and seeks truth for its own sake. One will be *just* when one has brought all one's drives and passions together into a harmonious whole where reason rules.

Plato tells us not to eliminate some part of our nature, but to develop it, to be a *person* in the fullest sense of the word. Not every individual can aspire to the same complete form. Individuals have different endowments. But all the ingredients of humanity are in all of us, and they can be harmonized in various ways. In attempting to define human excellence, Plato is setting forth his version of Greek humanism.

Plato's clearest description of falling short of the humanist ideal occurs when he discusses *usurpation* (in the state and the individual). The "timocratic man" is self-willed and only superficially cultivated. His only concern is for fame and honor. He is ambitious and often brutal. He may seek power for its own sake. He may think of nothing but athletic prowess. He may take on all the qualities of the "macho" male. His spirited nature has usurped the role of reason. The "oligarchic man" is even worse. He subordinates everything (including honors)

[1] Plato, *Republic* (trans. Cornford) IV, 427.

to the accumulation of money. Believing that money will enable him to satisfy any of his appetites, he soon forgets them and pursues the false security of wealth. His most "practical" appetite has taken over his whole nature. The "democratic man" makes no distinction between necessary and unnecessary pleasures. He gratifies whatever appetite happens to move him. His life is uncontrolled and inconsistent. He is continually subjected to a multitude of clamoring and conflicting desires. His life has no pattern, no point. His appetites have completely usurped the control that should be in the hands of spirit and reason. The "despotic man" is the worst. He has become obsessed with *one* appetite, and that an ignoble one. It has become a ruling passion, beyond law and reason. His whole nature has become enslaved to a frenzied craving for—what? It may be sex, drugs, alcohol. He is in the worst kind of slavery—to his own lower nature.

Plato expressed the classical view that the good life cannot be considered apart from the good state. Morality requires service to the state, and the human being achieves his or her highest good as a member of society. By the same token, the individual is cut off from his or her ideal development without a state to provide protection, nurturance, and education. A Socrates in a bad state is truly exceptional, and usually comes to a tragic end. Plato's ethical theory is not that of an isolated individual who achieves the highest good under any and all social circumstances.

It has sometimes been charged that Plato's ethics is incompatible with his politics. The one requires "well-roundedness," while the other requires specialization. In defense of Plato, it can be argued that rulers are not cut off from philosophic speculation, courage, and temperance simply because they rule. Soldiers, too, must order their appetites and attain at least enough wisdom to know what is worth fighting for. Workers are not restricted to ordering their appetites: They may be "spirited" as they do dangerous jobs and pursue ambitious projects, and "rational" so far as they attain true opinion. Each person will do what he or she does best for the sake of society as a whole, but at the same time aspire to the humanistic ideal that best expresses his or her own endowments.

Aristotle

Aristotle (384–321 B.C.) was an idealist, although he disagreed with Plato that ideal reality consisted of a realm of Forms removed from time and space. For Aristotle, the ideal was something that emerged from the natural: it was the end of a line of development. Everything in nature has the capacity for being better than it is. It can achieve its "true being" through a process of self-development. Aristotle, trained in biology, emphasized growth. An individual achieves its potential when it exemplifies its species. An acorn achieves its potential when it becomes a great oak tree; a person achieves his or her potential to the degree that he or she exemplifies humanity. A tree that is an oak in every sense of the word is a good oak tree; a person who is a human being in every sense of the word is a good person. Man is not to surpass man but to aspire to humanity.

To find out what humanity consists of is the work of the biologist, psychologist, sociologist, and historian, as well as of the philosopher (in the narrow sense) and the metaphysician. Aristotle was all these things and more. We cannot, of course, discuss very much of Aristotle's investigations of the human person, but we can mention some of the qualities he felt were essential in human nature.

As human beings we share with plant life the potential to take nourishment, grow, and reproduce. We share with animal life the potential to experience sensations and impulses. But the distinctive thing about us (shared only with God) is our rational capacity. Aristotle defines man as "a rational animal." One way in which this capacity functions is to control the impulses and appetites. Some may be encouraged; others must be inhibited. In doing this successfully, a person achieves *moral virtue.* Are there any guides? Accepting the Greek slogan "moderation in all things," Aristotle tells us we should choose "the golden mean." We will neither be ascetic, nor will we indulge every pleasure-urge that comes along. We will be neither rash nor cowardly; we will be courageous. We will be neither miserly nor extravagant; we will be generous. We are not born with moral virtue, but only with the potential for it. We must train ourselves. We must reach a state in which we experience the right feelings in the right degree at the right time. We must consciously develop those habits, attitudes, and dispositions that spare us from excess.

The pattern cannot be the same for all individuals. Some are more favored by fortune or nature than others. No one can be a perfect human, but each person can take in hand what aptitudes he or she has and put them together (over a period of time) in a way that approaches the ideal.[2] But the important point is to do so in a deliberate program of self-cultivation. One does not drift toward human excellence. One *strives* for it. It is a task presided over by the practical aspect of reason.

> From the same causes and by the same means that a moral virtue is produced, it may also be destroyed. This is equally true of the arts. It is by playing the harp that both good and bad harpists are produced, and so of builders and the rest; for men become good or bad builders according as they practise building well or badly. If this were not so, they would require no instruction, but would all have been born good or bad at their trades. So too in the case of the virtues. It is by our actual conduct in our intercourse with other men that we become just or unjust, and it is by our conduct in dangerous situations, accustoming ourselves there to feel fear or confidence, that we become cowardly or brave. So, too, with our appetites and angry impulses: it is by behaving in one way or another on the appropriate occasions that we become either temperate and gentle or profligate and irascible. In short, a particular kind of "moral disposition" *(hexis)* is produced by a corresponding kind of activities. That

[2]"We are to demand only so much of any theory as may be appropriate to its subject-matter, and in matters of conduct and expediency there are no fixed laws, any more than in matters of health." Aristotle, *Nichomachean Ethics* (trans. Wheelwright) 2, ii.

> is why we ought to take care that our activities are of the right sort, inasmuch as our moral dispositions will vary in accordance with them. It is no small matter, then, what habits we form even from early youth; rather this is of great, indeed of paramount importance.[3]

This is still quite vague. The golden mean has not taken us very far. Can reason not take us beyond this principle? Aristotle gives us some more guidance in his discussion of *prudence.* One is prudent when one can conceive and carry out actions that are advantageous to oneself and for the good life in general. One can calculate, find the right means, sacrifice instant gratification for long-range success. One learns from experience—one's own and others'.

But human nature is not entirely self-seeking. We are also *social* beings. We have an instinct toward community. An individual who existed apart from others would have to be a beast (or a god). The social instinct takes three forms: (1) The union of male and female to reproduce the race creates the family. The individual receives the necessities of life through the family and functions to preserve and strengthen it. (2) The union of families produces the village. The individual both benefits others in the village and is in turn benefited. His or her concerns have been extended. (3) The union of villages produces the state. Community is now fully developed. The individual is associated with others, not simply for food and companionship, but for the sake of a good life. He or she is involved with others in the task of creating conditions in which the moral nature of humankind can survive and grow. These three stages should be thought of as logical ones rather than historical periods. The family is the logical prerequisite for the village, and the village for the state. The state is an organic being in which both the individual and the community reach their highest realization.

Unless the state is badly out of kilter, the good person will be a good citizen and a good citizen will be a good person. The two are not identical, but each aids and abets the growth of the other.

Even more important for Aristotle than moral virtue is *intellectual virtue.* We not only must act, we must also *know.* Not only does reason prescribe the golden mean, discern genuine prudence, and recognize the social aspect of human nature; it also is the source of whatever understanding the individual has of human nature. But this is not enough. If we are to be intellectually virtuous, we must turn our reason to matters beyond the self and the species. We must acquire philosophic knowledge of the whole chain of being, from physical nature at the bottom to God at the top of the hierarchy. We must not only reason about what is best for ourselves and society, but also apprehend the first principles of reality itself. Aristotle prized theoretical knowledge at least as much as he prized practical knowledge. We fully express our human nature when we can find gratification in knowledge for its own sake.

[3]Ibid., 2, i.

The individual who has achieved a high level of self-realization will, according to Aristotle, be happy. Happiness is the supreme good—that for the sake of which everything else is done. No one can aspire to anything better. But happiness does not consist of a surfeit of pleasures; such a life is fit only for cattle. Nor does it consist of honor, for this is superficial and too much influenced by social contingencies. Nor does it consist of virtue in the narrow sense, because a person with virtuous habits can be miserable. Nor does it consist of wealth, for money is only a means and may be unwisely used. Happiness for Aristotle is *eudaimonia*—literally, "possession of a good demon." Happiness is the sense of vital well-being experienced when our human nature has been well attuned and is functioning in a natural way. As individuals we achieve satisfaction when we have harnessed and harmonized our capacities, when we feel that at last we have reached our potential. Under the guidance of reason, we seek to become truly human. Our happiness is the measure of how well we have succeeded.

Aristotle suggests that it is counterproductive to seek happiness directly. Although it is our aim, our *attention* must be directed toward those activities that are connected with our natural faculties and aptitudes. Happiness exists not in the abstract, but as the bloom on a healthy organism. It is the mark and by-product of a harmonious set of natural functions. Similarly, pleasure itself should not be our conscious aim, for we might pursue it in ways that distort our basic humanity. However, when we have accustomed ourselves to expressing our humanity rather than our beastliness, we will experience a more fitting pleasure. "It is pleasure which prompts us to base deeds, and pain which deters us from noble ones; and therefore men ought, as Plato observes, to be trained from youth to find pleasure and pain in the right objects—which is just what we mean by a sound education."[4]

In conclusion, it should be pointed out that Aristotle is not simply restating Platonic ideas. As we have seen, the germ for ideal development, according to Aristotle, is found within each organism. There is no realm of ideal essences (Forms) outside individuals and fully developed. Unlike Plato, Aristotle does not hold that ethical knowledge (or philosophic knowledge in general) requires contemplation of the Form of the Good. Aristotle tends to be more sympathetic to tradition and common sense. He believes in private property and marriage. In the political realm he is more concerned with the various *possibilities* (in the light of the actual circumstances) than with a perfect state that accurately reflects the Form of Justice. He does not submerge the individual in the state as Plato occasionally seems to do. Where in Plato's "republic," in which everyone serves the state, is any *happiness* to be found? Aristotle can even see some merits in democracy—a polity that was anathema to Plato. Aristotle's conservatism would not permit him to accept Plato's rejection of slavery and unequal status of women. Aristotle believes that a good state was essential for the moral development of most citizens, but it did not have to be as radical or as arbitrary or as comprehen-

[4]Ibid., 2, iii.

sive as Plato would have it. "It is strange," wrote Aristotle, "that the author of a system of education which he thinks will make the state virtuous, should expect to improve his citizens by regulation, and not by philosophy or by customs and laws.[5]

Hedonism

With the breakup of the Greek political order, the notion of self-realization in and through the city-state was abandoned by most philosophers. Paralleling the trend in religion toward cults that offered "salvation" to the individual, the movement in philosophy was toward theories that described personal excellence apart from public life. In contrast to Plato and Aristotle, the new philosophy held that self-realization was possible for the individual regardless of the political situation in which he or she is found. The good life was within reach of everyone. One had but to exploit the resources one found in oneself. One depended on nature rather than social institutions, custom, or convention. The hero of many of these schools of philosophy was Socrates—a man who somehow had preserved his integrity and equanimity in the face of very trying circumstances.

One such school was hedonism. The hedonists, perhaps drawing the converse of Socrates' dictum that the good man is happy, held a very simple theory: Pleasure is good, pain is evil. The wise person seeks to increase the former and decrease the latter.

Aristippus (435–356 B.C.) emphasized the positive side of hedonism. He would exploit the present for whatever joy it might contain. He preferred intense pleasures to mild ones, sensualism to intellectualism, excitement to repose. While Socrates had said that "an unexamined life is not worth living," Hegesias (a disciple of Aristippus) taught that a life without a great passion was not worth living.[6] Many of the stanzas of Edward FitzGerald's *Rubáiyát of Omar Khayyám* express the ideas of Aristippus and his followers. For example:

> Come, fill the Cup, and in the fires of Spring
> Your Winter-garment of Repentance fling:
>   The Bird of Time has but a little way
> To flutter—and the Bird is on the Wing.
>
> Ah, make the most of what we yet may spend,
> Before we too into the Dust descend;
>   Dust into Dust, and under Dust, to lie,
> Sans Wine, sans Song, sans Singer, and—sans End!

Epicurus (341–270 B.C.) emphasized the negative side of hedonism: freedom from pain. Too many pleasurable experiences had painful effects. Also, they

[5]Aristotle, *Politics* (trans. Jowett) 2, v.

[6]So effective was he that he was forbidden to orate. Too many listeners committed suicide.

required too much effort. Epicurus was a prudent man: He would anticipate consequences and would weigh costs. "Eat, drink, and be merry" occurs in the Bible; it was not said by Epicurus.[7]

The pleasures that he would seek were "pleasures of the soul" rather than those of the body. "It is not continuous drinkings and revelings, nor the satisfaction of the lusts, nor the enjoyment of fish and other luxuries of the wealthy table, which produce a pleasant life, but sober reasoning, searching out motives for all choice and avoidance, and banishing mere opinions, to which are due the greatest disturbances of the spirit."[8]

What Epicurus prized most was a state of serenity in which one is free from passion, fear, and pain. This condition of perfect calmness and contentment is called *ataraxia.* The achievement of this blessed state is a matter of self-cultivation. It requires discriminating among desires and controlling them. Epicurus distinguishes between "natural" and "unnatural" desires. Among the latter are desires for exotic food, fine clothes, wealth, fame, and political power. These can all be dispensed with. Another division can be made within the class of natural desires. Some are "necessary" (e.g., food and drink), and some are "unnecessary" (e.g., sexual gratification). These unnecessary natural desires can all be dispensed with. Among the necessary desires are those for life, for repose, and for happiness. These alone should be indulged. Those desires that support life are for moderate food, drink, and shelter. Those desires that foster repose are for the absence of fear and worry. Those desires that promote happiness are for knowledge and friendship.

The "fear and worry" point merits elaboration. Of all the ancient philosophers, Epicurus was the least superstitious. His view of the universe was objective and materialistic. Reality consisted of atoms, and events occurred according to laws of cause and effect. The miraculous and the supernatural have no place in Epicurus' philosophy. People do not, therefore, have to be afraid of religion. They do not have to worry about whether they are menaced or favored by divine power. If the gods exist, they are only configurations of atoms and have more to do with their time than to meddle in the affairs of men. In addition, people do not have to fear death. When the atoms that constitute their being become so disordered that consciousness is no longer sustained, that is the end of it. There is no "underworld," Hades, or shadowy realm in which their "spirits" wander. Death is simply the cessation of sensations and should not be dreaded. We neither lament the loss of the time *before* we existed, nor should we mourn the loss of time *after* we exist. Death, Epicurus says, does not come to any man, for when *he* is, death is not, and when *death* is, he is not. This kind of enlightenment so impressed the Roman poet Lucretius that he called Epicurus his "savior."

[7]See Ecclesiastes 2:24 and 8:15 and Luke 12:19. It was the nineteenth-century writer G. J. Whyte-Melville who said, "To eat, drink, and be merry, because tomorrow we die" *(The Object of a Life).*
[8]Epicurus, "Letter to Menoeceus," in Oates, ed., *The Stoic and Epicurean Philosopher,* p. 32.

It may be asked whether Epicurus' theory really belongs among those called "self-realization." It is indeed a self-realization theory, because Epicurus sought to foster a particular state of being from the human resources he possessed. He sought to achieve an inner condition that would make him content and free from external disturbances and at the same time would permit him to enjoy those pleasures within his reach. According to those who knew him, he succeeded.

Stoicism

Four great schools of philosophy were in existence in Athens by the end of the fourth century B.C. Joining the Academy of Plato, the Lyceum of Aristotle, and the Gardens of Epicurus was the Stoa, established by Zeno of Cyprus. Zeno was followed by Cleanthes of Assos, who was succeeded by Chrysippus of Cilicia. These early Stoics held beliefs that were similar to those of the Cynics, philosophers who expressed great contempt for civilization, politics, and the niceties of life. Both groups emphasized the heroic virtue of the self-reliant and independent individual.[9] The "middle Stoa" of Diogenes of Seleucia, Panaetius of Rhodes, and Posidonius of Rhodes became quite popular in Rome in the first century B.C. Its ideas were even further from those of the uncompromising and inflexible Cynics. The most well-known Stoics, however, were the Stoics of the Empire: the statesman Seneca (A.D. 4–65), the slave Epictetus (50–120), and the Roman emperor Marcus Aurelius (121–180). Stoicism is still a vital school of philosophy.

Although the theory has taken many forms through the years, its basic ideas may be expressed under three headings: independence, apathy, and harmony with nature.

The things that happen to us are beyond our control, but our reaction to them is not. We achieve *independence* when we can say with Marcus Aurelius: "External things touch not the soul, not in the least degree." We and we alone determine our attitude. "The great blessings of life," wrote Seneca, "are within us and within our reach. Tranquillity is a certain state of mind which no condition of fortune can either exalt or depress." The important consideration for us as individuals is not what we *have* but what we *are.* The trials of life call forth great fortitude. To master oneself in time of calamity is more important than to triumph over events. Socrates had said that "no harm comes to a good man." This is true—when we realize that pain and hunger, danger and death, are not really *harms.* "Invictus," by the nineteenth-century poet William Ernest Henley, expresses the Stoic ideal of independence:

Out of the night that covers me,
  Black as the Pit from pole to pole,
I thank whatever gods may be
  For my unconquerable soul.

[9]The founder of the Cynic school was Antisthenes. Other Cynics were Crates, Stilpo, and Diogenes of Sinope.

In the fell clutch of circumstance
  I have not winced nor cried aloud.
Under the bludgeonings of chance
  My head is bloody but unbowed.

. . .

It matters not how strait the gate,
  How charged with punishments the scroll,
I am the master of my fate:
  I am the captain of my soul.

This kind of heroic self-control is possible only if the individual can view things with a high degree of detachment. One must cultivate *apathy*: reduce desires, despise fortune, avoid strong passions. "Chastise your passions, that they may not chastise you. . . . It belongs to a wise man to resist pleasure; and to a fool to be enslaved by it."[10] Some Stoics were ascetics and withdrew from the world entirely. Others agreed to participate, but would not commit their whole being to any project fully and irrevocably. They would retain perspective by not taking their own role in history too seriously. Whatever happened, they could preserve their integrity, for this is all they desired and all that was worth desiring. The story is told of Stilpo, who emerged from his burning home, his toga in flames, his family and worldly possessions destroyed. "I have saved everything," he cried, "my good name, my integrity, my fortitude!"

This willingness to accept whatever happens, to avoid the emotions of envy, hate, ambition, pity, regret, and disappointment, is made possible for the Stoic by his belief that the universe is rational and that everything happens for the best. He can accept what befalls him because it is part of a great plan.

> Everything harmonizes with me, which is harmonious to thee, O Universe. Nothing for me is too early nor too late, which is in due time for thee.[11]

> Remembering then this disposition of things, we ought to go to be instructed, not that we may change the constitution of things—for we have not the power—but in order that, as the things around us are what they are and by nature exist, we may maintain our minds in harmony with the things which happen.[12]

The individual seeks to be *in harmony with nature* because it is providential.

For most Stoics, this rational and purposive principle of the universe, the *Logos,* was a divine force or God. Each individual is a "distinct portion of the essence of God." One can thus understand *why* things happen in both the factual and teleological sense. And one can also understand what part one is intended to play in the whole.

[10]Epictetus, *Enchiridion* (trans. Thomas W. Higginson) 106.
[11]Marcus Aurelius, *Meditations* (trans. Thomas W. Higginson) IV, 23.
[12]Epictetus, *Discourses* (trans. Thomas W. Higginson) I, 12.

Other people are also fragments of the Logos. Derived from the same God, we are all brothers and sisters. Our spiritual kinship transcends boundaries of race and state and social class. We are all members of the same cosmos; all citizens of the universe.[13] Stoic cosmopolitanism means that all people everywhere are subject to the same moral law. Our common humanity implies duties to one another that are *natural* rather than merely conventional. Roman lawyers, most notably Cicero, impressed with this vision of natural law, believed that the fundamental laws of Rome should reflect a universal standard of propriety. All persons are equal on this standard, and each has rights which other people and the state itself are obliged to respect. The doctrine of an ordered cosmos populated by people possessing a spark of divinity thus led to the doctrine of natural rights.

Let us conclude, however, by emphasizing the kind of nature each of us is to develop. Our self-realization will consist of a state of mind that enables us, calmly and gratefully, to accept whatever the Logos has in store for us. We will try to understand the necessity and purpose of every event. We will bear no malice toward anyone, excusing the other's imperfections, even as we try to correct our own. We affirm our own dignity and respect that of others, for all are fragments of the same divine Logos. The Stoics in their earnest discourses, letters, and manuals assumed that one could take oneself in hand and achieve a state or condition of existence that was true to the essence of one's own being. This essence, like the Logos itself, was free, rational, and moral. More than any other group, the Stoics emphasized self-discipline.

Conclusion

There are other ethical theories that can plausibly be said to fall under the heading of "self-realization." Baruch Spinoza (1632–1677) also urged that people develop their rational nature and accept their place in a natural system that is both rational and divine. G. W. F. Hegel (1770–1831) may be interpreted as holding that individuals should realize the potential of the Absolute Spirit that was the most important part of their being. Friedrich Nietzsche (1844–1900) argued that one should practice a "master morality," which meant that one should grow in power and refuse to be brought down to the level of the herd: "Maintain holy thy highest hope." The evolutionary theories of Herbert Spencer (1820–1903) and others emphasized the duty to struggle and compete. Progress of the species and society requires that each individual develop fully whatever qualities he or she has that serve the "length and breadth of life."

Some theories, to be discussed below under other headings, contain elements of the philosophy of "self-realization." John Dewey in his emphasis on growth, John Stuart Mill in his emphasis on the higher pleasures, and Immanuel Kant with his emphasis on the good will are examples.

[13]The Stoics not only got clear of the city-state, but went beyond the "sanctuaries" that provided refuge for various philosophic and religious groups who wished to drop out of society.

For Further Reading

Aristotle. *Nichomachean Ethics.* Many editions.
Aristotle. *Politics.* Translated by Benjamin Jowett. New York: Random House, 1943.
Cicero. *On the Commonwealth.* Translated by George Holland Sabine and Stanley Barney Smith. Indianapolis: Bobbs-Merril Co., n.d.
Whitney J. Oates, ed. *The Stoic and Epicurean Philosophers.* New York: Random House, 1940.
Plato. *The Republic.* Translated by Francis M. Cornford. London: Oxford University Press, 1945.

RELIGIOUS THEORIES

Judaism

It is impossible to present an accurate and balanced account of Judaism in a few pages. Judaism evolved over a long period of time. It rejected many external influences, accepted some, and transformed others. Many great leaders appear in Jewish history, and each has had his spiritual impact. The "Old Testament," the Talmud, and the Midrash provide a rich but not always consistent set of teachings about the nature of God (Yahweh) and the worshipers' duties to him. Traces of primitive views still exist in the Scripture, although most of it was written just before and during the Exile and compiled and edited afterward.

One important concept of Judaism is that of the *covenant.* At various times in history Yahweh revealed himself to humanity. He promised certain benefits in exchange for certain actions. These covenants tell us much about the nature of God: his power and his morality. The covenant with Abraham (around 1500 B.C.E.)[14] promised that this patriarch would be the source of a great people. Abraham and his descendants were to worship faithfully and conduct proper rituals and sacrifices. The covenant was renewed with Moses (around 1350 B.C.E.). Yahweh would lead the chosen people from slavery in Egypt, but expected in return not only conscientious observation of ritual but a very high standard of righteousness. Details of the human being's duty to Yahweh were revealed to Moses at Mount Sinai. Yahweh now promised that he would lead the Jews to the land of milk and honey and an independent state in Canaan. After a great deal of warfare, the Jews achieved security under King David (around 1000 B.C.E.). The Jews did not always live up to their promises and absorbed many of the

[14]B.C. stands for "before Christ." Some Jews prefer to use B.C.E.: "before the Christian (or Common) Era." A.D. stands for "anno Domini: "in the year of the Lord." Some Jews prefer to use C.E.: "Christian (or Common) Era."

idolatrous practices of the region. In 937 B.C.E. the kingdom split up into Judea and Israel. In 722 B.C.E. Israel was conquered and destroyed by the Assyrians. The book of Deuteronomy was probably written in the next century in order to recall the Judean people to the terms of the covenant and to halt the further corruption of the true faith. In 586 B.C.E. Judea was carried off into captivity by the Babylonians. During this exile, it was believed that Yahweh would yet keep his promise if the people returned to the way of life he had revealed to him. In 538 B.C.E. the "remnant" returned to Jerusalem and rebuilt the temple. A great effort was made to keep Judea faithful to God, to remember the lesson of the Exile. After a period of domination by Macedonia and Alexander's successors, the Jews maintained a perilous independence until conquered by Rome in 63 B.C.E. In 70 C.E. a fierce rebellion was ruthlessly put down and the temple utterly destroyed. Further dispersion of the Jews occurred, although many of them never gave up hope that their piety would eventually be rewarded by a restored homeland.[15]

Various conceptions of God are present in the writings of the legalists, chroniclers, poets, and prophets. How *powerful* is he? At times his power seems to be limited to a particular area. At other times he seems to be the most powerful god in the universe. Finally, his power is so great that he is set forth as the creator of the cosmos and a being who can cause whole nations to do his will. The Jews finally achieved the notion of monotheism, but it is apparent that the older traditions did not always subscribe to it. Animism,[16] totemism, polytheism,[17] and henotheism[18] finally gave way to the conviction that there is no god before or *after* Yahweh!

How *moral* is he? At times, he seems to be oblivious to moral concepts. He behaves as a jealous tyrant who acts in arbitrary, cruel, and unjust ways. More often, however, he is a just God, for he will live up to his promises in the covenants. And he frequently grants another chance to the Jews and to humanity in general. He finally comes to exemplify the most exalted principles of love, mercy, and forgiveness.

Corresponding to these various concepts of Yahweh's nature are various codes for human behavior. One constant factor, however, is obedience: the Jews are obliged to carry out the commands of Yahweh.

Why should people obey the commandments? One reason is that Yahweh has power and can harm or help them. Just as he punishes and rewards the Jewish nation (depending upon whether it has lived up to the terms of the covenant), he can punish and reward individuals. Adam, Abraham, Joseph, Noah, Saul, David, Solomon, Ahab, Samson, and many others fared well or ill depending upon their

[15]Even before the destruction, many more Jews lived outside Palestine than in.

[16]E.g., the worship of sacred oaks, stones, and springs.

[17]The gods of Abraham, Jethro, and Mount Sinai were coalesced into one god: Yahweh.

[18]The success of Jewish arms in Canaan proved that Yahweh's power was not limited to the area of Mount Sinai. Later a dramatic contest is recounted in 1 Kings 18 between Yahweh and the Ba'al of Jezebel.

obedience.[19] Related to this is the gratitude that people should have for a god who has provided them with the blessings of life, the bounties of the earth, and (in the case of Israel) freedom from captivity. A more compelling reason, perhaps, can be derived from the belief that Yahweh is good, knows perfectly what goodness is, and wants people to act morally. Yahweh took the leadership: he thrust himself into human history and revealed the nature of righteousness. This was an incalculably precious gift. Humanity no longer had to continue in its wicked ways. The response of humanity to this revelation varies. Some people will recognize their deepest ethical convictions set forth in authoritative terms. Some will not, and are destined to remain hopelessly enmeshed in sin. People can be co-workers with God, sharing his holy intent, in this, our true life on earth.

What is enjoined in this revelation? A great many things. The elements of the Mosaic Law (the Torah) number well over six hundred. At its heart are the Ten Commandments:

1. Do not place any gods above Yahweh.
2. Do not make or worship idols.
3. Do not curse.
4. Respect the sabbath.
5. Honor your parents.
6. Do not kill.
7. Do not commit adultery.
8. Do not steal.
9. Do not bear false witness against your neighbor.
10. Do not be covetous.

Other commandments specify just relations between people—often in a detailed way:

> When a man leaves a pit open or when a man digs a pit and does not cover it, and an ox or an ass falls into it, the owner of the pit shall make it good; he shall give money to its owner, and the dead beast shall be his.[20]

> When a man strikes the eye of his slave, male or female, and destroys it, he shall let the slave go free for the eye's sake.[21]

The concept of justice is based upon a sense of proportionality between offense and punishment: "Your eye shall not pity; it shall be life for life, eye for eye, tooth for tooth, hand for hand, foot for foot."[22] This is not retaliation in a vindictive

[19]A notable exception to this is the case of Job. This is why the book of Job is one of the most fascinating books of the Old Testament.
[20]Exodus 21:33–34. All Biblical quotations are from the Revised Standard Version.
[21]Exodus 21:26.
[22]Deuteronomy 19:21. See also Leviticus 24:19–20.

manner, but a case of reparation or "making good." Evil must be purged from society at the same time that the injured are given their due. The principle of justice applies to all: "You shall have one law for the sojourner and for the native."[23]

Some commandments impose severe penalties when the purity of religion is jeopardized:

> You shall not permit a sorceress to live.[24]

> If your brother, the son of your mother, or your son, or your daughter . . . entices you secretly, saying, "Let us go and serve other gods" . . . you shall not yield to him or listen to him, nor shall your eye pit him, nor shall you spare him, nor shall you conceal him; but you shall kill him; your hand shall be first against him to put him to death. . . . You shall stone him to death with stones. . . .[25]

A great many of the laws have to do with diet: what we may eat, how it is to be prepared, and the like. And a great many are concerned with details of sacrifice and ritual, holidays and feasts.[26]

It has been the task of commentators and casuists to say to what extent these laws are to be obeyed and what exceptions (if any) can be made to them. The problem is both logical and historical. And it is philosophical also, for it must be ascertained which laws truly reflect the will of a God who is good. Divisions of Judaism subscribe to different interpretations, and so do different individuals. Even Orthodox Judaism dispenses with injunctions that are irrelevant to conditions of modern civilization—or it tries to get around them.[27]

Existing side by side with the legalistic tradition, and often in conflict with it, is the prophetic tradition. The essential function of an Old Testament prophet was not to foretell the future, but to interpret the nature and will of God. The prophet was an inspired person who had his or her own version of God's revelation to proclaim. Often the prophet attempted to supplement the legalistic, priestly, or ritualistic insights with something else. Amos, for example, emphasized the justice of Yahweh and condemned the Jews for their rapaciousness. God will punish

[23]Leviticus 24:22.

[24]Exodus 22:18.

[25]Deuteronomy 13:6–10.

[26]It is easy to be critical of the ritualistic law, but, on the positive side, it can be seen to hallow special occasions, to celebrate life "in its unspeakable goodness," to reflect the divine source of goodness in even the smallest aspects of life. See Smith, *The Religions of Man*, pp. 281–285.

[27]In Israel many ingenious devies are being developed for dealing with the ancient prohibitions concerning the Sabbath: elevators that automatically stop at every floor so that the Jew will not have to push a button, electric ranges that will keep food warm without being turned on or off, a timer for flush toilets, electric-eye switches for turning on lights, an ink that will become invisible after a few days (which gets around the bar against making a "permanent record" on the Sabbath), fully automated electric plants, etc. See *Newsweek,* November 24, 1980, p. 114.

them for oppressing the poor, for taking bribes, for their pride in wealth and power. Yahweh said to Amos:

> I hate, I despise your feasts, and I take no delight in your solemn assemblies.
> Even though you offer me your burnt offerings and cereal offerings,
> I will not accept them, and the peace offerings of your fatted beasts I will not look upon.
> Take away from me the noise of your songs; to the melody of your harps I will not listen.
> But let justice roll down like waters, and righteousness like an everflowing stream.[28]

Hosea saved the Hebrews from complete despair when Israel was destroyed. He emphasized God's love and mercy, and he talked about the redeeming quality of that love. God says:

> I will heal their faithlessness; I will love them freely, for my anger has turned from them.
> I will be as the dew to Israel; he shall blossom as the lily, he shall strike root as the poplar; his beauty shall be like the olive, and his fragrance like Lebanon.
> They shall return and dwell beneath my shadow, they shall flourish as a garden, they shall blossom as the vine, their fragrance shall be like the wine of Lebanon.
> O Ephraim, what have I to do with idols? It is I who look after you.
> I am like an evergreen cypress, from me comes your fruit.[29]

Isaiah, a third prophet of the eighth century B.C.E., stressed the power of Yahweh (even greater than that of Assyria) and held that he was the moral ruler of the universe. Like Amos and Hosea (6:6), he called for righteousness instead of ritualistic sacrifice. "Bring no more vain offerings; incense is an abomination to me."[30] "Cease to do evil, learn to do good; seek justice, correct oppression; defend the fatherless, plead for the widow."[31] He recalled the chosen people to their mission, and predicted that a remnant would survive.

Jeremiah in the seventh century rather reluctantly accepted the Deuteronomic reform under Josiah, but urged the people to recognize the reality of Babylonian political power. He struck a new note when he emphasized the relation of individuals to God, instead of nation to God:

> In those days they shall no longer say:
> "The fathers have eaten sour grapes, and the children's teeth are set on edge."
> But every one shall die for his own sin; each man who eats sour grapes, his teeth shall be set on edge.[32]

[28]Amos 5:21–24.
[29]Amos 14:4–8.
[30]Isaiah 1:13.
[31]Isaiah 1:16–17.
[32]Jeremiah 31:29–30.

"Deutero-Isaiah" (chapters 40–55 of the book of Isaiah), the nameless prophet of the Exile, was joyful and optimistic. Yahweh is merciful and compassionate. Pardon is nigh. More important than the national greatness of Israel is its possession of a unique revelation. A servant of God, often a *suffering* servant, it has been chosen to reveal true religion to the world.

> I am the Lord, I have called you in righteousness, I have taken you by the hand and kept you;
> I have given you as a covenant to the people, a light to the nations, to open the eyes that are blind, to bring out the prisoners from the dungeon, from the prison those who sit in darkness.[33]
> It is too light a thing that you should be my servant to raise up the tribes of Jacob and to restore the preserved of Israel;
> I will give you as a light to the nations, that my salvation may reach to the end of the earth.[34]

It seems arbitrary to stop here, without mining the ethical riches of such books as Job, Jonah, Psalms, Ruth, and many others, and without pointing out some of the deeper insights of the law books themselves. But perhaps enough has been said of the curious mixtures of law and love, ritual and spirit, the priestly and the prophetic, that characterize the Judaistic tradition.

Jesus

Jesus, although no philosopher, was a person of great ethical sensitivity. He was also a highly successful speaker and teacher. His influence on those who knew him was tremendous. For almost two thousand years Western civilization has professed to follow his teachings.

The ethical views of Jesus are based on the concept of *love.* Love takes two forms, for it has two distinct objects. The first is love of God. We should love God because he is *worthy* of love. He is not only powerful (which would inspire respect), but a thoroughly moral being as well. He showers his blessings on mankind and heeds the call of those who turn to him. He is gracious and forgiving. He is a perfect being, but one who can be approached in worship and fellowship. A personal relation can be achieved with the "heavenly Father" that goes far beyond the perfunctory relation present in mechanical ritual and sacrifice.

The second kind of love is directed to other people. We love them, not because they are perfect, but because they need our love. This kind of love consistently places the concerns of others first. As individuals we claim nothing for ourselves, we are ready to give all. Love requires self-sacrifice—in the interest of the neigh-

[33]Isaiah 42:6–7.
[34]Isaiah 49:6.

bor. Love does not judge: it neither condemns nor compares. It would not be accurate to say that love gives others more than they deserve, for the question of just deserts does not come up. As God loves us, so must we love one another. If we love God, we must love his creatures. We love others not as a response to a commandment of God, but in the spirit of God. Obedience to God's will consists in emulating God in his love for mankind.

The love of other people goes beyond the principle of the Golden Rule, a principle of equity set forth not only in the Judaistic and Christian religions, but in most other religions as well. Rather than view others on a level of equality with ourselves, we should, according to Jesus, place them *ahead* of us. We return good for evil, turn the other cheek, accept unjust punishment, and accede to outrageous requests. Prudence and plain common sense are incompatible with this ideal of heedless and indiscriminate love. Seeking nothing for the self, the follower of Jesus lives a life of continuous service to others.

We are to love our neighbor, and everyone is our "neighbor": Samaritans, Roman officials, Pharisees, harlots, publicans, and tax collectors. There is no place in Jesus' outlook for enemies.

The Pharisees were the most liberal and enlightened teachers of the Mosaic law, but Jesus was relentless in his criticism of their views. Morality cannot be reduced to rules. Morality, according to Jesus, is a matter of inward feeling rather than outward action. The latter may be an indication of the former, but usually it is not. "Upright" people may obey the law but have *malice* in their hearts. They may be *proud* that they are so punctilious. They may respect the rights of their neighbors but *envy* their success. They may refrain from adultery but be consumed by *lustful passion.* Sinful people, on the other hand, may disobey the law but be *charitable* in their feelings for others. They may make the wrong sacrifice at the altar but *pray sincerely* for divine help.

The fact is that Jesus believed that law and love were quite different approaches to morality. Where there was one, the other could quite easily be absent. One could obey the law not to harm one's enemies, but this is not enough, for one should not even *want* to harm them. One should not strike another, nor even feel anger. One should not bear false witness, but should eradicate from one's heart all ill-will. Obedience to the law may be compared to a gleaming sepulcher: the agent is clean on the outside but unspeakably rotten on the inside. Love not only requires more than law, it requires less. Jesus violated the Sabbath. He associated with outcasts. He reduced the law to "two commandments."[35] Whatever is done in the spirit of love is good; whatever is done in the spirit of hate is bad. The law itself is quite irrelevant—except where it might set forth a humanitarian rule of thumb.

As Paul and others were quick to point out, this code of morality is very demanding. Indeed, for normal human beings, it is impossible. One may succeed

[35]"You shall love the Lord your God with all your heart, and with all your soul, and with all your mind. This is the great and first commandment. And a second is like it. You shall love your neighbor as yourself. On these two commandments depend all the law and the prophets." Matthew 22:37–40.

in not committing adultery, but can one avoid having adulterous thoughts? One may observe the law when one is harmed by a neighbor, but can one banish resentment? One may refrain from reprisals, but can one actively love those who wrong or attack one? Does this not demand more than human nature can provide? This is an ethical code for saints, not for flesh-and-blood people.[36]

Jesus would certainly agree. The human being alone must necessarily fall short. A radical transformation of the human nature is required, and this is something that the individual, with the best of intentions, lacks the power to achieve. Divine aid is necessary. The very personal relationship that Jesus enjoyed with God is the means by which true morality may be attained. One prays to God for assistance. One's spirit is perfected over a period of time through the grace of God. The Pharisees *resist* temptation. The follower of Jesus whose soul has been cleansed by God does not *experience* temptation.

Much has been attributed to Jesus concerning the kingdom of God. We shall not try to identify all the meanings that "kingdom of God" had for Jesus. The statements attributed to him are neither clear nor consistent. The Gospels were written many years after the events that they depict and are representative of many points of view. One of them, of course, is that of Paul (who never knew Jesus), who taught that Jesus was a savior-god and would return in glory. Jesus may have believed this. He may have believed that those who identified with him would triumph over death and live forever with God. But whether he believed in his own divinity, a kingdom of God on earth, or heavenly bliss in eternity is debatable. He assuredly believed he was destined by God to preach a new morality, to show by his action what this morality implied, and to give his life if necessary. And he doubtless believed in a kingdom of God in a spiritual sense, consisting of harmony and fellowship between the individual and God. This kingdom did not have to await the Second Coming or anything else: it began to grow in the soul of the individual who found God.[37] And he did believe that ethics was a miraculous affair: the surpassing of human nature by a divine infusion of grace. *This* kingdom of God he had personally experienced, and he wanted others to feel the same joy as he in being delivered from sin.[38]

Membership in the kingdom took precedence over ordinary concern and normal prudence. Jesus espoused a blithe heedlessness: "Do not be anxious about your life, what you shall eat or what you shall drink. . . . Look at the birds of the air: they neither sow nor reap. . . . Consider the lilies of the field, how they grow; they neither toil nor spin. . . . Therefore do not be anxious about tomorrow, for tomorrow will be anxious for itself. Let the day's trouble be sufficient for the day."[39]

[36] "You . . . must be perfect, as your heavenly Father is perfect." Matthew 5:48.

[37] "Being asked by the Pharisees when the kingdom of God was coming, he answered them, 'The kingdom of God is not coming with signs to be observed, nor will they say, "Lo, here it is!" or "There!" for behold, the kingdom of God is in the midst of you.' " Luke 17:20–21.

[38] The inner peace of Jesus, derived from his fellowship with God, inspired his disciples to say: "Lord, teach us to pray." Luke 11:1.

[39] Matthew 6:25–34.

Blessedness is available in this life. This is the "reward" that Jesus emphasized —not the reward of preferred seating in some earthly or heavenly realm. Actions done for the sake of a reward cannot possibly be acts of love. For Jesus, saintliness was its own reward, for it consisted of perfect accord between the human and the divine will. The soul, imbued with boundless love, at last is at peace.

Augustine

Learned in philosophy and history, Augustine (354–430), Bishop of Hippo and one of the Fathers of the Church, was the first great Christian theologian.[40] Drawing upon the Bible (especially the letters of Paul), faithful to the Nicene Creed, knowledgeable in the ways of the world, he set forth Christian orthodoxy in a systematic and plausible way. Where reason could help, he utilized it. Where it fell short, he appealed to faith.

Augustine perceived things in a historical framework. History for humanity began in the Garden of Eden. Adam and Eve (and the world in general) were excellent creations of God. Adam and Eve were free in the sense that they could, if they wished, obey God's will. From pride, however, they disobeyed. As a consequence, God withdrew his grace and banished them from the Garden. Their descendants inherited their deficient nature. Their nature was so diminished that they could only lead lives that were disordered and unhappy. The best of them could say with Paul: "What I would do, that I cannot do; what I would not do, that I do do." Human beings necessarily sin. Their love is misplaced: They are greedy and lustful. Human evil is not simply that of the flesh; it goes deeper than that. "Though from this corruption of the flesh there arise certain incitements to vice . . . it was not the corruptible flesh that made the soul sinful, but the sinful soul that made the flesh corruptible."[41] Augustine gave praise to God: "Thou didst set me face to face with myself, that I might behold how foul I was, and how crooked and sordid, bespotted and ulcerous."[42]

The world itself is deficient. Augustine describes the plagues, famines, earthquakes, tornadoes, and floods that inflict humanity. We are doomed to pain and suffering, tyranny and slavery, ignorance and disease. "What river of eloquence could ever suffice to set forth the wretchedness of this life?"[43]

All this raises the problem of evil. If God is great and good, why are his creatures so bad? And if they are so helpless, why are they so afflicted? And if

[40]The Fathers of the Church are the orthodox Christian writers of early times. One traditional grouping distinguishes eight that are especially eminent. In the Latin Church are Saint Ambrose, Saint Jerome, Saint Augustine, and Saint Gregory the Great. In the Greek Church are Saint Basil the Great, Saint Gregory Nazianen, Saint John Chrysostem, and Saint Athanasius. These eight are sometimes called "Doctors of the Church."

[41]Augustine, *City of God* XIV, 3. (trans. Dods), p. 444.

[42]Augustine, *Confessions* VIII, 7. (trans. J. C. Pilkington) (Cleveland: Fine Editions Press, n.d.), p. 135.

[43]See *City of God* 22. 22.

God is providential, why has he chosen to place us in this situation of "living death and dying life"? Augustine offers two explanations: (1) Nature (including human beings) is not evil in any positive way. Being creation, it is not perfect, for only the Creator is perfect. It has certain deficiencies or privations. That something "is a nature, this is because it is made by God; but that it falls away from Him, this is because it is made of nothing."[44] It is not unjust that people are unhappy, for the evil they do results from the deficiencies they possess. (2) Adam freely sinned. His children pay the price. Their wills stubbornly resist the moral sovereignty of God. They also freely disobey the commandments. They have earned their misery by their recalcitrant will. The first explanation is Neoplatonic: the will is deficient. The second explanation is Judaistic: the will is a positive evil. In any case, no divine injustice can be charged. If we cannot fully understand why God would have created a situation that in his foreknowledge he knew would lead to such misery, we must remember that the will of God, in some respects, is inscrutable.

The good news is that God has not completely forsaken humanity. He intends that his original high hopes be realized—at least for some of humankind. So he sent Jesus to proclaim the glad tidings of salvation. As all of humanity fell with Adam, they may rise with Christ. The kingdom of God will be more glorious than the Eden of Adam, and those who enter it will be blessed forever. Jesus came to teach a higher morality than the Law and to exemplify this morality in his own life. He taught that God will restore grace to those who are still stumbling in the footsteps of Adam. It was essential, according to Augustine, that Christ be crucified. The sins of humanity had to be paid for; Jesus was the perfect sacrificial lamb. Because he suffered, we do not have to. Moreover, Jesus triumphed over death, thus showing that we also (with God's help) can triumph over death. God's love for us is indicated by the fact that he sent "his only begotten son" to suffer and pay for our sins.[45]

Augustine accepted the Nicene settlement that Christ was both fully human and fully divine. Christ was God who became incarnate in man. This "sublime mystery" is logically necessary. Christ had to be fully human in order that his life be exemplary and his suffering real; but he had to be fully divine in order to atone for our sins and to triumph over death.

So, at last, there is hope. "From this hell on earth," writes Augustine, "there is no escape, save through the grace of the Saviour Christ, our God and Lord."[46] Those who are saved are saved through no merit of their own. All fall short of worthiness for salvation and eternal life. But some will be selected by God. He will create a distinction where none existed before. Some will be turned to Christ and the work of regeneration will begin. Where before they could not even obey

[44]Ibid., XIV, 13, p. 460.

[45]Augustine was not always comfortable with the Pauline idea of God satisfying his sense of justice by offering a divine sacrifice to himself. Augustine chose to emphasize the graciousness of God and the moral purity of Christ's life and teachings.

[46]*City of God*, XXII, 22, p. 848.

the Law, they now are "born again" and aspire to the highest expression of the morality of love.

Christ will return, a kingdom of God on earth will be established, the sheep will be separated from the goats, and finally the saints will go to dwell with God in heaven, while the sinners go to hell to be with the Devil whom they have served on earth. But before this dramatic triumph of God takes place, humans will live in a world that is a curious mixture of the good and bad. Augustine discussed this period between Christ's death and his return in terms of "the two cities."

The heavenly city or City of God is composed of all persons who serve God. It will endure through all time (including the fall of Rome) and culminate in heaven. The earthly city is composed of those who do not serve God. The people of both cities commingle in this life, those in the invisible city seeking to grow in grace, those in the visible city pursuing success and recognition in temporal enterprises. Loyalties in the two cities are in striking contrast. For every genuine value there is a counterfeit value. Citizens of the City of God seek peace in fellowship and security with the Lord; citizens of the other city seek peace by subjugating their enemies in war. The Christians seek glory through election by God and a seat in heaven; non-Christians seek glory through honors and political office. The elect practice the love taught by Jesus; the damned, consumed by lust, wallow in the filth of concupiscent love. The godly praise the beauty of the transfigured soul; the ungodly are moved by the beauty of physical nature. The righteous believe on faith; the unrighteous take pride in their scientific and philosophical attainments. Citizens of the heavenly city express their courage in humbleness, endurance, and steadfastness; the citizens of the earthly city express their courage by facing and overcoming dangers. Christians are only sojourners in this world; they are in it but not of it. Non-Christians lose their souls in worldly matters and know no other realm. This is the radical dualism that Augustine believed characterized human existence.

The supreme value is to draw nearer to God. Everything else is trivial; all other values are derivative or inconsequential. Everything except the love of God is a snare and a delusion. Christ has given humanity the opportunity to overcome the separation between itself and God that took place in the Garden. The good life is reunion with God—with all that that entails.

It would follow from this other-worldly view of Augustine's that human institutions are of little importance. Slavery is only one of the many evils to be expected in this "vale of tears"; but, since it does not prevent salvation, it may be tolerated. So too may poverty, disease, and injustice. Governments may be expected to be vicious and unjust. "What are kingdoms but great robberies?"[47] People, not content to rule over animals, seek to ape God by ruling over other people, "a reach of arrogance utterly intolerable." "There is nothing so social by nature, so unsocial by its corruption as [the human] race."[48] No longer able to

[47]Ibid., IV, 4, p. 112.
[48]Ibid., XII, 28, p. 410.

live naturally, people are, in their fallen condition, subject to government. Government is a punishment for sin.

Augustine, like Paul, taught obedience to government, for it is instituted by God as part of his plan. It may express the wrath of God. It may serve a positive social purpose by holding in check the lawless passions of the unregenerate.[49] But no one should make the mistake of confusing the "justice" of an unusually good state with divine justice, of which it is at best only an image. In any case, politics is irrelevant to Christians, who need no human institution for their salvation.

Augustine is a social and political conservative. He teaches obedience and endurance. No reform or revolution can cure the fundamental ills of humanity. The Christian will be a good citizen. The only limit to his obligation to obey is when the state issues commands that his conscience cannot accept. "As far as our souls and their eternal salvation are concerned, we must be subject only to God and not to any man who contravenes God's law."[50] The Christian may even be a good ruler, but citizen or ruler, the heavenly city commands his highest allegiance.

The only institution regarded as important by Augustine is the Church. This was founded by Christ and is the visible embodiment of the City of God. He defended the doctrine of apostolic succession and the authority of the bishops. The Church must preserve and interpret the true religion, keeping it free from heresy. It has the authority for the spiritual care and discipline of the flock. It administers the sacraments through which grace is restored and increased. Stressing a spiritual relation with God and an invisible kingdom above and beyond temporal and worldly institutions, Augustine was nonetheless a faithful churchman.

Thomas Aquinas

Europe had begun to emerge from the Dark Ages in the eleventh century. There was a revival of commerce and a revival of learning. More and more was learned about the culture, philosophy, and science of other times and other people. The Europeans realized how backward they were, how far they trailed the ancient civilizations and many contemporary ones as well. The scholars of the "little renaissance" sought to absorb and come to terms with ideas that were exciting in their freshness and challenging to their prejudices.

[49]It may conceivably serve the interests of the heavenly city—though this is unlikely. Augustine did, however, have a vision of a Christian Commonwealth, which the Middle Ages sought to enact. See Gerald Runkle, *A History of Western Political Theory* (New York: Ronald Press Co., 1968), pp. 86–88 and chaps. 6 and 7.

[50]Augustine, quoted in Herbert A. Deane, *The Political and Social Ideas of St. Augustine* (New York: Columbia University Press, 1963), p. 148.

By the time of Thomas Aquinas (1225–1274), many ancient manuscripts had been discovered and disputed in the new universities. One of the greatest discoveries was the work of Aristotle. His work, like many of the classical writings, displayed a worldly interest. He not only believed that the natural world was worthy of serious study, but also had confidence that reason, rational and empirical, could understand it.

The reception of Aristotle by the Church was not a friendly one. The reason is easy to see. He relied on reason; the Church traditionally relied on faith. He emphasized knowledge; the Church emphasized a state of grace. Aristotle seemed to be quite at home in a world that Augustine called "the earthly city." Furthermore, some of Aristotle's views in metaphysics, ethics, politics, and religion were in flat contradiction to Christian dogma. Church authorities forbade the teaching of his views on science in 1210 and soon banned most of the rest of his philosophy. This did not, of course, prevent Aristotle from being studied.

The characteristic philosophic activity of the little renaissance was *scholasticism.* The essence of scholasticism is to reconcile authorities. Even before the discovery of Aristotle, scholars had sought to reconcile the various parts of the Scripture, the creeds and traditions of the Church, and canon and Roman law. Greek, Roman, Byzantine, and Islamic ideas, if they possessed any truth, had to be reconciled with Christian doctrine. All sources of truth, it was assumed, could be put together into a harmonious whole, with the eternal verities of the Christian religion pervading and uniting the whole system. The task of Aquinas was to bring the greatest non-Christian authority, Aristotle, into this system, without doing violence to Christianity. He was judged to have succeeded. Although his synthesis was condemned in the year of his death, it was soon accepted by the Dominican order. Thomas Aquinas was canonized in 1323. In the sixteenth century the Church decreed that he was of equal rank with the four great Latin Fathers, and in 1879 Pope Leo XIII declared that Thomism was the basis of theological instruction in the Roman Catholic Church.

In the medieval debate over the claims of faith and reason, Aquinas defended reason, without discarding faith. The rational faculty, he argued, was given us by God, and God expects us to use it. As Aristotle showed, reason can discover important truths about the world and human nature. Knowledge about what God has created can in turn lead to knowledge about God. Aristotle made some mistakes, but most of what he said about nature is correct. Aquinas himself philosophized about ethics, politics, the nature of God, the existence of God, creation, immortality, and a great many other things. Reason is to be welcomed as a divine gift, not feared as a snare of the Devil and the source of pride. It could be used not simply to derive the consequences of authoritative doctrine (revealed theology), but to establish religious truth itself (natural theology).

Faith has an important role to play also. It can "correct erring reason." It must be relied upon by those who are not philosophers. But not even the philosopher can rationally establish all the doctrines of Christianity: "Then only do we know God truly when we believe Him to be above everything that it is possible for man to think about Him, for . . . the divine essence surpasses the natural knowledge of which man is capable."[51]

The important point is that faith and reason do not conflict. Truth is one. Faith comes to us directly from God; rational knowledge comes to us indirectly from God.

Aquinas accepted the views of Aristotle almost without change when describing the human being as a natural being. The goodness of human beings—their *summum bonum*—is as Aristotle demonstrated. We must realize our form, our humanity. Like everything else in nature, we are driven from within to seek our own fulfillment. The body is not something to be despised and rejected. Every human faculty has its proper use, and all natural desires aim at the good. Reason must be our guide, however, for it can grasp the notion of what is fitting for humanity. It sees the larger picture, controls the choice of the higher good over the lower, engenders the right habits, and forges the virtuous character. There are "natural laws" that the reason can grasp, and these laws define the lines of development that lead us to happiness. They reflect the inclinations implanted in all beings to seek their good, to achieve their true being, to realize their form.

Aquinas spelled out in great detail the various goods that natural urges pointed to and resolved every conceivable conflict that could arise. In an almost endless series of syllogisms he patiently demonstrated what was right and what was wrong. He drew on a host of authorities, interpreting most of them in a way that would be consistent with Aristotle ("the philosopher"). One section, for example, is called "The Payment of the Marriage Debt."[52] He raises and answers these questions: (1) Whether husband and wife are mutually bound to the payment of the marriage debt. (2) Whether a husband is bound to pay the debt if his wife does not ask for it. (3) Whether it is allowable for a menstruous wife to ask for the marriage debt. (4) Whether a menstruous woman should or may lawfully pay the marriage debt to her husband if he asks for it. (5) Whether the husband and wife are equal in the marriage act. (6) Whether husband and wife can take a vow contrary to the marriage debt without their mutual consent. (7) Whether it is forbidden to demand the debt on holy days. (8) Whether it is a mortal sin to demand the debt at a holy time. (9) Whether one spouse is bound to pay the debt to the other at a festal time. (10) Whether weddings should be forbidden at certain times.

Aquinas agreed with Aristotle that the greatest natural fuction of human beings was to reason, to discover truth—scientific and philosophical. The most gratifying kind of knowledge is of the forms themselves—especially the higher forms. The perfection of intellectual activity, therefore, is knowledge of God himself. Corresponding to Aristotle's mystical conception of pure form is Aquinas's beatific vision of the divine substance itself. Here we pass beyond the highest good to the

[51]Aquinas, *Summa Contra Gentiles* I, 5. (trans. Anton C. Pegis) (Garden City, N.Y.: Doubleday & Co., 1955), vol. 1, p. 70.

[52]See Aquinas, *Supplement to Summa Theologica,* Question 64.

supremely good end, the achievement of which brings bliss instead of mere happiness. Aquinas did not think that Aristotle, a pagan, had much to tell us on this point.

Aquinas's political theory agreed with that of Aristotle, although he gave short shrift to all polities but monarchy. "The fellowship of society being thus natural and necessary to man, it follows with equal necessity that there must be some principle of government within society."[53] Citizens need the state for their own natural development and are obliged to serve the state for the common good of all. The state and its rulers have a status in the natural order that cannot be abrogated by religion or the Church. Non-Christians may be good citizens and just kings.[54] A good state is one whose human laws reflect natural laws.

There is a third kind of law important in Aquinas's philosophy: *divine law.* Divine law is an expression of divine rule. It is enunciated in commandments rather than discovered by reason, a gift of God's grace rather than an achievement of philosophers. Much of divine law is concerned with the inner thoughts and feelings of humanity: its propensity to sin. Taken as a whole, divine law expresses the perfection that is pleasing to God. In carrying out its divinely appointed mission of securing obedience to divine law (saving souls), the Church can issue commands of its own: *canon law.* A person's spiritual development requires adherence to a revealed standard of excellence.

At the very heart of spiritual excellence are the "theological virtues." These are distinctively Christian, and Aristotle had nothing to say about them. The human being is more than a natural creature. Aristotle's moral and intellectual virtues enable persons to be as good as humanity can be, but Christ has made it possible for humankind to surpass itself. The ultimate goal of each person is to possess the theological virtues. These are infused in humanity by God through the channels of grace of Christ's Church. They are three in number:

> First, as regards the intellect, man receives certain supernatural principles, which are held by means of a divine light; and these are the things which are to be believed, about which is *faith.* —Secondly, the will is directed to this end, both as the movement of intention, which tends to that end as something attainable,—this pertains to *hope*—and as to a certain spiritual union, whereby the will is, in a way, transformed into that end—and this belongs to *charity.*[55]

These virtues perfect our natural ones, but are discontinuous with them. Faith gives us knowledge and understanding beyond the power of reason to grasp; hope assures us that the unattainable is attainable; and charity or love directs us to emulate Christ in his concern for all creatures of God.

[53]Aquinas, *On Princely Government* (trans. J. G. Dawson) in A. P. D'Entrèves, ed., *Aquinas: Selected Political Writings* (Oxford: Basil Blackwell, 1959), p. 5.

[54]Aquinas would, of course, insist that the Church be permitted to carry out its work. Sometimes he goes beyond this and requires the state to be a servant of the Church. See Runkle, pp. 137–140.

[55]Aquinas, *Summa Theologica,* Prima Secundae, Question 62, 3, in Anton C. Pegis, ed., *Basic Writings of Saint Thomas Aquinas* (New York: Random House, 1945), vol. 2, p. 478.

Fletcher

The most influential and eloquent proponent of "situation ethics" today is Joseph Fletcher, Professor of Christian Social Ethics at the Episcopal Divinity School from 1944 to 1970. In numerous books and articles he criticized legalistic theories of ethics and applied the Christian doctrine of love to concrete problems—often with surprising results.

The legalistic approach, he believes, has dominated Judaism, Catholicism, and Protestantism. These traditions have attempted to lay down prefabricated rules and regulations for solving all moral problems. For every situation, it would seem, there is a prescription. "Solutions are preset, and you can 'look then up' in a book—a Bible or a confessor's manual."[56] Catholicism has relied upon reason to derive its rules from the facts of nature; these rules are supposed to reflect "natural law." Contraception and abortion are thus always wrong. Protestantism has relied upon the Bible and other sources of revelation. It "has rarely constructed such intricate codes and systems of law" as Judaism and Catholicism, "but what it has gained by its simplicity it has lost through its rigidity, its puritanical insistence on moral rules."[57] Suicide and adultery are always wrong. Some Protestants would add drinking, card playing, and dancing.

The importance of rules in these traditions is surprising, in view of the recognition of the importance of love by their most distinguished spokesmen. As legalists became aware of the complications of life (and the claims of mercy and compassion), elaborate systems of exceptions and compromises developed: rules for breaking rules. "Casuistry is the homage paid by legalism to the love of persons, and to realism about life's relativities."[58] Some latitude is permitted. Homosexuals do not *have* to be burned at the stake. Adulterers do not *have* to wear a scarlet letter. "Having set out laws based on ethical absolutes and universals, love compels [legalists] to make more and more rules with which to break the rules."[59] But so long as love is bound by rules, the ethical theory is still a legalistic one.

The polar opposite of legalism is antinomianism, in which all rules are dispensed with. This takes many forms. Some of the early Christian converts, having embarked on a new life in Christ, dispensed with the law entirely, holding that anything done in the spirit of love is moral. This attitude is *libertism,* and Paul had to instruct its adherents on the real meaning of "Christian liberty." The Gnostics took the next step: they threw the "rule of love" out with all the other rules. They claimed to be possessed by the Holy Spirit. Their moral decisions, says Fletcher, were "random, unpredictable, erratic, quite anomalous."[60] This "inspiritation theory of conscience" is "intellectually irresponsible." Modern ethical theories that stress moral intuition or the conscience as a special faculty are similar to Gnosticism. A third form of antinomianism is existentialism. Jean-Paul

[56]Fletcher, *Situation Ethics,* p. 18.
[57]Ibid., p. 19.
[58]Ibid.
[59]Ibid., p. 67.
[60]Ibid., p. 23.

Sartre, for example, says that each individual at every moment must freely decide what to do in complete isolation from any guide, rule, or principle. Man is condemned at every moment to "invent man."

Somewhere between these two extremes, Fletcher places his own ethical theory, his own interpretation of Christian ethics. From legalism he accepts rules as "available sources of guidance" or "repositories of moral wisdom." They are not absolute, but may be useful rules of thumb. There is only one law that is exceptionless, and that is the law to love God and man. From this absolute, no other absolutes can be derived. From antinomianism he accepts the principle that love must determine our obligation in any situation. This love is directed toward persons, not principles. Principles may be set aside when, responding to love, the agent sees a course of action that serves the deeper interests of others. We must not be *indifferent* to others—in some ways this is worse than hate. We must choose the action which promotes the greatest good for others; we must "seek an optimum of loving-kindness."[61] The choice may sometimes be hard. Not only do we set aside some pretty good rules, but we must also, in such cases, be willing to do some harm for a greater good. Immediate ills may be produced for beneficial results; some people may be hurt in order to spare many others. "Love justifies its means."[62] This approach "can lead situationally to the most complicated, headaching, heartbreaking calculations and gray rather than black or white decisions."[63] But the guiding principle is love—rational and enlightened and far-sighted. "Our obligation is relative *to* the situation, but obligation *in* the situation is absolute."[64]

Fletcher makes several applications of his theory and alludes to others: (1) Judith, who sexually enticed the general Holofernes and killed him while he slept, in order to save Israel; (2) the prisoner of war who commits suicide in order not to betray his comrades; (3) the captain of a lifeboat who pitched many passengers into the sea so that some could survive; (4) the Jewish doctor who performed three thousand abortions in a concentration camp in order to prevent the women from being incinerated; (5) the mother who provided her promiscuous daughter with contraceptives;[65] (6) the pioneer mother who strangled her own infant child in order not to betray the whole group to the Indians; (7) males in a sexually unbalanced society who took several women as spouse; (8) the German Lutheran theologian Dietrich Bonhoeffer, who conspired to assassinate Hitler.

In none of these cases is Fletcher willing to say that the agent did evil (or chose the lesser evil) in order to produce a greater good (or prevent a greater evil). He or she did *not* do evil if the deed was done with loving concern. The doctor who assists in euthanasia has done a good thing, *not* an excusably bad thing, and it was loving concern for the suffering of the patient that made it good. "The

[61] Ibid., p. 61.
[62] Ibid., title of chap. 7, pp. 121–133.
[63] Ibid., p. 64.
[64] Ibid., p. 27.
[65] The mother was convicted in court of impairing the morals of a minor.

situationist holds that whatever is the most loving thing in the situation is the right and good thing. It is not excusably evil, it is positively good."[66]

For Further Reading

Thomas Aquinas. *Summa Contra Gentiles.* Many editions.
Thomas Aquinas. *Summa Theologica.* Many editions.
Augustine. *The City of God,* translated by Marcus Dods. New York: Random House, 1950.
Joseph Fletcher. *Moral Responsibility: Situation Ethics at Work.* Philadelphia: Westminster Press, 1967.
Joseph Fletcher. *Situation Ethics: The New Morality.* Philadelphia: Westminster Press, 1966.
The Holy Bible.
Huston Smith. *The Religions of Man.* New York: Harper & Bros., 1958.
Milton Steinberg. *Basic Judaism.* New York: Harcourt, Brace & Co., 1947.

CONSEQUENTIALIST THEORIES

The Utilitarianism of Bentham

Jeremy Bentham (1748–1832) held that the propriety of all actions is measured by their tendency to produce pleasure and pain. The principle of utility requires us to promote pleasure and decrease pain. Since pleasure is intrinsically good and pain intrinsically evil, morality consists of generating as much of the former and as little of the latter as possible. The principle of utility "approves or disapproves every action whatsoever, according to the tendency which it appears to have to augment the happiness of the party whose interest is in question."[67]

This is a very simple theory. After the *good* has been identified (pleasure), it would appear reasonable to measure *rightness* by the degree to which that good is promoted by the action in question. The theory has the advantage of being based on objective and measurable experience. How long is the pleasure (or pain)? How intense is the pleasure (or pain)? Bentham was confident that morals and legislation could be quantified and thus approached in the spirit of science.

But when we ask *whose* pleasures and pains are to be taken into account, complications arise. Bentham's psychological orientation was an egoistic one: individuals necessarily seek their own good, quite oblivious to that of others. Yet he wanted the principle of utility to be applied to society in general: "It is the greatest happiness of the greatest number that is the measure of right and wrong."[68] He goes beyond classical hedonism when he writes: "The dictates of utility are . . . the dictates of the most extensive and enlightened . . . benevo-

[66]Fletcher, *Situation Ethics,* p. 65.
[67]Bentham, *Introduction to the Principles of Morals and Legislation,* I, 2, p. 2.
[68]Jeremy Bentham, Preface to *A Fragment on Government.*

lence."[69] How can this universalistic viewpoint be squared with his egoistic psychology? Is it not absurd to require the individual to do that which he or she is incapable of doing?

Although Bentham points out that individuals possess in some degree the sentiments of sympathy and benevolence and can thus derive pleasure from actions that benefit others, his chief solution to the problem is contained in his theory of sanctions. A sanction is a source of pleasure and pain that is "capable of giving binding force to any law or rule of conduct."[70] The individual responds to these sanctions egoistically.[71] The *physical* sanction binds one to the observation of laws of nature: one may wish to leave a building quickly, but one will not jump out of a tenth-floor window. The *moral* sanction binds one to the observation of "laws" of public opinion: one does not cheat customers if one wants them to come back. The *religious* sanction binds one to religious "law": if one believes in heaven and hell, one will not blaspheme against God.

It was the *political* sanction that interested Bentham most. From fear of magistrates and the courts, individuals will refrain from killing and robbing. They will pay their taxes and do all the things the state requires.[72] Bentham had a vision of reforming the laws of England in such a way that the general welfare would result from each individual rationally seeking his own advantage. The rewards and punishments dealt out by a carefully conceived system of law would promote the greatest happiness of the greatest number. The question of who would be available for performing this great reformation of society was no problem for Bentham. *He* would do it! *Introduction to the Principles of Morals and Legislation* (1789) was only the preliminary work for the grand project.

Laws must serve the utilitarian ideal. Punishments attached to them should be mathematically evaluated on such standards as intensity, duration, certainty, proximity, fecundity, purity, and extent. Three examples from the many principles Bentham offers are: (1) No punishment at all should be inflicted in those cases in which it would be "unprofitable"—that is, when it would be greater than the evil it seeks to prevent. (2) No punishment at all should be inflicted in those cases in which it would be inefficacious—that is, it would not prevent the evil. (3) The magnitude of a punishment must be proportionately increased when it falls short of the profit of the offense in point of certainty and proximity. Specific applications of these and other principles are given by Bentham in his book.

[69]Bentham, *Introduction to the Principles of Morals and Legislation,* X, 36, p. 121.

[70]Ibid., XIII, 2, p.24.

[71]"It cannot but be admitted that the only interests which a man at all times and upon all occasions is sure to find *adequate* motives for consulting, are his own." Ibid., 17, 7, p. 313. "Men calculate, some with less exactness, indeed, some with more: but all men calculate. I would not say that even a madman does not calculate." Ibid., XIV, 28, p. 188.

[72]"Pleasures and pains are the *instruments* [the legislator] has to work with: it behooves him to understand their force . . . their value." Ibid., IV, 1, p. 29.

The judiciary system that was to enforce the system of law was needlessly complicated and often corrupt. Litigation was too expensive, time-consuming, and technical. "Where is the justice," Bentham would ask, "for a citizen who must hire an expensive lawyer to plead his case with respect to an all but unintelligible law before a corrupt judge after a delay of three years?"[73]

There were indeed a lot of laws in Bentham's day (and there are also in ours)[74] that could not pass the test of utility—many, indeed, had disutility. Examples: imprisoning people for not paying their debts, requiring membership in the Anglican Church for certain political offices, specifying capital punishment for such crimes as picking pockets, punishing individuals for drunkenness and fornication, prohibiting usury—the list is endless.

Although Bentham was committed to the greatest happiness of the greatest number, he was not himself a socialist. Indeed, he consistently argued for free trade—because of its utility. He also defended freedom of thought, speech, and press—not because they were "natural rights," but because they were useful for discovering, publicizing, and correcting social evils. Slavery was not a violation of abstract justice but an institution that ran counter to the principle of utility. He came to prefer democracy, not because every person has the right to count as one in the deliberations of the whole, but because it would be effective against "sinister interests."

Bentham, with his concern for consequences, was a great force for reform. He had the temerity to expose legal and philosophical "fictions,"[75] challenge the Blackstones and Burkes, criticize the Constitution,[76] and question every hallowed tradition. What the government should do (or not do) was in every case an empirical matter. He sought to expose the "fallacies" of his opponents, who resorted to such devices as the so-called Chinese argument ("Our ancestors are wiser than we"), the official malefactor's screen ("Attack us, you attack the government"), the snail's pace argument ("One thing at a time! Not too fast! Slow and sure!"), the quietist argument ("No one else is complaining!"), and many, many more. Bentham was truly a man of the Enlightenment. Of the many evils "endured by the people of this country only a small part is to be regarded as the natural and unavoidable lot of human nature."[77] He achieved some successes. The Reform Bill of 1832 became law the day after he died. "In a long succession of acts a thoroughgoing reform of the law and the courts was brought about, and

[73]Runkle, p. 418.

[74]According to Illinois law, a homeowner cannot be sued if someone slips and falls on his or her unshoveled sidewalk, for it is a public way for which the homeowner is not responsible. But if he or she *does* clear the walk and someone falls, the homeowner can be sued for doing a negligent job. It is therefore in the interest of the homeowner not to shovel at all!

[75]Natural rights, contract theory of government, representative function of the British Parliament, society as something more than a sum of its parts, etc.

[76]"It gives facility . . . security and continual increase to waste, depradation, and corruption in every variety of shape and in every department." Bentham, *Handbook of Political Fallacies,* p. 154.

[77]Ibid., p. 105.

in an astonishing number of cases the reforms followed the direction that Bentham's criticisms had indicated. Sir Frederick Pollock has said rightly that every important reform of English law during the nineteenth century can be traced to the influence of Bentham's ideas."[78]

Does this reformism have a sound theoretical basis? Is the principle of utility true? Bentham admits that no direct proof can be given, "for that which is used to prove everything else, cannot itself be proved."[79] Many people, however, accept it unconsciously. Even those who criticize it employ arguments that ultimately rest on the principle itself—for example, "It's a dangerous idea!" Bentham tries to show that all alternatives are unacceptable; so, if you dispense with the principle, you have no principle at all. He attacks intuitionism as despotic ("My sentiment is sounder than anyone else's") or anarchic ("Your sentiment is as sound as any other"). He has no patience with the "principle of sympathy and antipathy," theories of the "moral sense," or appeals to "natural law," the "immutable rule of right," or the "fitness of things." All their adherents manifest a "very pardonable self-sufficiency." These alternatives are all subjective, depending as they do on the random reactions of individuals. His greatest ire is reserved for the "principle of asceticism." *No one* really believes that pain is good and pleasure bad. Secular moralists steel themselves to deny themselves pleasure so that they can derive the *greater* pleasure of honor and reputation. Religious moralists court pain so that they will be rewarded in heaven for what they have suffered on earth. The conduct of ascetics toward others is not consistent with their theory. Although they do deprive a lot of people of pleasure, they have more sense than to deliberately promote as much pain as possible for others. "Let but one tenth part of the inhabitants of this earth pursue [asceticism] consistently, and in a day's time they will have turned it into a hell."[80]

The Utilitarianism of Mill

John Stuart Mill (1806–1873) was the protégé of Bentham and was expected to carry on the work of the "philosophic radicals" in reforming British society. Although he sought to retain the basic principles of utilitarianism, he found it necessary to make some significant changes in the Benthamite theory.

Since pleasure or happiness is the only thing that has value (and, therefore, ought to be produced), we should scrutinize the nature of pleasure. Mill found that pleasures differ *qualitatively* as well as quantitatively. The value possessed by some pleasures is greater than that possessed by others. The pleasures of the intellect, for example, are intrinsically more valuable than those connected with the gratification of the appetites. The lower pleasures would not satisfy a human being. No one would exchange his or her humanity, with all its trials, for the

[78]George H. Sabine, *A History of Political Theory,* 3rd ed. (New York: Holt, Rinehart and Winston, 1961), p. 685.

[79]Bentham, *Introduction to the Principles of Morals and Legislation,* I, 4, p. 4.

[80]Ibid., II, 10, p. 13.

contentment of a pig or a fool. "It is better to be a human being dissatisfied than a pig satisfied; better to be Socrates dissatisfied than a fool satisfied."[81] Although a thoughtful human being may be tormented by a great many things, the pleasures of the intellect outweigh the person's pain.

How does Mill know this? His belief is based on the same thing that supports his belief that pleasure is good and the only good: human experience. Just as people do in fact desire pleasure and find that it is the only thing they desire for its own sake, they also discriminate between the higher and lower pleasures. People who have experienced both kinds of pleasure find the one more valuable or preferable than the other.

Other higher pleasures are identified by Mill. The pleasure of the sense of freedom is one.[82] One feels pleasure when freed from slavery, from tutelage to one's parents, from racial and sexual oppression, and from economic regulations. One feels pleasure when one is able to think one's own thoughts, express one's own opinions, perform one's own actions, and vote one's own political convictions. Although Mill's utilitarian justification for freedom is justly famous, the sense of freedom has intrinsic value in itself—in addition to the greater happiness the exercise of freedom promotes for society in general. One also finds pleasure in certain elevated feelings: love, aesthetic enjoyment, imagination. And third, one finds pleasure in his moral sentiments and the feeling in one's own mind that one has acted conscientiously. These are all qualitatively different pleasures, and all rate high in the scale of values.

This is not to say that Mill looked with contempt upon the humbler sort of pleasure. He not only gave up royalties so the poor could afford to buy his books, he was also concerned for their physical well-being. He was appalled by the poverty of the many—"the wretchedness of present society." He sponsored legislation that would recognize the right of collective bargaining for workers. He was arrested as a young man for distributing birth-control literature. He worked to alleviate the pain of disease and poor health. He backed programs of public education. He defended the free enterprise system (with qualifications) because it tended more to bring the blessings of economic well-being to the many than did mercantilism or socialism.[83] His ethics was concerned not merely to glorify the values of the cultivated gentleman but to raise society in general from misery to a level where greater human development could take place.

Mill was more straightforward than Bentham in emphasizing that moral acts

[81]Mill, *Utilitarianism* (New York: Liberal Arts Press, 1948), 2, p. 10.

[82]"All restraint, *qua* restraint," says Mill, "is an evil." *On Liberty* in *The Six Great Humanistic Essays of John Stuart Mill* (New York: Washington Square Press, 1970), 5, p. 219. When people's conduct is determined by tradition and custom, they are deprived of "one of the principle ingredients of human happiness." Ibid., 3, p. 181.

[83]Mill wrote that the difficulties of socialism are as "dust in the balance" when compared with "the sufferings and injustices" of the present system. It is because the free enterprise system has "never yet had a fair trial" in any country that Mill pursued his lifelong endeavor of reform instead of enrolling under the flag of socialism. See Mill, *Principles of Political Economy* (London: Longmans, Green, and Co., 1909), II, 1, p. 210ff.

and measures must take into account the interests of *all.*[84] Not so dependent upon an egoistic psychology, Mill called for disinterestedness and benevolence. Utilitarianism has a "firm foundation" in the "social feelings of mankind."[85] He discussed other sanctions of morality, but believed that the "internal" sanction (conscience) was more effective than the external ones. People can, he said, respond to "the pure idea of duty."[86] He does not argue that people will automatically and necessarily seek happiness impartially, any more than that they seek their own happiness to the exclusion of others'. But people can be nurtured to heed the needs of others, and they can discipline themselves and develop a character that more and more responds to the call of duty.

Certain obvious criticisms can be made against utilitarianism. One is that since the individual must calculate before every action whether it will indeed promote the greatest good, he or she will be immobilized. Mill's answer consists, first of all, in pointing out that the sole motive of all we do does not have to be a feeling of duty. Many actions are morally indifferent. We may please ourselves and our friends. We need only assure ourselves that we are not harming others in the process. Moreover, many actions that *do* serve others may be done from ethically neutral motives. His second point is that even when we do seek to act dutifully, we are not performing in a vacuum. The history of the human species provides ample guides. We know a lot about the tendencies of actions. Not every situation is utterly unique. "There is no difficulty in proving any ethical standard whatever to work ill, if we suppose universal idiocy to be conjoined with it."[87] We should use landmarks and direction posts while improving and refining them. If we find that adherence to the rule does not, in a particular case, promote the greatest happiness of the greatest number, we may consider making an exception to it; but we do so in the interest of a *greater* rule (that of utility), not in order to further our own private purposes. Mill was quite aware of the possible consequences of the breaking of the rule itself: It is weakened, falls into disrepute, and makes later violation easier. It is conceivable, therefore, that one should obey a pretty good rule even when in *this* case the direct consequences of doing so work against the principle of utility. But there is ample evidence in Mill's writings that he was an "act" utilitarian rather than a "rule" utilitarian.[88]

[84]"The happiness which forms the utilitarian standard of what is right in conduct is not the agent's own happiness but that of all concerned." *Utilitarianism,* 2, p. 18.

[85]Ibid., 3, p. 33.

[86]Ibid., 3, p. 30.

[87]Ibid., 2, p. 25.

[88]For example: "To the judge, the rule, once positively ascertained, is final; but the legislator or other practitioner, who goes by rules rather than their reasons, like the old-fashioned German tacticians who were vanquished by Napoleon, or the physician who preferred that his patients should die by rules rather than recover contrary to the rules, is rightly judged a mere pedant, and the slave of his formulas. . . . By a wise practitioner, therefore, rules of conduct will only be considered as provisional . . . they do not at all supersede . . . (when circumstances permit) the scientific process requisite for framing a rule from the data of the particular case before us." Mill, *A System of Logic* (London: Longmans,1959), VI, 12, pp. 616–618.

A second important criticism of Mill's ethics is that it ignores special relations between individuals and the claims of justice itself. Such hypothetical cases as these are presented: A parent spends money to send a stranger to college because the stranger is a more promising student than the parent's own child. A judge suppresses a piece of evidence that exonerates the prisoner, who is a troublemaker and universally hated in the community. A debtor gives money to charity instead of to wealthy creditors. A reporter breaks a promise to a secret source because the tidbit would delight a lot of people. In every case, it would seem, an action is done that is wrong but quite in accordance with the principle of utility. One way to meet this criticism is to emphasize the utility of general rules: Look out for your loved ones, do not execute innocent people, pay your debts, keep your promises. Society is better off in the long run if these rules are upheld; to make exceptions to them is to weaken them and decrease the general happiness in the long run.

The answer that Mill prefers to make, however, is in terms of rights, obligations, and justice.[89] These are not abstractions for him, but entitlements based on the greatest happiness of the greatest number. Society in general is better off when certain claims are universally recognized as valid. People have a right to liberty —to mess up their own lives if they wish. "All the errors which [the individual] is likely to commit against advice and warning, are far outweighed by the evil of others to constrain him to do what they deem is good."[90] At the same time, others have a right not to be harmed. One may offend their taste or inconvenience them, but cannot violate "a distinct and assignable obligation." Children have the right to special treatment from their parents. People have a right not to be lied to. Innocent people have a right not to be punished. Recognition of these rights and others serves the general happiness of society.

Societies in which competence and merit are generally rewarded tend to be happier than those in which they are not. The same is the case with respect to the recognition of private property. Agreements should be lived up to. Some sense of equality is also an aspect of justice. Mill distinguishes between two classes of moral duties. It is moral to be charitable, but the form it takes is up to the individual. We do not have a specific duty to help Peter rather than Paul, and neither Peter nor Paul may claim our help at the expense of the other. But when someone has a specific claim on us as a result of a special relation he or she bears to us, then *justice* requires that the claim be met. When someone has a right, "he has a valid claim on society to protect him in the possession of it."[91] There is nothing optional about this. Just acts may be *exacted* by the claimant. Is this utilitarian? Mill says that justice is justified by an "extraordinarily important and impressive kind of utility."[92] He calls justice "the chief part, and incomparably

[89]See *Utilitarianism,* 5, and *On Liberty,* 4 and 5.
[90]*On Liberty,* 4, p. 201.
[91]*Utilitarianism,* 5, p. 57.
[92]Ibid., 5, p. 58.

the most sacred and binding part of all morality."[93] Prudence is fine, benevolence is praiseworthy, but justice is obligatory.[94] Why? When rights are preserved, people can enjoy security. Peace is preserved. Individuals can aspire to their highest development. Liberty flourishes. "Justice is a name for certain classes of moral rules which concern the essentials of human well-being more nearly, and are therefore of more absolute obligation, than any other rules for the guidance of life."[95]

There is some reason to suspect that Mill already had a pretty clear idea of what rights, obligations, and justice consisted of, quite apart from their utility. He does not always succeed in demonstrating that they are validated simply by utility, and he makes some judgments that seem to depart from utility.[96] He wrestled long and earnestly (in *On Liberty*) with the harm principle, but the principle of utility did not lead him to most of his conclusions.[97] He referred to utility in only one significant instance in *On Liberty,* and not at all in *Considerations on Representative Government.* Mill does not present mathematical calculations but, instead, presents acts, rules, and rights that accord in some vague way with our sense of social propriety.[98] Just as Mill seemed to have an independent notion of the intellectually developed individual and assumed that his or her consciousness would be suffused with pleasure, he perhaps also had a vision of an open society of freely acting people recognizing the rights of all and assumed that this would have a greater amount of pleasure in it than any other society.

Even Mill's progressivism was compromised. Like Bentham, he was interested in results, in consequences. But while he looked to the future, he repeatedly turned to the past and sought to preserve its heritage. He liked Bentham, but found much to praise in Coleridge. He welcomed all democratic trends, but feared the rule of the uninformed majority.[99] "The abiding impression left by Mill's

[93]Ibid., 5, p. 64.

[94]One must be puzzled about the consistency of Mill's theory when he can regard some kinds of utility as more important than others. It would seem to be more consistent to apply the principle of utility to *any* situation in which pleasure or pain is involved. And it is quite possible that the positive units produced by prudent or charitable acts could exceed those produced by an act of justice.

[95]Ibid.

[96]The principle of equality, for example, was highly prized by Mill, although it is obvious that to say that everyone has a legitimate claim to the means for happiness is quite different from holding that happiness is to be treated in a calculus in a way indifferent to the fact of who happens to experience it. Strict utilitarianism would countenance the misery of some for the sake of the greater good. Mill expressed confidence that the principle of utility would reconcile all the apparent conflicts between the common principles of justice, but he never himself carried out the task. Mill was not a calculator!

[97]Harm to others consists in a violation of their *rights,* not a decrease of their happiness. The harm principle is to protect others in the exercise of their freedom, not to maximize the good. Many of the actions that Mill would permit involve a *lot* of general welfare—on the surface, at least, negatively!

[98]Much more often he appeals to intuitively known rights, a sense of fairness, and the notion of the dignity of the individual.

[99]There is some reason to believe that Mill was too much of an idealist, individualist, equalitarian, and libertarian to employ the principle of utility consistently as the measure of justice or of morality in general.

work," wrote Brinton, "is that of a mind of transparent honesty in a state of extreme tension."[100]

Ideal Utilitarianism

The utilitarianism of Bentham and Mill is the theory that whatever produces the most pleasure or happiness is right. *Utilitarianism,* however, has come to have a more general meaning: "whatever produces the greatest good is right." A person who believes that there are things other than pleasure or happiness that have intrinsic value, and that whatever has value should be promoted, is a utilitarian, although not a hedonistic utilitarian. Such theories have been called pluralistic or *ideal utilitarianism.*

Most utilitarians recognize pleasure or happiness as one good among many. Among the other goods that have been recognized are knowledge, aesthetic sensitivity, humanity, conscientiousness, and purity. Their opposites, therefore, are intrinsic evils: ignorance, aesthetic insensitivity, cruelty, unscrupulousness, and licentiousness. Most ideal utilitarians insist that values are located in the sentient being as states of mind or qualities of character, although it is possible to hold that values may exist outside consciousness. The value of a beautiful but remote waterfall lies in the consciousness of the viewer who beholds it, although one might argue that the value resides in the beauty of the waterfall whether it is perceived or not.

The ideal utilitarian must disengage pleasure from other values. That the acquisition of a piece of knowledge by one who thirsts for it gives pleasure does not mean that the value of that piece of knowledge consists of the pleasurable gratification it produces. The pleasure of knowledge is not, as Mill would say, an especially valuable pleasurable experience, but a state of mind containing two distinctly different values. A knowledgeable state of mind—for example, awareness of one's own shortcomings—may be painful, but it still possesses value. Similarly, a feeling of vengeance may be very pleasurable, but contain a lot of intrinsic evil. Many of our mental states are complex wholes in which are found intrinsic goods and evils.

Many of the things that the ideal utilitarian regards as intrinsic goods have beneficial tendencies. That is, possession of them tends to produce pleasure for both the agent and others. A person who possesses moral virtue will experience the pleasure of a good conscience and will be a source of happiness for others. Someone who is sensitive to beauty will feel gratification when reading a great poem and perhaps will also create works of art that will please others. But the ideal utilitarian does not have to point out the extrinsic value of these things, believing instead that they possess value in their own right. Whether or not virtue and aesthetic sensitivity are productive of goods (pleasure or something else), they

[100]Crane Brinton, *English Political Thought in the 19th Century* (New York: Harper & Bros., 1962), p. 102.

have intrinsic value. The same kind of ethical judgment that can abstract happiness from human experience and pronounce it good can also abstract other things and find them good. One is saved the kind of special pleading that occurs when one has to seek extrinsic justification for something that one already believes has intrinsic value. A feeling of generosity, for example, is good in itself, whatever its consequences; and a feeling of selfishness is bad, whatever its consequences. Some useless things are good.

This does not mean, of course, that good feelings or character traits always can be trusted to produce the greatest good. From good things, evil things sometimes result; and the utilitarian must be alert to these possibilities. An act of impulsive generosity (such as giving all one's wealth to a beggar) may have bad consequences that outweigh the goodness of the feeling that inspired it. From bad things, good things may result; and the utilitarian must exploit these possibilities. An act of suppressing the truth (as when a doctor does not tell a patient that an operation will be very painful) may have good consequences that outweigh the evil of ignorance. The ideal utilitarian must be as scrupulous in anticipating consequences as the hedonistic utilitarian.

Indeed, the task of ideal utilitarians is more difficult. They cannot be satisfied with evaluating the amounts of pleasure that are produced or even, in the case of Mill, discriminating among qualities of pleasures; they must take into account *all* the goods involved. They must see these goods as *commensurable*—that is, measurable on a common scale.[101] To do this is often a difficult matter. They know, for example, that the knowledge of nuclear fission is more valuable than the pleasure of getting a birdie on the eighteenth hole, but they cannot easily specify how many birdies are equivalent in value to nuclear knowledge. When two sets of alternative consequences contain about the same amount of value with respect to goods *X* and *Y*, they may choose the one that produces value *Z* in addition, but how would they compare a set that produces *X* and *Y* with one that produces *A* and *B*? Should the good of *purity* give way to the good of procreating children under the tutelage of Masters and Johnson? Should the evil of *brutality* be engendered in recruits who are being trained to defend their country? Or in football players who are being trained to win the game?[102]

Ideal utilitarians would be the first to admit that matters become very complicated. But where simplicity distorts the ethical situation, it is a mistake to seek it. To ignore all values but pleasure is to adopt a narrow and doctrinaire position. And to assume that these other things can be shown to be hedonistically justified is just plain false and a case of wishful thinking. If we say that the value of a discovery of an historical event in the thirteenth century that sheds light on our

[101]For a defense of the commensurability of values by an ideal utilitarian, see Rashdall, *The Theory of Good and Evil,* book II, chap. 2.

[102]After a painstaking analysis of alternative ways of acting, Richard B. Brandt concludes: "If 'pluralism' is right, in some situations reliable comparative judgments of value can be made; but in other situations such judgments cannot be made. This is probably what we should have expected!" *Ethical Theory,* p. 350.

understanding of that period is good because it produces pleasure for the investigator and those who hear about it, we are misconstruing both the motive of the researcher and the social consequences of the discovery. To say that a hateful temperament is to be avoided simply because it tends to produce pain misses its intrinsic evil. Individuals may temperamentally be well fitted for taking life. They may be good executioners or abortionists; they may perform well in cases of infanticide and euthanasia. The consequences of their actions may serve the greatest happiness of the greatest number very well, but their insensitivity to human life is an intrinsic evil.

Suppose we have to choose between two worlds. They have equal amounts of pleasure, but the first is devoid of knowledge, love, enjoyment of beauty, and moral qualities, while the second abounds in these things. Hedonistic utilitarianism would hold that it does not matter which we chose. This is absurd. We would choose the second world, because we know it is better. Or suppose that the first had a tiny bit more pleasure in it than the second, but none of the other qualities. The hedonistic utilitarian would have to choose the first world—which is equally absurd.[103]

Rule Utilitarianism

As we have seen, Mill believed that the derivation of rules of thumb from the history of human experience facilitates the making of ethical decisions. We do not always have to ascertain the consequences of a particular case of assault if we know that cases of assault generally produce more evil than good. And Mill also held that certain rights should be accorded individuals because societies are generally happier when these rights are consistently respected. The principle of utility can serve as the basis for rules that are almost binding in all situations. We use the term *almost* because particular cases can easily be imagined in which the general good requires that these rules occasionally be set aside. We need not keep a promise to send a young man to college if he turns out to be an utter wastrel. We need not tell the truth when to do so would be humiliating. The theory that general rules are no more than rules of thumb and that they may be set aside in those cases where the general good is served thereby is called "act utilitarianism."

Act utilitarians are no more eager to shock ethical sensibilities than anyone else. So they may advise us to take a broad and impartial view of the consequences involved. Be on guard against rationalizing what is to your interest! Do not overestimate the importance of your own goods and evils! Take into account the effect on others when they see a valuable rule of thumb violated! Have you weakened a very useful social rule? What effect will violation of the rule have on you? Will you find it somewhat easier to violate it the next time it is applicable and there are no genuine grounds for dismissing it? These warnings and injunctions fall within the scope of act utilitarianism.

[103]See G. E. Moore, *Ethics,* pp. 146–147.

But suppose that the agent is perfectly impartial and has taken an unbiased view of the consequences of his or her possible actions. And suppose that there is no danger of discrediting the useful rule of thumb: The action will be done in secret and no one will know. And suppose, finally, that the deed will not corrupt the agent: he or she will die the second after performing it. There is no doubt, for example, that killing the innocent person at this time will have beneficial results, that breaking a solemn promise to one's mother on her deathbed will produce the greatest net good, that taking the money from the unguarded cash register will have positive utilitarian consequences. Some philosophers who share the utilitarian concern for the greatest good nevertheless believe that these acts are wrong.

They justify their belief by appealing to "rule utilitarianism." The advocates of rule utilitarianism ask a simple question: Adherence by all to what rules would best serve society in general in terms of producing the greatest good? They seek to provide a set of rules, obedience to which would best serve society.[104] The rules ideally would cover all voluntary actions. They would be consistent with one another. All exceptions and qualifications would be contained in the rules themselves or be covered by higher rules. No exceptions could be made *to* the rules. Everyone would be obligated to obey all the rules, for they are designed to produce the greatest good. If universal adherence to a rule serves the general good, the people who violate it are culpable. Even though they may see some utilitarian advantage in breaking it, they are not justified in doing what would be wrong if done by others. The rule enjoys a certain majesty, quite apart from the particular consequences of adhering to it in any particular situation.

If the rule says to vote, I should vote—although my vote will make no difference in the outcome and I could have used my time more profitably. If the rule says do not burn leaves, I should not burn leaves—although, since others are obeying the rule, I will not contribute significantly to air pollution if I do. In these cases, the purposes of the rules are being met (large turnout at the polls, sufficient reduction of pollutants in the air), and I *know* that they are being met. Nevertheless, I am *subject* to them—unless there is another rule that relieves me of responsibility in just these kinds of circumstances.

Quite the opposite situation may occur when the rule is so counter to ordinary practice that very *few* people adhere to it, and the agent would be in a decidedly disadvantageous position if he or she chose to obey. The system of rules might be quite idealistic and, though aiming at very good things for society (or humanity), require actions that most people are unwilling to perform.[105] The agent would still be obligated to obey the rule (although he or she might well resent the immorality of those who do not)—unless there were a special rule that relieved him or her in cases of real hardship.

[104]They may do this in the broad context of humanity itself or choose the narrower bounds of a particular society. Or they may have a general system for humanity with derivative systems for specific societies.

[105]An example might be: reduce consumption of gasoline to two gallons per week.

Finally, we will look at a situation devised by Richard B. Brandt.[106] A system might contain the rule that aged parents should be supported by the state instead of by their children. But suppose that the present social order does not provide for this care. May the child then abandon the parent? No. The system of rules would be defective if it did not prescribe an alternative or standby method for taking care of the aged, with perhaps another maxim that we should work to get the preferred method accepted by the social order.

Rule utilitarianism does not look for a perfect system to be delivered from on high. Individuals and groups of individuals devise their own rules. Whether they can get widespread support for them or not, they are obliged to act according to those principles that, if acted upon by everyone, would promote the greatest good. The strength of the theory is twofold: it is based on consequences, and it applies equally to all people. In dealing with *types* of actions instead of particular acts, it squares more with our sense of moral propriety. We are called upon to act on principles rather than on the particular exigencies of individual cases.

That Mill himself was friendly to such an interpretation of utilitarianism has been argued by some commentators. To the extent that moral rules become incorporated into legal statutes, they would have to have the quality of genuine rules rather than simply rules of thumb, for laws and courts cannot deal with people in any other way. And Mill (as well as Bentham) was concerned to reform English law on the utilitarian model. To do this, he would have to show that the law expressed a rule that rested on a utilitarian justification, that society would profit if everyone obeyed it, and no one can claim exemption from it. Courts are required to uphold the law (which one hopes is utilitarian); they are not required to produce certain consequences.

The Instrumentalism of Dewey

John Dewey (1859–1952), America's greatest philosopher, emphasized the consequences of human actions. Although he was not a utilitarian, he shared with Bentham and Mill the view that philosophy should be employed for the criticism and reform of social institutions. They, too, must be judged on the basis of what they accomplish.

As a pragmatist, Dewey believed that truth was achieved through the solution of concrete human problems. The mind is an instrument for gaining control of a troubled situation and enriching the significance of subsequent experience.

> *If* ideas, meanings, conceptions, notions, theories, systems are instrumental to an active reorganization of the given environment, to a removal of some specific trouble and perplexity, then the test of their validity and value lies in accomplishing this work. If they succeed in their office, they are reliable, sound, valid, good, true. If they fail to clear up confusion, to eliminate defects, if they increase confusion, uncertainty and evil when they are acted upon, then they are false. Confirmation, corroboration,

[106]See Brandt, p. 399.

> verification lie in works, consequences. Handsome is that handsome does. By their fruits shall ye *know* them. That which guides us truly is true—demonstrated capacity for such guidance is precisely what is meant by truth. The adverb "truly" is more fundamental than either the adjective, true, or the noun, truth. An adverb expresses a way, a mode of acting. Now an idea or conception is a claim or injunction or plan to act in a certain way as the way to arrive at the clearing up of a specific situation. When the claim or pretension or plan is acted upon *it guides us truly or falsely;* it leads us to our end or away from it. Its active, dynamic function is the all-important thing about it, and in the quality of activity induced by it lies all its truth and falsity. The hypothesis that works is the *true* one; and *truth* is an abstract noun applied to the collection of cases, actual, foreseen and desired, that receive confirmation in their works and consequences.[107]

Truth is a matter of agreement, not between thought and reality, but between intention and result. Dewey's position is not a middle ground between empiricism and rationalism, but a radical departure from both. The function of thought is not to copy reality but to reconstruct human experience. Dewey's definition of truth is a moral declaration.

The purpose of ethical thought is not to discover absolute standards of human perfection, describe intrinsically good states of mind, or identify exceptionless moral laws. Such standards are abstract and remote from the real problems of people. Since these standards make no appeal to us, we tend to ignore them (unless they are backed by strong institutions). A *genuine* moral ideal guides our action because it is connected with our actual strivings and aspirations. The kind of ethical idea that Dewey was interested in is the kind that conceives of a better future and is effective in bringing it about.

If values are not objective features of the universe which impose on human beings the duty to promote them, what are they? In answering, we must avoid the error of radical empiricism. We cannot simply say that a value is what is valued, desired, or found enjoyable. Values will be based on actual human preferences, but not everything that an individual happens to value is a value. While not "objective" in a way emphasized by normative ethical theories, values for Dewey must be ends that are *worth striving for.* They become values when we have made estimates and appraisals and conclude that they are not only desired but *desirable,* not only satisfying but *satisfactory.*

Since a value is a claim to future action, we have to ask such questions as these: Is it realistic—that is, are means available for its realization? Are the means too expensive in terms of time and effort? What other values will be produced or lost in working for the value in question? What changes will I undergo in working for it? How will this value fit in with other goods I have set for myself? What consequences will the achievement of the value have in my life? A student who aspires to a certain profession—say, accounting—could ask herself these questions. In the process of answering them, the student might find that the desire

[107]Dewey, *Reconstruction in Philosophy,* pp. 156–157.

to be an accountant was just a casual inclination, or might find that it was a value that could call forth an earnest effort. Similar questions are in order when an individual or group is selecting social values.[108]

Dewey emphasizes the interconnectedness of experience. Although distinguishing between means and ends is essential for effective action, one must see them in a continuum. Every means is an end, for we experience it. Life is not only a constant going toward, but also a constant arriving at. Every means chosen for a particular end will produce other ends. Every end attained becomes a means for something else. In solving problems, we create other problems and other opportunities.

In our concern for knowledge of conditions and consequences, we are not forsaking the moral for the merely prudential. Our failure to apply scientific thinking in ethical matters has been catastrophic. In consequence of our reluctance to examine the empirical connections within experience, "the existence of values that are by common consent of a secondary and technical sort are under a fair degree of control, while those denominated supreme and imperative are subject to all the winds of impulse, custom and arbitrary authority."[109]

We have been told that the moral problem consists in summoning the will to act on behalf of goods (or maxims) already known. For Dewey, the problem is to discover what these goods *are*. Individuals and societies must not be satisfied with those handed down from the past. There is nothing sacred. Family relationships, draft laws, public sector unions, academic requirements, energy use, and a great many other ideals and practices must be evaluated on the basis of how they in fact serve us and how they can be changed to serve us better in the future. Reliance on precedent is a poor substitute for active, deliberate, and reorganizing intelligence. What we have learned in the past should be tools for improving the future. Conservatism is more dangerous than reform, for conditions change whether we like it or not, and old practices, customs, and rules that may have served a purpose yesterday may work against us today. By the same token, reform directed to specific problems should be set aside when shown unsuccessful in the course of events.

Dewey calls for experimentation in ethical matters. Just as the scientific method has worked well in turning up ideas that help us control physical nature, it can work well in providing us with ideas that will exploit the potential of human life in both its individual and social dimensions. Tenets and creeds in the moral realm are hypotheses. They are not principles that should be fought for, but ideas that should be tested in experience. How well do they alleviate the problem? Does affirmative action really reduce racial discrimination? Does the right to strike help solve the problem of underpaid police officers? Are racial discrimination and low

[108]"At the present time," Dewey writes, "almost all important ethical problems arise out of the conditions of associated life." John Dewey and James H. Tufts, *Ethics*. See Joseph Ratner, ed., *Intelligence in the Modern World*, p. 765.

[109]Dewey, *The Quest for Certainty*, p. 269.

police salaries real evils? Some hypotheses are discarded in the testing process. Some are altered. But all indicate possible ways of transforming social institutions. Loyalty to moral laws and social institutions is no great virtue when, in Dewey's time and our own, humanity is beset by a host of identifiable problems.

Dewey likes to bridge chasms. He says, for example, that there is no sharp division between goods that are material and those that are "spiritual." Health and prosperity are pervasive goods that support other goods. Effective dealing with the physical world opens up great possibilities for the achievement of goods in education, art, friendship, and (humanistic) religion. The same method that works in natural science can work in social science and the areas where our highest aspirations are located. Success in the "lower" contributes to success in the "higher," and vice versa. While Dewey's approach is utilitarian, it is not narrowly so. "While reflective knowing is instrumental to gaining control in a troubled situation (and thus has a practical or utilitarian force), it is also instrumental to the enrichment of the immediate significance of subsequent experiences. And it may well be that this by-product, this gift of the gods, is incomparably more valuable for living a life than is the primary and intended result of control, essential as is that control for having a life to live."[110]

Dewey wants to take philosophy out of its ivory tower. He will not accept the world as it is, while finding "salvation" in a good conscience, a kingdom of God, or a realm of essences. The function of thought is neither to contemplate the world nor to flee from it. Its function is to direct the kind of action that will improve it. This injunction applies to individuals who pursue their own ends intelligently and to citizens who act with others to improve society. Thought, whether engaged in by philosopher or nonphilosopher, must grapple with the real world.

The ethical task is never completed. "The business of reflection in determining the true good cannot be done once for all, as, for instance, by making out a table of virtues in hierarchical order of higher and lower. The business of reflection needs to be done, and done over and over and over again, in terms of the conditions of concrete situations as they arise. In short, the need for reflection and insight is perpetually recurring."[111]

For Further Reading

Jeremy Bentham. *An Introduction to the Principles of Morals and Legislation.* New York: Hafner Publishing Co., 1948.

Jeremy Bentham. *Handbook of Political Fallacies.* Baltimore: Johns Hopkins Press, 1952.

Richard B. Brandt. *Ethical Theory.* Englewood Cliffs, N.J.: Prentice-Hall, 1959.

John Dewey. *Reconstruction in Philosophy.* Boston: Beacon Press, 1957.

John Dewey. *The Quest for Certainty.* New York: G. P. Putnam's Sons, 1960.

John Stuart Mill. *Utilitarianism.* Many editions.

[110]Dewey, *Essays in Experimental Logic.* See Ratner, p. 934.

[111]John Dewey and James H. Tufts, *Ethics.* See Ratner, pp. 773–774.

John Stuart Mill. *On Liberty.* Many editions.
George E. Moore. *Ethics.* London: Oxford University Press, 1912.
George E. Moore. *Principia Ethica.* Cambridge: At the University Press, 1956.
Hastings Rashdall. *The Theory of Good and Evil.* 2nd ed. London: Oxford University Press, 1924.
Joseph Ratner, ed. *Intelligence in the Modern World: John Dewey's Philosophy.* New York: Random House, 1939.

DEONTOLOGICAL THEORIES

Kant

The deontologist in ethics, as the term itself suggests, emphasizes duty.[112] Moral obligation is a primary concept, not one derived from knowing what is good or valuable. Unlike the utilitarian, the deontologist believes that an act can be right regardless of its consequences in terms of pleasure or anything else. This is a formalistic theory rather than a teleological one.

The most significant proponent of this type of ethics is the German philosopher Immanuel Kant (1724–1804). In his philosophical career, he addressed himself to three great questions. The first two are: What can I know? What ought I to do? "Two things fill the mind with ever new and increasing admiration and awe, the oftener and more steadily they are reflected on: the starry heavens above me and the moral law within me."[113]

Kant believes that there is a universal and objective moral law that issues its commands without promise of reward for the agent or beneficial consequences for others. The agent is required to obey for no other reason than the wish to perform his or her moral duty. The elements of the moral law are categorical rather than hypothetical. One such element may say: "Tell the truth." It does not say: "If you want to be trusted and respected in the community, tell the truth." Another element may say: "Do not commit suicide." It does not say: "If others are saddened by the act, do not commit suicide." If external reasons have to be provided for moral action, that action loses its moral quality. It becomes an act of prudence or benevolence instead. Only an act done for the sake of morality itself is moral. To ask the question "Why be moral?" is thoroughly wrong-headed.

Kant formulates this "categorical imperative": "Act only according to that maxim by which you can at the same time will that it should become a universal law."[114] This means that we must act in a way that is exemplary. Our actions must be consistent with what we require from others. All rational beings are subject to the same law. None can appeal to exemptions that suit his or her own particular predicament. What is fitting for one is fitting for all.

[112]The term is derived from the Greek word *deon,* which means "binding," "needful," or "obligatory."

[113]Kant, *Critique of Practical Reason,* in Beck, trans. and ed., *Critique of Practical Reason and Other Writings in Moral Philosophy,* p. 258.

[114]Kant, *Foundations of the Metaphysics of Morals,* in Beck, p. 80.

There is no need to spell out these elements of the moral law. Reason discerns the principles of moral duty.

> Without in the least teaching common reason anything new, we need only to draw its attention to its own principle, in the manner of Socrates, thus showing that neither science nor philosophy is needed in order to know what one has to do in order to be honest and good, and even wise and virtuous. We might have conjectured beforehand that the knowledge of what everyone is obliged to do and thus also to know would be within the reach of everyone, even the most ordinary man. Here we cannot but admire the great advantages which the practical faculty of judgment has over the theoretical in ordinary human understanding.[115]

As Kant showed in *Critique of Pure Reason,* it is difficult to determine what is the case; but this difficulty does not exist for the practical reason when it seeks to determine what *ought* to be the case.

Kant does, however, offer some help. If an act conforms to the agent's inclinations, it may have been done *from* inclination and thus have no moral value. But if it is done despite inclinations to the contrary, there is reason to believe that it is done from *duty.* These people have reason to believe they are acting *from* duty, not simply *in accordance with* duty: the merchant who can profitably cheat but does not, the person whose life is a burden but who maintains it nevertheless, the person who is temperamentally indifferent to the sufferings of others but still is benevolent toward them. Kant is not saying that action against our natural inclinations is either a necessary or a sufficient condition for morality. He is insisting that we resolutely keep our inclinations out of the picture when we ascertain where our duty lies.[116] A genuine moral law does not admit of exceptions.[117]

Additional help is provided by Kant in what has been called the second formulation of the categorical imperative: "Act so that you treat humanity, whether in your own person or in that of another, always as an end and never as a means only."[118] Rational beings have an absolute worth. They must be respected as subjects with dignity and freedom. The moral law forbids us to treat

[115]Ibid., p. 64.

[116]An action that accords with one's inclination can have moral import, but it is difficult for the outsider to ascertain the true motive.

[117]Kant applies the categorical imperative to particular situations in ways that are more puzzling than helpful. Promises should be kept and debts paid, for example, because if people did not do so, then no promises would be extracted or money loaned. Promises and loans would disappear. A maxim that excused not keeping promises or paying debts could not be a moral law because it would destroy itself. Other maxims seem to be rejected because they would in actual practice conflict with basic human drives that lead to happiness. Suicide cannot be right because it conflicts with the instinct of self-preservation; failure to employ one's talents cannot be right because it conflicts with the drive for self-realization. These appeals to empirical consequences and human drives do not seem to be consistent with Kant's conception of the moral law as a system of universal rules each of which is validated by its own inherent a priori propriety. If, in these applications, Kant is simply asking what would be the result if *everyone* did (or failed to do) a particular act, he is appealing to some desirable state of affairs. His theory, then, would be teleological rather than deontological.

[118]*Foundations of the Metaphysics of Morals,* p. 87.

them as objects for our own purposes. Slavery, economic exploitation, and freak shows would be wrong, and so would manipulating people in social situations or using them for sexual gratification.

The worth of a human being is related to the fact that he or she may be the locus of a *good will.* "Nothing in the world—indeed nothing even beyond the world—can possibly be conceived which could be called good without qualification except a *good will.*"[119] Good will does not mean for Kant a feeling of warmth toward others (although this is a praiseworthy thing to have). The Kantian good will is a character that is attuned to the moral law. One exhibits a good will when one heeds the moral law and carries out its injunctions. "Gifts of nature" (intelligence, temperance, wit, courage, etc.) and "gifts of fortune" (power, honor, wealth, health, etc.) are nice to have, but they may be put to "mischievous" uses. The good will, which is produced from concern for what is *right,* has absolute value. The goal of life is not to be happy, but to be *worthy* of happiness.

The will that acts for the sake of duty alone does not have to be effective in order to be good. The individual who seeks to provide care for an aged parent from a sense of duty, but fails despite his or her best efforts, yet manifests a good will.

> Even if it should happen that, by a particularly unfortunate fate or by the niggardly provision of a stepmotherly nature, this will should be wholly lacking in power to accomplish its purpose, and if even the greatest effort should not avail it to achieve anything of its end, and if there remained only the good will (not as a mere wish but as the summoning of all the means in our power), it would sparkle like a jewel with its own light, as something that had its full worth in itself.[120]

This goodness, then, is not dependent on circumstances; it is within the reach of everyone.

The function of reason in its practical aspect is to produce a good will. Practical reason overrides all desires and feelings—except the desire to obey the moral law and the feeling of reverence for the moral law. The function of practical reason is not to produce happiness—instinct would have been a more effective means—but to renounce happiness when morality is at stake. In governing and shaping the will, reason engenders good character.

What is the relation between Kant's ethics and Christian ethics? Kant distinguishes "pathological" love from "practical" love. The former is a feeling and cannot be commanded. The latter is an element of moral law and can be commanded. We do not have to love others in an emotional sense, but we are required to respect their rights and perform the duties we owe them. The former is praiseworthy, but the latter is obligatory ("morally estimable"). For the Christian, people are moral regardless of what they *do;* for Kant, they are moral regardless of what they *feel.* The respect that one owes others is for Kant also owed oneself. Some Christian viewpoints, by contrast, surrender all claims of the

[119]Ibid., p. 55.
[120]Ibid., p. 56.

self. For Kant, all people alike are under the same moral law and enjoy the same rights.[121]

Since Kant believes that the moral law applies to all rational beings, it applies to God also. Like people, God belongs to a "kingdom of ends" and is subject to the moral law in the same way that people are. God upholds an act because it is right; it is not right because God upholds it. Moral truths are not *created* by rational beings any more than are mathematical truths. They are eternal, and reason (human and divine) *apprehends* them.

Some of Kant's ethicoreligious views are indicated in his "moral postulates." These are in answer to the third question he asks himself: What may I hope? These postulates cannot be proved in any rational way, but the reality of ethical consciousness gives us grounds for hope. The first postulate is that *human beings are free.* They are not subject to the law of cause and effect in the same way other phenomena in the world of experience are subject. They feel that they can respond to moral principle in the face of psychological law. If the moral life indeed possesses the significance it seems to possess, the agent finds within himself or herself the power to override all inclinations and feelings. The second postulate is that *God exists.* There is obvious injustice in the world. The moral person is not always rewarded and the evildoer is not always punished. There is no correspondence between actual happiness and deserved happiness. If a supreme being existed, this imbalance would be corrected—somewhere, sometime. If, however, one is convinced that justice will prevail, one's motive must still be that of obedience to the moral law. To act *for the sake of* happiness (even of a supernatural kind) is to forfeit all claims for that happiness. The third postulate is that *the soul is immortal.* Since the good will is the only thing in the universe that is good without qualification, it would indeed be a tragedy if such a will were to be lost forever. The loss of a good will that has been earnestly and painfully cultivated over a lifetime is a loss not only for the individual but for the universe itself. We may hope that the good will would be preserved for its own sake and for its own greater development. If reality is what it should be, it contains autonomous beings, a just Ruler, and immortal souls.

Ross

The most effective exponent of modern deontological ethics is the late English philosopher W. D. Ross (1877–1971). His most important books are *The Right and the Good* (1930) and *Foundations of Ethics* (1939).

He quotes with approval a long passage from Joseph Butler's *Dissertation on the Nature of Virtue* (1736) in which it is argued that human beings are "constituted so as to condemn falsehood, unprovoked violence, injustice, and to approve of benevolence to some preferably to others, abstracted from all considerations,

[121]See Gerald Runkle, "Law v. Love," *Darshana International* 5:3 (July 1965), pp. 10–21.

which conduct is likeliest to produce an overbalance of happiness or misery."[122] The argument is thought by Ross to be a refutation not only of hedonistic utilitarianism but of ideal utilitarianism as well. Butler's examples include cases where the claims of gratitude, friendship, honesty, and justice are ignored in behalf of the greater good. Choice of the greater good in these cases, for Butler, conflicts with "moral understanding," "moral sense," or "conscience"; for Ross, they conflict with "what we really think on moral matters." Ross, like all deontologists, gives credence to the views of the "plain man," and he will not accept a theory whose implications run counter to what a person of good sense feels is his or her duty in a particular situation.[123] The demands of duty, according to Ross, are self-evident. They cannot be proved, but they do not *require* proof.

The chief difference between Kant's theory and that of Ross is indicated in the distinction Ross makes between "proper" or "perfect" duty on the one hand and "conditional" duty on the other. For Kant, certain duties are unconditional: they admit of no exception. For Ross, a duty, real and not illusory, is only one objective fact in a moral situation. There may be other duties involved also. "Whether an act is a duty proper or actual duty [rather than simply a conditional duty] depends on *all* the morally significant kinds it is an instance of."[124] The term that Ross chooses for conditional duties is *prima facie duties.* A prima facie duty is what our duty would be if there were no other prima facie duties of greater importance. A prima facie duty, then, is not a special *kind* of duty, but one that is relevant to a particular situation. Whether it becomes an *actual* duty will depend upon the circumstances of the particular situation. The determination is made on the basis of examination and analysis. It is worth repeating, however, that a prima facie duty is valid and real; it must be carried out if not outweighed by some other prima facie duty.

Ross lists six kinds of prima facie duties or obligations: (1) Some rest on previous acts of the agent. One subclass includes those that rest on a promise (explicit) to carry out an action, or a promise (implicit) to tell the truth in conversation and writing. These are the duties of *fidelity.* The other subclass includes those duties that rest on a previous wrongful act. These are the duties of *reparation.* (2) Some rest on previous acts done by others on behalf of the agent. These are the duties of *gratitude.* (3) Some rest on the relation of merit to the distribution of happiness. These are the duties of *justice.* (4) Some rest on the fact that there are other beings whose condition can be improved with respect to virtue, intelligence, and pleasure. These are the duties of *beneficence.* (5) Some rest on the fact that our own condition may be improved with respect to virtue

[122]Butler, quoted in Ross, *Foundation of Ethics,* p. 79.

[123]When moral decisions become more difficult, Ross tends to move from "the plain man" to "thoughtful and well-educated" people and "the verdicts of the moral consciousness of the best people."

[124]Ross, *The Right and the Good* (Oxford: Clarendon Press, 1930), pp. 19–20.

and intelligence. Pleasure could be added if we think of it as an objective good (which it is) rather than simply our own pleasure. But since the prospect of our own pleasure is usually experienced as a temptation to transgress our duty, Ross does not list it with virtue and intelligence. Strictly speaking, numbers 4 and 5 involve the same goods. But just as we are more aware of our duty to produce our *own* virtue, we are aware of our duty to produce the *other's* pleasure. "Produce the virtue of the other" is a difficult task to carry out; "produce your own pleasure" is superfluous. Thus Kant, oversimplifying somewhat, said: "Seek to make yourself good and other people happy." (6) Some rest on the fact that there are beings who can be injured by our actions. These are the duties of *nonmaleficence.*

Ross does not claim that this list is complete. What could be added, perhaps, are the prima facie duties that individuals owe members of their own family. This would be quite consistent with his recognition of "the highly personal character of duty." "If the only duty is to produce the maximum of good, the question who is to have the good—whether it is myself, or my benefactor, or a person to whom I have made a promise to confer that good on him, or a mere fellow man to whom I stand in no special relation—should make no difference to my having a duty to produce that good. But we are all in fact sure that it makes a vast difference."[125] At the same time, Ross's theory recognizes general duties also—beneficence, self-improvement, nonmaleficence—where the principle "Promote the greatest good" has limited application.

There is no ordering in this list of prima facie duties. Ross cannot say that any one of them always takes precedence over any others. If there is a conflict in particular situations between one prima facie duty and another, there is no easy way for deciding which duty is the proper one, the one that should prevail. Sometimes the first will prevail over the fourth; at other times the fourth will prevail over the first. If we have promised to keep an appointment with *X,* we may do so, despite the disappointment experienced by *Y* and *Z.* But we may break the promise in order to prevent a physical assault on *Q.* Generally, our duty not to harm others overrides the duty to promote good for others, even when doing the latter produces more good. But we can imagine situations in which we should produce *a little bit* of harm for some people when it produces *a great deal* of good for others. There is, however, no set of second-order rules prescribing the conditions under which each prima facie duty is to prevail.

What the conscientious person must do for any situation is to ascertain the prima facie duties that are involved, then determine which one (or ones) is (or are) most urgent, most pressing, most obligatory, most binding. This task of determining whether something that tends to be our duty (e.g., keeping promises) is in the particular case our *actual* duty is more difficult than the first. "Our judgements about our actual duty in concrete situations have none of the certainty

[125] Ibid., p. 22.

that attaches to our recognition of the general principles of duty."[126] After due deliberation, we come to a conclusion we hope is correct; then we act, realizing that we are taking a moral risk. "We are more likely to do our duty if we reflect to the best of our ability on the *prima facie* rightness or wrongness of various possible acts in virtue of the characteristics we perceive them to have, than if we act without reflection. With this greater likelihood we must be content." [127]

The agent cannot be blamed for doing an act that he had reason to believe was his duty and did for that reason. Morally good actions do not have to be right acts, and right acts may be done that are not morally good actions. Rightness is inherent in the act itself; moral goodness attaches to the motive. It is the former that Ross is more interested in. He has thus chosen the term *beneficence* instead of *benevolence* and *maleficence* over *malevolence* because he wants "to emphasize the fact that it is our duty to do certain things, and not to do them from certain motives."[128] He apologizes for using *fidelity* and *gratitude,* for they indicate feelings that motivate, but he can think of no better words. "It is not our duty to have certain motives, but to do certain acts."[129] Duty is objective; it can be commanded. Motivation and feelings are subjective; they cannot be commanded.

Ross points out that his theory, which requires judgment between degrees of urgency among prima facie duties, makes no greater demand on people's deliberative capacities than does ideal utilitarianism with its host of heterogenous (but commensurable) goods. Neither offers a simple and mechanical criterion for right conduct. But even if utilitarianism had the advantage on grounds of simplicity, Ross would have to reject it because he can easily imagine situations in which it is known intuitively that the *right* act is the one that happens to produce *less* good than an alternative act. If I keep my promise to *A,* I produce 1,000 units of good for him; if I break my promise to him, I produce 1,001 units of good for *B*, whom I do not even know. This is not so much a case of taking our duty as philanthropists too seriously as it is a case of taking "our duty as makers of promises too lightly."[130] Instead of producing 1,000 units of good for a very good person, should I produce 1,001 units of good for a very bad person? "Surely not. I should be sensible of a *prima facie* duty of justice, i.e., of producing a distribution of goods in proportion to merit, which is not outweighed by such slight disparity in the total goods to be produced."[131]

It is not, then, self-evident that the right and the optimific are coexistent. We may be sure that an act is prima facie right without having the faintest idea of

[126]Ibid., p. 30.
[127]Ibid., p. 32.
[128]Ibid., p. 23.
[129]Ibid., p. 22.
[130]Ibid., p. 35.
[131]Ibid. Actions that produce the greatest amount of good are called optimific.

whether it is optimific. This is how our moral judgments work, and we have nothing else to go on. That we have a prima facie duty to produce good does not mean that we have no other prima facie duties. That we have a prima facie duty not to produce harm does not mean that we should *never* produce harm.

Although utilitarians have attempted neither deductive nor inductive proofs that the observation of special duties is optimific, some have argued that the validity of a special duty derives from its optimific consequences. Keeping promises, for example, is a duty because it promotes the greatest good, and the system of mutual confidence that it upholds throughout that society in which it is practiced must be included in that good. Ross would agree on the general utility of promise-keeping, but would point out its occasional disutility. In such cases the duty to keep promises does not evaporate. "To make a promise is not merely to adopt an ingenious device for promoting the general well-being; it is to put oneself in a new relation to one person in particular, a relation which creates a specifically new *prima facie* duty to him, not reducible to the duty of promoting the general well-being of society."[132] "The strengthening or weakening the fabric of mutual confidence" has been greatly exaggerated. We can conceive of particular cases where the strengthened confidence is greatly outweighed by evils and the weakened confidence outweighed by goods, so promise-keeping would not always be a duty on utilitarian grounds. In any event, one who breaks a promise at the end of one's life in a situation where there are no effects on others or on "the general confidence" would have failed to do one's duty.[133]

"I conclude," writes Ross, "that the attributes 'right' and 'optimific' are not identical, and that we do not know either by intuition, by deduction, or by induction that they coincide in their application, still less that the latter is the foundation of the former. It must be added, however, that if we are ever under no special obligation such as that of fidelity to a promise or of gratitude to a benefactor, we ought to do what will produce most good; and that even when we are under a special obligation the tendency of acts to promote general good is one of the main factors in determining whether they are right."[134]

Although Ross's target is what we have called "act utilitarianism," much that he says can be urged against "rule utilitarianism" also. If, as Ross says, the agent apprehends his or her duty to others in a direct and personal way, quite apart from the consequences of the particular act, it would also seem to follow that this apprehension would be independent of the consequences of *the particular rule* that the act is an instance of. The agent knows that it is right to meet this obligation so long as other obligations do not override it in this particular situation. The deontologist would be pleased that a particular duty enjoys the support

[132]Ibid., p. 38.
[133]Both deontologists and rule utilitarians question the rightness of certain actions done in situations where there will not be significant social consequences. "Why," they ask, "should an act be acceptable when done in secret but be wrong when others know about it?"
[134]Ibid., p. 39.

of a general rule, but would object to the claim that this rule owes its validity to the contention that society would have more good if everyone obeyed the rule rather than some other one. It is conceivable that a society that ignored merit in distributing its goods would contain a greater total good than one that did not, but the deontologist might nonetheless adhere to Ross's third prima facie duty. It is conceivable that a society that ignored special duties between members of a family would contain more goods than one that did not (Plato thought so), but the deontologist would hold that an important duty had been discarded. Rule utilitarianism, in short, misconstrues the basis for the duties it accepts and threatens the existence of others that it should accept. For all deontologists, Kant, Butler, Ross, and others, the concept of *right* is fundamental, and it cannot be reduced to the good consequences of acts or rules.

For Further Reading

Lewis White Beck, trans. and ed. Kant's *Critique of Practical Reason and Other Writings in Moral Philosophy.* Chicago: University of Chicago Press, 1949.

Brand Blanshard. *Reason and Goodness.* London: Allen & Unwin, 1961. Chapter 6.

Joseph Butler. *Dissertation upon Virtue.* Edited by A. Selby-Bigge. *British Moralists.* Oxford: Clarendon Press, 1897. Vol. 1.

Oliver A. Johnson. *Rightness and Goodness.* The Hague: Martinus Nijhoff, 1959.

Immanuel Kant. *Foundations of the Metaphysics of Morals.* Many editions.

Herbert J. Paton. *The Categorical Imperative: A Study in Kant's Moral Philosophy.* London: Hutchinson's Universal Library, 1946.

W. David Ross. *Foundations of Ethics.* Oxford: Clarendon Press, 1939.

W. David Ross. *The Right and the Good.* Oxford: Clarendon Press, 1930.

Chapter 2

SEX

The individual must make many choices in his or her sexual life. Some choices have ethical significance. If one intends to lead an ethical life, one must make these choices on the basis of intelligent thought. They must be made in the light of what seems to be true and relevant ethical principles. In the area of sexual behavior, as in all areas of conscious behavior, Horace Mann's observation holds: "Virtue is an angel, but she is a blind one, and must ask of Knowledge to show her the pathway that leads to her goal."[1]

Why, in this task of examining our life, do we start with sex? Sexual behavior has traditionally been thought of as endowed with special moral significance. When someone is called "immoral," it is usually the person's *sexual* behavior that is being questioned. We never suspect that a person arrested on a "morals charge" has been discovered embezzling money. Whether sexual morality is the most fundamental aspect of ethics or not, it is a good place to start—simply because many people believe it is.

Perhaps a better reason to start with sex is that it is a very personal kind of conduct. As we move into other issues, we will find that they become increasingly social. We start with sexual problems and conclude with problems of war and peace.

Of the many sexual issues that could be cited, three have been selected for discussion here: premarital sexual intercourse, extramarital sexual intercourse, and sexual "perversions." Are actions of these types moral, immoral, or morally indifferent? For whom? Under what circumstances? Always? Sometimes?

For each issue, conflicting points of view are presented. The reader must, on the basis of his or her reasoning ability and knowledge, choose the point of view that seems to him or her to be closer to the truth. We are all, in some sense, sexual beings. The issues cannot be evaded.

[1]Horace Mann, *A Few Thoughts for a Young Man.*

PREMARITAL SEX

Premarital Sex Is Immoral

Early Christianity Christianity clearly teaches that premarital sexual intercourse is immoral. Jesus, Paul, the four great Fathers of the Latin Church, the medieval schoolmen, and the great Protestant reformers of the sixteenth and seventeenth centuries have agreed in condemning it. The Catholic Church and all major Protestant denominations today still condemn it.

Though it would be erroneous to construe the sixth beatitude ("blessed are the pure in heart")[2] in a narrowly sexual way, Jesus did oppose fornication. In the account added to the eighth chapter of John, Jesus saved the erring woman from stoning ("Let him who is without sin among you be the first to throw a stone at her") and told her that he did not "condemn" her. He is reported to have said, however, "go and sin no more." That Jesus was willing to forgive harlots and fornicators (and even argue that they were not as bad as the Pharisees) does not mean that he approved of their conduct. His view, rather, was this: Even the fornicators, *if they repent,* may enter the Kingdom.

The fighting edge of early Christianity was most often directed at the sexual promiscuity, not only countenanced, but celebrated by the pagan religions. The fertility rites of the Babylonian and Phoenician religions were widely practiced —sometimes by the Hebrews themselves. Nor were the Olympian gods known for their chastity. The temple of Aphrodite at Corinth utilized the services of hundreds of temple prostitutes. The Roman brothels were notorious, the word *fornication* deriving from *fornix,* the arch or vault of underground brothels. Against pagan permissiveness, the early Christians sought to establish a code of sexual purity. Matthew Arnold regarded chastity and charity as the distinguishing marks of early Christianity.[3]

Paul, in his letters to the churches throughout the Hellenistic world, inveighed against sexual transgressions:

> Therefore God gave [the pagan idolators] up in the lusts of their hearts to impurity, to the dishonoring of their bodies. . . .[4]
>
> Now the works of the flesh are plain: immorality, impurity, licentiousness. . . .
>
> But immorality and all impurity or covetousness must not even be named among you. . . .[6]

[2]Matthew 5:18. All Biblical quotations are from the Revised Standard Version.
[3]It is perhaps because of Christian denunciations of sexual immorality that "immorality" today in Christian countries nearly always means unethical *sexual* behavior.
[4]Romans 1:24.
[5]Galatians 5:19.
[6]Ephesians 5:3.

> Put to death therefore what is earthly in you: immorality, impurity, passion, evil desire. . . .[7]

> For this is the will of God, your sanctification, that you abstain from immorality; that each one of you know how to take a wife for himself in holiness and honor. . . .[8]

For Paul, the suppression of lust was an essential part of the Christian task to cast off the "old man" and grow in grace as a child of God. The sinful body, crucified with Christ, is to be replaced by a sanctified spirit, increasingly Christ-like, at peace with itself and with God. Only when the spirit triumphs over the flesh can the individual enter the kingdom of God.

Premarital sex is a conspicuous example of the triumph of the flesh over the spirit. To engage in it is to indulge our earthly passion instead of seeking our transcendent glory. It is to accept bondage to our bodily passions instead of living freely in the spirit. A person who engages in illicit sex cannot be the vessel of the Holy Spirit. He or she has embraced the world of time and death.

It is sometimes the case that "the spirit is willing but the flesh is weak." One may, despite one's best intentions, succumb to temptation. The demands of Christian morality are very high, and the transformation to spiritual righteousness is not easy. It is one thing to succumb and feel guilt and vow to sin no more. It is something else to seek sexual experience and make it an accepted part of one's life. One who sins, despite his or her best efforts, can be forgiven. One who sins with impunity cannot be forgiven. In short, whatever Christians manage to *do,* they must condemn in their hearts actions of unlawful sexual activity.

Augustine Saint Augustine, the greatest of the Church Fathers, had a clear and dramatic view of the immorality of sexual activity. He, like Paul and Jesus, chose to be celibate. Recognizing, however, the power of sexual lust, he permitted marriage for others. Paul supplied him with the reason: "It is better to be married than to burn."[9] Sex in marriage was to be for the purpose of procreation. Sex outside marriage was for Augustine the mortal sin of fornication.[10]

Augustine used the word *lust* in a very broad sense, to cover all unlawful yearnings. Lust first appeared in Eden as a punishment for Adam's and Eve's disobedience. It is the condition of a disordered soul, a soul without direction, unity, and peace. Lust in the narrower sense early manifested itself in the Garden when Adam in his nakedness found he could not control his sexual organs. For Augustine, sexual lust was always the most conspicuous and degrading form of that more general lust which is the human being's mortal condition as the result

[7]Colossians 3:5.

[8]1 Thessalonians 4:3–4.

[9]1 Corinthians 7:8.

[10]Sex in marriage when procreation is not the intent was merely a venial sin. A *mortal* sin results in spiritual death. A *venial* sin does not; it is more easily forgiven.

of the Fall from grace. Some phrases for it used by Augustine are "the disease of concupiscence," "the fire of lascivious indulgence," "the shame of nuptial pleasures," "the obscenity of mortal man."

But Augustine, like Paul, looked to salvation through Christ. The requirements of Christianity are indeed high and are beyond the power of mortals. How indeed can human beings practice the kind of boundless love for all taught by Jesus? How can finite beings become perfect as God himself is perfect? And how can healthy young men and women, their sexual drives strong and insistent, postpone intercourse until marriage? The answer to all these questions is that they cannot—unaided. The "good news" of the Gospel is that aid is available, supernatural aid. If faith can move mountains, it can calm the raging seas of human concupiscence.

Augustine sees the human condition to be that of membership in one of two cities. Some of us belong to the earthly city, where lust, pride, wealth, war, and glory are celebrated. These people carry their sins to the grave and to hell. Some of us, however, belong to the heavenly city, or the City of God, where chastity, love, humbleness, and peace are our ideals. These people are in the world but not of it. They are pilgrims on their way to an eternal kingdom. They seek God and grow in grace. Inhabitants of the visible city remain children of Adam. Inhabitants of the invisible city become children of God.

Procreation Why is sex in marriage permissible while sex before marriage is not? Certain obvious prudential and social reasons may be given (disease, unwanted pregnancy, public approbrium), but an adept libertine can deal with these. The real reason is that sexual intercourse is a natural function designed by God for the purpose of reproducing the species. Even before the Fall in the Garden, God intended that human beings reproduce. In his goodness, he has conjoined pleasure with this (and most other) natural functions. People who regard pleasure instead of procreation as the end err as foolishly as those who believe that royalties are the objective of the dedicated poet rather than the poem. They abstract an accompanying feeling from the act and ignore what the act essentially is. They pursue the shadow and forget the substance.

Now, if the true purpose of sexual activity is procreation, it must take place in a family unit. The fruit of the union will have a mother and a father. The parents are committed to one another for life, and to the family they head. People who marry have created a union that is consecrated by the church and the state. The man and woman have placed themselves in an institution where the natural result of their sexual activity finds a home, parental nurture, and social blessing. A new social unit has come into existence where the existence of all is enhanced. The feeling of love deepens, and the richness of life made possible by a permanent and intimate relationship develops. Sexual intercourse is only one part of a glorious whole. In short, when sexual intercourse contributes to a worthy institution, it is permissible. When, on the other hand, it is sought simply for its own delights, it is a falling away from our spiritual goal and is immoral.

The "angelic doctor," Saint Thomas Aquinas, insisted that sexual relations be confined to married couples, and recent popes have restated his position and his arguments. But the view that sexual intercourse is designed by God for procreation and that procreation fitly takes place only in marriage is found in the writings of the great Reformers as well. Martin Luther holds the view and offers some additional considerations as well:

> It is no slight boon that in wedlock fornication and unchastity are checked and eliminated. This in itself is so great a good that it alone should be enough to induce men to marry forthwith, and for many reasons. The first reason is that fornication destroys not only the soul but also body, property, honor, and family as well. For we see how a licentious and wicked life not only brings great disgrace but is also a spendthrift life, more costly than wedlock, and that illicit partners necessarily occasion greater suffering for one another than do married folk. Beyond that it consumes the body, corrupts flesh and blood, nature, and physical constitution. Through such a variety of evil consequences God takes a rigid position, as though he would actually drive people away from fornication and into marriage. However, few are thereby convinced or converted.[11]

> Many think they can evade marriage by having their fling for a time, and then becoming righteous. My dear fellow, if one in a thousand succeeds in this, that would be doing very well. He who intends to lead a chaste life had better begin early, and attain it not with but without fornication, either by the grace of God or through marriage. We see only too well how they make out every day. It might well be called plunging into immorality rather than growing to maturity. It is the devil who has brought this about, and coined such damnable sayings as, "One has to play the fool at least once"; or, "He who does it not in his youth does it in his old age"; or, "A young saint, and old devil." Such are the sentiments of the poet Terence and other pagans. This is heathenish; they speak like heathens, yea, like devils.[12]

Sexual Idealism Religious arguments are not the only ones that can be offered against premarital sex. Someone who believes that sexual experience is very valuable and not limited to generation may still hold that it should be reserved for sharing with a spouse. Sara Ruddick presents an excellent description of "complete sex" which goes beyond its hedonistic value. She speaks of a partner allowing himself "to be 'taken over' by an active desire, which is desire not merely for the other's body but also for his active desire." "Complete sex acts occur when each partner's embodying desire is active and actively responsive to the other's." They are "conducive to emotions that, if they become stable and dominant, are in turn conducive to the virtue of loving; and they involve a preeminent moral virtue—respect for persons."[13] "Complete sex" thus goes far beyond satisfying a localized itch: it opens up an ideal development for those who engage in it.

[11]Luther, *The Estate of Marriage* (1522), pp. 43–44.
[12]Ibid., pp. 44–45.
[13]Sara Ruddick, "Better Sex," in Baker and Elliston, eds., *Philosophy & Sex*, pp. 87, 88, 98.

Now, this does not in itself prove that sex should occur only in marriage (and Ruddick does not draw such a conclusion). But it does take it out of the realm of casual encounters. The tenderness and intimacy of sexual relations, the full embodiment of the sexual passion in oneself and one's reciprocating partner, the love and respect accorded the other, all these characteristic of "complete sex" are more likely to be found in a married state than in a relation where no great commitment has taken place. Those who seek "complete sex" apart from marriage may find it, but they may find instead simply a "one-night stand" or a succession thereof. This is not only disappointing but profoundly disillusioning as well.

To react against Augustine and others who preach of the evil of the flesh does not, then, necessarily place us in the position of defending premarital sex. It does place us in the position of seeing the sexual experience as something very pleasant, very good, and potentially ennobling. But the more we idealize it, the more reason we have to ask ourself whether it is something we would wish to share with a person who has not vowed to be our lifelong and exclusive partner.

The sexual impulse is not, after all, a drive that is uncontrollable. Its demands can be resisted and its satisfaction postponed. The sexual drive has too often been compared to the drive to eat and drink. But there is one great difference. One cannot live without food and drink, but one *can* live without sexual intercourse.

It was not a puritan but Freud himself who showed us how the sexual instinct can be transformed or directed into other outlets. Unmarried people can sublimate their sexual urges into more acceptable channels, such as artistic creation. The unsatisfied sexual drive does not have to "fester" and operate destructively. Even when individuals marry, they may want to ration their sexual expression if they intend significantly to contribute to civilization and culture.[14]

Premarital Sex Is Not Always Immoral

Christianity The chief moral argument against premarital sexual intercourse is based on Christian ethics.[15] But if one does not profess to be a Christian, one is not bound by Christian restrictions.

Even one who does profess to be a Christian does not have to be a Christian of the orthodox sort exemplified by Augustine and Martin Luther—or even by the apostle Paul. Jesus himself had very little to say about premarital sexual intercourse, and his few recorded remarks on sexual behavior in general are subject to varying interpretations. It is probably true that he lived a celibate life, but the fact that he did not choose to engage in sex does not mean that he thought it was wrong. He did not engage in chariot-racing either. Although the older tradition persists and underlies many of our institutions and mores, enlightened

[14]See Freud, *Civilization and Its Discontents*, 4.

[15]"The fact of having made sex into a 'problem' is the major negative achievement of Christendom." Comfort, *Sex in Society*, p. 54.

and liberal conceptions of modern Protestant Christianity have tended to move away from the "orthodoxy" outlined in the previous section.

One does not have to show that premarital sex is an *obligation* in order to defend it. One merely has to show that it is not wrong. It is simply one of many things that one may do if one so desires without having to believe that one has committed a mortal sin or violated a moral principle. Nor does one have to defend a life of promiscuity and profligacy. Seen in the light of the Aristotelian and Deweyan philosophies, premarital sexual intercourse practiced in moderation and with intelligence can be, for those who choose it, a rewarding experience free of stigma.

Humanism The sexual impulse is firmly rooted in human nature. Sexual intercourse is one of the functions of human beings. Thomas Aquinas, in returning to a naturalistic view of sexual intercourse, recognizes this; he counteracted the views of Paul and Augustine, who deplored it as the lust of "fallen humanity." But in restricting sexual intercourse to procreation, he looked to its results rather than to the experience itself. If sexual intercourse in order to be "natural" must have procreation as its conscious aim, very few people, in wedlock or out, would be behaving "naturally" when they engaged in it. The implication of Aquinas's restricted sense of "natural" is to brand most sexual acts as "unnatural."[16] Aquinas has returned to Aristotle only to emasculate him.

Performance of the sexual function, whatever its intended results, gives the individual a sense of vital well-being, *eudaimonia*, happiness. The pleasures of sexual intercourse accompany a natural activity the performance of which provides satisfaction and a heightened sense of biological and psychological health.

These pleasures are not to be lightly esteemed. They are important and beneficial. They do not, however, have to be conceived in a narrow sense. There is pleasure in eating and drinking also, but only the epicure or gourmet abstracts this pleasure and focuses on it as his prime target. The individual who can think only of the delight of foreplay and the ecstasy of orgasm misses much of the satisfaction and excitement that sexuality can provide. Sexuality involves the whole body, as well as the human personality with all its perceptions, memories, associations, sympathies, and ideals. "The experience of sensual pleasures, and particularly of sexual pleasure, has a pervasive effect on our perceptions of the world. We find bodies inviting, social encounters alluring, and smells, tastes, and sights resonant because our perception of them includes their sexual significance."[17]

[16]"Adultery in your heart is committed not only when you look with excessive desire at a woman who is not your wife, but also when you look in the same manner at your wife." Pope John Paul II, October 8, 1980.

[17]Ruddick, p. 87.

There is another way that commitment to sexual intercourse can distort Aristotle's humanistic ideal. This occurs when sexual intercourse is made the main objective in life to the exclusion of other vital potentialities. All-around self-development is forfeited, and the individual's life loses its balance and harmony. The man who makes a career out of getting girls into bed with him or the woman who bestows her sexual favors promiscuously falls short of the humanistic ideal. There are all kinds of natural functions. No one, unless it is that of rational development, should dominate all others.

The opposite kind of obsession is almost as bad. To try to inhibit a natural drive completely is to be at war with oneself: one incurs the pain of guilt and loss of self-esteem. In trying to destroy the drive, one gratuitously creates an enemy. One alienates part of oneself, a part that now threatens one as a satanic power. All this results from giving one natural drive more importance than it deserves. In trying to suppress our sexuality, we deny our humanity.[18]

Sublimation as a solution for sexual expression is too facile. Even Freud admitted that this was difficult for most people. Kinsey wrote:

> A great many persons have tried to establish their sexual lives on the assumption that sublimation is possible, and the outcome desirable.... Fundamentally apathetic persons are the ones who are most often moral (conforming to the *mores*), most insistent that it is a simple matter to control sexual response, and most likely to offer themselves as examples of the possibility of the diversion of probably non-existent sexual energies. But such inactivity is no more sublimation ... than blindness, deafness or other perceptive defects. If ... one removes those who are physically incapacitated, natively low in sexual desire, sexually unawakened in their younger years, separated from their usual sources of stimulation, or timid and upset by their repressions, there are simply no cases which remain as clear-cut examples of sublimation.[19]

In fact, most normally endowed individuals will seek some other sexual outlet (most often masturbation) when a sexual partner is unavailable.[20]

Between the excesses of overindulgence and total abstinence, Aristotle would recommend a "golden mean." Sexual intercourse in moderation has a contribution to make to the ideal of self-realization. One should not permit the sexual drive to take over one's life, but there are dangers, too, in trying to extirpate it. Somewhere between the extremes of a Casanova and Saint Simeon the lives of most of us should fall.

[18]For a discussion of the dangers of Christian morality for mental health, see Freud, " 'Civilized' Sexual Morality and Modern Nervous Illness," in James Strachey, ed., *The Standard Edition of the Complete Works of Sigmund Freud* (London: Hogarth Press, 1959), vol. 9. See also Reich, *The Sexual Revolution* (trans. Pol), part 1 ("The Fiasco of Compulsory Sexual Morality").

[19]Kinsey et al., *Sexual Behavior in the Human Male,* pp. 207–213.

[20]A related fallacy should also be corrected: People who do engage in sexual activity do not thereby reduce their artistic, academic, athletic, or professional output.

There are good reasons in our society for postponing marriage to a point well beyond the time when sexual urges manifest themselves. There is an education to be completed, a job to be acquired. Some people may decide not to get married at all, and society no longer frowns upon the single person. Are these individuals to be deprived of a normal sexual life and the humanistic ideal to which it contributes? According to the opponents of premarital sex, they would be obligated to live a celibate life.

The golden mean chosen by a single person might be somewhat different from that chosen by a married person, just as the golden mean selected by a person with extremely strong sexual urges might differ from that chosen by one with moderate sexual urges. But the single person, too, has a right to aspire to "vital well-being" and to make his or her sexual activity play a part in a harmonious life. Rather than sustain a marriage, the person's sexual expression may be the basis of an intimate relationship that benefits both parties. Or it may simply be a part of a friendship or several friendships or a succession of friendships, all of which contribute to the happiness of the people involved.[21] The kinds of rewarding life styles that sexual expression may contribute to vary. For Aristotle, every ideal has its natural base, but every natural base has several ideal realizations.[22]

Prudence An adherent of Dewey's ethics at this point would counsel intelligence. Few activities are fraught with so many potentially harmful consequences as sexual activity. This is especially true in a Christian society that condemns nonmarital sex. But Dewey would not say, "If you can't be good, be careful." And this is because being careful is *part* of being good.

The two most obvious dangers are disease[23] and pregnancy. It may seem strange that this is so at a time when protections and cures are available for venereal disease and contraceptives can be easily purchased in a drugstore. But the facts are that venereal disease has not been stamped out, that some individuals cannot recognize its symptoms, and that some do not seek treatment. And it is also true that hundreds of thousands of unwanted pregnancies occur annually in this country. It is not premarital sex that is wrong, but stupid premarital sex.[24]

There are some people who should not engage in premarital sex, not because of their stupidity, but because of their level of maturity. Lacking extensive experi-

[21]The stereotype of the rampant young man who wants to "score" does not have to be the model here.

[22]It is perhaps because the early Christians saw very little of the golden mean in the dissolute empire that they derogated sex per se.

[23]"The introduction of syphilis into Europe by the crew of Columbus's expeditions was perhaps the greatest godsend to the religious conception of sexual morality, history could possibly have provided." Comfort, p. 77.

[24]It should not be inferred from this that the problems of infection and pregnancy are always easily solved. Some strains of venereal disease have proved resistant to the usual cures, and some "new" diseases (e.g., nongonococcal urethritis) have appeared on the scene. And some contraceptives are not "foolproof" and/or have possible harmful side effects. But intelligent caution can relieve most of us from undue worry. "The role of technology is surely to make its [sex's] reproductive side more controllable and its play function more available." Ibid., p. 83.

ence in human relations, they are apt to expect too much or too little from their partners. They are also likely to misjudge the character and feelings of other people.

Young people seek peer approval. Some of them engage in sex because their friends do. Others refrain from sex because their friends do. Neither of these reasons is legitimate. People who indulge should do so because they are convinced that it is right (or not wrong), and those who refrain should also rely on moral principles. Young people should not become sexually active until they have given serious thought to the matter. Many young people, subject to peer pressure, engage before they really have reasoned out that it is right. They thus become victims of guilt and loss of self-esteem. Despite peer approval, they are going against parental upbringing and social mores, and they know it. A feeling of independence and responsibility must always precede unconventional behavior. No one can really condemn them for *not* having intercourse—even their peers will respect this behavior. So until they have thought about the ethical import of the whole issue, they would be far safer to refrain. Precisely what the real age of consent is, cannot be stated. Individuals progress to responsible adulthood at different speeds.

Once a person has decided that there are no compelling ethical reasons to refrain from premarital activity, he or she may assume there is no more need for responsible ethical thinking. This would be a serious mistake. The reasoned conviction that premarital sex is not in itself wrong provides no guidance to the question whether premarital sex with *this* person, at *this* time, and under *these* circumstances is wrong. To answer these more specific questions, questions even more specific have to be raised and answered. For example:

1. Do I like this person enough to share physical intimacies?
2. Will intercourse place me in a relationship I will not be comfortable in?
3. Will intercourse place the other in a relationship that is uncomfortable?
4. Will intercourse have an adverse effect on my reputation?
5. Will loss of virginity now embarrass me later when I marry?
6. Will intercourse with this person harm a valued relationship I have with someone else?
7. Am I being used by the other simply as a means for the expression of this person's lust?
8. Am I using the other simply as a means for the expression of my lust?
9. Will I remember this experience as joyous and beautiful or as furtive and tawdry?

The position here outlined, then, is that while premarital sex is not always wrong, it is not always right.

Conclusion This discussion has been very prosaic. It is indeed a far cry from the poetic view of the sexual union. Instead of talking about bliss, we have advised caution. Instead of emphasizing romance, we have employed causal reasoning. Instead of heeding the heart, we have recommended dispassionate thought. The whole approach sounds altogether too calculating. Leander would never have swum the Hellespont to spend the night with his beloved if *this* had been his philosophy!

But the fact is that to deal with the issue of sexual intercourse in any other way is to court disaster. Passion and feeling may exist, and if it does, it should be taken into account. But somewhere in the background, the mind must operate and see the affair in factual terms and issue its commands on the basis of reason. Too many times have individuals lived to rue the moment they plunged into a sexual relationship whose results were destructive. If the heart cannot distinguish the "satisfying" from the "unsatisfactory," the mind must.

Perhaps some of the excitement of premarital sex can be captured by recalling Dewey's basic approach to ethics. He tells us not to be bound by convention. We should look to the future instead of to the past. There are no certainties to guide us. The soundness of our choices are established by their success in action. Ethics is an experimental enterprise. In all our acts we take a chance. And in unconventional action, we take a greater chance. Maybe there is something wondrous to be gained!

Summary of the Issues

Premarital sex is condemned by orthodox Christianity as a case of indulgence of the flesh at the expense of spiritual development. The only purpose of sexual intercourse is procreation; and procreation should take place only in marriage, for children should be born in a family and reared by a family. A more liberal version of Christianity, however, might hold that premarital sex can be an expression of love and that procreation need not be its aim.

Premarital sex may be approved by humanism as a case of exercising natural capacities. For a healthy person to deny himself or herself this healthy outlet is to miss an important joyful experience and perhaps to court personality disorders. The sexual desire is a powerful one; that it can be handled by "sublimation" is improbable. Another version of humanism, however, stresses procreation as the purpose of sexual activity. Recreational sex, therefore, is natural or humanistic only in a very superficial way.

Both sides favor sexual relations between people who have made a commitment to one another and view the pleasures of sex as part of a richer legacy of understanding and shared experience. Neither condones the single-minded pursuit or casual appropriation of sexual pleasure in total disregard of the other values present in human intimacy. But the opponents of premarital sex believe that this condition can be met only in marriage, while the advocates of premarital sex believe that the condition can be met whenever individuals have affection and respect for one another.

Both sides are alert to the many dangers and disabilities for individuals in our society who engage in premarital sex. It is very difficult for the young and inexperienced to deal with the personal and social problems that premarital sex generates. The advocate of premarital sex, however, believes that people who are intelligent, cautious, and prudent can deal with them and find premarital sex a rewarding experience. If undesirable consequences provide the only argument against premarital sex, the individual who manages to avoid them has done nothing wrong.

Discussion Questions

1. Epicurus believes that sex, a natural but unnecessary desire, is more bother than it is worth. Do you agree?
2. If you were convinced that a sexual encounter would produce "the greatest happiness for the greatest number," would you necessarily choose it? Why?
3. What do you think a "rule utilitarian" would say about premarital sex? Would you agree? Why?
4. What do you think a high school course in sex education should teach? Why?
5. How strongly do you think Jesus felt about premarital sex?
6. Do you agree with Paul and Augustine that sex is inherently bad? Why?
7. Do you agree with Aquinas that sex (while good) should always be engaged in for purposes of procreation? Why?
8. Aristippus would engage in sexual relations solely for the pleasures involved. Is he right?
9. Do you see anything inherently wrong with recreational sex where there is no personal commitment between the partners? Explain.
10. In your opinion could Kant plausibly sponsor a categorical imperative against premarital sex? Explain.
11. Which do you think is a better injunction: "Express your humanity." "Surpass your humanity." Explain.
12. What prima facie duties do you think might become relevant in relations between two actual or potential sexual partners?
13. Can you think of any ethical theory that would justify the double standard in evaluating premarital sex? Explain.
14. Do you see any ethical difference between married and unmarried partners engaging in recreational sex? Explain.
15. Do you see any ethical difference between "committed" and "uncommitted" partners engaging in premarital sex? Explain.
16. Do you see any ethical difference between close friends and casual acquaintances engaging in premarital sex? Explain.
17. If you believe that premarital sex is wrong, how far down in the list of sins would you place it? Explain.
18. If you think that chastity is good, how high in the list of virtues would you place it? Explain.
19. What would an "ideal utilitarian" say about chastity? Do you agree? Why?
20. Is a rich and rewarding sexual relationship possible only when the partners are married? Explain.
21. To what extent do you believe that the sexual drive can be sublimated?
22. Do you believe that if the sexual drive is not expressed or sublimated, it could create personality disorders?

23. Under what circumstances, if any, do you believe that premarital sex would be ethically acceptable? Explain.
24. What ethical judgment do you make of your friends who engage in premarital sex?
25. Do you think that God prohibits premarital sex? Why do you believe this?

For Further Reading

(Works designated with an asterisk are relevant to all three sections of this chapter.)

*T. H. Adamowski. "Character and Consciousness: D. H. Lawrence, Wilhelm Reich, and Jean-Paul Sartre." *University of Toronto Quarterly* 43 (Summer 1974):311–334.

*Ronald Atkinson. *Sexual Morality.* New York: Harcourt, Brace & World, 1965.

Augustine. *On Continence.* In Philip Schaff, ed., *A Select Library of the Nicene and Post-Nicene Fathers.* Grand Rapids, Mich.: Wm. B. Eerdmans Publishing Co., 1956. Vol. 3.

Augustine. *On Marriage and Concupiscence.* In Philip Schaff, ed., *A Select Library of the Nicene and Post-Nicene Fathers.* Grand Rapids, Mich.: Wm. B. Eerdmans Publishing Co., 1956. Vol. 5.

*Derrick S. Bailey. *Sexual Ethics.* New York: Macmillan, 1963.

Robert Baker and Frederick Elliston, eds. *Philosophy & Sex.* Buffalo: Prometheus Books, 1975. See especially: Sara Ruddick, "Better Sex"; D. P. Verene, "Sexual Love and Moral Experience"; Bernard H. Baumrin, "Sexual Immorality Delineated"; Frederick Elliston, "In Defense of Promiscuity."

Robert R. Bell. *Premarital Sex in a Changing Society.* Englewood Cliffs, N.J.: Prentice-Hall, 1966.

D. G. Berger and M. G. Wenger. "Ideology of Virginity." *Journal of Marriage and the Family* 35 (November 1973):666–676.

Paul Blanshard. "Christianity and Sex." *The Humanist* 34 (March 1974):27–32.

*Edward M. Brecher. *The Sex Researchers.* New York: New American Library, 1961.

K. L. Cannon and R. Long. "Premarital Sexual Behavior in the Sixties." *Journal of Marriage and the Family* 33 (February 1971):36–49.

*D. R. Cartlidge. "I Corinthians 7 as a Foundation for a Christian Sex Ethic." *Journal of Religion* 55 (April 1975):220–234.

*J. T. Clemons. "Toward a Christian Affirmation of Human Sexuality." *Religion in Life* 43 (Winter 1974):425–435.

*Alex Comfort. "Sex in Society." Secaucus, N.J.: Citadel Press, 1975.

J. F. and A. R. D'Augelli. "Moral Reasoning and Premarital Sexual Behavior." *Journal of Social Issues* 33, no. 2 (1977):46–66.

*V. A. Demant. *Christian Sex Ethics.* New York: Harper & Row, 1963.

Evelyn Miller Duvall. *Why Wait till Marriage?* New York: Association Press, 1965.

*Albert Ellis. *Sex without Guilt.* New York: Lyle Stuart, 1958.

Sigmund Freud. *Civilization and Its Discontents.* Translated by James Strachey. New York: W. W. Norton, 1962.

*"Frontiers of Sex Research" (symposium). *The Humanist* 38 (March 1978):8–43.

*Chad Gordon and Gayle Johnson, eds. *Readings in Human Sexuality. Contemporary Perspectives*. New York: Harper & Row, 1976.

R. Haughton. "Towards a Christian Theology of Sexuality." *Cross Currents* 28 (Fall 1978):288–298.

P. Hebblethwaite. "Faith, Hope and Chastity." *Times Literary Supplement* no. 3879 (July 16, 1976):891.

M. E. Heltsley and C. B. Broderick. "Religiosity and Premarital Sexual Permissiveness." *Journal of Marriage and the Family* 32 (November 1970):647–655.

*Hans F. Hofmann. *Sex Incorporated: A Positive View of the Sexual Revolution.* Boston: Beacon Press, 1967.

*Alfred C. Kinsey et al. *Sexual Behavior in the Human Female.* New York: Pocket Books, 1965.

*Alfred C. Kinsey et al. *Sexual Behavior in the Human Male.* Philadelphia: W. B. Saunders Co., 1949.

Martin Luther. *The Estate of Marriage.* In Walther I. Brandt, ed., *Luther's Works*. Philadelphia: Muhlenberg Press, 1962. Vol. 45.

J. L. Lyness et al. "Living Together: An Alternative to Marriage." *Journal of Marriage and the Family* 34 (May 1972):305–311.

*R. M. Morantz. "Scientist as Sex Crusader: Alfred C. Kinsey and American Culture." *American Quarterly* 29 (Winter 1977):563–589.

*Herbert A. Otto, ed. *The New Sexuality.* Palo Alto, Calif.: Science and Behavior Books, 1971.

Norman Pittenger. *Love and Control in Sexuality.* Philadelphia: Pilgrim Press, 1974.

T. Platt. "Christian Sexual Ethics: The Incomplete Revolution." *Encounter* 35 (Winter 1974):58–68. Reply by R. Duncan, 35 (Summer 1974):262–267.

P. Ramsey. "Do You Know Where Your Children Are?" *Theology Today* 36 (April 1979): 10–21.

*Wilhelm Reich. *The Sexual Revolution.* Translated by Therese Pol. New York: Touchstone Books, Simon & Schuster, 1974. Part 1.

*J. A. T. Robinson. *Christian Morals Today.* Philadelphia: Westminster Press, 1964.

J. J. Teevan. "Reference Groups and Premarital Sexual Behavior." *Journal of Marriage and the Family* 34 (May 1972):283–291.

*Helmut Thielicke. *The Ethics of Sex.* Translated by John Dobenstein. New York: Harper & Row, 1964.

*C. Warren, ed. "Sexuality: Encounters, Identities, and Relationships" (symposium). *Urban Life* 5 (October 1976):267–396.

*John C. Wynn, ed. *Sexual Ethics and Christian Responsibility*. New York: Association Press, 1970.

S. Uroda. "Christian Considerations for Sexual Decision-making." *Encounter* 38 (Winter 1977):72–80.

EXTRAMARITAL SEX

Extramarital Sex Is Immoral

Jews and Christians The Judeo-Christian tradition of our society has consistently regarded extramarital sexual intercourse as immoral. The Seventh Commandment says: "You shall not commit adultery."[25] The Tenth Commandment enjoins the Jew and the Christian not to covet his neighbor's wife.[26] These are commands of God, and who has a better right to command than he? The penalty prescribed for adultery by Mosaic law is death for both persons.[27] King David was not executed for his adultery, but despite his repentance he was punished severely.

The great contribution of the Jewish tradition was to achieve a genuinely moral conception of God. Conceived in various ways, God finally emerged as a being committed to the highest ethical values that the prophets could imagine. The source of all power in the world is also the source of all goodness. God not only is good, but has at various times in history revealed to humanity what human morality consists of. God's intention is that the human being, created slightly lower than angels, live by moral principles, that instead of responding to instinct and passion he freely choose actions that are right. These principles are not simply principles for individual excellence. They have a social dimension. Society (and humans were made to be social beings) can survive in peace and happiness only if its members abide by certain regulations.

Few of us are willing to accept all elements of the law stated in the Old Testament (over six hundred in number), but the Ten Commandments are fundamental. For the individual, they define a certain basic level of decency; for society, they prescribe basic principles for people who live together. As Huston Smith says, "Taken over by Christianity and Islam, the Ten Commandments constitute the moral foundation of half the world's present population."[28] And if we emphasize those that condemn killing, lying, stealing, and adultery, we take in most of the rest of the world, for they are absolutely necessary for individual decency and social order.

Jesus, as we have seen, was less concerned to emphasize the temporal punishments for immoral actions, but his views on marital fidelity are perhaps even more demanding than those of the Mosaic tradition. In the first place, there is no double standard. The erring husband is just as guilty as the erring wife or single woman. And in the second place, he condemns not only the action but the feeling that may (or may not) give rise to it: "You have heard that it was said, 'You shall not commit adultery.' But I say to you that every one who looks at a woman lustfully has already committed adultery with her in his heart."[29] The seriousness of Jesus' opposition to adultery is shown in the same chapter when he makes adultery the only acceptable reason for divorce and when he utters this "hard saying": "If your right eye causes you to sin, pluck it out and throw it away; it is better that you lose one of your members than that your whole body be thrown into hell."[30]

[25]Exodus 20:14.
[26]Exodus 20:17.
[27]Leviticus 20:10.
[28]Smith, *The Religions of Man,* p. 270.
[29]Matthew 5:27–28.
[30]Matthew 5:29.

Paul, in his letters, consistently enjoined the faithful to steer clear of adultery and all forms of sexual immorality. Opposed as he was to "the law," he yet believed that its basic rules (that is, the Ten Commandments) are summarized in the gospel of love: "Love is the fulfilling of the law."[31]

Aquinas and Luther In the writings of Thomas Aquinas we find the philosophic justification for marital fidelity. He quotes the Bible: "They shall be two in one flesh." In matrimony the male and female come together to make "one family life" and to beget and bring up children.[32] "The joining of husband and wife by matrimony is the greatest of all joinings, since it is a joining of soul and body, wherefore it is called a conjugal union."[33] Both sin against marriage when they commit adultery, for they are engaging in an action whose proper function is the procreation of children, and children are rightfully conceived in a conjugal union and brought up in a family.

> Every emission of the semen is contrary to the good of man, which takes place in a way whereby generation is impossible; and if this is done on purpose, it must be a sin. . . . Likewise it must be against the good of man for the semen to be emitted under conditions which, allowing generation to ensue, nevertheless bar the due education of the offspring. . . . Now in the human species the female is clearly insufficient of herself for the rearing of the offspring, since the need of human life makes many demands which cannot be met by one parent alone. Hence the fitness of human life requires man to stand by woman after the sexual act is done, and not to go off at once and form connexions with any one he meets, as is the way with fornicators.[34]

If Aquinas were asked why a natural function such as intercourse necessarily has but *one* purpose, he would answer that any other use of it is "incompatible" with its basic use. The individual who has intercourse without intending to produce children is working against the good of preserving the species. "Hence, after the sin of homicide, whereby a human nature already in existence is destroyed, this type of sin appears to hold the second place, whereby the generation of human nature is precluded."[35]

Martin Luther, in *A Commentary on St. Paul's Epistle to the Galatians,* recognizes the epistle as the classic statement of Christian freedom from the law, but his antinomianism does not go so far as to overlook the sin of adultery. This, like other expressions of lust, is a case of the flesh winning a victory over the spirit. Christian love shows itself superior to the law when it succeeds against tempta-

[31]Romans 13:10.

[32]Aquinas, *Supplement to Summa Theologica,* trans. Fathers of the English Dominican Province (New York: Benziger Brothers, 1948), Question 44, p. 2722.

[33]Ibid., p. 2724.

[34]Aquinas, *Summa Contra Gentiles* (trans. J. Rickaby) III, 122. See Vernon J. Bourke, ed., *The Pocket Aquinas* (New York: Washington Square Press, 1960), pp. 220–221.

[35]Ibid., p. 222.

tion, and finally when it has no need of the law to show it its shortcomings. Christian liberty is not simply the power to overcome temptation, but the power of banishing it entirely.

In discussing the adultery commandment, Luther writes: "Let us carefully note . . . how God especially honors and commends wedded life, since he confirms it with a special command. Hence he requires us to honor, guard, and observe it as a divine and blessed estate. Significantly he established it as the first of all institutions, and with it in view he did not create man and woman alike. God's purpose, as is plain, was . . . that they be true to each other, beget children, and nourish and rear them to his glory."[36]

Marriage as a Valuable Institution We must ask ourselves whether the institution of marriage is good. For if it is, then anything that corrupts or weakens it is bad. The family is a partnership between the husband and wife, economic and social as well as sexual. They share common ends of health, wealth, and happiness. The spouse is thus the only person whom the individual can depend on always to support him or her, to rejoice in his or her success, and solace him or her in times of trouble. More comprehensive than most partnerships, marriage requires trust between its principals. The wedding ceremony usually alludes to these things. The bride and groom are dramatically made aware that they are embarking on a new enterprise in which they will function now as a team, living together in closer intimacy than ever before experienced. They have committed themselves, "for better or for worse," to a unique relationship.

The element of commitment is important. "To promise permanence means, in fact, to acknowledge that at his best man remains sinful and that sin may invade his best emotions, so that a man better not trust himself to remain trustworthy, much less ask another person to rely on him, without assuming for himself commitments realistically designed to remedy the element of sin in all human love."[37]

When two people feel they are ready to make such a commitment, they secure the appropriate legal papers, arrange to have a ceremony in which vows are publicly declared, and (often) have the union blessed by their church. Such a commitment, before the whole world, is usually a deeper and longer-lasting one than a pair of romantic lovers might declare to one another in the privacy of the bedroom. The "piece of paper," spurned by the romantics, is a symbol of this greater commitment.

A commitment is also made by people who embark on a common-law marriage or who decide to live together. While the commitment often is not so great as that made by couples who secure marriage licenses, it often is. The Bureau of the Census reports that in 1979 there were at least 1,137,000 unmarried couples living

[36]Luther, *The Large Catechism.* See Waldo Beach and H. Richard Niebuhr, eds., *Christian Ethics* (New York: Ronald Press, 1955), p. 255.
[37]Paul Ramsey, *Basic Christian Ethics* (New York: Charles Scribner's Sons, 1951), p. 330.

together—an increase of 117 percent since 1970. There are ministers who will perform "in the sight of God" ceremonies for couples who for good reason (such as tax or pension considerations) do not want to make their union legal. Perhaps, in the broad sense of the term, we could speak of such couples as "married."

What people want when they decide to get married (whether they get the "piece of paper" or not) is a deep and intimate sharing of their lives. Each has chosen a person whom he or she loves in a way no other can be loved. While benevolence and friendship may go out to others, conjugal love is unique. What is shared with people outside the union is no longer unique and special when accorded to the spouse. What others get, the spouse does not. In being benevolent toward some, we eliminate the possibility of being benevolent toward others. In choosing some individuals as friends, we curtail friendly relations with others. There is only so much of oneself that can be given. To an even greater extent, in choosing a spouse, we give up certain familiarities with others. Adultery (casual or serious) is destructive of that special and unique relationship sought in courtship and pledged in marriage.

Children may come from the union, and the parents then take on the responsibility of caring for them and rearing them. That children are entitled to the love and care of parents would seem to be undeniable. That they be members of a family, unless that family is vicious, is to their immense advantage. Generally, according to sociologists, the best context for young children (other things being equal) is life with two parents. The next best is life with one parent or close relatives. Worst is life in foster homes and institutions. When spouses are "alienated," separated, or divorced, the children suffer.[38]

And, finally, it can be said that it is in the family that children learn the virtues of love, respect, and consideration. Their natural egoism is gradually replaced by fellow-feeling—that is what it means to "grow up." Their parents, too, in the context of a family, see from the moment of marriage their own sympathies broadened, as their capacity for benevolence and altruism ("sharing") develops.[39]

There are, then, at least three things that can be said for the institution of marriage: (1) It forges a unique partnership. (2) It provides a setting in which children can be reared. (3) It creates a family, which provides a training ground for the moral development of its participants.

Adultery versus Marriage How would extramarital sexual activity weaken this institution? Let us call the adulterer *X,* his or her spouse *Y,* and the other man or woman *Z.* When *X* has intercourse with *Z, X* has performed an act of physical intimacy that *Y* believes is distinctive to the *XY* marriage. It is not merely that *X* has shared his or her body with someone else; *X* has shared it in a very personal way. This can only mean to *Y* that he or she is inadequate or has failed in some

[38] "It is clear that the stability or otherwise of the home in which childhood is passed is probably the most important single factor in character structure." Comfort, p. 90.

[39] See Gerald Runkle, "Some Considerations on Family Loyalty," *Ethics* 68 (January 1958), p. 131ff.

way. *X* may say that the encounter with *Z* "doesn't mean a thing," but it does mean that his or her attachment to *Y* was not as exclusive as both *X* and *Y* believed when they got married. And if it *does* mean something or develops to the point that it does, then the bonds of the union are broken or seriously strained. Even if *Y* does not become aware of the infidelity, *X* must realize that he or she has taken the first step in what may become a line of development destructive to the union. *X* will, at the very least, probably have to lie and deceive. Whether *Y* knows about it or not, *X* will know that the trust on which marriage is based is a misplaced trust. Although *X* was attracted to the institution of marriage in the first place because of its benefits, *X* is now acting in a way that will destroy it.

An ethical principle in addition to distinctively religious ones is thus involved: the utilitarian principle of acting in such a way as to support an institution that is productive of great benefits for oneself, one's partner, one's children, and society in general. Even if one's own marriage is not especially successful, the benefits are there if one will work at it. An institution that has for so long served the interests of society and been freely chosen by individuals pursuing their own happiness should be treated with respect.

There is still another point to be made against extramarital sex. *X* has made certain vows at the beginning of the marriage, but has broken them in the adulterous relationship. Where now is *X*'s integrity? And when we add the deceit that he or she may have to practice in carrying on the affair (or affairs), we must see *X* as living a lie. In not remaining faithful to *Y*, *X* has not only wronged *Y* but has corrupted his or her own integrity. So a second ethical principle is violated, that of the categorical imperative to tell the truth, keep your word, live up to your vows.

Using Another as a Means Some attention should be paid to *Z*. If *X*'s attraction to *Z* is a casual one, *X* is *using Z*. This is in violation of Kant's second formulation of the categorical imperative: treat others as an end, never as a means only. *X* has made an object of another autonomous human being. If *X*'s attraction to *Z* is or becomes serious, *X* has placed *Z* in a very unpleasant situation. *Z* loves *X*, but can never have *X*—unless, of course, *X* divorces *Y*. But it is not fair to *Z* for *X* to develop a meaningful relationship to *Z* unless *X* can carry through. That is, if *Z* is willing to give herself or himself wholly to *X*, *X* must be free to give himself or herself to *Z*. Someone once remarked that if a man had to choose to save either his wife or his mistress from drowning, he would save his wife—for his mistress would understand. In short, extramarital sex requires either the reprehensible use of human beings as objects or places all three of the triangle, *X*, *Y*, and *Z*, in a very uncomfortable position that is bound to be unfair to two of them.

In his *Lectures on Ethics* Kant specifically applies the second formulation to sexual intercourse. When one loves another "purely from sexual desire," good will and affection are absent. The lover seeks his or her own satisfaction, not the happiness of the other. "Sexual love makes of the loved person an Object of appetite; as soon as that appetite has been stilled, the person is cast aside as one casts away a lemon which has been sucked dry."[40] The other is degraded. It is not the human nature that attracts the lover, but the sexuality of the other. It is quite possible that both parties are using the other as means. "They make of humanity an instrument for the satisfaction of their lusts and inclinations, and dishonour it by placing it on a level with animal nature."[41]

Kant's discussion anticipates Sartre's view of the "other-as-object" in *Being and Nothingness.*[42] According to Sartre, subjectivity or consciousness fashions a world of meanings and values for itself. The "being-for-itself" treats (or tries to treat) others in the same way it treats shade trees, loaves of bread, and train stations. But since there are other free consciousnesses in the world doing the same thing, there is bound to be trouble. Each individual lives always under the threat of the other. The "other-as-object" may at any time become "object-as-subject," and one's own world collapses: one shamefacedly becomes object.[43] Thus the problems in trying to develop a social philosophy. Sartre describes the dynamics of the relations between the sexes, a thoroughly discouraging account. He points out the near impossibility of achieving genuine love in the face of the inevitable stages of masochism, indifference, desire, sadism, and hatred. "Conflict is the original meaning of being-for-others."[44]

Kant's solution is found in permanent marriage. "The sole condition on which we are free to make use of our sexual desire depends upon the right to dispose over the person as a whole—over the welfare and happiness and generally over all the circumstances of that person."[45] In marriage there is a total and reciprocal agreement between two persons that everything is to be equally shared. "Whatever good or ill, joy or sorrow befall either of them, the other will share in it."[46] The sexual relation, while only one of the relations between the two partners, cannot now be separated from the entire relationship. Neither party is *using* the other, for each already belongs to the other. Only in the *union of human beings* can sexual relations exhibit a moral dimension.

Conclusion Many "permanent" marriages do not, of course, turn out to be permanent. Perhaps it would be better to speak of marriages "for an indefinite

[40]Kant, *Lectures on Ethics,* trans. Louis Infield (London: Century Co., 1930), p. 163.

[41]Ibid., p. 164.

[42]The philosophy of Jean-Paul Sartre is discussed in the first and third sections of chapter 9.

[43]"The Other-as-object is an explosive instrument which I handle with care because I foresee around him the permanent possibility that *they* are going to explode and with this explosion I shall suddenly experience the flight of the world away from me and the alienation of my being. Therefore my constant concern is to contain the Other within his objectivity, and my relations with the Other-as-object are essentially made up of ruses designed to make him remain an object." Sartre, *Being and Nothingness: An Essay on Phenomenological Ontology,* trans. Hazel E. Barnes (New York: Philosophical Library, 1956), p. 297.

[44]Ibid., p. 364.

[45]Kant, *Lectures on Ethics,* pp. 166–167.

[46]Ibid., p. 167.

period" than of "permanent" marriages. Marriages, despite the high hopes of those who contract them, do not always remain the instrument for profound love between partners and a good context for rearing children. Divorce is often an appropriate action for people who no longer can perform in a way that genuine marriage requires. But the fact is that the incidence of marriage is increasing. Although divorce is increasingly popular and easy to obtain, more people are getting married now than was the case a generation ago. "Failures" (their own or others') hardly dissuade them. And marriages last longer also (if for no other reason than the lengthening of the life span). Many couples who dispense with the wedding license live together in a way that for all intents and purposes is marriage. Despite the "sexual revolution," monogamous marriage is recognized as a value by at least as many people today as was the case in generations past. And despite all the criticisms that monogamous marriage has been subjected to,[47] it is still a popular and respected institution.[48]

Extramarital Sex Is Not Always Immoral

Religious Assumptions Some of the arguments used against the position that premarital sex is immoral are applicable in refuting the position that extramarital sex is immoral. Since the Judeo-Christian tradition condemns nonmarital sex in general, one line of attack against the condemnation of extramarital sex consists in attacking that ethical tradition. And this is easy to do.

On what rational basis can one accept the notion that an omnipotent God exists and that he revealed to Moses the essence of human morality on Mount Sinai? And on what rational basis can one believe that Jesus and Paul were divinely inspired when they confirmed the law? Divine origin is a mighty support for a moral rule, but the difficulty of proving that the divine will operated in the first place makes the position a very shaky one.

Even if it were granted that God exists and forbids extramarital sex, an important problem remains: the problem of deciding whether God himself is moral, that his "revelation" indeed possesses ethical validity. Might, even when infinite, cannot make right. Conscientious individuals have to be convinced that God is indeed devoted to morality. They have to have some moral insights of their own to judge the supernatural being and its pronouncements. Unless they are willing simply to proclaim as right whatever seems to be based on power, they must rely on some ethical convictions of their own. Socrates asked the young man in Plato's *Euthyphro* whether an act was right because the gods declared it to be so or whether the gods declared it to be right because it *is* right. The implication here

[47]See, for example, John McMurtry, "Monogamy: A Critique," in Baker and Elliston, *Philosophy & Sex.*

[48]David Palmer argues that it is unfair to blame marriage for difficulties caused by religious, economic, and social factors quite extrinsic to the institution itself. Not even Marx was guilty of this. See "The Consolation of the Wedded" in Baker and Elliston, *Philosophy & Sex,* p. 178ff.

is that no appeal to religious beliefs about what is the case can deliver us from the need to discern what *ought* to be the case. Recognition of God's omnipotence is no substitute for ethical philosophizing.

What ethical philosophizing is relevant to the issue of adultery? Thomas Aquinas provided us with an argument based on the idea that natural functions have a purpose and should be exercised only on behalf of that purpose. The purpose of sexual intercourse is procreation, and so it should be employed only on behalf of procreation. This would condemn not only nonmarital sex (when conception is not the object) but most marital sex as well.

But that Aquinas's idea is true is far from obvious—even if we assume that a Creator endowed us with natural functions with purposes in mind. Why does there have to be but *one* purpose for each function? And why does this purpose have to be narrowly conceived? Many of our natural functions can be made to serve several purposes, and while these other purposes may be regarded as not fundamental (or not the "intended" purpose), their expression is not regarded as wrong. Humans have the faculty of reason, the exercise of which produces theoretical and practical truth. But no one regards it as wrong to use this reason in a recreational way to play bridge, solve puzzles, or debate competitively. Humans have the function to take nourishment, but no one regards it as wrong to use this function in a recreational way to sample wines, celebrate birthdays, or plan banquets at which people give speeches. That these things may not be our moral duty does not mean that they are wrong. To prescribe one specific and narrowly conceived expression for each natural function is to place ourselves in a straitjacket and to deny ourselves many forms of expression.

Sex and Pleasure Richard Wasserstrom suggests a "demystification of sexual behavior." One form that this demystification could take is to "encourage the enjoyment of sex more for its own sake."[49] Neither marriage nor deep commitment, neither love nor great affection, need to be present for two people to enjoy intercourse. The view (which Wasserstrom does not necessarily hold) is this: "The situation in respect to sexual pleasure is no different from that of the person who knows and appreciates fine food and who can have a satisfying meal in any number of good restaurants with any number of congenial companions."[50] The person who held such a view and had intercourse with a person other than his or her spouse would be no more "unfaithful" to that spouse than he or she would be in having lunch with a business associate. Where affection is present, both experiences would doubtless be more gratifying, but if the adulterer loves his or her spouse, he or she would value experiences with that spouse even more.

This argument may be employed to show that extramarital encounters are not bad, since they are seen as casual and unimportant: they do not threaten any of the real values of ethical life. Or it may be employed to show that some positive

[49]Wasserstrom, "Is Adultery Immoral?" in Baker and Elliston, *Philosophy & Sex,* p. 214.
[50]Ibid.

net good (enjoyment) is produced in these encounters. The desire for sexual variety (especially among men) does not end simply because one has acquired a spouse.[51] It is thus a hedonistic argument. That does not mean, however, that it is necessarily that form of hedonism that emphasizes physical pleasures to the exclusion of others. The way is left open for the "higher pleasures" that Epicurus and Mill prized and for high values in general.

There are, admittedly, two difficulties with this view. The first is that one's spouse may not agree with it. If that is the case, vows are broken, lies are told, and deception in general is practiced. These are all bad things, but not based on categorical imperatives as exceptionless as Kantians would have us believe. Very few (if any) moral rules hold for all cases, for all people, for all conditions. There are often "extenuating circumstances." The philanderer is adept at stating them and they are often entirely self-serving and specious. But sometimes they are not. The spouse may be unable or unwilling to have intercourse. The spouse may be absent for a long period of time. One of the partners may be more appreciative of the spouse because of occasional affairs with others; he or she does not feel trapped.[52] The marriage union may have become simply a financial partnership or one maintained only for the sake of small children. Where valid extenuating circumstances can be supplied, it may be the greater part of morality to practice deception instead of injuring the feelings of the spouse. Where such circumstances cannot be delineated, one is morally wrong to engage in extramarital sex against the wishes of one's spouse.

The best solution to this problem, however, is the establishment of an understanding between the husband and wife. It is not argued there that all spouses should adopt an "open marriage."[53] But those who do so will have eliminated important moral obstacles to extramarital sex: breaking vows, lying, undermining trust, and so on. With such an understanding there can be no infidelity. They will also have obviated the need for finding "extenuating circumstances." A spouse who wishes to engage in sex outside of marriage is on firmest ethical grounds when he or she does so with the consent of his or her spouse. An "open marriage" can be contracted at the beginning of the union or adopted later with the concurrence of both parties. In denying that extramarital sex is always wrong, we merely assert that sometimes (but not always) it is not wrong.

The second difficulty with the view that sexual liaisons outside of marriage are casual and unimportant instances of pleasure gathering becomes clear when we

[51]It has been said that the male is naturally polygamous. In view of the prevalence of monogamy in male-dominated societies, this would seem to be in error. Males are monogamous but *polyerotic*—and so too, probably to a lesser extent, are females.

[52]"It is highly probable that adultery today maintains far more marriages than it destroys. . . .A good many marriages, and a good many personalities, require an 'adulterous' prop to keep them on their feet. The need may be 'immature' but it is certainly widespread, and it seems inevitable that our culture, like so many others, will come to admit and accommodate it." Comfort, pp. 119, 126.

[53]"Open marriage" is a marriage contracted to achieve the goal of companionship. Each partner is free to engage in sexual relationships with others. For an explanation and defense of this permissive kind of marriage, see O'Neill and O'Neill, *Open Marriage: A New Life Style for Couples.*

recognize that such liaisons may in fact become important. Affection may grow, even devotion. The person may become more attached to a paramour than to his or her spouse. Or it may happen that the person is first attracted to another for reasons other than sexual. Affection grows and the relationship comes to take on a sexual aspect. What is probably usually the case is sexual attraction and affection grow together, each enhancing the other. However it occurs, the relationship is not now the kind of casual sex-for-fun we were discussing above.

Sex and Love Sexual intimacy can thus be conjoined with great affection. This brings us to a second form of demystification of sex—also noted by Wasserstrom. "The mistake lies in thinking that any 'normal' adult will have these feelings toward only one other adult during his or her lifetime—or even at any time in his or her life. It is the concept of adult love, not ideas about sex, that needs demystification."[54] When it is recognized that a person can love more than one partner at the same time, and when this is considered a good thing, extramarital sex begins to take on an aura of respectability, if not positive morality.

This kind of love, which includes sex but is more than sexual, is of great social importance. One's highest impulses are not confined to one partner, but go out to others. This love is not exclusive or jealous. It is perhaps what the saints would have preached if they had not been obsessed by the sin of copulation. "Love your neighbor"—yes, in all senses of the word.[55]

One is surely able to love more than one person at a time. Christianity prescribes it, and human nature enacts it. We love our friends and we love our family, and our love is not diluted by being disseminated. And if in some cases, where unrelated adults of opposite genders are involved, this love takes on an additional sexual dimension, no harm is done.

But once again, we have a problem, and it is the same problem noted above: the demands and expectations of the spouse. Just as the expression of casual love is seriously brought into question by an aggrieved spouse, so too is the expression of idealized sexual love brought into question. Indeed, a serious relation is more likely to be resented than a casual one. Extenuating circumstances can be cited here also, but they are rightly viewed with suspicion. One who expects primary loyalty from one's spouse is seriously wronged when it is compromised.

But again, the solution lies in open marriage. Here the form is somewhat different. The first permitted sexual liaisons but preserved primary loyalty and faithfulness to the spouse. The second permits serious loving relations with others and does not require primary loyalty and devotion to the spouse. The spouse who

[54]Wasserstrom, p. 215.

[55]One can oppose the institution of monogamous marriage or get around it by adultery. John McMurtry apparently chooses the former, saying: "It is difficult to conceive of a more thoroughgoing mechanism for limiting extended social union and intimacy. . . .The most compelling natural force toward expanded intimate relations with others is strictly confined within the narrowest possible circle for (barring delinquency) the whole of adult life." "Monogamy: A Critique," in Baker and Elliston, *Philosophy & Sex,* pp. 168, 169.

agrees to this kind of arrangement is willing to take his or her chances in an arena of human relationships that is likely to be quite competitive. Such an open marriage would have to be equitable—each partner has the same rights—in order for it to justify extramarital sexual love. Otherwise the philosophic principle on which it is based—the goodness of loving relations—has arbitrarily been compromised.

Altering the Institution of Marriage The view that open marriage gets around all rational objectives to extramarital sex is not quite true. What now becomes subject to controversy is the altered conception of marriage and the family. If the conventional conception of these institutions is correct, the right to extramarital sex has been purchased at too great a price. What changes would be made in these institutions and are they socially desirable?

The essential difference between conventional marriage and open marriage is the element of exclusivity present in the first and absent in the second. One or both of the partners have significant relations with others. If these relations are simply those of sexual intimacy, the person who has them does not depend wholly on his or her spouse for sexual pleasure. Perhaps not at all. This admittedly constitutes a weaker commitment. It is not, however, necessarily fatal to the union. There are many factors that make for a good union (similar artistic, recreational, and economic interests; shared politics or religion; children; companionability). Just as marriages can survive differences in politics and artistic interest, some can also survive the absence of sexual exclusivity. And as long as the union is strong, whatever the particular bonds may be that hold it together, the partners may function adequately as parents. Such a marriage would be preferable to one based on a hypocritical acceptance of exclusivity and a deceitful practice of adultery.

The second form of nonexclusivity is more destructive, for here not only sexual relations but the entire spectrum of human relations may be shared with one or more nonspouses. It is not easy to describe the nature of the marriage when partners are so free in forming bonds with others. At one extreme, the strength and frequency of other relations may be so low that the marriage is hardly affected. At the other extreme, a person might forge such meaningful relations with so many people that his or her relation with the spouse is only one of a number, and perhaps not even the most important one. In this case the marriage has become so different from conventional unions that it can be said to exist no longer. The place of children and their upbringing in such a radically different context is impossible to describe.

The adherent of a Deweyan approach to the problem of the form that marriage should take would point out that the institution is historically conditioned. It has taken several forms in the past and will take different forms in the future. No one form is perfect and none fully meets the needs of a particular society and all the couples in it. "You shouldn't have to buy marriage off the rack; like a tailor-made suit or dress, it should conform exactly to the contours of those who choose to lothe themselves in it."[56] Both parties to the marriage should agree on the form they have selected; they should be clear on its goals and requirements. Certainty in this area, as in so many others, is not to be obtained. People best serve their interests, however, when they dispense with absolutes and employ the experimental method. The marriage contract should be subject to revision with the consent of both parties.

Social scientists should study how various marital partnerships work in various contexts and with different kinds of persons. They should see these phenomena as blends of facts and values. Neither moralists (in the old-fashioned sense) nor detached and objective scientists, they should provide us with accounts that may be useful to private individuals, counselors, ministers, and legislators. Public opinion and law should be tolerant of alternative forms of marriage, realizing that nothing is either perfect or permanent. Individuals will act intelligently—that is, on the basis of what information they have and in the hope of a happier future for themselves, their contemporaries, and their children.[57]

The open marriage may indeed (for some people) be an improvement over conventional marriage, and there are doubtless still other forms. The open marriage itself admits of many variations. Since extramarital sex is desired by a great many people in today's society, we must either condemn it for its destructive effects or recognize it as a good and discover the institutional framework in which it can best occur. The open marriage is at least one promising possibility.

Conclusion One final point: The incidence of marital infidelity is just as often the *effect* of a troubled marriage as the cause of one. If conventional marriage is important, we need to find out from the social scientists what these *other destructive factors* are. Also, if conventional marriage is important, its defenders and participants should consider preserving it even in the face of an occasional infidelity. That adultery is a legal ground for divorce does not mean that it should always function as a moral ground for breaking up a union that is in other respects strong and mutually beneficial.

Summary of the Issues

One argument against extramarital sex is based on the Biblical condemnation of adultery. But it is possible to question the notion that the Bible consistently represents the word of God. It is thus possible to question the notion that God prohibits adultery—or even that God exists.

Another argument against extramarital sex is that it is a perverted expression of the sexual drive, for procreation is hardly ever the intention. But some have

[56] O'Neill and O'Neill, *Open Marriage*, p. 70.

[57] That there is some reason for hope of growing tolerance here is indicated by the fact that laws against adultery, fornication, and homosexual relations between consenting adults, as well as unmarried conjugal unions, are being repealed or are not enforced.

argued that sexual expression may quite naturally have other purposes. It may be engaged in as an aspect of our social relations with others, and it may be pursued for hedonistic purposes.

The opponent of extramarital sex may answer that adultery, regardless of the friendship it fosters and the pleasure it produces, violates at least three important duties: (1) the duty not to use others as means, (2) the duty not to inflict suffering —in this case, on the aggrieved spouse, and (3) the duty to remain faithful to the vows one has made. The adulterer has thus failed to meet his or her obligations to two parties. In answer it has been argued that sexual relations are not exploitative when both parties participate as equals, that the spouse does not suffer if the affair is carried on discreetly, and that vows are not broken if the married couple has established an "understanding" (or open marriage).

What may be at stake is the institution of marriage (legal or common law), which is thought to have proved itself on utilitarian grounds. This institution, say the foes of extramarital sex, forges a unique and valuable partnership, provides a salutary setting in which children can be reared, and creates a family that is a training ground for the moral development of its members. Adultery weakens this institution. The supporter of extramarital sex is not convinced of the utility of the conventional marriage. That one has a cherished spouse at home does not mean that he or she should be denied the pleasures of sex with others or the gratification of loving relations with others. If one believes that the duties of keeping vows and avoiding deceit are compelling, one can reach an understanding with the spouse: "You are my primary concern but not the only one" or "You are only one of my objects of love." The marriage relation should be thought of as equitable and reciprocal, but not necessarily exclusive. There are many forms of marriage that might equally well serve various utilitarian purposes, including that of rearing children. Marital infidelity is common. An honest restructuring of the institution of marriage is preferable to hypocrisy and deceit.

Both sides tend to look with disfavor on extramarital sex when it is practiced in deceit and contrary to vows. But while the one side condemns it as a matter of principle, the other side will entertain "extenuating circumstances." While suspicious of easy rationalizations ("My spouse doesn't understand me," "My spouse is unresponsive," "I'll appreciate my spouse more"), this side will permit extramarital sex when the spouse is unwilling or unable to have sex, when the couple is separated for a long period of time, or when the marriage has become simply a legal partnership.

Both sides take into account the dangers of extramarital sex to the participant (for whom a casual affair becomes an obsession), to the paramour (who may be placed in a distinctly disadvantageous position), to the spouse (who may be terribly hurt), and to the marriage itself (which may be diminished and finally ruined). For the advocate of extramarital sex, however, such considerations are not decisive. If they cannot be gotten around by some form of open marriage, they must be avoided through caution and intelligence.

Discussion Questions

1. Do you believe that adherence to the ideal of faithfulness in marriage has utilitarian value? Why?
2. Does the duty to keep one's promises ever admit of exceptions with respect to the marriage vows? Why?
3. Is Kant correct in saying that sexual relations can only evade the charge of exploitation when they take place in marriage? Why?
4. Does God prohibit extramarital sex? Why do you believe or disbelieve this?
5. Do you think that conventional marriage unjustly cuts the individual off from valuable relations with other people of the opposite sex? Explain.
6. If someone claims extramarital prerogatives for himself or herself, should he or she be willing to extend it to the spouse also? Why?
7. Would an extramarital affair be wrong if it gave great pleasure to both participating parties and was not discovered by the spouse? Why?
8. Do you think that the pleasure of sex is just as important an end as procreation? What implications, if any, does your answer have for the question of extramarital sex?
9. Do you think, on balance, that extramarital sex produces more pleasure than pain for the three members of the "triangle"? Explain.
10. Is extramarital sex ethically acceptable for those married couples who have an "understanding"? Explain.
11. If you were to get married (or remarry), would you want to dispense with the vow of sexual exclusiveness? Why?
12. Can you think of any circumstances in which extramarital sex would be ethically acceptable in a conventional marriage?
13. Does sexual infidelity necessarily poison the relations between marriage partners? What bearing, if any, would the fact of discovery have on the marriage relation?
14. How far do you think one can go in friendship with a member of the opposite sex without damaging the marriage relation?
15. The marriage relation has been called a unique one. Is this the most important or valuable relationship that one person can have with another? Explain.
16. In general, do you think that children of a more or less open marriage fare as well as those of a conventional marriage? Explain.
17. How would you rank the desirability of these forms of marriage?: (a) open marriage, (b) conventional marriage with occasional infidelity, (c) conventional marriage with frequent infidelity. Explain.
18. Do you believe there is one form of marriage that is obligatory for all couples? Explain.
19. Would you regard common-law marriage ("living together") as having as high a moral standing as legal marriage? Why?
20. Would you regard a civil wedding as having as high a moral standing as a church wedding? Why?
21. Which do you think is more frequent? Adultery leading to a bad marriage or a bad marriage leading to adultery. Explain.

22. Do you think that partners in a marriage that is irreparably damaged are justified in engaging in extramarital sex? Why?
23. Do you think that infidelity on the part of your spouse would give you the right to be unfaithful also? Would you exercise this right? Why?
24. Do you think that Jesus would have opposed adultery so vehemently if women in his society had had equal rights with men? Explain.
25. Do you think that the ancient Greeks would have been so tolerant of adultery in their society if women had had equal rights with men? Explain.
26. Can you think of any other prima facie duty that might take precedence over the prima facie duty to be faithful to one's spouse?
27. Which theory would you most rely on in settling the issue of extramarital sex?: (a) Judaism-Christianity, (b) hedonism, (c) utilitarianism, (d) deontological ethics, or (e) none of the above. Why?
28. Are there situations in which Fletcher would regard adultery as ethically acceptable? Obligatory? Explain.

For Further Reading

See also the citations with asterisks in "For Further Reading" at the end of the previous section.

Thomas Aquinas. *On the Truth of the Catholic Faith.* Translated by Vernon J. Bourke. New York: Doubleday, 1956. Book 3, Part 1.

Thomas Aquinas. *Supplement to Summa Theologica.* Translated by Fathers of the English Dominican Province. New York: Benziger Brothers, 1948. Questions 44–63.

Augustine. *On the Good of Marriage.* In Philip Schaff, ed., *A Select Library of the Nicene and Post-Nicene Fathers.* Grand Rapids, Mich.: Wm. B. Eerdmans Publishing Co., 1956. Vol. 3.

Robert Baker and Frederick Elliston, eds. *Philosophy & Sex.* Buffalo: Prometheus Books, 1975. See especially: John McMurtry, "Monogamy: A Critique"; David Palmer, "The Consolation of the Wedded"; Michael D. Bayles, "Marriage, Love, and Procreation"; Richard Wasserstrom, "Is Adultery Immoral?"

J. E. and M. A. Barnhart. "Marital Faithfulness and Unfaithfulness." *Journal of Social Philosophy* 4 (1973):10–15.

Peter A. Bertocci. *Sex, Love, and the Person.* New York: Sheed and Ward, 1967.

Morton M. Hunt. *The Affair: A Portrait of Extra-Marital Love in Contemporary America.* Cleveland: World Publishing Co., 1969.

Immanuel Kant. *Lectures on Ethics.* "Duties toward the Body in Respect of Sexual Impulse." Translated by Louis Infield. New York and London: Century Co., 1930.

Christopher Lasch. *Haven in a Heartless World: The Family Beseiged.* New York: Basic Books, 1977.

Gerhard Neubeck. *Extra-Marital Relations.* Englewood Cliffs, N.J.: Prentice-Hall, 1969.

Nena and George O'Neill. *Open Marriage: A New Life Style for Couples.* New York: Evans and Co., 1972.

Rustum and Della Roy. *Honest Sex.* New York: New American Library, 1968.

Rustum and Della Roy. "Is Monogamy Outdated?" *The Humanist* 30:19–26.

Gerald Runkle. "Some Considerations on Family Loyalty." *Ethics* 68 (January 1958): 131–136.

Donald P. Verene, ed. *Sexual Love and Western Morality: A Philosophical Anthology.* New York: Harper & Row, 1972.

M. L. Walshok. "Emergence of Middle-Class Deviant Subcultures: The Case of Swingers." *Journal of Marriage and the Family* 18 (Spring 1971):488–495.

"PERVERSIONS"

Most Sexual "Perversions" Are Immoral and/or Sick

Definitions There are a great many problems in trying to define sexual "perversion." The most common definition employs the concept of deviation from what is "normal" in sexual relations. If *normal* is construed in a moral sense, then it would follow that sexual perversions are immoral. If *normal* means healthy in some mental or biological sense, then it would follow that sexual perversions are manifestations of sickness. The determination of the morality or healthfulness of certain sexual practices thus rests on the meaning of *normal.* And to specify what normality means is not easy to do. But whatever it means, sexual perversion will be, almost by definition, *bad,* for it is nonmoral, abnormal, a falling short of a standard of morality and/or health. The question, then, is not whether sexual perversions are bad (for they are), but what sexual practices indeed *are* perversions.

There are a great many sexual practices that society (or some segment thereof) would regard as perverse. But practices are perversions only if they deviate from some defensible norm. Any statement of proper sexual relations is obviously discriminatory: It will by implication excuse some practices and condemn others. We will argue that most "perversions" are genuine perversions, that they are deviations from a worthwhile norm and are thus wrong.

The failure in practice to achieve a norm may not be immoral in the strict sense of the term. If the dynamics of human psychology are such that the individual is never really in a position to make a deliberate choice in the same way, for example, that one may decide to take a lover, then falling short of the norm would be more of a personality disorder than a case of immorality in the narrow sense. It may indeed be true that mental illness or "arrested development" is the cause of sexual perversity. Even if this is so, the performance of perverse practices still falls in the area of undesirable behavior and could be called immoral in a broad sense of that word. It is difficult to draw a line between a deliberate choice of evil and a psychological tendency to do so, to blame the one on a bad will and the other on a diseased personality. This is an important problem in ethics that cannot suitably be dealt with here. When we say that a sexual practice deviates from the proper norm, we conclude that it is immoral or sick—"immoral" in the broad sense.

Practices Commonly Believed to Be Perversions What does "society" (in some vague sense) consider to be sexual "perversions"? There seem to be two large classes of "perversions": those of *style* and those of *objects.* Under those of style would fall fellatio (oral stimulation of the penis), cunnilingus (oral stimulation of the clitoris or vulva), sodomy (anal intercourse), sadism (sexual satisfaction through inflicting pain), and masochism (sexual satisfaction through experiencing pain). Under those of the object are incest (intercourse with a near relative), pedophilia (intercourse with a child), fetishism ("intercourse" with nonsexual parts of the body or with an inanimate object), homosexuality (intercourse with a person of same sex), bestiality (intercourse with a lower animal), necrophilia (intercourse with a dead person), and group sex (intercourse with more than one person at a time). There is a third class of "perversions" in which sexual excitement is sought apart from intercourse with other objects: masturbation (gratification through the physical stimulation of one's own genitals), voyeurism (gratification through witnessing sexual actions of others), and exhibitionism (gratification through exposure in public of one's own genitals).

This admittedly is not a logical classification, for there is no single principle that creates the classes. There is, moreover, much overlapping. A "style" may be used with several "objects"; an "object" may be sexually subjected to several "styles." Sodomy, for example, may occur with both homosexuality and bestiality, as well as with heterosexuality. Voyeurism may be directed toward members of the same sex, and exhibitionism may express itself before children.

While this list of "perversions" is by no means complete, it provides us with many of the practices that large segments of society consider perverse. Our task now must be to decide whether they really are perverse. That is a large task indeed, for it requires a statement and defense of a norm in sexual relations as well as a comparison of each of the "perversions" to this norm. What we will do, however, falls short of this. We will present some conceptions of sexual norms without claiming to establish any one of them, and we will test only some of the "perversions." The reader will have to choose his or her own norm and apply it to the "perversions" that interest him or her.

A Naturalistic Norm One norm for sexual practices is a naturalistic one with strong moral overtones: they must be performed for purposes of reproduction. That people have sexual organs at all, as well as the urge to use them, serves God's plan or nature's intention that they reproduce. On this narrow conception of the norm, most of the "perversions" would indeed be perversions, for they either make reproduction impossible or unlikely. Indeed, on this ideal, anything but male ejaculation in the female vagina would be perverse. Fellatio or masochism might have a place in the mating process, but only as a means to the final result of ejaculation in the vagina. They and all other sexual practices from foreplay to postcoital caresses would have no standing of their own, and if they were engaged in for their own sake, they would be perversions. Indeed, any element of romance or tenderness or mutual delight would be superfluous and run the danger of being a case of perversion. On this standard, the very wish that the woman should have pleasure is perverse, for this is unnecessary for conception. Finally, even a case of sexual intercourse in the "missionary position," with no frills and with prompt ejaculation, would be a case of perversion if reproduction were not the aim. The difficulty with this first norm is that *most cases* of sexual intercourse would turn out to be cases of sexual perversion.

This norm could be made much more acceptable by specifying that while generation of life may not be the *intention,* the actions performed are such as *could* produce life. People who perform sexually in a way that could generate life are behaving naturally, whatever their purpose. Even the use of contraception would not disqualify their actions. This modified naturalistic norm would approve all foreplay that contributed to the performance of the life-generating act: ejaculation in the vagina. Anything that deviated from the norm would be unnatural, perverse, and wrong. On this view, many of the "perversions" listed above are perversions, although fellatio, cunnilingus, sadism, and masochism, if relegated to an auxiliary role, need not be perverse. Nor would incest and pedophilia unless they became obsessive and ruled out other objects. This norm permits recreational sex, but the pleasure is connected with or leads to the sort of action that generates life. Just as animals engage in sexual intercourse without intention to reproduce, so can human beings. The natural impulse is aroused and satisfied in a fitting biological way.

A Humanistic Norm Many people would be unhappy with the norm just described. It makes the behavior of lower animals our norm, and humanity needs a norm of its own. "The sexual behavior of animals is typically instinctive. It tends to be stereotyped, and it occupies only a limited place in the general pattern of behaviour, since it is evoked directly by hormonal changes, and follows, as a rule a limited cyclical pattern."[58] It is the human being, with his or her imagination, memory, complicated psychology, and symbol-making ability, who most easily and most obviously departs from any naturalistic norm. And the departure may be in a higher direction or a lower direction. Some of the human idealizing capacity should be built into a norm that goes beyond the naturalistic one and thus is more appropriate to humanity. What is a fitting expression of the sexual impulse in dogs is not necessarily fitting for people. The impulse operates in different ways in the two species, and with different manifestations.

A second statement of the human norm has a pronounced moral character going far beyond the "natural." It envisions the sexual relation as involving two adult human beings who have sufficient affection and respect for one another that neither sees the other as simply a means for gratification. It is based on natural functions, but is not limited simply to reproduction. Just as animals engage in sexual intercourse without intention to reproduce, so, too, can human beings. Also like animals, they employ the parts of their physiology in a seemly and fitting

[58]Comfort, p. 33.

way; they recognize sexual differences. Unlike animals, however, humans must take into account the special obligations created by family relationships.

On the basis of some such statement as this, fellatio and cunnilingus are not necessarily perversions, for they may express affection and respect. Sodomy is not necessarily a perversion, although it is difficult to imagine performing the act without brutality. Most of the other "perversions" indeed are perversions and should be avoided. Both sadism and masochism violate the principle that people should not be used as means or objects. Incest is a perversion since it ignores the special obligations members of a family bear to one another. Pedophilia, fetishism, bestiality, and necrophilia are perversions, since another living adult human being is not involved. Homosexuality is a perversion, since there is obvious misuse of physiology. Anyone, therefore, who engages in these perverse practices is immoral.

The case of seeking sexual satisfaction *apart* from an object is more difficult to evaluate. If we strictly apply the criterion that proper sexual expression requires a partner, then masturbation, voyeurism, and exhibitionism would seem to be perversions. But some indulgence can perhaps be mustered for the first two of the three, in which no one else is involved who can be hurt or shocked or insulted. And if an individual, for one reason or other, is cut off from normal intercourse, the resort to masturbation or voyeurism (when the right to privacy of others is not violated) can be understood and perhaps excused. Certainly these practices would not constitute as gross a deviation as some of the other perversions.

A Psychological Norm A third statement of sexual norms has a more psychological basis and is linked to some theory of normal psychological development. Many psychologists have tried to define this development, notably Sigmund Freud. In Freud's view, children progress from oral and anal sexuality to genital sexuality. They overcome the Oedipus complex and direct the libido to nonfamily members. They pass through the homosexual state to a heterosexual one. There are all kinds of snares along the way as a child moves toward sexual maturity and mental health. He or she may become victimized by "retrogressions," "fixations," "inversions," or "complexes." When development is arrested, it is the business of therapists to find out why and to restore health. On this statement of sexual function, the emphasis is on health/illness rather than morality/immorality. The psychiatrist eschews moral conceptions, and focuses attention on the successful function of the whole human being. He or she may even call the various errant actions and attitudes "normal" (in view of the causal factors involved), but is committed to an ideal of mental health in which they play no part.

Wilhelm Reich stresses the moralistic repression of normal sexual outlets as the cause of "perverted" sex. The "conditions of the sex-negating social order" makes victims of the healthiest—that is, those who have the strongest sexual drives. When the individual has been restored to emotional health, "the moral straitjacket drops off along with the damming up of his instinctual needs." The individual is "virtually without any impulses that would require a restraining morality." The result is this: "Sexual intercourse with prostitutes becomes offensive; any existing fantasies of murder or rape lose their force and significance. To force a partner into a love affair or to rape her becomes bizarre and unthinkable, just as do any impulses to seduce children that may have existed previously. By the same token, former anal, exhibitionist, or other perversions also recede, along with social anxiety and guilt feelings. The incestuous ties to parents and siblings lose their interest, freeing energies hitherto repressed."[59]

Both Freud and Reich view sexual repression as the cause of "perversions" and mental illness in general. But Freud emphasizes the biological factor and seeks through treatment to bring the (neurotic) repressed sexual desires into consciousness, and thence to have them renounced, brought under rational control, and perhaps sublimated, whereas Reich emphasizes the social forces. Whereas Freud tends to recognize the importance of culture and the realistic need to adapt to it, Reich would alter or defy it in the interest of healthy sex, arguing that "perverse" attitudes can be eliminated only when suitable sexual outlets are available. "One can give up infantile and pathogenic desires in adulthood only if the road to normal genital gratification is open and if such gratification can be experienced."[60] The most that Freudian analysis can achieve is recognition, say, of an infantile fixation of a girl for her father, and, if moralistic arguments prevail, renunciation of it. "Actually," says Reich, "the girl can resolve the fixation to her father only if she finds a satisfactory sexual partner and experiences real gratification. If this does not happen, the infantile fixation either is not resolved or else regresses to other infantile instinctual goals, while the problem remains!"[61] Freud would seek to find more or less conventional channels; Reich advises unconventional (but "natural") ones.

Both Freud and Reich (and many other psychologists) would view most of the "perversions" cited above as true perversions. At their root are sexual attitudes appropriate at various stages of childhood. Disguised and camouflaged by guilt-ridden human beings, they manifest themselves in adult life as forms of behavior that rule out normal genital sex. These "perversions" are illnesses to be treated, rather than moral transgressions. Like all illnesses, they have both external and internal dimensions. And also like illness, they are undesirable and should be eradicated.

Conspicuous among these illnesses is homosexuality. It is true that the board of trustees of the American Psychiatric Association resolved late in 1973 to remove homosexuality "per se" from the list of "psychiatric disorders." In a referendum conducted a few months later, 5,854 of the association voted to support the board, while 3,810 members voted not to. Almost half of the eligible

[59]Reich, *The Sexual Revolution,* pp. 6, 7.
[60]Ibid., p. 16.
[61]Ibid.

membership (17,910) did not vote at all. The board did, however, define homosexuality as "a sexual orientation disturbance." And in the association's *Diagnostic and Statistical Manual of Mental Disorders,* it continues to be listed, along with fetishism, sadism, pedophilia, and others, under the heading "Sexual Deviations."[62] Despite the new ideas on homosexuality and the influence of the National Gay Task Force, American psychologists are not yet ready to view homosexuality simply as a "sex preference."

Conclusion If any of these statements of sexual norms (the natural, the moral, and the psychological) is acceptable, it does indeed follow that most "perversions" are perversions, and their expression a sign of immorality or sickness.

Most Sexual "Perversions" Are Neither Immoral Nor Sick

Nature No Guide The chief argument against sexual "perversion" is based upon a normative concept of nature. "Mother *Nature*" has certain intentions. Physiological organs have certain *natural* functions. Certain actions are proper for human *nature.* Our sexual impulses have certain *natural* expressions. When the distinction is made between natural and unnatural, the "perversions" are easily condemned, for they are "unnatural"—they deviate from the "natural." As John Stuart Mill points out:

> That any mode of thinking, feeling, or acting, is "according to nature" is usually accepted as a strong argument for its goodness. If it can be said with any plausibility that "nature enjoins" anything, the propriety of obeying the injunction is by most people considered to be made out; and conversely, the imputation of being contrary to nature is thought to bar the door against any pretension on the part of the thing so designated to be tolerated or excused, and the word "unnatural" has not ceased to be one of the most vituperative epithets in the language.[63]

The connection, however, between "unnatural" and "immoral" (and between "natural" and "moral") is not obvious. The wine taster's act of spitting out the wine instead of swallowing it goes against the natural function of drinking (which could quench thirst), but it is not immoral. The angry employee who strikes his unfair boss has behaved naturally but not morally.

Mill's criticism, however, goes more deeply: the distinction between "natural" and "unnatural" cannot legitimately be made. If we think of "nature" as "the aggregate of the powers and properties of all things," it makes no sense to say

[62]For a valuable discussion of the association's concern with the medical status of homosexuality and the arguments it inspired, see Joseph Margolis, "The Question of Homosexuality," in Baker and Elliston, *Philosophy & Sex,* p. 288ff.

[63]Mill, *Nature,* in George Nakhnikian, ed., *Nature and Utility of Religion,* p. 8.

that we should conform to nature, because no one can possibly *avoid* doing what nature enjoins. The human being necessarily obeys the laws of nature. If, however, "the useless precept to follow nature were changed into a precept to study nature—to know and take heed of the properties of things we have to deal with, so far as these properties are capable of forwarding or obstructing any given purpose—we should have arrived at the first principle of intelligent action, or rather at the definition of intelligent action itself."[64]

There is for Mill a second acceptable sense of nature: "that which takes place without human intervention." This is "nature" as the opposite of art or contrivance. To follow nature in this sense would mean to refrain from altering or improving the spontaneous course of events. If nature were taken as a *norm,* it would be *wrong* to try to alter or improve things. Mill, of course, opposes this. "If the artificial is not better than the natural, to what end are all the acts of life? To dig, to plow, to build, to wear clothes are direct infringement of the injunction to follow nature."[65] Mill also cites bridges, dams, breakwaters, and lightning rods. We could add anesthesia, fluoridated drinking water, airplanes, and night baseball.

What about instincts? Since these are natural, actions in accordance with them would be natural also, and we thus have a criterion. Mill denies this. Instincts have a great many possible expressions, and some instincts should be eradicated. A particular "instinct" could be the germ of very much or not much at all: it could be encouraged or inhibited. Mill prefers to talk about human *capacities* instead of human instincts. We have many possibilities, and what we make of them is up to us. We are each born with a nature—that is, many capacities and possibilities. This nature is altered through intelligence and discipline. We thus develop a "second nature." The *artificial* nature, then, in contrast to the raw material from which it develops, may be *superior.* "The duty of man is the same in respect to his own nature as in respect to the nature of all other things, namely, not to follow but to amend it."[66]

Freedom of the Individual In *On Liberty,* Mill makes an eloquent plea for individual liberty. Liberty is valuable for the simple reason that one should be able to shape one's own nature as one sees fit. It is not finished and definite. There is not just one model. Mill laments the fact that "peculiarity of taste, eccentricity of conduct, are shunned equally with crimes."[67] "In our times, from the lowest class of society down to the lowest, every one lives as under the eye of a hostile and dreaded censorship."[68] "If a person possesses any tolerable amount of com-

[64]Ibid., p. 12.
[65]Ibid., p. 14.
[66]Ibid., p. 37.
[67]Mill, *On Liberty,* III, in Max Lerner, ed., *Essential Works of John Stuart Mill* (New York: Bantam Books, 1961), p. 310.
[68]Ibid., III, p. 309.

mon sense and experience, his own mode of laying out his existence is best, not because it is best in itself, but because it is *his own mode.*"[69] Individuality is an important element of happiness; it must be permitted expression. "Different strokes for different folks" is a better slogan than "Follow nature," for the latter simply means what custom wants it to mean and is the parent of collective mediocrity.

Mill does, of course, recognize limits to what an individual rightfully may choose to do. There is the moral limit: Does this action promote the greatest happiness of the greatest number? Where it injures this end, it is wrong. But no appeal to what is supposedly natural will answer the moral question. Where the action does not injure the end, it is either moral or not immoral. "Moral" and "immoral" do not, for Mill, form a dichotomy. Between the moral and the immoral is the permissible. There is also a social or political limit. "The only purpose for which power [political or public opinion] can rightfully be exercised over any member of a civilized community, against his will, is to prevent harm to others. . . . Over himself, over his own body and mind, the individual is sovereign."[70] "Free scope should be given to varieties of character, short of injury to others."[71] When the harm principle is violated, society is justified in restraining the individual. When the utilitarian principle is violated, society need take no action but that of deploring the immorality.

The implications for the question of "perversions" of this statement of Western liberalism are obvious. So far as a sexual life style is based on the individual's own decisions about how to shape his or her own character, it contributes to the free and fearless attitude recommended by Mill. The person is better off (in terms of his or her own happiness) in this exercise of individuality, and society in general is better off (in terms of its own progress) for the presence of such persons. "Perversions," on the face of it, are simply eccentricities that society should tolerate.

Since there is no norm for human development beyond that of seeking to develop a character that can be happy (and which can contribute to the progress of a happy society), there can be no "deviations" from the norm. The term *perversion* is thus misleading and should have no basic role to play in the discussion. There are, as we have seen, unusual or unconventional actions, but these cannot be condemned in themselves.

Harm to Self and Others With respect to the "perversions" cited above, it should be remembered that they may be acceptable without being obligatory (beyond the general injunction to assert one's individuality). They may thus be "not immoral." One may for reasons of personal taste decide not to engage in necrophilia or exhibitionism, but anything one decides to engage in must be

[69]Ibid., p. 315. Emphasis added.
[70]Ibid., I, p. 263.
[71]Ibid., III, p. 305.

subjected to Mill's limiting principles on its own merits. If one's "perversions" do not violate them, they are acceptable—that is, not wrong. Some, then, will be acceptable, some not.

It may, of course, be foolish or self-defeating to engage in certain "perversions." And if we bring in a prudential approach to ethics, such as Dewey's, such actions would be wrong. Judgment here requires certain factual knowledge that scientists should provide for us. That the "scientists" have not always been reliable is indicated by the disgraceful history of attitudes toward masturbation. Until very recently medical authorities were almost unanimous in portraying masturbation as productive of a whole array of evils, from pimples and cancer to insanity. A generation ago some doctors even made a good living from "treating" young men for "nocturnal emissions"! For those "perversions" that can be shown to be dangerous (and masturbation is not one of them), the danger lies in the external circumstances; it is not inherent in the practice itself (with the possible exception of masochism). "Straight" sex can be dangerous in some circumstances too. Alex Comfort touches both bases (self and others) when he writes: "No form of sexual behaviour can be regarded as inacceptable, sinful, or deserving of censure unless it has demonstrable ill effects on the individual who practices it, or on others."[72]

To what extent do "perversions" *harm others*? Some obviously do not: necrophilia, fetishism, masochism, masturbation, bestiality, and cunnilingus, fellatio, sodomy, and homosexuality between consenting adults. Some rather obviously do harm others: exhibitionism and pedophilia. Some, however, are arguable. In some cases, sadism, to be sure, is harmful to others, especially when the object of sadism does not welcome it. When he or she does, however, an argument could be made for its acceptability. Much so-called "sadomasochism" is playful and symbolic, not harmful to either party. Voyeurism is harmful when it violates the right to privacy of others, but is not when directed toward pictures, movies, or shows by willing performers. Incest in those cases where children are involved would certainly be harmful, for the children are not qualified to decide what is in their interest. In other cases incest would not be ruled out by the harm principle.

Richard von Krafft-Ebing, whose *Psychopathia Sexualis* appeared in 1886, did much to sensationalize "perversions." He emphasized the monstrous nature of these actions in both agent and victim. He was fond of expressions like "moral degeneracy," "abnormal," "pollution," "horrible deed," and "obscene," and tended to blame all these loathsome practices on early and chronic masturbation. The mistake the reader is likely to make is that the horrible consequences for the agent and others necessarily follow from the "perversions" and are in no way connected with "normal" sexual desires. Fetishism *can* become obsessive and disrupt one's life. But so can love of an unavailable woman or man. Sadism *can* lead to dismemberment of a sexual partner, but so can jealousy. Homosexuality *can* lead to the corruption and rape of the young, but so can heterosexuality. The point is that a sexual orientation, whether "perverse" or "straight," should be

[72]Comfort, p. 15.

evaluated on the basis of its actual effect on the agent and others, not on the basis of the overpublicized accounts of the exploits of a John Wayne Gacy or the equally lurid people in Krafft-Ebing's cases.

To what extent do these "perversions" *conflict with the utilitarian principle*? Particular cases of "perversion" can be imagined in which the greatest happiness of the greatest number is violated. A homosexual liaison could ruin a reputation and topple a ministry, but so could a particular heterosexual liaison. But it is difficult to imagine how any "perversion" per se could compromise the happiness of society in general. If we emphasize the "rule utilitarianism" in Mill's philosophy, we could argue that the tendency of a certain type of action to decrease happiness establishes the utilitarian soundness of a particular rule, and that to violate that rule would bring it into disrepute and would make easier consequent violation by the agent and others. But "perversions" almost by definition are engaged in by minorities: most people would not be tempted to engage in them simply because they know that others do. The widespread practice of homosexuality would threaten the survival of the human race, but the birth rate is no problem now. There is little danger that homosexuality will become so popular that optimal reproduction of the race would be imperiled. The widespread practice of incest might ruin the genetic inheritance of the race and destroy the institution of the family, but there is little chance that enough people will be attracted to this "perversion" to constitute a dangerous trend. Necrophilia has about as much chance of "catching on" as coprophilia.

It is proper to apply the principle of utility to these practices, but when this is done, none seems to be seriously compromised. The burden of proof lies on those who would condemn the practices as immoral. And this proof has not been forthcoming. Until it is, the individual's unconventional sexual behavior, when no one is harmed by it, must be viewed as we view most of his or her other actions: as the individual's own business, with no moral taint. If we do not condemn the person who chases a little white ball around a golf course, we should similarly not condemn the person who has a shoe fetish.

Mental Health The argument against "perversions" based on mental health is harder to deal with and impossible to deal with adequately. That some people decline to call "perverse" practices immoral and call them sick instead, is assuredly a condemnation. Pitying "perverts" is better than beating them, but it still constitutes an attitude of disapproval. Personalities are called "disordered" because we cannot imagine "healthy" personalities engaging in such loathsome activities.

But until there is much more agreement among psychologists and philosophers on what mental and emotional health consists of, as well as the identifiable steps in the growth of this condition in the adult human being, it will be difficult to condemn (or diagnose) people who practice "perversions." Many of us have the feeling that exhibitionists, sadists, masochists, necrophiles, and pedophiles are sick, as well as those who engage in bestiality and fetishism, but it is difficult to say exactly why. Perhaps there are data to indicate that they are associated with *other* personality disorders that prevent successful functioning. But there assuredly are no data to indicate that people who practice fellatio, cunnilingus, sodomy, or homosexuality are unable to function successfully. By all tests of normal behavior (apart from the "perversions" themselves), they compare favorably with their "straight" contemporaries.

It might be noted that some "perverts," such as homosexuals, have a heavy burden to bear in the form of public disapproval of their life style and disappointment by family and friends. If some of them stagger a bit, it may be attributable to these external factors quite as much as to the presence of the "perversion" in their mental and emotional outlook. An important component in personality disorder is the feeling of guilt or uncertainty in the individual's own mind because of conflict with society's values. In societies where certain "abnormal" actions are approved (such as homosexuality, forms of sadism, masochism, and fetishism), people who practice them are not so likely to be psychologically disturbed. Homosexuals seem to be no more deranged than many of the rest of us; and if they are, the explanation is obvious.

It is possible to argue that not all forms of behavior that are immature or even neurotic are indicative of severe mental or emotional illness. "Many sexual manifestations are indeed examples of what psychiatrists term regression—but so are smoking, praying, swearing, playing jokes or football, and going to the pictures —to say nothing of the fantasy pleasures we derive from art and literature. Shorn of all immaturities we would be equally shorn of most of our motivation."[73]

Most moral statements or "models" of sexual relations beg the question, for they include the very ethical concepts that are at issue. Nothing is proved if one condemns "perversions" simply because they conflict with a rather arbitrary conception of what sexual experience should be.

Body Language An interesting alternative to these moral "models" has been provided by Robert Solomon. His "model" for sexuality is "a means of communicating with other people, a way of talking to them, of expressing our feelings about ourselves and them. It is essentially a language, in which one can express gentleness and affection, anger and resentment, superiority and dependence far more succinctly than would be possible verbally. . . ."[74] Sexuality is one of the important body languages that human beings possess. Like verbal languages, body languages "are born and grow in a societal context, as means of communication."[75]

Some people employ the sexual body language well (creatively, forcefully, effectively, articulately, gracefully); some do not. It may be used to please, manipulate, offend, charm, and so on. It can be enjoyable not simply because of what

[73]Ibid., p. 16.

[74]Robert Solomon, "Sex and Perversion," in Baker and Elliston, *Philosophy & Sex,* p. 279.

[75]Ibid., p. 280.

it does, but because of what it *says.* "One enjoys not just the tender caress but the message it carries; and one welcomes a painful thrust or bite not because of masochism but because of the meaning, in context, that it conveys."[76]

Let us now apply Solomon's model to "perversions." Since sexuality as a body language lends itself to many kinds of expressions (some creative, some forced), it "admits of breaches in comprehension." And this is where we find "perversion." "Perversion" is not a moral term but a case of "sexual incompatibility" or "sexual misunderstanding."

Masturbation, for example, is a case of "speaking to oneself." It is not immoral, but it does not rate high on the communication scale, since the person is expressing himself or herself without an audience. "Masturbation is the sexual equivalent of a Cartesian soliloquy."[77] Sadism and masochism are perversions when "expressions of dominance and dependence turn into actions" that are not welcomed by the other: a breakdown of communication. "When sadistic actions are not expected, they are to sexuality as real bullets in a supposedly prop gun are to the stage."[78] It may take a person a while to realize what is going on because he or she is not very perceptive or because his or her partner is too subtle or inarticulate. Oral and anal sex are not necessarily perversions but different ways to communicate. "Sexuality conceived as a language of intimacy and feeling that calls for ever new variations and inventiveness has as its worst violators those who, unimaginative and illiterate themselves, attempt to force others to accept their limited and impoverished vocabulary."[79] "Subway exhibitionism" is offensive because it is a vulgar, blatant, and unsubtle way to use language. Fetishism may indicate "stupidity, poor vocabulary, or fear of communicating, but it might be extreme ingenuity in the face of an impoverished sexual field."[80] A voyeur is a person who does not have much to say, but who perhaps is a good listener. Pedophilia and bestiality would seem to be perversions, for the person is "conversing" with beings who lack the ability to understand. Group sex need not be a perversion, but it *is* difficult to carry on several conversations at the same time. And homosexuality, according to Solomon, is not in itself a perversion unless—as in cases of heterosexuality—there is a breach of communication.

On this "model" of sexuality, then, perversion occurs when sexual body language fails in its function of communicating effectively and sincerely. It is not the act itself that is offensive, but the use that is made of it. If we don't like what other people "say" sexually, we should avoid them instead of questioning their morals.

Conclusion The sexual mores of a particular society conflict with those of many other societies. Yet the conformists in every society are convinced that their own

[76]Ibid., p. 281.
[77]Ibid., p. 283.
[78]Ibid., p. 284.
[79]Ibid.
[80]Ibid., p. 285.

attitudes are right. Their own sexual practices are natural, moral, and healthy; deviations are unnatural, immoral, and unhealthy. It is important that we know the mores of our own society, not in order to adhere to them, but in order to know what is expected and what is condemned—and why some people are disabled by the requirements of their own culture.

Summary of the Issues

Actions may be called perverse when they deviate from the normal. If the norm for sexual behavior is a naturalistic one, sexual "perversions" that deviate from it are perversions (unnatural). If the norm is a moral one, sexual "perversions" that deviate from it are perversions (immoral). If the norm is a psychological one, sexual "perversions" that deviate from it are perversions (sick). Since the term *perversion* definitely has a connotation of strong disapproval, the question is whether so-called perversions really are perversions.

The *naturalistic norm* has been adopted by some people who would condemn sexual "perversions." It is based on the view that the human being is endowed by nature with a certain physiology and is required to employ it in an appropriate way. A narrow interpretation of the view is that the sexual organs are "designed" for reproduction and should be used for that purpose. When they are not, the action is perverted (and thus bad). A broader interpretation of the view is that sexual behavior is natural if it is the kind that *could* lead to reproduction, whether reproduction is the intention of the agent or not. According to this interpretation, a great many "perversions" are indeed perversions, but some of them are not. A third interpretation of the naturalistic norm is more humanistic. It seeks to bring out the qualities that distinguish humankind from the lower animals. The naturalistic norm, however interpreted, has strong ethical overtones. Its adherents say, "Follow nature."

Mill and others reject this norm, arguing that the distinction between "natural" and "unnatural" cannot be made. They point out that people, while necessarily obeying the *laws* of nature, can and should amend what they find in nature—in themselves as well as around them. There are many possibilities, and progress in general depends upon the intelligent exploitation of these possibilities. Since nature itself provides no norms, there can be no deviations. "Perversion of nature" is a nonsensical expression.

An avowedly *moral norm* is suggested by the humanistic approach. Here an attempt is made to specify the kind of relations that should obtain between sexual partners. Many versions of such a norm would indeed imply that most of the "perversions" are indeed perversions, for they deviate from the norm.

Some people, however, would view sexual behavior in the wider context of moral/immoral behavior itself. Appealing to utilitarianism, they might argue that the only moral limitation on what the individual can do lies in the harm that results for the agent and for others. According to this principle, a great many "perversions" are ethically acceptable and thus not perversions at all. That certain "perversions" generally conflict with the utilitarian principle is no more obvious than "straight" sexual behavior does so.

The *psychological norm* is derived from certain conceptions of healthy psychological development. Freud, Reich, and others have shown that "perversions" result from internal or external pressures that distort normal growth. Since these aberrations are instances of deviating from a norm, they indeed are perversions. It might be more appropriate, however, to call them mental disorders than simply to condemn them as immoral.

Opponents of this view, however, point to the disagreement among psychologists on what constitutes normal personality or mental and emotional health. A great many people who engage in sexual "perversions" do indeed function successfully in other areas of life. Much of the strain that they sometimes exhibit is due, not to their practices themselves, but to harsh public disapproval.

An attempt to remove the question of perversion from the field of morals is represented by the view that conceives sexual behavior to be a kind of body language. The model for sexual behavior is effective communication. Sexual behavior that falls short of the model is perverse to a greater or lesser degree. According to this approach, some "perversions" in some contexts are perverse, and some "perversions" in some contexts are not.

Discussion Questions

1. Which "perversions" (if any) do you think are symptomatic of mental illness? Explain.
2. Is it true, as Mill says, that sexual practices that do not harm the self or others are ethically permissible? Why?
3. Are there any prima facie duties that are relevant to "perversion"? If so, what are they and why?
4. Do you think that a "rule utilitarianism" case can be made against any "perversions"? If so, how?
5. Do you think that an "ideal utilitarianism" case can be made against any "perversion"? If so, how?
6. Which naturalistic norm (if any) is a suitable standard for sexual perversion? Why?
7. What kind of a moral norm (if any) would you defend as a suitable standard for sexual perversion? Why?
8. If you believe that someone is sexually perverted, would you blame him or her on moral grounds or feel sympathy on health grounds? Why?
9. Do you think that homosexuals are more emotionally disturbed than heterosexuals? What evidence would you adduce?
10. Which "perversions" (if any) do you think are morally wrong? Why?
11. Do you agree with the view that sexual behavior is a form of body language and that most perversions are ethically neutral? Why?
12. Which "perversion" do you think is least defensible? Which is most defensible? Why?
13. Do you agree with Reich that most sexual perversions are produced by society's repressive attitude toward sex? Why?

14. Do you agree with Freud that most sexual perversions result from the failure of the individual to grow out of certain infantile attitudes? Why?
15. Is homosexuality per se less moral than heterosexuality? Why?

For Further Reading

See also the citations with asterisks in "For Further Reading" at the end of the first section.

Robert Baker and Frederick Elliston, eds. *Philosophy & Sex.* Buffalo: Prometheus Books, 1975. See especially: Thomas Nagel, "Sexual Perversion"; Michael Slote, "Inapplicable Concepts and Sexual Perversion"; Robert Solomon, "Sex and Perversion"; Joseph Margolis, "The Question of Homosexuality."

M. J. Buckley. *Morality and the Homosexual: A Catholic Approach to a Moral Problem.* Westminster, Md.: Newman Press, 1960.

V. L. Bullough. "Is Homosexuality an Illness?" *The Humanist* 34 (November 1974): 27–30.

J. L. Clark. "Coming Out: The Process and the Price." *Christianity and Crisis* 39 (June 11, 1979):149–153.

F. Craddock. "How Does the New Testament Deal with the Issue of Homosexuality?" *Encounter* 40 (Summer 1979):197–208.

Sigmund Freud. *Three Contributions to the Theory of Sex.* Translated by A. A. Brill. New York: E. P. Dutton & Co., 1962.

A. H. Goldman. "Plain Sex." *Philosophy of Public Affairs* 6 (Spring 1977):267–287.

R. Gray. "Sex and Sexual Perversion." *Journal of Philosophy* 75 (April 1978):189–199.

J. P. Gump. "Sex-Role Attitudes and Psychological Well-Being." *Journal of Social Issues* 28, no. 2 (1972):79–92.

C. Heyward. "Coming Out: Journey without Maps." *Christianity and Crisis* 39 (June 11, 1979):149–153.

Martin Hoffman. *The Gay World.* New York: Basic Books, 1968.

E. Hooker. *Final Report of the Task Force on Homosexuality.* Bethesda, Md.: National Institute of Mental Health, 1969.

J. Kupfer. "Sexual Perversion and the Good." *Personalist* 59 (January 1978):70–77.

Donald Levy. "Perversion and the Unnatural as Moral Categories." *Ethics* 90 (January 1980):191–202.

S. McCracken. "Are Homosexuals Gay?" *Commentary* 67 (January 1979):19–29.

S. Marcus. "Freud's Three Essays on the Theory of Sexuality." *Partisan Review* 42, no. 4 (1975):517–534.

Judd Marmor, ed. *Sexual Inversion.* New York: Basic Books, 1965. See especially: Thomas S. Sasz, "Legal and Moral Aspects of Homosexuality."

John Stuart Mill. *Nature.* In George Nakhnikian, ed., *Nature and Utility of Religion.* Indianapolis: Liberal Arts Press, 1958.

John Stuart Mill. *On Liberty.* Many editions.

Jean-Paul Sartre. *Being and Nothingness.* Translated by Hazel E. Barnes. New York: Philosophical Library, 1956. Part 3 ("Being-for-Others"), pp. 221–431.

Anthony Storr. *Sexual Deviation.* Baltimore: Penguin Books, 1964.

Chapter 3

LIFE AND DEATH

In this chapter we will probe some questions of life and death.

There are many areas in which one must make some very important decisions concerning the lives of others and oneself. The very existence of life, as well as its biological quality and continuation, is well within human control. Here again it is obvious that a responsible ethical judgment can best be made in the light of knowledge of the relevant facts and sensitivity to ethical standards. Often the decision is not easy. The questions are so momentous, however, that we should be willing to give them the careful study and deep thought that they require.

The first topic is in the area of *genetic engineering.* Biologists have discovered many of the genetic principles that determine our physical characteristics. What one is at birth is increasingly subject to prediction and control. To what extent should this knowledge be used to prevent undesirable traits and to produce desirable traits? Should individuals who intend to have children subject themselves to genetic counseling and screening? Should a concerted effort be made to improve the human race or to prevent its deterioration?

Great advances have also been made in the scientific control of reproduction. Artificial insemination, fertilization in vitro, and surrogate motherhood are already feasible procedures for human beings, and gestation in vitro will soon be feasible. Cloning has been done with lower animals, and biologists are advancing to the point where it may be possible for human beings. The procedures of recombinant DNA makes possible the transplantation of genes into the germ cell itself (although not yet in that of human beings). As we shall see, this new technology inspires many difficult ethical problems.

The second area is that of *abortion*. Statute law and Supreme Court decisions tell us what we may legally do, but individuals (parents and medical personnel) must determine what on moral grounds they ought to do. Does the fetus have any rights? Is it a form of human life? Is it a person? Under what conditions, if any, should or may its life be terminated? Perhaps the law and the Constitution should be changed.

The third area is that of *suicide.* Under what conditions, if any, does the individual have the right to terminate his or her own life? The related issue of voluntary euthanasia (as well as nonvoluntary euthanasia) will be discussed in chapter 7 (under the topic "Freedom of Action"). The issue here is the general one: Is a person who wants to take his own life ever morally justified in doing so?

There are additional areas involving life and death that will not be dealt with here, just as there are areas of sexual morality that were omitted from discussion in the previous chapter. The issue of capital punishment is briefly discussed in chapter 6 (under the topic "The Justice of Punishment"). The issue of killing in war is discussed in chapter 8 (under the topic "The Draft"). And some issues (such as contraception) will not be discussed at all.

GENETIC ENGINEERING

The Efforts of Biologists to Enhance the Quality and Possibility of Life Should Be Supported

Genetics Genetic engineering is based upon the pure science of biology, especially that branch of biology called genetics. It seeks to apply this knowledge in at least two ways: (1) in the detection, treatment, and elimination of genetic disease and (2) in the artificial production of various forms of life. The definition of Laurence E. Karp covers both: "We might consider Genetic Engineering to represent any attempt to modify the structure, transmission, expression, or effects of the genes, the ultimate directors of heredity."[1]

Genes are composed of DNA (deoxyribonucleic acid) and subsist on chromosomes as beads on a chain. One can only estimate the number of genes carried by human beings (between 50,000 and 1,000,000), but the number of chromosomes is fixed at forty-six. Half of our genes (and chromosomes) come from each parent. Each cell of the human body normally contains a full complement of genes and chromosomes. What do the genes do? They *direct the production of particular proteins* or parts thereof. "Some of these proteins order embryonic development; others are enzymes (catalysts which control cellular metabolic reactions); still others become part of the body structure."[2] Some genes will direct the formation of one organ, others the formation of another.

Genes and chromosomes occur in pairs, a member of each pair inherited from each parent. Members of a pair of genes are called *alleles.* If both members are the same, the person is said to be *homozygous* for that gene. If, however, the alleles are different, the person is said to be *heterozygous* for that gene: one must prevail (dominant gene) and the other "remain silent" (recessive gene).[3] Presumably all

[1]Karp, *Genetic Engineering: Threat or Promise?,* p. xii. This section and the next are deeply indebted to Dr. Karp's excellent book.
[2]Ibid., p. 3.
[3]There are a few genes that are *co-dominant.* A person may inherit the gene for blood type A from one parent and the gene for blood type B from the other. Instead of one prevailing, they both operate and the person has blood type AB.

genes are either dominant or recessive, so the only way a recessive gene can direct matters is when the same recessive gene is inherited from *both* parents. Most observable manifestations of genetic action (traits or characters) are the results of several different genes and are called *polygenic.* A few traits, however, are linked to *one* gene (or a single allelic pair) and are called *monogenic.* Since the gene supply for any individual is large and the number of possible combinations for polygenic traits is vast, offspring can differ substantially from their parents despite the fact that all their genes are inherited. The only way that novelty can be introduced is by *mutation* of an inherited gene. This involves a structural alteration of the DNA and is nearly always unfavorable.

Chromosomes for sex determination operate differently from the others. Normal eggs have an X chromosome, while sperm have either an X or a Y chromosome. When an XX embryo is formed, it is a female. When an XY embryo is formed, it is a male. The Y chromosome carries no genes except those which determine sex, but the X chromosome carries others as well. In the female embryo, "one of the two X chromosomes in each cell enters a life of functional inactivation. The result is that both men and women are left with 45 identical chromosomes which carry the genes for general body functions."[4] The forty-sixth chromosome, in the case of males, is Y; in the case of females, it is the inactive X. The forty-fifth chromosome, present in both sexes, is the X.

Genetic Diseases The first great concern of genetic engineering is how to deal with genetic diseases. Karp has classified genetic diseases under three headings:

1. Chromosomal abnormalities. One subclass is that of errors of chromosome number. Instead of having a pair of a particular chromosome, an individual may have three (trisomy) or one (monosomy). Most of the victims die by miscarriage. Down's syndrome (mongolism) is an example of trisomy and is one of the few diseases of this subclass that is not necessarily fatal. The other subclass is that of errors of chromosome structure. This includes gene duplication and deletion, and translocation of chromosomes. There is a very high correlation of chromosomal abnormality and advanced age of the mother, perhaps because the eggs (all of which were formed when the mother was a fetus) become defective in time. But nothing is yet known about the ultimate cause of chromosomal aberration.

2. Single gene defects. One subclass consists of those diseases caused by the mutation of a dominant gene—either in a forebear or in the individual. A mutant gene directs the production of a somewhat different protein; almost none is favorable. A parent carrying a mutant dominant gene stands a 50 percent chance of passing on the trait to each offspring. Among the common diseases caused by single mutant genes are achondroplastic dwarfism, Huntington's disease, polycystic kidneys, and retinoblastoma. A second subclass consists of those diseases caused by mutant recessive genes. Unlike the former subclass, these are negative

[4]Ibid., p. 6.

in result, for "the normal allele compensates for the functional absence of its partner."[5] Disease results only when the offspring inherits a malfunctioning recessive gene from *both* parents.[6] When one parent is a carrier and one is not, there is no risk. But when both parents are carriers, probability indicates that one in four offspring will have the disease and two in four will be carriers. The probability that *their* offspring will have the disease is much smaller, since the incidence of mutant genes in the general population (or gene pool) is very low. While we all carry mutant recessive genes (estimated at three to seven), the chances of mating with someone who has the same ones are low. One common recessive disorder is sickle cell anemia. Most recessive diseases are caused by errors of metabolism—faulty or absent enzymes. Examples are phenylketonuria, Tay-Sachs disease, and cystic fibrosis. The third subclass consists of diseases commonly called "sex-linked," but more accurately "X-linked." Since males possess only one X chromosome, they have no normal allele to compensate for a negative mutant gene carried on their X chromosome. Females who receive the normal X chromosome and the abnormal X chromosome will not be diseased, but will be carriers. They will carry the disease to male offspring who are unfortunate enough to get the mother's abnormal X (along with the normal Y from the father). A son's chances of having the disease are thus fifty-fifty. The afflicted man cannot pass on the disease to his children. His sons will receive the normal X from their mother (along with the father's normal Y). His daughters, however, having inherited his abnormal X along with their mother's normal X, will all be unafflicted carriers. Common X-linked recessive diseases are color blindness, hemophilia, and muscular dystrophy.

3. Multifactorial diseases. Unlike diseases of the previous type, these are the results of the interaction of *several* pairs. They are thus polygenically determined. Among the human traits that are polygenically determined is intelligence, so congenital mental retardation is a multifactorial disease. Many common birth defects "are thought to be caused by a polygenically determined heightened sensibility of some individuals to a particular environmental factor that tends to interfere with normal fetal development."[7] For some reason, "the recurrence risk for multifactorial diseases increases progressively with the birth of each afflicted child."[8] This, of course, is not the case for the monogenic diseases discussed above. Examples of common multifactorial diseases are cleft lip and palate, club foot, congenital heart diseases, diabetes mellitus, and epilepsy.

Genetic Counseling These, then are some of the basic facts as presently understood by geneticists. Where does the "engineering" begin? Let us first look at ways of dealing with genetic disease.

[5]Ibid., p. 27.
[6]It is important to remember that not all recessive genes are bad—only those that have experienced a mutation. And not all mutations are harmful, although most are.
[7]Ibid., p. 31.
[8]Ibid., p. 32.

Here the opportunity for human betterment is enormous. On the basis of what is already known, doctors can treat and provide some relief for genetic diseases that in earlier times were hopeless. Also, on the basis of this knowledge, we can counteract the conception and birth of many genetically afflicted children. When the disease is severe, this is a boon to society, the family, and the children themselves. As the relatively young science of genetics advances, we will be able to identify and deal, positively or negatively, with more and more genetic diseases.

The very least that can be done is provide *genetic counseling*—that is, advice to families that have reason to believe that there is risk of genetic disease in their projected offspring. There are already several hundred counseling centers in the United States. There should be more, and they should be more aggressive in bringing individuals in for counseling. At present, most counselees are people who have already had genetic tragedy in their immediate families and want to know how likely it is to happen again. Had they come in earlier, they might have spared themselves and society a great burden.

Accurate knowledge (including diagnosis where possible) of all genetic disease in the family tree is helpful, as well as of all miscarriages in the immediate family. Counselors will also be interested in childhood deaths, many of which could have been caused by a genetic disorder. They will want to know about geographic and racial backgrounds, for many diseases are more common in particular ethnic groups. They will want to know the ages of the prospective parents, for that of the mother is relevant to multifactorial diseases and that of the father is relevant to some diseases of dominant gene mutation. It is hoped that great data banks containing extensive genetic information about the whole population will be established so that the counselor will have at his fingertips information about the family that his counselees may not be able to provide. It is also hoped that genetic science will continue to advance, so that it will be possible to state the genetic inheritance of each individual—especially with respect to deleterious genes. The greater the knowledge (and its availability), the more accurate will be the indication of risk that prospective parents face.

In cases where a deleterious recessive gene is known to be possessed by both parents, it is already possible to predict that the next child stands a one-in-four chance of being inflicted. If one parent is found to possess a deleterious dominant gene, the child has a one-in-two chance of being afflicted. In these cases, as well as X-linked diseases, simple mathematical probability operates. For multifactorial diseases and those caused by chromosomal abnormalities, empirical probabilities can sometimes be cited. Parents may well decide not to conceive a child if the probability is 0.25 or better that he or she will have a serious or untreatable genetic disease.

Genetic Screening A procedure that would greatly contribute to genetic health is genetic screening: "the systematic examination of populations, the purpose of which is to detect persons who carry hereditary abnormalities capable of producing disease in those persons themselves or their descendants."[9] The population may be general or selective—that is, a specific subpopulation known to be at high risk. Such a program would be feasible only if tests were available that were simple, inexpensive, and reliable. The program may be directed toward adults, children, newborn infants, or fetuses. The nature of the program would depend on the particular disease screened for, as well as the state of genetic science.

If examination of the genetic facts indicates high risk for a couple, birth control may be recommended. If an egg has been fertilized in the case of a high-risk couple, the presence of the disease in the fetus can sometimes be checked by the process of *amniocentesis.*[10] If the fetus is found to be afflicted, abortion should seriously be considered. All newborn babies should be examined, for some genetic diseases can be treated if detected early—if that is the wish of the parents. This kind of genetic screening thus makes possible a more intelligent decision by parents and prospective parents.

Phenylketonuria (PKU) is a terrible genetic disease involving severe mental retardation, seizures, and skin lesions. About one person in fifty in the United States carries the recessive gene for PKU. It can be detected by amniocentesis. Most states require screening for this disease in all newborn infants. If detected early, treatment can correct the error of metabolism that is at the root of the trouble. But the child remains a carrier and should be so identified.[11] Other errors of metabolism, such as galactosemia, can also be screened for.

Although the presence of the PKU gene cannot be detected in healthy carriers, other recessive genes can be.[12] That for Tay-Sachs disease (TSD) is an example. There is no cure for this disease, death usually occurring at age three or four after a painful period of pervasive deterioration. If a couple both carry the recessive gene, they stand a one-in-four chance of conceiving an afflicted child. If they decide to go ahead anyway, they still have another option, for TSD can be detected by amniocentesis. Surely at this point abortion is in order. Since TSD is much more common among Ashkenazic Jews than any other group, selective screening is indicated.

Sickle cell anemia (SCA) is common among American blacks, approximately one in twelve being a carrier and one baby in 600 being a victim, so this disease also lends itself to selective screening. Sickled cells block small blood vessels

[9]Ibid., p. 65.

[10]This procedure involves withdrawing a sample of the amniotic fluid surrounding the fetus by means of a needle. The cells of the fetus can then be examined. It is not a completely safe procedure, however, so it should be employed only when there is some reason to suspect the occurrence of the disease. Over fifty diseases can be identified by this method.

[11]Moreover, if the child later becomes a mother, an additional precaution is in order. Since she discontinued her special diet designed to keep down her level of phenylalanine after her brain was formed (around age six), the chemical began to accumulate again. Although it is by this time harmless to the adult, it can pass into the fetus causing irreparable injury to the brain. A woman who realizes that she has PKU should resume the special diet (which is unpalatable) from the very moment of known pregnancy.

[12]Tests are available for detecting carriers of over fifty recessive gene diseases.

(preventing the flow of oxygen) and produces clots in bone, lung, and spleen tissue. All this is very painful and eventually produces death, usually in the twenties. There is no known cure or prenatal test for SCA. But there are methods of determining its carriers (as well as its victims). So these individuals might well choose their mates carefully. If a couple are both carriers, contraception would seem to be advisable. With SCA, amniocentesis does not provide a second chance as it does with PKU.

It would be very beneficial if carriers for such X-linked diseases as hemophilia and Duchenne muscular dystrophy could be detected, but no tests are as yet available. But since we know that all daughters of victims are carriers, they can be identified, as well as all victims' mothers. The victim himself will know that all his daughters will be carriers. This is surely useful information for some people who want to have children.

Multifactorial diseases do not yet lend themselves to screening. One possible exception is the anencephaly/spina-bifida complex of serious birth defects of the nervous system. They may soon be detectable in the fetus. Diabetes mellitus and hypertension are multifactorial diseases but cannot be detected in utero or perhaps even in infancy.

Screening programs for various chromosomal disorders have been useful. "Chromosomal diseases are relatively new to our recognition, and the first step in dealing with them is to delineate precisely which clinical abnormalities are associated with which chromosomal abnormalities."[13] Much progress has been made through studying karyotypes (photographs of a set of chromosomes from a cell, arranged for study in a standardized fashion). Screening is not only useful in anticipating the future, but also for suggesting early treatment and relief for such diseases as Klinefelter's syndrome (XXY) and Turner's syndrome (XO), the symptoms of which are not manifest until the late teens.

Screening has been objected to because it is expensive and so far deals only with "rare" diseases. But rare diseases add up.[14] And it is assuredly more expensive to take care of the unfortunate individuals who are afflicted than to prevent their birth in the first place. Where screening can assist in the making of informed choices on whether to conceive or, once having conceived, to abort, it would be foolish not to employ it. As techniques are improved, more diseases can be brought under scrutiny and expenses will go down.

When screening programs are planned for the population or a subpopulation, should they be compulsory or voluntary? Those who argue for the latter say that most people who have been educated to the need will take part voluntarily. But this is dubious. The rationale for some programs is difficult to convey. Moreover, some groups resent being singled out and "stigmatized." Public health officials

[13]Karp, p. 79.

[14]By the mid-seventies around 2,300 genetically related disorders had been identified. "It has been estimated that more than 25 percent of the hospitalizations of children are for illnesses with a major genetic component." Theodore Friedmann, "Prenatal Diagnosis of Genetic Disease," in Beauchamp and Walters, eds., *Contemporary Issues in Bioethics,* p. 572.

should make recommendations to legislatures and request compulsory screening programs when they are indicated. As Francis Crick said, "If we can get across to people the idea that their children are not entirely their own business and that it is not a private matter, it would be an enormous step forward."[15]

Eugenics Because genetic disease is harmful to individuals and to the society that has to take care of them, we should go much further than merely explaining to families the probable consequences of conception and childbirth. We should educate them to the value of eugenics and influence them, for the good of their offspring and society, as well as for their own good, to avoid producing genetically damaged children.

We have now entered the controversial area of eugenics. Since we have been discussing the avoidance of the birth of defective offspring, our concern has been with *negative* eugenics. Negative eugenics contributes to the aim of producing healthy children and a healthy population. It also reduces the drain on society of money and personnel required to take care of genetically diseased people. We should indeed utilize our expanding knowledge of genetics and our ability to quantify the risk faced by prospective parents. Negative eugenics is espoused by anyone who has any concern for future generations and problems of health care.

There are still two questions that should be raised and answered: (1) Should negative eugenics be compulsory? (2) What should be the status of *positive* eugenics? The emphasis of positive eugenics is not simply to avoid defective specimens but to foster increasingly better ones in the future.

Negative eugenics should be compulsory for *some* genetic diseases. Which ones? Those that require institutionalizing for their victims *and* that can be predicted with reasonable accuracy *and* that meet a prescribed minimum of probability of risk (say, 0.25). The first requirement would exclude those diseases that can be treated (such as PKU). The second would exclude many diseases that are multifactorial. The third would exclude those for which the risk is less than 25 percent (such as those that result from the marriage of first cousins whose family trees are healthy). As additional treatments are discovered, the list of diseases would tend to drop; but as more knowledge is acquired about genetic causes and screening becomes more widespread, the list would tend to increase.

How would compulsory negative eugenics be carried out? Abortion suggests itself, but there are important moral issues here. Most of us would not impose abortion against the will of a pregnant woman whose expected child is believed to have a good chance of being defective. Contraception suggests itself. But the trouble here is that contraception is not completely reliable and many people who should practice it will not do so (or will do so carelessly). This leaves sterilization. For carriers of mutant dominant genes, sterilization should be a prerequisite for obtaining a marriage license. For a couple who both carry a deleterious recessive gene, sterilization of one of them should be a condition for marriage. Women who

[15]Quoted in Joseph Fletcher, "The Ethics of Genetic Control," in Beauchamp and Walters, p. 587.

carry X-linked deleterious genes should also face sterilization as a condition for marriage. Couples who have had offspring with chromosomal or multifactorial diseases that reach the 0.25 figure should have to submit to sterilization for one of its parties.[16] The obvious rebuttal to the premarital sterilization proposal is to point out that many lovers who cannot get marriage licenses for genetic reasons will simply decide to live together and produce their defective children anyway. Perhaps nothing can be done with people who choose this route. However, we might believe it advisable to sterilize one of the couple as soon as a defective child has been born. This seems cruel, but the offending couple has, in the face of good advice and clear public policy, already injured the next generation and should not be permitted to do so again.[17]

Positive eugenics is in a somewhat different situation. There is, for example, greater disagreement among citizens as to what constitutes biological fitness. Should we try to produce more blue-eyed blondes? Or rock stars? Or athletes? Or geneticists? And what kind of balance in the population would we want to achieve? We would not want to have so many philosophers that most have to drive taxicabs (as many do), or so many chemists that most have to tend gas pumps. And even if we agree on the "mix," would we think it right to try to produce enough dim-witted people with enough patience to do menial jobs uncomplainingly? In any case it would appear to be a great infringement on individual liberty to require a prospective parent to mate with someone who had the desirable genetic makeup. While we can agree that some genes are bad and legitimately take steps to prevent their occurrence, we cannot certify those that are "good" and properly require matings that reproduce them. Finally, there is a serious practical problem. Most of the "good" traits, such as strength and intelligence, are multifactorial. They are thus much more difficult to create than diseased traits are to prevent.

So positive eugenics should be left to the individuals who want to practice it. While there is nothing wrong in seeking an egg or sperm that will tend to produce the kind of offspring desired, it should not be a matter of public policy required by law.

Reproduction: Artificial Insemination The second general type of genetic engineering is that which has to do with reproduction. Artificial means for conceiving, bearing, and delivering offspring have been and are being developed.

[16]Where empirical probabilities are reliable, they should be utilized when they reach 0.25 whether or not there have been previous births.

[17]"To go right ahead with coital reproduction in many couples' cases is like walking down a line of children blindfolded and deliberately maiming every fourth child. It is cruel and insane to deprive normal but disadvantaged children of the care we could give them with the $1,500,000,000 we spend in public costs for preventable retardates. . . . Ideally it is better to do the moral thing freely, but sometimes it is more compassionate to force it to be done than sacrifice the well-being of the many to the egocentric 'rights' of the few. This obviously is the ethics of a sane society." Ibid., pp. 585–586.

There are several ways to produce offspring that do not require sexual intercourse. Although most of these ways are still experimental as far as human life is concerned, artificial insemination is available for almost any woman who wants it. Semen, obtained through masturbation, is introduced into or near the woman's cervix (the constricted lower part of the uterus) at about the time of ovulation. If conception does not take place, the procedure is repeated during later cycles. The success rate is very high.

Artificial insemination is a boon to couples who cannot conceive children naturally. If the husband's semen contains sperm in insufficient quantity, several of his specimens can be pooled and concentrated. Or there may be certain anatomic abnormalities in one or both of the partners that prevent natural insemination. Or the husband may want to freeze and preserve his sperm for use at a later time, believing, perhaps, that it is of better quality now than later, or because he intends to get a vasectomy.

In cases where the husband is sterile, artificial insemination by a donor (AID) may utilize the semen of an anonymous male. Several sperm banks exist in this country, providing fresh or frozen semen to doctors and prospective parents. A single woman who does not wish to marry or cohabit but wants to have a child may employ the services of AID. The donors, paid for their semen, are usually medical students and interns. And while their blood type and general physical appearance are revealed to doctor and parents, their identity is not.

Sterility or the lack of a husband is not the only reason for AID. A husband may carry a deleterious dominant gene, and the couple wisely refuses to take the 50 percent risk. It may be that both partners carry the same deleterious recessive gene and wisely decline to take the 25 percent risk. Or they may have incompatible blood types. Recently some Nobel laureates in California made their semen available for eugenic purposes. AID, then, may be employed not only to have children, but to avoid producing defective children (negative eugenics), to produce outstanding children (positive eugenics),[18] and to prevent harm to the mother. These are worthy ends.

Another possible benefit from artificial insemination is the determination of sex. Many parents would like to know the gender of their future children for family planning. Some couples have six or seven children before they get the girl or boy they want, and some never do get their choice. For genetic reasons also it is sometimes important to know the sex of the child. This obviously holds for X-linked genes. Female carriers would want to have daughters (none would be afflicted, though half would be carriers), but not sons (half would be afflicted). An afflicted man would opt for sons, none of whom would be afflicted. Presumably, hemophilia and muscular dystrophy could eventually be eliminated. The sex of a fetus can be determined by amniocentesis, but this must take place in the

[18]Some positive eugenicists urge husbands to step aside so that their wives may get genetically superior sperm from outstanding scientists, athletes, or artists. This approach is called eutelegenesis. Confidentiality of donor may or may not be required.

sixteenth week of pregnancy, and abortion (if decided on) has its risks—as does amniocentesis itself. This is the only reliable method at present, though it is hoped that an easier and earlier method of fetal detection will become available. But if a method for separating the X- and Y-bearing sperm in the semen could be discovered, artificial insemination would be the means for determining the gender *in advance*—before conception takes place. Perhaps some of us will live to see this.

The logical counterpart to donor insemination is "surrogate parenting." If a wife is infertile, her husband's sperm is used to impregnate a surrogate mother. The surrogate bears the child and turns him or her over to the natural father and adoptive mother. Surrogate Parenting Associates, Inc., of Louisville, which observes very strict screening and legal procedures, offers a fee of around $10,000 to suitable surrogates (who are never permitted to meet the couple). The first baby was born in November 1980, and the company has many clients.

Reproduction: Ectogenesis The next type of artificial reproduction is more controversial: *ectogenesis,* methods of permitting an egg or embryo to perform some of its development *outside* the female reproductive tract. Growth in vitro (literally, "in glass") at some or all of the stages replaces development in vivo ("in something alive"). There are several possibilities (some *only* possibilities) for human reproduction: removal of an egg from the ovaries, fertilization in the laboratory, and gestation in an artificial womb; removal of an egg, fertilization in the laboratory, and implantation of the embryo in the mother or surrogate mother; removal of an embryo and full or partial gestation in an artificial womb or a surrogate mother. These have all been done with lower animals. In the case of humans, two great achievements are on record. On July 25, 1978, Louise Brown, the first "test tube baby" was born. Dr. Patrick Steptoe and Dr. Robert Edwards had removed an egg from one of Mrs. Brown's ovaries and fertilized it in vitro with Mr. Brown's semen, and two days later had implanted the embryo in Mrs. Brown's womb. The other achievement was similar, but it involved implanting the embryo in a woman other than the one who supplied the egg.

The possibilities for human betterment in these and similar techniques are tremendous. (1) Women who are infertile because of such abnormalities as blocked fallopian tubes may have children of their own. (2) Women who can conceive children but not bear them may have gestation take place in the laboratory or in another woman's body. (3) Study of developing fetuses in vitro would yield important knowledge about the cause of birth defects, many of which occur very early in gestation. (4) Prenatal development in vitro might be more healthy than in vivo, because the fetus would not be exposed to the harmful effects of drugs, radiation, and viruses. (5) Amniocentesis would not be necessary in the case of fetuses developing in vitro; genetic disease could rather easily be detected. The trauma of abortion could be avoided. (6) Frozen "egg banks" could be set up, analogous to sperm banks. If a man's wife did not have eggs in her ovaries, he could have someone else's egg fertilized by his own sperm and placed in his wife's womb (or an artificial one) for gestation.

John Stuart Mill, in his profound essay *Nature,* demonstrated that the "natural" is not always good and that the "unnatural" is not always bad. "The undeniable fact," according to Mill, is "that the order of nature, in so far as unmodified by man," conflicts with all his concepts of justice and benevolence.[19] Progress in improving the human condition has always consisted of *amending* nature, not by violating its laws (which is impossible), but by utilizing them to create a better world. We are not still living in caves, and we have advanced beyond the food-gathering stage. Joseph Fletcher echoes Mill when he writes: "To be civilized is to be artificial, and to object that something is artificial only condemns it in the eyes of subrational nature lovers or natural law mystics."[20] To those who would call artificial methods for the purpose of eutelegenesis "inhuman," Fletcher would point out that the "willed, chosen, purposed, and controlled" engendering of life is more human than the emotional or accidental way so often associated with sexual intercourse.[21]

"We do not create life in the test tube," says Patrick Steptoe.

> Life is already there in the living egg and the living sperm. When some diseases prevent them from getting together in the customary way, we merely provide the opportunity for them to come together in a different setting. Some people say you should only have conception occur as the result of some sexual act, otherwise there isn't any love attached to it. This is absolute nonsense. People making this decision (to try for a test tube conception) are making a very difficult, responsible decision. But they're making it in love, great love, and there's no doubt about it because they have to make many sacrifices.[22]

If it is acceptable for couples to have sex without conception, it is also acceptable for them to have conception without sex.

Reproduction: Cloning A third type of artificial reproduction is even more controversial: cloning. A clone consists of all the individuals produced asexually from one cell of a living being. Since each cell contains a full complement of chromosomes, members of the clone ("clonees") will be genetically identical to the animal from which the cell was taken. The usual method of cloning consists of transferring the nucleus of a cell to the interior of an egg from which *its* nucleus has been removed. This procedure has been successful in the case of frogs, some of the embryos developing into tadpoles and eventually adult frogs. It has not yet been successful for mammals. Another method, sometimes called cloning, is that of embryo fission. This consists of separating the cells of an embryo by instruments or chemicals. It has been carried out with mice. With both methods, several

[19] Mill, *Nature,* in George Nakhnikian, ed., *Nature and Utility of Religion,* p. 18.

[20] Fletcher, *The Ethics of Genetic Control* (Garden City, N.Y.: Anchor Books, 1974), p. 15.

[21] Fletcher, "Ethical Aspects of Genetic Controls."

[22] Steptoe, quoted in Loretta McLaughlin, "Test Tube Babies—Last Hope for the Barren," *St. Louis Post-Dispatch,* November 30, 1980, p. 1E.

generations of clones have been produced by cloning a clone. Each individual is genetically identical to the animal from which the cell has been taken (nuclear transfer) or the embryo that has been separated (embryo fission).

It is simply a matter of time (perhaps a long time) before cloning of humans can be done. When this is a reality, scientists will be able to produce genetic duplicates of people with very precious genetic endowments. Einstein is often given as an example, but it is much too late for him. When people have made great contributions to society, they can be cloned and some will be expected to distinguish themselves. Why should a one-in-a-million genetic complement be lost for all time? In saying that a member of a clone will be genetically identical to the cell or embryo from which he or she was derived, we are not saying that the *person* will be identical to the original. The environment will shape the person in a different way. Indeed, a clonee will be similar to the original in the same way that identical twins are similar to one another. Such twins rightly insist upon their own uniqueness. Genes aren't everything!

While waiting for the advent of human cloning, we can enjoy the benefits of cloning the lower forms of life in order to increase our food supplies "through rapid mass-production of high-quality grains, vegetables, and food animals."[23]

Recombinant DNA Finally, we will look at a form of genetic engineering popularly called recombinant DNA. This is a new field of research but has made some startling achievements. Researchers have taken genes from one simple organism and planted them in another. Most of the work has consisted of placing genes from bacteria, viruses, and cells (plant and animal) into the bacterium called *Escherichia coli.* The DNA of the former is cut and the removed pieces are inserted into a plasmid (ring of DNA) of *E. coli.* The ring of DNA is closed with an annealing enzyme, and the plasmid is then placed back into the bacterium. A hybrid has resulted and it reproduces itself quickly, passing the new genetic inheritance to all its descendants.

Much has been claimed for this research. If all human genes could be identified and transplanted at will, all genetic disease could be eliminated, for the germ cell itself is altered.[24] As Robert Sinsheimer put it, the new technique in principle "makes available to us the gene pool of the planet, all the genes developed in the varied evolutionary lines throughout the history of life—to reorder and reassemble as we see fit."[25] The slow workings of *natural* selection can be replaced by the "overnight" operations of *deliberate* selection. Humanity at last will be in control of its own evolutionary destiny.

[23]Karp, p. 206.
[24]This would be more satisfactory than what Karp calls "second-level genetic therapy," which consists of administering to the patient "normal gene products designed to do the work of the nonexistent or defective substances coded by the patient's own genes" (p. 96). These products (usually enzymes) are introduced into the body cells and are neither inherited nor permanent.
[25]Quoted in Howard and Rifkin, *Who Should Play God?,* p. 18.

A more immediate goal is to use the host bacteria to produce vital medical substances such as serums and vaccines to pit against diseases like hepatitis and cancer. David Baltimore of M.I.T. says, "Anything that is basically a protein will be makeable in unlimited quantities in the next fifteen years."[26] Other goals are to produce proteins for food (making us less dependent on cattle), to produce bacteria designed to consume oil spills before dying and dropping to the ocean floor, to manufacture insulin in quantity (making diabetics no longer dependent on the pancreas of cattle—often impure), to produce interferon (a natural substance that fights viruses and is very useful in combating cancer),[27] and to produce the pituitary growth hormone (doctors will no longer be dependent on the pituitary glands taken from cadavers—400 to 800 of which are required for each patient).

The first case of successfully transferring genes to animals was reported in 1980. Researchers at UCLA "isolated genetic material from mice, including the gene that confers resistance to an anti-cancer drug" and managed to transfer it to the bone marrow cells of other mice. If this technique can be applied to human cancer victims, their resistance to Methotrexate could be greatly increased. "Methotrexate, a common chemotherapy drug, kills tumors but also weakens the patient by destroying bone marrow cells." Massive doses could be given without toxic side effects.[28]

In addition to these and many more practical benefits, research into recombinant DNA may be expected to solve many theoretical problems: Why do some cells become malignant? What regulates or "turns on" genes?[29] What causes genes to mutate?

" 'There has been a golden age of chemistry and a golden age of physics,' says Peter Farley, president of Cetus Corp., one of the young companies organized to capitalize on recombinant DNA's potential. 'Now it's biology's turn.' "[30]

The Efforts of Biologists to Enhance the Quality and Possibility of Life Should Be Critically Scrutinized

The Morality of Caution Those of us who believe that knowledge is good should be very grateful to scientists. But sometimes values are produced at too high a price. Knowledge acquired by means of certain kinds of experimentation on human beings, for example, may not be worth the price. The utilization or

[26] *Newsweek,* March 17, 1980, p. 62.

[27] "The interferon made by gene-splicing will be 100 per cent pure, whereas the substance now extracted from blood cells is only one-tenth of 1 per cent pure." A course of interferon treatment at present costs as much as $50,000. See "The Making of a Miracle Drug," *Newsweek,* January 28, 1980, p. 82.

[28] "Curing Disease with Genes," *Newsweek,* April 21, 1980, p. 80.

[29] In a given cell, most genes do not do anything.

[30] See *Newsweek,* March 17, 1980, p. 62.

application of scientific knowledge (technology) intends to produce more concrete benefits for humanity. But we should scrutinize cases of scientific application and ask: Are the presumed benefits *genuine* benefits for humanity? What results are produced *in addition* to the intended results? What are the *long-range* consequences of beneficial applications? Cutting across the utilitarian criterion is another one: The obligation to observe certain moral laws, sometimes at the expense of beneficial consequences.

Genetic engineering is fraught with many dangers, some of which will be set forth here. Many of these dangers are real; some are hypothetical. These latter should not lightly be dismissed. When we do not have a clear idea of the consequences of a course of action, caution should be our watchword. The value of any end can be canceled out by unforeseen consequences. Leon Kass, who has written very perceptively on the moral aspects of genetic engineering, says that his own attack on the enterprise "has not been directed against science, but against the use of *some* technologies and, even more, against the unexamined belief—indeed, I would say, superstition—that all biomedical technology is an unmixed blessing."[31]

Science is conducted by scientists, and they are not less moral than any other group. Where their actions do not harm others, they may be permitted to do their work according to their own moral standards. But when there is the chance that other people may be harmed, peer pressure, public opinion, and legislation in the public interest may be required.

> The regulatory institutions should be encouraged to exercise restraint and to formulate the grounds for saying "no." We must all get used to the idea that biomedical technology makes possible many things we should never do.[32]

> The scientist on his side must both act and appear to act in a manner that justifies the layman's faith. He must therefore not only show a concern for the advancement of his discipline, but also for its bearing upon the communal good. Among other things this means that the scientist must allow for the possibility that the communal good might at times override scientific advance.[33]

Scientists are as prone to ethical error as anyone else. Some are so enthusiastic in carrying their work forward that they do not perceive certain ethical issues, or they ignore them when they are raised. Some are so convinced of the ultimate value of their research that they underestimate the importance of any ethical consideration that would delay it. The view of some is so restricted that they are oblivious to possible harmful consequences in other areas. A few scientists (like

[31]Kass, "The New Biology: What Price Relieving Man's Estate?" in Beauchamp, ed., *Ethics and Public Policy,* p. 390n.

[32]Ibid., p. 393.

[33]Martin P. Golding, "Ethical Issues in Biological Engineering," in Beauchamp, *Ethics and Public Policy,* p. 406.

some philosophers and artists) are concerned only with academic recognition and enhanced income from private sources such as pharmaceutical companies.

Knowledge indeed is power, and power is in the hands of those who possess it. Many will exercise it wisely, but some will not. When that power is so vast and impinges on the rights of society itself, it becomes a matter of public concern. Individuals in a democratic society must be sufficiently aware of what genetic engineers are doing, can do, and might do in the future so that they can control it in the public interest.

Ethical sensitivity must also be present in the thinking of the individual who decides whether to take advantage of the "benefits" of genetic engineering. Should one avail oneself of the opportunity to ascertain the sex of a fetus by means of amniocentesis, have an egg fertilized in vitro, abort a defective fetus, procreate with someone who carries the same recessive gene?

Not all the ethical issues can be raised here, and even fewer can be settled. Perhaps the most we can do is show that there *are* issues and that they cannot be settled as easily as some advocates of genetic engineering would lead us to believe.

Prolonging and Creating Life One issue involves the prolonging and creation of life. Medical science has already succeeded in prolonging the lives of grievously ill persons by means of cardiac pacemakers, kidney machines, organ transplants, radium treatments, and, in the last days, life-support systems. Geneticists are now unveiling the mysteries of the aging process. In a few generations, it may be possible to add several decades to the active life span of individuals. It is already possible for women who are otherwise infertile to conceive through artificial insemination. In the future, women who cannot bear or give birth to a child may turn to artificial wombs or have their embryo implanted in a surrogate mother. Men with low sperm count can have their seed concentrated and used for fertilization in vitro. When cloning becomes available, sterility in either male or female will be of no relevance. Any individual's cells may be used for producing "children" for himself/herself or for others. In a world where population is increasing at an alarming rate, should we not emphasize *preventing* life rather than prolonging and creating it?[34]

Genetic Screening Another area of concern is genetic screening. It is surely wise and beneficial for couples to seek genetic counseling if there are genetic disorders in their family histories. But if everyone with "bad genes" refrained from procreation, the human race would die out, for we all carry deleterious genes. Screening

[34]"Population-control advocates point out that while there are nearly four billion people in the world today, it took from the beginning of human history until 1830 to produce the first billion, a century more for the second billion, thirty years for the third billion, and a mere fifteen years to produce the last billion." Howard and Rifkin, p. 165.

also has the danger of increasing racial distrust or hatred, for some particular "bad genes" are more prevalent in some racial groups than in others. If genetic screening is imposed on some groups (such as blacks, for sickle cell anemia) with the intent of discouraging risky procreation, it may look like an attempt at genocide. Great care is needed here.

Should individuals be sought out and informed that they may be carriers of a genetic disease, or do they have the right "not to know"? Should parents be told that their child carries an extra chromosome (XYY), a condition that is more prevalent among criminals than the general population? Is compulsory screening a legitimate form of infringement of freedom?

The question of confidentiality enters the picture also. The problem is that of *using* the data while at the same time *protecting privacy.* Certain data could be used against job applicants (some airlines do not hire carriers of SCA because of their supposed vulnerability to rarefied air); some data could be used by insurance companies to raise premiums; some could be used criminally for extortion; some could be used by zealous counselors to shame individuals into not having children. It is easy to sympathize with individuals who maintain that their own and their family's genetic makeup is their own business. Neither the individual nor the ethnic group wishes to be stigmatized as carriers of a "dread disease."

How far should we go in compulsory genetic screening? Shall we test all groups (fetuses, newborns, and adults) for all disorders as soon as tests become available? What priority should screening have in relation to other claims on public health services? There is a point of diminishing returns (not always recognized by geneticists) where expenditures for the expensive screening of rare genetic diseases should give way to efforts to eliminate infectious diseases, build more public hospitals, clean up the air and water, and the like.

Negative Eugenics A third area of concern is negative eugenics. Couples with high risk may be counseled not to have children, but counseling may turn into strong public pressure. Some diseases are less severe than others, and some can be treated. Where should the line be drawn between degrees of severity and degrees of probability? And who should draw that line? The United States had a disgraceful period about fifty years ago when several states legislated compulsory sterilization for people with certain undesirable traits—even though their genetic basis was not always apparent.[35] It is not inconceivable that in the future, as genetic science advances, another movement for compulsory sterilization will develop. Some individuals are already calling for it for people who are afflicted

[35]Indiana passed the first sterilization law in 1907, calling for compulsory sterilization of "confirmed criminals, idiots, imbeciles, and others in state institutions when approved by a board of experts." Dozens of states followed. Well-known people in the forefront of the movement were Earnest A. Hooton, Alexander Graham Bell, Margaret Sanger, David Starr Jordon (president of Stanford University), Charles R. Van Hise (president of The University of Wisconsin), Harry H. Laughlin ("eugenics expert" for the House committee that drafted the nation's first immigration law), Luther Burbank, Theodore Roosevelt, and many others. See Howard and Rifkin, pp. 47–73.

or who carry deleterious genes. In some otherwise enlightened countries in Europe, sterilization of one partner is required in some cases for a marriage license. If this practice is wrong, it should be attacked now, before it is too late.[36] It was no less a liberal than Justice Oliver Wendell Holmes who wrote in 1927 in defending the constitutionality of compulsory sterilization:

> We have seen more than once that the public welfare may call upon the best citizens for their lives. It would be strange if it could not call upon those who already sap the strength of the state for these lesser sacrifices, often felt to be such by those concerned, in order to prevent our being swamped with incompetence. It is better for all the world, if instead of waiting for their imbecility, society can prevent those who are manifestly unfit from continuing their kind. . . . Three generations of imbeciles are enough.[37]

If the carriers cannot be sterilized, advocates of negative eugenics will favor killing the afflicted fetus. The morality of abortion is discussed in the second part of this chapter, but it must be touched on here. While a fetus afflicted with a very severe disease for which there is no treatment (e.g., Tay-Sachs disease) may morally be aborted, there are some diseases that are borderline (e.g., hemophilia, Down's syndrome, PKU) and a great many more that would clearly seem not to justify abortion. Some people with sickle cell anemia live to age fifty. Most men with XYY chromosomes live a normal and productive life. Diabetics and epileptics have made enormous contributions to our culture. Zeal to avoid bringing any but a genetically perfect specimen into the world might well lead to an unconscionable pattern of wholesale abortion. It is not beyond the realm of possibility for parents to abort a fetus simply because it is not of the "right" sex. And it is also possible that legislators will want to *require* abortion in certain cases. These are wild cases, but we need to face up to them now before they become realities. We must be morally sensitized before we fall into a pattern. And we must be ready with legislation or constitutional amendment to protect in advance whatever rights we think the fetus possesses.

The trouble with trying to eliminate deleterious dominant genes is that many of them are not discovered early enough to prevent reproduction.[38] Others eliminate themselves, either killing or sterilizing their carriers. The trouble with trying to eliminate bad recessive genes is that there are so many of them. We *all* carry them. Some varieties, moreover, are so rare that if one were singled out for

[36]The renewed interest in eugenics is spurred not only by recent genetic discoveries but the recognition in some quarters of the limitations in controlling the environment for the production of intelligent and law-abiding behavior. Schools cannot educate, and prisons cannot rehabilitate. Certain races, say scientists like A. R. Jensen and William Shockley, are genetically limited in their mental development.

[37]*Buck* v. *Bell,* 274 U.S. 200, 207 (1927).

[38]Huntington's disease, for example, can only be detected at onset—usually between ages thirty-five and forty-five. It is incurable.

sterilization, hundreds of generations would be required before an appreciable difference could be made in the number of people afflicted.

Successful negative eugenics itself poses significant risk. It reduces the gene pool. Who knows what *other* genes would be eliminated in eliminating the bad ones? They may be valuable now or in the future. Not knowing what the future holds, we should preserve our genetic diversity. Martin Golding cites the Swedish law that has banned the marriage of endogenous epileptics since 1757. The law is now attacked on the ground that the chances for an epileptic to have epileptic children are not high, and many epileptics are very intelligent and valuable members of the community. He also cites a blind poet, a deaf musician, a consumptive novelist, and a hunchback physicist who have been geniuses in their fields.[39] When a disease is not disabling or can be treated successfully, it would be foolish to eliminate its genes (and those that accompany it) from the population. Some "bad" genes are themselves beneficial—for example, carriers of sickle cell anemia are better able to resist malaria.[40]

A far more rewarding and feasible goal than trying to prevent the bequeathing of deleterious genes is that of preventing their occurrence in the first place. New defective genes are produced by mutation. Scientists know something about the causes of mutation and will in the future know more. "It seems prudent to attempt to prevent unnecessary contamination of our surroundings by radiation and mutagenic chemicals."[41] It is thus important not only to preserve our present genetic diversity, but, since almost all mutations are deleterious, to prevent increased diversity.

Positive Eugenics A fourth area of concern is the area of positive eugenics. Although there appears to be no threat of government insistence that society improve its genetic future, there may well be significant public pressure for individuals with "good" genes to seek similarly well endowed partners and to reproduce. It is better for future generations, we are often told, for superior people

[39]Golding, in Beauchamp, p. 405.

[40]"Can we really forecast the consequence for mankind, for human society, of any major change in the human gene pool? The more I have reflected on this the more I have come to doubt it. I do not refer here to the alleviation of individual genetic defects—or, if you will, to the occasional introduction of a genetic clone—but more broadly to the genetic redefinition of man. Our social structures have evolved so as to be more or less well adapted to the array of talents and personalities emergent by chance from the existing gene pool and developed through our cultural agencies. In our social endeavors we have, biologically, remained cradled in that web of evolutionary nature which bore us and which has undoubtedly provided a most valuable safety net as we have in our fumbling way created and tried our varied cultural forms. To introduce a sudden major discontinuity in the human gene pool might well create a major mismatch between our social order and our individual capacities. Even a minor perturbation such as a marked change in the sex ratio from its present near equality could shake our social structures—or consider the impact of a major change in the human life span. Can we really predict the results of such a perturbation? And if we cannot foresee the consequence, do we go ahead?" Robert Sinsheimer, "Troubled Dawn for Genetic Engineering," in Beauchamp and Walters, p. 611.

to beget in greater number than inferior ones. If one's partner is no great shakes, one can avail oneself of a sperm bank specializing in Nobel prize winners (or an egg bank specializing in Shakespearean actresses).

It is generally known that most of the traits that seem favorable are determined by the interaction of several gene pairs. They cannot be correlated with a single pair of genes as many genetic diseases can be. The environment plays an important role also in the development of such good traits as bodily strength, artistic talent, and intelligence. There are thus theoretical difficulties in producing "higher" types. There would be failures—"good" matings can have "bad" offspring, just as "bad" matings often have "good" offspring.

Another theoretical difficulty stems from ignorance of how traits are correlated. If society should breed for intelligence, what other valuable trait might it lose in the process? In addition to certain physical or organic traits, some eugenicists have called for moral traits in their progeny. Julian Huxley stresses altruism. Hermann J. Muller favors moral courage and integrity, as well as a sense of fellowship and appreciation of art and nature. Others like devotion to duty and a sense of discipline. If we cannot yet breed intelligence in any quick and certain manner, the production of these moral attributes remains far in the future.

Several practical difficulties would remain even if all these theoretical ones were solved by the advance of genetic science. If society seeks to produce better people, by means of public opinion or law, what good qualities will it select and in what proportion? Do we want a nation of Julius Ervings or a nation of Einsteins or a nation of Bette Midlers? Or some mixture? Who decides these matters? If the program is to be successful, it will have to be adhered to and be carried out consistently over a period of years. This would constitute a form of tyranny very few people (especially those of childbearing age) could accept. Moreover, the selection of various human specimens for a future society must be based upon a clear vision of what this society will be. Artistic appreciation would be useless in a society where there is no art. Physical agility could have no expression in a society where sports do not exist. What kind of society will give free play to altruism, discipline, and prudence? Since engineering human qualities must take into account the way these qualities can be used in a society, a blueprint of human society is required that is consistent with the various blueprints of its members. We can only engineer the part in the light of a clear conception of the whole. Leaders of society, in order to carry out eugenics, would have to go beyond mere tyranny; they would have to practice totalitarianism.

The alternative is voluntary eugenics, which would be on an individual basis and without clear direction. Both Huxley and Muller opt for voluntary eugenics. Muller writes:

> If we are to preserve that self-determination which is an essential feature of human intelligence, success and happiness, our individual actions in the realm of genetics must be steps based upon our own personal judgments and inclinations. Although

> these decisions are all conditioned by the mores about us, these mores can be specifically shaped and channelized by our own distinctive personalities.[42]

If voluntary eugenics were practiced on a small scale, there would be little effect, for good or ill, on future generations. If done on a grand scale, there could be great effects, but no one knows what they would be. It would be wise, therefore, to discourage social plans to improve the race in some vaguely grand way. The *personal* decision to avail oneself of genetic knowledge to improve one's progeny depends on several factors. It is more justifiable when done to avoid defects than to enhance strengths.[43] We all want healthy babies, but the wish to beget superbabies seems a little sick. What inadequacy is the parent trying to compensate for? What pressure would he or she already have placed on the child in having deliberately endowed it with good genes? To begin to constrain the growth and nature of a child before its conception seems in some strange way a violation of the child's freedom. Would not a more healthy parental outlook be to take whatever child the fates decreed and provide it with love and encouragement to follow its own bent?

Artificial Insemination A fifth area of concern is artificial insemination. We may criticize resort to AID in order to produce superior progeny, the practice called eutelegenesis. We may also criticize it, from the other direction, when a danger exists that the donors have not been carefully screened. Not only can genetic diseases be carried by donated semen, but infectious ones as well—gonorrhea, for example. There is a possible danger, too, in frozen sperm. It works, but not so well as fresh sperm. Karp raises several unanswered questions: "Which cellular metabolic functions are altered by low temperatures, and in what fashion? Which effects are permanent, and which reversible? A variable proportion of sperm in different samples are killed by freezing: what are the factors that favor survival?" Does freezing sperm induce gene mutation? "Our knowledge of sperm cryobiology is extremely limited."[44] One additional problem faced by practitioners of eutelegenesis who use sperm of famous or "superlative" men is that older men's sperm is more frequently defective through mutation.

Artificial insemination has been criticized on moral grounds, first, because it requires masturbation, and second, when the sperm of a nonhusband is used, because it is a case of adultery. These criticisms do not seem plausible to this writer.

Another question sometimes raised is psychological. Will the husband be disturbed by the knowledge that the sperm of someone else has fertilized his wife's egg? How will he feel toward the offspring? How will the child feel, knowing that

[42]Hermann J. Muller, quoted by Golding in Beauchamp, p. 401.

[43]And it is more justifiable when practiced naturally (that is, by choice of mate) than when practiced artificially—for reasons that are given later in this chapter.

[44]Karp, p. 141.

his or her "real" father is a test tube in a sperm bank? How will he or she relate to the legal father? How does the donor feel, knowing that he may have a host of unknown children somewhere out there? Why does he sell his sperm in the first place? For the money? Out of pride? In order to help childless couples? The problems that certain psychological attitudes may produce should be taken into account by people who are involved in artificial insemination. Serious questions must arise concerning the motives of the intelligent women who patronize the sperm bank of Robert K. Graham, whose donors are all Nobel prize winners.[45]

Surrogate parenting has pitfalls also. What if the pregnant surrogate changes her mind about giving up the child? If she keeps it, does the father pay child support? What are his interests in the matter? What if the child has birth defects? How does the husband of the surrogate mother feel? Is it moral to use one's body for a fee? Is it moral for single men to employ this service? Some surrogate parenting operations are not so strict as the Louisville one. Some do not even employ artificial insemination: A surrogate is introduced to the couple and has sexual relations with the husband until pregnancy occurs. How does the wife feel? Is it moral to commit adultery for the sake of producing a child or earning a fee?

Ectogenesis The most serious objection to artificial insemination is one that can be made to the whole present and future course of ectogenesis. The objection is based on a preference for natural procreation over mechanical processes, for warm bodies over laboratory equipment, for physical love over chemical reactions. Ectogenesis is a materialist approach to life. "In vitro" is itself a chilling expression. Leon R. Kass eloquently makes the point:

> Procreation is not simply an activity of the rational will. It is a more complete human activity precisely because it engages us bodily and spiritually, as well as rationally. Is there perhaps some wisdom in that mystery of nature which joins the pleasure of sex, the communication of love, and the desire for children in the very activity by which we continue the chain of human existence? Is not biological parenthood a built-in "mechanism," selected because it fosters and supports in parents an adequate concern for and commitment to their children? Would not the laboratory production of human beings no longer be *human* procreation? Could it keep human parenthood human?[46]

For those who choose "test tube babies" as the second best but only feasible way to produce the desired children, there is perhaps some justification; but for those who go the "in vitro" route to avoid having a sexual partner, to produce superior genetic types, to be sure of getting the desired gender, or to avoid the inconveniences of pregnancy, there is no justification whatever. The latter have chosen to depersonalize human relations, while weakening the social institutions

[45]The identity of Graham's five donors is known in only one case—that of William Shockley.
[46]Kass, pp. 384–385.

of marriage and the family. They have turned to scientists to perform a service they are unwilling to perform for themselves: the making of a baby. They are buying a manufactured product instead of procreating a new life.

There is still another consideration. Ectogenesis is, of course, a new science. Its methods are not yet perfected. A great deal of experimentation must still be done. Presumably, this will be done with animals before being conducted on human mothers and fetuses. Actually, however, much has already been done on mothers and fetuses. In any case, no amount of success with animals will ever prove the safety of the method for humans. Is it not immoral to engender life at one stage in order to experiment with its survival at later stages? Even when a technique has been "proved" successful for humans, as in the case of the production of Louise Brown, can we be sure that no physical damage has been done to the emerging person as a result of its treatment as an embryo? It will be a great many years before the full risk of ectogenesis to mother and baby is fully known. The human race is not so desperate for reproduction that we should experiment on human subjects and court great risks—both of which are inseparable from ectogenesis.

The great publicity given to artificial reproduction has resulted in the great willingness of some people to take part in experiments that are physically and psychologically dangerous. Some childless women beg for the opportunity. It has also created great hopes that cannot, in most cases, be realized. The fact is that by the end of 1980 only three "test tube babies" have been born in the world—none in the United States. Perhaps the Steptoe-Edwards Bourne Hall Pavillion near Cambridge will help a few, but most of the millions of infertile couples in the world are doomed to disappointment.

Cloning The seventh area of concern is cloning. Again, we should not wait until the method is perfected before adopting a moral stance. By then, it may be too late to do anything about it. There are so many moral issues here that we can raise but a few: Is it not a sign of inordinate pride for an individual to want to produce an identical copy of himself or herself? Is it fair to place on a clonee the pressure to equal the achievements of his or her "parent"? Is there a danger that cloning will be used for widespread positive eugenics with the attendant danger of reducing genetic diversity? Whom will a young clonee regard as his or her parent, and what kind of relationship with that parent will he or she have? Will clones of people who did well in one society be able to do well in an entirely different society?[47] What social standing will clones have and what treatment will they be subjected to? Will we someday want to create clones of ourselves in order to have compatible "spare parts" always available for transplantation?

Recombinant DNA Finally, let us consider "recombinant DNA." Many of the humanitarian and eugenic concerns expressed above apply here also. Even now,

[47]Karp speaks of the possibility of saddling ourselves with "groups of Xeroxed has-beens" (p. 204).

however, long before the application of recombinant techniques on human DNA, there is a tremendous risk in the research itself. Researchers in universities, government, and private industry have recognized the need to take extraordinary precautions. For a brief period in the seventies they even called a moratorium on continued research. The Asilomar Conference of 1975 brought an end to the moratorium and produced a set of guidelines for research.[48] These guidelines were taken up and superseded by others, that of the National Institutes of Health coming out in 1976. They attempt to state the form of safety required for containment in various kinds of experiment and to differentiate levels of minimal, low, moderate, and high risk. Moderate-risk containment, for example, according to the Asilomar statement, is "intended for experiments in which there is a probability of generating an agent with a significant potential for pathogenicity or ecological disruption." In addition to the stipulations for experiments of lesser risk, the following are required: laminar flow hoods, vacuum lines protected by filters, and "negative air pressure within the laboratory itself, to ensure that particles would not escape on air currents."[49]

One obvious risk stems from the fact that most research utilizes *E. coli,* a normally benign bacterium that lives in the human intestine. A great many genetic changes have been produced in its nucleus, many of which could cause terrible things to happen to man and his surroundings should the altered bacterium escape the laboratory. The bacterium reproduces every twenty minutes, so it would not take long for a host of virulent organisms to arise. Since the organisms are new, antibiotics are unknown. A newer form of it, designed to die outside the laboratory, *E. coli* K12, is supposed to be acceptable in moderate-risk experiments. But apparently no impaired bacterium is safe enough for such highly pathogenic organisms as those that produce the botulinum and diphtheria toxins. In the absence of perfect containment (which is probably impossible), a "safe bug" must be found. The most troubling aspect of the whole problem is that the scientists admittedly have not been able to state fully the nature and scope of the dangers in their work: there are "unknowns." It is impossible to take steps to prevent dangers when the dangers are not known. There have already been serious and fatal accidents, but not yet on a scale to alarm the public. The public interest is clearly involved here, and society cannot afford to permit the scientists to police themselves. Most of their guidelines are advisory only, and the chief penalty feared is withdrawal of supporting government funds from university laboratories. Private laboratories seem to be in a class by themselves. "Until Congress passes a law that extends the provisions of the NIH guidelines to industry and makes dangerous experimentation in recombinants a federal offense," scientists in private industry will not have to be especially careful. "For there is not a single federal statute or law which covers the conduct of recombinant DNA research."[50]

[48]See Hutton, *Bio-Revolution: DNA and the Ethics of Man-Made Life,* pp. 75–80.
[49]Ibid., p. 76.
[50]Ibid., p. 210.

Again, we must urge caution in research with human subjects. There is no assurance that what is successful in animals will also be successful in people. Often what has taken place in experimentation on animals is not clearly known. In the case of genetic transplant involving mice, the researchers could not say with certainty where in the bone marrow cell the gene ended up. Did it enter the correct chromosome—or does it simply float around within the cell? "A gene outside the chromosomes isn't subject to normal genetic regulation. Without such regulation the gene might run wild, producing a surplus of products as dangerous as a deficit."[51]

"To impose any limit upon freedom of inquiry is especially bitter for the scientists whose life is one of inquiry," writes scientist Robert Sinsheimer. "But science has become too potent. It is no longer enough to wave the flag of Galileo."[52]

One other problem should be noted: commercial use of recombinant DNA. Dozens of patents are pending for living organisms developed through this process. In 1980, the Supreme Court by a vote of 5–4 upheld the right of scientists to patent new forms of life. Some fear that when these processes are in the hands of private individuals and companies, not only will caution be dispensed with, but the free exchange of ideas itself. Competition will breed secrecy. Genentech, a San Francisco-based gene-splicing company, began selling stock publicly in 1980.[53] Harvard University is considering (1981) founding a company to exploit the commercial uses of its own recombinant DNA research as a way of increasing its revenues. "They like to say the university is a marketplace for ideas," says Harvard biologist Richard Lewontin. "With this, it will become a marketplace—period." Another fear is that emphasis on commercial use will take resources away from basic research. "What would be expected of the faculty member?" asked Gerald J. Lieberman, dean of graduate studies and research at Stanford (which is also considering going into business). "Would he now be expected to develop patents for the company?"[54]

Summary of the Issues

The basic issue in genetic engineering turns on a matter of degree. Some of its potential should be exploited, but other aspects of that potential should not. Which is which? One side to the debate emphasizes the benefits of genetic engineering; the other side is alert to its dangers. One side seeks the immediate advantage; the other side is concerned with long-range consequences, known and unknown. One side embraces the principle of utility; the other side appeals to

[51]*Newsweek,* April 12, 1980, p. 80.

[52]Sinsheimer, p. 610.

[53]Genentech is now (1981) testing a human growth hormone on young children stunted by pituitary deficiencies.

[54]See "Harvard as Entrepreneur," *Newsweek,* November 10, 1980, pp. 93–94.

individual rights and other deontological principles, as well as to God's will. One side expresses confidence, the other caution.

The positive side favors genetic screening as a means to prevent the conception or birth of children with serious genetic defects, as well as to ensure the prompt recognition and treatment of afflicted infants. For some diseases and for some populations, screening should be compulsory. The negative side asks whether such concern with rare diseases is worth the financial expenditure, whether the program would intensify racial tensions, and whether the program would be a legitimate infringement of the rights of freedom and privacy.

The proponents of negative eugenics would employ strong pressure on couples with unfortunate genetic combinations not to have children and to abort fetuses that are deemed likely to be defective. Some, for good utilitarian reasons, would make some measures that serve the cause of negative eugenics compulsory. The other side again appeals to freedom, and fears that compulsory programs will go too far. It also points out that many people with genetic defects can lead a rewarding and productive life. There is the danger of loss of respect for life (unless it is genetically "perfect") and wholesale abortion. There are also dangers in tampering with the population's gene pool. Although the proponents of positive eugenics have not yet called for compulsory measures, they do, say their foes, tend to overlook certain theoretical and moral difficulties.

Several artificial techniques are now available for fostering the conception, bearing, and delivery of children. Artificial insemination is of great benefit for couples who cannot conceive naturally or who, for good reason, choose not to do so. Ectogenesis is of great benefit for the woman who cannot conceive children but who can carry them. If the natural mother cannot carry or deliver the baby, surrogate mothers are available. The negative side argues that artificial insemination and ectogenesis are materialistic techniques rather than human processes. Psychological problems are pointed out. Finally, it argues that these methods are often employed by people for ignoble purposes.

Advocates of cloning point to the blessings of reproducing outstanding individuals, while its opponents point to various social, psychological, and ethical problems that success in this technology would give rise to.

With respect to all three of the productive technologies, the positive side is charged with failure properly to assess the dangers of experimenting with human subjects and with contributing to the population explosion.

Throughout the whole enterprise of genetic engineering, we encounter conflicting attitudes on supplementing natural processes or replacing them with artificial processes. The positive side stresses intelligence, control, and the need to amend "nature" for human purposes. The negative side tends to view such technology as tampering with nature (perhaps to our eventual disadvantage) or exhibiting "hubris" in playing God.

This basic difference is nowhere more apparent than in the debate on recombinant DNA, a process in which the germ cell itself is altered. Divine and/or natural selection is in principle replaceable by deliberate human selection. Although the technique has already produced practical gains, and many more are on the horizon, the negative side urges great caution. Not only are there known dangers to the world in this research, there are unknown results as well, which could be even more dangerous.

Discussion Questions

1. Would you be in favor of compulsory screening for sickle cell anemia? Why?
2. For what other genetic diseases (if any) would you favor compulsory screening? Why?
3. Do you think everyone should seek genetic counseling before marriage? Why?
4. If a man finds out that his fiancée's father is a hemophiliac, should he marry her? If so, should he have children? Why or why not?
5. If you have good reason to believe that the chances are good that your children would have genetic diseases detectable in the fetus, would you (a) decide not to have children, (b) resort to abortion if the disease is found to be present, or (c) go ahead and have children, hoping for the best? Why?
6. Do you believe that carriers of bad dominant genes should be sterilized before marriage? Why?
7. Do you believe that carriers of the same bad recessive gene should be permitted to marry without sterilization of one of the parties? Why?
8. Is there any acceptable way, in your opinion, to counteract the conception of genetically diseased children by couples who do not marry?
9. Do the utilitarian arguments in favor of compulsory requirements with respect to negative eugenics outweigh the principle of freedom of choice? Explain.
10. Do you think that feeble-minded people should be permitted to reproduce? Why?
11. Do you think that individuals should try to improve the quality of the human race by choosing marriage partners with "good" genes? Why? Would you criticize those who did? Why?
12. Even if you and your spouse could conceive children with no genetic defect, would you consider artificial insemination from a sperm bank of Nobel prize winners (or a transplanted egg from a Nobel prize winner)? Why?
13. Do you think that artificial reproduction goes against the will of God? Explain.
14. Do you think that surrogate mothers should be praised or criticized? Why?
15. If your child were the product of AID, would you tell him or her? Why?
16. If a safe and efficient artificial womb could be developed, would you recommend its use by all parents? Why?
17. If it could somehow be arranged for you or your wife to give birth to a clone of Robert Redford (or some other celebrity or accomplished person), would you jump at the chance, hesitate, or decline? Why?
18. Do you think that the marvels of artificial reproduction should be made available to single parents? Why?
19. Do you think that research on human cloning should be supported? Explain.
20. How important is "freedom of scientific inquiry"? Should society impose any limits on it?

21. Do you think that scientists working in areas in which catastrophic accidents can occur (e.g., recombinant DNA) can be trusted to police themselves? Why?
22. Do you think that scientists who experiment with human subjects can be trusted to police themselves? Why?
23. What duties, if any, do we owe the unborn? Explain.
24. Do you think the goal of genetic transplants for human beings is morally desirable? Are there any limits that should be imposed on such a technology? Why?
25. Do you see any danger in the technology of human reproduction and recombinant DNA being in the hands of private profit-making organizations? Or do you think it should be handled by universities or public institutions? Explain.
26. Do you favor the development of a technology that could control the sex of a child? Why? How about one that could control the intelligence of a child?
27. Do you regard the advances in creating and prolonging life as contributing to the problem of overpopulation? Explain.
28. What is your opinion of these injunctions: "Do not tamper with nature!" "Do not play God!"

For Further Reading

W. E. Anderson. "The Future Shock of Genetic Medicine." *Medical Opinion* 4 (1975): 54–61.

Tom L. Beauchamp, ed. *Ethics and Public Policy.* Englewood Cliffs, N. J.: Prentice-Hall, 1975. Chapter 7.

Tom L. Beauchamp and Leroy Walters, eds. *Contemporary Issues in Bioethics.* Belmont, Calif.: Wadsworth Publishing Co., 1978. Chapter 12.

Daniel Bergsma, ed. *Ethical, Social and Legal Dimensions of Screening for Human Genetic Disease.* Miami: Symposia Specialists, 1974.

Daniel Callahan et al., eds. *Ethical Issues in Human Genetics.* New York: Plenum Publishing Corp., 1973.

S. N. Cohen. "The Manipulation of Genes." *Scientific American* 233 (1975):25–33.

Theodosius Dobzhansky. *Genetic Diversity and Human Equality.* New York: Basic Books, 1973.

Joseph Fletcher. "Ethical Aspects of Genetic Controls." *New England Journal of Medicine* 285 (1971):776–783.

Joseph Fletcher. *The Ethics of Genetic Control.* New York: Anchor Books, 1974.

Charles Frankel. "The Specter of Eugenics." *Commentary,* March 1974.

F. C. Fraser. "Genetic Counseling." *American Journal of Human Genetics* 26 (1974): 636–659.

Theodore Friedmann. "Prenatal Diagnosis of Genetic Disease." *Scientific American,* November 1971.

Martin P. Golding. "Ethical Issues in Biological Engineering." *UCLA Law Review* 15 (1968):463–479.

D. S. Halacy, Jr. *Genetic Revolution.* New York: Harper & Row, 1974.

M. P. Hamilton, ed. *The New Genetics and the Future of Man.* Grand Rapids, Mich.: Eerdmans Publishing Co., 1972.

H. Harris. *Prenatal Diagnosis and Selective Abortion.* London: Nuffield Provincial Hospitals Trust, 1974.

Ted Howard and Jeremy Rifkin. *Who Should Play God?* New York: Dell Publishing Co., 1977.

Richard Hutton. *Bio-Revolution: DNA and the Ethics of Man-Made Life.* New York: Mentor Books, 1978.

Laurence E. Karp. *Genetic Engineering: Threat or Promise?* Chicago: Nelson-Hall, 1977.

Leon R. Kass. "The New Biology: What Price Relieving Man's Estate?" *Science* 174 (1971):779–788.

Joshua Lederberg. "DNA Splicing: Will Fear Rob us of Its Benefits?" *Prism,* November 1975.

Joshua Lederberg. "DNA Splicing: Will Fear Rob Us of Its Benefits?" *Prism,* November 34 (1971):9–12.

Paul Ramsey. *Fabricated Man.* New Haven: Yale University Press, 1970.

Robert Sinsheimer. "Genetic Engineering: The Modification of Man." *Impact of Science on Society* 20 (1970):279–291.

Robert Sinsheimer. "Troubled Dawn for Genetic Engineering." *New Scientist, London, Weekly Review of Science and Technology,* October 16, 1975.

J. M. Smith. "Eugenics and Utopia." *Daedalus* 94 (1965):487–505.

ABORTION

Abortion Is Immoral Except When Done in Order to Save the Life of the Mother or Prevent the Birth of a Grossly Defective Child

Legality and Morality It was in 1973 that the Supreme Court of the United States ruled that the Texas law making it a crime to procure an abortion except for the purpose of saving the life of the mother was unconstitutional.[55] This decision in effect invalidated dozens of other state anti-abortion laws.[56] Grounding its decision on a woman's "right to privacy" as protected by the Bill of Rights and the Fourteenth Amendment, the Court declared that a woman had the constitutional right to get an abortion during the first two trimesters of pregnancy. During the first, she had only to find a willing physician. During the second, when danger to herself was greater, states could regulate abortion procedures in the interest of safety. It was only in the third trimester that the interest of the fetus was recognized. Since the fetus is now viable (capable "of meaningful life outside the mother's womb") and the state had a "compelling" interest in protecting life, it may "proscribe abortion during that period except when neces-

[55] *Roe* v. *Wade,* 410 U.S. 113 (1973).

[56] The laws in some states were somewhat more liberal than that of Texas, permitting abortion in some cases before "quickening." Mississippi and New York, for example, had fairly liberal laws before *Roe* v. *Wade.* It must be admitted, however, that Mrs. Sherri Finkbine, expecting a "thalidomide baby," could not get a legal abortion anywhere in the United States in 1962.

sary to preserve the life or health of the mother." The right to privacy is limited when the mother's life or the "potential life" of the fetus becomes "significantly involved."

That abortion is now legal for all trimesters and without special justification for the first two does not settle the ethical problem. Whether the individual woman and her doctor behave morally when they accomplish an abortion is still to be decided. An act may be wrong without being a crime.[57] The pro-abortion people have achieved almost complete legal recognition of their basic principle: Whether an abortion is to be performed should be determined simply by the consciences of the parties to the act. According to the decision of a case a few years later, the woman and physician are not even bound by the wishes of the husband or the parents of minors.[58] But a free decision is not necessarily a *moral* decision. Given the legal freedom of a woman to have an abortion, the question we must now ask is whether the woman and doctor are *moral* when they act on this freedom.[59]

The Meaning of Human Life The majority view in *Roe* v. *Wade* itself suggests that they are not. It recognizes the right of the fetus in the third trimester, for it is sometime during this period that it becomes viable. If the state has a "compelling" interest to protect the life of the fetus at all, it would seem arbitrary to pick viability as the point where that interest is to be recognized. Clearly the fetus is alive during the whole gestation period—from the moment of conception. Why should the desires of the mother, which are ignored after viability, prevail *before* this point? If *life* is important, any moral distinctions based on the stages of its development are impossible to justify.

The development of human life from the fertilized egg (zygote) to adulthood occurs on a continuum. We may talk about embryo, fetus, infant, child, and adult, but they are all forms of human life, and the lines between them are not clearly drawn. No one can say precisely at what point an infant becomes a child, when a child becomes an adult, or when a fetus is capable of existence *ex utero.* People in the middle ages speculated about the point where the embryo became "ensouled" (some held at conception, others forty or eighty days afterward). In more recent days, some believe that "quickening" (movement of the fetus in the womb) is the beginning of a significant new stage, although movement surely took place before it was detected by the mother. Others cite brain activity or response to stimuli as a significant plateau. All this is idle. The fetus at all levels is a form of human life. It is of the human species. And long before viability or quickening, the fetus has the body and all the physical characteristics that are associated with

[57]It is important to make this distinction because, as R. J. Gerber says, for some people "removal of a law is tantamount to approving what the removal sanctions." See R. J. Gerber, "Abortion: Parameters for Decision," in Struhl and Struhl, *Ethics in Perspective,* p. 239.

[58]See *Planned Parenthood of Central Missouri* v. *Danforth,* 428 U.S. 52 (1976).

[59]About 29 percent of the pregnancies in the United States in 1979 were aborted.

human life. Life is life: it has a prenatal phase and a postnatal phase. If, at a late stage, the fetus is "potentially able to live outside the mother's womb,"[60] it has this same potentiality *early* in pregnancy also. The only difference is that in one case, the fetus is closer to *achieving* its potentiality than in the other.

If one defines *persons* in a particular way, it will turn out that the fetus is not a person. Justice Blackmun apparently defined it to mean forms of human life that have been *born,* for he denies the unborn the right to life guaranteed by the Constitution. Admittedly, fetuses cannot hold property, participate in the census, or count as dependents on income tax forms. But all this is legalistic and has no bearing on the moral issue. If we define *persons,* as some psychologists do, as forms of human life that have become "socialized" or have a clear sense of their own identity, infants are not persons and would also be denied the right to life. A theologian may define *person* as any form of human life possessing a soul and argue that the fetus is such a form. How can we resolve this definitional dispute? We do not have to. Somewhere along the line, sooner or later, life achieves personhood. Even if we do not believe that the fetus is a person, it has in all of its stages the *potentiality* of becoming a person. If we value personhood, we must value that which has the potential for achieving personhood.

The crucial consideration against abortion, then, is that the fetus is a form of human life, a person or a potential person, and thus has the right to survival. It is immoral to deprive such a being of life.

Richard A. Wasserstrom summarizes a view that places the fetus in "a distinctive, relatively unique moral category" somewhat lower than persons but superior to animals:

> This view sees the value of human life in the things of genuine value or worth that persons are capable of producing, creating, enjoying, and being, for example, works of art, interpersonal relations of love, trust and benevolence, and scientific and humanistic inquiries and reflections. Correspondingly it sees the distinctive value of the fetus as being alone the kind of entity that can someday produce, create, enjoy and be things of genuine value and worth.[61]

This is instructive and should give anyone pause who is considering the destruction of a normal, healthy fetus. But it does not go far enough. The fetus has value beyond its potential for a productive career in society. It has value in itself as a form of human life—whatever success the future holds for it. If human life itself did not have intrinsic value (as a person or potential person), we would be justified in dispatching unpromising infants, hopelessly insane adults, and old people who have already made their contribution. If we value human life per se, we will value it at all stages of its development, from conception to burial, and we will value it regardless of its achievements. Can ethical philosophy justify a respect for life?

[60]Justice Harry A. Blackmun, *Roe* v. *Wade.*

[61]Wasserstrom, "The Status of the Fetus," in Rachels, *Moral Problems,* p. 121.

Religious Considerations Paul Ramsey recounts the story of Dr. Bernard N. Nathanson, who after a year and a half as director of the Center for Reproductive and Sexual Health, at that time "the largest abortion center in the Western world," resigned for reasons of conscience. He had presided over 60,000 fetal deaths. In an article recanting his previous views, Dr. Nathanson said:

> This issue is human life, and it deserves the reverent stillness and ineffably grave thought appropriate to it. . . . There is a danger that society will lose a certain moral tension that has been a vital part of its fabric, . . .[and that we will] permit ourselves to sink to the debased level of utilitarian semiconsciousness.[62]

There is, as Ramsey argues, a great similarity among American religions on respect for life. The Jewish tradition, despite the view that "individual human life" begins only after the head or the main part of the fetus emerges from the birth canal, has such great respect for the life-bearing fetus that it holds that it can be destroyed only to save the mother's life and that holy days may be violated to preserve it. Roman Catholicism, believing the fetus is "ensouled," regards it as a person who cannot be permitted to die except in efforts to save the mother's life.[63] Protestantism is beginning to end its "apostasy . . . from the common Christian tradition concerning the sanctity of unborn life."[64]

> Life is sacred because God has placed great value on it:
> Before I formed you in the womb I knew you, and before you were born I consecrated you. . . . [65]
>
> O Lord, thou hast searched me and known me! Thou dost beset me behind and before, and layest thy hand upon me.[66]
>
> For thou didst form my inward parts, thou didst knit me together in my mother's womb.[67]

"A man's dignity is an overflow from God's dealings with him, and not primarily an anticipation of anything he will ever be by himself alone."[68] We are all, fetuses and "persons," forms of life chosen by God and created in his own image. Apart

[62]See Ramsey, *Ethics at the Edge of Life,* p. 45.
[63]Catholicism opposes *taking* the life of either mother or fetus, but permits "indirect" or "passive" death of the one when it is possible to save the other.
[64]Ibid., p. 48.
[65]Jeremiah 1:5.
[66]Psalms 139:1, 5.
[67]Psalms 139:13.
[68]Ramsey, "The Morality of Abortion," in Abelson and Friquegnon, *Ethics for Modern Life,* p. 66.

from God, we are nothing. With God, we are everything. God's concern for man is as great in man's nascent stages as in his adult stages.[69]

God wishes people to love and support one another, and at no time is this love and support more needed than during infancy and gestation. Quoting the Protestant theologian Karl Barth, Ramsey says: "Respect for life means that a man should 'treat as a loan both the life of all men with his own and his own with all men.'"[70] Again, quoting Barth:

> The unborn child is from the very first a child. It is still developing and has no independent life. But it is a man and not a thing, nor a mere part of the mother's body. . . . He who destroys germinating life kills a man and thus ventures the monstrous thing of decreeing concerning the life and death of a fellow-man whose life is given by God and therefore, like his own, belongs to him. . . .[71]

Christians have a special reason to stand in awe of human life. That God became man in the person of Jesus, says Barth, "unmistakeably differentiates human life from everything that is and is done in heaven and earth. This gives it even in its most doubtful form the character of something singular, unique, unseparable and irreplaceable. This decides that it is an advantage and something worthwhile to be as man. This characterizes life as the incomparable and nonrecurrent opportunity to praise God."[72]

Convenience Christians were early horrified at the low regard for life held in pagan societies. Abortion and infanticide were common. Plato recommended both practices for eugenic reasons in *Republic.*[73] Aristotle recommended them in order to keep the population down and avoid poverty.[74] In ancient Sparta, infants were examined by state inspectors; those who were "defective" were killed. Often, however, abortion and infanticide were practiced simply for reasons of convenience to parents. Children require time, money, and attention, and they were often dispatched for purely selfish reasons. In the Hellenistic period, abortion and infanticide were practiced on such a scale that underpopulation problems developed in many cities. In the days of the Roman Empire, children were often regarded as obstacles to sexual license. In the cities especially, divorce was common, and couples did not want to be burdened with children. The widespread disrespect for early forms of human life was linked with the sexual debauchery prevalent in Rome.

How is this relevant to the issue of abortion today? Unless women and their doctors view the Supreme Court decision as an opportunity for moral judgment,

[69]Ramsey suggests that we are all "fellow fetuses." "From womb to tomb ours is a nascent life." Ibid., p. 62.

[70]Ibid., p. 68.

[71]See ibid., p. 69.

[72]See ibid., pp. 68–69.

[73]See Plato, *Republic* V, 460–461.

[74]See Aristotle, *Politics* 1265b.

they may undertake an abortion for the flimsy reasons that obtained in the Hellenistic period. If we find its practices abhorrent, we should find the idea of "abortion on demand" abhorrent also. That women and doctors are legally required to give no justification for abortion in the first two trimesters does not mean that they are not subject to the requirement of *moral* justification. In one respect, women have even more latitude than they did in classical times. Now, as the result of the 1976 decision, they are not even legally required to secure the consent of husband or parent. Women can get an abortion simply for their own *convenience,* if they can find a doctor and a clinic to cooperate. Convenience is not a sufficient moral reason for killing a fetus.[75] A woman facing an abortion decision must examine her deepest moral convictions. In trying to make the right decision, she will consult with anyone who can be of assistance on both the factual and the ethical aspects of the problem.[76] Hers is a far more serious decision than that to employ contraception, for life is already in existence.[77] If abortion is chosen, it should be the *last* resort, rather than the first.

"Grounds" for Abortion Perhaps few pro-abortion partisans would rest their case on convenience. Other grounds are cited: (1) Abortion is necessary for the physical health of the mother. We should take this argument seriously, but most conditions of ill health can be ameliorated with professional treatment. Only when ill health has a good chance of leading to death does it constitute a legitimate moral excuse for abortion. (2) Abortion is necessary for the mental health of the mother. "Mental health" is a very vague term. It may range all the way from irritability to psychosis. Mental health is a condition difficult to identify. "Pro-life" organizations as well as public agencies provide counseling for people who feel that a birth would be psychologically damaging. We should also recognize that there is the possibility of emotional disturbance for the woman who has an abortion and knows that she has taken an innocent life. (3) Abortion is necessary to prevent the birth of a defective baby. This is also a serious consider-

[75]"The Court," wrote Justice Byron R. White in his dissenting opinion in *Roe* v. *Wade,* "apparently values the convenience of the pregnant mother more than the continued existence and development of the life or potential life which she carries. . . ."

[76]The counseling offered at abortion clinics should be infused with the need to respect human life in all its forms. Too often it is perfunctory.

[77]"A respect for the sanctity of human life should, I believe, incline [women] toward a general and strong bias against abortion. Abortion is an act of killing, the violent, direct destruction of potential human life, already in the process of development. That fact should not be disguised, or glossed over by euphemism and circumlocution. It is not the destruction of a human person—for at no stage of its development does the conceptus fulfill the definition of a person, which implies a developed capacity for reasoning, willing, desiring, and relating to others—but it is the destruction of an important and valuable form of human life. Its value and it potentiality are not dependent upon the attitude of the woman toward it; it grows by its own biological dynamism and has a genetic and morphological potential distinct from that of the woman. It has its own distinctive and individual future." Daniel Callahan, *Abortion: Law, Choice, and Morality.* See Abelson and Friquegnon, *Ethics for Modern Life,* p. 99.

ation. But "defective" infants can and often do grow to be productive and happy persons. Indeed, some of the world's greatest geniuses have been born with physical defects. It is only when the fetus is judged to be so grossly defective that the infant would have to be institutionalized for life that killing it could be condoned. The so-called thalidomide babies are examples. As a result of pregnant women taking the drug, many children were born with severe deformities. Aborting fetuses with Down's syndrome (mongolism) is somewhat different, for such children can be taught to take care of themselves. The principle here is that the potential for active and independent life is present in some defective fetuses, while the potential in seriously deformed fetuses is for human life only in the biological or vegetative sense. A very high standard of morality requires the protection of all forms of human life, but individuals who could not respond to such a high standard and aborted a truly monstrous fetus should not be condemned. While their action was not exemplary, it cannot be called immoral.

(4) Abortion is necessary because the fetus is the result of rape or incest. (5) Abortion is necessary because the family is not able to support another child. (6) Abortion is necessary because the mother is unmarried and/or a minor. The answer to these three situations is a simple one. If the mother is psychologically, economically, or physically incapable of caring for the child, it can be given up for adoption at birth. That there are good reasons for the mother not to attempt to care for the child should not in itself deprive the fetus of the right to live. We do believe that people who have sexual intercourse must bear some responsibility for its consequences, but this principle does not apply when intercourse was forced on the female. And even if it was not forced, a concern for resulting life may well dictate that the child would have better prospects in an adoptive family. That babies are often conceived in unfortunate circumstances should not be a death sentence for the babies when there are families and agencies that are willing to take on the care and upbringing that the natural parents feel they must conscientiously decline. What the mother *can* provide the fetus is care during gestation. For this the child can be grateful, whether he or she ever sees the mother or not.

The Value of Human Life The "respect for life" argument is not exclusively a religious one. One does not have to believe that God generated life, that he made the human being in his image and forbids the taking of human life. One may directly intuit the great value that life has, not only because of what it may do, but because of what it is. Atheists and agnostics for the most part are also opposed to the taking of innocent life. They do not regard life as divinely ordained, but they can still regard human life as the greatest thing that has so far evolved in nature. If they are consistent in valuing life, they will be opposed to any act that destroys it. In the case of the fetus, we have not only human life, but human life that is thoroughly innocent. It has done absolutely nothing to merit its own extinction. It is at the start of a human career and should be permitted the development that persons at all other stages of life demand for themselves. What is more important than life that life must give way to it?

If human life does have value, there are obvious utilitarian reasons for protecting it. No one would want to live in a society where human life is not valued. One would be in constant danger of losing one's own life and seeing friends and loved ones losing theirs. A society is happier when all of its members, secure in the possession of their own lives, can go about their business. "Respect life" is a rule whose habitual and exceptionless observance serves human societies better than any other rule that could be devised.

Exceptions to the rule tend to weaken it. Warfare, capital punishment, and euthanasia have this effect, and those of us who do not want to cheapen human life are very fearful of the effects of war, capital punishment, and euthanasia on moral sensibility. We therefore either oppose them outright or try to confine them to the most necessary occasions. Nothing could weaken the rule more than unnecessary ("nontherapeutic") abortion. When mother and doctor can, for the flimsiest of reasons, terminate a life at any time during the first six months of its existence, the rule is weakened and our sensibilities are brutalized. We are thus prepared to compromise the rule in other cases.

This is not the "slippery slope" fallacy that advocates of abortion sometimes charge. The rule has been violated. Life itself is no longer a paramount value. If we are morally responsible, we must reformulate the rule to exclude abortion, or build exceptions into the rule itself. If we do so, we are committed not to life itself, but to life *in certain prescribed forms and circumstances.* This rule may be so cumbrous or so vague that neither we nor society can really respond to it in every case where it becomes relevant. If we cannot reformulate the rule or choose not to do so, we are reduced to not *acting on principle,* which is the end (cessation) of ethical life. If the *reason* for not killing no longer applies, or applies only in a qualified and special way, then it may not be called upon at all in a great many cases where life is at stake. In weakening the rule, in the eyes of ourselves and society, we are left with no rule at all or one that is so vague and subjective that it leaves the way open for further compromise.

It is quite possible that we have already begun to slide down the slippery slope in condoning abortion in cases where the fetus is grossly defective. This is a case of taking human life, deformed though that life may be. And if our principle here is that such a life will be unhappy, unproductive, and a constant drain on the resources of others, it is difficult to see why it would not apply to grossly deformed infants and horribly injured adults as well. We might make the distinction that the latter are *persons* while fetuses are a form of life that has not yet achieved personhood. But this seems arbitrary and ignores the fact that the development of human life takes place on a continuous spectrum. Another difficult line to draw is that between fetuses that are grossly defective and those that are simply defective. Our attempt to draw a line above was probably a failure. It is possible that sometime in the future, the state, rather than *condone* the termination of defective fetuses, will *require* it. Some years ago, it may be remembered, the Supreme Court permitted compulsory sterilization of mental defectives.[78]

[78]See *Buck* v. *Bell,* 274 U.S. 200, 207 (1927).

One other danger should be noted. Suppose that a doctor, in performing a legal abortion, finds a live fetus in his hands. It is against the law to kill it or permit it to die. But the doctor may reason that since his goal was to terminate the pregnancy—that is, to kill the fetus—the fact that it was ex utero rather than in utero is a technicality that he can morally overlook.[79]

Hare and the Golden Rule The philosopher R. M. Hare has provided us with a "Golden Rule" argument against abortion. We might note that the Golden Rule is not limited to Christianity. It is an important part of Judaism, Islam, and most other world religions. It is not crucial in the ethics of Jesus, who, while espousing it, goes far beyond it. The Golden Rule simply enjoins us to do toward others what we would want them to do toward ourselves. It is thus a secular rule of fairness: we place ourselves and everyone else on a plane of equality. It is much closer to Kant's categorical imperative, which enjoins us to claim nothing for ourselves that we would not grant to others, than it is to the sacrificial love taught by Jesus which makes no claim whatever for the self.

How ought we to treat a fetus? Is there anything about it or the person it will become that would make it wrong to kill it? We do know that if the pregnancy is not terminated, a baby will be born and in all likelihood become a mature person like the rest of us. It is the potentiality "that the fetus has of becoming a person in the full ordinary sense that creates the problem," says Hare.[80] The potentiality also suggests the answer. "If we are glad that nobody terminated the pregnancy that resulted in *our* birth, then we are enjoined not . . . to terminate any pregnancy which will result in the birth of a person having a life like ours."[81] Even if we are unhappy, we would in a fetal state have wanted to be spared so that we would have the opportunity to be glad we were alive.

Hare's argument does not imply that all cases of abortion are immoral, but it does establish that abortion "is prima facie and in general wrong in default of sufficient countervailing reasons."[82] The same argument would militate against contraception, and continence as well. Hare is pleased that his parents had intercourse and conceived him, and presumably does his part in creating new life (limited by due appreciation of the question of possible overpopulation). The "countervailing reasons" would be such as the fetus being so defective that its chances of becoming a person glad to be alive are slight. If a mother and doctor abort a normal fetus, they are eliminating the chances of producing a baby. And they are doing so in a much more decisive way than the parents would if they practiced contraception on one occasion or decided to be continent for a given period of time. The probability of producing a happy person from a normal fetus is much greater than that of fertilizing an ovum in an act of intercourse. Furthermore, "if a general duty to produce children be recognized (as the view I have

[79]See *Commonwealth* v. *Kenneth Edelin,* 359 N.E. 2d 4 (1976).

[80]Hare, "Abortion and the Golden Rule," in James Rachels, *Moral Problems,* pp. 157–158.

[81]Ibid., p. 159.

[82]Ibid., p. 173.

suggested requires), to kill a fetus means the nonfulfillment of this duty for a much longer period (the period from its begetting to the begetting of the next child, if any); whereas if you do not beget a child now, you may five minutes later."[83] We can harm persons by preventing them from coming into existence!

Hare finds the Golden Rule useful in dealing with the question of overpopulation. "There would be a point at which the additional member of each of these units [world, societies, families] imposed burdens on the other members great enough in sum to outweigh the advantage gained by the additional member."[84] If we imaginatively thrust ourselves into these lives and nonlives, we might sense some point where the gladness of those who are glad to have been born is outweighed by the sorrow of those who feel crowded and insecure.

Although Hare's theory is an odd one indeed, and we have omitted some of its odder points, it does provide a sound moral basis for permitting fetuses (at least, normal ones) to survive. He recognizes no more rights for the fetus than he does for separated semen and egg, or coitus itself; but he would protect it because it is further along to personhood than these other things and statistically has a better chance of making a mature person. Presumably he would be even more protective of the infant than of the fetus. And he does recognize that parents become fond of the fetus in the womb, and rightfully do not consider contraception as being as sinful as abortion. It is not that the fetus has certain "rights." Hare's crucial point is that we are living persons, and since we are glad that others protected and nursed us to living parenthood, we should do the same thing for other helpless fetuses.

Medical Personnel and Facilities Whether to abort or not is obviously a moral decision for doctors and medical personnel as well as for women and the friends and family who advise them. If the ethical autonomy of a woman, family, and friends is to be respected by law, that of medical personnel should be also. The law seems to recognize this. *Roe* v. *Wade* did not give women the right of "abortion on demand." Medical people must be found who can *conscientiously* assist her. If conscience is to determine whether an abortion is to be performed, that of doctors, nurses, and hospital officials is relevant also.

Paul Ramsey gives several examples of medical personnel who have been discriminated against by their hospitals for conscientiously refusing to assist in abortions. He also discusses the difficulties encountered by students and potential students in the medical schools because of their moral stance against abortion. There is a federal statute and many state statutes that forbid coercing and requiring "individual or entity" to perform abortion procedures when they are contrary to the religious beliefs or moral convictions of that individual or entity. The better laws, according to Ramsey, will be *even-handed.* That is, they will protect the person who has assisted in abortion just as they will protect those who refuse to

[83]Ibid., p. 165.
[84]Ibid., p. 169.

do so on grounds of conscience. They should also protect a public hospital if that "entity" for reasons of its own declines to offer abortions. Yet in 1976, in *Doe* v. *Bridgeton Hospital Association,* the supreme court of New Jersey declared that not only public but nonsectarian private hospitals were obliged to offer elective abortions![85] In 1977 the U.S. Supreme Court refused to review the *Bridgeton* case. The U.S. Court of Appeals had declared in a case involving a Kentucky hospital that *any* private hospital could be protected by the antidiscriminatory legislation, and that public hospitals, while they could not deny abortion on ethical grounds, could not, each and every one of them, be *required* to perform abortion if their facilities are inadequate.[86] The U.S. Supreme Court did deal with public hospitals in 1977.[87] The policy of the mayor and the director of Health and Hospitals of St. Louis was not to offer abortion in city hospitals "except when there was a threat of grave physiological injury or death to the mother." The Court found "no constitutional violation by the city of St. Louis in electing, as a policy choice, to provide publicly financed hospital services for childbirth without providing corresponding services for nontherapeutic abortion."[88]

Ramsey's concerns, expressed in his chapter "Abortion after the Law," are valid ones. Now that *Roe* v. *Wade* has made abortion a matter of conscience, we must be on guard against the possibility of private and public agencies invading the realm where conscience is to perform. Laws must be enacted to protect the conscientious choice of medical personnel (students and practitioners), and they must be *enforced.* And hospitals, public and private (sectarian and nonsectarian), must be protected in choosing what kinds of services they will provide (while not discriminating against their personnel). If the decision of public hospitals cannot be based on ethical reasons *(Wolfe)*, it can be based on reasons of "public policy" *(Poelker)*. In any event, no hospital, not even a public one, is obliged to offer *all* forms of health care. The *Wolfe* and *Poelker* decisions seem to be in agreement on that. And Ramsey would join them. *Roe* v. *Wade* does *not* require medical personnel and hospitals to provide "abortion on demand."

Abortion May Be Justified on Grounds Other Than Saving the Life of the Mother or Preventing the Birth of a Grossly Defective Child

Legality and Morality The U.S. Supreme Court took a great step forward in *Roe* v. *Wade* in legalizing abortion during the first two trimesters. It is to be hoped that the restrictions placed on the third trimester will eventually be removed. One reason the Court gives for this restriction is that abortions in this

[85]See *Doe* v. *Bridgeton Hospital Association,* 71 N.J. 478, 366A 2d 641 (1976).
[86]See *Wolfe* v. *Schroering,* 388 F. Supp. 613 (1974), modified, 541 F. 2d 523 6th Cir. (1976).
[87]See *Poelker* v. *Doe,* no. 75–442, 45 LW (1977).
[88]See Ramsey, *Ethics at the Edges of Life,* p. 77.

period are especially dangerous for the mother. If the mother and doctor are willing for reasons of their own to take the risk and conduct the operation according to the medical standards set forth for the second trimester, it is difficult to see how this should be a matter of further concern to the state. Another reason the Court gives for the restriction is that it is during the third trimester that the fetus becomes viable. The distinction is an arbitrary one, for if the fetus has no rights of a person (conceded by the Court), it is difficult to discern any rights it begins to bear when it is *almost* a person. The case of a fetus having gradually passed over into a viable stage (no one knows precisely when) is not materially different from the case of a fetus that could live outside the mother's body if given a bit more time to gestate. If the Court is willing to let people decide whether a five-month fetus will be carried to term, it should also let people decide whether a seven-month fetus will be carried to term. If medical science were to develop to the point that a five-month fetus could be removed and sustained in an artificial womb until birth, would it be accorded the same protection the Court affords the seven-month fetus?

At any rate, individuals are now able to exercise their own moral judgments (for six months) without fear of being treated as criminals.[89] And when they begin to think about the ethical consequences of an abortion for themselves or their patients—assuming always good medical facilities and treatment—they will be able to take into account certain benefits that may accrue for the mother, the family, and society itself.

Benefits and Costs Among the possible benefits are the following: The unmarried mother is spared the disgrace of bearing a child; the weak mother is spared a deterioration of health brought on by full-term pregnancy or birth; the woman who has been the victim of rape or incest is spared the anguish of carrying a child she loathes. The family that is financially unable to support another child is able to spend its money on the children it already has; the family is spared the time, money, and energy required in caring for a defective child; the family that needs the earning capacity of the mother will retain it. Society will have another factor operating against the always-present danger of overpopulation; society will be spared the expensive care of defective children (who often live to an advanced age); society will be spared the expense of providing aid to families who have more children than they can support.

Against these possible gains, what must be taken into account as possible losses? Here the only relevant factor is the health and life of the mother. An abortion is a surgical operation, so there is risk. But if the operation is done according to medically prescribed standards, it is not a grave risk. According to

[89]Daniel Callahan, in criticizing highly restrictive abortion laws, wrote: "If they succeed in keeping down the overall number of abortions, they do so at too high a price. Unenforced and unenforceable, they bring the law into disrepute." Callahan, *Abortion: Law, Choice, and Morality.* See Abelson and Friquegnon, p. 89.

a study conducted by the Federal Center for Disease Control of almost two million legal abortions between 1972 and 1974, the fatality rate (3.9 per 100,000 operations) was far less than that for childbirth (15) and appendectomies (352). It was even less than for tonsilectomies (5)![90] The Supreme Court itself contrasted the safety of modern techniques with those of the recent past. The horrific connotation that the word *abortion* still has in some quarters today is a result of the dangers in the operation as practiced a generation or so ago. We might also add that many were illegal, done with improper facilities, and performed by quacks and amateurs. One of the great benefits the Court ruling makes possible is that women today do not have to resort to the butchers and fumblers they once had to turn to.

What about the financial cost of abortions? Unless there are serious complications, the cost of an abortion is less than that of normal childbirth. It is, nevertheless, more than some women can afford. It is strange that maternity wards exist in some public hospitals while abortion wards do not. According to the ruling in *Poelker* v. *Doe,* this is not unconstitutional. But it does seem strange that public hospitals do not have to provide facilities for nontherapeutic abortion when that operation is as legal as delivering a baby. On the same day the Court ruled that Title XIX of the Medicaid program does not require participating states "to finance the costs of both medically necessary and nontherapeutic abortions for needy individuals."[91] It also ruled that the equal protection clause does not "require a state welfare program to subsidize nontherapeutic abortions if it pays for childbirth and medically necessary abortions."[92] States *may* fund nontherapeutic abortions, but they do not have to. Congress *could* make willingness to fund nontherapeutic abortion a condition for a state's participation in the federally subsidized Medicaid program, but it has not done so. In fact, the Henry Hyde amendment to a Medicaid bill in Congress (1976) barred Medicaid spending for abortions except in certain specified cases. It was ruled unconstitutional by a federal court.[93] But in June 1980, the Supreme Court (in *Harris* v. *McRae*) by a 5–4 vote upheld an even more restrictive amendment barring Medicaid spending for abortions except in cases where the woman's life would be endangered by childbirth or where rape or incest had been promptly reported. Individual states are not barred from paying for abortions, but they will get no help from the federal government. Prior to 1976, about one-third of the million or so legal abortions performed in the United States were for women on welfare. This figure

[90]See Leiser, *Liberty, Justice, and Morals,* p. 106.

[91]*Beal* v. *Doe,* 432 U.S. 438 (1977). See Bruce E. Fein, *Significant Decisions of the Supreme Court, 1976–1977 Term* (Washington: American Enterprise Institute for Public Policy Research, 1978), pp. 49–50.

[92]*Maher* v. *Roe,* 432 U.S. 464 (1977). See Fein, pp. 50–51.

[93]Judge John F. Dooling, Jr. (U.S. District Court for the Eastern District of New York), a practicing Catholic, stated that the Hyde amendment interfered with women's free exercise of religion (protected by the First Amendment), for many "mainstream" religions do not proscribe abortion. He also said that Hyde was inconsistent with a statutory right established when Medicaid was instituted in 1965: that of the poor to have "medically necessary" health care—not simply life-preserving health care.

dropped sharply after the Hyde amendment, and will remain very low now that the Supreme Court has made its decision. The fault, however, lies with Congress. It is doubtful that the states will pick up the financial burden. It is regrettable that so many of the indigent will not be able to avail themselves of the options the more prosperous have at easy reach.[94]

The Rights of the Fetus We must now confront the question of the rights, if any, of the fetus. Though utilitarian benefits of abortion are substantial, it is possible that they may be overridden by the rights of the being whose life is sacrificed.

Can the "right" of the fetus to life itself be justified in utilitarian terms? No plausible case could be made against abortion on utilitarian grounds if we stuck with the consequences of the act itself. The benefits for the mother, the family, and society of an act of abortion freely chosen and medically carried out would not be exceeded by the problematical happiness of the fetus were it to enter life ex utero. This is especially true if the future life would be severely handicapped by physical or mental deformity, if it was unwanted by the parents who created it, or if it was begun in a crowded and poverty-stricken home. It is the more general loss of respect for life that is supposed to follow from general moral acceptance of killing fetuses that is the problem. We are, say the anti-abortionists, on a "slippery slope." That some may slide into infanticide, euthanasia, and generally murderous action if abortion became respectible is possible. But most people can see so clearly the difference between terminating a fetus and killing a child or adult that a better analogy would be falling off a precipice than clawing futilely on an icy slope. That abortion was associated with infanticide in Greek and Roman times does not mean that the two attitudes necessarily occur together or that the one leads to the other. Both were aspects of a *general disrespect for life* that characterized those violent times. Today we must do what we think is right and only so long as we think it's right. To question our own moral judgment because it may pave the way for future error is to espouse a form of ethical skepticism that could be greatly destructive of moral values in the long run. And to fear that the masses will plunge into mindless sin if we liberalize our own standards is a form of ethical elitism that is contemptible.

We are now ready to face the crucial question: Does the fetus have inviolable or indefeasible rights such that abortion, when the life of the mother is not at stake, would be immoral?

[94]Justice Marshall, dissenting in the *McRae* case, said: "By definition, these [poor] women do not have the money to pay for an abortion themselves. Denial of a Medicaid-funded abortion is equivalent to denial of legal abortion altogether." Justice Brennan, also dissenting, said of the majority: Their "fundamental flaw . . . is [the] failure to acknowledge that the discriminatory distribution of the benefits of governmental largesse can discourage the exercise of fundamental liberties just as effectively as can an outright denial." Justice Stewart, speaking for the majority, said: "Although government may not place obstacles in the path of a woman's exercise of her free choice, it need not remove those not of its own creation. Indigency falls in the latter category."

The answer may depend on whether the fetus is a *person.* Presumably, it is easier to justify killing a nonperson than killing a person, for it is more plausible to deny rights to the former than to the latter. It is, however, very difficult to specify whether a fetus is a person or not without begging the question. We will have to be very careful not to stipulate a definition that is simply verbal and sidesteps the moral qualities of the concept itself.

The Fetus as a Nonperson Let us first look at the pro-abortionist arguments based on the belief that the fetus is *not* a person.

One form of this argument is that the fetus is nothing more than a part of the mother's body, a piece of tissue growing on, and sustained by, the rest of the pregnant organism. Perhaps this view was held by Dr. Thomas Szasz when he said: "There ought to be no special laws regulating abortion. Such an operation should be available in the same way as, say, an operation for the beautification of a nose."[95] The fetus may be living, but has no life of its own. This argument need not detain us. As the anti-abortionists insist, the fetus does have a distinct genetic composition of its own from the moment of conception and very soon has in miniature most of the physical attributes of human beings. We need not study the pictures they thrust before our eyes to realize that there is something wrong with the idea that the fetus is nothing but a parasitic growth.

Another form of the argument, while denying personhood, admits that the fetus is an individual manifestation of life, but not yet human. The admonition to spare human life does not apply because the fetus lacks qualities that we ordinarily associate with humanity: rationality, feelings, self-consciousness. If we have no great compunctions against killing nonhuman forms of life such as cattle, insects, and fish, we should have none here. This is unsatisfactory too, for it is not absurd to hold that life may still be human though lacking in its early stages those qualities that it will exhibit later.

A third form of the argument is that the fetus is human life but lacks the additional characteristics that would make it a person in some physical or legal sense. It is not a person until it physically has emerged from the womb. This view is found expressed in Talmudic writings. It is also assumed in *Roe* v. *Wade* by Justice Blackmun when he asserts that there is no tradition in this country of regarding the fetus as a person entitled to equal protection of the law. Emergence of the fetus is not an arbitrary line to draw in human development. The continuum has indeed been interrupted. The being now breathes air. The umbilical cord is cut. The fetus is "on its own" now. It has become a baby, violently and traumatically. Childbirth is Marx's model for a social revolution where a new society with its own unique and essential structure begins its troubled life. As a form of human life, the fetus may have rights, but they must be less commanding than those possessed by a being living outside a womb and recognized as a person

[95]Szasz, "The Ethics of Abortion," *Humanist,* July 22, 1966.

by every court in the land. We would not want to subject the fetus to cruelty or casually put it to death; but in the interests of those who are indisputably human, we can legitimately deny it further development.

There is a fourth form of the pro-abortionist argument based on nonpersonhood which sets an even more restrictive definition on "person." Ashley Montagu, for example, a pro-abortionist, writes:

> The embryo, the fetus, and newborn of the human species, in point of fact, do not really become functionally human until humanized in the human socialization process. . . . Humanity is an achievement, not an endowment. The potentialities constitute the endowment, their fulfillment requires a humanizing environment.[96]

Where Montagu writes "humanity," read "person." Michael Tooley distinguishes between "person" and "human being," and argues that to be a person is to have a serious right to life. "An organism possesses a serious right to life only if it possesses the concept of a self as a continuing subject of experiences and other mental states, and believes that it is itself such a continuing entity."[97] Now, this surely goes too far. For on this view not only do fetuses lack the right to life, but infants do as well. Tooley is a conspicuous example for anti-abortionists of individuals who have begun the slide down the slippery slope. Tooley would say that just as it would be wrong to torture a newborn kitten (it can feel pain), but not wrong to kill it (it has no sense of selfhood); so too it is wrong to torture an infant, but not necessarily wrong to kill it.

The Fetus as a Potential Person Whichever way we view the fetus's lack of selfhood (and the third view seems most plausible),[98] the pro-abortionist still has to come to terms with this argument: Although the fetus is not a person, it has the potential of being one. If the life of a person is valuable, that which is potentially a person is valuable also. If persons have the right to life, potential persons do also.

Ordinarily we would not want to say that if *X* has the potential for being *Y*, he will have the same rights as *Y*. Cadets at West Point have the potential for being officers, but they do not have the same rights as officers. A middle-aged woman has the potential for being a senior citizen, but does not have the rights of a senior citizen (Social Security checks, discounts at theaters, etc.). A rookie baseball player has the potential for being a "six-year man," but does not have

[96]Montagu, quoted in R. J. Gerber, "Abortion: Parameters for Decision," in Struhl and Struhl, eds., *Ethics in Perspective,* p. 241.

[97]Tooley, "Abortion and Infanticide," in Abelson and Friquegnon, p. 81.

[98]Tooley is correct that if we draw a line between stages of human life for purposes of determining the right to live, it must be based on "morally relevant differences." The line drawn in the third view seems more relevant when life is at stake than the one Tooley draws. His may be relevant to other decisions, but not to the one whether to kill.

the right of "free agency." It may be answered that the fetus is already living and what is at stake is whether it has a right to retain that which it already has. Again, it is not the case that if *X* already has *Z* and has the potential for becoming *Y*, which clearly has the right to *Z*, then *X* has that right also. A professor has a position and has the potential for tenured status, but her right to the position is conferred only after she wins tenure. It may be answered that we should at least value things that have a potential for something that is clearly valued. If *X* has the potential to be *Y* and if *Y* is valued, then *X* should be valued also. There is some truth in this, but it certainly does not follow that *X* should be regarded as having the *same degree* of value as *Y*. The difference in value is crucial here. We may place great value in a stately oak tree, but very little on the acorns. We may prize a masterpiece, but look with contempt on the paint on the artist's palette.

The argument of Hare "abjures" the two positions usually taken in anti-abortionist arguments, the rights of the fetus and the status of the fetus as a person, and condemns abortion because it is counter to the Golden Rule. But it seems to be based on the intuitive value we place on human life—as we experience it in our own existence. In answer one can argue that the two forms of life (in utero and ex utero) do not necessarily have the *same value*. Hare recognizes the problem of overpopulation, but quotes *King Lear* with some approval: "Let population thrive!"

Hare and the Golden Rule Nevertheless, let us look at the application of the Golden Rule in Hare's argument. Since we are glad to be alive, we should demand for the fetus the same thing we would demand were we a fetus, namely, survival and an opportunity for existence ex utero. It does seem strange to apply the Golden Rule to a prior stage of our own being, a stage at which we could not possibly want *anything*. Moreover, the Golden Rule is generally thought to apply to persons only, and Hare does not want to have to try to prove that fetuses are persons. Indeed, he applies the Golden Rule to ova and semen and decisions to have sexual intercourse. He is glad his parents had intercourse and conceived him precisely when they did, and presumably places himself in the position of the ovum (he would want to be impregnated) and that of the sperm (he would want to impregnate). On his application of the Golden Rule, contraception is wrong (though not as bad as abortion); and this is ridiculous.

A sounder application of the Golden Rule would be on behalf of humanity itself. People find that life is good, so a goodly number of fetuses should be brought to term. As an individual who was once "a gleam in my father's eye," I would not have wanted to see universal continence, nationwide contraception, or wholesale abortion. But how could I expect to have or arbitrarily choose the particular congeries of events that produced the unique fetus that became me? If I had not been produced, someone else would have been—by my parents or someone else. Pro-abortionists do not argue for an end to conception. Lear's injunction is really superfluous. The issue is selective abortion, and what particular claims I might have for a "happy union" cannot take precedence over claims that other hypothetical lives might have for a fruitful union made impossible by the union that produced me. Indeed, the creation of me *ruled out* the creation of others. Perhaps I should put myself in their place and demand my own nonexistence. It is true, as Hare points out, that the chances of a fetus already conceived are somewhat greater than those of a future hypothetical fetus, but it is far-fetched to suppose that this slender statistical edge should settle the moral issue of all fetuses. The most the Hare argument can establish is this: If humanity in general is glad to be alive, it may employ the Golden Rule collectively and recognize a joint duty to procreate a new generation.

Hare's approach actually provides a better argument for abortion than against. If we can forget about the egg, sperm, and intercourse decisions and think only of the fetus, we can perhaps reasonably ask whether, if we were a fetus, we would want to be born. If we are defective, deformed, or about to be thrust into an unhappy or indigent family, we might well decline the honor. Moreover, as long as we are granting all this awareness to the fetus, we might expect it to invoke the Golden Rule also and ask whether, if *it* were the mother, would it (or she) want to have a child placed in its hands in this particular situation? The least we can do is to estimate the fetus's chance for a happy life on the basis of the information we have. Medical science is now able to detect certain congenital diseases in the fetus by means of examining amniotic fluid taken from the sac surrounding the fetus. Among the afflictions that can be discerned in this way are Down's syndrome, microcephaly, cystic fibrosis of the pancreas, Turner's syndrome, Klinefelter's syndrome, and Tay-Sachs disease (amaurotic idiocy), and others.[99] Doubtless medical science will extend the present list. Would *we* want to be born and live the life of an amaurotic idiot?

Where the prospects are not so bleak, for either the baby or the family, a happy life may be lost through the abortion. But there will be other fetuses and other lives, and their chances for happiness will be just as good.

Assuming That the Fetus Is a Person Finally, let us look at an argument for abortion that accepts the principle (for the sake of argument) that the fetus *is* a person. Judith Jarvis Thomson concedes this point and maintains that it is sometimes not immoral to kill an innocent person.

She asks you to imagine waking up one morning to find yourself attached to a violinist—unconscious but possessing great talent. It seems that he has a kidney ailment and the use of your circulatory system is the only way his life can be sustained. The violinist is a person, you are told, and since to remove the apparatus would kill him, you must remain attached to him for nine months (or nine years or indefinitely). According to Thomson, it would be an act of great generosity on your part to agree to this, but you would not be immoral if you did not. The parallel to pregnancy is obvious.

[99]See Leiser, pp. 106–107.

If it is the case that remaining plugged in would eventually kill you (by putting additional strain on your own kidneys), the Catholic would say that since pulling the plug would *directly kill* the violinist, while leaving it in would only *result* in your death, the connection must be maintained. To agree would indeed be praiseworthy, says Thomson, but not obligatory. Moreover, argues Thomson, the decisions as to who will be saved cannot be left to the impartial judgment of a third party. If *your* body is equally necessary for the life of two persons, it would *not* be an act of impartiality to assign it to someone else. "If a human being has any just, prior claim to anything at all, he has a just, prior claim to his own body."[100]

Even if your life is *not* threatened by your attachment to the violinist, you do not owe him the use of your body. That he has a right to life may be conceded, but this does not mean that everyone else is obligated to do all the things that are required to sustain it. Others have rights also (e.g., you, to your own body), and they may respect his, and out of kindness support it, but they are not obligated to give up their rights to satisfy his.

It may be objected at this point that a fetus *acquires* the right to use the mother's body, that the mother's voluntary act of intercourse in effect has invited the fetus to come into her body. She is thus at least partly responsible for its presence there. A fetus produced this way has a better claim than one engendered by rape. Here Thomson provides us with another analogy. Suppose you open a window at night (the air is stuffy) and a burglar crawls in. Although you provided him with the means to enter, you did not invite him in. He cannot claim the right of using your house. Suppose you take very prudent steps against the burglary menace, say, install bars on the windows, the fact that they proved defective does not give the successful burglar any rights. "It seems to me that the argument we are looking at can establish at most that there are *some* cases in which the unborn person has a right to the use of its mother's body, and therefore *some* cases in which abortion is unjust killing."[101]

An excellent point that Thomson makes is that what may be an act of kindness or generosity on your part is not necessarily morally obligatory. If you permitted the violinist to remain plugged in for ten years, you would be doing a very praiseworthy act, but it would not have been unjust or immoral to refuse. If he needed your kidneys for just one hour, it would be indecent to refuse (and perhaps immoral), but it would not have been unjust.

Summary of the Issues

Since the Supreme Court decision in 1973, responsibility for choosing abortion has rested largely in the hands of pregnant women and medical personnel. Many pro-abortionists, however, oppose the restrictions retained for the third trimester,

[100]Thomson, "A Defense of Abortion," in Rachels, *Moral Problems,* p. 138.
[101]Ibid., p. 143.

while many anti-abortionists lament the decision and favor a constitutional amendment to prohibit abortion in all but very special circumstances.

The anti-abortionists stress the value of human life and invoke religious and secular arguments for their contention that life ought to be cherished and protected—especially when it is totally innocent of wrongdoing. They also employ utilitarian grounds to show that disregard for fetal life can lead to disregard for life in general. The pro-abortionists, on the other hand, seem to be more concerned with the quality of life than with life itself. They use the utilitarian approach to show how unwanted children, families, and society itself will suffer when certain fetuses are permitted to survive. The anti-abortionists try to show how these evils can be mitigated.

There is a great difference in the two sides on the question of what fetuses should be permitted to be born. At one extreme are the people who would resort to abortion only when necessary to save the life of the mother or to prevent the birth of a grossly defective child. Even in these cases, it would be an act of superior morality to preserve the child—but it is not required. At the other extreme are the people who favor abortion "on demand" and would stretch the principle of the mental health of the mother to cover cases of simple inconvenience. Not only must the pregnant woman and her family, friends, and counselors attempt to draw the line between ethically acceptable and unacceptable abortion, but medical people also. Doctors and other medical personnel must decide the conditions under which they can conscientiously assist in abortions. Hospitals also must decide how best to represent the collective conscience of their constituency. Public health programs on both the national and local level must establish the conditions under which abortion will be paid for from public funds.

Underlying much of the debate is disagreement on the meaning of such expressions as *human life, self,* and *person.* The anti-abortionists may concede that the fetus, according to most definitions, is not a self or person, but they will insist that it is a form of human life and is a *potential* person. The fetus is simply the prenatal phase of a continuous life span; it should not be dispatched any more than should infants and old people who might not qualify as selves or persons. If we value life, we should value it in all of its stages. The pro-abortionists may concede that the fetus is a form of human life; it does not become a person, however, until it has experienced the trauma of birth. Only then does it acquire the rights of personhood. That the fetus has the potential for becoming a person does not confer upon it the *rights* of a person. Since life in utero and life ex utero possess different values and different rights, it is often moral to subordinate the interests of the former to those of the latter.

Hare believes that these distinctions are irrelevant and offers an interesting argument against abortion based on the Golden Rule: "Would you have wanted *your* mother to have had an abortion?" The pro-abortionists utilize the Golden Rule also, but with opposite conclusions.

Finally, Thomson argues that abortion can be morally condoned even if we assume that the fetus is a person and has the rights of a person. Since the application of this argument is not restricted to abortion to save the life of the mother or to prevent a monstrous birth, the anti-abortionists must find a way to refute it.

Discussion Questions

1. Do you think that medical personnel and institutions are morally obligated to provide whatever assistance in abortion does not conflict with the law? Explain.
2. Do you agree with the legal dictum that a fetus is not a person? Why?
3. Do you agree with many pro-abortionists and anti-abortionists that the line drawn by the Supreme Court between the second and third trimesters is artificial and arbitrary? Explain.
4. Do you believe that it is moral to abort a fetus that is found to have Down's syndrome? PKU? Tay-Sachs disease? Why?
5. Ignoring the legal question, do you believe that it is moral to kill a newborn child who is afflicted with Down's syndrome? PKU? Tay-Sachs disease? If your answer differs from the one you gave to the previous question, what made the difference?
6. What prima facie rights do you believe a fetus has? What rights, if any, do you think would take precedence over them?
7. How would you assess the utilitarian argument in favor of abortion? How would you assess the utilitarian argument against abortion?
8. In speculating about the value of life, would you be more impressed with the value of life itself or with the value of the quality of the lives in question? Explain.
9. Granting that innocent persons have the right to live, how would you evaluate the argument that the fetus, being a *potential* person, has the same right?
10. What is your opinion of the view that human life is a continuum and that all stages, prenatal and postnatal, are entitled to the same rights?
11. How would you assess the Catholic argument that neither the life of the fetus nor that of the mother may legitimately be *taken,* but that the one may be *permitted* to die in order to save the life of the other? If you were pregnant, would you choose a Catholic obstetrician?
12. Do you believe that it is right to take the life of the fetus in order to save the life of the mother? Why?
13. Assuming that the mother will survive in any case, do you believe that the physical health of the mother is a legitimate reason for abortion? Explain.
14. Do you believe that the emotional health of the mother is a legitimate reason for abortion? Explain.
15. Do you see any possible misuse of the principle that abortion is permissible in cases where it is necessary for the physical or emotional health of the mother? Explain.
16. Do you agree with the soundness of the Supreme Court opinion that permission of the father of the fetus and the family of the pregnant woman is not required for abortion? Explain.
17. Do you think that abortion could ever be carried out in the spirit of love? Explain.

18. What do you think of the adoption recourse recommended by the anti-abortionist for pregnancies caused by rape? By incest?
19. Is it reasonable, in your opinion, to assess the degrees of responsibility to the fetus on the basis of whether the unwanted pregnancy was the result of rape, ineffective contraception, or no contraception at all? Explain.
20. Do you believe that the indigent are entitled to the same medical assistance for abortion that the well-to-do can afford? Why?
21. Do you think it is the legitimate role of the state to "protect" the pregnant woman who wants an abortion in her third trimester? Why?
22. Do you think an unmarried woman is entitled to abortion "on demand"? Why?
23. What is *your* opinion of Hare's "Golden Rule" argument?
24. What is *your* opinion of Thomson's argument?
25. What do you think an ethics of self-realization would have to say about abortion? Is such a view sound?
26. Have you ever known anyone who had an abortion and regretted it afterward? Have you known anyone who decided not to have an abortion and regretted it afterward? Discuss.

For Further Reading

Raziel Abelson and Marie-Louise Friquegnon, eds. *Ethics for Modern Life.* New York: St. Martin's Press, 1975. Chapter 1.

Clifford E. Bajema. *Abortion and the Meaning of Personhood.* Grand Rapids, Mich.: Baker Books, 1974.

Sissela Bok. "Ethical Problems of Abortion." *Hastings Center Studies,* 2 (1974):33ff.

R. B. Brandt. "The Morality of Abortion." *Monist* 56 (1972):503ff.

Baruch A. Brody. "Abortion and the Sanctity of Human Life." *American Philosophical Quarterly* 10 (1973):133ff.

Daniel Callahan. *Abortion: Law, Choice, and Morality.* New York: Macmillan Publishing Co., Inc., 1970.

Marshall Cohen, Thomas Nagel, and Thomas Scanlon, eds. *The Rights and Wrongs of Abortion.* Princeton, N.J.: Princeton University Press, 1975.

John F. Dedek. *Human Life: Some Moral Issues.* New York: Sheed & Ward, 1972.

Jane English. "Abortion and the Concept of a Person." *Canadian Journal of Philosophy* 5 (1975):233ff.

Joel Feinberg, ed. *The Problem of Abortion.* Belmont, Calif.: Wadsworth Publishing Co., 1973.

John Finnis. "The Rights and Wrongs of Abortion: A Reply to Judith Thomson." *Philosophy and Public Affairs* 2 (1973):117ff.

Norman Fost. "Our Curious Attitude toward the Fetus." *Hastings Center Report* 4 (1974): 4ff.

D. Gerber. "Abortion: The Uptake Argument." *Ethics* 83 (1973):80ff.

R. J. Gerber. "Abortion: Parameters for Decision." *Ethics* 82 (1972):137ff.

David Granfield. *The Abortion Decision.* Garden City, N.Y.: Doubleday, 1969.

Germain G. Grisez. *Abortion: The Myths, the Realities, and the Arguments.* New York: Corpus Books, 1970.

Group for the Advancement of Psychiatry, Committee on Psychiatry and Law. *The Right to Abortion: A Psychiatric View.* New York: Charles Scribner's Sons, 1970.

R. M. Hare. "Abortion and the Golden Rule." *Philosophy and Public Affairs* 4 (1975): 201ff.

T. Hilgers and D. J. Horan, eds. *Abortion and Social Justice.* New York: Sheed and Ward, 1973.

Marvin Kohl. *The Morality of Killing: Euthanasia, Abortion, and Transplants.* New York: Humanities Press, 1974.

J. M. Kummer, ed. *Abortion, Legal and Illegal: A Dialogue Between Attorneys and Psychiatrists.* Santa Monica, Calif.: Kummer, 1967.

Nancy Howell Lee. *The Search for an Abortionist.* Chicago: University of Chicago Press, 1969.

Burton M. Leiser. *Liberty, Justice, and Morals.* 2nd ed. New York: Macmillan Publishing Co., 1979. Chapter 3.

Anne Lindsay. "On the Slippery Slope Again." *Analysis* 35 (1974).

Thomas A. Mappes and Jane S. Zembaty, eds. *Social Ethics: Morality and Social Policy.* New York: McGraw-Hill Book Co., 1977. Chapter 1.

Joseph Margolis. "Abortion." *Ethics* 84 (1973):51ff.

Ashley Montagu. *Life before Birth.* New York: New American Library, 1964.

Frances Myrna. "Abortion: A Philosophical Analysis." *Feminist Studies* 1:49ff.

Jan Narveson. "Semantics, Future Generations, and the Abortion Problem." *Social Theory and Practice* 3 (1975):461ff.

John T. Noonan, ed. *The Morality of Abortion: Legal and Historical Perspectives.* Cambridge: Harvard University Press, 1970.

Robert L. Perkins, ed. *Abortion: Pro and Con.* Cambridge, Mass.: Schenkman Publishing Co., 1974.

Pope Pius XI. *Casti Connubi.* New York: Paulist Press, 1941.

Malcolm Potts et al. *Abortion.* Cambridge: At the University Press, 1977.

James Rachels, ed. *Moral Problems.* 3rd ed. New York: Harper & Row, 1979. Part 2.

Paul Ramsey. *Ethics at the Edges of Life.* New Haven: Yale University Press, 1978. Part 1.

Evelyn Reed and Claire Moriarity. *Abortion and the Catholic Church: Two Feminists Defend Women's Rights.* New York: Pathfinder Press, 1973.

Joel Rudinow. "On the 'Slippery Slope.'" *Analysis* 34 (1974):173ff.

Betty Sarvis and Hyman Rodman. *The Abortion Controversy.* 2nd ed. New York: Columbia University Press, 1974.

George Sher. "Hare, Abortion, and the Golden Rule." *Philosophy and Public Affairs* 6 (1977):185ff.

Society and Friends, American Friends Service Committee. *Who Shall Live?* New York: Hill & Wang, 1970.

Karsten J. and Paula Rothenberg Struhl, eds. *Ethics in Perspective.* New York: Random House, 1975. Part 2, section 2a.

L. W. Sumner. "Toward a Credible View of Abortion." *Canadian Journal of Philosophy* 5 (1974):163ff.

Judith Jarvis Thomson. "A Defense of Abortion." *Philosophy and Public Affairs* 1 (1971): 47ff.

Michael Tooley. "Abortion and Infanticide." *Philosophy and Public Affairs* 2 (1972):37ff.

Mary Anne Warren. "On the Moral and Legal Status of Abortion." *The Monist* 57 (1973): 43ff.

Richard Werner. "Hare on Abortion." *Analysis* 36 (1976):177ff.
Roger Wertheimer. "Understanding the Abortion Argument." *Philosophy and Public Affairs* 1 (1971):67ff.

SUICIDE

Suicide Is Always Wrong

The Christian View Christianity, born at a place and time in which suicide was commonly accepted as an honorable departure from life, early placed itself in opposition to the practice.

The commandment "Thou shalt not kill" was interpreted categorically. While exceptions were made for warfare and the administration of justice, both legitimate functions of duly ordained governments, none was made in the case of killing oneself. Suicide is homicide, murder. Nowhere in the Bible is there precept or permission to take one's own life. Just as Christians are to uphold and respect the life of others, they are to uphold and respect their own.[102] Although our life is "given" to us by God, we are God's creatures and still belong to him. "Hence whoever takes his own life sins against God, even as he who kills another's slave sins against that slave's master."[103]

There would seem to be some exceptions to the Christian stance against suicide: The Old Testament hero, Samson, pulled down the building, killing himself along with his enemies. But Samson, says Augustine, was justified on the ground "that the Spirit who wrought wonders by him had given him secret instructions to do this."[104] Perhaps the holy women who threw themselves into the river to avoid ravishment during the persecutions, and are today venerated as martyrs, are also exceptions. Perhaps they too were "prompted by divine wisdom"; Augustine does not know. Abraham, when he set out to kill Isaac, was prepared to violate the injunctions against private execution (moreover, of an innocent person), but he certainly was responding to a direct order from God. These cases, indeed, are very exceptional. "He, then, who knows that it is unlawful to kill himself, may nevertheless do so if ordered by Him whose commands we may not neglect. *Only let him be very sure that the divine command has been signified.*"[105] Jesus consistently urged his followers to flee persecution to preserve their lives, never once advising them to "lay violent hands upon themselves." The members of the Jim Jones cult in Guyana who took their lives were probably deceived—by their own feelings and by the monstrous man who gave the orders.

[102]Thomas Aquinas says that "one owes the greatest love" to oneself. *Summa Theologica,* Secunda Secundae, Question 64, Article 5. Translated by Fathers of the English Dominican Province (New York: Benziger Brothers, 1947), vol. 2, p. 1469.
[103]Ibid.
[104]Augustine, *City of God* (trans. Dods) I, 21, p. 27.
[105]Ibid., I, 26, p. 31. Emphasis added.

Augustine, who had a vivid conception of the dangers, trials, and temptations of human existence, inveighed against suicide. Christian women who have been raped by barbarians should not commit suicide, for the sin was not theirs. And even if they did sin by assenting in some sense to the act, suicide would be wrong. For here, as in all cases of moral disgrace (including that of Judas), suicide precludes the opportunity to repent. Those who commit suicide for fear that they *will* do an immorality have foolishly chosen a *certain* sin over an *uncertain* sin.[106] The pagans mistakenly extol the purity of Lucretia, the noble matron of ancient Rome who destroyed herself after having been raped by King Tarquin's son. Her act "was prompted not by love of purity, but by the overwhelming burden of her shame."[107]

Christians may expect many tribulations in this "vale of tears" through which they must pass. If some are relatively fortunate in this life, they need only look at the misfortunes of others now and in times past—or read the account of Job in the Old Testament.[108] The recourse of the Christian is not to take his or her life but to call on God for help during times of distress. God does not inflict anything on us that we cannot, with God's help, bear.[109] Misery may be the occasion for a closer union with God. And there is the ultimate consolation that we are members of a higher realm than the "earthly city": We belong to the "city of God," where there is infinite and everlasting peace. One of the great Christian virtues is *hope.* Paul wrote: "We know that the whole creation has been groaning in travail together until now; and not only the creation, but we ourselves, who have the first fruits of the Spirit, groan inwardly as we wait for adoption as sons, the redemption of our bodies. For in this hope we are saved. Now hope that is seen is not hope. For who hopes for what he sees? But if we hope for what we do not see, we wait for it with patience."[110] It is through hope that another great virtue is sustained: fortitude.

That there is another world to look forward to does not mean that Christians should take the initiative and flee to it through suicide. Their situtation is not like that of the pagan who read Plato's *Phaedo* and committed suicide in order quickly to enjoy the blessing of immortality. The Christian's soul must be perfected, and part of this process takes place in this world where he or she obeys God's will and grows in grace. Part of God's will is that people utilize this worldy experience and cling to the life that makes it possible.

[106]The most fantastic form of this kind of thinking is to commit suicide immediately after forgiveness is received for past sins—in order to depart life in a blessed condition!

[107]Ibid., I, 19, p. 25.

[108]The part where Job is restored to health, wealth, and happiness may be ignored, for that was added by scribes who could not accept the truth that endless suffering is sometimes the lot on earth of good persons.

[109]"No temptation has overtaken you that is not common to man. God is faithful, and he will not let you be tempted beyond your strength, but with temptation will also provide the way of escape, that you may be able to endure it." 1 Corinthians 10:13.

[110]Romans 8:22–25.

Stoicism It is difficult to understand the logic of the Stoic philosophy, which also believes in a cosmic providence and teaches fortitude. The Stoics have written persuasively on the need to accept whatever occurs as part of a divine plan and to accept uncomplainingly what the plan holds for us. We should not lament the loss of honors and friends, the diseases that touch not the soul, or the end of life's drama (when we would wish to declaim a few more lines from the stage). Yet many of them countenanced suicide—which would appear to be an obvious rejection of the role decreed for the individual to play. Augustine had much to say about Cato, the Roman soldier, statesman, and Stoic. Cato committed suicide because he could not endure the victory of Julius Caesar. This is not, says Augustine, an act of fortitude. Much more admirable was the conduct of Regulus, who, after defeat and imprisonment by the Carthaginians, did *not* avail himself of suicide. "Patient under the domination of the Carthaginians, and constant in his love of the Romans, he neither deprived the one of his conquered body, nor the other of his unconquered spirit. Neither was it love of life that prevented him from killing himself. This was plainly enough indicated by his unhesitatingly returning, on account of his promise and oath, to the same enemies whom he had more grievously provoked by his words in the senate than even by his arms in battle."[111]

The Stoics hold two beliefs that do not go well together: that nothing is evil in itself and that life requires a lot of fortitude. Yet neither goes well with suicide. On the first, "unreal" evils may become so grievous that the individual may escape them through suicide. "O happy life," says Augustine sarcastically, "which seeks the aid of death to end it!"[112] On the second, fortitude wavers just at the point where it is most needed. "It has yielded, it has succumbed, it has been so thoroughly overcome as to abandon, forsake, flee this . . . life."[113]

The Stoics would have been much more consistent (and closer to the truth) if they had forbidden suicide. Prizing the strength of will that is proof against outward calamity, the steadfastness that enables the individual to grow in power with every adversity, the courage that inspires one to do one's best so long as life and limb shall last, they could have provided a definitive case against suicide. "It matters not how strait the gate, how charged with punishment the scroll," wrote William Ernest Henley centuries later; "I am the master of my fate; I am the captain of my soul." Epictetus was the true Stoic hero, not Seneca, for he did not commit suicide, while Seneca (as a result of Nero's generosity) did.

One does not have to be a Christian to accept the immorality of suicide, as this interpretation of Stoicism indicates. The causes of suicide are often ignoble, exemplifying the very things that Stoicism despises: *cowardice* in facing physical pain or dishonor; *weakness* in not being willing to make the best out of a bad situation; *loss of integrity* in declining to carry out one's duty in uncomfortable

[111]*City of God,* 1, 24, p. 29.
[112]Ibid., XIX, 4, p. 678.
[113]Ibid., p. 679.

circumstances; *irresponsibility* in not being willing to accept the consequences of one's own action; *selfishness* in seeking peace for oneself while leaving problems to one's survivors. Many decisions to commit suicide are made when the mind is clouded by excessive grief, drunkenness, and drugs. They are made in conditions when clear thinking is impossible, but these conditions are states of mind that the wise person will avoid like the plague. They are conditions of his or her own life that the person has some control over. Although the Stoics will in their breadth of understanding be able to sympathize with the person who for reason of one failing or another embarks upon suicide, true Stoics cannot condone the action on the part of others or themselves.

Rationality The ultimate form of irrational action is that taken by the person who is insane or temporarily mad. Many suicides are committed when people are in this state. While the person cannot, perhaps, be held morally blameworthy for an act done during insanity, the fact that insanity and suicide so often go together is an indication of its basic irrationality.

Despite the fact that the suicide rate has remained fairly constant in the United States over the past fifty years, that of young people between fifteen and twenty-four is on the increase. Since 1955 it has quadrupled.[114] Various causes have been suggested: The anxiety of adolescence (self-doubt, search for identity and peer acceptance), a sense of isolation (parents are engaged in their own lives), and competitive pressure (for grades, jobs). Most of these suicides are not rational. Many are impulsive, done in a moment of deep despair. It has been estimated that the number of attempted suicides among the young is one hundred times the number of successful suicides, which suggests that many young people are concerned not so much with dying as with getting some attention or punishing an authority figure. "A suicide attempt," says Dr. Calvin J. Frederick of the National Institute of Mental Health, "is a cry for help, a cry for someone to care." This is said to be why the rate of attempted suicide among females is much higher than among males, while the rate of actual suicide among males is much higher than among females: "Men don't feel free to cry for help. Women do."[115] But each "cry" must be taken seriously, for the next attempt may succeed. Young people who take a bleak outlook on life must be treated and counseled. Suicidal acts by young people are signs of psychological disturbance. Unable to see a way out of difficulties, often overestimated in importance, they seize an irrational alternative. If they were more experienced in life and more objective about their predicament, they would not take this desperate action.

What the potential suicide must realize is the finality of the act. Most mistakes can be corrected or atoned, but not this one. Desperate though one may be, it is possible that the situation will be different tomorrow—or next year, or in ten

[114]"Accidents" with alcohol, drugs, and automobiles are not counted as suicides, although many of them are suicidal.

[115]See "Teen-Age Suicide," *Newsweek*, August 28, 1978, p. 76.

years. One should not, as a matter of prudence if nothing else, cut oneself off from the brighter days that almost certainly will arrive. Unsuccessful suicides often do not try again; they were lucky. Successful suicides are forever dead.

Kant Let us take a case in which these brighter days will surely not arrive. An individual is dying a painful death. No good accrues to his loved ones through his survival. He is not a religious man and does not believe that suicide violates a commandment of God. He can take an overdose of his medicine and bid adieu to his misery once and for all. Would it be moral for him to do so? According to Immanuel Kant, it would not be.

> It is a duty to preserve one's life, and moreover everyone has a direct inclination to do so. But, for that reason, the often anxious care which most men take of it has no intrinsic worth, and the maxim of doing so has no moral import. They preserve their lives according to duty, but not from duty. But if adversities and hopeless sorrow completely take away the relish for life; if an unfortunate man . . . wishes for death, and yet preserves his life without loving it and from neither inclination nor fear but from duty—then his maxim has a moral import.[116]

"Do not commit suicide" is a categorical imperative, and like all such imperatives it offers no rewards beyond morality itself. To shorten one's life from love of oneself could not be universalized as a law of nature. "One immediately sees a contradiction in a system of nature, whose law would be to destroy life by the feeling whose special office is to impel the improvement of life."[117] The maxim would contradict "the supreme principle of all duty."[118] The second formulation of the categorical imperative (use humanity as an end, whether *in your own person* or in that of another) also condemns suicide.[119]

What does one accomplish by being moral? One achieves a "good will." This development is open to the wretched man in our example. By committing suicide, he corrupts it. By adhering to the moral law and living, he enhances it. He therefore makes himself *worthy* of happiness. Kant states certain "moral postulates" that are answers to the question "What may I hope?" Two of these are the existence of God and the immortality of the soul. If a person is worthy of happiness, he or she may hope that a supernatural power exists that will provide the rewards so lacking in this life. If a good will has been achieved, one may hope that it will not be terminated by death and will have an endless duration for its continued development. These are merely hopes and have no bearing on the ethical decisions themselves. But one who feels that the moral enterprise is real

[116]Kant, *Foundations of the Metaphysics of Morals* (trans. Beck), p. 59.

[117]Ibid., p. 81.

[118]Ibid., p. 87.

[119]Thomas Aquinas also views suicide as a violation of a "law of nature" in a somewhat different sense: "Everything naturally keeps itself in being, and resists corruption so far as it can." *Summa Theologica,* Secunda Secundae, Question 64, Article 5, vol. 2, p. 1469.

and who has any sense of a just and reasonable universe, may to that extent indulge his or her hopes.

Some Distinctions Finally, let us make a distinction between suicide and some other kinds of acts that are sometimes confused with it. (1) People who are hopelessly ill and choose not to avail themselves of extraordinary life support systems (voluntary "passive" euthanasia) are not suicides. They do not take their own lives but permit nature to take its course. (2) People who perform an act of great courage in the midst of great danger are not suicides. Their intention was not to die themselves but to save someone else. The soldier who falls on a live grenade or drags a fallen comrade from the battlefield, the mother who snatches her child from the path of an onrushing car, and the citizen who goes to the aid of a person being mugged may all die, but they would have preferred to live. (3) Humanitarians who endanger their lives in medical research or their health in incessant labor to produce benefits for others (say, cures for disease, beautiful poems, or labor-saving inventions) are not suicides. Even if one is not a humanitarian but is so engrossed in work that one is careless of one's health, one is not a suicide if death was not part of one's intention. (4) Adventurers who like to climb mountains, explore the Amazon, jump out of airplanes, and do other dangerous things are not suicides if death comes not from design but in the course of pursuing their love of excitement. (5) Reformers or revolutionists who take great risks to change the political structure of society are not suicides if death should befall them. Condorcet and Nathan Hale are examples. (6) Men and women of principle who refuse to save their own lives by betraying others or compromising their principles are not suicides. Antigone, Jesus, Christian martyrs, Socrates, and Joe Hill are examples. In all these categories, with the possible exception of the first, the individual did not despise his or her life, but put other things ahead of it. Perhaps in many cases the person was foolish or immoral, but he or she was not guilty of suicide.[120]

Suicide Is Not Always Wrong

Although we may have been "given" our life by God, by the forces of nature, and/or by our parents, the fact remains that it is our life. "Obviously there is nothing to which every man has a more unassailable title than to his own life and person."[121] Our life was not "loaned" to us on condition that we protect and cherish it. We did not ask to be born. Life was thrust upon us, free and clear, with no consent or discussion on our part.

Once we are in existence, however, we can exercise some control. We can choose our actions and can espouse certain moral principles. We can make plans

[120]These cases are cited to forestall a defense of "suicide" based on taking it in a wide (and illegitimate) sense.

[121]Arthur Schopenhauer, "On Suicide" (trans. Saunders), in *Essays of Arthur Schopenhauer,* p. 399.

and project a career. *That* we live was not of our doing; *how* we live is. But there are restrictions. One is that our life (at least on earth) will be of finite length. It is said that of all the animals, man is the only one who knows that he will die. The "gift" of life, which the person did not seek, will be taken away sooner or later. But here, the individual has some control. As Pliny said, "The chief remedy for a troubled mind is the feeling that there is no greater blessing than an opportune death; and that every one can avail himself of."[122] It is fitting that the freedom that the individual did not have at one end of his or her existence is present at the other. "Life," says Pliny, "is not so desirable as to be protracted at any cost."[123]

Religious Considerations There are arguments against this view. Some say that it belongs to God or providence to decide when the time is opportune, that the individual who takes matters into his or her own hands thwarts the will of God. Now, if God is omnipotent, it is impossible to thwart his will. Whatever is done must be consistent with his intentions. If God is good, whatever comes to pass is part of his providence. We flatter ourselves too much if we think that we can change the course of divinely appointed events. Perhaps it is God's will that a person *does* commit suicide.[124]

A more naturalistic (or deistic) view of God, espoused for the sake of argument by David Hume, holds that the universe was created by God to operate according to natural law and that humanity, which performs in it, is given certain powers of body, passion, and reason that have their natural expression also. God neither ordains nor interferes.

> Every event is alike important in the eyes of that infinite Being, who takes in at one glance the most distant regions of space, and remotest periods of time. There is no event, however important to us, which he has exempted from the general laws that govern the universe, or which he has peculiarly reserved for his own immediate action and operation.[125]
>
> Shall we assert that the Almighty has reserved to himself, in any peculiar manner, the disposal of the lives of men, and has not submitted that event, in common with others, to the general laws by which the universe is governed? This is plainly false.[126]

The human being has been given powers and has full authority to employ them as he or she sees fit.

[122]Quoted in ibid., p. 400.
[123]Ibid.
[124]Dr. Henry Pitney Van Dusen, a prominent Protestant leader, and his wife committed suicide several years ago. Their suicide note referred to the practice of modern medicine of keeping people alive into old age and infirmity, implying that some people live past the time allotted them by God. Suicide may be, not an attempt to "take things out of God's hands," but an act of adjusting to his plan. See George R. Plagenz, "What's Christian: Euthanasia or Prolonging Agony?" Edwardsville *Intelligencer,* July 3, 1980, p. 5.
[125]Hume, "Of Suicide," in *Essays: Moral, Political and Literary,* p. 588.
[126]Ibid., p. 589.

God may wish that humans be more prudent, that they be more ethical, that they serve their Creator more faithfully, but he does not exert pressure from on high that they do so. These things he leaves to their inherent natures. If God controls everything, he does it indirectly, and he does not reveal the details of his plan.

If we held back from action because of our concern that God's plans not be interfered with, we might think it wrong to build dams, drain swamps, inoculate for disease, and play night baseball. Any active person daily invades "the prerogatives of nature" and with no sense of guilt.

Superstitious people say that it is impious "to put a period to our own life and thereby rebel against nature." "And why not impious," asks Hume, "to build houses, cultivate the ground, or sail upon the ocean? In all these actions we employ our powers of mind and body to produce some innovation in the course of nature; and in none of them do we any more."[127]

To cultivate the ground is not to find fault with the Creator, but to use the resources he has given us. To take one's life is in the same category. The person who commits suicide may, according to Hume, say: "I thank Providence, both for the good which I have already enjoyed, and for the power with which I am endowed of escaping the ill that threatens me."[128] On the face of it, that person is no more guilty than the one who seeks means to *prolong* life.

In summary, then, the "will of God" argument does not establish the immorality of suicide. Recognition that God is the ultimate cause of the universe and the lives that exist in it does not lead to any particular conclusion about the proper behavior of any part of it.

What we need is an argument to show, not that God's will be done, but that he specifically forbids suicide. We need to know that he judges individuals who commit suicide to have used their powers in an undesirable manner. Various religions will have different notions about what these divine judgments are. In the case of Judaism and Christianity, we find no "revelations" in the sacred writings that suicide is wrong. To bank everything on the injunction "Thou shalt not kill" seems to be a strategic mistake in view of all the exceptions that Jews and Christians have been willing to make to it. If we believe that God is good, we can infer that it is his will that we be moral. It is thus appropriate to shift our attention from God to the morality of human action.

Prudence and Responsibility Although we hold that our lives belongs to ourselves, it does not follow from this that there are no limitations on what we do with or to them. Prudence would indicate that one use a net when sleeping in the jungle where anopheles mosquitoes abound. Ethics would indicate that one not destroy the net if someone else is sleeping in the same tent. There is nothing

[127]Ibid., p. 592.

[128]Ibid., p. 591.

intrinsically right or wrong about employing or destroying mosquito nets, but circumstances can make a great difference.

What prudential factors are relevant to the decision whether to commit suicide? Positive factors are: the prospect of a lingering, painful, and incurable illness;[129] the expectation of a disgrace or imprisonment that will make the rest of one's life miserable; the expectation of an unbearable humiliation or torture at the hands of one's enemies. Negative factors are: the possibility that a cure may be found for an unsupportable disease; the possibility that the future will look brighter tomorrow; the opportunity to grow in spiritual strength through surviving the crisis; the recognition that additional thought and effort may turn up a solution to the problem. These are a few of the factors that the prospective suicide would be wise to consider. But the decision is the person's own, and where other people are not significantly involved, that decision, even if it is in favor of suicide, must be judged as wise or foolish, not moral or immoral. The individual has done to the life to which he or she has title what has suited himself or herself best.

It is quite pointless to call suicide "the coward's way out." It may be the prudent person's way out. Instead of despising the absence of courage to face the consequences of a bad situation, we might just as often marvel at the courage of one who has been able to act against the strongest instinctive urge: to survive.

EXIT, a British organization dedicated to "the right to die with dignity," has published a suicide manual called "A Guide to Self-Deliverance." When doctors cannot practice euthanasia, the individual must do it himself.[130] EXIT recommends that people suffering from painful and incurable disease commit suicide only after examining other options. But if they have made a rational judgment, they should carry it out efficiently and with as few bad results for others as possible. The manual shows how. Socrates said that an unexamined life is not worth living. This may be true. But it does not follow from this that an examined life *is* worth living.

The ethical dimension of suicide manifests itself when others are significantly affected. What ethical factors are relevant to the decision? Positive factors are: the belief that continued life will be a crushing burden on one's loved ones; a prisoner's expectation of breaking under torture and betraying comrades; the belief that death will spare one's family and friends the misery of an exposé of one's secret crimes. It is said that Frederick the Great carried a little vial of poison during the Seven Years' War, intending to use it if captured so that his country would not have to pay a ransom. Themistocles committed suicide rather than help the Persians (who had given him refuge) mount a campaign against the Greeks

[129]It was a feature of Thomas More's *Utopia* (1551) that suffering patients in hospitals had the right to kill themselves and even to demand help from officials in this task. In 1935, More was canonized by the Roman Catholic Church.

[130]Euthanasia is discussed at greater length in the first section of chapter 7.

(who had banished him). "Who will dare to reproach him for this, or who can tell what else he ought to have done?"[131]

Negative factors are: knowledge that one's loved ones will experience great misery from one's untimely demise; knowledge that the insurance company will not pay off in cases of suicide; recognition that one will have broken a promise or placed oneself in a position of being unable to keep a promise. When the interests of others are seriously harmed (not simply inconvenienced), the individual is immoral to commit suicide. Where they are not, the individual is not immoral in that action.

Obligatory Self-Sacrifice Whether one is ever *obligated* to commit suicide—that is, one would be immoral *not* to—is difficult to ascertain. One may argue that morality sometimes requires an act of great danger, but it is something else to say that there are situations when one ought deliberately to take one's own life. Many people criticized the morality of the American reconnaissance flyer Gary Powers, who some years ago crashed in Russia, for not consuming his cyanide tablet before he was taken prisoner. And we do praise the person who does an act known to be fatal in order to save others. But do they have a *right* to his or her sacrifice? Probably not. I may give up my last kidney to save the life of my twin brother, but I am not obliged to. Such actions are *supererogatory*—they are admirable, but go beyond the requirements of duty.

It may appear that we are extending the meaning of suicide beyond its normal limits. The cyanide-swallower and the kidney-donator do their deeds in order to serve other ends: sacrificing their lives is simply the only available means. Literally, it is said, these are not acts of suicide. In answer, it may be argued that the sacrifice of one's life is nearly always performed for the sake of other ends (although not always so noble). When one sacrifices one's life to avoid pain, it is not life that one abhors, but pain. When one sacrifices one's life for a child, it is not death that one loves, but the child. When one takes great risk, for oneself or others, one places oneself in the position of *perhaps* sacrificing one's life. In all these cases, the person has placed a value on his or her own life, on sheer existence, which is less than the *quality* of that life which he or she desires or the interests of others whom he or she serves. Hume is closer to the truth on this issue when he writes: "If my life be not my own, it were criminal for me to put it in danger, as well as to dispose of it; nor could one man deserve the appellation of *hero,* whom glory or friendship transports into the greatest dangers; and another merit the reproach of *wretch* or *miscreant,* who puts a period to his life for like motives."[132]

Schopenhauer One of the great pessimists in the history of philosophy is Arthur Schopenhauer. The cause of our misery, he says, is the blind and insatiable will

[131]Friedrich Paulsen, *A System of Ethics* (New York: Charles Scribner's Sons, 1899), p. 588.
[132]Hume, p. 591.

at the heart of human nature. We all feel ourselves to be the center of the world and desire everything for ourselves, destroying everything in our way. There is no relief, no satisfaction. "Unrest is the mark of human existence. We are like a man running down hill who cannot keep on his legs unless he runs on."[133] Our life swings between the pain of unsatisfied desire and the boredom of satiation. "Life presents itself as a task to be performed." In an attempt to find a spot "not too exposed to the fire," Schopenhauer examined several forms of "salvation": The life of reason is promising, for here we are only spectators, but relief is only temporary, for the will reexerts itself. The enjoyment of beauty takes us outside ourselves for a while, but this is of short duration. Religions that teach selflessness, the Nirvana of Buddhism or the absorption of Atman in Brahma, are correct in their goal, but the total asceticism they demand is beyond the power of most of us to achieve. It would appear that suicide is the only escape for a person who, as Schopenhauer, believes that human life is "some kind of mistake." Religious teachers "tell us that suicide is the greatest piece of cowardice, that only a madman could be guilty of it; and other insipidities of the same kind."[134] But Schopenhauer, after having presented the most persuasive case for suicide in philosophical literature, advises against it. His reason: The individual has not destroyed life, but only an individual manifestation of it. It is a "vain and foolish act," for the thing-in-itself (the species, life, the will in general) "remains unaffected by it, even as the rainbow endures however fast the drops which support it for the moment may change."[135] Schopenhauer lacked the courage of his convictions (and also logical consistency). For of what concern would the survival of the larger will be to a selfish individual will? Getting out of the rat race is all *he or she* cares about!

The Ancients The ancient Stoics and Epicureans had a more reasonable view of suicide. When a point is reached when one can no longer lead one's life with dignity, one should depart. Death is inevitable in any case. Why should not the individual choose the best time? Marcus Aurelius "even defended the right of the individual to emancipate himself from the danger of 'intellectual decrepitude.' "[136]

Seneca wrote:

> How terrible is death to one man, which to another appears the greatest providence in nature, even toward all ages and conditions! It is the wish of some, the relief of many, and the end of all. It sets the slave at liberty, carries the banished man home,

[133]Schopenhauer, quoted in Alburey Castell, *An Introduction to Modern Philosophy* (New York: Macmillan Co., 1943), p. 146.

[134]Schopenhauer, *Essays,* p. 399.

[135]Schopenhauer, *The World as Will and Idea,* in R. B. Haldane and J. Kemp translation (London: Routledge & Kegan Paul, 1964), vol. 1, p. 515.

[136]O. Ruth Russell, *Freedom to Die* (New York: Dell Publishing Co., 1976), p. 54.

and places all mortals upon the same level: insomuch, that life itself were punishment without it. When I see tyrants, tortures, violences, the prospect of death is a consolation to me, and the only remedy against the injuries of life.[137]

In the meantime Epicurus will oblige me, with the following saying: "Rehearse death", or—the idea may come across to us rather more satisfactorily if put in this form—"It is a very good thing to familiarize oneself with death." You may possibly think it unnecessary to learn something which you will only have to put into practise once. That is the very reason why we ought to be practising it. We must needs continually study a thing if we are not in a position to test whether we know it. "Rehearse death." To say this is to tell a person to rehearse his freedom. A person who has learned how to die has unlearned how to be a slave. He is above, or at any rate beyond the reach of, all political powers. What are prisons, warders, bars to him? He has an open door. There is but one chain holding us in fetters, and that is our love of life. There is no need to cast this love out altogether, but it does need to be lessened somewhat so that, in the event of circumstances ever demanding this, nothing may stand in the way of our being prepared to do at once what we must do at some time or other.[138]

If I can choose between a death of torture and one that is simple and easy, why should I not select the latter?—Why should I endure the agonies of disease—when I can emancipate myself from all my torture?—I will not depart by death from disease as long as it may be healed and leaves my mind unimpaired—but if I know that I will suffer forever, I will depart, not through fear of pain itself, but because it prevents all for which I live.[139]

When the time was right, Seneca did commit suicide. According to Tacitus, he first cut his veins, but bled slowly. Then he called for poison, but it had no effect. Then he was carried to a vapor bath, where he suffocated. Through the ordeal, he was cheerful and philosophical.

Summary of the Issues

One issue in the suicide controversy is the meaning of the term. Those who oppose suicide often take a narrow view that would exclude dangerous acts done on behalf of ends other than the termination of life. Those who condone suicide take a broader view and regard acts that are believed to be fatal as suicidal, even though they were undertaken for reasons other than the termination of life. Both sides, however, would regard a self-destructive act done for the purpose of evading anticipated suffering on the part of the agent as suicide.

[137]Seneca, *Of a Happy Life,* in Walter Clode, ed., *The Morals of Seneca* (London: Walter Scott, n.d.), p. 89.

[138]Seneca *Letters from a Stoic,* Robin Campbell translation (Baltimore: Penguin Books, 1969), XXVI, p. 72.

[139]Seneca, Letter LXX. See Russell, p. 54.

Those who condone suicide argue that while we have no power over whether we are born, we do have the right to control the kind of life we lead and the time that it will end. Various circumstances can be imagined in which suicide would be a rational and prudential course of action. Although granting to the other side that suicide is often the act of a grief-stricken, emotionally disturbed, or intoxicated personality, the proponent of suicide insists that this is not always the case.

Those who condemn suicide on religious grounds deny that one's life belongs to oneself alone. God has given us life in order that we may use it to grow in grace, whatever tribulations we may have to face. God prohibits suicide. Some Christians on the basis of their interpretation of the Scriptures and early tradition would, however, dispute the view that God never condones suicide.

The "will of God" argument holds that the suicide has usurped a prerogative of God. Instead of persevering in the hope of better things to come and trusting in divine providence, the suicide has taken desperate measures of his or her own. Hume, on the other hand, argues that God's will is achieved through human feelings and thoughts, and from these the decision to commit suicide may sometimes fittingly be made.

Stoicism shares several important ideas with Christianity: providence and fortitude. This philosophy has been utilized by both sides in the suicide debate. One side emphasizes the Stoic virtues of courage, strength of character, integrity, responsibility, and concern for others in arguments against suicide. The other side points out the actual behavior of Stoic notables who committed suicide in the interest of personal dignity.

Schopenhauer's is another philosophy that can be used both ways. If the world is as bad as Schopenhauer claims and the individual is not especially fortunate, there may be ample reason for suicide. On the other hand, Schopenhauer did not in the end (for metaphysical reasons) recommend suicide.

On the deontological level, Kant holds that the duty to preserve one's life (however miserable) is a categorical imperative. In addition, suicide often violates certain duties we owe others. The other side will not condone suicide when other people are seriously harmed by it, but grief and inconvenience are not enough. Moreover, there might be duties involved that do more than condone suicide: suicidal actions may sometimes be obligatory.

Discussion Questions

1. A man recently parachuted to the top of the Gateway Arch in St. Louis. He slid off and died. Was he a suicide? Was Antigone? Was the war hero who saved seven lives before being shot down? Was the woman who declined special life-support systems in the hospital? Explain.
2. Do you believe that God categorically prohibits suicide? Why?
3. Do you believe that one is ever obligated to commit suicide? Why?

4. Do you think that the decision to commit suicide is ever a completely rational one? Explain.
5. Do you believe that the duty not to commit suicide is categorical or only prima facie? Explain.
6. Would Socrates' death have been ethically more acceptable if he had been bound and beheaded instead of drinking the hemlock? Why?
7. Which interpretation of Stoicism, prosuicide or antisuicide, is more consistent with its basic tenets? Explain.
8. In what sense, if any, is it possible to act against the will of God?
9. In your opinion, is suicide always an act of cowardice? Explain.
10. Under what circumstances, if any, should one seek to prevent someone else from committing suicide?
11. Have you ever contemplated suicide? Why didn't you go through with it?
12. What is the scope and meaning of the Sixth Commandment?
13. Do you think that Schopenhauer, in deciding not to commit suicide, was consistent with the fundamental tenets of his own philosophy? Explain.
14. Some people in Britain have prepared a "suicide kit." Do you think its circulation in the United States should be banned by law? Do you think it is morally right to offer such a product on the market? Why?
15. Is it true that most attempted suicides do not try again? Is it true that people who threaten to commit suicide seldom do so?
16. What utilitarian arguments could be advanced for suicide?
17. It is said that even in hell, "the common damned" shun the society of suicides. Do you agree?
18. Caesar said of Cleopatra, "Bravest at the last, She levell'd at our purposes, and being royal Took her own way." Brutus, after running on his sword, said, "Caesar, now be still: I kill'd not thee with half so good a will." And Antony called Brutus "the noblest Roman of them all." In your opinion, is there any truth to these Shakespearean sentiments?
19. Spinoza said: "Those who commit suicide are powerless souls, and allow themselves to be conquered by external causes repugnant to their nature." Comment.
20. Thomas Browne said: "We are in the power of no calamity while death is in our own." Comment.
21. Under what circumstances do you believe that suicide is clearly immoral?

For Further Reading

Thomas Aquinas. *Summa Theologica.* Translated by the Fathers of the English Dominican Province. New York: Bensiger Brothers, 1947. Secunda Secundae, Question 64, Article 5 (Vol. 2).

Augustine. *The City of God.* Translated by Marcus Dods. New York: Random House, 1950. Book 1.

David Hume. "Of Suicide." *Essays: Moral, Political and Literary.* London: Oxford University Press, 1963.

Arthur Schopenhaur. "On Suicide." Translated by T. Bailey Saunders. *Essays of Arthur Schopenhauer.* New York: A. L. Burt, n.d.

Seneca. *Letters,* especially 26 and 70. Many editions.

Chapter 4

BUSINESS: PRIVATE AND PUBLIC

In moving from abortion and suicide to the realm of business, we seem to be leaving a realm where *personal* decisions must be made to one where only *collective* decisions are important. Here we are concerned with what corporations, governments, and unions ought or ought not to do. But obviously, these collective units are themselves responsible to the individuals who are their constituencies. At the same time, the policies and practices of these collective units are also subject to the critical appraisal of those of us who are affected by their policies and practices.

We cannot, of course, scrutinize all the aspects of private and public business in these pages. We will discuss advertising, although that is not the only merchandising practice that has important social consequences. Price setting, market dominance, and credit practices are other possible topics. We will discuss government regulation of business so far as it applies to product safety, occupational safety, and protection of the environment, while ignoring those kinds of regulation that deal with monopolistic practices, stock market swindles, and use of the airwaves. We will discuss public sector strikes, while omitting questions of labor relations, rights, and duties in the private sector.

In discussing advertising, we will try to assess its impact on social values. What goods does it serve? What evils does it promote? As we would expect, there is a great disagreement in the answers to these questions. One side views advertising as a reprehensible enterprise with very little redeeming value, while the other side views advertising as so essential for economic well-being that its occasional excesses can be excused.

In discussing government regulations, we will compare the social benefits produced by regulation with its social costs. Everyone believes that some regulation is necessary. But how strict should it be? How extensive should it be? Do we have too much or not enough? Are there any principles by which warranted interference with business can be distinguished from the kind that is undesirable?

In examining public sector strikes, we will raise the question whether they are ethical and discuss the attitude that government should take toward such strikes. There is something disconcerting about strikes of schoolteachers, firefighters, and police officers, yet we respect the right of automobile workers and electricians to strike. Are there principles that distinguish one from the other, or are they basically the same kind of collective action?

We will return to the realm of business when we examine distributive and compensatory justice in chapter 6. Business considerations will also be relevant to our discussion of freedom of expression in chapter 7 and foreign aid in chapter 8.

ADVERTISING

Advertising Is a Reprehensible Enterprise

Advertising is a reprehensible enterprise because it deceives, exploits, and produces harmful effects in society as a whole. Not all advertisements are deceptive, but most of them are. Not all advertisements seek to exploit people, but most of them do. Not all of advertising's social effects are harmful, but on balance they are. Let us look at each of these charges.

Deception There are at least three areas in which deception operates. First is *effectiveness* or quality. We are induced to believe that the product will perform a function satisfactorily, or at least as satisfactorily as any of its competitors and better than most. Next is *price.* We are induced to believe that the product is a bargain, that we will get more for our money than we would if we made an alternative purchase. Third is *need.* We are induced to believe that our happiness requires the ownership of the product. We cannot be well groomed without a certain suit of clothes, smell like a man without Aqua Velva aftershave, protect our family without a certain insurance policy, educate our children without a set of *Encyclopaedia Britannica,* be safe on the highway without Firestone tires, enjoy our vacation without a Caribbean cruise, experience good health without vitamin supplements, or live a gracious life without a plethora of convenience foods and labor-saving devices.

Advertisers employ many methods to perpetrate these deceptions. One is that of the flat-out lie. The car dealer is *not* giving you the "best deal anywhere." The loan at "10 percent interest" is *not* at 10 percent if you make monthly payments on the entire principal. You are *not* receiving books or records "free" if you are obligated to buy others. Renault automobiles are *not* the easiest cars to park. A healthy skin will *not* make you popular. "To know us is to love us" is *not* true for Early Times Bourbon Whisky. The *Wall Street Journal* does *not* "provide all the business news you need—when you need it." Löwenbräu beer, as distributed in the United States, in *not* a foreign beer. "For travel and shopping," Visa is *not* "the most widely recognized name in the world." A healthy woman does *not* need a vaginal deodorant in order to avoid giving offense. People on a normal diet do *not* need iron, zinc, and vitamin supplements. Vaginal contraceptive suppositories (Semicid, Encare, S'Positive) are *not* as effective as the pill or IUD, nor is the spermicide they contain (nonoxynol 9) new.[1]

Sometimes the claims that advertisers make are called cases of "puffery." This is a euphemism for "hyperbole" or "exaggeration." But exaggeration is still contrary to the truth and thus a case of deception. *Does* Lancers bring out "the beauty in simple things?" *Is* Loews Warwick "the best of the West"? *Was* "photography invented for people" who, like us, cannot draw? *Is* Ultra Fine Flair "precisely right for people who write precisely"? *Would* Beethoven, if he were alive today, record on Scotch Brand tape? *Is* it the case that "wherever you go," Lord Calvert "is making a splash"? *Is* it "better in the Bahamas"? Is it *true* that in Saronna, "all we think about is love"? *Is* Southern Comfort "the grand old drink of the South"? Are we *really* "saving money" when we buy a product? *Does* one sip of Erlanger Beer tell us that it is a classic?

Even when advertising contains no statements that are false, it can misrepresent its product by declining to include some relevant facts. As aspirin company can proclaim the effectiveness of its product in superlative terms, without stating that half a dozen other products are equally effective. A real estate ad can list all the assets of a particular house without mentioning its leaky basement and faulty plumbing. An ad for an insurance policy will point out all the forms of protection it provides, but will not cite the situations that are not covered. An ad may state that a certain product is on sale for $100 less, without pointing out that the product never did sell for the higher price or that competing products are also available at the lower price.[2] Mattress ads tell about the low prices of "regular" models, revealing only in small print that "firm" and "extra-firm" are more expensive. Defenders of this method will say that the sellers are simply putting their best foot forward. There's nothing wrong with that! The sellers would be foolish to pay an ad agency money to publicize their shortcomings! The answer is that whenever facts are selected in such a way as to create a false belief, there is misrepresentation. In deliberately withholding or obscuring pertinent facts, the advertisers are practicing deception. They are presenting *one* side in such a way that it appears to be the whole story.

Other ways of misrepresenting are use of suggestion, vagueness, and ambiguity. One may make two or more statements that *suggest* by their juxtaposition that there is a connection between them. A cosmetics company proved the effectiveness of this device many years ago with its famous ad: "She's beautiful! She's engaged! She uses Ponds." A simple statement may itself be suggestive. "Borgia Pizza is as inexpensive as it is delicious" suggests that it is both inexpensive and

[1]The FTC charged the three companies with "false, deceptive or misleading" advertising early in 1980.

[2]Many products are distributed with the "sale" or "reduced" price printed on the package itself!

delicious. "We're building a reputation, not resting on one" (Ramada Inn) suggests that competitors are coasting along on their past achievements. Questions (rhetorical) suggest statements: "What is more luxurious than a Belchfire-8"? suggests that nothing is. One may also misrepresent by using vague terms. Cigarettes are *mild,* hotels have *spacious* lobbies, cars are *sporty,* pastries are *fresh,* prices are *low,* and savings are *big.* The strategy behind the use of vagueness is to avoid being pinned down. Since no one knows the dividing line between the application and nonapplication of the adjective, advertisers are really not saying much when they use a vague word. Cigarettes that do not dissolve the lining of one's mouth may be said to be "mild." Hotels that have anything more than a desk in a broom closet may be said to have "spacious" lobbies. Cars whose style is not that of a hearse may be said to be "sporty." The hope, however, is that the reader or listener will think of things clearly at the other extreme, the area of certain application. When a man tells his beloved that she is beautiful, he is only saying that she is not ugly; but she, on hearing that she is not in the area where the term clearly does not apply, will perhaps place herself with famous movie stars clearly in the area of certain application. Amoco employs an ambiguous statement, which is perhaps true in one sense but surely false in another: "America runs better on American oil." Datsun screams, "We are driven!" Through use of suggestion, vagueness, and ambiguity, the advertiser can and does create a false impression without making a false statement.

Finally, we should note the use of visual materials to misrepresent. A TV commercial may tout a home permanent set by showing a permanent achieved by another product. A fast-food chain may display a hamburger that is much larger than the one it sells. A paint company may use someone else's product in its demonstration. A few years ago the U.S. Supreme Court considered a case involving the Federal Trade Commission and the Colgate-Palmolive Company. The company's television commercial demonstrated the effectiveness of Rapid Shave by spraying it on sandpaper, then shaving the substance clean. During the demonstration the announcer said: "To prove Rapid Shave's supermoisturizing power, we put it right from the can onto this tough, dry sandpaper. It was apply ... soak ... and off in a stroke." Investigators for the FTC found that the "sandpaper" was actually plexiglass to which sand had been applied, and that a soaking period of about eighty minutes was required before the razor would work. The Court found in favor of the FTC and against the company: there was misrepresentation.[3]

Obviously, not all statements that are false are lies. Not all discourses that create a false impression are intended to deceive. Not all uses of fakery are for the purpose of misrepresenting the facts.[4] The storyteller, the dramatist, and the

[3]See "Opinion in Federal Trade Commission v. Colgate-Palmolive Co. et al" in Beauchamp and Bowie, *Ethical Theory and Business,* p. 452ff.

[4]Using mashed potatoes in TV commercials in place of ice cream (which would melt under the lights) is not deceptive unless the advertiser seeks to emphasize the texture.

poet are not foisting lies on us. Myths and metaphors are not literally true, but they are not intended to deceive. Advertisers, however, are usually doing something else. They seek to make us believe that reality is something that it is not and which they *know* it is not. They seek to make the mediocre appear great, the bad appear good, the expensive appear inexpensive. They try to convert the desire into a need, spending into saving, appearance into reality. They deliberately mislead us.

Is this morally objectionable? Obviously not all cases of deception are wrong. We tell our children about Santa Claus and the Easter Bunny. We praise the dinner, though the vegetable was overcooked. We tell the mugger we have no money. Even a Kantian can be persuaded that morality does not always require telling the truth. The case of advertisers is different. They deceive, not to entertain children, avoid offending people, or preserve what is theirs, but *in order to make a profit* for themselves and their client *at our expense.* This indeed is reprehensible. Deception may be regarded as wrong on Kantian terms as a violation of an injunction not to lie for the purpose of advancing oneself at the expense of others.

Deception may also be censured for the effect it has in our economic system. Deception is inconsistent with the free-enterprise system, which manufacturers and the advertisers they hire profess to support. In this system, the consumers are supposed to be sovereign. They make intelligent choices, thereby encouraging efficient producers and discouraging the others. They express their needs and desires, and producers immediately spring up to satisfy these needs and desires. When supply and demand are equal, a situation the market always seeks to achieve, the buyer pays a fair price and the seller makes a legitimate profit. Producers compete to supply buyers with the best products at the lowest prices to satisfy their wants. Everyone benefits.

But if the buyers do not *know* which is the best product, if they cannot make *correct* price comparisons, if they do not know what their *real* wants are, they cannot perform the crucial functions the system assigns them. Advertising, far from assisting buyers, confuses them, making intelligent choice almost impossible for most. Deceived about quality, price, and need, we are not in a position to encourage good producers and enhance the material dimension of our happiness. Lacking factual knowledge, our choices are not that of a sovereign but are responses to forces outside us. Alfred Sheinwold, whose bridge columns contain perceptive philosophy as well as impeccable logic, expressed the point succinctly: "It was once believed that the wealth of nations depended on each person doing what was good for him or her. The theory breaks down when we don't know what is good for us."[5]

Remedies What is the remedy for misrepresentation in advertising? One answer is to emphasize *Caveat emptor:* "Let the buyer beware." Since ancient times, from the very beginning of trade, people who entered the marketplace had to be on

[5]Alfred Sheinwold, "Bridge," *St. Louis Globe-Democrat,* June 20, 1980, p. 15D.

guard against fraud and sharp practice. They were warned to examine the product carefully, to decline to take at face value what was said about it, and (somewhat later) to read carefully all the fine print in the sales agreement. Buyers still need to heed these warnings. When they do not, they deserve what they get. Deception is part of the rules of the game (as it is in bridge), and if you're victimized by it, you have only yourself to blame. Next time, perhaps, you will not be so hasty, so careless, so greedy, so gullible.

This is not a good answer, for these reasons: (1) That people may be warned about predators and in many cases avoid being victimized does not provide a *moral justification* for the predators. That one may exercise caution to avoid falling into the clutches of a rapist does not mean that rape is an acceptable action. If deceptive advertising is immoral, it remains immoral no matter how often warnings against it succeed. Moreover, to label something morally wrong does not eliminate it. (2) Modern life is too complicated to permit intelligent buyers to make all the investigations necessary for an intelligent choice. They have too many things to evaluate, and changes in products and pricing occur too frequently. Publications of consumer groups help, but only brush the surface of the bewildering sea of products that buyers are confronted with. (3) Economics is not a game played for sport or amusement. It is a necessary institution of our social life. In a game, we win or lose, smile or frown, and go on to something else. In economics, we prosper, languish, or are wiped out. Our very happiness is at stake, as well as that of society in general.

A better remedy is stringent government regulation and strict enforcement at the state and national levels. Not everything that is immoral should be legislated against, but when a practice harms society and can be clearly identified, it should be forbidden by law. Deliberate deception for the purpose of making a profit is a form of fraud, and there is ample precedent for interdicting fraud. "Let the buyer beware" is always a prudent warning, with or without regulation, but it is not a principle permitting advertisers to do whatever they want in bilking the public. Even if it were true (which it is not) that most reasonable people can see through deceptive claims, the purpose of law is to protect the not-so-intelligent as well. While, as we will argue later, truth in advertising will not afford us full protection, it would go a long way. To require advertising to eschew false claims in its print copy, electronic commercials, billboards, and packaging is a basic protection for consumers. To oppose it in the name of "free speech" is to assert "the right to lie" in the public marketplace. Here the consumers' right not to be systematically and deliberately lied to takes precedence over the sellers' right of free speech.

Many laws are already on the books, nationwide and statewide. The Federal Trade Commission and the Food and Drug Administration seek to protect the consumer. The Federal Communications Commission has a role to play also. Their resources are limited, however, and loopholes in the laws exist. The power of consumer groups is exceeded by that of lobbies for the producers. Only the most blatant forms of misrepresentation are dealt with at present. Although "flim-flam men" can no longer sell "snake oil" from the backs of wagons as a cure for everything from nervousness to syphilis, there is still a long way to go before consumers can be assured that what they hear in an advertisement is true.

Exploitation The second charge that can be made against advertising is that it exploits. It seeks to manipulate people, to condition them to buy the goods and services it touts. Deception is only one of its techniques for doing this.

Advertising aims not just at satisfying desires, but at creating them. Real or imagined improvements in products must be displayed to consumers in such a way that a desire for them is produced. New products must be brought to their attention in such a way that they feel they must have them. The contentment they may have experienced before they had ever heard of the improvement or product must be shattered by a sense of discomfort or deprivation. Often these desires are intensified to the point where they are experienced as urgent needs. The consumers feel that they must have the product for the sake of their very happiness. They "owe it to themselves," say, to have a video-tape attachment for their television set. Doubts about personal grooming and cleanliness instilled by advertisers have created desires for a vast panoply of junk from vaginal deodorants to expensive soap. "Don't you wish everyone" used Dial? "Advertisements keep us in a state of perpetual dissatisfaction with what we do have."[6]

The producer sometimes says, "We only give the public what it wants." David Braybrooke offers six reasons for believing that this claim is "less than fully warranted": (1) The buyer is often not aware of the alternatives. (2) The "wants" are not spontaneous, but instilled through advertising campaigns. "Half a century of dilation on speed, power, and thrills [by automobile companies] has fostered and intensified wants that now seem questionable to many. . . ." (3) The public is deliberately confused by advertisers in order to make misjudgments about relative values. (4) Sellers "obstruct institutional remedies for the lack of information" the buyers suffer from: consumer research, consumer advocacy in government, truth-in-packaging laws, truth-in-lending laws, laws against misrepresentation, and so on. (5) The big companies that dominate the market "have a considerable amount of discretion respecting innovation." Consumers cannot choose what has not been offered to them, although they may desire it more than what is. (6) Producers ignore wants that are real but can only be satisfied "by concerted action, not in the market."[7] This last point will be expanded on below.

Desires are produced, of course, in order in turn to produce action: the transaction. People must be moved, trained, or indoctrinated to make the right purchase.

[6]Gerald F. Cavanagh, *American Business Values in Transition* (Englewood Cliffs, N.J.: Prentice-Hall, 1976), p. 119.

[7]David Braybrooke, "Skepticism of Wants, and Certain Subversive Effects of Corporations on American Values," in Beauchamp and Bowie, pp. 504–507.

No sizable segment of the population is immune to the barrage: children,[8] adoles cents, young marrieds, singles, men and women on the rise, old people. Each has its problems, for which advertisers offer solutions. The appeal may be loud or barely audible; it may employ a large billboard or a tiny insert; it may drum the message home by monotonous repetition or continually change slogans to capture attention; it may be in bad taste or employ the highest order of acting, art, and sentiment; it may employ original tunes or take over old favorites to plant the message in our consciousness along with the melody. The standard is simply this: *What will work?*

What has been found to work is a vast array of emotional appeals. Logicians call them "fallacies of relevance." They are really not fallacies, for they have no similarity to rational argument—deductive or inductive. They do not represent aberrations in logical thinking but are *substitutes* for thinking itself. They seek to *circumvent* rationality by offering considerations that are utterly without relevance to the conclusion or action they seek to produce.

Specific Emotional Appeals Although only a few of these appeals have been identified by name (sometimes going back to ancient times), every human emotion can be the basis for an emotional appeal. The appeals that are discussed below are far fron constituting an exhaustive list of the nonrational appeals employed by advertisers to impel their victims to the prescribed course of action.

1. Appeal to fear. People have active imaginations and can be made to feel fear without being shown that there is reason to be fearful. If they are desperate (or even worried), they can be expected to seize whatever "solution" is offered. "The cosmetics industry has made millions of dollars from appeals to fear. Are you safe or only half safe? Do you have dry and itchy scalp? Can your makeup pass the close-up test? Do you have an affliction that not even your best friends will tell you about? On such profound matters as these, we can't take chances. So we buy liquids, pastes, and sprays in order to be *sure.* Fear is used to sell insurance (fires and accidents occur), automobile tires (cars go out of control), and travelers' checks (money is lost or stolen). It is used to sell soap: Do you have 'pink toothbrush' or 'ring around the collar'?"[9]

2. Appeal to hope. Our hopes may be aroused by a description of what might be. Matchbook ads arouse and cater to our hopes to be artists, songwriters, or speedy readers. Women can lose weight and/or achieve a bigger bust. A puny

[8]Aldous Huxley points out how susceptible children are to propaganda. He calls them "television fodder." They not only can be made to harass their parents to buy the latest sugar-coated cereal, but are seen as the buyers of tomorrow: " 'Think,' writes Mr. Clyde Miller ecstatically, 'think of what it can mean to your firm in profits if you can condition a million or ten million children, who will grow up as adults trained to buy your product, as soldiers are trained in advance when they hear the trigger words, Forward March!' " Huxley, *Brave New World Revisited* (New York: Harper & Row, 1958), p. 68.

[9]Gerald Runkle, *Good Thinking: An Introduction to Logic,* pp. 303–304.

young man can become a Charles Atlas. The old can look young: "A woman faces so many things," says Helena Rubinstein. "Why should looking her age be one of them?" People with complaints or serious illness are offered relief in many forms. "In a state of hope, one doesn't ask the right questions. One is in a hurry to embark, to realize one's hopes before the opportunity is snatched away. A possibility is converted mentally to a probability, and a probability into a virtual certainty."[10]

3. Appeal to sex. In a state of sexual excitement people are vulnerable to business offers. Travel brochures feature alluring pictures of scantily dressed women who can hardly wait till you arrive. "Come and get it!" says one such brochure. Cars are sold by means of "hidden persuaders" and some not so hidden. A beautiful woman perched on the hood of an Austin Healey Sprite suggests, at the very least, an improvement of one's sex life. Television commercials employ handsome creatures of both sexes to sell shaving cream, swimming pools, perfume, and lipstick and other cosmetics. Not only are their words and actions provocative, but so are the names and even the shapes of their products.

4. Appeal to the people. People can be made to feel uncomfortable if they are separated from the great majority. They must be part of the crowd. They will read any book—so long as it is a best seller. They will be impressed by Gordon's Gin because it is the largest seller in the world. If they're too young for gin, they'll want to be part of the "Pepsi generation." They will be prompt to change the width of their neckties or the length of their skirts when "fashion" dictates. They want to do the things that are "in," to avoid those that are passé. The *ad populum* appeal operates not only to induce people to *select* what others presumably have selected, but to feel they are entitled to have *as much as* most people seem to have. People are made to feel deprived (in need) if they do not snap up the latest camera, TV attachment, or kitchen appliance. No one wants to drop out of the great middle class.

5. Appeal to flattery. Those who are immune to the appeal to the people may be pushovers for the appeal to flattery. Claims are pitched toward the *discriminating* smoker, the *conscientious* parent, the *fastidious* dresser. "If Gordon's Gin is the big seller, then House of Lords is used for the *gentleman's* martini and Beefeaters by those who spare no expense. Those who want to 'rally 'round the fun with young America' will flock to Harley Davidson, while the *connoisseur* will select a Ducati."[11] Budweiser's current campaign flatters workers in all fields: "For all you do, this Bud's for you!" Rodney Dangerfield speaks for all of us when he says, "I don't get no respect." When we are complimented, when someone has the perceptiveness to recognize our good qualities and the kindness to point them out, we may be all too ready to accept uncritically whatever offer is made.

[10]Ibid., p. 308.
[11]Ibid., p. 299.

6. Illegitimate authority. People respect certain individuals for their achievements in their fields. Athletes, actors, and singers are national heroes. Astronauts, authors, and musicians are not far behind. Their names and faces are instantly recognized. Advertisers seek to transfer our respect for them to the products they are paid to endorse. If Brut is good enough for Joe Namath, it's good enough for me! Jim Lovell endorses an insurance company, Bill Russell endorses telephones, and Nancy Lopez is pushing a particular camera. The strangest instance of this appeal "occurred in an advertisement extolling the merits of a recording tape. The 'authority' appealed to is dead and was dead before tapes were even invented, yet: 'If Beethoven were alive today, he'd be recording on Scotch brand recording tape.' The ad goes on to say that Beethoven was a genius. 'But he was even more than that. He was a pro.' Like Russell and Namath, presumably."[12]

7. Appeal to humor. Much advertising is funny, or intended to be. This is disarming, for it seems to be entertainment rather than a hard sell. People who can amuse us will not cheat us. Advertisements for low-calorie beer rely on humor. Volkswagen has had many amusing ads—one depicting a VW as a police car. The Stiller-Meara ads are already classics. Perhaps it all began with 'I can't believe I ate the whole thing!" Products involved in such good fun must be O.K.!

But good fun or not, this appeal, like the other six, as well as other appeals not discussed here, serves the simple purpose of arousing and exploiting a particular emotion for the purpose of producing an intended action. These appeals, devoid of logical structure, are potent in psychological impact. They are the acceptable form of a technique we instinctively recoil from: brainwashing.

Exploitation and Morality That this kind of exploitation is morally wrong is obvious. It is a clear case of using human beings simply as objects. They are viewed by advertisers simply as potential buyers, automations that can be impelled, if the conditioning is right, to reach for the billfold and say the magic words. The science and art of human motivation have no more assiduous students than the creators of ads. It is difficult to imagine a more appropriate example for Kant's second formulation of the categorical imperative than advertising.

What the advertisers do would be very distasteful to Plato and Aristotle also, for it seeks to corrupt human rationality. To destroy, subvert, or circumvent reason is an affront to the humanistic ideal. Reason must rule in the just human being, but advertising arouses the spirit and the appetites, encouraging these elements of the human soul to usurp the role assigned to the rational element. This desire is stirred to clamor for satisfaction, then that. The spirit too is aroused, as zeal, pride, and ambition claim their illegitimate due. The individual is not proof against these social pressures. The chances of being a good person in a bad society, as Plato and Aristotle knew, are very slight. Reason cannot control the soul, it cannot foster harmony, it cannot impose its own pattern in the face of all these pressures from the outside. The result of the permeation of our conscious-

[12]Ibid., p. 296.

ness by the ceaseless bombardment of advertising is, for many of us, a disordered personality.

There are no easy remedies. One hesitates to call in the law to punish purveyors of persuasive appeals. Misrepresentation is relatively easy to recognize, but the seduction typical of emotional appeals is often quite subtle and blends gradually into rather harmless forms of enchantment. The attempt to control persuasive discourse would be an infringement of freedom that to many of us would seem totalitarian. We have the right to call on government to protect us from flat-out deceit, but not from bad argument (or substitutes for argument).

It is the human condition in modern times, when sophisticated and far-reaching communication systems exist, to be threatened by con artists in many fields. Advertising is only one of these fields. Politics and religion are others. Individuals must somehow find the resources to resist the incessant campaigns of opinion makers, to think their own thoughts. Education will help. At all levels of education, in all subject areas, individuals must be taught to distinguish bad argument from good argument and argument from nonargument. An introductory course in logic is not enough. Only when individuals can recognize that a claim is badly supported do they have a chance of prevailing rationally against the powerful forces to which they are subjected.

Social Effects Finally, we will look at the third charge: Advertising has harmful results for society as a whole.

First of all, advertising promotes the sale not only of useless products but of harmful and dangerous ones as well. Cigarettes, guns, and motorcycles instantly come to mind. We can add drug paraphernalia, some hair straighteners, and some hair dryers. Burton Leiser reports that in 1973, "vitamins and mineral supplements accounted for more than 5000 cases of poisoning among children under five years of age. . . ."[13] Drug companies advertise their products among doctors in some cases without adequate tests for their safety. Defective tires and dangerous automobiles are heedlessly advertised: sometimes they are "called back"; sometimes they are not. Pornographic books and movies, as well as just plain trashy ones, are promoted with great skill. Many toys (all heavily advertised) have been found to be so dangerous or hazardous to health that a special law had to be passed in 1969 (Federal Child Protection and Toy Safety Act).

Second, advertising promotes an artificial and false standard of happiness. Society is led to believe that money, when spent for the right products, will guarantee contentment. The insurance salesperson is selling not a policy, but security. The cosmetics company is selling perpetual youth. Beer and soft drink companies sell a rousing good time. The real estate salesperson never shows a house—it is always a "home." The telephone company sells love and friendship. Luxuries of all kinds serve the cause of gracious living. But *la dolce vita* is not really "the good life"—it is a life of material possessions. Our sense of value gets

[13]Leiser, *Liberty, Justice, and Morals,* p. 286.

turned upside-down. We believe that the good life consists not of what we are or what we do, but of what we *have.* Advertising thus is guilty on two counts. It identifies the good life with the happy life, and it identifies happiness with manufactured products.

We have already seen how advertising creates desires and converts them to "needs." People expect their standard of living to continue to rise. They are shown how others live—their new cars, TV sets, boats, vacations in exotic places, leisure suits—and believe that society is unjust to them if *they* cannot have all these things too. Rising expectations generate excessive spending and debt, social unrest, and strikes. Nowadays unskilled workers believe they should have a two-bathroom house and a new station wagon every three years.

Finally, advertising is wasteful. It not only promotes waste by persuading people to buy useless products and to replace what they already have, but is wasteful in itself. Billions of dollars are spent every year, not to produce products, but to produce appeals designed to *move* products.[14] Some very good talent is attracted to advertising because the economic payoff can be very rewarding. And some people whose talent is irrelevant (e.g., endorsers) receive very good fees also. Surely these talented people could make a more concrete contribution to society. Plato had little respect for merchants, but they did perform the social function of getting the products of artisans into the hands of people who would use them. What would he have thought of people whose profession was *persuading* people that they *needed* certain products? To inform consumers what products are available and what those products in fact can do is one thing. To expend money and talent to persuade people to acquire them is something else. In the first, consumers may be expected to make their choices in the light of their own desires and needs; in the second, they are *conditioned* to acquire them.

There is something profoundly wrong with a system in which a company finds it necessary to spend more money touting the qualities of its product than actually to manufacture it. Surely the cost of advertising must be covered by the retail price charged for the product. When we buy a bar of a nationally advertised soap, what percentage are we paying for advertising it? Apologists for advertising claim that the great savings from increased volume more than compensates us for the advertising we pay for.[15] Perhaps in some cases this is true. The figures are hard to get at and analyze. One study, however, conducted among 5,200 toy and hobby retailers by Pepperdine College and directed by Consultants to Management, Inc., showed that most of them

> dislike national television advertising despite the fact that such advertising of toys by manufacturers has increased the retailer's business. According to the report, the reason for the toy retailers' dislike of television is their suspicion that the cost of

[14]In 1976, Proctor and Gamble spent about $340 million for advertising, while the total figure for the industry was well over $33 billion!

[15]This is the defense of the telephone company (a monopoly), which begs us to make more and more long-distance calls.

television advertising is so high that manufacturers are forced to put exorbitant prices on toys, counting on the appeal of television to children to force the sales to the ultimate disappointment of child and parent and the resentment of the latter against the retail store which sold him the overrated merchandise. Of those surveyed, 77 percent of the toy store retailers and 81 percent of the discount department store and chain drugstore managers felt that television advertising increased prices.[16]

There is another aspect to wasteful advertising. John Kenneth Galbraith discusses it in his theory of the "dependence effect" and social balance. Advertising is so successful in creating desires and "needs" that more and more of people's income must be spent in satisfying them. This money is spent in the private sector, for it is here that the products are most insistently advertised. The result is that people have very little left to support goods and services in the public sector. Everyone thus has cars, but society has bad roads. Children have calculating machines but poor schools and teachers. People have three bathrooms in their houses but obnoxious air to breathe outside. People have electronic games to play on their TV sets but no clean and safe parks to retire to.[17] "A politician or public servant who dreams up a new public service is a wastrel."[18] Producers who coax people to absorb their frivolous, dangerous, or useless goods are respected business leaders. "It is scarcely sensible that we should satisfy our wants in private goods with reckless abundance, while in the case of public goods, on the evidence of the eye, we practice extreme self-denial."[19]

What is the remedy? Regulation of some kind may be a partial answer to the problem of harmful or dangerous goods, but the other social evils of advertising are so pervasive that they cannot be significantly eliminated without eliminating advertising itself. To do this by law seems rather too drastic in a free society. The best we can do is to acquaint ourselves with the enemies and their *modus operandi.* If we do this we can resist and mitigate the harm that they produce. In the last analysis, this applies also to the deception and exploitation exerted by the advertisers on individuals' minds. We may have to *tolerate* advertising, but we do not have to be its victims.

It is sometimes argued that effective advertising is necessary for continued prosperity, high production, and employment. "From this it follows that in order for our economy to continue in its present form people must learn to be fuzzy-minded and impulsive, for if they were clear-headed and deliberate they would rarely put their hands in their pockets. . . . If we were all logicians the economy could not survive, and herein lies a terrifying paradox, for *in order to exist economically as we are we must try by might and main to remain stupid.*"[20]

[16]David Loudon and Albert Della Bitta, "Case Study—Hasbro Industries, Inc.," in Donaldson and Werhane, *Ethical Issues in Business,* p. 292.
[17]These examples are not Galbraith's but are offered in his spirit.
[18]Galbraith, *The Affluent Society* (Boston: Houghton Mifflin Co., 1958), p. 261.
[19]Ibid., pp. 259–266.
[20]Jules Henry, "Advertising as a Philosophical System," in Beauchamp and Bowie, p. 471.

Advertising Performs a Valuable Social Function

Professionalism No profession is beyond reproach. A one-sided "description" can make any group look bad: ministers, professors, lawyers, and doctors. All that needs be done is select the "bad apples" and focus on the bad practices. The advertising profession is just as concerned about its shortcomings as any other profession. It joins with consumers in protesting unethical practices. It exhibits a sense of responsibility in policing its own actions.[21] It has come a long way from the days when Listerine, Postum, and Lydia Pinkham's were blithely offered as panaceas for all ills. Today people have as much confidence in the truth of statements issued by reputable advertising agencies as they do in that of statements made by ministers, professors, lawyers, and doctors.

In 1971 the Advertising Code of American Business was announced:

1. TRUTH. Advertising shall tell the truth, and shall reveal significant facts, the concealment of which would mislead the public.
2. RESPONSIBILITY. Advertising agencies and advertisers shall be willing to provide substantiation of claims made.
3. TASTE AND DECENCY. Advertising shall be free of statements, illustrations, or implications which are offensive to good taste or public decency.
4. BAIT ADVERTISING. Advertising shall offer only merchandise or services which are readily available for purchase at the advertised price.
5. GUARANTEES AND WARRANTIES. Advertising of guarantees and warranties shall be explicit. Advertising of any guarantee or warranty shall clearly and conspicuously disclose its nature and extent, the manner in which the guarantor or warrantor will perform, and the identity of the guarantor or warrantor.
6. PRICE CLAIMS. Advertising shall avoid price or savings claims which are false or misleading, or which do not offer provable bargains or savings.
7. UNPROVABLE CLAIMS. Advertising shall avoid the use of exaggerated or unprovable claims.
8. TESTIMONIALS. Advertising containing testimonials shall be limited to those of competent witnesses who are reflecting a real and honest choice.

This code was sponsored by the American Advertising Federation, the American Association of Advertising Agencies, the Association of National Advertisers, and the Council of Better Business Bureaus.[22]

[21]An elder statesman of the advertising industry pointed out in 1960 several continuing concerns of the profession: (1) "The technical literature of advertising is currently filled with the kind of 'good-and-bad' criticism advertising needs." (2) "Advertising people have promoted and secured the adoption of 'Truth in Advertising' laws in over half our states, and have supported the work of Better Business Bureaus in policing these laws." (3) "They have supported the purposes, if not always the methods" of the FTC. (4) "In their various trade and professional organizations advertising men have drafted any number of codes of 'ethical' practices." (5) "Many important advertising media refuse to accept advertising for certain classifications of products." James Webb Young, "Wanted: Responsible Advertising Critics," in Girvetz, ed., *Contemporary Moral Issues,* p. 255.

[22]See Beauchamp and Bowie, p. 198.

The Advertising Council spends millions of dollars every year for causes, not connected with profit, but in service to the public interest. Private corporations have financed advertising campaigns for such worthwhile causes as international friendship, preservation of natural resources, better schools, safer highways, crime prevention, and health care. Advertising should not be judged simply on the basis of its noble efforts any more than by its more ignoble ones. Advertising should be judged by its overall record. Critics who dwell on isolated "horrible examples" in advertising are no better than those "shoot-from-the-hip" critics who denigrate a profession by exposing a greedy minister, a venial professor, an unethical lawyer, or a drunken surgeon. This essay is an attempt to place the issue in a fairer perspective.

"Deception" and "Exploitation" Let us look first of all at the charge of deception and exploitation. In contemporary society no group committed to getting a particular point of view across is held rigorously to a standard of literal truthfulness: politicians, the American Medical Association, labor groups, or educational associations. They are all expected to present the facts that make their point, exaggerate somewhat, and utilize statistics for their own purposes. This takes place without threat of public censure or legal repression. Where a "statement of fact" is a deliberate and bare-faced lie, advertising is culpable. But this is no more frequent in advertising than in any other field that wants to influence public opinion.

Sometimes an advertising appeal is misleading to some people. No discourse, however, is immune to human stupidity. Someone is bound to misinterpret what is said. An instructor who had just made a seating chart for his class asked the students to stay in the same seats for the rest of the semester. After class was over, one student remained at his desk—because, as he said, the semester was not over yet. If this sounds far-fetched, consider the case of Clairol and its claim that its dye will "color hair permanently." The FTC believed that this was deceptive, for some people would think that their hair would grow from the scalp for the rest of their life in the Clairol color. The federal circuit court agreed with the FTC. Ivan L. Preston cites several examples of ads believed by the FTC to be deceptive —not because they would deceive the reasonable consumer but because they would deceive the ignorant consumer: The joke-beer produced every Christmas by Pittsburgh Brewing Company, called Olde Frothingslosh, was claimed to be the only beer with its foam on the bottom; a circus claimed that it was "the greatest show on earth"; an encyclopedia company claimed that its volumes were "free" to the buyer who agreed to pay a certain sum of money for updating supplements; Ayds candy mints claimed that their use made weight reducing "easy"; Ipana toothpaste claimed that it produced the "smile of beauty"; a manufacturer of an inflatable buoyant device ("Swim-Ezy") to be worn under a bathing suit claimed that it was "invisible."[23] Some of these charges of deception

[23]See Ivan L. Preston, "Reasonable Consumer or Ignorant Consumer? How the FTC Decides," in Beauchamp and Bowie, p. 485ff.

made by the FTC were upheld in the courts, and some were not. The government is not obliged to protect sensible and intelligent consumers: people who will not misinterpret, who can recognize puffery, who can get the point of a joke, who can distinguish between literal and figurative discourse, who can do simple arithmetic. There is no way to protect people who do not recognize that "three for a dollar" is no savings for cans of soup that retail for thirty-three cents apiece, or who believe that a toothpaste will straighten crooked teeth or that automobile tires will prevent skidding under all circumstances. To try to protect them through a misguided sense of paternalism would bring not only advertising, but all projects of public-opinion formation, to a screeching halt.

Advertising, and all other kinds of opinion formation, should be viewed as an attempt to make a point in the great marketplace of ideas. People are not exploited, but are given persuasive appeals that are partisan in nature. The people are respected, for it is left to them to decide which partisan position has made the best case. Most of them will be able to distinguish the better from the worse. Protected only against outright and deliberate falsehood (which is rare in advertising), they have the responsibility and ability to discern whether an advertisement presents the whole truth, to be on guard against suggestiveness, to recognize and discount puffery and vague terms, and to be alert to tricks their emotions may be playing on them. The situation may be compared to a case in court. Every party has a right to the best case that can be made for him, her, or it. Even a confessed murderer is entitled to a skilled advocate. When all the testimony has been taken, the examination and cross-examination of witnesses conducted, and the opening and concluding speeches made by the attorneys, the jury renders a verdict. On the market, the consumers, after hearing strong advocacy from all sides, render their verdict.

Desires and Needs Advertising is frequently charged with "creating" desires and needs. It is doubtful that critics really know enough about the generation of these feelings to speak very confidently on the matter. What people desire and feel they need is a very complex matter involving a great many factors. These factors include people's inherent natures, their lifetime experiences, their present situation, and their present experience. The pitches of the advertisers are surely significant influences, but are only a small part of the daily welter of things that affect people. Advertisers compete with one another, and advertising itself competes with other pressures and social expectations. The feelings that people experience as desires and needs will be conditioned not only by what they are, where they are, and the stimuli they are subjected to, but also by their own goals in life and sense of values. The model of consumers being trained and conditioned by a particular set of factors, like isolated rats in a laboratory, is a case of oversimplified psychology. To believe that human beings can successfully be treated as "means only" by diabolical advertising copy is to ignore too much, not least of which is human autonomy. That advertising has some effect cannot be denied—it did sell the sizzle and not the steak. But that it is the overriding cause of consumer decision is false—it did not sell the Edsel.

But however the desires and felt needs are produced, they are, after all, t individual's own. If one experiences a desire, it is a real desire; if one feels a need, it is a felt need. One confers, consciously or unconsciously, the degree of urgency or importance on whatever inclinations arise in one's consciousness. John Dewey is correct in saying that people do not react willy-nilly to whatever stirs them in this moment and that. The human being has evolved as a higher organism whose experience is not simply passive but redirective. It is human nature to utilize experience for enriching experience.

If we recognize certain desires and needs as real and worth satisfying, who is to say they are otherwise? Tom may err in buying *Penthouse* instead of the *Times;* Laura may be short-sighted in buying a sports car instead of saving her money for another year of college; the Joneses may be vain in buying a wrinkle remover instead of a badly needed set of cookware. But these people have made their decision and have spent their own money. If we do not like their decisions and blame advertising, we ignore the fact that the desires, however they were produced, were experienced *as* desires and freely acted upon.

Friedrich von Hayek disputes the contention that wants are not urgent when they have been created. Few of our desires are "spontaneous." Most are generated from without: We see others enjoying things, we emulate, we learn. "To say that a desire is not important because it is not innate is to say that the whole cultural achievement of man is not important." More specifically, it is a mistake to demean those wants "which are created by the process by which they are satisfied." If a company were barred from producing desires for those things which it produces, then producers of music, painting, and literature would be barred. The desire and satisfaction that cultivated people experience from works of art are possible only because they *are* cultivated—that is, they have been exposed to works of art that were produced before the desire was felt. Public education "seems to regard it as one of its tasks to instill a taste for literature in the young and even employs producers of literature for that purpose. Is this want creation by the producer reprehensible?"[24] So far as advertising is concerned, we return to the sovereignty of the consumers: Let *them* decide which desires to satisfy—however they are generated.

Some people arrogate for themselves the decisions that in any free society belong to the people. From their Olympian heights they pronounce certain products useless, frivolous, or dangerous.[25] To limit or dictate consumers' choices is an outrageous infringement of freedom (except, of course, when a desired commodity is in short supply over a long period of time). Reformers may plead or reason with foolish consumers and provide them with pertinent facts, but they

[24]Friedrich von Hayek, "The Non Sequitur of the 'Dependence Effect,'" in Beauchamp and Bowie, pp. 509–510.

[25]Any product that is legal to sell should be legal to advertise. That guns, poison, and cigarettes may be put to dangerous uses should not disqualify them. "Blunt instruments" like hammers, bricks, and fireplace pokers can be used dangerously also.

… when they presume to specify how individuals may spend …

… at individuals in a democratic society cannot empower their … uce the schools, parks, health facilities, clean air, and public tra… …ar to the heart of Galbraith. Such a movement to a welfare or socialist state is certainly within their rights. If they believe that their money can be more beneficially spent on public goods than on private goods, they have the means to alter what Galbraith regards as an imbalance in the two sectors. Advocates of the Galbraith position are just as eloquent and persuasive as those for private enterprise. Apparently most people believe they will be happier by making individual choices of their own from what private industry offers than by giving up more of their money in taxation to support public projects.

Benefits Turning from the negative or defensive posture, proponents of advertising can cite many positive benefits.

First, they can point to the *information* conveyed to consumers by advertising. This often is hard fact. Ads for clothes in Sears catalogues provide material, color, and size. Cigarette ads provide accurate statements of tar and nicotine content. Automobile ads give us EPA gas-mileage estimates, horsepower, and engine size. Photo-development ads indicate the price for each film size and length of wait. Above all, ads provide pictures of the product. A "consumer hero" can do a great deal of shopping without leaving home. It is quite possible that lawyers, doctors, and dentists who object to advertising in their professions fear that *too much* information would be revealed about their fees and services.[26]

But most important, the vast majority of the purchasing public would never even hear of a really excellent product or service unless if it were not advertised. New drugs, appliances, and fabrics must be advertised before they can find their way into the hands of the people who benefit from them. We look for ads for movies, plays, and concerts in order to find out what is available when we want to go out at night. The very professors who jeer at advertising are pleased to see brochures advertising the texts they have authored (and seldom object to the puffery).

Second, the success of advertising in print and electronic media has substantially reduced the price of newspapers and magazines. Most of the publications would have to fold were it not for their advertising revenue. Television is free for those of us who do not contract for cable. Now, it is true that someone has to pay for these good things, but it does not have to be the people who use the products that are advertised. We may deliberately choose to boycott companies that "waste" their money (and ours) in advertising, but most of us find that

[26]"Two medical associations appealed a rule [of the FTC] striking down 30 state laws that kept optometrists and ophthalmologists from publicizing prices. (Studies showed that where ads are prohibited, eyeglasses cost 25 to 40 per cent more than where they are not.) Jane Bryant Quinn, "Regulating the Regulators," *Newsweek,* January 21, 1980, p. 73.

somewhat higher prices for commodites are a rather painless price to pay for cheap papers and newspapers and free television and radio. Moreover, the high volume of sales made possible by advertising reduces the unit cost of the product. In a great many cases, advertising makes possible a *lower* price for the product than what would prevail had it not been advertised.[27] And some products, of course, would not even *get* produced unless, through advertising, a market could be created.

This brings us to the third social benefit of advertising: a rising standard of living. People can afford more and more products. Why? Mass production. Unless commodities were *sold,* there would be no mass production. And without advertising, these commodities would *not* be sold. It has been found feasible for a great many products to produce them in great quantity, simply because advertising has convinced a great many people of their value. The rising standard of living in America (the envy of the world) is in large part due to advertising.

The high production of a great many products (the sale of which is ensured by advertising) suggests a fourth benefit: a high rate of employment. A free enterprise system succeeds only when money circulates and products are exchanged. Transactions must take place. Transactions are what advertising exists to bring about. If products are moving, people will be needed to manufacture them. The resulting high employment will put money in the pockets of more people. Advertising will encourage them to spend it and further keep the wheels of industry spinning. "Nothing happens until something is sold" is a business slogan that contains a lot of truth. Advertising makes sure that things, a lot of things, will be sold.

Finally, we will argue that the rising standard of living is a good thing. More people can live better than their ancestors did, with respect to comfort, diet, drudgery, entertainment and recreation, mobility, and just about everything else. That these goods and services are often material does not mean that those who purchase them are materialists or that advertising engenders a materialistic view of life. Material things are properly seen as means for valuable experiences, some of which could be called "spiritual." Typewriters facilitate the production of valuable literature. Telephones contribute to friendship. Travel deepens international understanding. Automobiles transport police officers and social workers. Well-constructed homes enhance the possibility of happy family life. Labor-saving appliances make possible greater leisure for study. New drugs and over-the-counter remedies serve the cause of health. So do the maligned soap products. Television sets provide entertainment for invalids. The invention of the printing press put Bibles in nearly every home. That some people sometimes become obsessed with acquiring and displaying material goods does not mean that we

[27]Even in inflationary times, consumers can buy a lot. Though the value of their dollar is lower, they have more dollars. Inflationary trends, when kept within reason, have generally been accompanied by a *rising* standard of living. Compare the thirties, when the dollar was powerful, with the sixties, when it was less so.

are all doomed to lose our sense of values in an affluent society. The wise will be grateful for the help that material goods provide them in their quest for the good life, but they will keep them in their place as means for other things.

As the standard of living goes up and advertising shows to one and all the many good things on the market, there is indeed a sense of rising expectations by the great middle class. They want their share of the good things, and they want their children to fare better than themselves, just as they fared better than their parents. The lower classes, too, will want a "piece of the action." There is nothing wrong with these sentiments. They may inspire greater ambition and effort on the part of individuals. They may produce a campaign for a more just distribution of goods. They may produce more effective bargaining by labor organizations. They may provoke a more careful examination of political candidates and government policy. There is nothing in any of these results to fear. They occupy the middle ground between apathy or "malaise" on one side and revolution on the other.

Conclusion In summary, it can be maintained that advertising is not fundamentally deceptive or exploitative, that advertising is only one force of many that produce desires, that created desires are sometimes good and sometimes bad and it is the responsibility of consumers to know the difference, and that advertising has positive benefits in terms of the dissemination of information, the inexpensiveness of media products, the supply of affordable goods in general, high employment, and an increasingly high standard of living for all.

Summary of the Issues

While the critics of advertising can put together an impressive list of evils, the defenders answer that this sort of one-sidedness is possible for any profession and describes the concern for standards within the advertising profession.

One charge made against advertising is its propensity to deceive—to deliberately create false impressions in order to sell a product. This deception takes many forms. Although defenders remind us of the slogan "Let the buyer beware," the fact remains that deception is immoral. While defenders do not condone blatant misrepresentation (and there is not much of that anymore), they recommend a more tolerant attitude for opinionmakers in all fields. Individuals must distinguish the good "pitches" from the bad and make up their own minds. The critics, however, believe that advertisers should be compelled by law to stop misleading the public. The rejoinder of the defenders is that no set of laws can protect consumers from their own stupidity.

A second charge is that advertising creates desires instead of simply showing that its products satisfy the desires that people happen to have. It possesses an imposing and effective set of techniques for conditioning people to buy products. Advertising is a form of brainwashing that is employed to exploit the consumer. This kind of action is in clear violation of Kant's ethics, for it treats the other as a means only. It is also contrary to the ideas of Plato and Aristotle, for it seeks to corrupt or bypass human reason. No easy remedy is in sight.

The defenders of advertising detect a certain paternalism in the critics' point of view. The critics, they argue, have underestimated the autonomy of consumers and their ability to make rational choices. Advertising is only one influence that consumers have to deal with, and advertising itself does not speak with a consistent voice. No one and no institution can claim the authority to tell the people what desires they should have and on what basis they should make their choices.

The third major issue is an utilitarian one. The critics emphasize the bad effects of advertising: (1) Advertising promotes the sale of useless, inferior, harmful, and dangerous products. To the extent that its nonlogical appeals work, the assumed ability of the consumer to make wise choices (a staple of the free-enterprise ideology) is called into question. (2) Advertising promotes a standard of happiness that is artificial and false. (3) Advertising is wasteful of human talents and materials, and the consumer is forced to foot the bill. (4) Advertising induces us to spend our money in the private sector instead of in the public sector where it will do us more good. For many of these claims, the defenders of advertising have plausible rebuttals.

The defenders of advertising can point to utilitarian gains: (1) Advertising conveys a lot of free and important information about products. (2) Advertising subsidizes the print and electronic media. (3) Advertising boosts sales, which reduces the unit cost of production, often resulting in lower prices for the consumer. (4) Advertising contributes to rising employment, a rising standard of living, and rising expectation among the people—all good things. The critics of advertising can mount plausible rebuttals to most of these claims.

Discussion Questions

1. About what percentage of the price of soap covers the cost of advertising it? Is there any way to discover whether advertising has really increased the price or, by creating a large market, has decreased it?
2. In your own experience, have you found that advertising has made you make purchases that you later realized were foolish? Explain.
3. Suppose there are two products equally priced and you know nothing about the quality of either. You have, however, seen advertisements for Brand A, but not for Brand B. Which would you buy? Why? Suppose that Brand A cost 10 percent more than Brand B. Which would you buy? Why?
4. Do you believe that most advertising misrepresents the product? Or does it merely exaggerate? Explain.
5. Do you think that deceptive advertising is immoral or is simply one of the facts of the business world? Explain.
6. How far do you think that government should go in protecting the public from its own gullibility or stupidity? Explain.

7. Do you think that advertising in seeking to make "consumer heroes" of us all has inculcated a false conception of happiness in many of us? Explain.
8. Do you agree that advertising is exploitative and seeks to use human beings as means? Explain.
9. Granting that advertising has some harmful effects, would you hold that they are outweighed by the beneficial effects? Explain.
10. Would you buy a product that an advertising agency has paid a sports celebrity $200,000 to endorse? Explain.
11. Can you think of any advertisements that are, in your opinion, in bad taste? Explain.
12. Can you think of any advertisements that have provided accurate and useful information about a product? Describe them.
13. Would you agree that a great many good things would never catch our attention if they had not been advertised? Explain.
14. Would you agree that a great many good things could not be produced economically had their sales not been boosted by advertising? Explain.
15. Comment on this bit of doggerel:

    The codfish lays ten thousand eggs,
      The homely hen lays one.
    The codfish never cackles
      To tell you when she's done.
    And so we scorn the codfish,
      While the humble hen we prize,
    Which only goes to show you
      That it pays to advertise.

16. Do you share Plato's contempt for the person who sells the product instead of creating it? Why?
17. Would you argue that anything done by advertising that is immoral should also be made illegal? Why?
18. Do you think that advertisers in general have a high sense of professionalism? Why?
19. Do you think that doctors and dentists should advertise? Why?
20. Suppose that a toothpaste ad claims that the product would give you a beautiful smile and that some people buy it to straighten their teeth. Who is to blame? Why?

For Further Reading

Tom L. Beauchamp and Norman E. Bowie, eds. *Ethical Theory and Business.* Englewood Cliffs, N.J.: Prentice-Hall, 1979. Chapter 7.

Richard T. DeGeorge and Joseph A. Pichler, eds. *Ethics, Free Enterprise and Public Policy.* New York: Oxford University Press, 1978.

Thomas Donaldson and Patricia H. Werhane, eds. *Ethical Issues in Business.* Englewood Cliffs, N.J.: Prentice-Hall, 1979.

David M. Gardner. "Deception in Advertising: A Conceptual Approach." *Journal of Marketing* 39 (January 1975).

Harry K. Girvetz, ed. *Contemporary Moral Issues.* 2nd ed. Belmont, Calif.: Wadsworth Publishing Co., 1968. Chapter 10.

Leslie Gould. *The Manipulators.* New York: David McKay, 1966.

Nat Hentoff. "Would You Run This Ad?" *Business and Society Review* 14 (Summer 1975).

John G. Keane. "On Professionalism in Advertising." *Journal of Advertising,* Fall 1974.

Burton M. Leiser. *Liberty, Justice, and Morals.* 2nd ed. New York: Macmillan Publishing Co., 1979. Chapter 9.

John T. Lucas and Richard Gurman. *Truth in Advertising.* New York: American Management Association, 1972.

W. G. Magnuson and Jean Carper. *Dark Side of the Marketplace: The Plight of the American Consumer.* Englewood Cliffs, N.J.: Prentice-Hall, 1968.

Sidney Margoulis. *Innocent Consumer vs. the Exploiters.* New York: Simon & Shuster, 1967.

Dexter L. Masters. *The Intelligent Buyer and the Telltale Seller.* New York: Alfred A. Knopf, 1966.

David Ogilvy. *Confessions of an Advertising Man.* New York: Atheneum, 1963.

Vance Packard. *The Hidden Persuaders.* New York: Pocket Books, 1957.

Ivan L. Preston. *The Great American Blow-up: Puffery in Advertising and Selling.* Madison: University of Wisconsin Press, 1975.

Gerald Runkle. *Good Thinking: An Introduction to Logic.* 2nd ed. New York: Holt, Rinehart and Winston, 1981. Chapter 10.

Charles H. Sandage and Vernon Fryburger. *Advertising Theory and Practice.* 9th ed. Homewood, Ill.: Richard D. Irwin, 1975.

Frederick Stuart, ed. *Consumer Protection from Deceptive Advertising.* Hempstead, N.Y.: Hofstra University, 1974.

GOVERNMENT REGULATIONS

The Public Interest Requires Stricter Regulation of Business

Regulation: Old and New In the thirties, in response to the Depression, the Congress of the United States enacted many laws regulating business and established many agencies to carry them out. Examples of such agencies that still survive are the Civil Aeronautics Board, the Federal Deposit Insurance Corporation, the Federal Communications Commission, the Federal Home Loan Bank Board, the Federal Maritime Commission, the Federal Power Commission, the Food and Drug Administration, the National Labor Relations Board, and the Securities and Exchange Commission. These took their place with a few agencies that had been established earlier, such as the Interstate Commerce Commission (1887) and the Federal Trade Commission (1914). These agencies serve such purposes as preserving competition and, where that is unfeasible, regulating prices and licensing in such a way as to protect the consumer. Their main function is economic, and generally each agency deals with a specific kind of business. The

ICC deals with railroads and trucking, the CAB with airlines, and the FHLBB with banks.

There is much that can be said for and against extending government activity of this kind, and about the effectiveness of these agencies, but the concern here is with a different kind of government regulation: that which aims at social goods that are not primarily economic. Although this new form of regulation has important economic consequences, the change has "included less concern with economic growth and employment and more emphasis on equity and the quality of life both on and off the job."[28] This concern has been marked by the creation of the Environmental Protection Agency (1970), the Consumer Product Safety Commission (1972), and the Occupational Safety and Health Administration (1973). It has also been marked by more extensive efforts on behalf of the consumer by older agencies such as the FCC, the FDA, and the FTC.[29] "In the decade since the first Earth Day, the Federal government alone has passed more than 80 laws aimed at safeguarding air, water, land and public health."[30] Although the discussion here deals mostly with the federal government, state and local governments are assumed to bear certain responsibilities also for safe products, occupational safety, and environmental protections.

Product Safety In 1969, just before the CPSC was set up, the National Commission on Product Safety reported that 600 household products posed safety problems and that most of the millions of injuries in the home were caused by these products.[31] Products designed for children are now scrutinized more closely: toys that may be harmful and clothing that may be very inflammable. Medicine containers must now be made so that they cannot easily be uncapped by children (or anyone else). "Star Wars" rocket launchers and steel darts for backyard horseshoes have been banned. The automobile industry has had to provide seatbelts as standard equipment in all cars. Cars have been called back to remedy various unsafe features from faulty brakes and transmission systems to loose fans. Radial tires have also been called back in great numbers for safety reasons. Lawn mowers have been improved. Hair dryers that might cause cancer have been taken off the market. The National Highway Traffic Safety Administration has completed a three-year study and concluded that most of the Fords manufactured in 1972–1979 have a tendency to slip from park to reverse when the engine is running.[32]

[28]Murray L. Weidenbaum, *The Future of Business Regulation,* p. 58. This section is indebted to Professor Weidenbaum's excellent book.

[29]The Equal Employment Opportunity Commission is another important new agency. Its function is discussed in chapter 6.

[30]*Newsweek,* May 5, 1980, p. 80.

[31]See *Final Report of the National Commission on Product Safety* (Washington: Government Printing Office, 1970).

[32]NHTSA attributed 6,000 accidents, 1,710 injuries, and 98 fatalities to this defect. See *Newsweek,* June 23, 1980, p. 65.

The FDA has banned cyclamates because tests have shown that they are carcinogenic. It has required warning labels for food containing saccharin and posters for stores that sell it. A few years ago Red No. 2, an industrial dye used in soft drinks and candy (and many other products), was banned. The FDA has insisted on careful tests before drugs can be prescribed or sold over the counter.

Attempts to protect the health and safety of consumers may take four forms: (1) Issue requirements for the design of products that would otherwise be hazardous. (2) Ban the manufacture and sale of clearly harmful products. (3) Require that clear instructions for safe use accompany products that could be misused. (4) Require the printing of warnings on products that are dangerous. What these measures accomplish is significant decrease in danger for the consumer. The fact is that individuals are often unable or unwilling to investigate the product themselves. The resources of the government (which exists to serve them) are utilized in order to supplement the normal market forces. Certain matters cannot be left to the decision of companies, for their fundamental aim is to increase sales and to keep the unit cost of production down. The number of lives of children that have been saved by safety lids on aspirin bottles alone testifies to the appropriateness of the regulatory approach.

Occupational Safety Occupational safety and health have also been areas of concern in recent years. Although some efforts of protection had been made early in the twentieth century (mostly on the state level), workers were generally believed to have assumed known risks when they accepted certain employments. Miners, railroad workers, construction workers, and electric line workers especially were expected to die and be injured on the job. Moreover, their accidents were often blamed by courts and employers on their own negligence or that of fellow workers. Still, more progress was made in the field of safety than in that of health. The reason for this is easy to see. Knowledge of industrial disease was more difficult to acquire. That certain diseases were occupationally related was often not obvious. Many diseases occur after a more or less long period of exposure, and not all workers in a particular industry will get a particular disease, nor will all who get the disease be found to have worked in the same industry.[33]

The OSHA exists under an assistant secretary of labor and has the power to inspect work areas and levy penalties on employers who countenance the existence of unsafe conditions.[34] The Labor Department can issue standards that

[33]Luminous Processes, Inc. (formerly, Radium Dial Co.), of Ottawa, Illinois, operated for several decades before it was closed down by the Nuclear Regulatory Commission. The workers painted radium dials on the faces of timepieces. From 1920 to 1973 it used radium 226. Forced to switch to tritium in 1973 and observe certain elementary safeguards, the company was fined in 1977 and lost its license the next year. It required many years before the connection between the radioactive materials and the high incidence of cancer among workers was recognized.

[34]Many of the agencies, however, are "independent regulatory commissions." They are not housed in executive departments, and their members are appointed by the president on a nonpartisan basis for terms that do not coincide with the presidential term.

have the force of law. The OSHA "was criticized in its initial years for moving too slowly both in enforcement and in the setting of standards. However, it did force many companies which had not previously done so to take a systematic approach to managing safety and health matters. A poll of 1,143 business executives conducted jointly in 1975 by Lou Harris and the Wharton School. . . showed that 36 percent of the companies surveyed had instituted safety programs as a result of OSHA. Seventy-two percent said that OSHA had been a factor in causing them to intensify safety efforts."[35]

The Occupational Safety and Health Administration (OSHA) has enforced noise standards in the steel industry, required protection against lead exposure in battery companies, and prescribed the number of exits for factory buildings. It has issued rules and guidelines for safer machinery and electrical systems. Its main concern, however, has been with identifying diseases that are occupationally related and taking steps to prevent them. Frederick D. Sturdivant relates a horrendous tale of the Bridesburg Plant of Rohm and Haas Company.[36] The company refused to admit until 1974 that its product, BCME (bis-chloro-methyl), was instrumental in the cause of cancer. Twenty-five percent of the deaths of Bridesburg employees between 1954 and 1971 had been by cancer, and many of the victims had been fairly young. In 1971, Dr. Norton Nelson, a leading cancer expert, reported to the company that his studies showed that BCME was the most potent carcinogen he and his colleagues at New York University had ever examined. The OSHA inspectors continued to give the company a clean bill of health, reporting as late as 1974 that medical opinion could not establish that BCME or CME (a substitute for BCME) was the cause of deaths—they could be attributed to smoking, heredity, air pollution, or something else. This rather meek performance by the OSHA may be contrasted with its posture a few years later: In 1977 it proposed "that if a substance has a harmful effect on the physiology of the lower mammals, then it should be at least suspected of a comparable effect on human beings, whose body chemistry is not so very different from that of other mammals."[37] If a substance has been shown to be a carcinogen in experimentation with laboratory animals, then it is indeed a carcinogen and should be regarded as such; aside from the question of amount, it is different from noncarcinogenic substances. There is little doubt today that benzidine and asbestos are carcinogens from which workers should be protected.

A tremendous job faces society and the agencies that seek to protect workers in ascertaining the possible hazardous effects of many substances employed by industry. Not only are we ignorant of the effect of many that have been in use for some time, but a host of new ones appear on the scene every year. The OSHA and other agencies should be supported in their attempt to find the answers and take the proper preventive steps.

[35]Sturdivant, *Business and Society,* p. 161.

[36]See ibid., pp. 162–166.

[37]Greenwood and Edwards, *Human Environments and Natural Systems,* p. 274.

One important area that requires close scrutiny is the safety and health of workers employed in places where unusual radioactivity is present. We are all subject to radiation, *particulate* (protons, neutrons, alpha particles, and beta particles) and *electromagnetic* (vibrating waves of electrons). The former can be contained by very thin shields, but the latter require thick shields of lead. Particulate radiation is not dangerous except when the radioactive substance is inhaled or ingested.[38] Danger from electromagnetic radiation depends simply on exposure and is determined by the amount of exposure. A single high dose or accumulated low doses can cause death and genetic damage. This kind of radiation may come from radio, television, and radar waves, as well as from visible and ultraviolet light, and X-rays. It also comes from naturally radioactive substances such as uranium and from some of the radioisotopes produced from nuclear fission, such as Cerium 144; waves from such substances are called gamma waves. Much of the natural background for radiation exposure cannot be avoided, but society has it within its power to protect people from gamma rays. Exactly how much radiation the human body can tolerate over and above the natural exposure is not known for certain.

It would seem to follow from this that great care should be taken to protect the health of workers in nuclear energy installations (as well as those who work with X-rays). People employed in nuclear facilities may be protected very well from high-level radioactivity, but may be badly injured by accumulation of low-level radiation. Thus it is important not only to shield them and constantly monitor radiation levels on the premises, but also to keep account of the annual radiation they are exposed to. "The fact that background radiation is unavoidable makes health physicists wary of anything that adds to it."[39]

Until the disaster at Three Mile Island in the spring of 1979, corporations had been quite successful in protecting their workers. In March 1980, a similar incident occurred at the Crystal River nuclear power plant in Florida. Radiation monitors suddenly began to register rems per hour far above the acceptable level. The automatic safety controls immediately began to operate, cutting off the atomic chain reaction and rushing extra cooling water through the reactor. Disaster was presumably avoided, although a lot of radioactive water had to be drained from the quench tank under the reactor vessel and from the floor of the containment area. In both cases, the Nuclear Regulatory Commission denied that dangerous radiation existed for nearby communities, but no one can say with any confidence what injuries were sustained by workers in the plants themselves.

There is risk, of course, in all occupations. Some schoolteachers complain of "white lung disease," from inhaling chalk dust. One has to try to determine what

[38]Strontium 90, for example, is a radioisotope produced by nuclear fission. It emits beta particles. Much of it appeared as a fallout from nuclear explosions some years ago. Cows ate grass upon which it had fallen, and people drank milk from the cows. Result: accumulation in, and damage to, their bones.

[39]Greenwood and Edwards, p. 299.

level of risk is "acceptable." Where the risk is clearly known, workers can perhaps be permitted to make their own choices, but only within these strictures: (1) The employer does everything that is feasible to reduce the risk, and (2) the workers are clearly informed about what risks still exist. Where the degree of risk is not clearly known (as is often the case with some forms of carcinogenity and radioactivity), the workers should not be permitted to work at all.

The Environment: Air Perhaps the greatest responsibility for the welfare of individuals is borne by the Environmental Protection Agency. Armed with dozens of federal laws, the EPA is charged with issuing regulations and guidelines on behalf of the environment and bringing violators to trial. It also may require "environmental impact statements" for new projects planned by a company. It is also expected to cooperate with and assist local jurisdictions.

Only a few aspects of environmental concern can be discussed here. One has to do with the atmosphere. Despite a series of national, state, and local laws, the United States faces a grave problem in air pollution. In many localities and most cities, human activities have polluted the atmosphere beyond its power to regenerate. What is done in one area, because of the flow of air masses, affects conditions in other areas. So the problem is both national and global. The EPA estimated that the United States was responsible for 222 million tons of air pollution in 1970, over one-fourth of the world total.[40]

Among the pollutants are the following:

1. Carbon monoxide. This gas results from incomplete combustion—mostly from automobile engines. "Normal background levels of atmospheric CO range from .025 to 1 ppm. However, in a typical American city the range is from 10 to 50 ppm."[41] Immediate effects on humans: blurred vision and dizziness. Long-range effects: unknown. About 90 percent of the CO in the air is man-made.

2. Sulfur oxides, especially SO_2. This gas results from the burning of fossil fuels. When it combines with oxygen and water vapor in the air, the result is sulfurous acid (H_2SO_3) and sulfuric acid (H_2SO_4). "Either acid can do considerable damage to vegetation, fabrics, metals, paintwork, and even stone."[42] Effect on humans: irritation of throat and lung tissue, along with bronchial constriction. About 66 percent of the sulfur oxides in the air are man-made.

3. Particulates. This is a generic term and includes such particles as fly ash, coal dust, insecticide dust, metallurgical fumes, and oil smoke.

4. Hydrocarbons. These include paraffins, olefins, acetylenes, benzenes, naphthenes, and anthracenes. Most of them are caused by the combustion of gasoline and oil. Some of them react in sunlight with ozone and nitrogen oxides to cause

[40]Greenwood and Edwards, p. 204. This subsection is greatly indebted to this fine book.

[41]Ibid., p. 202. *Ppm* stands for "part(s) per million." Ronald Reagan said in his 1980 presidential campaign that most air pollution is caused by natural biological processes. Presumably he knows better now.

[42]Ibid., p. 203.

photochemical pollution. One of these resulting pollutants is called PAN (peroxyacetyl nitrate), and it is a major irritant.

5. Nitrogen oxides. NO is the direct product of combustion—mostly coal and oil. It may pick up another atom from the air and become NO_2, which often appears as a reddish-brown haze. More dangerous are such pollutants as PAN that result when NO_2 combines photochemically with hydrocarbons. Although only about 6 percent of nitrogen oxides are man-made, the balance is upset. Nitrogen oxides released at high altitudes react with ozone (O_3), reducing it to O_2. This is serious, for the ozone layer (15 to 35 kilometers above the ground) shields us from deadly ultraviolet radiation. "An MIT study indicated that a fleet of 500 SSTs flying regularly in or near the ozone layer would reduce the ozone by 12 percent in twenty-five years."[43]

6. Fluorocarbons. One of them, Freon, also contributes to the breakdown of ozone when it is wafted to the high altitudes. Freon is used as the propellant in aerosol sprays. When the FDA announced in 1976 the phasing out of aerosol sprays, one of its commissioners said: "The known fact is that fluorocarbon propellants used to dispense cosmetics are breaking down the ozone layer. Without remedy the result could be a profound adverse impact on our weather and on the incidence of skin cancer in people."[44]

At times, of course, the air we breathe is more polluted than at other times. When weather conditions and/or geographic features permit pollution levels to accumulate in a given area, the people who inhale the air are in trouble. Two of these phenomena are *urban heat island* and *temperature inversion.* The latter can be deadly. The smog (coal smoke and fog) that was trapped over London in 1952 cost thousands of lives. Photochemical "smog" (formaldehyde and PAN), common to Los Angeles, is caused mainly by automobile emissions and, given the climate and geography, is virtually impossible to eliminate. Los Angeles has succeeded in eliminating pollution from stationary sources, but until the exhaust problem in cars can be solved, Angelenos are destined to breathe very unhealthy air.

In 1975 the EPA estimated the cost of air pollution as $16 billion per year—$6 billion for sickness and death, $10 billion for property damage.[45] In a study published by the Harvard Energy and Environmental Center, it was estimated that 53,000 Americans a year die from industrial air pollution.[46]

How can these losses be reduced? (1) Improve combustion: Use low-pollutant fuels, increase heat and oxygen to achieve more complete combustion, use afterburners. (2) Pass all air from a combustion process through mechanical filters. (3) Pass polluted air through water or oil to remove certain pollutants ("scrub-

[43]Ibid., p. 207.
[44]Ibid.
[45]See Sturdivant, p. 306.
[46]See *St. Louis Post Dispatch,* February 3, 1981, p. 7A.

bing"). (4) Subject polluted air to chemical treatment—for example, reduce sulfur oxides to sulfur. These procedures are all expensive. But unless government at all levels takes strong steps, very little will be done. A company cannot be expected to accept an added cost unless its competitors must do so also.

The Environment: Water A second area of concern is water. The water requirement in the United States is already very close to the total fresh water supply—a little more than 500 billion gallons a day. Water needs are expected to rise to 900 billion gallons by the year 2000. Since neither the need nor the supply is uniform throughout the country, great attention must be paid to transporting water, recycling water, and reducing pollution. These efforts require government regulations at all levels, including cooperative arrangements between different jurisdictions. Not only do jurisdictions purify and distribute water, but they also seek to control the impact on the water supply by individuals and businesses. Businesses use enormous amounts of water (especially for cooling in industrial processes) and return it in one form or another to the environment.[47] "Government agencies estimate that between 40 and 70 billion dollars will be needed to restore water quality and control pollution by the year 2000. This estimate is certain to be raised as costs increase, and work on the problem has scarcely begun."[48]

The key to the solution appears to be that of reducing waste. One way is to capture more of the rainfall for human use, but care must be taken here not to rob plant and animal life of their needs. Another way is to husband more carefully the water we take from rivers, lakes, and underground sources. This would include better storage and conveyance, in which losses by seepage and evaporation are lessened. It would also include better use of water for domestic purposes, such as drinking, cooking, hygiene, sewage dilution, air conditioning, fire protection, recreation, and sprinkling. There is no reason, for example, for water used for flushing toilets (five gallons per flush) to be of the same quality as that used for drinking. Moreover, when "return flow" water is treated properly, it adds to our water supply when dumped into streams and lakes.

The greatest threat, however, comes from pollution. It also provides the greatest opportunity. Pollution is indirect waste, for it makes recycling difficult or impossible, and recycling is absolutely necessary if we are to meet our water needs. And, obviously, pollution harms the quality of the water of streams and lakes into which it is dumped.

Some kinds of pollutants, such as sewage and other organic substances, are biodegradable—that is, they can be broken down by bacterial action. But if we do not treat them, they are "treated" by the streams and lakes: this kind of treatment causes reduction of oxygen in these bodies. When oxygen is exhausted,

[47]The breakdown is: industrial use, 57 percent; agricultural use (irrigation), 35 percent; domestic use, 8 percent. See Greenwood and Edwards, p. 230.

[48]Ibid., p. 231.

the river or lake is "dead." Other pollutants, however, such as heavy metals like mercury, hard detergents, and pesticides like DDT, are much more resistant. Oil is a dangerous pollutant also. It not only kills aquatic plants and animals, but by reducing the oxygen content of water into which it has been spilled, it hinders the natural decomposition of organic wastes.

By far the greatest cause of pollution is industry. Unless its practice of dumping or spilling pollutants into our waterways is sharply curtailed, most of our rivers and lakes will be dead or poisoned in a few years. The Cuyahoga River caught fire a few years ago, and the Great Lakes are almost dead right now. The EPA had to go to court in 1974 to stop the Reserve Mining Company from dumping wastes containing asbestos fibers into Lake Superior.[49]

A great many toxic substances are man-made and enter both the water and air supplies, as well as the land. Many of them are carcinogenic. They are mobile and persistent, and accumulate in living tissue. The chlorinated hydrocarbons include DDT, DDE (the first stage in the breakdown of DDT), and other pesticides. Although they destroy insects (at least until resistant strains develop), they seriously harm the nervous and productive systems of all animals, including humans.[50] Most of our food is contaminated by pesticides, and we are accumulating the substances in our bodies.[51] Cancer victims and people who have died from liver and central nervous system diseases have been found to contain a much higher residue of chlorinated hydrocarbons than people who died from other causes. By 1973, DDT had been largely banned in the United States, but exports to other countries continued—so we will reap that harvest. In 1974, aldrin and dieldrin were also banned. Even with a *worldwide* ban (which is unlikely), these pesticides would be around for a very long time. Safer pesticides, such as the organic phosphates and carbonates, have been developed, but they are not without risk also. Various herbicides have also been under scrutiny by the EPA.

Some progress toward clean air and water has been made. According to the EPA, "the sulfur-dioxide level in America's air has been cut by 17 per cent since 1972, and carbon-monoxide levels have fallen an average of 7 per cent a year. Combined data from 25 major metropolitan areas show that the number of 'very unhealthful' days dropped by one-third between 1974 and 1977. EPA research also shows demonstrable improvement in U.S. water quality. The amount of key industrial pollutants in the nation's waterways has been cut in half since 1972."[52]

The Environment: Waste Disposal A third area of environmental concern is that of solid waste disposal. Included here are nontoxic materials, toxic materials,

[49]The daily discharge of taconite tailings was 67,000 tons. The asbestos, a carcinogen, was finding its way into the drinking water of neighboring cities.

[50]The significance of Rachel Carson's 1962 book *Silent Spring* is that there were no birds singing—they were all dead from insecticides.

[51]The average amount of DDT in the human body is already greater than the amount that is permissible in food.

[52]*Newsweek,* May 5, 1980, p. 80.

and radioactive materials. These materials pollute not only the air and the water, but the land as well.

The average individual generates about eight pounds of junk a day: paper, garbage, metals, glass, plastics. What do we do with it? Most of it has been sent to open dumps. This is unsatisfactory because the fires pollute the air, the soil and water become contaminated, and the dumps themselves are eyesores. The EPA has tried to close them, without much success. A better solution is incineration, but this, too, pollutes the air unless the equipment is modern and expensive. Government efforts here have also been resisted. Some optimists look forward to the time when heat from incinerators will be used to create electricity.[53] Another solution is the sanitary landfill, but such questions arise as whether we have enough land to bury the junk in, whether filling ravines will harm water drainage patterns, whether use of estuaries and tidal flats will seriously harm the balance of nature, and whether we can be sure that a given landfill really is "sanitary."

Another concern here is the waste of waste. How long can we take raw material from our environment for manufacture and return it in the form of junk? Conservation dictates "resource recovery." Much of the material burned or buried could be recycled (e.g., paper and aluminum cans) or reclaimed (e.g., by making tile out of crushed glass). This sort of solution merits more support from government. Used copper, lead, tin, iron, and rubber do not have to be lost to us forever. Many materials could be used in road building: rubber (well over 100 million tires are thrown away each year), pulverized glass, "supersludge," and others.

A special problem exists with respect to plastics. They cannot be incinerated, for hydrogen chloride gas (which is very corrosive) is produced. They should not be buried, for they are not biodegradable. And no one has yet perfected a plastic container that can be recycled. Junked cars are another problem. It is not economical to separate their parts and to recycle the metals. And they are too big to bury—so there they sit.

Far exceeding in quantity the solid waste generated by individuals is that generated by agriculture and mining. An example of the first is the manure produced by livestock—which amounts to ten times that of human sewage. The EPA has tried to set standards for its disposal, and attempts are being made for greater utilization of the manure in making composts and fertilizers,[54] as well as methane gas. The most obvious waste in mining occurs in strip mining, which, if unregulated, desolates the land, destroys habitats, contributes to erosion and floods, and exposes substances that pollute streams. "Between 3.5 and 4 million acres in the United States have been mutilated by all forms of surface mining, and about two-thirds of this acreage had not been reclaimed."[55]

[53]"According to Arsen Darnay of the EPA's Office of Solid Waste Management Programs, the energy locked in the nation's municipal refuse could light all its homes and commercial establishments." Greenwood and Edwards, p. 260.

[54]It is impractical simply to spread it over the fields, for each head of feed-cattle produces over 2.5 tons of manure a year.

[55]Ibid., p. 265.

Toxic materials are also a problem in solid waste disposal. Asbestos, mercury, and lead are well-known examples. Noxious waste, if improperly disposed of, can be a real hazard to health for a long time. Some years ago Hooker Chemicals & Plastic Corporation dumped 21,000 tons of it in the Love Canal area in Niagara Falls, New York. In 1978, officials declared a health emergency and moved 237 families from their homes nearest to the contamination site. In the spring of 1980, the EPA revealed a study showing that several residents had damaged chromosomes. This explained the fact of miscarriages and birth defects among residents far in excess of national averages. There was also evidence of nerve damage and cancer. Although the evidence is not without its skeptics, the president signed an emergency order and a federal agency released several million dollars to temporarily relocate the people in other quarters. But the people *never* want to go back. " 'I want a fair market value for my house and to get this nightmare over with,' said Jo Ann Kott, who had suffered a miscarriage and a stillbirth."[56]

In 1979, thirty-five million tons of hazardous waste were produced in this country. The EPA estimates that less than 7 percent of it was disposed of properly.

Over one thousand barrels of chemical wastes were found in an illegal landfill south of Belleville, Illinois, and a warehouse in East St. Louis in the spring of 1980. The Illinois EPA brought suit against several companies and began supervising the removal of dangerous materials. Earlier in the same year the federal EPA had to employ a new ultraviolet process to clean up an area polluted by waste oil containing the deadly chemical dioxin. Three years earlier the EPA had to "excavate 247,000 gallons of PCB-contaminated soil and divert a creak 3,000 feet around" an unlicensed disposal pit in Jefferson County, Missouri, containing chemical wastes. Several cases of companies paying farmers to permit dumping or burial of hazardous waste have been reported in Illinois and Missouri. One result was new regulations on both sides of the river: "New regulations require hazardous waste producers in Missouri to register with the state, keep records of waste generated and shipped, notify the state Department of Natural Resources of what is happening to it, use a department-licensed hauler for moving it, and use a permitted disposal site. Under the new regulations . . . landfill operators must accept only state-approved waste, monitor groundwater nearby, post a bond or liability insurance, and set aside funds to close and maintain filled sites. Violations carry a maximum penalty of $10,000 per day." Illinois regulations are similar. In some respects, the state laws are stricter than federal rules. The federal EPA has established toll-free numbers in the two states that citizens can dial to report dumping—and hundreds of calls were received in the spring of 1980.[57] A subcommittee of the House Interstate and Foreign Commerce Committee had identified fifty-two potential hazardous waste sites in Missouri in the fall of 1979.

[56]*Newsweek,* June 2, 1980, p. 56.

[57]See Bill Anderson and Mark Edgar, "Hazardous Waste," *St. Louis Globe-Democrat,* July 2, 1980, p. 11A.

A year later, the EPA had inspected only five of the eighteen in the St. Louis area.[58]

One problem in dealing with toxic waste is that most people do not want hazardous waste disposal sites of any kind—chemical or radioactive—in their neighborhoods. Many citizens do not believe that the regulations of the EPA and NRC are strict enough in themselves or their application to protect the area. Illinois passed a bill (and overrode the governor's veto) in December 1980 that bars the importation of highly radioactive waste from any state that does not accept a like amount from Illinois. Illinois is the state with the most nuclear power plants.

Let us now look at the problem of radioactive waste. Grave as the problem is in protecting workers at atomic energy plants and the residents in their environs, that of *disposing* of waste is a greater one—perhaps an unsolvable one. If nuclear power plants are to solve the energy crisis, however, it must be solved. The crux of the problem is the duration of radioactivity—in some cases millions of years. The minimum length of time that has to be dealt with is 800 years. "Low-level" waste is handled by private companies licensed by the federal commissions. Some of it has been sealed in drums and dropped into the Pacific Ocean. Some is buried in the ground on sites approved by the states. According to the EPA, this has not always been satisfactory—many of the drums in the ocean, for example, have burst and are leaking radioactivity. As sites are filling up, technology is trying to develop a relatively inexpensive method for neutralizing the radioactivity of low-level wastes.

"High-level nuclear wastes are still in the custody of the Nuclear Regulatory Commission (NRC), which took over the responsibility from its predecessor, the AEC."[59] These wastes, from military and commercial projects, come to several million gallons a year; they have been stored in steel tanks underground. There have been several instances of leakage, so plans are to convert the liquid to solids and store the solid material—somewhere. Various suggestions have been made, including abandoned salt-mines, orbits around the sun, oceanic trenches, Antarctica under the ice, caverns created by underground atomic bomb tests. None is perfectly safe, and all are expensive.

Ethics Not all the concerns of environmentalists have been touched on here. Omitted have been such concerns as the conservation of natural resources such as coal, oil, and minerals, the protection of animal and plant life, and the reduction of noise pollution. But perhaps enough has been said about air, water, and solid waste to support the quite innocuous thesis that government agencies (EPA and others) must be supported and their efforts intensified if the quality of life on spaceship earth is not to deteriorate badly in the years ahead.

[58]See Terry Ganey, "Politics and Hazardous Waste," *St. Louis Post-Dispatch,* September 14, 1980, p. 3D.

[59]Greenwood and Edwards, p. 313.

No great ethical argument is necessary to support the contention that government regulation of business in an extensive and intensive way is necessary to protect the public interest. This is especially obvious with respect to the products Americans buy, the conditions under which they work, and the environment that sustains them. If government exists to serve the people, these are fundamental ways it can serve them, for they relate to their health, safety, and ultimate survival. If we can convert the utilitarians' happiness to interests, these are the strongest interests of virtually everyone in the nation, the ones to which other interests must give way.

It is not denied here that free enterprise in many of its actions also serves the greatest interest of the greatest number. But one of its motives, to enhance profits, sometimes gets in the way of this social good. A company, operating under the best of intentions, must penalize itself if it takes steps, say, to reduce its emission of particulates if its competitors do not do so also. Even voluntary programs adopted by all members of a particular industry will not be as stringent as is desirable, for this industry is itself in competition with other industries for the consumer's dollars. Only government action throughout the whole community of business and industry can properly safeguard the public interest. If the public interest cannot adequately be protected by government *regulation* of private property, socialism offers itself as an alternative.[60]

It may well be the case that the "standard of living" in the sense of material possessions will go down if regulatory powers are pushed to the point they should be, but that is an acceptable price to pay for safe products, healthful working conditions, and clean air. If an effective catalytic converter can be found for automobiles, they will cost more, but we may decide to drive them longer. If the safety problems of nuclear energy cannot be solved, we should be ready to resort to coal. And if emission standards for coal burning make electricity more expensive, we must resolve to get by with less.

The Public Interest Requires a Reduction in the Regulation of Business

Financial Costs The first argument that can be offered for a reduction in the amount of government regulation of business is a prima facie one. If it is true that there already is a great amount of regulation, and that this regulation costs us dearly, it is quite possible that we have enough—perhaps too much. The burden of proof would thus lie with those who would increase it—and perhaps with those who would retain it. In any case, the first thing that must be taken into account is the amount and cost of the present system (if we can use that word) of regulation.

[60]The prominent environmentalist Barry Commoner advocates this in his book *The Closing Circle* (1971).

The most obvious cost of regulating business is found in administration itself. Well over $3 billion were spent in 1976 to pay the salaries and operating expenses of federal bureaucrats. The figure is much larger today. When we add the cost of maintaining bureaucrats on the state and local levels, we get a figure that is even more alarming.

But the expense of supporting government agencies is only a fraction of the expense borne by the country in *complying* with their regulations. Professor Robert DeFina of the Washington University Center for the Study of American Business has conservatively estimated this figure as $63 billion for 1976.[61] This means that for every dollar paid to support agencies, twenty are generated in expenses for private business. DeFina estimates that administrative costs will be around $5 billion in 1980 and compliance costs around $100 billion. Last year the nuclear industry alone spent around $7 billion "for safety studies, new equipment at the nation's other [not Three Mile Island] nuclear-power plants, retraining for reactor personnel. . . ."[62] "The Council on Environmental Quality . . . estimates that between 1973 and 1978, the United States spent $91.8 billion meeting Federal environment standards alone. Between 1978 and 1987, the CEQ predicts, legally mandated national spending on environmental protection will approach $500 billion."[63]

The Clean Air Act cost more than $53 billion between 1972 and 1978. Compliance costs are estimated at $37.5 billion annually by 1987. Exactly how much is each added percentage point of improvement worth? The 1977 amendments sought not only to reduce pollution, but to protect clean air from *becoming* polluted. The implication of the formulas is that relatively clean areas can be prohibited from adding pollution—even when the total pollution would be well within the standards set for other areas! Another strange feature of the legislation is that incremental emissions are measured on a one-day basis instead of annually. The Reagan administration is pledged to attack the whole system of federal regulation. The Clean Air Act is due for reauthorization by Congress in 1981, so this will probably be the first big test for his policy.[64]

Paul W. MacAvoy, professor of economics at Yale University, estimates that the amount of investment that must be spent for complying with regulations reduces the GNP by about one-half a percentage point a year. This means that in ten years the economy is "running 6 or 7 percent below its capacity because of these controls alone."[65] More and more new capital must be spent in compliance, which means that less is available for innovation, expansion, and improved productivity. This "is most evident in the environmental and safety areas, in which government-mandated outlays account for almost one-tenth of new capital formation."[66] Moreover, decisions in use of capital must be made in a spirit of

[61]See Weidenbaum, p. 22.
[62]*Newsweek,* April 7, 1980, pp. 33–34.
[63]*Newsweek,* May 5, 1980, p. 80.
[64]See "Reagan's Big Cleanup Fight," *Newsweek,* December 8, 1980, pp. 69–70.
[65]See *Regulating Business: The Search for an Optimum,* p. 5.
[66]Weidenbaum, p. 23.

uncertainty: What new government regulations will appear tomorrow? What will be the effect of present regulations on new products and processes? Finally, we should note that many companies succumb and many installations close down because they do not have sufficient capital to meet new regulations.[67] And some, of course, never get started because of the existence of these requirements. These are not costs simply for capitalists, but to society in general in terms of decreased productivity and loss of jobs.

The Consumer Most of the costs of compliance are passed on to the consumers. One way that they pay is through higher prices. Regulations on the manufacture of automobiles between 1968 and 1978, having to do with safety and environmental factors, added about $665 to the cost of each car. American car buyers thus spent $6.7 billion for compliance in 1978.[68] If the Fords with the "defective" transmissions had been called back, the cost to the company (and the consumer) would have been about $360 million. American home buyers had to pay about $2,000 more per house for compliance in 1975 than they did in 1970. There is another $4 billion. Despite the function of some agencies to *control* prices, permission has been given to raise them because of the added cost of compliance to standards imposed by other agencies. The fields of transportation, communication, electric power, and natural gas provide examples.

The consumers pay in another way. Because of the capital need for compliance, less is available for research and development. Their expectation of new or improved products is thus reduced. Weidenbaum offers these indicators: The amount spent for R&D increased at a much lower rate after 1967 than before. Fewer scientists and engineers were employed by industry in 1975 than in 1968. Fewer patents were issued in 1973 than in 1963, while in the rest of the world the number doubled.[69]

Another, more direct factor is at work in depriving consumers of new and better products. Regulations may make the process of getting approval so long or costly that the producer decides to shelve the whole project. If the product is approved, it comes to the consumer after a delay. The rules of the FDA are so stringent that the United States, no longer the leader in introducing new medicines, was "the thirtieth country to approve the anti-asthma drug metaproternol, the thirty-second to approve the antituberculosis drug refampin, the sixty-fourth to approve the antiallergic drug cromolyn, and the one hundred sixth to approve the antibacterial drug co-trimaxazole."[70] Some good products never get on the market at all, and some, like cyclamates, are taken away from us. Had it not been for a special act of Congress, we would have been deprived of saccharin also.

[67]Chrysler's complaints are well known. "Several hundred foundries . . . were closed down during 1968–1975 in part because they could not meet requirements such as those imposed by" EPA and OSHA. Ibid., p. 24.

[68]See Ibid., pp. 12–13.

[69]Ibid., p. 25.

[70]Ibid., p. 26.

Freedom Finally, we should note the great loss of freedom experienced in a situation where directives from regulators rain down in ever-increasing volume. Every business decision is in effect a joint decision, with the government the not-so-silent partner. Forms must be filled out, studies made and reported, licenses and permits obtained. The federal government prints thousands of different forms, and individuals and companies spend 143 million man-hours (71,500 man-years) a year (1978) filling them out. Not only must business do what government approves, but it also has to do it *in the way* prescribed by the government. In 1977, the Dow Chemical Company, after having spent over two years and $4 million in trying to comply with environmental standards for building a new plant in California, abandoned the idea. It had gotten only four of the sixty-five permits it needed from various jurisdictions. Inspectors from agencies may appear unannounced at any time on company premises. It required a Supreme Court decision (1978) before OSHA could be made to secure a warrant first, but it is doubtful that fearful managers would turn away OSHA inspectors even if they did not have a warrant.

Milton Friedman points out that much of the power possessed by big business dervies not from market forces but its ability to influence government. "Airline fares were kept high and service limited, not through the market but through the Civil Aeronautics Board, as has been demonstrated since the partial deregulation of air travel. The trucking industry imposes billions of dollars of extra cost each year on all of us, not through the market but through the Interstate Commerce Commission. Opposition to the deregulation of trucking comes not from the trucking industry's customers or potential competition but from big business, big labor (the Teamsters) and the trucking firms themselves." Chrysler could not have obtained its loans and U.S. Steel could not have forced American consumers to pay prices higher than those charged by foreign steel producers without the assistance of the government.[71] With respect to the newer controls, business is about as helpless as the rest of us, for it has not yet made the alliance with government. The shoe is on the other foot—and it hurts! Not wanting freedom in the one area, it has lost it in the other.

The general argument presented above does not prove that regulations should be reduced, but it should create the suspicion that we are overregulated and place the burden of proof on those who believe otherwise.

Useless Regulation: Occupational Safety A better argument against regulations would be to examine some of them to see whether they work. Here we would be selective and approve of those that serve their purpose (which is the public good) and call for the repeal of those that do not. If we find that a great many do not pass this test, we can conclude that reduction of regulations is in order. *These* at least should be eliminated. Whether they should be replaced by new ones will be dealt with below. Since the greatest rash of regulations in our time and the recent

[71]Milton Friedman, "The Corporate Clout," *Newsweek,* May 5, 1980, p. 82.

past has been in the areas of safety, health, and environment, we will confine our attention to those areas.

MacAvoy makes an astonishing statement about such controls in general: "In the case of health, safety, and environmental controls, there are no findings of benefits whatsoever. Rivers are not cleaner, nor is the air of significantly greater quality."[72] How is this possible? The accident rate has increased since the OSHA came into existence! According to MacAvoy, this is because its guidelines deal merely with specific physical characteristics of equipment and working areas. The real cause of accidents is the *behavior* of workers rather than the physical things around them. He suggests that better results would be obtained through an incentive scheme in which companies that had fewer accidents would pay less to the workers' compensation program in which they participate. We might add that companies could award concrete benefits (say, a trip to Las Vegas) for workers who have maintained a good record over a stated period of time.[73] In any case, the company itself could do more in achieving safety by means of its own programs than by blindly following the detailed guidelines imposed by "experts" from the OSHA.

The OSHA requires portable toilets for outside work, even when facilities are already available. It mandates controls in smelters and battery factories that reduce the presence of lead to 100 micrograms per cubic meter or air, although the figure of 200 micrograms is safe. And it issues silly and useless pamphlets such as this (for farmers):

> Be careful around the farm. . . . Hazards are one of the main causes of accidents. A hazard is anything that is dangerous.
>
> Be careful when you are handling animals. Tired or hungry or frightened cattle can bolt and trample you. Be patient, talk softly around cows.
>
> Don't move fast or be loud around them. If they are upset, don't go into the pen with them.
>
> Cows are more dangerous when they have new calves. Be careful if you have to reach into their pen. Try not to go into the pen with them. Keep pets and children away, too.
>
> A bawling calf can cause all the cows to be upset. If that happens, stay out of the feedlot. They could bolt and knock you down.
>
> Always try to keep a fence between you and your cattle. Never try to handle a bull alone. Always have a helper. . . .

[72] *Regulating Business,* p. 5.

[73] The Mueller Company (a fire hydrant manufacturer) of Decatur, Illinois, does just that. Officials say they have "reduced their accident rate and their workers' compensation costs by having drawings for cash prizes and trips, including trips to Las Vegas." Only employees with excellent safety records are eligible for the drawings. See Associated Press story by Susan J. Smith, *Edwardsville Intelligencer,* June 30, 1980, p. 4.

DON'T FALL.

Be careful that you do not fall into the manure pits. Put up signs and fences to keep people away. These pits are very dangerous. . . .

Put away tools, equipment and feed when not using them. . . . When floors are wet and slippery with manure, you could have a bad fall. . . . If your ladder is broken, do not climb it. . . .

Wear clothes that fit right.[74]

Do we really need directives stating how often spittoons should be cleaned?

The OSHA has been operating on the principle that just about any exposure to carcinogens is unsafe. A few years ago it reduced the allowable benzene exposure limit from 10 ppm to 1 ppm. The petroleum industry, the major user of benzene, challenged the standard in federal court and won. The Supreme Court, in upholding the decision in July 1980, said in the words of Justice John Paul Stevens that the OSHA had failed to establish that the benzene rules were "reasonable, necessary and appropriate" to remedy a "significant risk of material health impairment." It had insufficient evidence that benzene at or near 10 ppm had ever caused leukemia. Charles J. DiBona, president of the American Petroleum Institute, said: "The court's landmark decision recognizes that health regulations in this country must be made on the basis of scientific facts, rather than pure speculation."[75] "OSHA had estimated that the benzene rule, if upheld by the court, would have required industry to invest about $266 million in plant modification, with first-year operating costs of up to $205 million and recurring costs of $34 million annually. The capital costs of protecting an individual worker would have been about $1,390 in the rubber industry and $39,675 in the petrochemical industry."[76]

Sometimes the industry knows what is best—and nearly always what is more economical. The steel industry showed that it could achieve the same protection against noise, required by the OSHA, by different means. The OSHA's program cost about $1.2 million per worker; the industry's program cost $42.[77]

Useless Regulation: Product Safety As far as safe products are concerned, here again more attention should be paid to behavior than to physical characteristics. Detroit will never be able to build a car that is perfectly safe. People drive cars. If their driving habits are bad, they will kill themselves no matter how many safety belts are installed and regardless of the location of the gas tanks. Safety devices are, of course, desirable, but the market should decide which ones the consumer feels are important enough to pay for. Guns and poisons are clearly

[74]Printed in *Omaha World-Herald,* June 15, 1976. See Weidenbaum, p. 105.
[75]Quoted in article by Martha Shirk in *St. Louis Post-Dispatch,* July 6, 1980, p. 1–I.
[76]Ibid., p. 3–I.
[77]See Donald Ubben, "OSHA Noise Standards Stir Debate," *Washington Report,* December 19, 1977.

unsafe, but they are offered on the market in the hope that those who buy them will use them wisely and carefully. It might be pointed out that the millions of Ford cars and trucks that were thought by the National Highway Safety Administration under Joan Claybrook to have faulty transmission systems were *not* recalled in 1980. She was overruled by Secretary of Transportation Neil Goldschmidt, and warnings were mailed to owners instead. Owners may reasonably be expected to place their vehicles firmly in park—especially when the motor is running.

The Consumer Product Safety Commission (CPSC) banned a certain kind of aerosol spary adhesive in 1974 because it was mistakenly believed to cause birth defects. By the time the ban was rescinded about seven months later, at least nine women had undergone abortions. Certain materials in children's pajamas were banned recently because they were inflammable. Manufacturers treated them with a chemical (Tris) to make them flame-resistant. The CPSC found this to be carcinogenic and again banned the pajamas. Perhaps the kids should be sent to bed naked—provided, of course, that the bedclothes have been certified to be safe. The CPSC did back down and lowered its flammability standards.

The FDA does an important job on behalf of consumers. To its credit, it never approved thalidomide. But its excessive caution has cost ailing individuals drugs that could have spared them hours of suffering, and perhaps death. Sodium valproate, the most effective remedy for myoclonic epilepsy, was not available in the United States until eleven years after it was marketed in France—and then only after extensive media pressure had been applied. The average time required for getting FDA approval is twenty months, but it often takes six or eight years.[78] Other very useful drugs (isoprinosine, propranolol, and dimethyl sulfoxide, for example) have had uphill battles with the FDA for acceptance. "It takes 25 times as much paperwork and twice as long to get a drug approved in the U.S. as in England," the AMA's Dr. Ray W. Gifford, Jr., told the U.S. House of Representatives. According to Gifford, an innovator can expect to spend seven to ten years and $30 million from the time a drug is discovered to its approval by the FDA. Increasingly, he says, the FDA's detailed regulations may be discouraging the best scientists from participating in a new drug research.[79] The recent permission for the use of marijuana for glaucoma patients was too long in coming. Some states are now permitting the use of marijuana in reducing nausea resulting from chemotherapy. That insufficiently tested drugs are often unavailable for people who are already so close to death that they have nothing to lose is unconscionable.

Despite the needs of diabetes sufferers and overweight people for a calorie-free sweetener, the FDA has banned cyclamates and almost succeeded in driving saccharin off the market. It seems that almost every week we hear of another

[78]See Karen Feld, "Does FDA Hold Helpful Drugs Off the Market Too Long?" *St. Louis Globe-Democrat,* July 24, 1980, p. 5B.
[79]See *Parade,* September 14, 1980, p. 24.

product that has been found to be carcinogenic. That laboratory rats cannot survive massive doses of a particular substance does not mean that it is dangerous in relatively smaller amounts for human beings. One researcher is supposed to have discovered that wearing leisure suits contributes to cancer, because a test group of white rats showed a higher incidence of the disease than the control group, which dressed as it pleased.

Useless Regulation: The Environment No one can quarrel with the importance of protecting the environment and the need for strong laws and agencies for that purpose. Air and water are crucial to our very existence, and other resources are crucial to our standard of living. That people must be protected against noxious chemical and radioactive waste is undeniable. But one can quarrel with the means often chosen by government regulators to achieve these ends.

The requirement that steel plants install "scrubbers" reduces the emission of iron oxide dust, but, since the scrubber is run by electric power, the utility plant that produces it spews out even more sulfur and nitrogen oxides and other pollutants.[80] If we make the power companies themselves employ scrubbers, there is again an unintended side effect: "In extracting the pollutants from coal," the Pennsylvania Power Company "produces 18,000 tons of sludge a day."[81] What do you do with it? Toxic waste may become a problem. "Ironically, many of the 32,000 to 50,000 dump sites for hazardous materials are filled with the by-products of the cleanup of the 1970s: huge quantities of pollutants filtered from the nation's air and water."[82]

The federal government is generally stricter with private industry than it is with its own operations. Weidenbaum gives many examples and says: "By conservative estimates, 25 percent of all federal facilities in the country failed to comply with regulations intended to develop and maintain clean water."[83] Moreover, it permits the export to foreign countries of radioactive materials and pesticides barred in this country, when it is obvious that air and water movement will bring much of the material back to the United States. A recent death "triggered a Congressional investigation into widespread complaints about job hazards in the Postal Service, which has one of the worst safety records in the Federal government. Its 645,000 employees sustained 36,510 job-related injuries" in 1979.[84] It is not held to the safety standards laid down by the OSHA. " 'If we were a private outfit, they'd close us down in a minute,' says William Quinn of the New England mail handlers' local."[85]

The Endangered Species Act requires environmental studies on the consequences of construction for the wildlife of the area. Sometimes vast undertakings

[80]See Armco Steel Corporation, *1975 Annual Report,* p. 3.
[81]Weidenbaum, p. 21.
[82]*Newsweek,* May 5, 1980, p. 82.
[83]Weidenbaum, p. 133.
[84]*Newsweek,* January 21, 1980, p. 41.
[85]Ibid.

are halted because the habitat of an obscure and worthless species seem to be threatened. The concern of environmentalists for all members of the animal kingdom is touching, but we do not have to be fanatics.

Private business is not opposed to the goals of the EPA and the legislators who make the laws. It can be argued, however, that many of the regulations are badly thought out, arbitrary, and unreasonable. Concerns for deadlines has created problems. *Can* automobile emission be reduced by 90 percent in five years? *Can* the air be made 25 percent cleaner by 1987?[86] *Can* the discharge into water of all pollutants be ended by 1983? The Water Pollution Act of 1972 set various stages of progress toward clean water, using such terms as "best practicable" and "best available" technology. The EPA explained what these terms mean:

> Congress intends "best practicable" to mean a level of control already achieved by the least-polluting plants in any given industry. Thus, if several chemical plants have achieved a high level of waste control, then every chemical plant in the country will be required to have a similar technology by 1977. . . . "Best available" technology goes one step further. If only one plant in a given industry has a highly advanced waste control system, then that becomes the best available standard for all plants in that industry.[87]

It is easy to see why industry so often challenges the EPA. "I feel that industry, more and more, is finally coming to the realization that if it's convinced that a particular set of standards is just completely erroneous and unachievable and that they have a strong technical and legal position, they ought to just stand pat and litigate some of these things."[88] So said Bernard M. Kostelnik, Environmental Affairs Officer of Anaconda Company. At the time, there were well over four hundred court cases pending between the EPA and private business.

The EPA, however, enjoys the support of the public—just as the other regulatory agencies do. They appear to "protect" the health and safety of consumers and people in general against the "selfish" interests of big business. People seem more concerned to increase controls than to cut back. Illinois already has effective legislation on disposal of chemical waste (EPA is satisfied), but the General Assembly got "carried away" just before the end of the session in 1980 and passed a rash of proposals that would (1) make it the duty of the state to clean up toxic chemical sites when those who had dumped the wastes could not be found, (2) change the criminal code to make "midnight hauling" a felony carrying a three-year sentence, (3) require land deeds to provide information about any waste

[86]The states of the high-polluting twenty-nine that do not set up inspection programs for the exhaust systems of cars are threatened by the EPA with loss of federal money for highways and sewage and air treatment. The motorist under such programs would have to pay for the inspections and the needed repairs. Deadlines have been set for the end of 1982 (for state-run programs) and 1981 (for licensed private programs).

[87]See Sturdivant, p. 302.

[88]Bernard M. Kostelnik, quoted in Sturdivant, p. 323.

buried there, and (4) ban the storage of certain radioactive material. The governor, a moderate in environmental matters, is in a dilemma, according to political writer Bill Lambrecht. He knows the legislation is misguided but does not want to affront the public.[89] The benefits of regulation are immediate and easily seen by the public; the costs are not.[90]

The Utilitarian Test The third (and best) argument against regulation is to question the utilitarian net gain that seems so obvious to its sponsors. If the moral justification for regulation is a utilitarian one—that is, it promotes the greatest interests of the greatest number—then it should be shown for each proposed regulation that its benefits will outweigh its harm. This usually is not done. Either the harm (or cost) is ignored completely, or it is discounted as simply a decrease in profit for unprincipled barons of industry. In July 1980, the EPA banned the spraying of the Lake of the Ozarks (a popular recreational area in Missouri) with light diesel oil. This had been done for forty years to kill mosquitoes, but the EPA claimed that the practice violated the Clean Water Act. The businesses of the region, facing loss of revenue, protested, pointing out that the amount of oil was tiny compared with that produced by outboard motors.

There is a suggestion in proregulation literature that the goods promoted—health, safety, and so on—are incommensurable with possible harm (or cost). That is, nothing could conceivably outweigh in value such things as protecting the environment and shielding people from deadly hazards. Factors that really *are* incommensurable with one another cannot, of course, be compared, for there is no common measure. But when there is, the utilitarian calculus is inapplicable and no appeal should be made to it. We do not, however, want to dispense with utilitarianism, for this is the best technique we have for determining public policy. We want to be able to assess a public measure in terms of *who* is affected by it, *how much* they are benefited, and *how much* they are harmed. Thus we will want to view the goods envisioned by regulators as of great value indeed, but not so great as to rule out the possibility of being outweighed by harms.

Arguments are often conducted in an emotional way. Proponents of regulation paint vivid pictures of all kinds of things that endanger our survival. We are in immediate peril. People are being contaminated by poison, the air is unfit to breathe, deleterious genetic changes are occurring, and so on. Placed in a state of fear, we ask, "What must we do to be saved?" In our panic, we are ready to accept any solution. Having just seen a picture of a river on fire, we demand that it be cleaned up—whatever the cost. The kind of sober and careful analysis that utilitarianism requires seems out of place when we imagine a "silent spring" or

[89]See *St. Louis Post-Dispatch,* July 6, 1980, p. 5B. He signed the bill in September 1980.

[90]That private industry can and does take some steps of its own is indicated by the action of Wes-Con, a private concern specializing in hazardous-waste disposal. It bought the underground silos in Idaho that formerly housed the Titan I missiles. These silos, under the nose of the government since 1975, are perfect for disposal.

ponder the half-life of Carbon 14. The people in the environs of Three Mile Island in 1980 reacted hysterically to the prospect of venting the krypton gas from the containment building—although scientists are agreed that the amount of radiation experienced by anyone in the two month process would be equivalent to less than one chest X-ray.

We do, somehow, make "cost-benefit" analyses of situations in ordinary life that involve gains and losses that cannot be weighed against one another so easily as different quantities of wheat. We believe that a chance to do well in the Great Falmouth Road Race is more valuable than a beer party the night before, that a contribution to the Cancer Society is more valuable than the purchase of a lottery ticket, that the creation of a beautiful poem is better than the production of soap bubbles, that saving two hours of traveling time is better than saving twenty dollars, that acquiring a true belief about a political candidate is better than reading the latest novel by Harold Robbins. We place not only abstractions like beauty and truth on the scales, but life itself. Although lives would be saved by reducing the expressway speed limit to forty miles per hour and banning transoceanic air travel, we do not demand that these things be done. Lives would be saved also by banning cigarettes, liquor, guns, and motorcycles, but do we really want to take this step?

There is also the factor of likelihood. We generally will accept the risk of a grave calamity if the likelihood of its occurring is low—even for a rather small gain. We will change a tire on the side of a busy highway rather than have the car towed in. We will eat a meal cooked by strangers, although they may be trying to poison us. We will board an elevator on the fortieth floor, although we see no safety-inspection sticker on the wall.

Some things we know are made available on the market at the price of lost health and lives. Yet we do not feel guilt when we buy coal, tuna, car batteries, or asbestos siding. We feel that accidents and disease are inseparable from life, and the fact that some people suffer in most occupations is outweighed by the good their products and services provide for others.

It is the failure to *apply* utilitarianism that permits regulators to increase their domain. Though they talk about results, they fail to view the *whole situation.* They focus on the evils that are avoided and ignore the greater ones that are produced. Nuclear power, for example, has certain hazards, but it is far cleaner than processes that rely on fossil fuels.

Let us look at some examples of problems in utilitarian thinking. A few years ago it cost about $200 million a year to reduce the percentage of sulfur in fuel burned in New York City from 0.6 to the 0.3 prescribed by government. Is the gain in respiratory health worth $200 million a year? Another way to put it is to ask whether this money could have been used more effectively for human goods.[91] A major corporation decides not to expand by building a new plant in

[91]See Michael Sterne, "Environmentalist Questions Priorities," *New York Times,* July 13, 1978. Weidenbaum, p. 64.

an area of unemployment. Reason: the cost of meeting all the environmental-impact requirements is prohibitive. Is the infinitesimal rise of effluent in the river more important than additional jobs for workers? Safety requirements on the manufacture of American cars inflate their price to the point where foreign imports can undersell them. Is the slightly safer level of American cars worth the rise in unemployment? A certain drug helps most sufferers of a particular disease, but is fatal to one patient in 50,000. Should it be made available (with proper warnings) despite the fact that some people will die? Air bags in cars will save lives. How many lives would have to be saved in order to justify the immense capital funds and consumer expenditures that mandatory air bags would entail? Several small paper companies will collapse if forced to meet waste disposal requirements. Which is more important, several stretches of pure water or a competitive situation in the paper industry?

As Almarin Phillips states, "Regulation is appropriate whenever the aggregate gain in social welfare from regulation exceeds the aggregate cost of regulation, with all side effects considered."[92] This is not always easy to ascertain. There is much that has to be anticipated and many comparisons to be made. But, as was argued above, the burden of proof lies with those who would regulate. They must show, not simply the good their proposals will do, but also that it will *exceed* the ills involved in all the other consequences. The Supreme Court did *not* believe that the OSHA had shown that the costs of its benzene regulations were matched by their social gains. A workplace need be only "reasonably safe"; it does not have to be "risk-free." That a species may be endangered does not in itself mean that a project that threatens it should be barred. That some fish die in a river is significant only if the value of those fish exceeds the cost of preventing the activity that kills them. It may be cheaper to find other sources of drinking water than to prevent a particular source from being polluted. Plastic containers may not be biodegradable, but how much would it cost to replace them?

Until the regulators are required to provide specific and responsible statements of the impact of *their* regulations, we will continue to see government regulating remain, as it has for the last ten years, among the fastest-growing "industries" in America. It is not sufficient to talk in the abstract about clean air, clean water, worker safety, consumer safety, and the like. We never had, and we never will have, perfection in these areas. If regulations are justified utilitarianistically, let the regulators show the utility of every regulation they would impose.[93]

[92]Almarin Phillips, "Regulation and Its Alternative," in *Regulating Business,* pp. 165–166.

[93]The applicability of utilitarianism to cost-benefit analysis has been challenged in an incisive article by Alastair MacIntyre: "Utilitarianism and Cost/Benefit Analysis: An Essay on the Relevance of Moral Philosophy to Bureaucratic Theory." The contention in this subsection, however, is that if the proregulation adherent can appeal to utilitarianism, the antiregulation adherent can also. While a perfect utilitarian analysis is impossible, some analyses are better than others. Tom L. Beauchamp criticizes MacIntyre in an article entitled "Utilitarianism and Cost/Benefit Analysis: A Reply to MacIntyre." Both articles are printed in Beauchamp and Bowie, *Ethical Theory and Business,* see pp. 266–276 and 276–282. Readers are urged to examine these articles and decide for themselves the appropriateness of utilitarianism in judging social issues.

Summary of the Issues

Most people agree that the government should regulate product safety and occupational safety and health, and control the impact of business and industry on the environment—all for the sake of the public good. There is, however, disagreement on the scope and strictness of this regulation.

One side emphasizes the gains that have already been made and the problems that remain to be solved. The campaign against hazardous products, improper working conditions, and the polluted environment must be vigilant and continuous. New products appear on the market; methods of production and waste disposal change. Unless the government strictly monitors business, the concern to increase profits will result in an ever-increasing number of practices that harm the general welfare.

The other side emphasizes the *cost* of regulation—both in administering it and complying with it. These costs are borne not only by business, but also by taxpayers and consumers. And the costs in terms of dollars are substantial. There is also a price to pay in the loss of freedom. These costs are not always compensated by the social gains that regulation is supposed to promote. Many regulations are useless, arbitrary, unreasonable, counterproductive, and just plain silly.

Both sides take utilitarianism as their standard. An indisputably legitimate function of government is to regulate private practices in the interests of the general population. Government is the means by which society can protect itself against those who for mercenary reasons would flood the market with unsafe products, employ workers in unhealthful jobs, and destroy the environment of all.

Those who are critical of contemporary regulative policies would replace rhetoric and emotional appeals with a more sober application of utilitarianism. Anticipated consequences of regulation (or nonregulation) should be weighed on the same scale as *commensurable* values. The *likelihood* of anticipated consequences must also be a factor. The question of *priorities* should also be dealt with—could the expenses incurred in eliminating *x* be better applied to eliminating *y* or promoting *z*? What is required for each proposed regulation is a comprehensive and long-range cost-benefit analysis. The proposed regulation should be imposed only if the anticipated aggregate gain in social welfare exceeds its aggregate cost in money, jobs, new products, and the standard of living. While many people who call for stricter regulation of business would accept these strictures in theory, they ignore them in practice.

The rejoinder of the proregulation people is that the complexities of cost-benefit analysis ofter permit private industry to delay or halt restrictive programs that are badly needed.

Discussion Questions

1. Do you think that it is realistic to expect *all* regulations to be worth their cost? Why?
2. How would you balance the benefits of nuclear power with its dangers?

3. Do you believe that the production of nuclear energy is regulated too tightly or not tightly enough? Explain.
4. Select an industry that you know something about. Do you think that the safety and health of its workers are underregulated or overregulated? Explain.
5. Do you resent the fact that you must pay for the seatbelts and catalytic converters in the cars you buy? Why?
6. Do you resent the fact that cyclamates have been taken off the market? Why? Was Congress right in preserving saccharin?
7. Do you believe that clean air and clean water are adequately protected by existing regulations? Why?
8. Are there any prima facie rights that should be taken into account to supplement the basic utilitarian approach assumed above?
9. In your opinion, would private industry have adequately policed itself if the extensive regulations of the seventies had not been imposed? Why?
10. What do you think of Ralph Nader?
11. Was your appraisal of Reagan in 1980 influenced by his views on deregulation? Explain.
12. Why, in your opinion, was Barry Commoner, an eminent environmentalist, almost ignored as a presidential candidate in 1980?
13. If this country is to err on the side of overregulation or underregulation, which would you choose? Why?
14. If the establishment of a paper-clip factory in El Paso would create 10,000 additional jobs but bring about the extinction of the blue-tailed titmouse, would you be in favor of it? Why? What if it cost five human lives in the construction process? Explain.
15. Do you have any solution for the problem of storing radioactive material? Explain.
16. Check with the weather bureau of your nearest big city on the air quality for the last two weeks. What is your reaction?
17. Are you distressed or pleased that medicinal drugs require much more time to be approved for use in the United States than in other countries? Why?
18. Having read many quotations from the writings of Murray Weidenbaum, are you distressed or pleased that President Reagan in 1981 appointed him chief economic adviser (chairman of the Council of Economic Advisers)? Explain.
19. Where would you place the burden of proof when regulation is being debated? On those who favor it or those who oppose it? Why?
20. Would you ban plastic containers? Why? Throw-away bottles? Why?
21. What kinds of recycling programs are you aware of in your area? What other kinds, in your opinion, would be feasible? Why?

For Further Reading

N. A. Ashford. "Worker Health and Safety: An Area of Conflicts." *Monthly Labor Review* 98 (September 1975).

Tom L. Beauchamp, ed. *Ethical Theory and Business.* Englewood Cliffs, N.J.: Prentice-Hall, 1979. Chapter 4.

Michael H. Brown. *Laying Waste: The Poisoning of American by Toxic Chemicals.* New York: Pantheon, 1980.

Thomas Donaldson and Patricia H. Werhane, eds. *Ethical Issues in Business: A Philosophical Approach.* Englewood Cliffs, N.J.: Prentice-Hall, 1979. Part 3.

Ned J. Greenwood and J. M. B. Edwards. *Human Environments and Natural Systems.* 2nd ed. North Scituate, Mass.: Duxbury Press, 1979.

Regulating Business: The Search for an Optimum. San Francisco: Institute for Contemporary Studies, 1978.

Peter H. Schuck. "Why Regulation Fails." *Harper's* 251 (September 1975).

Frederick D. Sturdivant. *Business and Society: A Managerial Approach.* Homewood, Ill.: Richard D. Irwin, 1977. Chapters 7, 12, and 13.

Murray L. Weidenbaum. *The Future of Business Regulation: Private Action and Public Demand.* New York: AMACOM, 1979.

Murray L. Weidenbaum. "The High Cost of Government Regulation." *Business Horizons* 18 (August 1975).

William B. Werther, Jr. "Government Control vs. Corporate Ingenuity." *Labor Law Journal* (June 1975).

Harrison A. Williams, Jr. "Legislation and Responsibility: The Occupational Safety and Health Act." *Journal of Current Social Issues* 12 (Spring 1975).

PUBLIC SECTOR STRIKES

Strikes in the Public Sector Are Wrong in Principle

All workers have the right to organize themselves and to bargain collectively with their employers on matters of mutual concern. As individuals they would not have much leverage against their employers. It was not believed a generation or so ago that federal, state, and local employees were entitled to the rights of collective bargaining granted to private sector employees by the National Labor Relations Act (Wagner Act) of 1935. Since 1935, however, the number of civilian government workers has grown steadily, and there are well over fifteen million of them today. Workers in the public sector are no longer simply spoils system appointees or do-gooders in public service; they are employees who, like their comrades in the private sector, have a legitimate interest in the conditions of their employment. Prevailing public opinion today recognizes their right to some kind of collective bargaining also.

Collective Bargaining: Federal Level On the federal level, recognition was officially granted through a series of executive orders and an act of Congress. In 1962, President Kennedy, in response to a report by a task force that had studied employee-management relations in the federal service, issued Executive Order 10988. This required federal employers to recognize union organizations and to bargain with them if they met the requirements for "exclusive" recognition. The order did not give unions all the rights protected in the private sector by the

Wagner and Taft-Hartley (1947) acts,[94] but it had taken an important step. While negotiation regarding the federal agency's mission and structure and affecting salaries and wages established by Congress was barred, there were many areas in which meaningful discussions could take place.[95] The order also provided a grievance procedure. Two other orders were issued the next year, establishing a "Code for Employee Organizations,"[96] and a "Code of Fair Labor Practices."[97] Executive Order 11491, issued by President Nixon, became effective in 1970. It established central machinery for making and interpreting labor policy and for dealing with appeals and disputes that could not be settled within the employing agency. "Since under the new order, as was true under the original order, federal employees [were] not permitted to strike, the system for final and binding arbitration [was] equitable and realistic."[98] The order also contained stipulations strengthening the negotiating process and ensuring bargaining in good faith. This order was amended by orders 11616, 11636, 11838, and 11901.

All these orders were replaced by Title VII of the Civil Service Reform Act of 1978, which in 1979 became the basic law governing labor relations between federal employees and employers. Although many of the provisions of the orders were repeated, the new law advanced the cause of collective bargaining a bit further. In the first place, this was a *statute,* not merely an executive order that could be easily changed or rescinded. In the second place, it set up the Federal Labor Relations Authority (FLRA) to replace the Federal Labor Relations Council. The FLRA is an independent agency consisting of full-time, nonpartisan members, who serve staggered terms and can only be removed for cause.[99] The FLRA is similar, then, to the National Labor Relations Board (which deals with the private sector) in its autonomy. "The major functions of the FLRA are to decide representation and unfair labor practices cases, negotiability disputes, appeals from arbitration awards, and to provide leadership in establishing policies and guidelines under the statute."[100] Third, the statute provides for judicial review and enforcement of the orders of the FLRA. Fourth, the law makes "profound changes . . . in the area of negotiated procedures. First, negotiated procedures, which must be included in all agreements negotiated in the Federal sector, will be *required* to provide for binding arbitration as the final step. Under the Executive Order, arbitration has been optional. Second, the negotiated grievance procedure must also provide for the settlement of "questions of arbitratability." No longer will these questions be referred to the Assistant Secretary of Labor. This one change should substantially speed up the resolution of grievabil-

[94]For example, federal employees could not be required to join a union as a condition of employment, and no union could advocate the right to strike.

[95]See Arthur A. Sloane and Fred Witney, *Labor Relations,* 2nd ed. (Englewood Cliffs, N.J.: Prentice-Hall, 1972), p. 513.

[96]Unions must observe democratic processes and be free of corruption.

[97]This extends additional private sector rights (but not that of striking) to public sector unions.

[98]Sloane and Witney, p. 519.

[99]The FLRC consisted of the chairman of the Civil Service Commission, the secretary of labor, and an official named from the president's Executive Office—all serving at the pleasure of the president.

[100]Frazier, "Labor Management Relations in the Federal Government," p. 132.

ity and arbitratability issues. Third, the scope of negotiated grievance procedures has been significantly broadened."[101]

Collective Bargaining Below the Federal Level In view of these elaborate provisions on the federal level, the rights of labor would seem to have been properly recognized. The situation on the state and local levels is not quite so favorable, although more and more states are recognizing the right of collective bargaining in some sense. Most states have some legislation mandating collective bargaining for public employees, but only sixteen have "comprehensive bargaining statutes patterned after the National Labor Relations Act." At one extreme is Virginia, the supreme court of which unanimously ruled in 1977 that "public employees could not enter into collective bargaining agreements with local governing bodies or school boards,"[102] and at the other extreme are eight states that permit a limited right to strike for some employees. Most of the states that do not mandate collective bargaining do have meet-and-confer statutes and/or permit union membership.

It is the contention here that collective bargaining is the right of all workers, and that is produces greater understanding between management and labor, settles many disputes in a peaceful and orderly way, and tends to avert ruinous strikes.[103] If this is so, the states in general have a way to go in their legislation. It is foolish to forbid strikes while failing to mandate equitable procedures to deal with labor problems. In 1970 the Twentieth Century Task Force on Labor Disputes in Public Employment stated: "The members of the Task Force are of firm opinion that inaction in developing and initiating basic policies for employee relations in any government unit is short-sighted at best. We believe that policies that will provide for the orderly participation of employees and their organization in matters affecting their welfare are essential in all areas of government and should be inaugurated where they do not now exist."[104]

Some people have recommended the passage of a congressional act that would apply to state and local workers—either a "National Public Employment Relations" act or the extension of the NLRA to state and local employees. This is not a sound strategy, for these reasons: (1) Both these measures would grant the right to strike to public employees, although the former could grant a limited right. (2) In view of the diversity of state institutions and interests, it would be better if each state formulated its own legislation guaranteeing unionization and good-faith collective bargaining. (3) A federal law would be an unconstitutional encroachment on states' rights. The U.S. Supreme Court, in the case of *National Cities et al.* v. *Usery* (1976), ruled that Congress could not impose the regulations of the Fair Labor Standards Act on states and their subdivisions. If the interstate commerce clause was an improper "peg" for this extension, it would certainly be

[101]Ibid., p. 136.
[102]Miller, "The National Labor Relations Act," p. 637.
[103]Many strikes are simply to obtain recognition!
[104]Twentieth Century Task Force on Labor Disputes in Public Employment, *Pickets at City Hall* (New York: Twentieth Century Fund, 1970), p. 2.

deemed improper for collective bargaining laws, which go more deeply into states' economic affairs.[105]

It is important that collective bargaining laws provide procedures to avert strikes arising from an impasse between bargaining parties. After all means (including mediation and fact-finding) have been tried in attempting to prevent an impasse, procedures must be available for dealing with it once it has arisen. Since in the public sector, "cessation of work has not been considered a viable public policy," means must be found to head it off.[106] *Arbitration* is one. Here a third party studies the issues and renders a *binding* decision. It is often somewhere between the last offers of the two parties. One problem with arbitration is that it sometimes tends to discourage good-faith bargaining. Neither party will offer much, because it wishes to preserve a lot of distance between the two offers when arbitration begins. The party will concede much less than it is prepared to accept. Another means is *"final offer" arbitration.* The arbitrator cannot compromise but must choose the last offer of one of the parties. Both parties make the best offer they can, one that is calculated to seem fair to an arbitrator. This gets around the problem of conventional arbitration and is becoming increasingly popular among the states. This procedure also has a problem: If both parties have indeed gone as far as they can, one of them will be faced with an unworkable "solution."[107]

Many observers are optimistic and believe that the states will rather quickly follow the good example set by the federal government in mandating procedures for effective collective bargaining and for dealing with impasses when bargaining has taken place. If this were already the case, it would be much easier to argue against the propriety of strikes. There would be no excuse whatever for a strike. But even so, the arguments against strikes by public employees are so strong, whether the laws are as they should be or not, that strikes must stand condemned.

The Public Interest In the first place, such a strike is a serious blow to the greatest interests of the greatest number. It is an act that produces dreadful harm to the public.

A postal workers' strike would bring business to a halt.[108] Social Security checks would not be delivered. The flow of commercial paper, as well as newspa-

[105]Bruce A. Miller suggests other constitutional pegs: The Fourteenth Amendment could be invoked, for public employees do not enjoy "equal protection of the laws." The taxing clause could be used to deny federal funds to all jurisdictions or institutions that do not have adequate collective bargaining procedures. See Miller, p. 640ff.

[106]Rynecki and Gausden, "Current Trends in Public Sector Impasse Resolution," p. 274.

[107]See ibid., pp. 273–276.

[108]The first nationwide strike of federal employees was that of the postal workers in 1970. It involved 150,000 employees and lasted about a week. "The walkouts prompted the passage of the Postal Reorganization Act of 1970, which established the Postal Service as an autonomous mail agency, prohibited strikes, and provided for compulsory arbitration." See Shannon, "Work Stoppage in Government," p. 14ff.

pers and magazines, would be stopped. A strike by armed services personnel would threaten the security of the nation. On the local level we have already seen the effects of many kinds of work stoppages. Transit workers have shut down a city's public transportation system, crippling its commerce and industry as workers try unsuccessfully to get to their places of business. Sanitation workers create unhealthy conditions for all when they strike. Schoolteachers at all levels interrupt the instruction of children when they walk off the job. Medical personnel (doctors, nurses, orderlies, technicians) threaten lives when they leave their stations in state and municipal hospitals and clinics. These people are all engaged in *essential* public services. Although they may have legitimate grievances, they are obligated to stay on the job while working for redress. It is because state legislatures believe this that none has accorded public employees the same right to strike that is accorded to employees in the private sector. Even where a right to strike is admitted, it is limited to so few people and such special circumstances that the legislation can generally be said to forbid strikes.[109] President Franklin D. Roosevelt rightly called public sector strikes "unthinkable."

No state permits strikes by employees whose job is to protect the public safety. Although police and firefighters' strikes have occurred, they are always illegal—and wrong. As Governor Calvin Coolidge said during the Boston police strike of 1919, "There is no right to strike against the public safety by anybody, anywhere, anytime." A strike by police places us back in the state of nature, and this condition is just as bad as Thomas Hobbes said it was. Boston almost immediately became a cauldron of violence and looting in 1919. In Montreal in 1969, people were afraid to go outside their homes, and thousands acquired weapons for self-protection.[110] As experience during police strikes has shown, it is not simply the lower classes or the criminal element that performs lawless acts, but middle-class and "respectable" people as well. The result of firefighters' strikes are almost as bad. Fires are untended, buildings burn down, and lives are lost. Arsonists (often strikers) have a field day.

But all this is to labor the obvious. Public employees exist in the first place because the public singled out certain services that it regarded as so vital to its interests that they could not be consigned to the contingencies of private enterprise. It instituted them because they were deemed essential, and retained control of them for the same reason. We may seek to assign degrees of "essentiality" to these services, but the degree would range from "essential" to "absolutely essential."

[109]Among the restrictions cited by the states are: It should pose no danger to the health, safety, or welfare of the community; mediation, fact-finding, and arbitration must first be tried; written notice must be given well in advance of the strike date. See Barrett and Lobel, "Public Sector Strikes—Legislative and Court Treatment," in Rowan, *Readings in Labor Economics and Labor Relations,* p. 333ff.

[110]For vivid descriptions of the Boston and Montreal experiences, see John F. Burton, Jr., and Charles Krider, "The Role and Consequences of Strikes by Public Employees," in Rowan, p. 329.

Are Public Workers Underpaid? Some defenders of public sector strikes emphasize the depressed economic plight of public employees. For example: "The growth of [public sector] unionism and rank-and-file militancy is attributable to a number of factors . . . but the main reasons spring from the fiscal crisis itself. State employees . . . increasingly are aware that they are subject to a gradual erosion of material standards because of budgetary priorities . . . the tax revolt, inflation, and state policies designed to restrain inflation."[111]

What *is* the plight of public employees? Professors Walter Fogel and David Lewin tried to answer the question. A summary of their findings is this:

> There is a growing body of evidence that government employment is attractive in terms of both wages and job security. A recent U.S. Bureau of Labor Statistics survey found that clerical, data processing, and manual workers employed by municipalities in 11 large urban areas were substantially better paid than their counterparts in private industry. In most cases, federal employees in the same cities were also paid more than comparable private sector workers. Fringe benefits in the public sector are also as good or better than those in the private sector, according to a national survey of U.S. municipalities. Futhermore, job hiring and tenure practices provide considerable security to public workers: In 1971, 57 percent of nonfarm private employees worked a full year, whereas in the public sector, the proportion was 77 percent. Attractive wages and salaries, steady demand for public services, and tenure practices all combine to produce low rates of employee turnover—19 percent in state and local government and 22 percent in the federal service in 1970, compared to 58 percent in private manufacturing.[112]

In addition to supplying evidence for these surprising findings, they also try to account for them. They offer five factors that tend to give an upward bias to wage determination in the public sector: (1) When government employers survey private sector wages for a comparable occupation, they only contact large firms (which tend to pay more than small firms). (2) Private industry will pay only as much as is necessary for unskilled and immobile workers, while government will pay a decent wage—and impose a shorter work week. (3) Government pays at least union wages ("prevailing wages") for workers in the various crafts, which usually are substantially higher than the average wage for those kinds of work. Moreover, it usually pays the higher "construction rate," whether the worker is engaged in construction or not. (4) The government tends to offer more fringe benefits and security than the comparable private employers, but it does not take this into account when comparing its wages with private wages. (5) The government pays too much for unique public sector positions, because it has nothing in the private sector to compare them with. So it compares one jurisdiction with another, thus creating "circular wage escalations," Or it compares one public occupation with another—for example, firefighters and sanitation workers with

[111]James O'Connor, *Fiscal Crisis of the State* (New York: St. Martin's Press, 1973), p. 238.
[112]Fogel and Lewin, "Wage Determination in the Public Sector," in Rowan, p. 337.

police—which results in overpayment for firefighters and sanitation workers. These factors, which are still at work today, have this general result: "Public sector wages tend to exceed those of the private sector for all occupations except high level managers and professionals."[113]

The Uniqueness of Public Employment Although public employees have many of the same problems, aspirations, and rights that private employees have, there are significant differences in the two kinds of employment and in the conditions under which they conduct their bargaining. In view of these differences, it is by no means arbitrary to deny the right to strike to the public worker while granting it to the private worker.

Professors Harry H. Wellington and Ralph K. Winter concede that three of the four arguments for collective bargaining in the private sector apply to such bargaining in the public sector also: the need for industrial peace, industrial democracy, and effective political representation. "Much less clearly analogous to the private model, however, is the unequal bargaining power argument."[114] If someone in the private sector charges "unfairness," he or she can appeal to economic factors in the market, but the charge in the public sector usually applies to political decisions. In view of the people's needs and desires, are they or are they not spending enough money on, say, teachers' salaries? Moreover, in the private sector, a raise in wages will produce a raise in price for the commodity and usually a reduction in sales (and eventual loss of jobs), but the demand for the products and services provided in the public sector is "relatively inelastic." The public employer that grants a pay raise must make a political decision to cut back the service in question (e.g., decrease the size of the police force), cut back some other service (e.g., sanitation), or seek an increase in taxes. A mayor, unlike a corporation head, seeks not to maximize or retain profits or stay in business, but to implement programs and get reelected or move to a better position. "What he gives to the union must be taken from some other interest group or from taxpayers. His is the job of coordinating these competing claims while remaining politically viable."[115] Nonmonetary issues also are more difficult matters in the public sector, for these may inspire politically powerful advocates—for example, how schoolchildren are to be disciplined or how police protection is to be assigned. In short, the market (economics) operates to control (positively or negatively) the concessions made to labor in the private sector, but in the public sector it is politics that prevails.

The pressures that public officials are subject to stems not only from direct loss of services, but also from the indirect consequences of works stoppages: The police strike in New Orleans at Mardi Gras time in 1979 cost business millions of dollars; the transit strike in Chicago (where the transit workers were already

[113]Ibid., p. 341.

[114]Harry H. Wellington and Ralph K. Winter, "The Limits of Collective Bargaining in Public Employment," in Rowan, p. 312.

[115]Ibid., p. 315.

the highest paid in the nation) in December 1979 cost downtown merchants an estimated $15 million a day; the transit strike in New York in 1980 cost the city millions in tax revenues. There are many other financial costs to both private and public interests when services are disrupted. Though these indirect effects are economic, they have to be dealt with in a political context.

If public sector bargaining is viewed as primarily political rather than economic, is this not consistent with the "normal American political process" of trying to respond to and recognize various political pressures? If the right to strike is part of the collective bargaining process, the answer must be no. The strike exerts *extraordinary* pressure on officials; the union possesses a *disproportionate* share of political power. The strike (or threat thereof) will induce officials, not limited by the market forces, to "press for a quick end to the strike with little concern for the cost of settlement."[116] Strikes are simply too effective. To transplant the right to strike from the private to the public sector would "institutionalize the power of public employee unions in a way that would leave competing groups in the political process at a permanent and substantial disadvantage."[117] The public simply does not want to be deprived of essential services, and its officials, not subjected to the need to make a profit, "cave in" to their constituencies.[118]

A strike not only distorts the normal political process but is an attack against the government and the will of the people it is supposed to reflect. It challenges the ultimate authority of the people and their sovereignty. It flouts the will of the majority that has made the decisions and approved the budget. "Organized labor threatens the orderly, legal, representative process by introducing demands on the budget which are not a part" of the intention of the people who created it.[119]

There are certain other peculiarities in public employment that strike adherents often ignore. In the private sector, management can consider its assets, profit margin, and competition and decide whether it can accept a proposed settlement. Herbert Lahne says, "The union wants to meet with someone who says 'I will' or 'I won't,' rather than 'I can't.'"[120] This is usually not the case when talking to a mayor, a school board, or a board of regents. Local budgets are uncertain and fluctuating things. Can money be found? Does the budget have to be balanced? Can taxes be raised? What will the tax receipts be? What will be the effects of inflation? Can a "supplementary budget" be passed?[121] The Board of Regents of the University of California agreed to faculty raises of seven percent for 1970–1971; the governor agreed to 5 percent. But the legislature voted zero. The

[116]Ibid., p. 317.
[117]Ibid., p. 319.
[118]The weakness of public officials and their concern with short-run consequences (political and economic) are exemplified in the bankruptcy of the City of New York.
[119]Choi, "Collective Bargaining in the Public Sector," p. 226.
[120]Quoted in Alan Balfour, "Appropriate Bargaining Units for State Employment," *State Government* (Autumn 1976), p. 213.
[121]See Kearney, "Municipal Budgeting and Collective Bargaining," p. 108ff.

state court of appeals upheld the legislature.[122] More recently the teachers and the board of regents in Florida agreed on an 8.85 percent raise. When the legislature only supplied 7.1 percent, the teachers insisted that the board make up the difference from other lines of the budget. In the case of *United Faculty of Florida etc.* v. *Board of Regents* (1979), the district court of appeals stated: "That statute [which reserves the right of the legislature to provide less than the amount requested to fund a collective bargaining agreement] operates to make all collective bargaining agreements subject to the approval, through the medium of appropriations, of the legislative body. That the Legislature might not provide full funding for the collective bargaining agreement was a contingency well known to the parties before, during, and after negotiations."[123] In view of these political realities, it is unreasonable for unions to charge employers with "bad-faith" bargaining when they cannot get a certain answer and to strike in reprisal.

Remedies For the sake of its safety, health, and welfare, as well as to protect the integrity of its democratic institutions, society must adopt a strong stance against strikes by its employees. If collective bargaining with mediation and fact-finding does not work and if the union does not accept some form of binding arbitration, the government should avail itself of legal remedies to prevent the strike or end it. The most effective remedy is the court injunction. If the court injunction does not bring the strikers back to their jobs, the strikers can be found in contempt of court and fined and/or jailed.

The Norris-LaGuardia Act (1932) established federal restrictions on the use of court injunctions in private labor disputes, but it does not apply to federal employees.[124] This was clearly established by the U.S. Supreme Court in the case of *United States* v. *United Mine Workers* (1974). Nor do the "little" Norris-LaGuardia acts in the states extend beyond the private sector. The California Supreme Court so ruled in *City and County of San Francisco* v. *San Francisco Building and Trade Council* (1977). The court stated that injunctions do not violate the First Amendment and "reiterated that an illegal strike did not carry with it constitutionally protected activities."[125] A few years before, the Illinois Supreme Court had held that the state's anti-injunction statute did not apply when the public health, safety, and welfare were threatened.[126]

The Taylor Law (1967) of the State of New York is an excellent piece of legislation. It *requires* injunctions to stop or prevent strikes in the public sector. The public employer does not have to prove to the court that the work stoppage

[122] *California State Employees Association* v. *Flourney* (1973).

[123] See Henkel, "Collective Bargaining in Higher Education," p. 353ff.

[124] Even in the private sector, the Norris-LaGuardia Act does not categorically forbid injunctions in all cases. The U.S. Supreme Court declared in *Boys Market, Inc.,* v. *Retail Clerks Union* (1970) that where a union has violated the arbitration and no-strike provisions of its contract, injunctions against it can be issued.

[125] See Douglas, "Injunctive Relief in Public Sector Work Stoppages," p. 409.

[126] See *City of Pana* v. *Harold Crowe* (1974).

is illegal or demonstrate that it threatens the public health, safety, or welfare. In answer to the charge that the act violates the "involuntary servitude" provisions of the Thirteenth Amendment, its defenders can point out that the employees know that strikes are illegal in New York and if they don't like to work in such a situation, they don't have to. The Appellate Court of New York, in upholding the law in the case of *Yorktown Central School District No. 2* v. *Yorktown Congress of Teachers* (1973), stated: "In conclusion, the court approached the issue of 'right versus wrong in a free society.' The Taylor Law, rightly or wrongly, represents the public policy of this State. Its object is to prescribe such as that herein. . . . So long as it is the law, no individual or group of individuals, no matter how well motivated, may, by breaking the law and thereafter willfully disobeying a court order to comply with it, complain if he or they are compelled to suffer the sanctions which in advance of their defense they knew the law provided." A few years before, the New York Court of Appeals, in ruling that the denial of "little" Norris-LaGuardia rights to public employees was not unconstitutional, recognized the legitimacy of seeking to bring a quick end to strikes in the public sector: "Prompt determination unencumbered by the long, drawnout procedures involved in jury trials are needed in criminal contempt proceedings under the Taylor Law in order to deter the continuance of paralyzing public strikes by visiting speedy punishment on the offenders. It is not unreasonable to assume that the Legislature, which prohibited strikes by public employees, would provide every reasonable means for enforcement of that prohibition by giving the courts the powers necessary to bring about their early termination."[127]

There were 136 injunctions issued under the law, through 1978, and dozens of contempt citations. Fines have been in the hundreds of thousands of dollars, and stiff jail terms have been handed out.[128] With this powerful weapon available, mayors and other officials in New York are guilty of "playing politics" in the lowest sense when they accept a quick and expensive settlement in labor disputes.[129]

Another weapon available for use against illegal strikers is to discharge them. In *Hortonville School District* v. *Hortonville Education Association* (1976), the U.S. Supreme Court ruled that school boards could discharge and otherwise discipline teachers who struck during a collective bargaining dispute in violation of state law. Police have been fired in Baltimore and New Orleans and firefighters in Kansas City.

[127]See *Rankin* v. *Shanker* (1968).

[128]For an illuminating discussion of the Taylor Law, see Douglas, pp. 340–352.

[129]During the transit strike in New York City (April 1980), unions and union members were fined about $36 million. The strike lasted a little more than a week. See Andy Logan, "Around City Hall: Settling," *New Yorker*, April 28, 1980, p. 121. That the New York police, firefighters, and sanitation workers accepted the package offered in July 1980 instead of striking was determined largely by fear of losses under the Taylor Law.

Conclusion The fact is that unions harm their own cause by striking. They arouse the indignation of the public, which feels that it already bears too heavy a tax burden and that tactics of extortion are being used. The trend toward effective collective bargaining legislation in the states may well be deterred by the propensity of public sector employees to strike. If the right to strike seems to be linked to the right to bargain collectively, the public may well bar the latter in order to prevent the former. This would indeed be unfortunate, for public employees have the same rights to associate, organize, and work for gains that private employees have. They, too, want to bargain for more money and better conditions, and they want to participate in management decisions and be treated with dignity. In both sectors, collective bargaining tends to foster cooperation and avoid impasses. But the peculiarities of public employment, as explained above, disqualify the public employee from striking.

Strikes in the Public Sector Are Not Wrong in Principle

Catastrophe or Inconvenience? There can be no discounting the inconvenience to the public produced by public sector strikes. Many of them go beyond inconvenience and are disruptive and catastrophic. That is why the strike is such an effective weapon in labor disputes. But in this respect, strikes are often no more calamitous to the public than are many private sector strikes. A strike by a teacher union in Peoria is no more destructive to the public interest than a strike by the nation's steelworkers or airline pilots. Even a nationwide teachers' strike would be as endurable as a strike by the nation's meatpackers. The Taft-Hartley Act (1947), whatever its imperfections, provides the federal government with means to deal with private sector strikes that constitute a national emergency. When a strike is judged to imperil the "national health or safety," certain settlement procedures are prescribed. Analogous procedures could be prescribed for public sector strikes when it has been duly established that they are truly catastrophic and not merely inconvenient. The point is simply that strikes in *both* areas *may* be catastrophic, in which case extraordinary procedures can be resorted to. But just as strikes are not regarded as wrong *in principle* in the private sector, they should not be regarded as wrong in principle when they occur in the public sector.

The resourcefulness of the American people has made it possible to endure strikes that would at first glance have appeared disabling. During sanitation workers' strikes, Americans have hauled their own refuse to disposal areas. During transportation strikes, they have formed car pools, donned roller skates, or walked. The employers have also demonstrated resourcefulness in maintaining essential services through the use of supervisory personnel and agencies (public and private) outside their jurisdiction. It would be difficult to show that lives were lost by such public sector strikes in the health area as the nursing home strike in New York City (1976), the strike by interns and residents in the public hospitals of New York City (1978), or the physicians' strike in Los Angeles County (1976).[130] Montana has a curious law that permits nurses to strike provided there is no other health care facility strike within 150 miles! Municipalities may even deal with strikes by firefighters and police (which are illegal in all states). In the case of the former, they may rely heavily on supervisory personnel, contract with neighboring fire units ("mutual assistance pacts"), press police officers into duty, and/or activate volunteer units.[131] In the case of the police strikes, municipalities again can rely on supervisory personnel. They can also call in the National Guard or hire private security personnel. It would be helpful if certain rules were in force: (1) Supervisory personnel (say, sergeants and above on police forces) cannot be members of the same union as the "workers."[132] (2) Contracts for firefighters and police do not end at the same time.[133] Advance notice (say, twenty days) of a strike must be given.[134]

In view of their resources, officials do not have to "cave in" to the demands of strikers. They resisted the firefighters in Dayton. They did not resort to binding arbitration, for the settlement might have been more than the city could afford to pay. They did not invoke the tough laws of Ohio (e.g., automatically firing all strikers), but utilized their local ordinances instead—which left open the possibility of amnesty and did not require that injunctions be issued. They did not request the presence of the National Guard, for that would have seemed to be an "anti-union" act, as well as an admission that they could not manage their own affairs.[135] The city of Palo Alto successfully waited out a strike of all city employees except those in public safety and management in 1975. About 450 people walked off the job. "During the 23-day strike, management and part-time employees operated all essential city services (including water, gas, and electric utilities, a sub-regional water quality control plant, and a centralized communications system) without interruption. In addition, many non-essential services such as recreation and library were provided on a curtailed basis. The net savings to the city during this period was $85,000."[136] In the same year, the city of Berkeley survived a twenty-five-day strike of firefighters. It did not surrender to the device of binding arbitration, call for injunctions, or dismiss anyone. The city manager

[130]See Samuel Wolfe, "Strikes by Health Workers: A Look at the Concept, Ethics, and Impacts," *American Journal of Public Health* (May 1979), p. 431ff.

[131]See Perry Moore, "Lessons from the Dayton Firefighters Strike," p. 33ff.

[132]A police union was advised by a labor attorney: "So, don't overlook any facet of the police department. Remember, the fewer members in your bargaining unit, the more officers there are available to do your work if you should choose to strike." See Richard M. Ayres, "Police Strikes: Are We Treating the Symptoms Rather Than the Problem?" *Public Management* (April 1977), p. 13.

[133]This is well within the control of the locality.

[134]Some of the handful of states that have recognized the limited right of strike require written notice, ranging from ten to thirty days. See Barrett and Lobel, "Public Sector Strikes—Legislative and Court Treatment," in Rowan, pp. 333–335.

[135]See Moore, p. 33ff.

[136]Sipel, "Breaking Barriers," p. 4.

declared: "The city can come out the winner in a settlement."[137] The city of Kansas City survived a firefighters' strike in 1975 with the aid of police personnel, citizen volunteers, and National Guard troops. Chicago had its first firefighters' strike in February 1980, and after seventeen days had survived without a major disaster. The city asked for recruits, signing up 677 at $16,524, and relied on supervisory personnel and sanitation workers. In cases like these, public opinion can grow in support of management. Public support for the police strike in New Orleans in 1979 dropped from 67 percent to 17 percent in two weeks.[138] Inconveniences will be endured with some grace, for management is, it would seem, saving the public from additional tax burdens.

The teachers' strike in Levittown, Long Island, finally ended late in the fall of 1978 after a loss of thirty-four school days. The taxpayers, many of whom had to pay property taxes of more than $200 a month for their modest homes, resisted stubbornly, and the gains of the teachers were very small. They were to get no raises for a year and a half, and could look forward to only 5 percent in each of the following two years. Mayor Edward Koch of New York City professed to have wanted to hold out in the transit workers' strike in 1980, which shut down the city's subways and most of its buses for eleven days. He criticized his predecessors (Lindsay and Beame) for having capitulated to union demands. But since a state agency (the Metropolitan Transportation Authority) now runs the city's transit system, it was Governor Hugh Carey who had the authority to make the settlement. Koch told reporters, "We were coming back to life in this city. Then the M.T.A. folded." He stated, "The city won the battle in the streets. The Metropolitan Transportation Authority lost it at the bargaining table." The *New York Times* headline said, "On the Strike's Last Day, Difficulties Were Not Dire."[139] When the police in Memphis struck in the summer of 1978, the city held out for only eight days before meeting most of the strikers' demands—although there had been little lawlessness. Workers who had been fired were reinstated without penalty.

The point here is not to show that management is right and the strikers wrong. It is simply to show that the public is not utterly helpless against public sector strikes. It has its resources. Even strikes by public safety personnel do not automatically result in a "defeat" of the public.

Motives The motives of public sector strikers are often maligned. It is true that they often seek higher pay, better working conditions, and fringe benefits. But surely this is a motive anyone can understand and sympathize with. Are their

[137]Taylor, "Fire Fighters Strike," p. 6.
[138]See *Time,* March 5, 1979, p. 18.
[139]See Logan, pp. 102–122. Koch himself was accused of "caving in" a few months later when he settled with the police, firefighters, and sanitation workers in order to avert a strike. The benefits were greater than those won by "civilian" workers two weeks before. Base pay went to $21,832 for 1980–1981 (for police and firemen) and to $23,518 in 1981–1982. "Sanitmen" are not far behind. The $1 billion budget gap continues to widen.

demands excessive? Obviously no comprehensive answer can be given, but certain observations may be made.

In the first place, the willingness of government (on the state and local levels especially) to keep pace with double-digit inflation by offering appropriate wage hikes is certainly no greater than that of private industry. The call nowadays is usually for a "cost of living" raise. If the annual inflation rate is 14 percent, and private workers get around 10 percent, how does the public employee feel who is grudgingly offered 3 percent? "We went through an era in the early 1970s when public wages caught up with the private sector, even exceeding them in some places. Now, the public sector is lagging again."[140] Even in 1970 when the postal workers' strike occurred, the top pay for a letter carrier with twenty-one years of service was $8,442. According to the Bureau of Labor Statistics, a family of four in New York City (where the strike began) required $11,236 for a moderate standard of living in 1970.[141] "Union leaders view the strikes as a national consequence of the economic squeeze on public workers caused by inflation and a revolt by citizens against high taxes. 'We're going to see more of these strikes,' says W. Howard McClennan, president of both the International Association of Fire Fighters and the AFL-CIO public-employee department. 'We are tired of being made the scapegoat of the plight of the cities.' "[142]

In the second place, certain kinds of public employment are hazardous (e.g., police and firefighting) and merit special consideration. When the police went on strike in New Orleans late in the winter of 1979, the base pay for patrolmen was $11,964.[143]

In the third place, salaries for professional and managerial workers are (and have been for a long time) far less than for comparable workers in the private sector. In federal employment nearly all professional classifications above GS 12 provide salaries averaging less than those paid in comparable private employment.[144] In 1972, "the highest pay schedule in government, that for the federal executive branch, contained salaries ranging from $36,000 to $60,000—well below the $144,000 median salary then paid to the chief executive officers of America's 774 highest paying corporations."[145] A study in 1974 of 100 government jobs in Los Angeles showed that all sixteen of the top positions had salaries less than 90 percent of comparable private sector positions.[146] Salaries for chief administrative officers in American cities are incredibly low. Since this is usually the top salary, compression takes place throughout the municipal structure. In 1980, the highest salary permitted for any employee in the city of St. Louis was $25,000.

[140]Roger E. Dahl, labor relations expert for the U.S. Conference of Mayors, quoted in *U.S. News & World Report,* March 17, 1980, p. 73.
[141]See Shannon, p. 15.
[142]*U.S. News & World Report,* August 7, 1978, p. 65.
[143]*Time,* March 5, 1979, p. 18.
[144]See Fogel and Lewin, pp. 350–351.
[145]Ibid., p. 350.
[146]See ibid.

This applies to the mayor, comptroller, building commissioner, hospital administrator, physicians, and everyone else.

Social workers and schoolteachers are in a class by themselves. Although it is difficult to find a comparable occupation for social workers, it is nevertheless true that their salaries are far lower than those of people with similar college degrees and experience in the business world. Although the salaries of public school teachers generally compare favorably with their counterparts in the private sector, they range far lower than those of nonteachers with similar degrees in the private sector. In both sectors, teachers' degrees and experience are inadequately rewarded. The discrepancy between supply and demand in these professions is surely a factor accounting for the low salaries, but social workers and schoolteachers should not be criticized for seeking professional salaries for professional work.

Public workers no longer have an advantage over private workers in such fringe benefits as pensions. They are playing "catch-up." Nor do they have a great advantage in security. "Policemen are laid off. Firefighters are laid off. They've cut back on city employees, schoolteachers and sanitation workers."[147] It is difficult not to sympathize with the striking Chicago schoolteachers who "took their action only after enduring four delayed paydays, including a payless Christmas recess."[148]

Public employees bargain and strike for aims that go beyond their own financial advantage. Teachers may strike for better schools, smaller classrooms, safer buses, and modern classroom equipment. They often awaken the public to important needs and win its support. "During the Bridgeport strike hundreds of parents and students bused forty miles to demonstrate outside the gates of the temporary concentration camp for striking teachers."[149] Two hundred and sixty teachers had been arrested. The strike in New York City by the young doctors in 1978 was for the purpose of improving care in the municipal hospitals (which were in bad shape). At least one of the aims of the sanitation workers' strike in Memphis at the time of the King assassination in 1968 was to end racial discrimination in job assignments.

Genuine Collective Bargaining President Kennedy's Executive Order 10988 (1962) "reversed the philosophical view that unionism in the public sector was inconsistent with governmental sovereignty."[150] Many states have not yet come around to the view that public employees have the right to form a union, to have that union recognized, and to engage in collective bargaining. Meet-and-confer laws are not even a poor substitute. In 1980, nineteen states did not provide for collective bargaining by faculty in higher education, and none of those that did

[147] W. Howard McClennan, "Let Public Workers Strike?" *U.S. News & World Report,* September 25, 1978, p. 81.

[148] See *Time,* February 11, 1980, p. 53.

[149] Thompson, "More on 'The Promise of Public-service Unionism,' " p. 55.

[150] Moschos, "Management in Police Labor Relations," p. 9.

required its legislature to come up with the money to finance the "settlement." Some states recognize unions, but do not permit them to bargain![151] It is difficult to call all strikes wrong when many are simply for the purpose of getting recognition of a union as a bargaining agent. Some union leaders are willing to *give up* the right of police and firefighters to strike, *provided* that their right to bargain is recognized and that impasses be settled by binding arbitration![152] This is generally opposed by public employers. Thomas E. Huebner, city manager of San Antonio, said: "Binding arbitration places the responsibility for making critical decisions in the hands of someone other than an elected public official. It perverts the form of government that this country has had for over 200 years."[153]

But we must go further and ask whether *genuine* collective bargaining can be said to exist when the possibility of a strike is ruled out. The answer is no. As long ago as 1966 the American Federation of State, County and Municipal Employees stated:

> AFSCME insists upon the right of public employees . . . to strike. To forestall this right is to handicap free collective bargaining process. Wherever legal barriers to the exercise of this right exist, it shall be our policy to seek the removal of such barriers. Where one party at the bargaining table possesses all the power and authority, the bargaining becomes no more than formalized petitioning.[154]

The employer may request binding arbitration, but it may be to the union's interest to decline. The union may request binding arbitration, but it may be to the employer's interest to decline. As Theodore W. Kheel, a respected labor arbitrator, said, "Collective bargaining cannot exist if employees may not withdraw their services or employers discontinue them."[155]

The union often has no legal recourse when an impasse is reached except to accept the latest offer or resort to such tactics as "blue flu" or slowdowns. When the employer bargains in bad faith or is not backed by the body that supplies the funds, the union is helpless. The police in Albuquerque refrained from striking in 1973, then found that striking firefighters and blue-collar workers got better contracts than they did. It was understood that the discrepancy would be eliminated in a later contract. But when it was not, they struck in 1975. The police in Oklahoma City had been negotiating for a raise. The city asked for advisory

[151]In *Vorbeck* v. *McNeal* (1976), the U.S. Supreme Court ruled that it is unconstitutional to prohibit union membership by police, but not to exclude them from the state's public employee bargaining laws!

[152]W. Howard McClennan is an example. See *U.S. News & World Report,* August 7, 1978, p. 66.

[153]See *U.S. News & World Report,* September 25, 1978, p. 82.

[154]International Executive Board AFSCME, *Policy Statement on Public Employee Unions;* Rights and Responsibilities 2 (July 26, 1966). See Rowan, p. 329.

[155]Quoted in Burton and Krider, p. 323.

arbitration. The arbitrator recommended a 10 percent across-the-board raise. When the city council unanimously voted for 7.5 percent, the police struck (1975).[156] Who can blame them? What else could they have done?

Neither labor nor management wants a strike—it is costly for both parties. But the blame for not reaching a settlement may fall on either side (or both). Where is the justice in preserving the status quo when it is desired by only one party? If management and labor "agree to disagree," the bond between them is broken. Management loses the services of labor, and labor loses the wages from management. A strike is the public acknowledgment that the two parties can no longer work together. Collective bargaining must be conducted in the realization that this may be the outcome and that concessions must be made by both parties to avert it. Without the possibility of a strike, management holds the trump card: relations will be preserved on its own terms. Bargaining by the union consists simply in appealing to the good will and sense of fairness of management. The right to strike does *not* give the trump card to labor, for it will be hurt by a work stoppage also. It does, however, ensure that both parties will be faced with some very unpleasant consequences if a settlement is not reached.

Professors Burton and Krider refute the contention that in the public sector, unlike the private, there are no market restraints. First, and most obvious, is the fact that wages lost during a strike are felt by employees. Second, the public will be concerned about rising taxes. Third, the prices the public pays for such services as water, sewage, and sanitation may be raised. And fourth, there is always the possibility of the government's subcontracting services to the private sector (sanitation, transportation, postal service, for example). These are all economic constraints that must be taken into account when the union considers the wisdom of going on strike.[157] To these we can add the possibility of fines for unions and officials. The striking teachers in Levittown, for example, were fined two days' pay for every day on strike, with an average loss per teacher of $5,000.[158]

"Democratic Processes" This brings us to the most serious argument against the right of public employees to strike: that it usurps the decision-making power properly possessed by elected officials, that it distorts the democratic processes. As has been argued above, the public authority is not helpless. States and cities have survived strikes and have resisted the demands of strikers. The officials who back down and make ruinous concessions are acting in a way they believe is politic, but the voters who retain them in office are short-sighted or stupid. Very few strikes seriously threaten the public health, safety, or welfare; and when they do (usually because of the absence of contingency plans), there are legal remedies available.

[156]See Ayres, p. 10ff.
[157]See Burton and Krider, p. 325.
[158]See *Time,* November 27, 1978, p. 9.

A political unit must decide the kinds of public services it desires, their nature and scope, and how much it is willing to pay for them. A city might decide that it can get along with badly trained police and a few broken-down fire trucks. A state might decide that its complement of social workers can be halved and that it will not compete with other states for well-qualified professors. The federal government may be content with inefficient bureaucrats and slow mail delivery. All units must set their aims and fix their priorities—theoretically, at least, in response to the will of the voters. They are assisted in this by the demands of their own employees. Officials are indeed subjected to a great many pressures, and some of them are strong. But they have the final say (subject to the indirect approval of their constituencies), and are responsible for the decisions made. When unions succeed, they have merely been a factor in increasing and/or redistributing public expenditures. This may or may not benefit the consumers of the services affected. One of the realities of political life is the need to deal with competing claims in ways that best serve the public welfare. Harry Truman made a remark on this point that has become famous.[159]

There is really no point in trying to distinguish "pure" political pressure (which is supposed to be all right) from economic, or "impure," political pressure (which is supposed to be wrongly exerted by unions). If only the former were countenanced, then most lobbying and petitioning would have to be barred along with strikes. The conduct in big cities of craft unions that allied themselves "politically" with the dominant "in" political groups and eschewed the strike (e.g., in Chicago under Mayor Daley) was really not so "pure." And it was much less open and manageable than collective bargaining (with the possibility of strikes) would have been. As Burton and Krider argue, this sort of thing subverts the "normal" American process of decision making just as clearly as do strikes.[160] So we come back to our position that pressures—of all kinds—are constants in political life. The public authority may react to them more or less well.

Union demands are not always sound and strikes are not always justified, but public employee unions are often the whipping boys for errors and shortcomings in other areas: the belief that a proposed strike would be devastating, the opportunism of political leaders, the inefficiencies of administrators, the short-sightedness of budget preparers, the misplaced values of taxpayers, the fear of the people that they may be inconvenienced, and the wastefulness, greed, and corruption of "public servants." When a governmental unit faces a collective bargaining crisis, it is too easy to point the finger at the union, when the union is, at most, only one part of the problem. As far as public opinion is concerned, the union is often in a "no win" situation. If it succeeds in achieving its demands, it has cost the taxpayer money. If it does not succeed and goes on strike, it is disrupting society.

[159]"If you can't stand the heat, stay out of the kitchen."

[160]See Burton and Krider, p. 328.

Injunctions As public indignation builds, the cry goes out, "Seek an injunction!" We will conclude this essay with a discussion of the role of injunctions in labor disputes.

Just as public sector strikes should not be condemned in principle, so too should the resort to injunctions not be condemned in principle. The Taylor Law of the State of New York does the former—for all strikes—and calls for automatic injunctions. This is unique. Most states ban strikes but do not mandate seeking injunctions. A few states outlaw strikes only in the areas of safety and health. The position of Theodore Kheel on this issue recommends itself: the right to strike cannot be determined in advance of the strike itself. Procedures for ending strikes should be exercised *only after* it has been demonstrated that public safety and health have been seriously endangered. The injunction is a legitimate means for protecting the public when a strike has been shown to be destructive.[161]

But it should not be employed indiscriminately—as some would do for all public sector strikes and many would do for strikes of safety and health personnel. There have been some instructive court cases in recent years that confirm the proposition that injunctive relief is in order only in cases of real emergency: (1) *School District for the City of Holland* v. *Holland Education Association* (1968). Even though the strike was against state law, the Michigan Supreme Court overruled a lower court that has issued an injunction against the teachers, declaring that an injunction could not be issued without "a showing of violence, irreparable injury, or breach of the peace." (2) *School Committee of the Town of Westerley* v. *Westerley Teachers Association* (1973). Rhode Island has a no-strike law, but its supreme court ruled that it is not so that "every time there is a concerted work stoppage by public employees, it should be subject to an automatic restraining order." (3) *Armstrong Education Association* v. *Armstrong School District* (1972). Pennsylvania has a limited right-to-strike law and limits injunctive relief to cases "where the court finds that the strike constitutes a clear and present danger or threat to the health, safety, or welfare of the public."[162] The Commonwealth Court of Pennsylvania quashed the injunction of a lower court because the grounds offered for it (disruption, harassment, and possible loss of state subsidies) were insufficient. (4) *Timberlane Regional School District* v. *Timberlane Regional Education Association* (1974). The Rockingham County Superior Court has denied an injunction, holding that collective bargaining implies the right to strike! The Supreme Court of New Hampshire upheld the decision and declared: "The injunction is an extraordinary remedy which is only granted under circumstances where a plaintiff has no adequate remedy at law and is likely to suffer irreparable harm unless the conduct of the defendant is enjoined."[163]

[161]See Theodore W. Kneel, "Resolving Deadlocks without Banning Strikes," *Monthly Labor Review*, July 1969, pp. 62–63.

[162]Douglas, p. 409. This whole paragraph is indebted to Douglas's excellent essay.

[163]Some of these cases are also discussed in Barrett and Lobel, pp. 335–336.

Sometimes the injunction is not used when it should be, because it seems to have adverse political consequences. Sometimes it is not used because it would expose the government's lack of good-faith bargaining before the strike. Sometimes it is not used because to do so would make a settlement more difficult.[164] The effectiveness of the injunction is a matter of some controversy. Joel Douglas writes: "The prevalent practice of enjoining most work stoppages contributes very little to meaningful labor relations. The widespread disregard of injunctions, the inconsistent use of contempt of court citations, and the jailing of union leaders have not served to prevent work stoppages in government."[165] Others, however, see it as a panacea. Perhaps if it were used with discrimination and carried stiff penalties for disobedience, it would be more effective in stopping strikes in those cases where the public interest requires that they be stopped. In any case, it provides the best solution yet devised for those of us who are opposed to barring strikes in principle yet have some concern for public safety and health.

Conclusion If we view collective bargaining as a right possessed by private sector employees, we must recognize it also for public sector employees. Both groups view the strike as a fundamental adjunct of collective bargaining. Both operate under constraints. The "political" act of the public employees is constrained by economic factors in society, and the "economic" act of private employees is constrained by political factors in society. The liberty of both groups is limited by the deeper concern of the public. The private employee is limited by the procedures stipulated by the Taft-Hartley Act in cases of national emergency. The public employee is limited by the injunction remedy when public safety or health is threatened. Those who would invoke Mill's "harm principle" against strikers must be prepared to show that the harm they produce is of sufficient scope and severity to limit their right to act collectively for their own interests.

There were 413 public employee strikes in 1977, compared with fewer than 50 a year before 1966. The year 1980, at midpoint, seemed sure to break the record of 2.5 million lost workdays. There are many more to come. Most municipal strikes occur after June 30, for that is when many contracts expire. There were 215 teachers' strikes during the first half of the 1979–1980 academic year. Is it plausible to argue that each of these is wrong in principle?

Summary of the Issues

Both sides in this debate applaud the progress made by government employees in the field of union activity and collective bargaining. States and municipalities, however, are far behind the federal government in recognizing these basic rights

[164]Even when an injunction is found to be invalid, employees who have violated it are still found to have been in contempt of court. This is not the case, however, in all states. See ibid., p. 336.
[165]Douglas, p. 415.

of workers. Some states permit "unions" but prohibit collective bargaining. Some people favor congressional action to achieve this goal; others oppose it. One good result of guaranteed collective bargaining is that issues could be settled without resort to a strike. If an impasse does develop, some form of binding arbitration could then be turned to.

One group would make arbitration compulsory in order *always* to prevent the strike, while another group argues that collective bargaining can be genuine only when there is the threat of a possible strike. Both parties must bargain in the light of a possible loss of services or a loss of wages. While binding arbitration may sometimes serve the interests of both parties and be entered into on those occasions, it may take the last weapon out of the hands of the workers—as well as the last weapon from the employer.

The antistrike people emphasize the evils of public sector strikes. These interrupt services that have been deemed so essential that they are operated by the public itself. It is right and proper that most jurisdictions prohibit public sector strikes and no jurisdiction permits strikes that threaten the public safety. The prostrike people argue that public sector strikes are not necessarily catastrophic. Many of them are less destructive of the general welfare than private sector strikes. If jurisdictions are far-sighted and resourceful, they can protect their constituents from many of the expected calamities—even when police and firefighters strike. If an emergency situation *really* develops, public employers have recourse to the same relief that is available to private employers.

The antistrike people argue that public employment is unique in another way. Striking public workers have unfair leverage, since they are dealing in essential services and are in a situation where market factors do not operate. Settlements tend to be political rather than economic, thus bypassing normal democratic processes. When they apply the ultimate pressure, officials usually "cave in." It is not, therefore, unjust and arbitrary to deny public workers the rights enjoyed by workers in the private sector. The prostrike people answer that a lot of politics takes place outside normal processes—much of it not so open as when a strike occurs. In any case, the strikers are expressing a point of view that officials and voters have to come to terms with. This is just another competing claim that must be assessed.

What can a jurisdiction do when it has a strike on its hands? One remedy is to hold out: Public opinion will be on its side. Another is to get a court injunction. The antistrike camp likes the Taylor Law because it *mandates* injunctions whenever a public sector strike occurs. Fines and imprisonment will bring an end to the strike—if officials have the courage to impose them. Finally, of course, striking workers can be discharged. The prostrike camp also would advise the jurisdiction to hold out if it believes that its cause is just. But the indiscriminate use of injunctions is opposed. Injunctions become legitimate *only* when a strike has been shown to seriously endanger public safety, health, or welfare. Most public sector strikes do not meet these criteria, but when one does, the jurisdiction can seek a remedy similar to the one available in the private sector. Many court cases can be cited to back the contention that injunctive relief is in order only in cases of real emergency.

Another issue in the debate centers on the grounds for striking. One side argues that the pay of public workers compares well with that of private workers, especially when security and fringe benefits are considered. The other side argues that public workers have fallen behind private workers, especially in the professional and managerial positions. In view of inflation and the tax revolt, this condition is bound to deteriorate—unless they act militantly. It also points out that many of the things that workers strike for have nothing to do with their own economic status.

Discussion Questions

1. Under what conditions would you seek an injunction against striking teachers? Sanitation workers? Firefighters? Police? Explain.
2. Do you believe that every worker has the prima facie right to strike? Why?
3. Would you lose respect for a teacher you saw on a picket line? Explain. Would you lose respect for a teacher you saw cross a picket line? Explain.
4. Do you think that members of the armed services have the right to form a union? Engage in collective bargaining? Strike? Why?
5. Do you believe that citizens have a prima facie right to police protection? What if they are not willing to pay police more than the minimum wage? What is "fair pay" for police?
6. Do you agree that all employees have the right to belong to a union and engage in collective bargaining? Why?
7. Do you believe that college professors in general are underpaid? Why? (Be careful on this one!)
8. Is it true that the work of public employees is more essential to the safety, health, and general well-being of society than the work of private employees? Explain.
9. Would you prefer to live through a strike of postal workers or one of meatpackers? Firefighters or plumbers? Public librarians or movie projectionists? Explain.
10. Do you think that injunctions should be issued automatically or only when sought on prescribed grounds? Why?
11. What would your response be to a nationwide strike of physicians in private practice? To a strike of physicians employed in public institutions?
12. Do you think that private sector employees have been more successful than public sector employees in keeping up with inflation? Why?
13. Do you think that recognized bargaining rights for public employees tends to increase strikes or avert them? Why?
14. Which do you think is a more practical kind of binding arbitration: when the arbitrators can choose their own figure or when they must select one of the "final offer" figures? Why?
15. Would you be in favor of national legislation that would protect the rights of state and local employees to organize unions and bargain collectively? Why?

16. Would you be in favor of national legislation which would give public sector unions the same right to strike as that possessed by private sector unions? Why?
17. Do you think that taxpayers are too tight-fisted in their attitudes toward wages for public employees? At the national level? The state level? The local level? Explain.
18. Do you think that managerial and professional people in public employment are underpaid? Explain.
19. Do you think that repressive state and local laws have prevented or encouraged the occurrence of strikes? Explain.
20. Do you think that the loss of public esteem experienced by striking public workers injures their cause in the long run? Explain.
21. Do you agree that state and local public employees unfairly lag behind federal employees in their collective bargaining rights? Explain.
22. What is the law in your state on public sector strikes? Would you alter it in any way? Explain.

For Further Reading

B. Aussicker. "Incidence and Impact of Faculty Union Strikes." *Labor Law Journal* 28 (December 1977):277–284.

Richard M. Ayres. "Police Strikes: Are We Treating the Symptoms Rather Than the Problem?" *Public Management* 59 (April 1977):10–13.

Jerome T. Barrett and Ira B. Lobel. "Public Sector Strikes—Legislative and Court Treatment." *Monthly Labor Review* 97 (September 1974):19–22.

Tim Bornstein. "Legacies of Local Government Collective Bargaining in the 1970s." *Labor Law Journal* 31 (March 1980):165–173.

Yearn H. Choi. "Collective Bargaining in the Public Sector: Where Are We?" *State Government* 51 (Autumn 1978):225–229.

R. Theodore Clark, Jr. "Injunctive Relief: Some Practical Considerations." *Public Management* 58 (February 1976):12–14.

Joel M. Douglas. "Injunctive Relief in Public Sector Work Stoppages: Alternate Approaches." *Labor Law Journal* 30 (July 1979):406–415.

Joel M. Douglas. "The Labor Injunction: Enjoining Public Sector Strikes in New York." *Labor Law Journal* 31 (June 1980):340–352

Walter Fogel and David Lewin. "Wage Determination in the Public Sector." *Industrial and Labor Relations Review* 27 (April 1974):410–431.

Henry B. Frazier III. "Labor-Management Relations in the Federal Government." *Labor Law Journal* 30 (March 1979):131–138.

C. R. Greer. "Public Sector Bargaining Legislation and Strikes: A Case Study." *Labor Law Journal* 29 (April 1978):241–247.

Stafford Hansell. "Role of the Legislature in Collective Bargaining." *State Government* 49 (Autumn 1976):221–223.

Jan W. Henkel, "Collective Bargaining in Higher Education: State Legislatures Still Hold the Purse String." *Labor Law Journal* 31 (June 1980):353–367.

Paul Johnston. "Promise of Public-service Unionism." *Monthly Review* (September 1978), 1–17.

Richard C. Kearney. "Municipal Budgeting and Collective Bargaining: The Case of Iowa." *Public Personnel Management* 9 (March–April 1980):108–115.

Bruce A. Miller. "The National Labor Relations Act: Should Amendments Cover Public Employees?" *Labor Law Journal* 30 (October 1979):637–642.

Perry Moore. "Lessons from the Dayton Firefighters Strike." *Public Personnel Management* 8 (January–February 1979):33–40.

D. M. Moschos. "Management in Police Labor Relations: Where Art Thou?" *Public Management* (April 1977).

James Perry. "Strikes in State Government Employment." *State Government* 49 (Autumn 1976):257–262.

Richard L. Rowan, ed. *Readings in Labor Economics and Labor Relations.* 3rd ed. Homewood, Ill.: Richard D. Irwin, 1976. Part 4.

Steven B. Rynecki and Thomas Gausden. "Current Trends in Public Sector Impasse Resolution." *State Government* 49 (Autumn 1976):273–276.

Stephen C. Shannon. "Work Stoppage in Government: The Postal Strike of 1970." *Monthly Labor Review* 101 (July 1978):14–21.

George A. Sipel. "Breaking Barriers." *Public Management* (February 1976).

David T. Stanley. *Managing Local Government under Union Pressure.* Washington: Brookings Institution, 1972.

John L. Taylor. "Fire Fighters Strike." *Public Management* (February 1976).

William W. Thompson II. "More on 'The Promise of Public-service Unionism.' " *Monthly Review* 50–60 (March 1979).

Chapter 5

EDUCATION

In this chapter we will discuss three of the many problems encountered in the field of education. They are legal and institutional problems, but they are also moral problems. The individual in each case must make ethical judgments that involve concepts of justice, rights, desired results, and ultimate values. It is judgments like these when applied in a collective way that determine major social commitments. Even when one's judgments fail to make a difference in how the world turns, the individual at least has arrived at a basis for evaluating institutions and their policies.

The first problem is one that has been hotly debated since 1954 and will be with us for many years to come. Is integrated education required by the Constitution? Is it a worthwhile objective apart from legal requirements? Is failure to achieve integration a denial of the rights of minority children? What good results can be expected from integration? Are they worth the costs? What evil results from integration? Does the good outweigh the bad or the bad outweigh the good? Is forced busing the only way to achieve integration? Should we support the practice of forced busing? What should be done in those urban school districts in which even forced busing would produce schools that are predominantly black or Hispanic? What is the relation between housing patterns and racial mix in the schools? What bearing should the difference between de facto and de jure segregation have on forced busing and redistricting?

The second problem is one that is now being debated in many colleges, governing boards, and state legislatures: What are the legitimate aims of undergraduate education? What should colleges in general or our own college in particular seek to achieve for its students? For many years the ideal of liberal education provided the answer: inculcate a sense of moral responsibility, provide understanding of the major fields of knowledge, and promote artistic sensibility. In the twentieth century this ideal was challenged by the notion that education should be practical and in its undergraduate stage should train the student for a profession. College was no longer the refuge of the aristocrat but a place for young people to "gear up" for jobs in the real world. Which view better expresses the real nature and needs of man?

The third problem is a contemporary one also. Have colleges gone too far in trying to assemble winning athletic teams? Has intercollegiate athletics been carried to a point where the educational integrity of colleges has been compromised? Are colleges guilty of hypocrisy? What is, or should be, the relation of athletic aims to educational ones? Is there an educational value in intercollegiate athletics, sports, or game playing?

Students who read both sides on these problems should be able to come to ethical conclusions of their own.

BUSING

Forced Busing Is an Inappropriate Means for School Integration

Integration: The First Seventeen Years The U.S. Supreme Court moved this society into a new era when in 1954 it unanimously ruled that state laws which set up separate systems of education for white and black children violated the right of equal protection under the law guaranteed by the Fourteenth Amendment. The decision in *Brown* v. *Board of Education* set aside an earlier ruling requiring only that the systems be equal.[1] Chief Justice Earl Warren, writing for the Court, stated: "To separate them [Negroes] from others of similar age and qualifications solely because of their race generates a feeling of inferiority as to their status in the community that may affect their hearts and minds in a way unlikely ever to be undone." He quoted from the finding of a lower court with approval: "A sense of inferiority affects the motivation of a child to learn. Segregation with the sanction of law, therefore, has a tendency to [retard] the educational and mental development of Negro children and to deprive them of some of the benefits they would receive in a racial[ly] integrated school system." Warren concluded that "in the field of public education the doctrine of 'separate but equal' has no place. Separate educational facilities are inherently unequal." In 1955, the Court ordered that school desegregation take place "with all deliberate speed."

One may question whether in fact black children develop a feeling of inferiority in a segregated school, but it is undeniable that in segregating them, the states were treating them *as if* they were inferior. And this itself would be sufficient today (if not in 1954) to constitute a violation of the Fourteenth Amendment—to say nothing of conflicting with scientific fact and "simple justice."

The response of the South was at first one of defiance. The state of Virginia, for example, ordered all schools that desegregated to be closed and cut off funds to those that refused to close.[2] Governor Orval Faubus of Arkansas, on the

[1]*Plessy* v. *Ferguson* (1896). In upholding a Louisiana statute requiring "equal but separate accommodations" for white and black railway passengers, the *Plessy* court upheld the whole system of segregated facilities.

[2]This was ruled unconstitutional by a federal district court in January 1959.

pretext of preventing disorder and violence, used state troops to bar the entry of nine black students to Central High School in Little Rock in 1957. President Eisenhower, reluctantly upholding the federal district court's order to integrate, sent federal troops, and the students entered. About a year later, the Supreme Court emerged from its hibernation and unanimously declared that "it is emphatically the province and duty of the judicial department to say what the law is." And the law is not to bow to violence provoked by politicians. "The constitutional rights of respondents are not to be sacrificed or yielded to the violence and disorder which have followed upon the actions of the Governor and Legislature."[3]

The most successful response of the South was tokenism, and that was countenanced for several years by the federal courts. It was at least a step forward, and no one had imagined that the school system could be overhauled in one day. Some southern legalists had argued that the *Brown* decision had not called for integration, but simply prohibited segregation. If states permitted mixed schools, they could not be accused of enforcing segregation. Moreover, "gradualism" could be claimed, for the second *Brown* dictum, "with all deliberate speed," was vague. So blacks were admitted in a trickle to southern schools. The dual system was officially dismantled, but only those blacks who cut all the red tape and passed all the legal hurdles were admitted to white schools—and often were made to suffer for it. This was not gradualism but obstructionism. "The Court's great error lay not in the formulation of 'all deliberate speed,' but in not monitoring 'deliberate speed' after *Brown* to ensure that some genuine progress actually took place."[4] It simply refused to review any cases that upheld the obstructionist tactics.

The Supreme Court finally spoke out in two cases in 1963.[5] Two other cases were concluded in 1965.[6] Its opinions expressed the Court's exasperation. " 'By 1965, in *Bradley,*' the Court fumed, 'more than a decade has passed since we directed desegregation of public facilities *with all deliberate speed.* Delays in desegregating school systems are no longer tolerable.' "[7] The *Griffin* case had begun in 1951 (the school board had been the defendant in one of the companion cases to *Brown*), and Justice Black lamented that the original plaintiffs had all passed high school age by now. In the ten years following *Brown,* only slightly more than 2 percent of the black children in the South had been integrated.

The year 1964 began a period in which integration proceeded much more rapidly. The reason is simple: the federal judiciary no longer stood alone. It was now joined and supported by the executive and legislative branches. The Civil

[3] *Cooper* v. *Aaron* (1958).

[4] Wilkinson, *From Brown to Bakke: The Supreme Court and School Integration, 1954–1978,* p. 86.

[5] *Goss* v. *Board of Education* and *McNeese* v. *Board of Education.* The first was in Knoxville, the second in Illinois; both were concerned with pupil-placement statutes.

[6] *Bradley* v. *Richmond School Board* dealt with bias in teaching assignments. *Griffin* v. *County School Board* finally put an end to the last holdout in Virginia, Prince Edward County, which had closed its public schools and supported private schools with "tuition grants."

[7] See Wilkinson, pp. 95–101.

Rights Act of 1964 not only forbade discrimination in all public accommodations, but also empowered the Department of Justice to bring suit "for the orderly achievement of desegregation in public education." The NAACP no longer had to carry the costly burden of litigation. Just as important was the decision to empower the Office of Education of HEW to formulate guidelines for desegregation and to cut off federal funds from districts that did not comply.

The Supreme Court case of *Green* v. *Board of Education of New Kent County* (1968) marked another great step forward. The Court rejected the theory of voluntary choice with all its busing, forms, and placements in favor of a genuine one-system approach. Integration was to be compulsory; simply the absence of statutory segregation was not enough. So long as "voluntarism" prevailed, schools would be identifiable as black or white, with a few patient and courageous blacks serving as tokens in the white schools. The Court charged school boards "with the affirmative duty to take whatever steps might be necessary to convert to a unitary system in which racial discrimination would be eliminated root and branch" and to do it *now*. The effect of this decision in rural counties of the South was to reduce busing. Since there was little residential segregation, the ideal of the neighboring school (serving both races) could be (and was) implemented. Despite strong political efforts to delay integration, but assisted by several important (and unanimous) Supreme Court decisions,[8] it now moved forward at a very respectable pace. "By 1971, according to HEW estimates, 44 percent of Negro pupils attended majority white schools in the South as opposed to 28 percent who did so in the North and West. The South, seventeen years after *Brown* (and in the midst of President Nixon's 'southern strategy'), became America's most integrated region."[9]

The Busing Decisions Most of this integration, however, had taken place in rural areas. The situation in the cities—northern as well as southern—was another matter. For in the cities, residential areas were themselves segregated. Adherence to the principle of a unitary system based on neighborhoods would result in schools that were largely segregated. The Charlotte-Mecklenburg school system, for example, had a school population that was only 29 percent black, but most of these students lived in one quadrant of the city. Although the district was technically not segregated, since there was a unitary system and opportunity for voluntary transfer, most blacks attended schools that were overwhelmingly black and staffed by black teachers. In *Swann* v. *Charlotte-Mecklenburg Board of Education* (1971), the Supreme Court unanimously declared the court-approved desegregation plan of 1965 unconstitutional and ordered this large metropolitan district to assign students throughout the district in such a way that each school

[8] *United States* v. *Montgomery County Board of Education* (1969) dealt with racial ratios of faculty. *Alexander* v. *Holmes County Board of Education* (1969) and *Carter* v. *West Feliciano Parish School Board* (1970) reversed lower courts that had granted delays.

[9] Wilkinson, p. 121.

would approximate the racial composition of the district. The schools had to be integrated no matter what the residential patterns in the county were. This would require busing, lots of busing, and it would be forced. The Court declared that the Constitution required "the greatest possible degree of actual desegregation" and said that there was a constitutional "presumption against schools that are substantially disproportionate in their racial composition."

The Charlotte plan was imposed on many southern cities in the months to follow, and it spread to border and northern cities. Denver, the first northern city affected, had a school population about the same as Charlotte's and an Anglo majority of about 66 percent. Its school district was a city unit rather than a consolidated city-county unit like Charlotte's. It was ordered to bus students on behalf of racial balance in *Keyes* v. *School District No. 1, Denver, Colorado* (1973). Distances were not so great, but children were to be taken from their neighborhoods. Plaintiffs did not have to show discrimination in a particular school assignment. It was enough, held the Court, to show that one part of the district was segregated to cast doubt over the whole district. "Once guilt was established in part of a district, the courts could desegregate the entire system unless local officials could prove that the remaining segregation was not limited to school system policies."[10] In 1974, a federal district judge ordered busing for the city of Boston. Here, too, the white school population was about 66 percent, but most of the blacks were in predominantly black schools. Judge W. Arthur Garrity said that given "the racial concentrations of its population, Boston is simply not a city that can provide its black schoolchildren with a desegregated education absent considerable mandatory transportation."[11] The plan adopted was to attempt to affect as few schools as possible and to keep busing to a minimum. Many students were therefore bused from Roxbury into nearby South Boston. Roxbury is the city's worst ghetto; South Boston a white working-class neighborhood.

Neighborhoods With the mandating of busing, the federal courts have come a long way from the legitimate position staked out in *Brown.* Where the original intention was to bar statutory segregation, the position now is to require statutory integration—at whatever cost. Instead of simply protecting minority children from insulting and demeaning policies that would keep them in their own schools, the courts are now requiring that they be placed in schools where they will have the educational "advantage" of studying side by side with whites. If the assumption here is that they will be deprived of equal opportunity to learn if not placed in an integrated school, the present policy is just as insulting as the old. Before *Brown,* children were bused from their neighborhoods in the rural South in order to achieve segregation; after *Swann,* children are bused from their neighborhoods in urban cities (northern and southern) in order to achieve integration. Busing,

[10]Gary Orfield, *Must We Bus? Segregated Schools and National Policy,* p. 16. This section is indebted to Orfield's excellent book, as well as to that of J. Harvie Wilkinson.

[11]See Wilkinson, p. 206.

the early foe of the integrationists, is now their greatest ally. Instead of defending the neighborhood school, they are destroying it.

Something should be said on behalf of the neighborhood school. It is supported by local taxes and is the visible embodiment of the expenditure of those taxes. It is the focal point of local interests, which are not merely educational but social and recreational as well. It often gives the neighborhood a sense of identity and fosters public spirit. Children walk to school with their neighbors. Their friends at school are their friends at home. Parents who associate in educational enterprises associate also in neighborhood matters. Both students and parents have a sense of belonging and sharing in common causes. What busing does is divide the neighborhood and thus destroy it.

Children living in one world are made to function during their school hours in another world. They are thrust into an alien situation and expected to thrive. Whoever is bused, white and black, must live a dual existence. The children cannot even count on being at the same school for more than a year or two. The adjustment is even more difficult for Hispanic people who have problems due to language and cultural differences. It is said, but nevertheless true, that minority students are often not welcomed by Anglos in the school to which they have been bused. The reception of blacks at South Boston High School is only the most conspicuous case among several ugly situations precipitated by busing. Busing has seldom proceeded smoothly, especially in the first few years. Racial harmony is a fine ideal, but it is simplistic to think that it can be achieved by forcing children from different neighborhoods to study together. And it is unfair to make our children guinea pigs in a social experiment.

Where integrated education has taken place in the context of integrated neighborhoods, it has gone smoothly. Where there has been segregation (de facto or de jure) in the school district, it has not. It is true that much residential segregation that has been regarded as de facto is really de jure. The courts have required that de jure be proved, and this is usually not difficult to do. Zoning ordinances, restrictive covenants, FHA and VA loan procedures, as well as unequal police protection, have all had the backing of government and have contributed to segregrated housing patterns. Laws have indeed fostered the growth of ghettos and barrios. But this is the reality of urban life today. It is unfair to ask the children of today to atone for the sins of the dominant white majority of the past.

What we should do instead is to look for ways of integrating housing in the future. We must make sure that political connivance and support for segregated housing have been stopped. We should provide easy housing loans for disadvantaged people. We should build public housing in the suburbs and small towns. We should increase the chances of economic progress for minority groups so that they will be able to escape the ghettos and barrios. The goal will be integrated housing, from which integrated education will naturally follow. If, for a time, we must have schools in the cities that are not integrated, we should make sure that they are at least equal to those that are integrated. What the minority students learn in their "separate" schools may provide them with the means later in life to move out of the ghetto once and for all. The enormous amount of money that is spent on busing students away from their local schools could be put to much better use in *improving* those schools.

Dubious Gains The prominent sociologist James S. Coleman, an early advocate of forced busing, had supported the underlying sociology of the *Brown* decision in a study in 1966, arguing that "if a minority pupil from a home without much educational strength is put with schoolmates with strong educational backgrounds, his achievement is likely to increase," while that of the latter will be little effected.[12] An important study by David Armor, however, failed to show any increase of learning by minority students in integrated city systems but did show an increase of race consciousness.[13] Recent studies have confirmed this. Martin Patchen and his associates concluded: "Contrary to much of the thinking in the literature, attending predominantly white classes did not benefit black students most when their white peers came from high-status families or had high academic values."[14] A study by Daniel S. Sheehan of the achievements of 1,115 blacks who had attended segregated schools and 810 who had attended desegregated schools showed that "after controlling for previous achievement level, student sex, prior school experience, social status, parental involvement, and attitude toward education," the former had higher "adjusted language arts, reading, and mathematics posttest scores."[15] A few reported cases of improvement of performance can more easily be explained by presence in a better *school* than by association with a "better" class of students.

What about racial attitudes?

> Many of the social scientists who testified in the 1954 Supreme Court case of *Brown* v. *Board of Education* believed that school desegregation would lead to more positive racial attitudes. . . . However, the evidence indicates that this optimistic prediction was unwarranted. Studies on the effects of desegregation on radical attitudes indicate that it leads to negative racial attitudes more often than it leads to positive ones. Since 1954, 13 studies have focused on the effects of school desegregation on the racial attitudes of whites toward blacks. In four studies, it was found that desegregation had predominantly positive effects on racial attitudes. . . . In seven studies, predominantly negative results were obtained . . . and in two, desegregation had no significant effect on attitudes. . . .[16]

[12]Coleman et al., *Equality of Educational Opportunity*, p. 22.

[13]See Armor, "The Evidence on Busing," p. 90ff.

[14]Martin Patchen et al., "Academic Performance of Black High School Students under Different Conditions of Contact with White Peers," p. 33.

[15]Sheehan, "Black Achievement in a Desegregated School District," p. 185.

[16]Stephan and Rosenfield, "Effects of Desegregation on Racial Attitudes," p. 795ff.

The study of Stephan and Rosenfield of white elementary schoolchildren tended to confirm the majority view.

What about the "sense of inferiority" referred to in *Brown*? A careful study of 194 high schools led to the conclusion that "cross-racial exposure apparently has a deleterious effect upon the self-concept of blacks." Their average "residual self-esteem is lower in racially balanced schools than in predominantly black schools."[17]

White Flight In a great many cities, busing has had a counterproductive effect on integration. It has contributed to "white flight." This, of course, makes it more difficult to preserve racially balanced enrollments in the schools. And when the balance has tipped to a situation where "minority" students are in a majority and the principle of proportionate representation is made to prevail, black or Hispanic students find themselves in a school that seems to be as segregated as it was before busing took place. There are fewer whites in the district to integrate *with.*

In most northern districts, urban whites who do not want to integrate with minorities can simply flee to the suburbs. This is not so easily done in the South, for the suburbs are themselves part of the consolidated district—as in Charlotte, Miami, or Tampa. These people, unless they want to find new jobs, are locked into the system. They can, however, like whites in the North, send their children to private schools—if they can afford to.

How much integration are whites willing to accept? Will they accept 15, 20, 30, 40, or 50 percent minority classmates for their children? Suppose that most will accept 15 percent. But there are some who won't, and they will leave. This raises the percentage of minority students in an integrated district to 20 percent. Those who accept only 15 percent leave. This increases the minority presence a little more, so other whites leave. When the figure gets beyond 50 percent, most of the white families with children want to leave. When it gets to 75 percent, only the poorest whites will remain. Those white families that favor integration do so only up to a point. They do not want their children to be a minority in a black school. The black school itself is stigmatized as one offering inferior education in culturally backward surroundings.

The phenomenon of "black flight" should also be noted. In the years 1970–1974, declines in black enrollment have been noted in most cities. Cleveland by 14 percent, St. Louis by 11 percent, and San Francisco by 10 percent are examples. Between 1969 and 1977, black enrollment in Washington, D.C., dropped by over 25,000 students. "Brown flight" has also been noted in such cities as San Francisco, which lost 14 percent of its Hispanic enrollment in 1970–1974. "The flight of middle-class black families from the central city schools may bring about

[17]Drury, "Black Self-Esteem and Desegregated Schools," p. 100. See also Simmons et al., "Self-Esteem and Achievement of Black and White Adolescents," p. 86ff.

some suburban desegregation but it also robs the schools of one of their most important assets. . . . The remaining minority children attend schools stigmatized as inferior not only by whites but also by the successful members of the minority communities."[18]

It would be a mistake to attribute these "flights" solely to the racial composition of the schools—there are many other reasons to flee decaying cities—but it is a factor.

The results, at least, are undebatable. Between 1968 and 1974, the following reductions of Anglo enrollment were reported: Atlanta from 38 percent to 15 percent, Boston from 68 percent to 59 percent, Chicago from 38 percent to 29 percent, Dallas from 61 percent to 45 percent, Detroit from 39 percent to 26 percent, Memphis from 46 percent to 29 percent, New Orleans from 31 percent to 19 percent.[19] Although all groups are fleeing, whites are fleeing in greater numbers. The five largest school districts in the country had enrollments in 1974–1975 in which Anglos were in the minority: New York, 34 percent; Chicago, 29 percent; Los Angeles, 41 percent; Philadelphia, 34 percent; and Detroit, 26 percent. To these may be added the following where "minority" enrollment (1974–1975) is the majority: Baltimore, Cleveland, Dade County (Miami), Denver, District of Columbia, Gary, Houston, Kansas City (Missouri), Newark, and St. Louis.[20] The trend continues, and the contemporary scene is one in which concentration of non-Anglos is even greater than was the case in 1975.

In recent years even Coleman has opposed forced busing in city districts as counterproductive, for it accelerates white flight.[21]

The Futility of Forced Busing in the Cities How do you integrate a district that is preponderantly black and/or Hispanic? If the aim is simply to reflect in each school the racial ratios that exist in the district, busing can do it. But what would it accomplish? If the purpose of integration is to bring the minorities into contact with the dominant white race with its greater advantages and middle-class values, the purpose would not be realized, for the whites are too low in number and are probably just as disadvantaged as the others. If the purpose is to break down white prejudice, it would probably not be realized either, for the whites would themselves be a resentful handful in a stigmatized school. It is difficult to think of any educational purpose that would be served by, say, an 80/20 mix in an inner city school.

By default, then, if nothing else, the segregated residential patterns should be permitted to determine the composition of the city's schools.

[18]See Orfield, p. 74.

[19]See ibid., p. 72.

[20]See ibid., p. 68. Some 1980 figures: Chicago, 18.3 percent; St. Louis, 19 percent; Los Angeles, 28 percent (projected to 14 percent by 1987).

[21]See James S. Coleman, "Liberty and Equality in School Desegregation," p. 9ff. See also Coleman et al., *Trends in School Segregation, 1968–1973.* For a vigorous defense of Coleman, see Ravitch, "White Flight Controversy," p. 135ff.

In districts where there are not enough whites to go around, officials may do what they can, adhering to residential patterns. This was done, for example, in Atlanta in 1971. As part of the "Atlanta compromise," more black administrators were appointed and no great attempt was made through busing to attain proportionate racial mixtures in the schools. "Atlanta simply pronounced the city desegregated and said that further busing would lead to rapid flight from the city by the remaining whites."[22] The plan was strongly supported by Governor Jimmy Carter and Judge Griffin Bell, and upheld by the court of appeals.[23] Sometimes, however, federal courts have ordered extensive busing in an urban district, knowing full well that nothing much will be accomplished. The judges of the Sixth Circuit Court, for example, stated that "genuine constitutional desegregation can not be accomplished within the [Detroit] school district boundaries."[24] The court should have used the term *integration* instead of *desegregation.*

Rejection of forced busing in the cities should not imply, however, that nothing should be done on behalf of quality education and integration. Among the things that can be done are the following. (1) Greater state and federal aid to the city schools.[25] The tax base of the cities is being eroded by decreasing property values and the removal of business and industry. They need money. If their schools are, in a sense, "separate," they must at least be made "equal" to those around them. Senator William Roth, Jr., put it well: "As an alternative to busing, I favor the development of first-rate, high quality, neighborhood schools for all children, regardless of race."[26] (2) Preservation of some white schools, with voluntary admission of some minority students. This would counteract "white flight" and provide *some* integration. (3) Creation of "magnet" schools in the inner city. These schools would offer attractive and specialized programs and would be made available to whites on a voluntary basis. (4) Development of special programs aimed at helping the disadvantaged minority children. This was one of the purposes to be served by the "Atlanta compromise." It can also serve the Spanish-speaking students.[27] None of these measures would require forced busing.

[22]Orfield, p. 25.

[23]*Calhoun* v. *Cook* (1971).

[24]*Bradley* v. *Milliken* (1976). This decision came after the Supreme Court struck down cross-districting in *Milliken* v. *Bradley* (1974).

[25]In "Milliken II," the Supreme Court ordered the state of Michigan to pay for remedial programs, counseling, and other improvements in the Detroit system (*Milliken* v. *Bradley,* 1977). Three years before, the Court had denied a metropolitan system (*Milliken* v. *Bradley,* 1974).

[26]See Orfield, p. 105.

[27]Indeed, this sort of approach was mandated by the Supreme Court in *Lau* v. *Nichols* (1974). Chinese students were entitled to a correction of their language deficiency. "Under these state-imposed standards there is no equality of treatment merely by providing students with the same facilities, textbooks, teachers, and curriculum; for students who do not understand English are effectively foreclosed from any meaningful education." In 1980 there were about 3.6 million students whose English was inadequate for regular classrooms (over 70 percent are Spanish-speaking). The federal government spent $167 million to support bilingual teaching. The main debate today centers on two issues: (1) Are these programs to be "transitional" or "maintenance"? (2) Is the federal government to continue to pay for them?

Creation of Metropolitan Districts Another solution to the problem of desegregating the cities has been suggested by the approach of Charlotte and other metropolitan districts. Where a city district (mostly black) is surrounded by suburbs (mostly white), district lines can be redrawn in such a way that a new and larger district results that encompasses the city and some or all of the suburbs. This new district will have a school population in which white students are at least equal in number to black students. Through a system of forced busing, racial integration is achieved in all schools.

This approach was almost successful in the city of Richmond. The school population of the district was about 65 percent black, so a district court ordered it joined to the white suburbs of Henrico and Chesterfield. The order was reversed, however, by the Fourth Circuit Court, which pointed out that a district judge cannot "compel one of the States of the Union to restructure its internal government for the purpose of achieving racial balance in the assignment of pupils to the public schools."[28] The Supreme Court considered the case a year later. The vote was 4–4, Justice Lewis Powell having disqualified himself as a former chairman of the Richmond School Board. The decision of the Circuit Court was thus left to stand, and the people of Richmond set out to "integrate" its schools—with the usual white flight and search for private schools.

The suburbs around Detroit were similarly spared in the case of *Milliken* v. *Bradley* (1974). The lower courts had ordered the preparation of a desegregation plan that would combine the district of Detroit (overwhelmingly black) with fifty-three suburban districts (overwhelmingly white). This would have produced an enormous district and required extensive busing. The courts were correct at least in their judgment that no real integration could take place in the city itself. When the case reached the Supreme Court, Justice Powell did sit, and the vote was 5–4 to overrule the lower court. While the Supreme Court reaffirmed its rule in *Keyes* that segregation anywhere in a district was prima facie evidence of a segregated district, it refused to apply it to a region or metropolitan area. In rejecting the lower court's "vast new super school district," Chief Justice Warren Burger wisely stated: "No single tradition is more deeply rooted than local control over the operation of schools; local autonomy has long been thought essential both to the maintenance of community concern and support for public schools and to the quality of educational process."

The suburbs, however, cannot relax, for despite the *Milliken* ruling, district lines were redrawn in the Louisville and Wilmington areas in 1975. In the first city, when a lower court had ordered metropolitan integration, the Louisville school board voted to dissolve. The surrounding county system then was required by state law to take over the city system. The Supreme Court, considering the matter moot, took no action. In the second, the Supreme Court upheld a lower court, which had found that the state of Delaware had contributed to segregation

[28]*Bradley* v. *Richmond School Board* (1972).

in the metropolitan area and ordered the formation of a metropolitan district.[29] So whenever the courts find that residential segregation is de jure in a metropolitan area, it can order new districting.

The Supreme Court, unanimous in its early decisions, has been split on cross-districting. The future of metropolitan busing, the only means for genuine integration in city schools, would appear to depend on court appointments. Some judges, believing in the integrity of state districting, tend to oppose it. Some judges, believing that de facto segregation is virtually the same as de jure segregation, will require it. And a few, perhaps, will make their decisions after a careful examination of the contribution of government power in the creation of segregated residence.

Public Opposition to Forced Busing One thing at least is clear. The American people are opposed to forced busing. They oppose it within the old district, and they oppose creating new districts in which it can take place. This opposition is reflected in the legislative and executive branches of the national government. The federal courts have had to stand alone. They have had to oppose public opinion. Relying on their own rather special interpretation of the Fourteenth Amendment, they have taken the power away from the people. The U.S. Supreme Court has not, since the early seventies, spoken with a unanimous voice. American policy has often had to depend on the thinking of *one* Justice. A peculiar legalism has taken precedence over democratic processes.

We do not have to point to the vociferous protests and public demonstrations in places like Louisville and Boston to show the majority opposition to forced busing. A Harris Survey in 1973 showed that three out of four Americans were opposed to forced busing.[30] Gallup polls in the early seventies showed fewer than one in five favoring busing from one district to another.[31] A national poll conducted by the *New York Times* and CBS showed that 71 percent were opposed to "racial integration of the schools . . . if it requires busing."[32] A *Washington Post* survey a little later had the figure at 76 percent.

A great deal of opposition is found in the black and Hispanic communities. Polls taken of minority families in St. Louis in 1980–1981 showed a solid majority of black parents opposed to forced busing. Black and Hispanic educators often oppose creation of metropolitan districts from fear that control will end up in the hands of white administrators with the result that minority children will receive an inferior education.

Elected political officials have overwhelmingly opposed busing—either from conviction or to please their constituency. President Nixon opposed busing. In his 1972 message to Congress, he said that the school bus, once a "symbol of

[29]See *Evans* v. *Buchanan* (1975).

[30]See Peter Gall, *Desegregation: How Schools Are Meeting the Historic Challenge* (Arlington, Va.: National School Public Relations Association, 1973), p. 7.

[31]See Orfield, p. 113.

[32]See *New York Times,* February 13, 1976.

hope," was becoming a "symbol of social engineering on the basis of abstractions."[33] In the Nixon administration, the efforts of the Justice and HEW departments on behalf of forced busing were almost eliminated. In some cases, lawyers from the Justice Department even testified against it. Nixon managed to get a provision into the Emergency School Aid Act of 1973 forbidding use of integration money for busing. President Ford, who as House Republican leader had supported legislation and a constitutional amendment prohibiting forced busing, carried on the Nixon program. The Republican platform in 1976 favored antibusing legislation and a constitutional amendment. Ford in his campaign promised to restrain the courts. This was not a partisan issue. In the Democratic primaries, Edmund Brown, Frank Church, and Henry Jackson were critical of forced busing. Even the liberal Morris Udall recognized an "emerging consensus" against it and supported voluntary plans. Jimmy Carter, still proud of the "Atlanta compromise," said: "This well-intentioned idea [busing] has contributed little to the equalization of educational opportunity, has often resulted in a decreased level of integration over the long term, and has divided and sidetracked our efforts toward improving education of all children."[34] His message to Congress in 1977 made no mention of busing. In looking at the party platforms in 1980, we find that the Republicans opposed forced busing, while the Democrats did not mention it.

The House of Representatives, always more in tune with the feelings of the voters, passed several antibusing measures in the seventies: that no district be forced to bus until its case had been appealed to the Supreme Court, that no children could be bused beyond the nearest school, that HEW could not cut off funds to districts that defied court-ordered busing, that no gasoline could be allocated to districts carrying out forced busing, that no federal-aid money could be used for defraying the expenses of busing (even when requested by local school officials), that no federal court could order busing for integration unless a prior determination had been made that a *discriminatory purpose* was an important motivating factor in the situation that the busing is supposed to correct, that cross-districting could not be imposed against the wishes of the state in question, and many more. Not all of these measures became law, for the Senate had to concur.[35] But the antibusing sentiment was strong in the Senate, and some of these measures were halted only by filibustering. The liberals who had criticized the use of this tactic in years past for obstructing civil rights and other popular programs are using it now to counteract a national sentiment against busing. This is not to say that all liberals defend busing. Senator Thomas Eagleton said in 1975: "Looking at the experience of the last decade, I find no compelling reason to maintain busing as a congressionally authorized procedure in school desegrega-

[33]See Orfield, p. 103.

[34]See ibid., p. 107.

[35]A law that was passed (1975) says that HEW cannot threaten loss of federal funds to force a school district to bus students beyond the school closest to their homes. The Eagleton-Biden amendment (1979) would continue this kind of prohibition.

tion cases when . . . in a great many cases, the social problems created by busing now outweigh the social advantage to be derived from bringing black and white students together."[36]

An amendment to a $9.1 billion appropriations bill providing for the operations of the State, Justice, and Commerce departments for 1981 was passed in December 1980. This amendment prohibits the Justice Department from bringing any sort of court action "to require directly or indirectly the transportation of any student to a school other than the school which is nearest the student's home." If Carter vetoes such a law, it is unlikely that Reagan will.

Conclusion The case against forced busing is thus twofold: (1) the inappropriateness of the means to the end and (2) the conflict between dubious court interpretations and the public will.

1. If the end is an integrated school where the educational potentials of minority children are realized through harmonious association with whites representative of the dominant American culture, forced busing is a singularly inept means. Those who stubbornly insist on forced busing have abandoned the basic common sense in means/end thinking so patiently explained by John Dewey. In the first place, it is ineffective. Schoolchildren who have been bused do not always experience feelings of racial concord when forced to be a minority in an integrated school, nor do they, when a majority, welcome the entry of another race into their schools. A busing scheme, which is so patently racial in inspiration, tends to emphasize the differences among students rather than their common humanity. Nor is there any compelling evidence that minority children learn better in an integrated situation or that their self-esteem is heightened.

Forced busing not only does not produce the desired end, but would be too expensive even if it did. Among the costs, in addition to the obvious one of funds for buses, maintenance, gasoline, and wages, are the following: The resentment aroused in the hearts of white and minority citizens, the elimination of the neighborhood schools, the loss of local and state control (especially in the case of cross-districting), the disruption of family life resulting from double shifts in busing schedules, and the emphasis on racial balance at the expense of educational concerns. The money spent in buying and maintaining buses and in carrying out litigation in federal courts would go a long way in rectifying the shortcomings in city schools.

Elliot Richardson, Secretary of HEW in 1972, in opposing forced busing, spoke of the "widespread belief that remedies have been imposed that harm more than they help."[37]

2. It is incontestable that segregated education mandated by law is unconstitutional. But it does not follow from this that all school boards must, through forced busing, impose a system of racial balance throughout their districts. Even less

[36] *Congressional Record,* September 24, 1975.
[37] See Orfield, p. 104.

does it follow that they are to overcome the patterns of residential segregation—somehow *negate* them—by such a districtwide educational system. Whether the residential segregation is de facto or de jure is really beside the point. If integrated schools are the commanding concern, they should be achieved even where the segregation is only de facto. And if they are not the commanding concern, they need not be achieved even where the segregation is de jure. The fact is that a great deal of residential segregation exists. It is pointless to dispute whether it developed naturally (de facto) or with the connivance of the law (de jure). That the present generation of schoolchildren is required by the Constitution to pay for the social or legal sins of the past is far-fetched indeed. That integrated education is a remedy for segregated housing seems to put the cart before the horse. And that districts must be joined to achieve it (in cases where residential segregation of a whole region is found to be de jure) is not only an affront to states' rights, but an indication that some court personnel have lost all concern for what the Constitution actually says.

If the sort of social engineering favored by those who would wish to integrate all students regardless of the nature of their neighborhoods and cities is in order, the legitimate remedy is to be found, not in the courts, but in the legislatures. The Constitution does not mandate integration, but the people may require it by law and empower the executive departments to carry it out by whatever means it chooses—including forced busing. But the people evidently are not now ready to do this. Yet, though they live in a "democracy," they are being made to do so on the basis of rulings by appointed federal justices and a badly divided Supreme Court.

Forced Busing Is an Appropriate Means for School Integration

The End: Constitutional and Moral Whether the U.S. Supreme Court is correct in saying that the Constitution requires positive integration rather than merely an end to state-supported segregation may be difficult to say. But the fact is that it has spoken on the matter several times in a unanimous and unequivocal way. Integration of all districts, together with the busing that that requires, is now the law of the land. Short of a constitutional amendment, all branches and agencies of the government, as well as school boards, are obligated to obey that law. The actions of Congress, presidents, and executive departments during the seventies are unconscionable.

The constitutional argument is not implausible. If minority children, because of the income and social position of their parents, are at a disadvantage when they do not have children of more fortunate parents in their schools, then the laws that countenance the situation are not affording them "equal protection." And if forced busing is the only means for remedying the situation, then a system of forced busing is mandatory for all school districts. It is true that this argument goes beyond that of bringing an end to the invidious and thoroughly racist practices of dual school systems, but it does perhaps draw a legitimate corollary.

The legal argument depends, of course, upon the factual truth that integration does indeed have a beneficial effect on minority children. *Brown* in a famous footnote cited several empirical studies to show that this is indeed the case. Recent studies have all shown that integration does not have an adverse educational effect on learning for either minority or Anglo children. And some have shown a beneficial effect.[38] Studies made by the National Assessment of Educational Progress in the mid-seventies showed significant gains by black children in the integrated South. A national study by Robert L. Crain and Rita E. Mahard in 1977 also showed significant gains, especially when integration began early in the students' career.[39] Willis D. Hawley of the Institute for Policy Studies at Vanderbilt University says: "In spite of America's reluctance to integrate its schools, all the evidence shows that minority students do better in integrated schools than they do in segregated schools and that race relations improve."[40] These studies, of course, are not conclusive, but we can conclude from them and others that no one is *hurt* by integration.

Where the evidence is most unmistakable is in the case of the Hispanic minorities. Granted that Spanish-speaking people need special programs and some instruction in the Spanish language, it is nevertheless the case that their English improves in an educational setting where Anglos are present. So does their progress in subjects involving American culture.

What some studies have turned up is an improvement in racial attitudes by children in integrated schools.[41] This is just as important as academic improvement. If, as some people believe, America has for a long time been *two* societies, confronting one another in resentment, distrust, and fear, genuinely integrated schools would tend to break this down and thus serve the cause of community

[38]See Christopher Jencks et al., *Inequality: A Reassessment of the Effect of Family and Schooling in America* (New York: Basic Books, 1972); Meyer Weinberg, *Desegregation Research: An Appraisal,* 2nd ed. (Bloomington, Ind.: Phi Delta Kappa, 1970); Nancy H. St. John, *School Desegregation: Outcome for Children;* Thomas F. Pettigrew et al., "Busing: A Review of 'The Evidence,' " in Nicolaus Mills, ed., *The Great School Bus Controversy.*

[39]See Crain and Mahard, *Desegregation and Black Achievement.* In a later article they argued that while "southern black achievement is not related to school racial composition," northern "black achievement, college attendance and college survival are all higher in predominantly white high schools." See "School Racial Composition and Black College Attendance and Achievement Test Performance," p. 81ff.

[40]See Robert Lindsey, "School Integration Looks More than Ever Like a Lost Horizon," *New York Times,* August 24, 1980, p. E5.

[41]See, for example, Sheehan, "A Study of Attitude Change in Desegregated Intermediate Schools," p. 51ff. This study is especially illuminating, for it deals with the Dallas Independent School District, which contains 13 percent Mexican-American as well as 45 percent black students. No loss of "self-esteem" was reported. See also Falk, "School Desegregation and the Educational Attainment Process: Some Results from Rural Texas Schools," p. 282ff. The Stephan and Rosenfield study (1978) cited above did show that desegregation could under some circumstances lead to more positive racial attitudes.

and common purpose. Actually, of course, when we take into account the Hispanic (Chicano, Puerto Rican, and Cuban) populations, as well as Indian and Oriental, America is *several* societies. It is not argued here that the Constitution *requires* us to do those things which break down the walls between the nation's racial groups. But to do so would be a worthwhile goal. It cannot be done overnight. And integrated schooling cannot do it all, but it would be a splendid step toward the Stoic ideal of human brotherhood.

Whatever limitations the Supreme Court places on *constitutional* need for integration, the legislatures and executives of the country can push for integration in the schools—just as it has done so successfully in the area of public accommodations. While the courts seem concerned only with requiring bused integration in districts or regions where there is evidence of de jure residential segregation, elected officials can and should move toward it even when residential segregation is only de facto (if that ever is the case!).[42] Rather than berate the courts for insisting on constitutional protection for our minorities, we should go beyond what is legally necessary toward what is socially and morally desirable.

Forced Busing as the Only Efficacious Means If integration is a worthy end, we must choose efficacious means. Not only does forced busing produce integrated schools, but it is the *only* thing that will. Voluntary busing does not work. A few blacks go to white schools, but virtually no whites opt for black schools. Magnet schools do bring a few Anglos into the minority neighborhoods, but the list of black applicants is usually much longer than that of whites. It is often the case in cities that not all the magnet schools can be filled if the ratio is kept to fifty-fifty. Before another black is admitted from the long list, a qualified white must apply. Some magnet schools (e.g., "classical academies") have insufficient applications from *both* races. Active recruitment is necessary.[43]

Busing by itself does not produce integration. Even in cities where magnet schools are successful, the other schools will be overwhelmingly minority. Genuine integration is not achieved, because (1) there are not enough Anglos to go

[42]One can, however, take a legalistic attitude against the viability of the distinction. Irving Ferman, for example, states: "The Supreme Court's adoption of segregative intent establishing the *de facto/de jure* distinction is unmindful and insensitive to what *Brown* was all about: the relation of equal protection against the harmful consequences of racial segregation as it impacts upon the psychological and educational makeup of an individual." He quotes with approval and would "build on" an opinion of the Sixth Circuit Court of Appeals in *Oliver* v. *Michigan State Board of Education* (1974): "When constitutional rights are involved, the issue is seldom whether public officials have acted with evil motives or whether they have consciously plotted with bigotry in their hearts to deprive citizens of the equal protection of the laws. Rather, under the test for de jure segregation, the question is whether a purposeful pattern of segregation has manifested itself over time, despite the fact that individual official actions, considered alone, may not have been taken for segregative purposes and may not have been in themselves constitutionally invalid." See Irving Ferman, "*Brown* v. *Board of Education*—Actions Necessary to Effect Its True Meaning," *Howard Law Journal* (1980), pp. 58–59.

[43]Despite this, magnet schools in St. Louis were 26 percent underenrolled when desegregation began in the fall of 1980.

around, and (2) most of the Anglos are as impoverished and disadvantaged as the minority children.[44] The South was fortunate in its development toward integration in having metropolitan districts in which just the opposite was the case. But most northern cities have an insoluble problem: The city *is* the school district. Officials may bus the children all over town, but the schools will still be "minority" schools.

Busing will produce genuine integration in the cities only if new school districts are formed in which the city is simply a part. The four dissenting justices in the *Milliken* case (1974) "argued that the practical effect of the decision was to elevate the prerogatives of the suburbs above the constitutional rights of the black children. They insisted that integration would be both meaningless and temporary without suburban involvement."[45] Justice Thurgood Marshall, sitting in a case twenty years after *Brown,* in which he had been the NAACP attorney, stated:

> The Court's answer is to provide no remedy at all for the violation proved in this case, thereby guaranteeing that Negro children in Detroit will receive the same separate and inherently unequal education in the future as they have been unconstitutionally afforded in the past. . . . Under a Detroit-only decree, Detroit's schools will clearly remain racially identifiable. . . . Schools with 65 percent and more Negro students will stand in sharp and obvious contrast to schools in neighboring districts with less than 2 percent Negro enrollment. Negro students will continue to perceive their schools as segregated facilities and this perception will only be increased when whites react to a Detroit-only decree by fleeing to the suburbs to avoid integration.[46]

What before was a segregated school has now become a segregated district.

The metropolitan approach is surely feasible for all but one or two cities in the United States. New York, with over 700,000 minority schoolchildren (1974–1975), is in a class by itself. Several studies have shown, however, that integration by means of the metropolitan approach is feasible for the other large cities: Los Angeles, Chicago, Philadelphia, and Detroit.[47] Racial balance can be achieved, whites will not be outnumbered, and bus rides will not be unreasonably long. If it can be done in these four cities, it can be done anywhere—and indeed it has been successfully carried out in many middle-sized cities in the southern and border states.

It is not, of course, necessary to create gigantic districts. Cities and suburbs could be carved up in ways to produce two or more districts, or subdistricts within the larger one. School districts need not be citywide or countywide, or follow *any* political boundaries. They are creatures of the state government and can be

[44]"In older central cities, the entire school system may serve children from a narrow social and economic range, thus minimizing the possibility of academic benefits from desegregation." Orfield, pp. 69–70.

[45]Ibid., p. 34.

[46]*Milliken* v. *Bradley* (1974).

[47]See Orfield, pp. 179–192.

whatever the states select for them. The fiscal independence of school districts is already a thing of the past—state and federal moneys are depended upon. The cities, once rich in tax receipts, are now, in their decline, facing grave problems. The question has been raised whether the cities can *afford* school systems of their own.[48] From the fiscal point of view, the most feasible thing to do would be to combine a poorer district with a more affluent one.

If the federal courts *want* integration, they will have to order cross-districting. They will have to take a more strict view of "de facto" segregation than the Supreme Court did in *Milliken.* As 1980 began, metropolitan integration since *Milliken* had been achieved only in Louisville and Wilmington, but two Supreme Court decisions in 1979 provided encouragement by ordering districtwide desegregation in two Ohio cities.[49] These rulings not only constituted an affirmation of *Keyes,* but required extensive busing and turning thumbs down on a de facto plea. The Court had previously said that smaller districts could be created out of larger ones only if that action contributed to desegregation.[50] If the right of states to control their own districts must give way to the Fourteenth Amendment where districts are *reduced,* why not appeal to the same principle where districts are *retained*? If the courts or the people want integration in the cities, they will have to form metropolitan districts.

In St. Louis the school board and the NAACP have filed suit for a new metropolitan district that would include the suburbs. In order to forestall this, some Missourians have advocated a *voluntary* plan for desegregation across district lines. U.S. District Judge James H. Meredith ordered the State of Missouri to submit a more specific revision of an earlier proposal for such a plan by February 2, 1981 (since extended). The plan would provide for magnet schools serving several districts and the voluntary busing of urban students to suburban schools that are underenrolled. The state would pay half the expense. It is hoped that suburban districts, fearing that de jure segregation might be proved against them, will join such a program rather than risk a court-ordered metropolitan district.[51] That such a voluntary plan would be upheld in the higher courts cannot

[48]City schools in financial straits have had to reduce to half-days, cut back sports, music, and activities programs, discharge employees, close while seeking emergency funds, and conclude the school year early.

[49]See *Columbus Board of Education* v. *Penick* (1979) and *Dayton Board of Education* v. *Brinkman* (1979).

[50]See *U.S.* v. *Scotland Neck Board of Education* (1972) and *Wright* v. *Council of the City of Emporia* (1972).

[51]The St. Louis school board believes that it can indeed show that de jure residential segregation has led to school segregation. It cites the dictum in the Detroit case (*Milliken* v. *Bradley,* 1974): "An interdistrict remedy might be in order where the racially discriminatory acts of one or more school districts caused racial segregation in an adjacent district, or where district lines have been drawn on the basis of race." The top officials of the state are, of course, opposed to the creation of a metropolitan district. The attorney general has advised three legislators who planned to introduce bills that would forbid state financing of busing across district lines to withdraw them, for such action could be used against the state in federal courts later.

be guaranteed. The St. Louis school board and NAACP are willing to consider a voluntary plan, but the state legislature seems to be in no hurry to provide a plan that would take substantial steps toward metropolitan integration. And the suburban school districts are almost unanimously opposed. On March 3, 1980, the Court of Appeals in ordering desegregation for the St. Louis district, stated: "Voluntary techniques will not effectively desegregate the St. Louis school system." It is quite possible that the voluntary plan for the metropolitan area would receive a similar judgment—even if something acceptable to the lower court (William L. Hungate has replaced Meredith) is forthcoming from Missouri and the suburban districts.

Many people say they want integration, but are opposed to forced busing. It is difficult to know what this means. If they are sincere, they mean that they want integration only when enough individuals freely decide to take part and make it a reality. Or they mean that if the residential patterns were different, they would favor it. But these are counterfactual conditions. Anyone who favors integration now or in the foreseeable future must seriously consider accepting forced busing, for integration cannot be achieved in any other way. Unless integrationists do entertain the idea of forced busing and examine its pros and cons objectively, we can be somewhat cynical and suspect that it is not, after all, the bus ride they object to but what happens at the *end* of the ride.[52] Let us, then, look at two general questions: Do the people favor integration? Is forced busing too high a price to pay for it?

Public Opinion Several studies and polls have been conducted on the acceptability of integration. The pattern is one of growing acceptance. In the South, the percentage of white adults objecting to integration where only a "few" of the students were black decreased from 72 percent to 15 percent in the years 1959–1975. The corresponding figures in the North were 7 and 3 percent. Where the school makeup was half and half, the figures for acceptance went from 83 percent to 38 percent in the South and from 34 percent to 24 percent in the North.[53] "People continue to support school desegregation and to oppose busing, refusing to recognize the incompatibility of their values and believing that there is some other way to achieve integration."[54]

Opposition to forced busing is often very strong in districts at the beginning and through the first year or so. In Charlotte, Louisville, and other districts,

[52]Many who say they favor integration have not in their own housing decisions chosen desegregated neighborhoods or schools. Their opposition to busing is a natural extension of their opposition to integration expressed in their choice of residence. See Ronald S. Edari, "White Attitudes toward Busing: Segregation and the Life Cycle," p. 98ff.

[53]Gallup polls, reported in Orfield, p. 109. Similar but more specific results were reported by Alston and Crouch, "White Acceptance of Three Degrees of School Desegregation, 1974," p. 216ff. Although the authors lament that only 32 percent of southern whites and 43 percent of northern whites "would not object to any form of integration," the fact is that only 32 percent "object only when blacks form more than one-half of the population."

[54]Orfield, p. 108.

public opinion was very strong (and widely publicized). Busing is proceeding smoothly today in many places where dire predictions once were made. Often political leaders will stir up trouble for their own political purposes—as Orval Faubus did in Little Rock when token integration was at stake. Instead of carrying out the directives of federal courts as responsible officials should, they seek to become local heroes through defiance. Sometimes the integration plan is faulty. In Boston, instead of busing throughout the district, blacks from Roxbury were bused in great number into South Boston simply because its high school was nearest. Sometimes opposition is strong when integration is attempted in a district where the number of Anglos is very small. Often the "education" of the parents is incomplete; they are not adequately informed about what will take place and prepared for it. These obstacles are not insurmountable, and the evidence is that where they have been avoided or surmounted, public acceptance of forced busing becomes greater as time goes on.[55]

Four important antidesegregation bills were defeated in Congress in 1979: The Collins amendment, "prohibiting the Justice Department from using federal funds to require busing"; the Walker amendment, "invalidating the use of any ratio, quota or other numerical requirement"; the Mottle constitutional amendment, prohibiting busing to a public school other than the school nearest to the student's home"; the Ashbrook amendment, "prohibiting the new Department of Education from issuing regulations, rules or guidelines requiring busing as a condition to receive federal funds."[56]

Integration is a good example of how enlightened views favored by a minority have come to be accepted by the majority if, somehow, they can be put into practice somewhere. Few people now favor slavery, but a great many did in 1860. Few people now favor de jure segregation in housing, the military, and public accommodations, but many did in 1954. Few people now favor depriving minorities of the vote, but many did in 1964. The growing acceptance of equal rights for women has taken place over two generations, and the old attitudes strike most of us today as thoroughly wrong-headed. Constitutional law and statutory law have succeeded in bringing the majority view (often a thoughtless kind of prejudice) in line with the convictions of a fair-minded minority.[57]

At times in our history, we believed that the insane were proper objects of ridicule, that painless childbirth was irreligious, that a murderer was not entitled to legal counsel, that contraception should be prohibited by law, that books

[55]"In most communities desegregation has gone peacefully and smoothly—for every Boston and Louisville there are dozens of other communities, which have received no headlines and attracted no television coverage, where desegregation is proceeding without major incident." *Report of U.S. Commission on Civil Rights* (Washington: Government Printing Office, August 1976).

[56]See Randal Alonzo Mangham, Introduction to Symposium Commemorating the 25th Anniversary of *Brown* v. *Board of Education, Howard Law Journal* (1980), p. 4n.

[57]"The Supreme Court of the United States is really the schoolmaster of the Republic and if it cannot command, it can at least educate the American people about what they need to do to improve the educational systems of the country." Philip Kurland, "Equal Educational Opportunity or the Limits of Constitutional Jurisprudence Undefined," in Charles U. Daly, ed., *The Quality of Inequality* (Chicago: University of Chicago Press, 1968), p. 65.

containing four-letter words should be banned, that people were poor because they were lazy and should be the recipients of private charity only, that children of nine could work for ten hours in a factory—the list is endless. Our social views have changed for the better. We have become more civilized. Sometimes we have to be dragged, kicking and screaming, to a higher level of human justice. There is every reason to believe that public attitudes will continue to grow in support of integration—and that which makes integration a reality: forced busing.[58] In time, the word *forced* may be dropped. In preintegration days, busing was forced also. In rural areas in the North and South, this was the only way to get to school, and in some cities also, but it was not called "forced." It was *education* that was forced, and busing was understood to be the appropriate means for it.

The Costs of Forced Busing Let us now look at the *costs* of busing. Are they really disproportionate to the acknowledged gains that it makes possible?

In many districts, busing for integration is not a new system imposed on an area where busing did not exist before. It is simply a matter of replacing one busing plan with another one. In many cases, the new busing will be *less* extensive (and less expensive) than the old. This was often true in those districts where busing had been used to carry out the dual school system. Just as people now sometimes complain that a bus carries their child past the nearest school to one across town, minorities once lodged the same complaint. In many cases the cost of busing for integration will be about the same as it was before.

Admittedly, integration will occasionally require a greater outlay for busing than would have been required otherwise. How much more? In Jackson, Mississippi, operating expenses rose from 0.6 percent to 1.8 percent of the annual budget. Richmond went from 0.4 to 1.1 percent, Winston-Salem from 1.8 to 4.0 percent. In the Charlotte system, 400 square miles, the costs went from 0.8 to 1.6 percent. In other metropolitan systems, Jacksonville and Tampa, costs went from 1.3 to 2.2 percent and from 1.35 to 1.7 percent, respectively. It cost Prince Georges County, Maryland, ninth largest district in the country, an additional 0.6 percent to bus. The expenses for Clark County, Nevada (8000 square miles), was only 2.3 percent of the annual budget, and that included buying thirty additional buses![59] Denver was able to integrate at an additional cost of 1.6 percent of its budget.[60] A great many cities that did *not* integrate showed an increase in busing costs. The major cost of busing, if there is an additional cost

[58]A study of desegregation in Milwaukee refuted the "proximity resistance" argument that those most immediately threatened are strongest in their protest, finding instead: "Parents of children in the public schools became more supportive of integration and busing on several different measures. On the other hand, people without children in the schools became more resistant, and parents of children in parochial schools showed the most negative attitude change." Jacobson, "Desegregation Rulings and Public Attitude Changes," p. 698.

[59]Commission on Civil Rights, *School Desegregation in Ten Communities* (Washington: Government Printing Office, 1973).

[60]See Orfield, p. 133.

at all, is in the first year, when additional buses are purchased. Federal and state funds should be made available to ease the financial burden of districts in the transitional stage. The Emergency School Aid program has often *prohibited* grant money from being used to defray busing expenses!

A second "cost" that is often cited in antibusing arguments is the additional time that students must spend sitting on the bus. This does not hold water at all. Busing for integration seldom results in a higher average riding time than existed before integration took place, and in rural areas it is usually much less. Very few busing plans require any student to ride for more than thirty minutes, while forty minutes seems to be the top figure.[61] Where hardship occurs is in those districts that for reasons of economy have to use the same buses for an early school shift and a late school shift. Children in the same family are coming and going from sunrise to sunset. This could be averted by grants from state and federal sources —always reluctant to support busing.

A third "cost" is supposed to be violence that is characteristically intensified in integrated schools. The amount of violence attributable to forced busing has been grossly exaggerated. Where it occurs at all, it is usually the result of ignorant and strident parents and demogogic politicians.

> A survey of almost a thousand school superintendents by the Commission on Civil Rights turned up little evidence of serious violence accompanying desegregation. Only one district in fifteen had required additional police help, and most of them were back to normal within two months. Very few educators reported that educational activities had been disrupted for more than two weeks. Problems are apt to be greatest during the first year when older, formerly segregated children are first brought together in a school. Attention from the media and the public usually focuses on such schools.[62]

White students are in no danger even when bused to a ghetto. Their work takes place in a *school,* which is (or should be) insulated from the city around it.

A fourth "cost" is supposed to be the demise of the neighborhood or "walk-in" school. Actually, of course, this kind of school has been exceptional for many years. It began to disappear in rural areas when the one-room schoolhouse was deemed inadequate. Most children could not attend elementary schools within a mile of home, and only about one in four could attend high school within a mile of home—*before* integration began. In 1976, Secretary William T. Coleman, Jr., reported that the annual increase in the number of school buses in the five years after *Swann* was the same as the annual increase in the five years before *Swann.* It should also be noted that many students are driven to school, drive themselves to school, or utilize public transportation. A great many more bus to parochial schools. With all this transportation taking place (none of which is connected

[61]The busing required for private schools ("segregation academies") is generally far more than for public schools—proving again that for many people it is not the busing itself that is the issue.
[62]Orfield, p. 127.

with integration), there cannot be many students left who walk to the good old neighborhood school.

There is something disingenuous in blaming segregated schools on segregated housing. The causal relation is a two-way one. Segregated education has done much in fostering and retaining segregated housing. This reciprocal interplay raises the question of "incremental segregative effect." The Supreme Court and lower courts have recently shown an interest in the matter.[63] A good, white school, staffed with white teachers, can be used to "preserve" a neighborhood. White schools are built for white neighborhoods, black for black neighborhoods. Continued residential growth around them is calculated to follow racial patterns. Attendance lines are gerrymandered and pupil assignments manipulated. Schools of the right type are built where the particular race is expected to live, and draw accordingly from the appropriate group—with the help of real estate people, of course.[64]

It is certainly easier to bus than to eliminate segregated residential patterns, whether they are de jure or de facto, whether brought about by personal choice, political connivance, unscrupulous real estate operators, school boards, or chance. "Ever since Africans were brought to these shores, whites have either determined the conditions of propinquity or exercised the option of separating themselves to the extent that this was possible. That whites, to varying degrees, have a desire to separate themselves from blacks and that, therefore, varying numbers of whites will exercise this option under certain circumstances has to be accepted as a given in race relations. . . ."[65] Integrated neighborhoods are a thing of the remote future, at best; integrated schools can be produced *now.*

A fifth "cost" of busing is supposed to be the stimulus it gives to "white flight" from the cities. There are so many factors contributing to flight (white, black, and brown) that it is impossible to ascertain the relative importance of integration. The flight was well under way in the South before *Swann* and in the North before *Keyes,* and the *Milliken* decision has not reversed it. The fact is that the cities have had tremendous problems in the last few decades. The houses are old and the neighborhoods are decaying. Industries are moving out. Employment opportunities are dwindling. The populations are older and not of childbearing age. The declining tax base results in poorer public services—including fire, police, sanitation, and education. Political leadership is inefficient and corrupt. The successful middle-class families are leaving for good and sufficient reason. Each case of such a family leaving in effect provides more reason for the remaining families to leave. As long as people have cars, good roads, and plenty of gas, they can move

[63]See *Dayton Board of Education et al.* v. *Brinkman* (1977) and *Amos* v. *Board of School Directors of the City of Milwaukee* (1976).

[64]See Taeuber, "Housing, Schools, and Incremental Segregative Effects," *Annals of American Academy of Political and Social Science* (January 1979), p. 157ff. The whole issue is entitled "Race and Residence in American Cities" and edited by Wade Clark Roof.

[65]Erber, "White Flight and Political Retreat," p. 54.

from the cities quite easily, without even changing jobs. If the fear of integrated education is now a factor, it is only one of several.[66]

It is difficult to see what was accomplished for integration in the Atlanta settlement. Keeping 10 percent of the students from fleeing did not make the city integrated, nor did it directly serve the educational needs of the students, black or white. The NAACP suspended its Atlanta chapter for accepting the plan, for it surrendered the goal, integration, in order to prevent white flight (and to get more black control of the school system). If a metropolitan school system had been set up, however, one comprising the white suburbs, there would have been integrated education with very little white flight. None was reported from the schools or state of Florida when statewide desegregation took place.[67]

As far as student enrollment is concerned, an important study of sixty districts in ten southern states showed that "districts less than roughly 30% black experienced only moderate white enrollment instability which was unrelated to the level of black concentration. . . . By combining high percent black districts, the overall black concentration can be reduced and the problem of white withdrawal reduced correspondingly. Failing the adoption of multiple district plans or other successful compensating strategies, desegregation of districts with high percent black enrollments is predicted to be costly in terms of white withdrawals."[68]

Conclusion If the above argument is sound, forced busing is an appropriate means for a social goal that is both worthwhile and increasingly popular. Busing is not without its costs, but these costs are not disproportionate to the goods it serves. Without busing, there will be no integration. As Edmund Burke said, "The only thing necessary for the triumph of evil is for good men to do nothing."

Summary of the Issues

Both sides accept the Supreme Court decision of 1954. The dual school system is wrong and the laws which prescribe it are unconstitutional. Children are denied their rights when made to attend segregated schools. "Separate but equal" is self-contradictory. As a result of this decision, together with executive and legisla-

[66]Ernest Erber masterfully refutes the Coleman-Ravitch thesis by showing that there is no correlation between percentage of minority gain and white loss. Some cities (1968–1976) experienced great white loss and low minority gain, and some even experienced great white loss at the same time that minority *loss* took place. If it is argued that white flight is from particular integrated schools, Erber has only to cite the case of Chicago. White enrollment dropped by over 40 percent, "though it remained the most segregated large-city system in the country." The whites were not bused—but still they fled. And a great many departing whites did not even *have* children! He also cites other social scientists who have also sharply criticized Coleman's theory. See Ibid., p. 53ff.

[67]See Armor and Schwartzbach, *White Flight, Demographic Transition, and the Future of School Desegregation,* p. 17.

[68]Giles, "White Enrollment Stability and School Desegregation," pp. 862–863.

tive action in Washington, segregation in education in the South was for the most part ended by 1971. What separation of the races still existed, in the North as well as the South, was due more to residential patterns than to educational design. This separation was (and is) more characteristic of urban areas than rural ones.

In the early seventies, the federal courts declared that racial *integration* in the schools was required. Ending segregation and the dual school system is not enough. The separation of the races resulting from residential patterns within the school district was to be overcome by forced busing within the district. Busing was to be employed to achieve racial balance in each of the schools. It is on this point that our controversy turns.

The probusing side argues that "equal protection" for schoolchildren entails genuine integration, not simply the absence of deliberate segregation. A moral principle is also involved that is so important that legislatures and school boards should go beyond what a narrow construction of the Constitution might imply and insist on racially balanced schools for the sake of brotherhood and racial accord. Since integration can be achieved only by busing and since voluntary measures do not work, forced busing is the only available means.

The antibusing side disagrees with most of these contentions. The Constitution does not require integration. Courts, executives, legislatures, and school boards should not try to achieve it by forced busing. Among the consequences of such a program is the loss of the neighborhood school and the social values it supports for all races. Another is the fact of "white flight" from districts with a large minority population—which is obviously counterproductive to integration. Empirical studies are also cited to show that integration achieved by forced busing has not produced educational and emotional benefits for minority children, nor has it contributed to racial harmony. The probusing side has rejoinders for each of these consequentialist arguments.

Other issues are: (1) The cost of busing in dollars and time. One side emphasizes it; the other side minimizes it. (2) Public acceptance of integrated schools. One side emphasizes the militant opposition; the other side argues that the initial public outcry is usually followed by peaceful acceptance. (3) Popular support for forced busing. One side shows that it lacks democratic support; the other side points out that an enlightened minority can lead the others toward a state of understanding and support. (4) The fact of segregated housing. One side would have integrated education follow integrated residence; the other side believes that the values of integrated education are too great to postpone.

The existence of urban school districts with a majority of "minority" population poses a peculiar problem. The antibusing side points out the futility of trying to achieve genuine integration in a district where there are not enough white Anglos to go around. The probusing side calls for redistricting so that there *are* enough white Anglos to go around. The Supreme Court has not spoken clearly on the issue, but the key consideration seems to be whether racial patterns of residence in metropolitan areas are de facto or de jure. The antibusing side tends to view the patterns as de facto, while arguing for the merits of local control and defending the right of states to draw their own boundary lines. The probusing side tends to view the patterns as de jure, while arguing that the Constitutional and moral rights of minority children should take precedence over existing residential patterns regardless of how they have developed. Those who sincerely believe in integrated education must accept not only forced busing but the creation of metropolitan school districts as well.

Discussion Questions

1. Do you think that the *manner* in which authorities carry out the integration of a district has much bearing on its success? Explain.
2. Do you accept the distinction between *nonsegregation* and *integration*? If so, which is required by the Constitution? Explain. Or do you think that *neither* is required by the Constitution? Explain.
3. Would you agree that forced busing to achieve integration in a district that is 80 percent black is futile? Explain.
4. Do you see much hope for voluntary integration within a district—say, in "magnet" schools? Why? What about voluntary integration *across* district lines?
5. Do you agree that people who oppose forced busing are really objecting, not to the ride, but to what happens at the *end* of the ride? Why?
6. If you were a white parent in an integrated school district, at what point would you move from the district because of the racial composition of the schools? 10 percent black? 25 percent black? 50 percent black? 75 percent black? 90 percent black? Not at all? Why?
7. Substitute "black parent" for "white parent" in the preceding question.
8. If you were a black or Hispanic parent, would you prefer to see your children in an integrated school filled with tension and distrust or in a peaceful neighborhood school?
9. If you favor integrated education, would you favor redistricting for purposes of bringing in the white suburbs? On moral or Constitutional grounds?
10. Do you think that integrated schools should wait for integrated residence patterns? Why? Or do you think that integrated schooling may in time work against segregated residence? Why?
11. Consider the racially separate residential patterns that you are familiar with. Do you think they just naturally developed that way (de facto segregation), or do you think they developed with the aid and connivance of law (de jure segregation)? Explain. In attempting to distinguish de facto and de jure, where would you place the factor of the pressure of public opinion? Why?
12. What financial arguments could be given against forming metropolitan school districts? Are they valid? Why?
13. Integration is usually defended on moral grounds that are deontological and attacked on moral grounds that are utilitarian. Do you think there are significant utilitarian arguments that could be mounted for integration? What are they?
14. Do you think that minority children are educationally handicapped if they spend their learning years in schools that are not integrated? Why?

15. Do you think that integrated schooling will ultimately contribute to racial accord? Why?
16. Many black parents oppose forced busing. Why? Do you think that they are misguided? Explain.
17. Would you vote for a political candidate who opposed forced busing? What if he or she was for integration? What if he or she was against both integration and forced busing? Explain.
18. Would you favor forced busing in a large school district where white Anglos formed a majority? Why? What if the white Anglos were a minority? Why?
19. Suppose that the facilities and instruction in two schools are the same. One has a racial composition similar to that of the state. The other is racially homogeneous. Which one would you prefer that your child attend? Why?
20. Evaluate Nixon's "southern strategy."
21. Evaluate Carter's "southern strategy."
22. To what extent is Reagan utilizing the resources of the executive department to achieve integration through forced busing?
23. What is the position of your senators and congressman on forced busing?
24. Would you favor a constitutional amendment against forced busing? Why?
25. Do you think that people who resort to white flight (or black or brown flight) should feel guilty? Why?

For Further Reading

Jon P. Alston and Ben M. Crouch. "White Acceptance of Three Degrees of School Desegregation, 1974." *Phylon* 39 (September 1978):216–224.

David J. Armor. "The Evidence on Busing." *Public Interest* (Summer 1972).

David J. Armor and Donna Schwartzbach. *White Flight, Demographic Transition, and the Future of School Desegregation.* Santa Monica, Calif.: Rand Corp., 1978.

Ronald Aronson. "Is Busing the Real Issue?" *Dissent* 25 (Fall 1978):409–415.

"Brown v. Board of Education: Twenty-five Years Later" (Symposium). *Crisis* 86 (June 1979):189–273.

R. Stephen Browning, ed. *From Brown to Bradley: School Desegregation 1954–1974.* Cincinnati: Jefferson Law Book Co., 1975.

James S. Coleman. "Liberty and Equality in School Desegregation." *Social Policy* 6 (January–February 1976):9ff.

James S. Coleman et al. *Equality of Educational Opportunity.* Washington: Government Printing Office, 1966.

James S. Coleman et al. *Trends in School Segregation, 1968–1973.* Washington: Urban Institute, 1975.

Robert L. Crain and Rita E. Mahard. *Desegregation and Black Achievement* (Santa Monica: Rand Corp., 1977).

Robert L. Crain and Rita E. Mahard. "School Racial Composition and Black College Attendance and Achievement Test Performance." *Sociology of Education* 51 (April 1978):81–101.

Darrel W. Drury. "Black Self-Esteem and Desegregated Schools." *Sociology of Education* 53 (April 1980):88–103.

Ronald S. Edari. "White Attitudes toward Busing: Segregation and the Life Cycle." *Journal of Black Studies* 10 (September 1979):98–118.

Ernest Erber. "White Flight and Political Retreat." *Dissent* 26 (Winter 1979):53–58.

William W. Falk. "School Desegregation and the Educational Attainment Process: Some Results from Rural Texas Schools." *Sociology of Education* 51 (October 1978):282–288.

Reynolds Farley et al. "Barriers to the Racial Integration of Neighborhoods: The Detroit Case." *Annals of the American Academy of Political and Social Science* 441 (January 1979):97–113.

Michael W. Giles. "H.E.W. versus the Federal Courts: A Comparison of School Desegregation Enforcement." *American Politics Quarterly* 3 (January 1975):81–90.

Michael W. Giles. "White Enrollment Stability and School Desegregation." *American Sociological Review* 43 (September 1978):848–864.

Norene Harris et al., eds. *The Integration of American Schools: Problems, Experiences, Solutions.* Boston: Allyn & Bacon, 1975.

Amos Isaac. "The Issue Is Not Busing but the Fourteenth Amendment: Strategies for Evasion." *Education and Urban Society* 9 (May 1977):259–276.

Cardell K. Jacobson. "Desegregation Rulings and Public Attitude Changes: White Resistance or Resignation?" *American Journal of Sociology* 84 (November 1978):698–705.

Cardell K. Jacobson. "School Racial Composition Effects on Avoidance, Separation, and Integrationist Attitudes of Adolescents." *Sociological Quarterly* 20 (Spring 1979):223–235.

David L. Kirp. "Law, Politics, and Equal Educational Opportunity: The Limits of Judicial Involvement." *Harvard Educational Review* 47 (May 1977):117–137.

David L. Kirp. "School Desegregation and the Limits of Legalism." *The Public Interest* 47 (Spring 1977):101–128.

Florence Hamlish Levinsohn and Benjamin Drake Wright, eds. *School Desegregation: Shadow and Substance.* Chicago: University of Chicago Press, 1976.

Joel A. Lieske. "Group Disorders in Urban Schools: The Effects of Racial Desegregation and Social Emancipation." *Urban Affairs Quarterly* 14 (September 1978):79–101.

J. Dennis Lord. *Spatial Perspectives on School Desegregation and Busing.* Washington: Association of American Geographers, 1977.

Nicolaus Mills, ed. *The Great School Bus Controversy.* New York:Teachers College Press, 1973.

G. W. Nobit and T. W. Collins. "Order and Disruption in a Desegregated High School." *Crime and Delinquency* 24 (July 1978):277–289.

Gary Orfield. *Must We Bus? Segregated Schools and National Policy.* Washington: Brookings Institution, 1978.

Martin Patchen et al. "Academic Performance of Black High School Students under Different Conditions of Contact with White Peers." *Sociology of Education* 53:33–51.

"Public School Desegregation" (Symposium). *Washington University Law Quarterly* (Spring 1979):309–434.

Diane Ravitch. "Color-blind or Color-conscious?" *The New Republic* 180 (May 5, 1979): 15–20.

Diane Ravitch. "White Flight Controversy." *The Public Interest* 51 (Spring 1978):135–149.

J. L. Regens and C. S. Bullock III. "Congruity of Racial Attitudes among Black and White Students." *Social Science Quarterly* 60 (December 1979):511–522.

Christine H. Rossell. *The Unintended Impacts of Public Policy: School Desegregation and Resegregation.* Durham: Duke University, Institute of Policy Sciences, 1978.

Christine H. Rossell. "White Flight: Pros and Cons." *Social Policy* 9 (November 1978): 46–51.

Nancy H. St. John. *School Desegregation: Outcome for Children.* New York: John Wiley, 1975.

"School Desegregation: Lessons of the First Twenty-five Years" (Symposium). *Law and Contemporary Problems* 42 (Autumn 1978):1–183 and 42 (Autumn 1978): 233ff.

D. O. Sears et al. "Whites' Opposition to Business: Self-Interest of Symbolic Politics." *American Political Science Review* 73 (June 1979):369–384.

Daniel S. Sheehan. "A Study of Attitude Change in Desegregated Intermediate Schools." *Sociology of Education* 53 (January 1980):51–59.

Daniel S. Sheehan. "Black Achievement in a Desegregated School District." *Journal of Social Psychology* 107 (April 1979):185–192.

Roberta G. Simmons et al., "Self-Esteem and Achievement of Black and White Adolescents." *Social Problems* 26 (October 1978):86–96.

Walter G. Stephan and David Rosenfield. "Effects of Desegregation on Racial Attitudes." *Journal of Personality and Social Psychology* 36 (August 1978):795–804.

Symposium Commemorating the 25th Anniversary of *Brown* v. *Board of Education. Howard Law Journal* 23 (1980):1–133.

Karl E. Taeuber. "Housing, Schools, and Incremental Segregative Effects." *Annals of American Academy of Political and Social Science* 441 (January 1979):157–167.

J. Harvie Wilkinson III. *From Brown to Bakke: The Supreme Court and School Integration, 1954–1978.* New York: Oxford University Press, 1979.

Franklin D. Wilson. "Patterns of White Avoidance." *Annals of American Academy of Political and Social Science* 441 (January 1979):132–141.

K. L. Wilson. "Effects of Integration and Class on Black Educational Attainment." *Sociology of Education* 52 (April 1979):85–98.

THE AIMS OF EDUCATION

The Chief Purpose of Undergraduate Education Is the Cultivation of the Arts and Sciences

Human Concerns The three chief concerns of humanity are the good, the true, and the beautiful. Our success as human beings is measured by our ability to recognize and promote moral values, distinguish fact from falsehood, and enjoy the marvels of nature and art. Our life should consist of a steady growth in the understanding of these sublime concepts. They should increasingly suffuse our consciousness and heighten our experience as we move from the irresponsibility, ignorance, and insensitivity of infancy into the blessedness of maturity.

Most young people of college age are beyond childhood and on the verge of adulthood. They have begun to take a lively interest in values and the world around them. They want to make sense of things and come to terms with the universe. Their intellectual powers are strong and their aesthetic sensitivities are acute. Their experience is limited, but they have intimations, not of immortality, but of wisdom. They are groping for meaning. They want to move up to a higher plateau. They want to become more fully human.

The means to facilitate this kind of growth are present (or potentially present) in the American college or university. The faculty are individuals who have committed their lives to the mastering of a particular branch of learning. The library is full of good books and journals. The art building houses paintings and sculptures. Cocurricular activities in music, drama, and literature abound. Distinguished visitors to the campus present concerts, speeches, symposiums, and plays. Clubs exist for political, religious, and philosophical interests. All these resources and activities serve the quest for the good, the true, and the beautiful. In some schools, even the curriculum serves these ends.

Not only can the university offer students precisely what they need at the very time they need it, but their attendance will be the last occasion in their life when they can advance their deepest concerns over a sustained period of time under professional guidance in the company of peers. The university experience is the last best chance for laying the foundation for a lifetime of truly human growth. Since courses and classes are the chief part of undergraduate life, the curriculum especially should be fashioned in such a way as to produce humanistic insights and lay the basis for more.

The Good Study of "the good" is the most practical enterprise that people can engage in, for it deals with those principles that ultimately must justify their actions and the course of their lives. As Socrates told Callicles: "There is no question which a man of any sense could take more seriously than this which we are now discussing: what course of life one ought to follow. . . ."[69] Since the practical is that which is concerned with action, nothing can be more practical than the examination of principles that one can accept as the guideposts for *all* one's actions.

What is good? What is just? What is right? Such questions are inescapable. We must answer them whether we want to or not. To refuse to answer them is itself an answer, for it is tantamount to saying that it is right to act in a way oblivious of any conscious recognition of the principle of rightness. To refuse to seek theoretical foundations for maxims according to which we ordinarily act is to act as if these maxims certified their own truth. To say that these questions are meaningless is to say that life is meaningless. We will necessarily make value judgments. Wisdom consists in making them on as reasonable a basis as possible.

The search for the good manifests itself when one seeks to distinguish what is the case from what ought to be the case. One will judge one's own actions, character, and habits, as well as those of others. One will examine the laws and mores of society. One will evaluate the performances of political leaders. One will

[69]Plato, *Gorgias* 500C.

question the existence and efficacy of institutions. One will formulate standards of excellence while trying to improve the quality of human life.

How many college courses contribute to the search for the good? Obviously, courses in ethics will be very helpful. They may emphasize ethical theory or seek to relate ethical theory to contemporary problems. They may concentrate on personal ethics or social ethics—or attempt to combine the two approaches. There may be courses in business ethics, legal ethics, and medical ethics, all valuable applications of theory to specific situations. Courses in religion, Christian and otherwise, also serve the students in their quest for deeper knowledge of the good.

Courses in literature also provide material for ethical scrutiny. What ethical principles did Hamlet seek to respond to, and were they valid? Is the pessimism of *Shropshire Lad* sound? Is there any excuse for the behavior of the characters in the Updike novel *Couples*? Good biographies are also useful. Here we see the growth or atrophy of moral concerns, the changing of standards, and the complexity of human life.

Courses in the social sciences often expose ethical issues: segregation, distributive justice, affirmative action, treatment of law-breakers, relative merits of political systems, and so on. History recounts events produced by individual and public decisions, all of which may be examined from the ethical point of view.

Even courses in natural science are useful in ethical judgment. Physics and chemistry tell us about radioactivity, its promises and dangers. In other courses, we learn about the environment and the threats to it. In biology, we learn about human life and gain important knowledge for dealing with such ethical problems as genetic engineering, euthanasia, and abortion.

This is just a brief indication of some of the possibilities. Most ethical problems require *facts* for their solution. One cannot evaluate the soundness of compulsory genetic screening without knowing something about genetics. An opinion about educational desegregation will have no value unless it is held in the light of demographic realities. A viewpoint on atomic power will be useless apart from knowledge of the availability of certain natural resources. A theory on the treatment of criminals must take into account the facts of recidivism. If nothing else, courses in the social and natural sciences will provide the student with knowledge of (1) the various disciplines and their relations to one another, (2) where to find information later needed for ethical judgment, and (3) the basic concepts and vocabulary. It is unfortunate that requirements in science have dwindled so much in our universities. It is also ironic. The further science and technology advance in our society, the less demand there is that citizens know anything about them.

College students, in short, should confront in the subject matter of their courses aspects of the universe that should be treasured, enhanced, improved, or eliminated.

The True There is nothing that philosophers through the ages have expressed more agreement on than the value of knowledge.

When Socrates said that "knowledge is virtue," he may have meant, first of all, that knowledge of the good is a prerequisite for doing good. Plato, Aristotle, and Thomas Aquinas carried the idea a little further and held that one always acts on the basis of one's idea of the good, that the difference between a virtuous person and a scoundrel lies in the greater ethical insight of the former. Socrates may have meant that knowledge of the way experiences are connected, their consequences and causes, is the key to the good life. Bentham and Dewey would agree with this. Or Socrates may have meant that knowledge has value in itself. It is this third sense that we will be concerned with here.

Plato and Aristotle prized knowledge for its own sake. There was value for them in having a comprehensive and theoretical understanding of the universe quite apart from the practical use that this understanding could be put to. The Aristotelian gentlemen required leisure to study, and Plato's "philosopher kings" had to have a little time to themselves for communing with the realm of Forms. The Stoics thought it was more important to know *why* things happened than to exert themselves to bring about certain things. Mystics through the ages have celebrated the ineffable knowledge attained in their visions. In a more pedestrian manner, the *philosophes* of the Enlightenment were proud of the new knowledge that was at last dissolving the ignorance and superstition of the past.

Epicurus and Mill preferred to base their theories on the undeniable goodness of pleasure, but both so exalted the superior goodness of intellectual pleasures that knowledge seems to function for them much in the way of a value all its own. In ideal utilitarianism, knowledge is an intrinsic value whose presence is desirable "from the point of view of the universe." It is a quality of human experience: a *knowing* state of mind is superior to an *erroneous* state of mind.

In our curiosity to know the world, we testify that we desire that which is desirable. Until this curiosity is blunted by more pressing concerns of life, we want to comprehend reality—if not in the metaphysical sense, at least in the scientific sense. We want to know *what is what:* the structure and forces of matter, the characteristics of organic and animal life, the nature of human beings. We want to know what humanity has done in the past as well as the kinds of societies it sustains in the present. The person who has employed reason to achieve understanding, according to Aristotle, experiences *eudaimonia*—literally, "possession by a good demon," but more accurately, a sense of vital well-being. To the degree that one *knows,* to that degree one has expressed the most unique aspect of one's humanity.

This is what it means to be liberated. You are not merely liberated or emancipated from ignorance. You are liberated in the sense that you are functioning as a person: it is *your* nature that has prevailed. You are not simply another object caught up in the forces of nature, you are a center of consciousness that is *aware* of these forces.

Whether we look at knowledge from a hedonistic, utilitarian, or humanistic point of view, it is the value we may most appropriately expect our universities to foster. Students should emerge from their four years of higher education with a basic understanding of mathematics, physics, chemistry, earth science, political science, sociology, economics, anthropology, history, biology, and psychology. This is a large order, but this is a rich and varied universe we live in. No one can be called educated who has not worked seriously, at least for a short time, in each of the major fields of knowledge.

The Beautiful In going from the good and the true to the beautiful, we move into an area of sheer delight. For in aesthetic enjoyment we are moved to the depths of our being. In morality we achieve virtue, uprightness, and a sense of direction, in knowledge we experience deep gratification, but in the appreciation of the fine arts we are transported and occasionally moved to tears.

Who can forget the surpassing joy experienced upon first gazing on the actual paintings of Van Gogh, hearing Handel's *Messiah,* witnessing a performance of *Othello,* reading Housman's "Loveliest of Trees," looking up at the spires of the cathedral at Chartres, reading *Raintree County,* hearing Wild Bill Davison play "Sleepy Time Down South," or seeing *Treasure of the Sierra Madre* on the screen?

Something of this joy is experienced by many through the more popular products of art. But those who have experienced both the "high" and the "low," if we may be permitted to use these terms, generally testify to the superiority of the former. They know that Robert Frost surpasses Edgar A. Guest, that George Gershwin is better than Elton John, that Picasso is better than Norman Rockwell, that James Thurber is funnier than Bennett Cerf, that Marie Sandoz is better than Jacqueline Susann, and that just about anybody is better than Harold Robbins. What a college education can do is to bring students into a deeper appreciation of art by exposing them to what have been accepted as works of genius. Students learn what to look for, what to listen for, and to apply the canons of artistic achievement. Some of this will "take," some will not. They will at least have had the chance to be rescued from the tawdry standards of mass culture and popular taste. If, after hearing Mozart, they still prefer the Grateful Dead, so be it. But the opportunity of rising above "Hee Haw" and *Smoky and the Bandit* should be theirs. A person who enjoys a dirty limerick may enjoy T. S. Eliot at least as much, and Robert Browning is not that far from Robert Service.

So, in recognition of the beautiful and life-long delights it promises us, the universities should require extensive courses in art appreciation, music appreciation, and literature in all its forms. They have only four years to open these new worlds to their students. If they fail, most students will live the rest of their lives in a state of stunted development, their taste for the marvelous atrophied, and their sensitivities brutalized by mass culture.

Professional Education What is the place of professional education in a four-year program? In view of the demands made above for liberal education in the arts and sciences, little room is left in the curriculum for professional learning. Most of this must be deferred to the graduate level.

The professions of law and medicine have long been aware that preparation cannot be achieved within the limits of a four-year program. Business administration, education, and engineering have yet to learn that students cannot be both educated as persons and trained for a profession within the four-year structure.

This does not mean that they cannot "major" in one of the arts or sciences. Just as a prospective doctor may major in biology and a prospective lawyer in government, the business person, educator, and engineer can choose appropriate majors—perhaps economics, psychology (or the teaching field), or physics, respectively. But in each case, they will be working with ideas instead of techniques.

Let students learn the theory first, then go on to professional applications. Let them rely on advanced courses or work experience to teach them what they need to know on the job, instead of surrendering the academic training they can get no other place than in the undergraduate university. It is wrong to seize freshmen and place them in a rigidly structured professional program. Constricted in their education by occupational concerns, they do not have time to smell the flowers —they don't even know that the flowers exist.

This is not to say that relevance for life is to be kept resolutely out of the picture, that students are to be locked in an ivory tower for four years, then released to sink or swim in the real world. Science courses may show some applications for their principles, as may economics and sociology courses. As we have seen, the ethical bearing, the potentialities for human betterment, should always hover over courses of instruction. But the university is a sanctuary of a kind, and the *fundamental* concern should be with the effect of education on the mind—its tendency to produce a mind that is attuned to the search for the good, the true, and the beautiful. There will be ample time afterward to learn a trade or "do high deeds in Hungary."

The college years are the halcyon years in which students have their last intensive and extensive opportunity to pass from adolescence into maturity by engaging themselves with the ideas and insights of the most successful adults the world has known. They become civilized by discovering what civilization is. They become truly human by pursuing those truly human concerns: the quest for the good, the true, and the beautiful.

The Chief Purpose of Undergraduate Education Is Preparation for a Career

Practical Considerations The proponent of a four-year undergraduate experience devoted chiefly to the study of liberal arts and sciences is asking for something that very few students can afford. College is expensive. Most students, for very good reasons, want to qualify for a job as soon as possible. Postponement of professional training adds another one to three years—at about $7000 to $10,000 per year. If the student could be working in each of those years, say for

$13,000, the cost is about $20,000 per year. This may be an acceptable price to pay in the case of a student favored by fortune, but it is too steep for most young men and women.

The program is designed for aristocrats. Such people can remove themselves from real life and cultivate their intellectual and aesthetic sensibilities. They can acquire polish, build up their vocabulary, and "broaden" themselves, with no concern for how they are to make a living. The whole scheme is that of providing a "finishing school," a form of education that was concocted for people who never would have to work.

A liberal arts education is a carryover from the days when it was assumed that a diligent student could master all the fields of knowledge. This has not been possible for several centuries. The "Renaissance man" or polymath is a creature of the past and will be seen no more. Most of us must be satisfied with being conversant with only one part of one field of knowledge, while modestly deferring to others in other parts and other fields. The best of us, those who in a lifetime of study have gone beyond this, did not achieve their competence (or even a small component of it) in a four-year undergraduate career.

What students get in liberal arts education is breadth and very little depth. But the breadth is phony, for it is derived from minimal exposure to a lot of things. It is shallow. The students have dabbled but never mastered. They have been shoved into a lot of courses and learn less and less about more and more.

The extensive requirements represent the interests of the various academic departments that, to secure their continued existence, have struck a political bargain. To hide their sins, they speak of the "well-rounded individual." What they have produced instead is at best a dilettante, at worst a poseur.

A Strange Interlude The liberal arts advocate evidently assumes that college freshmen have not learned anything in high school; that if college does not expose them to history, science, or psychology, they not only will be ignorant in these fields but will not even know what they are. This surely is to slight the efforts made in secondary education. Colleges blithely continue to duplicate what the high schools have done. They offer (or require) a foreign language, a course in American history, a course in European history, a survey in English literature, a course in natural science, and a course in American government. If these subject areas did not "take" in high school, will they "take" in college? If a "foundation" is valuable and effective for life, why does the foundation have to be repeated in college? Isn't it about time for students to go on to something new?

Some subjects are deemed so useful to other studies that they cannot be assumed to have been mastered in high school. So colleges require "skill courses" in English composition, logic, and speech. There is justification for requiring early competence in writing, thinking, and speaking, and if it is not achieved in high school, it should be taught early in the college career. But most of the courses that colleges require and that duplicate high school studies are not so fundamental. It is difficult, for example, to see what purpose is served by requiring a voice major to take a course in earth science or a business administration major to take a course in art appreciation.

Another assumption made in arguments for liberal arts is that nothing will be learned afterward. If students are not instructed in the arts and sciences in college, they will be forever cut off from these accouterments of the educated person. Although it is said that college provides the foundation for activities and interests that will be built upon throughout life, it is denied that the beginning can be made anywhere but in college. This is not true. Beginnings in all these "basic" areas can be made in places other than the four-year college. They can be made *before* college and they can be made *after* college. College is not an oasis that we finally reach after a wasteland of high school and where we take on all the supplies we will need before setting out to cross the desert of ordinary life.

The liberal arts ideal is an artificial structuring of human life and has very little relation to the real needs and motivations of people. As John Dewey would argue, education is a lifelong activity. We build on what we know and we also branch out in new directions—throughout our lives. We may cultivate new interests—in college and out. We study best when we are pursuing *our* interests, when we are engaging material that is relevant to *our* concerns, when we are trying to solve *our* problems. There is ample time after college for study in areas we find promising. And it does not have to be a structured or institutional form of instruction (although it may be). By the time a person reaches three score years and ten, he or she has added a great deal to what was learned in college. And most of this additional learning has been far more useful to the person.

While in college, students may choose a few electives from the field of liberal arts that interest them. Professional programs will not preempt *all* their time. Having *chosen* the electives, they can be expected to profit from them (most of the time). This is preferable to a system in which students are *required* to take a host of "general studies" courses that have little relevance to their present interests. It is doubtful that they will "profit" from this or even remember very much. This force-feeding, far from creating an interest, just as often prejudices students against the subject for the rest of their lives. Many courses based on the liberal arts and sciences can be given a practical focus, thus serving both the theoretical and the professional interests of the student. Examples: chemistry for nurses, medical ethics, psychology of education, philosophy of science, business ethics, mathematics for accountants, and history of legal traditions.

Education is continuous, beginning at birth and ending at death. It is not limited to the four years from age eighteen to age twenty-two. That is an important period, however, for that is when students must learn the skills that they can offer on the job market. They will soon be *employees.* And their employers and clients rightly will be more concerned with what they can *do* than with how deeply they have penetrated the mysteries of "the good, the true, and the beautiful."

"Knowledge for Its Own Sake" "Knowledge for its own sake," as John Dewey endlessly argued, is a completely wrong-headed ideal. It is based on an erroneous notion both of the nature of thought and the nature of reality.

Thought is an active function of a biological organism that seeks to survive and to reconstruct its own experience. It seeks not to understand what is the case but to produce desirable states of affairs. Thought serves a purpose—as do all faculties that have evolved. It is useful and practical. The purpose of thought, Dewey says, is not to behold "reality" but to change it. Our task is not to make our ideas conform to reality, but to make reality conform to our ideas. We are not passive spectators of things that come to pass but are ourselves a factor, often a potent one, in what comes to pass.

The conventional idea of truth is that ideas, opinions, or beliefs must conform to, correspond to, mirror reality. If we could somehow step out of our consciousness and view our idea and the thing-in-itself, we would pronounce that idea true if it "copied" that thing, if it actually grasped the essence of the thing that is known. A modern contextual definition of truth is this: A statement is true if and only if what it asserts is the case. Truth in this sense is supposed by some to be gratifying, even productive of "higher" pleasures. "It fortifies my soul to know," wrote Arthur Clough, "that though I perish, Truth is so."

Dewey radically alters this conception of truth, changing knowledge from a contemplative stance to an operative activity. Ideas must have consequences for life. They must lead us to results that we value and away from those we do not. Ideas are means for clearing up difficulties. They guide action. When they do so successfully, they are true. The individual thinks truly when his ideas prove useful for ordering and controlling his experience.[70]

The second erroneous assumption is that reality is permanent. Just as Plato sought the absolute forms and the Aristotelians sought the changeless essences in nature, their followers have assumed a timeless structure in the universe that philosophers and scientists should seek to capture once and for all. This "quest for certainty" ignored the flux of experience, empirical contingencies, and the uncertainties of common life in order to find and rest secure in an absolute conception of what (forever) is the case. For Dewey, *experience* is the only reality we will ever know. We seek to understand its patterns in order to predict its future. We seek to predict its future in order to control the quality of our personal and social lives.

If Dewey is right, education (in all its myriad forms) consists of learning more and more effectively how to deal with experience. There are concrete problems to be solved. The educated person is one who has the imagination and facts to devise hypotheses that will work in clearing up real difficulties. He or she is the one whose actions make a difference, not the one who treasures an insight into reality. If truth is a matter of correpondence, it is not correspondence between thought and reality, but between intention and result.

[70]See "The Instrumentalism of Dewey" on page 43.

The consequences of this outlook for education (at all levels) is that students will study those topics that make a difference in life and that they will study them in such a way that these differences are manifest—if possible, in their own lives. Undergraduate life is not too soon to prepare for a profession—indeed, even before, the student is preparing for the profession of life itself. Both senses of "profession" suggest an active and practical activity in which various ideas for intended and beneficial results are tried out. The professional has its academic side, but that is pursued only because of its relevance to the practical side, and its relevance must be unmistakable. Students will have other interests besides the professional in the narrow sense, but in most cases they have made a tentative decision on the kinds of jobs they will seek, and they should be allowed to plunge into the kinds of activities they think will constitute their life work. Instead of being forced to *know* in several areas, they will be trained to *be effective* in a chosen field.

Two fundamental mistakes are made in traditional education.

1. The belief that people must first learn the theory or principles of a discipline before they can apply or use that discipline. On the contrary, the theory is true (if indeed it is) *because* it can be applied. This is how we know that it is true. Successful applications suggest new applications, which in turn alter the theory. Theory guides practice and practice suggests theory. The two are not separate concerns but different aspects of the same activity of controlling experience. The engineer does not have to wait until graduate school to see the effectiveness of the science of physics. The notion of learning a science first, whether it is physics, psychology, or economics, and then applying it is based on a mistaken notion of the learning process. In education, the usefulness of what one learns does not have to be postponed to some remote and questionable future.

The Good 2. The belief that one can think of "the good" apart from "the true." The good is experienced as a feeling of dissatisfaction with what is the case. Ends are not written on the stars, to be grasped by a philosopher and held up to show how wrong we are or society is. They are realistic hopes of what the present situation can be transformed into. How they are produced is an experimental matter, and whether they will suffice, once they are realized, is an experimental matter also. Students should indeed raise the question about "the good," but it would be better to speak of "goods" than of "the good." And these goods should be sought, not as absolutes, but as relative to the real interests of individuals and societies, and the times and conditions under which they live. Students, then, must make value judgments, but they must be *their* value judgments, not "judgments" derived from ideals imposed by others and passively accepted.

When we bring (1) and (2) together, we have the essence of Dewey's philosophy. Human values are suggested in scientific inquiry and guide scientific inquiry. We study in order to improve our life and in the process get glimpses of still higher improvements. "Reconstruction can be nothing less than the work of developing, of forming, of producing (in the literal sense of that word) the intellectual instrumentalities which will progressively direct inquiry into the deeply and inclusively human—that is to say, moral—facts of the present scene and situation."[71] The purpose of ethical thought is not simply to make judgments but to devise effective action.

Education for Dewey is a process that is one with the moral process. In school students learn to change experience from the worse to the better. Somewhere along the line they prepare for *entry* into a profession. They now have marketable skills, but their education will continue and their professional powers will increase. They function as citizens also, and as they mature, they become more *useful* to society—which is to say they become more effective as moral beings.

We conclude this essay with three provocative quotations from Dewey's *Experience and Education:*

> Admit that traditional education employed as the subject-matter for study facts and ideas so bound up with the past as to give little help in dealing with the issues of the present and future. Very well. Now we have the problem of discovering the connection which actually exists *within* experience between the achievements of the past and the issues of the present. We have the problem of ascertaining how acquaintance with the past may be translated into a potent instrumentality for dealing effectively with the future. We may reject knowledge of the past as the *end* of education and thereby only emphasize its importance as a *means.* When we do that we have a problem that is new in the story of education: How shall the young become acquainted with the past in such a way that the acquaintance is a potent agent in appreciation of the living present?[72]

> What, then, is the true meaning of preparation in the educational scheme? In the first place, it means that a person, young or old, gets out of his present experience all that there is in it for him at the time in which he has it. When preparation is made the controlling end, then the potentialities of the present are sacrificed to a suppositious future. When this happens, the actual preparation for the future is missed or distorted. The ideal of using the present simply to get ready for the future contradicts itself. It omits, and even shuts out, the very conditions by which a person can be prepared for his future. We always live at the time we live and not at some other time, and only by extracting at each present time the full meaning of each present experience are we prepared for doing the same thing in the future. This is the only preparation which in the long run amounts to anything.[73]

> It thus becomes the office of the educator to select those things within the range of existing experience that have the promise and potentiality of presenting new problems which by stimulating new ways of observation and judgment will expand the area of future experience. He must constantly regard what is already won not as a fixed

[71]Dewey, *Reconstruction in Philosophy,* pp. 20–21.
[72]Dewey, *Experience and Education,* p. 11.
[73]Ibid., pp. 50–51.

> possession but as an agency and instrumentality for opening new fields which make new demands upon existing powers of observation and of intelligent use of memory. Connectedness in growth must be his constant watchword.[74]

The best kind of education is that which teaches the student how to solve a specific problem in such a way that he can more efficiently deal with the next one.

Summary of the Issues

The chief issue in this debate is whether the college experience should deepen students' awareness of the good, the true, and the beautiful or whether it should perfect their ability to solve problems. Those who favor the former emphasize what students can *be;* those who favor the latter emphasize what students can *do.*

One side believes that concern for the good, the true, and the beautiful is the essence of humanity. Much of traditional philosophy can be cited in support of this claim. It shows how college courses in the liberal arts and sciences contribute to human growth. Its proponents insist that the college years provide the best (and perhaps the last) opportunity for becoming adults, for passing from adolescent barbarism into civilized maturity. While not denying the importance of practical education and training, they regard it as secondary and favor postponing most of it.

Proponents of the other side argue that professional training may well begin in the undergraduate years. One who intends to be a gentleman or lady of leisure may dabble in the arts and sciences in these crucial years, but most people neither want to wait nor can afford to. It is only when we assume that individuals have no intellectual development before college or afterward that we can conclude that failure to pursue the arts and sciences in college cuts them off forever from artistic and theoretical interests.

The difference between the two sides goes more deeply than this. One side stresses devotion to an objective good already in existence and the contemplation of timeless beauty, as well as knowledge for its own sake. Individuals become civilized by discovery and conforming to standards outside themselves. The other side perceives individuals in a more active stance. They confer value and create beauty in interaction with their natural and social environment. They seek "truth" as a means for controlling experience. The mark of an education person is not the ability to appreciate the distinctions in the good, the true, and the beautiful, respectively, but the ability to solve practical problems.

If the goal of education is to instill sensitivity, the arts and science approach wins out. If the goal of education is to increase effectiveness, the professional approach should be chosen. In developing our intellectual nature, we become

[74]Ibid., p. 90.

civilized in the humanistic sense. In developing our practical nature, we become civilized in the pragmatic sense. In doing the former, we encounter another realm in which we will find gratification throughout our life, whatever profession we eventually enter. In doing the latter, our life is of one piece, for we enhance our ability to reshape the world around us in both our professional and nonprofessional efforts. Both approaches claim to build on what is natural in humanity. Is the human mind something that should be enlightened or is it an instrument to reshape the world?

Discussion Questions

1. Do you think that colleges should require a course in music or art appreciation? Why?
2. Who do you think is a better educated person, the philosophy major with an A.B. degree or the mechanical engineering major with a B.S. degree? Why?
3. Do you think that the "general studies" requirements are too extensive at your school? Why?
4. Why do you think that traditional philosophy tends to favor the first essay above rather than the second?
5. Are you impatient to take practical courses in your major? Is this a good thing?
6. Do you think you received adequate formal exposure to the arts and sciences in secondary school? Explain.
7. Do you think that the person in professional undergraduate education is being shortchanged? Why?
8. Do you think that it is important to know the place of Charlemagne in history? Why?
9. Is it possible to *understand* a situation without being able to control its outcome? Is it possible to *control* a situation without understanding it? Do your answers have anything to do with the present controversy?
10. Which, in your opinion, is the most valuable college course you have taken? Explain.
11. Do you think that college faculties are qualified to establish graduation requirements? Explain.
12. Do you agree with Socrates on the importance of studying ethics? Why did you register for this course?
13. Do you think that adequate attention is paid to ethical issues in your other courses? Explain.
14. One student said to another: "Are you a business major, or are you here for an education?" Do you agree with the assumption behind this question? If you were a business major, how would you have answered?
15. Do you believe that "high culture" is really superior to "popular culture," or is the former simply a matter of snob appeal? Explain.
16. Aristotle, when asked how much superior the educated are to the uneducated, answered, "As much as the living are to the dead." What did he mean? Do you agree with him?
17. What could Ezra Pound have meant when he said: "Real education must ultimately be limited to men who insist on knowing that the rest is mere sheep-herding." Do you agree?

18. "The goal of female education," said Adolf Hitler, "has invariably to be the future mother." Discuss.
19. "Education," said George Trevelyan, "has produced a vast population able to read but unable to distinguish what is worth reading." Discuss.
20. The cultured person, according to Matthew Arnold, is one "who knows the best that has been said and thought in the world." And he said that the pursuit of the perfect "is the pursuit of sweetness and light." Discuss.
21. If you were an employer, would you hire a liberal arts graduate? Why?

For Further Reading

R. D. Archambault, ed. *John Dewey on Education: Selected Writings.* New York: Modern Library, 1965.

Theodore Brameld. *Philosophies of Education in Cultural Perspective.* New York: Dryden Press, 1955.

John Dewey. *Democracy and Education.* New York: Macmillan Co., 1916.

John Dewey. *Experience and Education.* New York: Macmillan Co., 1938.

John Dewey. *Reconstruction in Philosophy.* New York: Mentor Books, 1950.

Robert M. Hutchins. *The Higher Learning in America.* New Haven, Conn.: Yale University Press, 1936.

Lewis B. Mayhew, ed. *Higher Education in the Revolutionary Decades.* Berkeley, Calif.: McCutchan Publishing Corp., 1967.

Alexander Meiklejohn. *The Liberal College.* New York: Arno Press and the New York Times, 1969.

John Stuart Mill. "Inaugural Address at Saint Andrews." In Albert W. Levi, ed., *The Six Great Humanistic Essays of John Stuart Mill.* New York: Washington Square Press, 1963.

John D. Millett. *The Liberating Arts: Essays in General Education.* Cleveland: Howard Allen, 1957.

John Henry Cardinal Newman. *The Idea of a University.* New York: Holt, Rinehart and Winston, 1960.

William G. Perry, Jr. *Forms of Intellectual and Ethical Development in the College Years.* New York: Holt, Rinehart and Winston, 1970.

Huston Smith. *The Purposes of Higher Education.* New York: Harper & Bros., 1955.

A. N. Whitehead. *The Aims of Education and Other Essays.* New York: Macmillan Co., 1929.

INTERCOLLEGIATE ATHLETICS

Intercollegiate Athletics Should Be Deemphasized

The Function of Athletics Robert M. Hutchins said, "There are two ways to have a great university. It must have a great football team, or a great president." Whether this is true or not, it is undeniable that one way to be *thought* to have a great university is to have great athletic teams. The public reads more about the institution's athletic affairs than its academic affairs, and coaches and athletes are more famous than faculty members and scholars. The average person will be much more likely to know the name of a school's coach than its president. Under whom did Woody Hayes, Bear Bryant, and Adolph Rupp serve?

The athletic program is expected to bring publicity to the school, attract students, foster student unity, and encourage alumni giving. "The traditional American affinity for sports and reverence for education combined to form an unbeatable attraction. Every Saturday, educated sports heroes performed for an appreciative audience. Fanfare, combat, and hope of victory assured public identification and loyalty."[75] The most conspicuous function of athletic competition is to enhance the image of the institution.

We may want to question the appropriateness of this public relations function. Publicity is not necessarily a good thing. If this publicity is scandalous (or even negative), the school has not benefited. There is a university on the banks of the river that sponsors a "Mississippi River Festival" every summer. The "festival," for the most part, consists of rock concerts. Unfortunately, since these festivals have been plagued with violence, rape, drunkenness, drug dealing and usage, and automobile accidents, the publicity has been counter to the kind the festival was designed to produce. With respect to athletics, the public is finding out more about the universities than they would wish.

Does athletic fame attract students? Perhaps it does, but it would be a stupid engineering student who chose Georgia Tech over M.I.T. because of its athletic prowess. Some serious students are "turned off" by a school's athletic record. Notre Dame, which has an excellent academic program, is unjustly viewed by many as simply a sports mill. Does athletic success foster student unity? Here again, the case is not clear. Often students' enthusiasm is tepid in comparison with that of alumni and townspeople—especially when they have difficulty in getting tickets, have to pay a handsome price, or are relegated to seats in the end zone.

Does athletic success arouse public support? Do legislators tend to reward successful schools with more generous appropriations? They may have done so in the past, but today, with the closer scrutiny of tax dollars, there are signs that funds will be more available for activities closer to the heart of the academic mission.[76] What about alumni giving? Certainly alumni will contribute money for *athletic* purposes in the case of a few successful universities, but the overall record for alumni giving exhibits no such pattern. A careful study of 138 "big-time" schools from 1960 to 1976 yielded this conclusion: "Our statistical analysis has revealed that there is simply no relationship between success or failure in football

[75]Christine H. B. Grant, "Institutional Autonomy and Intercollegiate Athletics," *Educational Record* (Fall 1979), p. 411.

[76]If taxpayers are now willing to reduce expenditures for athletics and other "frills" in the high schools, they may do so also for universities—even the "successful" ones.

and basketball and increases and decreases in alumni giving."[77] "In the final analysis, however, the lack of any relationship between success in athletics and increased alumni giving probably matters a great deal less than the fact that so many people believe that such a relationship exists."[78]

Since sport is a major college effort and is taught to and engaged in by students, the proper question is not whether the public relations purpose succeeds, but what the *educational* function of sport should be. Intercollegiate sports can legitimately serve two classes of students: those who intend to make a profession out of sports and those who do not. Both learn to play the sport under professional guidance and compete with the best athletes of other schools. They learn to discipline themselves, make great demands on their bodies, and (in team sports) to cooperate with others on behalf of a common end. They are zealous to win but are generous in defeat. They learn what the rules are and how to play by the rules. Sport is thus an intrinsic good and an extrinsic one. It is exciting and pleasurable, but it also fosters valuable human characteristics. It is clearly a worthwhile activity and quite within the province of higher education. Those who major in physical education will learn to teach others, and a tiny minority will join the pros. Those who do not major in physical education will have experienced a pitch of excitement and a controlled regimen not to be found in intramurals or informal sports. But both will have to keep the competition in a proper perspective, for the credit hours earned in varsity sports are but a small fraction of those required for graduation.

If something like this is the function of intercollegiate athletics, we need to raise several questions: Does the importance of this function justify the amount of money spent by the university? Does the university employ ethical means in administering the athletic program? Does the university deal fairly with its athletes and potential athletes?

Finances The amount of money spent annually for intercollegiate athletics in 1980 is probably something over half a billion dollars.[79] The actual figure would doubtless be higher if it included indirect university support in such areas as facilities, office space, and utilities. Where does this money come from? Gate receipts, media fees, students fees (with or without admission), general institutional funds, and contributions from private organizations and individuals. The revenue pattern varies a great deal, depending on the program of the school. Division I (NCAA) programs do well at the gate, for example, while Divisions II and III depend more on institutional funds. The use of student fees in the latter

[77]Sigelman and Carter, "Win One for the Giver? Alumni Giving and Big-Time College Sports," p. 293.

[78]Ibid. See Frederick Klein, "Bring in the Brawn: Recruiting of Athletes Intensifies as Colleges Seek Prestige, Money," *Wall Street Journal,* April 11, 1967, p. 1.

[79]See Robert H. Atwell, "Some Reflections on Collegiate Athletics," *Educational Record* (Fall 1979), p. 367.

is declining, as schools are finding that students are resisting and that they can get more from gate receipts. They derive very little, however, from television and contributions.[80]

What is the money spent on? Salaries and wages of personnel who administer and carry out the program (athletics directors, coaches, assistant coaches, trainers, office staff, statisticians, publicists, equipment people, groundskeepers, etc.), uniforms and equipment, supplies, travel, recruitment, and scholarships ("grants-in-aid"). The last is a sizable figure, for in many cases a scholarship covers not only tuition and fees, but room, board, and incidental expenses as well. Another major expense is payment on outstanding loans.

It is widely believed that the great revenue-producing sports, football and basketball, usually pay for themselves and in some cases support the "minor" sports as well. The fact is that 81 percent of all football programs do not even pay for themselves. This is true of 69 percent of all men's athletic programs. Although there are many schools that require the athletic program to pay for itself, 37 percent of such programs do not. The total deficit for NCAA schools in 1977 was $537 million.[81] The pattern for the past decade is one of increasing deficits, going beyond inflationary increases, so the future does not look good. Schools are in a dilemma: If they hold the line, they will be at a competitive disadvantage—which will indirectly cost them money; if they spend more, they will increase their deficits. When we take into account Title IX of the Higher Education Act of 1972, which requires equal treatment of women in all areas of higher education, including sports, the prospect is bleak indeed. If men's athletics must be run at a loss, what will the deficits be when colleges spend an equal amount on women?

There are, to be sure, a few universities that show a profit on their football and basketball programs. The perennial powers bring in the fans, inspire private contributions, and receive television fees. But even the Division I schools showed a net loss of $151 million in 1977. Despite the practice of channeling some of the television and bowl game receipts of the more fortunate schools to the less fortunate ones, Robert Atwell can conclude: "Fewer than one hundred institutions dominate the NCAA and their interests are largely oriented toward big-time football and basketball. They have a monopolistic hold on revenue sources—both at the gate and through television—that virtually assures second-class status to other athletics programs."[82] Even those few enterprises that seem to show a profit would at best break even were it not for student fees, general university resources, and private donations.[83] It is doubtful whether *any* school can show a profit, in

[80]For a detailed report on financing athletics, see Raiborn, *Revenues and Expenses of Intercollegiate Programs: Analysis of Trends and Relationships, 1970–1977.*

[81]See Donna A. Lopiano, "Solving the Financial Crisis in Intercollegiate Athletics," *Educational Record* (Fall 1979), p. 394ff.

[82]Atwell, p. 372.

[83]The Sun Angel Foundation, an organization boosting Arizona State, has raised about $2.5 million for athletic scholarships and $4.5 million for expansion of the stadium. See Ron Reid, "There's the Devil to Pay," *Sports Illustrated,* October 29, 1979, p. 26.

the strict sense of that word, on the basis of the operation of the sport itself. Although we speak of football and basketball as cases of "big business," they are not, even when most successful, *profitable* businesses.

Win, Win, Win For every winner, there must be a loser. The pressure is very great, especially in the major sports, to be a winner. A great deal of money is involved, and the winners tend to get the greater share in gate and television revenue. In a sense, the investment must be recouped and the future assured. The athletic department is under great pressure to produce a winner, and the jobs of coaches are at stake. Slogans from professional sports increasingly are applied to collegiate programs: "Winning isn't the main thing—it's the *only* thing." "Winning isn't everything, but losing is nothing." "Show me a good loser, and I'll show you a loser."

If the main function of sports were educational, winning would not be so important. The athletes would play their hearts out and learn a lot even if they lost. But when the function is public relations, only a winning season can be a successful one. Having invested in a huge staff, joined a big-time conference, and built a stadium to hold 100,000 fans, schools cannot even *consider* sports as educational. They have embarked on a program in which only winning can keep the program afloat both financially and in terms of public relations.

Under the great pressure to win, the athletics department, off the field as well as on, strives to do everything possible within the rules to build a successful program. It will recruit athletes from all over the country (and the world), offering "free rides" and the opportunity for national recognition. It will bring young people to the campus who haven't a chance to complete a degree. If their high school grades and test scores do not meet NCAA requirements for athletic eligibility, it will wait until the athletes have attended junior college. There they can compete and pile up enough credit hours in "snap courses" to be able to enroll and compete at the four-year institution. Once they are on the university campus, they can be kept eligible by taking meaningless courses like "Theory of Coaching," "Current Events," "Aerobatic Dancing," and "Rules of Basketball." "Academic counselors" in the athletics department make sure the minimum is attained in the classroom so that coaches can get the maximum on the practice field.[84] All this is within the rules, although it has little to do with the conception of athletics as one of the components of an educational experience.

The pressure to win unfortunately induces many institutions to *break* the rules. A few years ago the American Council on Education conducted an inquiry into the need for and feasibility of a national study of intercollegiate athletics. In its "partial listing" of documented violations, the inquiry team reported the following:

[84]Academic adviser John Rehfield of Arizona State said that the head football coach had told him "my job was to get our players eligible or I'd be fired." See "Scorecard," *Sports Illustrated,* November 26, 1979, p. 25.

Altering high school academic transcripts.
Threatening to bomb the home of a high school principal who refused to alter transcripts.
Changing admissions test scores.
Having substitutes, including assistant coaches, take admissions tests.
Offering jobs to parents or other relatives of a prospect.
Promising one package of financial aid and delivering another.
Firing from a state job the father of a prospect who enrolled at other than the state's university.
"Tipping" or otherwise paying athletes who perform particularly well on a given occasion—and then on subsequent ones.
Providing a community college basketball star with a private apartment and a car.
Providing a quarterback with a new car every year, his favorite end with a "tip" and the interior linemen with nothing.
Getting grades for athletes in courses they never attended.
Enrolling university big-time athletes in junior colleges out-of-season and getting them grades there for courses they never attended.
Using federal work study funds to pay athletes for questionable or nonexistent jobs.
Getting a portion of work study funds paid to athletes "kicked back" into the athletic department kitty.[85]

Athletic competition is singularly governed by rules, and so is the conduct of an athletic program. They are explicit and spelled out in great detail. It would seem to be the minimum in moral behavior to adhere to these rules. Although members of athletic associations are pledged to abide by the rules that govern the operation of programs, many seek an unfair advantage over others by violating them. It is, in a sense, a form of immorality discussed by Kant in his theory of the categorical imperative. It is not, however, each athletic rule that is an imperative, but the duty to live up to a promise voluntarily made. The moral violation is that of violating a *code* that is accepted for oneself and expected of others.

Papers and magazines have carried many items in recent years of unethical behavior by officials who profess to teach sportsmanship.

In 1979 Frank Kush, long-time coach at Arizona State, was suspended after a former player had brought suit for $1.1 million, claiming that Kush had struck him, humiliated him, and pressured him to quit and give up his scholarship. Kush was fired when a cover-up was discovered. One of the sworn statements of an assistant coach had Kush saying: "Things are getting tough. We better close the circle, and we might have to lie, steal or cheat." Kush himself had publicly stated: "My joy is to win football games, put people in the stadium and make money for the university."[86] The same fall, Arizona State had to forfeit several games for using eight ineligible players. It seems that they had gotten grades

[85]George H. Hanford, "Controversies in College Sports," *University Record* (Fall 1979), p. 357. See also Hanford et al., *An Inquiry into the Need for and Feasibility of a National Study of Intercollegiate Athletics,* pp. 74–76.
[86]See Reid, p. 26.

of B in a summer extension course taught in the Los Angeles area by Rocky Mountain College (Billings, Montana). Conference officials charged that they neither attended class nor did any work. The academic adviser in the athletics department had signed them up and told them that everything had been taken care of.[87]

A few months later, officials in the basketball program at New Mexico were faced with federal indictment for bribery and for mail and wire fraud. This was called a case in which "NCAA action apparently is the least of the university's worries."[88] Forged transcripts from junior colleges were also involved.[89] A little later, six players were declared ineligible for receiving credit for a summer extension course they did not take. This also was in the Los Angeles area. It was offered by Ottawa University of Kansas. Someone had forged their names, paid the tuition, come to class, and taken the examination—but not those students.[90] Head coach Norm Ellenberger and some assistants were fired.[91]

Five universities in the Pacific-Ten Conference were barred from football championships (1980) and postseason play by the conference. The University of Southern California admitted in the fall of 1980 that 330 athletes who were admitted to the school (by the athletic department!) were scholastically deficient. A USC report also admitted that athletes were signed up for courses that they did not attend. A sprinter, Billy Mullins, attended four junior colleges *simultaneously* in the fall of 1977 in order to compete in the 1978 track season at USC. Chuck Muncie, a great running back at the University of California, "never went to class at all," according to his roommate. "I never saw him all week except when we got taped up for practice."[92]

Sports Illustrated quotes a "knowledgeable source": "For the NCAA to cite every instance in which a junior college manipulates a player's grade to make him eligible for transfer to a four year school would be like the police ticketing every person who drives over 55 miles per hour or arresting every person who enters an office football pool."[93] In most cases, it is not necessary to falsify junior college transcripts. All one has to do is get the student into the right courses with the right teachers. Many junior colleges willingly function as "feeder schools." The athlete is placed there by the big school and is "looked after" until he is eligible to compete in the "big-time."[94]

[87]See "Scorecard," *Sports Illustrated,* November 26, 1979, p. 25.

[88]John Papanek, "Now New Mexico Feels the Heat," *Sports Illustrated,* December 10, 1979, p. 33.

[89]Eight of the "eligible" players were junior college transfers.

[90]See "New Mexico: More Tremors," *Sports Illustrated,* December 17, 1979, pp. 75–76.

[91]Ellenberger himself was acquitted on the federal counts, but still faces several state charges having to do with fraudulent travel vouchers. Assistant coach Manny Goldstein pleaded guilty to some federal counts. Ellenberger admitted "he knew that NCAA rules were being broken, but did not intend to defraud any one or commit a crime." "Scorecard," *Sports Illustrated,* June 30, 1980, p. 9.

[92]See Associated Press story in *Edwardsville Intelligencer,* August 13, 1980, p. 13.

[93]*Sports Illustrated,* December 17, 1979, p. 76.

[94]See David Condon and Linda Kay, "Scandal: How the Junior-College Railroad Works," *St. Louis Globe-Democrat,* August 29, 1980, p. 4B.

The NCAA simply does not have the resources to keep all its members honest. It also lacks the subpoena power. What we hear about is just the tip of the iceberg. One FBI agent working on the New Mexico case said: "We are doing what the NCAA is supposed to do."[95] It was not the NCAA, for example, that uncovered the case of seven University of Oregon football players (including the two top quarterbacks) who received "extra benefits" in the form of airline tickets "through a secret account at a local travel agency that dealt with the athletic department." Nor was it the university. "The gingerly handling of the situation suggested to some observers that university officials had hoped to hush up the ineligibility of the seven players so as not to hurt the sale of season tickets, which had begun just a few days earlier. And after the news broke, the Oregon coach, Rich Brooks, did his best to prevent an erosion of ticket sales. Betraying little visible remorse over the apparent rules violations by the seven players, Brooks seized the occasion to accuse newspapers covering Oregon's scandal of having somehow 'slandered' his team. Of an ongoing Lane County grand jury probe into possible athletic department wrongdoing, Brooks said, 'It's a matter of how far some people will go to prove a point. Some people just don't want to let it die.' "[96]

The NCAA holds universities responsible for the conduct of "independent" booster organizations. Cases of "slush funds" are periodically reported. These operate under-the-table payments for athletes and coaches. Sometimes the payments are out in the open. When the University of Colorado hired coach Chuck Fairbanks away from the New England Patriots, the Flatirons Club paid $200,000 to settle a suit brought by the Patriots against Fairbanks for not honoring his contract.[97] A booster organization in Columbia is helping the Missouri football coach, Warren Powers, pay off his obligations in running out of a contract at another school. The universities seek this kind of private support. Many schools, including Missouri, require a "donation" to the athletic fund before choice season tickets can be obtained.

A scandal brewing in early 1981 involves a midwestern basketball team. A copyrighted newspaper story reports that the coach had arranged for an abortion for the girlfriend of his star player; that players received thousands of dollars in cash, clothes, and airline tickets, and were forgiven loans from coaches and boosters; that the mother of the star player, previously indigent, had acquired an expensive home and two new cars since moving to the college area. Denials have been made by the institution, and investigations are being conducted.[98]

One final example from the athletic chamber of horrors illustrates the use that can be made of "independent study": "A former University of Oregon football

[95]See "Scorecard," *Sports Illustrated,* February 25, 1980, p. 13.

[96]"Scoreboard," *Sports Illustrated,* July 14, 1980, p. 16.

[97]Fairbanks "remarked that he had previously broken three other legal contracts and saw nothing wrong with breaking another one." Ewald B. Nyquist, "Win, Women, and Money: Collegiate Athletics Today and Tomorrow," *Educational Record* (Fall 1979), p. 375.

[98]The development of this story and its outcome can be followed in the *Kansas City Times,* beginning in February 1981.

player, Derrick Dale, earned instant eligibility in 1978 by 'taking,' as independent study, a jogging course at nearby Lane Community College; he was credited for running he had done in football practice."[99]

Exploitation If intercollegiate athletics often violates the Kantian principle to live according to the rules, it also violates another Kantian principle—about using humanity as an end. It too often sees athletes as simply objects to be exploited for the glory and profit of the university. It is of little concern to the university whether the athletes grow in stature, preserve their physical health, or even get a degree. A clear indication of this attitude is the widespread practice of withdrawing financial support from athletes who want to quit the team and stay on as students. The athletic department has purchased them body and soul for use on the playing field.[100] A similar practice is "red-shirting," whereby athletes are kept out of competition for a year, thus saving a year of eligibility while they learn and mature.

What happens when the eligibility years have been used up? A few, very few, athletes join professional teams. Many who complete their degrees go into coaching. What about the many who have not completed their degrees? They have perhaps enjoyed a few years of glory, but they have learned little that will help them get a job. The carryover value of throwing blocks and making jump shots is not very great. So far as learning marketable skills and knowledge are concerned, their college experience has been a waste of time. Perhaps it has even been harmful. No longer acclaimed and idolized, coddled and privileged, they exchange their status as "big man on campus" for one of unprepared job seeker. A faculty committee investigating the abuses as USC stated: "Failure to confront a student-athlete early with the realities of his or her true potential for academic survival is unethical. Such practices are tantamount to exploitation. . . ."[101]

Perhaps the greatest harm done to student-athletes is the deadening of whatever conscience they have. A big-time basketball player was accused of stealing a bicycle. "I didn't steal it," he said. "I took it." School officials, says Pete Axthelm, "owe the kids more guidance than direction to the hoop."[102] The student is also cheated on a realistic level. "When you tell a kid that college is just a charade," said Bob Knight, Indiana basketball coach, "you do him a terrible disservice. You tell him you can give him a good deal in a no-show

[99]"Scorecard," *Sports Illustrated,* February 25, 1980, p. 11.

[100]That the athlete is an employee was recognized in the case of *Taylor* v. *Wake Forest University* (1972). An athlete had been awarded a four-year football scholarship on the condition that he maintain eligibility. After the first year he dropped out of sports and his scholarship was terminated. His parents sued. The state court upheld the university, declaring that the scholarship was a contract, since the athlete had agreed "in consideration of the athletic award . . . to maintain his athletic eligibility, and this meant both physically and scholastically." At that time the university's policy of terminating aid to nonparticipating athletes was not yet a written one! See Cym H. Lowell, "The Law and Collegiate Athletics in Public Institutions," *Educational Record* (Fall 1979), pp. 485–486.

[101]See *St. Louis Globe-Democrat,* October 14, 1980, p. 3D.

[102]Pete Axthelm, "Scandal on the Court," *Newsweek,* December 24, 1979, p. 77

summer job, or a soft deal in the classroom. Then he goes out into the world without a degree or an education. And what the hell does he do when he discovers that life doesn't have any more deals for him?"[103]

This is especially true of the black athlete. Only about thirty percent of them are graduated. None of the five black starters on the national basketball championship team of Texas–El Paso (1965) ever got a degree. Eight black former athletes recently sued the California State University at Los Angeles for $14 million. "The athletes claim they were channeled into meaningless physical education courses that did not lead to graduation and that they were given credit for uncompleted courses to retain their eligibility. They state that the university arranged for other students to take admissions entrance tests, persuaded high schools to change athletes' grades, operated a fraudulent loan system, and did not fulfill promises of a free education. The athletes never graduated and charged the university with failing to give them adequate education, academic counseling, and remedial work."[104]

There is a much higher percentage of blacks in athletics than in higher education. Whether blacks are athletically superior to whites is not the question. The facts indicate that white society is more concerned to get blacks into athletic squads than into student bodies. "If you are black and can play some ball, your chances of gaining access to a college education are greater than if you have only limited athletic ability, but have the potential for a significant intellectual contribution to society."[105] Harry Edwards and others have spoken of the tragedy of urging young blacks to view athletics as the only route to success. If they are shooting for the pros, most of them will be disappointed.[106] These young people should be encouraged to pursue other interests as well, and to take seriously the other educational opportunities. The famous and wealthy professional star is just not a realistic model. It may be difficult for the star to point this out to young blacks without seeming to be ungrateful, arrogant, or presumptuous, but he should say to them, "I made it in sport, but most of you are wasting your time."[107]

What is true for blacks is true for the disadvantaged and academically unprepared of all races. Athletes are lured into collegiate sports with promises of fame and fortune. They are urged to concentrate on sport to the exclusion of everything else. From an early age they learn to become cogs in athletic machines and very little else.

It is inevitable that injuries will occur in intercollegiate athletics—just as they do in intramurals and physical education courses. A comprehensive study of

[103]See ibid.

[104]Nyquist, p. 380.

[105]Edwards, "Sport within the Veil: The Triumphs, Tragedies and Challenges of Afro-American Involvement," p. 122.

[106]There were fewer than 900 blacks in professional football, basketball, and baseball in 1979.

[107]See Edwards, p. 120.

athletic injuries in 1975–1976 conducted by HEW showed that 4 percent of all collegiate athletes received a major injury.[108] If we include minor injuries (causing the athlete to miss one to twenty days), the total figure was about 160,000. Do the schools adequately deal with the reality of athletic injury? Do they employ the services of physicians and certified trainers during practices and games? Not usually. More often than not, the coaches not only have total control but serve as medical "experts" also.

> Despite the expectation of injuries in any sport, many colleges seem ill-prepared for minimum readiness; that is, the presence of a person delegated and qualified to render emergency first-aid care. The most surprising statistic from the entire HEW survey may be the admission by seventy-five two-year colleges and sixty-five four-year colleges that they have no one immediately responsible for emergency health care. Also, far too many schools which responded that they had an emergency health care person relied on a coach or assistant coach for this service.[109]

In their ignorance and pressure to win, head coaches will often encourage an injured athlete to "play hurt."

What Should Be Done If the universities and colleges wish to regain their integrity as institutions of higher education, they should immediately begin the process of deemphasis. What should be done will seem drastic to the "big-time" schools, but virtually all schools are obliged to make changes. The competition for athletes is just as fierce among the smaller schools (they just do not aim at the "blue-chippers"), and the special favors accorded athletes are just as prevalent. That most of the publicity has been directed toward the major powers should not conceal the fact that just about any school that competes feels it must take extraordinary measures to get and retain the young men and women who will enable it to compile a respectable record. Among the steps in deemphasis are the following:

1. Eliminate the favoritism that benefits the major sport athlete over athletes in the minor sports, and that benefits athletes in general over the nonathletes. Award scholarships and campus work on the basis of academic promise and financial need. Robert Lipsyte speaks of the "varsity syndrome." "This process of selection begins in youth sports and culminates in professional sport events, or high level amateur competition, which are limited to a very few individuals. Those who do make it in sports are given deference that far exceeds their worth or importance to society. This further isolates them from the mainstreams of the population and, in fact, creates an elite group. . . .Athletes are waved, as it were, through the toll-

[108] A "major" injury was defined as one requiring the athlete to miss more than twenty days of participation.

[109] Robert Calvert, Jr., and Kenneth S. Clarke, "Injuries and Collegiate Athletics: Taking Their Measure," *Educational Record* (Fall 1979), p. 463.

booth of life. And then, as celebrities, they are given a whole new identity as heroes."[110]

2. Eliminate recruiting of athletes. It is not only demeaning for university officials to beg high school students to opt for their institution, but also unhealthy ego-building with respect to the athlete.[111] The ideal should be that of athletic teams chosen from the student body—those who have freely chosen to attend the school for reasons of their own. In many cases today, the athletes who "represent" the school have been flown in from miles away and have little interest in the school itself. The "walk-on" who makes the team is an oddity.

3. Reduce the expenses of major sports so that more money can be spent on minor sports and intramurals. Some schools might well consider giving up football—a notorious drain on most athletic budgets. Deemphasis would also require the reduction of coaching staffs in football and basketball, as well as of scholarships and recruitment. Travel expenditures can also be reduced. There is little reason for teams to travel across the country to engage in contests involving sixty or forty minutes of playing time.

4. Return sports to the students. Provide more opportunities in intercollegiate athletics and intramurals. Make the facilities available to students other than those on the glamour teams. Let them into the stadium as spectators.

> Of all the forms of cheating on college campuses today, one of the most outrageous is the way many students themselves are being cheated out of enjoying sports. The intercollegiate jockocracy has been depriving many students of sports facilities and then charging them twice for the privilege of not participating. The athletics fee entitles students to attend home games—if enough seats are available in the student section. On the other hand, the limited availability of intramural facilities clearly discourages extensive use of them by the student body.[112]

5. Extend equal opportunity in sports to women. Many schools are fighting a desperate rearguard action against the Department of Education, which is trying to implement Title IX. They have argued against the application of the principle of equal opportunity to "revenue-producing" sports (as if there were any!), and 300 institutions have hired a public relations firm to lobby against Title IX in Washington. "This action presents the absurd spectacle of institutions of higher education spending campus dollars—often public funds—to lobby for maintain-

[110]Lipsyte, "Varsity Syndrome: The Unkindest Cut," pp. 15, 19.

[111]Kris Jenner, age seventeen, an intelligent and talented athlete at Mascoutah (Illinois) High School, was wooed by dozens of big universities. He was brought to campuses every weekend (after football season ended) until he made his selection. "The pressure was really something—nearly unbearable," Jenner said. "Calls to my home, coaches wanting me to visit their schools' campuses. Having people become closer to me personally, to the point where it was getting hard to tell them no." See *St. Louis Post-Dispatch,* January 27, 1980, p. 2C.

[112]Neil D. Isaacs, "The Losers in College Sports," *Washington Post,* October 16, 1977.

ing sex discrimination in sports."[113] The real danger is that women's athletics will run aground on the same "big-time" insanities that have ruined men's athletics.[114]

6. Form new conferences and associations. If schools believe they would be at a competitive disadvantage as a result of cutting back on scholarships, recruitment, and the like, they should pull out of their conferences or associations and schedule games with schools upholding standards similar to their own.[115]

Deemphasis requires more than living up to the rules (although that would help); it requires adopting a *new* set of rules.

Weakness of Leadership In the midst of the Arizona State scandal, President Schwada is reported to have said, "I just want to get back to running the university." *Sports Illustrated* commented: "Trouble was, insofar as athletics were concerned, there was no evidence he had really begun."[116]

Even the well-intentioned chief executive has difficulty in carrying out reforms.

One of the great obstacles is public opinion. "A university president tampers with athletics at his peril in the face of alumni and state legislators who take more pride in the prospect of a bowl game than a Nobel prize."[117] Presidents need to do some educating of their own.

A second obstacle in many cases is the organization of the university. "On several campuses, the governance and control of intercollegiate athletics, particularly football and basketball, are independent of the usual lines of presidential authority. As one university president has remarked, they are 'frequently far more autonomous and unrelated to the campus than such tyrannical and cussedly independent siblings as Medicine and Law.' "[118] Paul Hardin received an education of his own when he served as president of Southern Methodist University, stating:

> I didn't realize that there are a tremendous number of schools in this country where the president or chancellor does not run the athletic program. Where it is treated as none of his business by an athletic board or a totally independent athletic director. . . . Most of them [the presidents] are under incredible pressure to look away. In some schools, by either explicit understanding or tradition, the chief executive officer has

[113]Ellen W. Gerber, "The Legal Basis for Regulation of Intercollegiate Sport," *Educational Record* (Fall 1979), p. 474.

[114]The number of schools offering athletic scholarships to women increased from 60 in 1974 to over 500 in 1978. See Hanford, p. 363.

[115]It is not unthinkable to give up intercollegiate athletics entirely. Only about 60 percent of schools field athletic teams, and some that do not are quite distinguished!

[116]See Reid, p. 30.

[117]Harold Howe II, "Sex, Sports and Discrimination," *Chronicle of Higher Education,* June 18, 1979, p. 72.

[118]Nyquist, p. 378.

> absolutely no control over athletics. In these schools he can run the English Department and the cafeteria but he better not try to run the football or basketball team. There is a de facto passiveness.[119]

Alumni and booster groups often have more input than the president; and the governing board, when it is not directly interfering itself, is content with the arrangement. Somehow, the presidents must regain the reins of leadership. They are, after all, the ones who are responsible to the governing board for the conduct of the university. They are the ones who must balance the budget and defend the institution's policies to the public and the courts.

A third obstacle is the control exercised by such athletic associations as the NCAA, AIAW, NAIA, and NJCAA, as well as particular conferences. We have already seen how a school, in order to be competitive, tends to do all that its membership permits. Sometimes legitimate interests of the school conflict with the rules of the association—for example, eligibility requirements, foreign student participation, due-process procedures. If a school believes in the educational soundness of what it is doing and resents "dictation" by the association, common sense would suggest that it leave the association and associate with schools that have similar viewpoints. Leadership that blames all its woes on external agencies is guilty of bad faith.

In view of the erosion of educational integrity, the acute financial problems, and the win-at-all-costs attitude present in many of our colleges and universities, strong leadership is urgently needed.

Intercollegiate Athletics Should Not Be Deemphasized

The Need for Selective Criticism The case for deemphasis per se is not conclusive. Schools that can support quality sports may well continue to do so, while those whose financial resources cannot keep up with inflation and increasing costs may well decide to compete at a more modest level. The term *deemphasize* is itself misleading and not very helpful. It denotes action against a policy of emphasizing sports, and it is unclear what *emphasize* means. If it means placing sports in a position of primary importance in a school's program, few if any schools would admit that they emphasize sports, and the question of deemphasizing thus becomes meaningless. The real question is simply the lengths to which schools can legitimately go in fielding athletic teams. And the answer to the question must lie in the nature and condition of the particular institution itself, as well as the educational goals it sets for itself.

The blanket denunciation of intercollegiate athletics for misspending educational funds is not plausible, in view of the fact that less than one percent of the

[119]See William E. Davis, "The President's Role in Athletics: Leader or Figurehead?" *Educational Record* (Fall 1979), p. 426.

money spent in higher education goes to sports.[120] Whether the money is misspent is relative to how well it serves the purposes of particular institutions. Can *this* school afford to do what it is doing, and does it get a fair return for its expenditures? Is its athletic program consistent with its educational aims?

It almost goes without saying that schools should abide by their own rules and the rules of the associations and conferences of which they are members. The few that do not have unfairly discredited the rest. That some have cheated in recruiting and eligibility does not mean that the entire enterprise is shot through with dishonesty and therefore ripe for "deemphasis." That some coaches cannot control their tempers does not mean that Frank Kush, Woody Hayes, and Bobby Knight are representative of the profession. There are ethical athletic departments and estimable coaches, but they do not make sensational news stories. Those that do, lead the unthinking reader to condemn athletics in general and to call for "deemphasis." It would be desirable if all programs were beyond reproach. But since they are not, fair play would indicate that we should punish those that are found guilty and at least withhold judgment on the others.

"Exploitation" To view athletes as an exploited class is to make a very one-sided appraisal of the actual situation. In receiving a scholarship, athletes have an opportunity—which might otherwise be denied them—of attending an institution of higher education. The athletic program brings them to the campus and keeps them on the campus. Many athletes may not be enthusiastic about the academic side of education, but in this they are no different from many other segments of the student body. A great many athletes benefit from their whole collegiate educational experience. And a great many complete their degrees. What should be noted is that about half the football players in the NFL *did* complete their degrees, although their futures clearly lay in professional competition. Of the five starters for the 1965 NCAA basketball finalist, University of Kentucky, *all* graduated with their class. And by no means all of the student-athletes major in physical education—although this is an honorable profession for which no apology is required.

Athletic departments, concerned with grades and eligibility, closely monitor the academic progress of their athletes—much more so than do the advisement and counseling offices of the university. Although this interest is partly self-serving, it does benefit the student-athletes. The practice of pushing them into meaningless courses is not typical; where it exists, it should be stopped. It would be a fine thing if there were agencies in the university that monitored the academic work of *all* students as carefully as the athletic department does for its people. An effort should be made to keep everyone "eligibile," whether he or she sets foot on the playing field or not.

The case of the black athlete is a difficult one. Those who have not learned to study in the lower grades, or who are victims of poverty and poor schools, may

[120]See Atwell, p. 367.

fail on the college level. But this is not unique to the sports scene. Blacks in general have a lower rate of graduation than whites. The encouraging statistic is that fully 30 percent of black athletes complete their degree. The counseling and tutoring they receive through the athletic department can often serve as a model for what their nonathletic counterparts could receive. It is true, as Jesse Jackson points out, that we should not hold the prospect of athletic greatness out to black youth to the exclusion of other educational values, but the fact is that athletic success is possible for a great many blacks, and professional success to a few. Whether they make it in the pros or not, they will have had the opportunity for a college education.

Perhaps recruiters are too optimistic about the academic prospects of some of the high school graduates they sign up, but so too are some of the admissions officers of our universities. Acceptance based on the hope that they will succeed is quite different from the cold-blooded buying of bodies. The university standards for admission are often lower than those for athletic eligibility. And the academic standards for continued athletic participation are usually higher than those for continued enrollment in the university. The university that will reduce requirements (GPA or standardized test scores) to bring in and retain minorities is not criticized so severely as the athletic department that, according to association rules, is held to a high standard. Both, however, are willing to take a chance with marginal students and supply advice and special programs to remedy their disadvantage. If it is laudable when the university does it, it is no less laudable when the athletic department does it. It is, in either case, an attempt to attract and retain students for an educational purpose. Sometimes the students succeed, and sometimes not.

The extent of athletic injuries has been exaggerated. Only one college football fatality was reported in 1975–1976, and none in 1977–1978. Spinal cord injury in football was about one per 10,000 participants in the three-year period 1973–1975; in men's gymnastics the incidence was eight times this figure. The figure of 160,000 collegiate athletic injuries in 1975–1976 is not so alarming when we realize that seven-eighths of them were minor (loss of participation for twenty days or less) and note that about 50,000 injuries were reported in intramurals and physical education courses in the same period.[121]

Educational Values Intercollegiate athletics serve several educational values. The most obvious is that of the all-but-indispensable supplement to the academic major of physical education. A person who is preparing to teach physical education or to coach athletic teams should have the personal experience of competition and of being coached. This experience is comparable to that which prospective teachers of music, debating, dramatics, and journalism receive in various cocurricular activities. Those who intend to teach an activity should have *participated* in that activity at the college level.

[121]See Calvert and Clarke, pp. 444, 450, 455.

Some writers, actors, and musicians become professional performers in their fields, and their experience in college has helped educate them for their work. The few athletes who become professional performers have similarly been educated for their work.

Many graduates who participated in such activities as writing, dramatics, music, and athletics do not pursue professions where these activities directly benefit them, but they may be helpful in many socially important endeavors. Writers may be better business people for their ability to express themselves well. Actors may take part in amateur theatrics. Musicians may participate in municipal bands or part-time musical groups. Athletes may coach Little League teams or officiate at local athletic contests. In addition, these people will have acquired skills and interests that are gratifying to them as performers for many years.

We may grant that these collegiate experiences do not have to be "big-time" in order to produce educational results. But where the instruction is better, the time spent more extensive, and the caliber of competition higher, the benefits for the individual fortunate enough to participate would surely tend to be greater. Athletes learn more in some situations than in others. Just as they learn more in intramurals than in pickup games, they learn more as members of a Division I team than of a Division III team. To ask a school to "deemphasize" is to ask it to offer less than it might for a gifted athlete. The goal of athletics is not simply to win (if it were, schools would schedule as many "patsies" as they could), but to do well against worthy competition.

It is a mistake to take the term *education* in a very narrow sense and restrict it to what happens in the classroom, library, and laboratory. Though the academic life is the heart of the educational experience, it is only part of it. The university has a student for four years—perhaps the most important four years of his or her life. The student is growing and maturing in many ways: socially, physically, emotionally, ethically, as well as intellectually. The school should be concerned not only with the student's academic education but with his or her education as a human being in all the ways of the world. Those who have competed in sports know well the benefits that they derived from it and continue to derive.

Lou Little, long-time football coach at Columbia University, said it well:

> I think football is valuable because it develops in the young men qualified to play characteristics wholly useful to any man. Every boy who can should play football or one of the other rugged sports that test will against will, body against body. He'll learn to work with a group, to discipline himself and to pick himself off the seat of his pants after he has been knocked down. He will develop a priceless asset—competitive desire. Are there any more valuable things than these that a young man can learn to complement his formal classroom, library and laboratory education?
>
> In my coaching years, I felt I was a teacher fully as much as the teachers of anthropology, zoology or any of the several hundred other courses. My classroom

did not have four walls. My laboratory did not have test tubes or scientific equipment. Our examination period came on almost any Saturday afternoon during October and November. These were noisy tests, usually exciting, sometimes happy, often heartbreaking. My students were in a tough course leading not, as the professors say, to "specialization," but to a richer experience of living.[122]

Although he was talking about men's football, much of what he says applies also to other sports and to women's athletics.

If competitive sport has significant educational value, it should not be limited to varsity and intercollegiate competition, nor should it be limited to a handful of "major" sports. A broad array of sports should be made available on both the intercollegiate and intramural levels. The extent to which an institution can provide these educational values will depend upon its own resources and particular aims. Uniformity is neither possible nor desirable. In some manner, shape, or form, sport has an important role to play. There is room in this country for both the University of Alabama and the University of Chicago. The indiscriminate call for deemphasis exhibits a bias against the kind of school that seeks a particular kind of excellence and assumes that success in one area precludes success in others.

Philosophy of Competition James W. Keating, a professor of philosophy and physical education, offers a definition of competition: "An attempt (according to agreed-upon rules) to get or keep any valuable thing either to the exclusion of others or in greater measure than others."[123] Competition is a pervasive part of ordinary life. We compete in the marketplace for sales, jobs, and promotions. We compete in schools for admission and grades. We compete in politics for political office. We may even compete with others for a marital partner. It is difficult to find a society in which there is not some form of competition—though it may not be economic. Keating believes that competition is "an ineradicable trait of human nature."[124] Within limits, competition is a fine thing. "Without a powerful stimulant such as competition human potentialities remain as such, potentialities which will never be actualized."[125]

Athletic competition may take on several ethical attributes. First, it must take place according to the rules. True competitors cannot avail themselves of an advantage through cheating. This holds for all kinds of competition. Though they may lose, they preserve their integrity and dignity as competitors. In sports, these rules are clearly spelled out for all contestants—more clearly than in other areas where prizes and rewards are sought. The competitor responds to the principle of fairness—a principle of utmost importance in all walks of life. Second, athletic

[122]See Davis, p. 430.
[123]James W. Keating, "The Ethics of Competition and Its Relation to Some Moral Problems in Athletics," in Osterhoudt, *The Philosophy of Sport,* p. 159.
[124]Ibid., p. 165.
[125]Ibid., p. 164.

competition is an exciting activity that is immediately gratifying to contestants. They want to win and must do all they can for victory. What an athlete wins is not nearly so important as what a competitor wins in economics, politics, or courtship, but the medal or recognition is a symbol that on a given day or season the athlete triumphed in a contest of skill. This is profoundly gratifying. Even in defeat athletes have enjoyed the zeal of all-out effort. They savor the battle, and though they lose, they can thank their opponents for a thrilling contest. The athlete should not compete to prove that he is a "better man" (or person) or to counteract inner doubts he may have about his manhood (or personhood), but to experience the joy of combat and, on occasion, the additional joy of victory. Good sportsmanship consists not only of abiding by the rules but of respecting the opponent whose best efforts are required to make a good contest.[126] The third ethical component of athletic competition is the self-discipline that is called for in training for the contest and in engaging in it. This may be greater or less, depending on the seriousness that athletes bring to the sport. Dedicated athletes will make sacrifices so that they will be able to bring out the best in themselves. They will learn how to use their entire set of physical and mental and emotional resources for their chosen purpose, for that maximum effort that may lead to victory. The fourth ethical component is the willingness to continue to strive, though victory may be eluding the athlete's grasp. Athletes will give their all until the final gun goes off. They will "hang in there." They will be tenacious. Tired and in pain, they will have the fortitude to sprint that last hundred yards in a race. The fifth ethical component is apparent in team sports. Athletes will learn how, and be willing, to cooperate with others on behalf of a common goal. In basketball, they will pass off to the open player and play some defense. In baseball, they will bunt when the situation calls for it. In football, they will block for the running back and on defense will help out in another pass reception zone.

These are indeed genuine ethical attitudes: to play by the rules, to love the game, to get the most from one's ability, to continue to strive, and to subordinate oneself for the success of the team.

In sports we see most clearly the essentials of competition. The objective is victory and its immediate results. The situation is not cluttered up by considerations of a better job, more money, or acceptance by others. Defeat is not a catastrophe, for the competitors have experienced the zest of full commitment. One of respect for their opponents and in consistency with their own engagement, they have played to win. Whether they win or lose, they have used their bodies and minds to full capacity and can look forward to the next contest.

What competitors learn in athletic competition can serve them well in other situations of life. Having learned to play by the rules, enjoy the excitement of competition, discipline themselves, persevere against the odds, and cooperate, they will be more likely to win in other areas of competition: economic, profes-

[126]Friedrich Nietzsche said that he respected the enemy who was as aggressive and "masterful" as himself.

sional, political, and social. Having learned to demonstrate excellence in athletic competition, they can demonstrate excellence in other forms of competition.

Albert Camus "said that it was from sports that he learned all that he knew about ethics." Henry Steele Commager "argued that it was on the playing fields that Americans learned the lessons of courage and honor which distinguished them in time of war." Lyman Bryson is quoted as saying: "It could be established, I think, that the next best thing to the rule of love is the rule of sportsmanship. This virtue, without which democracy is impossible and freedom uncertain, has not yet been taken seriously enough in education."[127] Henry C. Link said: "Sportsmanship is probably the clearest and most popular expression of morals. Morals are the rules of the game, and sportsmanship means that cooperation according to the rules is more important than ruthless competition."[128]

It should be remembered, however, that athletes are not competing in "life" at the moment they are competing on the field. They must give themselves wholly to the game. Athletic competition, in school and beyond school, is a disinterested activity that has its own charm and rewards. Victory does not mean a better job, a killing in the market, or higher political office. In itself, it is much less important but more personal. The contestants want to succeed because they want to succeed, and that, within the context of the sport itself, is sufficient.[129]

Playing Games Competition considered on its own merits—that is, when results beyond the activity itself are ignored—is a form of play. It may be, and often is, engaged in because it is immediately satisfying. It is not the only form of play, for parents may romp with their children in a way that is not competitive. A person may volley on a tennis court, ride a bike along a forest path, caress another person, or strum on the guitar for sheer enjoyment. Competitive play requires the urge to win; noncompetitive play does not. Both share the quality of gratifying a human need.[130] Competitive play thus occurs in the context of a game with rules explicit enough to indicate a winner when the game is over. Games themselves can be broken down into physical (football, track, tennis, golf, baseball) and nonphysical (bridge, chess, Monopoly, "Stop the Music"). The former we call sports or athletics, the latter simply games. When we play a game (in the broader sense), we are engaging either in sports or games (in the narrow sense).

[127]See Keating, p. 166. The theory outlined above is not that of Professor Keating, but it employs his definitions and reflects, I think, his general point of view.

[128]See Jan Broekhoff, "Sport and Ethics in the Context of Culture," in Osterhoudt, p. 222.

[129]The Scythian Anacharsis had difficulty understanding the point of the Olympic games in the sixth century B.C. and said to Solon: "So these athletes are all the more ridiculous if they are the flower of the country, as you say, and yet endure so much for nothing, making themselves miserable . . . to get an apple and an olive-branch when they have won!" See ibid., p. 221.

[130]"Sport that lacks the element of competition and does not emphasize performance, is no longer sport; sport, however, which has lost the element of playfulness has degenerated into mere production, has become toil, according to" Klaas Rijsdorf. "Sport is the development of antithetical play in the direction of competition." Broekhoff, p. 221.

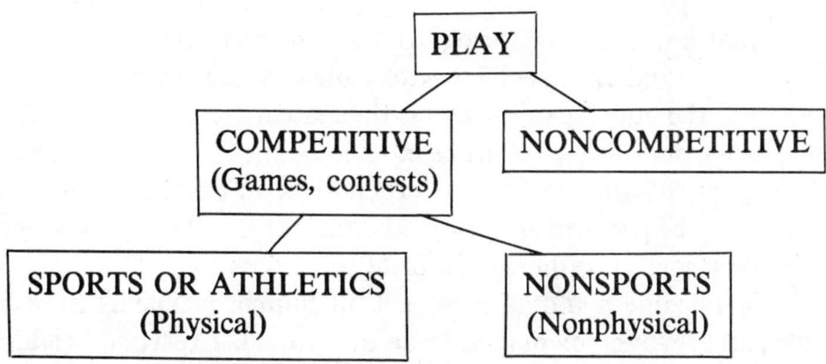

To avoid confusion in what follows, we will employ the term *game playing* in the broad sense to include contests that are both physical and nonphysical.

Although the essence of game playing is to produce a winner, there is a sense in which one may be said on occasion to compete with oneself. On the golf course, a player whose "opponent" is not in his class may try to shoot a better score than he did the previous week. A solitary high jumber may try to top six feet for the first time, or a jogger try to better her time over a certain course. The bridge player, with the match already in hand, may try for overtricks through the use of a type of endplay not yet mastered. The player today is competing with the player he or she was on some other day.

Bernard Suits supplies a useful definition of game playing: "To play a game is to attempt to achieve a specific state of affairs, using only means permitted by rules, where the rules prohibit more efficient in favor of less efficient means, and where such rules are accepted just because they make possible such activity."[131] This definition is deficient only because it leaves out the elements of competition and victory, but these perhaps are implied. It does bring out some important points. The goal of the high jumper is not simply to get beyond the barrier, or he or she would walk around it. The runner can get to the finish line more quickly by cutting across the oval. The football player can seize the ball during a time-out and place it in the end zone. And the bridge player can grab every trick on the table. Nongolfers cannot understand the pains that golfers take to get a little white ball into a cup four hundred yards down the fairway. But at bottom all games are as irrational as this. The gamesman has imposed rules on himself for no reason but to heighten an activity, to supply a challenge, to make competition possible. These rules are thus quite different from traffic rules, which serve a clear utilitarian end. "Playing a game is the voluntary attempt to overcome unnecessary obstacles."[132]

In a fanciful but persuasive essay, Suits suggests that game playing is what makes life worthwile, that it comes very close to being the *summum bonum.* All

[131]Bernard Suits, "The Grasshopper; A Theisis Concerning the Moral Ideal of Man," in Osterhoudt, p. 203.

[132]Ibid., p. 204.

the other values that humanity has recognized are instrumental to leisure time and are thus derivative and extrinsic. The grasshopper in his account is right in believing that play is the purpose of life and is thus much closer to the truth than the "workaholic" ants, but this view must be modified somewhat to include Suits's contention that "game-playing performs a crucial role in delineating that ideal – -a role which cannot be performed by any other activity, and without which an account of the moral ideal is either incomplete or impossible."[133]

Suits asks us to imagine a utopia in which all human problems have been solved. No one has to work, for machines do everything. Everyone has all the material goods he or she wants. Those interpersonal problems that might remain after the economic problems have been solved have been banished by a science of psychology that actually cures people. "There is no longer any competition for love, attention, approval or admiration, just as there is no longer any strife in the acquisition of material goods."[134] There is no longer any need for such virtues as self-sacrifice, benevolence, industry, fortitude, and truth-seeking. "Morality is relevant only to the extent that the ideal has not been realized, but there is no room at all for morality in the moral ideal itself, just as there is no room for revolution in the ideal which inspires revolutionary action."[135]

What, then, will the people in this blessed condition *do*? Art? No, because art is based on utility (for which there is no need) or is an expression of hopes, fears, frustrations, triumphs, and tragedies (which are unknown). Friendship? No, for there is nothing of any importance to be shared. Sex? Perhaps, but only as pleasure comparable to other physical pleasures.[136] Pursuit of knowledge? No, because the limits of human knowledge have already been reached. Philosophy and science have achieved their ends in both the theoretical sense and the sense of controlling the environment. Their instrumentality has been fully realized. There is nothing left to know.

"What we have shown thus far is that there does not appear to be anything to *do* in Utopia, precisely because in Utopia all instrumental activities have been eliminated. There is nothing to strive for precisely because everything has already been achieved. What we need, therefore, is some activity in which what is instrumental is inseparably combined with what is intrinsically valuable, and where the activity is not itself an instrument for some further end. Games meet this requirement perfectly. For in games we must have obstacles which we overcome *just so that* we can possess the activity as a whole, namely playing the game. Game-playing makes it possible to retain enough effort in Utopia to make life worth living."[137] Admiration and sharing become possible again, as well as striving and

[133]Ibid., p. 205.
[134]Ibid., pp. 206–207.
[135]Ibid., p. 208.
[136]"Sex, as we have come to know and love it, is part and parcel with repression, guilt, naughtiness, domination and submission, liberation, rebellion, sadism, and masochism, romance and theology. But none of these things has a place in Utopia." Ibid., p. 211.
[137]Ibid., pp. 211–212.

the emotions of victory and defeat. And the crowning morality will be sportsmanship. "The notable institutions of Utopia . . . will not be economic, moral, scientific, and erotic instruments [all based on scarcity]—as they are today—but institutions which foster sport and other games."[138]

Conclusion Some, as Suits admits, will not like this. They will say they are not games-people. They want to build dams and push back the frontiers of knowledge. But in Utopia they could do these things only *as* games, for all these serious aims are already achieved. They would have to conceal from themselves the fact that the dams can easily be built by machines and all knowledge easily retrievable from the memory banks of computers. They would have to function as golfers who, instead of simply dropping the ball into the cup, assign themselves the pointless task of hitting from the tee with a selected club and flailing through rough and sand trap. But "strivers" and "seekers" would still not be satisfied. Their actions must be truly productive. "People like to be building houses, or running large corporations, or doing scientific research to some purpose, you know, not just for the hell of it."[139]

If it is true that these people can find contentment only in doing things that serve a useful purpose, they don't belong in Utopia. Perhaps, Suits admits, Utopia is really not a utopia at all. He leaves the issue open. The strivers and seekers, feeling that life as game-playing is hardly worthwhile, would see Utopia as an empty dream and dismantle it. Games would once again be "relegated to the role of mere pastimes useful for bridging the gaps in our serious endeavors."[140]

But if we have returned at the end to the reality where "life is real, life is earnest," recalling what was said above, we can still argue that games in general and sports in particular are not only pleasant interludes but valuable and ethical training experiences for the jobs that are to be done.[141]

If this is to be achieved, deemphasis is not the course that universities necessarily should take with respect to intercollegiate competition. They should instead, in a way consistent with the rules and their own resources and goals, pursue an aggressive policy of fielding teams of the highest quality.

Summary of the Issues

We may perhaps agree that intercollegiate athletics, since it is administered by a university or college, should have an educational function for those who engage in it, and that it should be judged on this basis rather than on its tendency to enhance the institution's image or to attract contributions.

[138]Ibid., p. 217.

[139]Ibid.

[140]Ibid., p. 218.

[141]Those who would reject Suits' Utopia are willing to see life itself as a game, for they have chosen to have obstacles rather than assured success.

Some people would deemphasize athletics: eliminate favoritism toward student athletes; terminate the recruiting of athletes, reduce expenditures for major sports so that more money could be spent on intramurals and minor sports, extend equal opportunity to women, form new conferences and associations, legislate suitable rules, and so forth. Their opponents stress the value of big-time competition under qualified coaches. The educational values possible for the athletically gifted cannot be fully realized unless they are in a good program and face comparably gifted opponents. Deemphasized programs, it is charged, choose mediocrity over excellence. They may also espouse a philosophy of competition that puts sports in the forefront of the educational mission instead of the merely ancillary position it officially occupies. Some go even further and argue that sports are a form of game-playing and that game-playing ultimately is what makes life worth living. Those who call for deemphasis thus appeal to fairness, while their opponents appeal to utility, often of an ideal kind.

But the utilitarian approach is also employed by the side that favors deemphasis. It points out the great expense of athletics. In most schools, the financial loss is great; in only a very few does the sport pay for itself; in none does it show a profit. The other side disputes the figures. A second utilitarian debit is the pressure to produce winners. Schools are forced to do everything within the rules to remain competitive, and many of these things are clearly incompatible with the stated aims of either amateur sport or education. Very often they violate the rules. A real chamber of horrors can be furnished from the exposed conduct of various departments of athletics. The other side points out that stories of cheating are sensational and thus newsworthy; most schools do not cheat. A third result of the emphasis on winning is the tendency to exploit the athlete. Various forms of exploitation are described, from red-shirting to playing hurt, but the worst is to send the athlete into the world (after eligibility has been used up) unfit to cope with life or a profession. The other side emphasizes the opportunity for an education provided to athletes who could not otherwise go to college. They also argue that the college experience has often contributed to the athlete's success after college.

The two sides agree that sports have value. The basic issue is whether these values can be more successfully, more extensively promoted, and done so with fewer bad effects, in a setting where athletics is emphasized than in one in which it is not.

Discussion Questions

1. Do you believe that sports "build character"? Does intercollegiate sport build *more* character? Does big-time competition build still more? Explain.
2. Where would you place most of the blame for the sports scandals of recent years? Explain.
3. Do you think the college athlete who has no chance to earn a degree has been exploited? Why?

4. Do you think the famous athlete who enjoys a position of privilege on some campuses has earned that position? Explain.
5. Would you be in favor of prohibiting the recuitment of athletes? Why?
6. Do you believe that young blacks have been harmed by the prospect of athletic fame and fortune dangled before them? Why?
7. Do you think that college athletic programs discriminate against women? Explain.
8. Do you agree with Suits's argument on behalf of the supreme value of game playing? Why?
9. Do you believe that the competitive "instinct" is an important one and should be cultivated? Why?
10. How would you compare the educational value of sports with such other extracurricular activities as dramatics, debating, music, and writing?
11. How highly would you rate intercollegiate athletics as a means for promoting "school spirit"? Is school spirit important? Why?
12. Do you think that your school overemphasizes intercollegiate athletics? Explain.
13. Do you think it would be better for schools that want to compete on the big-time level to hire their own athletes openly and forget about academic requirements? Why?
14. What kind of a case do you think can be made by the ex-athlete who sues a school for not providing him or her with an education?
15. Since women's sports have now been admitted to the NCAA, do you expect that they will produce the same kinds of excesses that have been reported in men's sports? Why?
16. Do you know of any "snap courses" at your school that athletes gravitate toward? How do you feel about this?
17. Assess the moral impact of television on intercollegiate athletics.
18. Do you think that the cost of the athletic program at your school is justified in terms of the educational values it promotes? Explain.
19. If you add the school spirit and publicity promoted to the educational values, do you believe that the cost of the athletic program is justified? Explain.
20. Thinking only of educational values, do you have greater respect for M.I.T. or the University of Alabama? Why? Would you rather be a student at the University of Southern California or the University of Chicago? Why?

For Further Reading

Ed Cowan. "Why Sport?" *Humanist* 39 (November–December 1979):22–28.

Educational Record 60 (Fall 1979). Whole issue.

Harry Edwards. *Sociology of Sport.* Homewood, Ill.: Dorsey Press, 1973.

Harry Edwards. "Sport within the Veil: The Triumphs, Tragedies and Challenges of Afro-American Involvement." *Annals of the American Academy of Political and Social Science* 55 (September 1979):116–127.

George H. Hanford et al. *An Inquiry into the Need for and Feasibility of a National Study of Intercollegiate Athletics.* Washington: American Council on Education, 1974.

Neil D. Isaacs. *Jock Culture U.S.A.* New York: W. W. Norton & Co. 1978.

Robert Lipsyte. "Varsity Syndrome: The Unkindest Cut." *Annals of the American Academy of Political and Social Science* 455 (September 1979):15–23.

Robert G. Osterhoudt, ed. *The Philosophy of Sport.* Springfield, Ill.: Charles C. Thomas, 1973. Part 2.

Mitchell H. Raiborn. *Revenues and Expenses of Intercollegiate Programs: Analysis of Trends and Relationships, 1970–1977.* Shawnee Mission, Kans.: National Collegiate Athletic Association, 1978.

George H. Sage, ed. *Sport and American Society: Selected Readings.* 2nd ed. Reading, Mass.: Addison-Wesley Publishing Co., 1974.

Lee Sigelman and Robert Carter. "Win One for the Giver? Alumni Giving and Big-Time College Sports." *Social Science Quarterly* 60 (September 1979):284–294.

Sports Illustrated. Many issues.

John T. Talamini and Charles H. Page, eds. *Sport and Society: An Anthology.* Boston: Little, Brown & Co., 1973.

Chapter 6

JUSTICE

The concept of justice is fundamental in ethical thought. When other people are affected by our action (and they nearly always are), we have to ask whether to do the action would be just to them. Would the action violate their rights? Is it just to smoke in the presence of others who claim the right to clean air? Is it just to shout down a radical political speaker? What about a reactionary speaker? Is it just to reward children of vastly different merit equally? Is it just to prevent some adult citizens from voting? Is it just to deny medical care to people unable to pay? Is it just to execute a murderer? When we recognize that other people (and society in general) have legitimate claims on us, we have accepted the basic principle of justice.

Not only are individuals required to act justly toward others, but states and their governments are also required to act justly in their dealings with citizens. The tax rate should be equitable. Officials should not be permitted to take bribes. Judicial procedures should guarantee a fair trial for all. Everyone is entitled to the equal protection of the laws.

Some claims that individuals have on the actions of others are regarded as so important that they should be recognized and enforced by the government itself. It is thought to be unjust for *X* to steal from or do physical injury to *Y,* so the powers of government are employed to preserve *Y* in his or her legitimate claims against theft and injury. This, then, is another way in which the state can be just: ensure just relations *among* its citizens.

Such terms as *legitimate claim, equitable, entitled,* and *fair* are indispensable in talking about justice, but adequate understanding of the concept of justice requires knowledge of what *constitutes* legitimacy, equity, entitlement, and fairness. This issue will be with us throughout this chapter.

We cannot, however, address ourselves here to all the areas in which justice is to prevail. Nothing will be said, for example, about the just limits of free speech and free religious worship. We will also ignore the question of just procedures in the courts. And we will not have anything to say about the relative justice of various forms of government. Instead, we have selected these three topics from the broad field of justice: (1) *Distributive justice.* According to what principle should we as members of society seek to distribute the material goods of that society? (2) *Preferential justice.* Are there legitimate ways by which employers and educational institutions can compensate members of certain classes that have been discriminated against in the past? (3) *Criminal justice.* According to what principle should we punish violators of our laws?

These would appear to be political questions, for the task of securing just distribution, providing compensatory justice, and dispensing just punishment falls mostly on the shoulders of the government. Success in all of them would seem to be dependent on what the government is willing to do. The state is just to the degree that it conducts itself in these areas in a way that justice requires. But the role of the citizens is very important. They must judge the state on the basis of their own concepts of justice and, if they are responsible citizens, seek to get their concepts of justice reflected in formal rules that are enforced by their government. Some of these rules may be negative, for in some cases justice may be better served by excluding political action.

Our discussions will for the most part be conducted from a political viewpoint, but it should be noted that our three topics are not exclusively political ones. Individuals often face problems of distribution, compensation, and punishment, quite apart from the government. They will want to act on the basis of their sense of justice whether the law has anything to say on the matter or not. One may, as a private individual, decide to bequeath equal sums of money to all one's children, take part in a United Fund campaign, or give the physical worker in the family a larger portion of meat at dinner. Presumably, one is acting according to a sense of distributive justice. Someone else may decide to hire a black applicant over a slightly more qualified white applicant, seek out a woman to admit to an auto mechanics course, or lend the car more often to a sickly teenager than to a robust one. Presumably, that person is acting according to a sense of compensatory justice. Someone else may decide to punish a child more severely for a third offense than for a first, vote as a jury member for capital punishment, or refuse to speak to a friend on the street who has failed to invite him or her to a recent party. Presumably, this individual is acting according to a sense of just punishment. In short, while this chapter is essentially political, it is not exclusively so, for all these issues come up in private life and quite apart from prevailing law.

DISTRIBUTIVE JUSTICE

Society Should Guarantee Only a Minimal Standard of Living for All Its Members

There is no distributive problem concerning fresh water on an island containing half a dozen bubbling springs and inhabited by four people. But there is such a problem in a lifeboat equipped with one quart of water and containing eight people. In a society consisting of several million people living in an area with limited natural resources, factories and machines, and technical skills, it is obvious that not everyone can have all of what he wants. We are all in a "lifeboat." And if we want to think of the matter globally, we could think of our planet as a spaceship. Who gets what and how much?

Need and Merit We might invoke the principle of *need:* Everyone is to get what he or she needs. This is unsatisfactory for two reasons: (1) *Need* is a relative word. A musically inclined person may feel she needs a harp, expert instruction, and funds for travel, if she is to develop her talent. This could be very expensive. Someone else might feel he needs a yearly vacation in the Bahamas if he is to retain his sanity in this stressful world. It is impossible to state legitimate human needs in a way that would satisfy everyone. (2) *Need* is a vague word. Some things (e.g., food) are clearly needs, and some things (e.g., a seven-bathroom home) are clearly not. But most things fall somewhere between these extremes. Is travel (with its broadening effect) a need for all? Are color television sets and tickets to cultural or athletic events genuine needs? How about the sense of security for our old age? The trouble with "need" as a criterion is that cases could be made for so many "needs" that they would exceed society's productive capacities.

We might next invoke the principle of *merit.* Not everyone should have the opportunity to have harp lessons, vacation trips, color television sets, and tickets to the Rams' games, but only those who *deserve* them. Since the resources of society are limited, they should be apportioned on the basis of merit. If Helen has talent, she will get the music lessons denied to Alice; and if Horace works hard he will get to watch the Rams play football in Anaheim. One merits things because of what one is or does, for what one is or does benefits society in certain predictable ways. But there are difficulties here also. Some people would appear to have no merit. That is, they have not earned any portion of society's wealth. Small children, skid-row bums, the feeble-minded, the insane, and the disabled do nothing for society. Others who will not work, or will do so only sporadically, deserve only a very small portion. Some people, whether it is their own fault or not, hardly contribute enough to society to merit the basic necessities of life. According to Herbert Spencer and other social "Darwinists," they should be permitted to perish. But we are more humane.

Individual Rights John Locke believed that everyone has the natural right to *life,* and Jefferson called the same right an "inalienable" one. Since this right is natural rather than conventional and inalienable rather than something that must be earned, it represents a claim that anyone in any condition can legitimately press. Since it is a legitimate claim, justice requires that we recognize and honor it. Any society with any resources at all is obligated to provide the basic necessities of life (food, shelter, clothing, and some health care) to all its members regardless of merit. We must provide these things to minors, loafers, defectives, and criminals.

So we have returned to the principle of need, but in a very restricted sense. Justice requires that people do what they can in providing the basic necessities of life for the "less fortunate." This can be done through private charity or through state programs of aid. And it does not matter what it costs. Before anyone can own a Lincoln Continental, everyone must have sufficient food, clothing, shelter, and basic medical care to survive.

For anything beyond these basic needs we can go back to the principle of merit —but, again, with a difference. It is not the state's function to determine who merits something more than someone else. That it is, is the assumption of every totalitarian system from Plato's "republic" to the Union of Soviet Socialist "republics." We need a more objective criterion of merit and one that preserves the freedom of individuals to wrest what they can from society's supply of goods. We do not have very far to look. This criterion is implicit in the workings of the free enterprise system.

In a free-market economy, individuals are motivated to work in order to acquire what they want over and above what society guarantees them. They compete with others for their share of the wealth. Some will work longer, harder, and with greater ingenuity. Some will take chances; others will "play it safe." All will spend their earnings on what they want—that is, they will choose their own goods. In some rough measure, what they get will be proportional to what they do. The second of Locke's natural rights, *liberty,* thus provides the philosophic support for a theory of just distribution of goods over and above those required for sheer existence.[1]

The third of Locke's rights, *property,* recognizes the claim that everyone has to the fruits of his or her labor. Individuals are entitled to keep most of what they have earned. They will, of course, have to give up some of it in order to support a police force and national defense that protect the lives, liberties, and property of all. This third right validates the claim of individuals to private ownership.

These three rights constitute the basic claims of individuals. Nothing is so obviously counter to the requirements of justice than an action by an individual, a group, or a government that deprives a person of life, liberty, or property, so long as the person respects these rights of others.[2] Such an action is resented and protested against in a spirit of righteous indignation. We may hope that our neighbors will treat us with kindness, but we cannot *demand* that they do so. We can, however, demand that they respect our life, liberty, and property. Governments exist to enforce this demand. The basic rights not only are important in themselves, but best serve the ideal of just distribution.

[1]Milton Friedman, after refuting arguments "against the so-called capitalist ethic," admits that this does not prove that it is correct. "I find it difficult to justify either accepting or rejecting it, or to justify any alternative principle. I am led to the view that it cannot in and of itself be an ethical principle; that it must be regarded as instrumental to some other principle such as *freedom*. . . . I find it hard, as a liberal, to see any justification for graduated taxation solely to redistribute income. This seems a clear case of using coercion to take from some in order to give to others and thus to conflict head-on with individual *freedom.*" *Capitalism and Freedom,* pp. 164–165, 174. Emphasis added.

[2]This is what the Fifth Amendment of the American Constitution was getting at when it stated: "No person shall be . . . deprived of life, liberty, or property without due process of law. . . ."

Our conception of distributive justice is perhaps not quite complete. The third right claimed by Jefferson in the Declaration of Independence is the *pursuit of happiness.* Exactly what this adds to life and liberty is not clear, but it does suggest some additional rights for all members of a civilized society: rights to an education and to a job. Surely individuals who are denied these things cannot realistically aspire to happiness or earn their fair share of society's goods. Society therefore owes to all its members the opportunity to be educated and to hold a job. Through private or public means, distributive justice requires that these things be guaranteed.

In summary, then, the requirements of distributive justice are the basic necessities of life, education, and a job. What an individual is permitted to acquire beyond these will depend on his own exertions and talents, under the protection of the rights to liberty and property. When this is the case, the goods of society may be said to be distributed justly. This theory of justice is unmistakably based on the rights of individuals.

The Good Society It is when philosophers conceive of a grand and glorious state that they lose sight of justice. They concern themselves with what is useful for society as a whole rather than with what protects the rights of individuals. The Greeks had no conception of individual rights, and it was easy for Plato to subordinate everything to his conception of a good state. His ideal state has a unity, perfection, and destiny quite apart from the lives of its members. It possesses all the virtues, while those of individuals are derived from the part they can play in the whole. It turns out that reason is possessed by a small class of philosophers—who do the ruling. Courage is the highest virtue of the warriors —who do the fighting. And temperance is the only virtue that workers can aspire to. "Justice" consists in each segment performing the function for which it is best fitted and which will preserve the kind of state Plato wants. *Distributive* justice consists in granting to individuals what they need in order to carry out their prescribed functions. This also is what they deserve, for it is appropriate to their supposed basic nature and to the role they are expected to play. But these natures and these roles have no objective basis. They are derived from a vision of a harmonious society unique to Plato and made to serve that society. Other visionaries may have different visions, but they, too, will identify various aspects of human nature and press them into service. In starting with the organic whole instead of the individual, they all miss the essential character of justice.

It might seem to be the mark of fanaticism to insist upon rights apart from the good of the whole—or even the actual institutions of a society and the way they work. Perhaps something should be said in favor of the Platonic approach, where the emphasis is on society. Even if it is granted that a society possesses enough wealth and organization to guarantee basic rights to all, how do we know that enterprising action under the aegis of liberty and private ownership will produce much or any of the goods that will raise the lot of some people above that of subsistence? Shouldn't a theory of distributive justice not only properly divide what is available, but also take into account the potential of society to increase the *amount* that is to be divided? Would a society that recognized the claims of individuals to life, liberty, property, education, and employment have anything to divide beyond the basic necessities?

The Free Enterprise Ideal Here we are struck with a remarkable fact, one that amazed and gratified most eighteenth-century philosophers from John Locke to Adam Smith: The "wealth of nations" grows in a society in which free enterprise prevails. When the restraints of paternalism and mercantilism are broken, when each individual is permitted to pursue his or her own economic advantage, when people find that their resourcefulness and energy are rewarded in the marketplace, production increases and the standard of living rises. In Smith's words:

> The uniform, constant, and uninterrupted effort of every man to better his condition, the principle from which public and national, as well as private opulence is originally derived, is frequently powerful enough to maintain the natural progress of things toward improvement, in spite of the extravagance of government, and of the greatest errors of administration.
>
> Every individual is continually exerting himself to find out the most advantageous employment for whatever capital he can command. It is his own advantage, indeed, and not that of society, which he has in view. But the study of his own advantage naturally, or rather necessarily leads him to prefer that employment which is most advantageous to the society.
>
> The natural effort of every individual to better his own condition, when suffered to exert itself with freedom and security, is so powerful a principle, that it alone, and without any assistance, is not only capable of carrying on the society to wealth and prosperity, but of surmounting a hundred impertinent obstructions with which the folly of human laws too often encumber its operations; though the effect of these obstructions is always more or less either to encroach upon its freedom, or to diminish its security.[3]

The amazing fact is that the "natural order" is such that when individuals seek their own advantage intelligently and freely, they contribute to the advantage of society. Egoism, prudence, and selfishness are in no way incompatible with public virtue, benevolence, and social values, provided that they are enlightened. Alexander Pope expressed this almost divine harmony:

> Thus God or nature formed the general frame
> And bade self-love and social be the same.

Recognition of individual rights, far from harming society, is the very best way to benefit it.

[3]Adam Smith, *An Inquiry into the Nature and Causes of the Wealth of Nations,* 5th ed. (New York: Random House, 1937), pp. 326 (II, 3), 421 (IV, 2), 508 (IV, 5).

The French *philosophes,* imbued with the ideals of reason, reform, and progress, emphasized individualism and natural rights. Some of them were also utilitarians (e.g., Helvétius and D'Holbach) and saw no conflict between a theory which held that the individual has certain rights and another theory which advocated promoting the greatest happiness for the greatest number. They, like Smith, were convinced that the best way to increase the happiness of all was to permit individuals freely to pursue their own happiness. Once again, then, rights and social good are far from incompatible.

Rights and Utility It was Jeremy Bentham (1748–1832) who broke the alliance between the two theories. Recognizing that "rights" (real or imaginary) could be pressed into service on behalf of any social theory, he regarded the rights theory as "nonsense on stilts" and placed all his confidence in "the greatest happiness of the greatest number." But it is significant that *on terms of utility* alone he supported the free enterprise system. He accepted the liberalism of Adam Smith, declaring that in economics Smith "has not left much to do, except in the matter of method and precision."[4] Bentham even retained the egoistic psychology prevalent in the older utilitarianism. Bentham's successor, John Stuart Mill, espoused the free-market economy on utilitarian grounds, although later editions of *Principles of Political Economy* contained revisions that compromise the doctrine of laissez-faire in some respects. Both Bentham and Mill, after banishing "rights," reinstate them as rules of justice possessing especially powerful utilitarian support![5]

It is not claimed here that natural rights and utility complement one another philosophically. The "harmony" envisioned by the men of the Enlightenment may have been a lot of wishful thinking. Just as insistence on one set of rights may conflict with social happiness, so too have some applications of utilitarianism in welfare-state or socialistic theories conflicted with individual rights. The point here is simply that a utilitarian justification for institutions based on the idea of rights can plausibly be developed. In view of the material success of nations that have adopted the free enterprise system, it is fair to argue that recognition of rights (upon which justice is based) is not necessarily at the expense of the social good.[6]

It should also be noted that for Bentham and the other utilitarians, society is conceived of as an aggregate of individual persons. If it is good, it is because its members are happy. The notion that society is something over and above the people who make it up was a philosophic "fiction" that the utilitarians would not abide. Their notion of society was far different from that of Plato and Hegel, who conceived society in organic terms. For them, the individual was an abstraction;

[4]See Elie Halevy, *The Growth of Philosophic Radicalism* (Boston: Beacon Press, 1960), p. 108.

[5]See above, pp. 33, 35, 37–38.

[6]The United States Constitution contains both a Bill of Rights and (in the Preamble) a commitment to "promote the general welfare."

for utilitarians, society is an abstraction. Our theory of distributive justice thus derives another confirmation from the utilitarians. Both emphasize that it is *individuals* to whom justice is due, not the needs of a state.

One final observation: The disparities of wealth and income in a free enterprise society are not so great as is commonly believed. We often hear it said that 5 percent of our population get 20 percent of the income, while the bottom 20 percent of the population get only 5 percent. In can be argued, however, that such figures fail to take into account the fact that great disparities exist *in the life of one individual.* When one is young, one may be near the bottom of the scale; in later years, as the result of one's own efforts, one may be near the top of the scale. A guarantee of virtually equal income would deny individuals the material rewards that they as business people, professors, or carpenters, may look forward to as they master their professions.[7] A fairer index of the distribution of wealth would be based on the *lifetime* earnings of individuals. It may also be pointed out that the differences in capitalist states are not nearly so great as those in status societies (e.g., India), backward countries (e.g., Egypt), or Communist countries (e.g., Russia).[8] But even if there *were* great disparities in America, this would not mean that the theory of justice outlined above is erroneous. If some people believe that justice is not enough, they can supplement the institutional guarantees for it with their own philanthropic efforts.

Society Should Guarantee a High Standard of Living for All Its Members

The problem of distributive justice is not so simple as some would have us believe. There are a great many cases where we need to know how justly to distribute goods, and each case is different. How much of a company's profit should justly be distributed to its workers in the form of wages? How much to the people who supplied the capital? How much of an oil company's profits should go to research and development? How much of the tax receipts of a city, county, state, or nation should go for parks, for medical care, for the treatment of mental illness, for the rehabilitation of criminals, for educational facilities, for the salaries of government workers? No theory of distribution will easily settle all these and many other problems. But we need some theory if we are to address these problems at all. The least we can do is to identify the grosser forms of unjust distribution.

Problems of "Merit" The typical solution is to specify the minimal needs of everyone and to guarantee them on the basis of the right to life, then to divide the rest of society's output on the basis of merit. Everyone is to get something, but how much above this each person gets will depend upon the contribution he

[7]For a few individuals, such as professional athletes, the "big money" is possible only in their early years.

[8]See Friedman, p. 169.

or she makes. The merit side of the solution is handled by a system of free-market economy, welfare state, or socialism. The first holds that merit is roughly rewarded when government does not intervene. The second holds that extensive legislation and government programs are necessary in order for true merit to be recognized and rewarded. The third holds that only by extensive collective ownership can anything like proportionate reward be achieved.

The French socialist/anarchist Pierre-Joseph Proudhon argued that capitalism permitted stockholders to receive rewards disproportionate to their contribution, and coined the expression "Property is theft." Karl Marx, who derived more from Proudhon than he cared to admit, argued that the proletariat were denied the "surplus value" their labor created, and accepted the slogan "To each according to his work," for "the lower phase" of Communism. Both emphasized due return on work, the one believing this was possible in small groups where people worked together on the basis of "mutual aid" and "reciprocity," the other in an organized socialist state where the bourgeoisie had been dispossessed. Proudhon would eliminate government, which functions to preserve unearned benefits; Marx would take over government to ensure that all benefits would be earned. At the other extreme we have the defenders of "free enterprise" who emphasize the contributions made by entrepreneurs. Milton Friedman provides them with a slogan: "To each according to what he and the instruments he owns produces."[9] Somewhere in between is the group that advocates restrictions on the "wheeling and dealing" of entrepreneurs, protections for labor organizations, minimum wage laws, graduated income tax, and so forth. Despite these differences, there is general agreement that society should reward individuals on the basis of what they have contributed to society. There must be something very plausible in a position that can be accepted by Proudhon, Marx, Friedman, and Franklin Delano Roosevelt.

Let us, however, look more closely at the concept of merit. What, exactly, does *merit* mean? If it means the qualities necessary to make a good living, then it follows in tautological fashion that a free-market economy will most accurately reward merit, and the problem of distributive justice would seem to have been solved. But such a meaning is clearly unsuitable. We can think of people succeeding grandly on the market with less than glorious merit, and we can think of other people with a lot of merit who have not prospered.

What are the human qualities and actions that we tend to call meritorious? Intelligence, artistic sensitivity and creativeness, ingenuity, ambition, mechanical talent and skill, courage, and persistence are human qualities that can lead to monetary rewards, but they often do not express themselves in lucrative occupations. A professor of Greek may be very intelligent but can only earn a salary that is near the poverty level. Vincent Van Gogh sold just one painting in his lifetime. The discoveries of many inventors are exploited by others. A professional soldier may be very brave but unable to afford to rent a home for his family. Harry Fletcher has been trying for years to build a better mousetrap.

[9]Friedman, pp. 161–162.

Some people are willing to work longer and harder than others. Example: the unskilled worker who holds two jobs. Some people achieve for themselves higher levels of education. Example: the hopeful schoolteacher who acquires three master's degrees and one doctorate in a vain attempt to get a job. Some people's efforts are more productive of social value. Example: the social worker who is especially effective. Such people are not necessarily rewarded in the marketplace for their superior efforts. By contrast, we have the clever young copy writer on Madison Avenue whose salary is in six figures because he or she has a knack for writing advertisements that induce people to buy cigarettes.

Many of the meritorious qualities one is born with, and it is possible to argue that even when they lead to a substantial contribution to social goods, the individual is not justified in claiming greater rewards than those received by individuals who are less favorably endowed. Why should a scientific genius who works no harder than a common laborer be supported in great luxury while the laborer lives in a tenement? Why should the genius be blessed again by society for having been blessed by nature? Many human qualities, such as industriousness, would seem to be within the reach of all. Some people *choose* to work hard, seek an education to the limits of their ability, and save their money for sound investments. Others *choose* to loaf, frequent pool halls, and spend their money on whiskey and fast cars. But the latter (as well as the former) are doing what they do because of what they *are*—over which they have little control. We no longer penalize people for their race or sex, but many of the qualities that are regarded as meritorious and productive (and thus deserving of reward) are just as far beyond the individual's control as race and sex. One is or is not a child of fortune.[10]

A second kind of fortune is the *situation* into which one is born. If character and habits are shaped to any great extent by external factors, the kind of environment in which one is born and reared is a matter of utmost importance. Family, friends, and neighborhood are crucial influences for any young person, and these are elements over which one has little or no control. If one was fortunate enough to have loving and supportive parents, if one grew up in a home where values were respected, if one had the benefit of estimable role models, if one lived in a neighborhood where law was respected and life and property were secure, if one happened to be assigned to a good school with educated and dedicated teachers, one's chances of developing a meritorious character and habits are greatly enhanced. If, in addition, one is so fortunate in birth that one can be sent to an expensive school, helped out by tutors, and inherit a lot of money or the family business, one's cup indeed runneth over. We no longer feel that we need to reward people "of good birth" (nobility, gentry, "established family"), but in effect we do the same thing when we reward those who have had the opportunity to develop

[10]Kant has spoken of "the niggardly provision of a stepmotherly nature" (*Foundations of the Metaphysics of Morals,* first section) and Hume of blind nature "pouring from her lap, without discernment or parental care, her maimed and abortive children" (*Dialogues Concerning Natural Religion,* part 11).

the qualities we admire and penalize others who through no fault of their own have been born into environments that stifle their development. The race is not always to the swift when, through the luck of birth, the runners start at different points.

Finally, we should note the factor of sheer contingency or "blind luck" during the course of life. One person may gain fame because she had an idea for which the time happened to be ripe. Another person may have gotten a job because the employer liked the tie he happened to be wearing when he was interviewed. Another person may have gone to college because a local branch of the state university happened to open its doors in her own neighborhood. A bridge player occasionally remarks, "I'd rather be lucky than good."

Does all this mean that we should opt for a system of government by experts, people who in their wisdom and unlimited power will redress all the violations of distributive justice? Such a regime would address itself to the problem of ascertaining what *real* merit consists of, then strictly apportion benefits accordingly. Nothing would be left to chance. But this would be a totally controlled society, and most of us (unless we were sure that our particular merit was generously evaluated) would be loath to accept it. An alternative course of action would be this: The regime, still absolutist, would decide that the job of ascertaining real merit was either too difficult or, because of the element of luck in people's nature or nurture, impossible.[11] It would then, in the absence of objective criteria, impose as much equality as is possible in view of the need to maintain sufficient incentive to produce the conveniences of life. If no one *deserves* more, everyone should receive the same. But we would want to reject this solution also, because, while we might grant that "merit" is overemphasized, we feel there should be a place in society where *some* reward for *some kinds* of merit is accorded. Also, we might believe that the principle of need should operate. Some people need more than others: A teacher needs books, a person with an operatic voice needs lessons, an artist needs paint, a paralyzed person needs a wheelchair, an athlete needs steak, a mother needs food for her children, and so on.[12]

A Theory of Justice The correct solution to the problem of distributive justice is a theory that recognizes the difficulty of determining merit, the duty of society to meet the various needs of people beyond that of sheer survival, and the

[11]Walter Kaufmann, for example, in trying to specify the requirements of distributive justice, lists eight basic categories (what one is, has, has done, is doing, needs for himself, needs for his dependents, desires, and has contracted to do) and a host of subcategories, concluding that the whole project of sorting out the claims and weighing them is impossible. See "Doubts about Justice" in Kiefer and Munitz, *Ethics and Social Justice.* See also Bowie and Simon, *The Individual and the Political Order,* p. 97ff.

[12]It may be possible to treat need in an equalitarian manner. That is, an effort is made by society to meet the needs of *everyone* to the degree that the resources of society make possible. This ideal is expressed in Marx's slogan for "the higher phase": "From each according to his ability, *to each according to his need.*" On this interpretation, the second objection becomes irrelevant. The first, however, still holds.

existence of a government that goes far beyond the phantom structure favored by eighteenth-century liberals.

Having said enough about the first point, we will go at once to the other two. What a society, in the interest of distributive justice, can guarantee its members depends upon the resources of that society, its ability to exploit them, and the number of people it contains. What would be just in societies of extreme scarcity would be quite different from justice in comfortable or affluent societies, and even subsistence societies.[13] If the United States is an affluent society, the rights that Americans can claim are much more extensive than those claimed by members of a poor and backward society. One situation is like being in a supermarket, the other is a crowded lifeboat.

This approach will require a "busy" political apparatus, but not an omnicompetent or omnipresent one. While preserving an area of free economic activity, it demands for all a much higher standard of living than that of minimal needs. The government will foster a situation in which everyone has a balanced diet, lives in a spacious home, possesses most of the conveniences of life, has access to low-cost transportation, receives free education to the limit of the ability to perform, has complete health care (medical, dental, and mental) from the cradle to the grave, has free use of parks, amusement areas, libraries, and museums, can look forward to a paid vacation every year (if he or she works the rest of the year), and is protected against the catastrophe of unemployment. These are expensive indeed, but we should remember that our society is blessed with immense resources.

The means by which this fair distribution is to be made cannot and should not be stated in doctrinaire terms. It is insisted here, however, that government be democratic.[14] There will have to be a leftward move toward a genuine welfare society and perhaps beyond it. Government will indeed regulate, and it will administer programs and property. It will play its role as a "countervailing power" in the midst of other great powers—capitalistic, military, educational, and labor. It will operate pragmatically and experimentally, in the best sense of John Dewey's philosophy.

Certain general actions, however, would seem to be obvious. Government will raise the minimum wage-rate, it will socialize medicine (or sponsor national health insurance), it will raise taxes on higher incomes, it will administer housing programs, it will support education at all levels, it will impose a vigorous program of energy production and conservation, it will finance public transportation, it will protect the environment and natural resources, it will build libraries and museums, it will set aside land for parks and recreation areas, it will strengthen the social security system, it will guarantee full employment—all these things it will

[13]See Bowie and Simon, pp. 205–212.

[14]Here we must be dogmatic. Whether democracy is preferable to other forms of government is itself a question of justice. But this is an aspect of justice we have chosen not to discuss in this chapter.

do, directly or indirectly, on a national scale or a regional one, these things and many more.

Galbraith, Bentham, and Rawls John Kenneth Galbraith long ago spoke of "an implacable tendency" in our society "to provide an opulent supply of some things and a niggardly yield of others."[15] In his "theory of social balance" he lamented the fact that so much of our gross national product is in the form of inane or harmful goods and services, and so little in the form of things that really improve the quality of life. Is it reasonable to spend more money to advertise cigarettes than in cancer research? Galbraith strikes a utilitarian note when he writes:

> By failing to exploit the opportunity to expand public production we are missing opportunities for enjoyment we might have had. Presumably a community can be as well rewarded by buying better schools or better parks as by buying bigger automobiles. By concentrating on the latter rather than the former it is failing to maximize its satisfactions. As with schools in the community, so with public services over the country at large. It is scarcely sensible that we should satisfy our wants in private goods with reckless abundance, while in the case of public goods, on the evidence of the eye, we practice extreme self-denial. So, far from systematically exploiting the opportunities to derive use and pleasure from these services, we do not supply what would keep us out of trouble.[16]

What is called for here is a reallocation of our productive efforts, a task that only government can perform.

Defenders of free enterprise often cite its utilitarian value, and appeal to Jeremy Bentham to show that it fosters the greatest happiness of the greatest number. Perhaps in its day it did. In the eighteenth century it was a progressive system that promised (and delivered) to the people more benefits than the system of mercantilism and special privilege which it supplanted. But no one can fail to notice the utilitarian language used by Galbraith above in defending increased government (or collective) enterprise. The term *maximize* itself was coined by Bentham. If we believe in progress, in reform, in beneficial consequences for society as a whole, we must apply the principle of utility to the *contemporary* situation and take a rather skeptical view toward certain "rights" of individual property. A society in which goods are distributed according to the principle of a decent or high standard of living for all may be not only fairer than the alternatives but happier as well.

Galbraith did speak of "social balance," so he stops short of thoroughgoing socialism. And, above, so did we. Somehow, the efforts of government to build a good society and the efforts of entrepreneurs to realize a profit must be seen as compatible. It is difficult to draw boundaries around private enterprise beyond which social enterprise cannot encroach. What is considered a "decent" or "high"

[15]Galbraith, *The Affluent Society,* p. 250.
[16]Ibid., pp. 259–260.

standard of living today is quite different from what was the case in previous periods. In 1920 a family could be regarded as doing well even if it did not have an automobile. Not so in 1950; but then it could enjoy a high standard of living without owning a color television set. Not so in 1980. What the legitimate expectation will be in 1995 no one can say.[17] One vague way to state the principle that relates social action and private enterprise is this: The "right" to private property can be recognized only to the degree that it is consistent with a high standard of living for all—that is, a just distribution of society's goods.

This theory of justice is quite different from that of John Rawls. He asks us to imagine ourselves behind a "veil of ignorance": we do not know what our position or talents will be in some hypothetical society. Forced to be impartial and objective, we can now pronounce what distribution of goods would be just. According to Rawls, we would regard ourselves as justly treated in material wealth if this principle prevailed in society: No one has any more than anyone else except in those cases where this position of advantage would improve the position of the disadvantaged. "The higher expectations of those better situated are just if and only if they work as part of a scheme which improves the expectations of the least advantaged members of society. The intuitive idea is that the social order is not to establish and secure the more attractive prospects of those better off unless doing so is to the advantage of those less fortunate."[18] Our theory, however, would permit economic inequality whether it benefited the least favored or not—provided, of course, that the least favored enjoy a high standard of living. Rawls's "veil of ignorance" is a useful device to help us conceive of fairness in an impartial way, but it is not obviously true that we will all come up with the same intuition. *This* writer would be willing to take his chances in a society where his own sense of fairness prevailed, whether he was one of the lucky ones or not.

Conclusion Aristotle defined justice as treating similar cases in a similar manner. To treat equals equally is to guarantee fairness. Now, all people are similar in that they are human beings. Any differences they may have are not relevant to their common humanity. Their humanity makes them equals. On the basis of this equality, it is fair to reward them equally from society's supply of material goods. People display differences also, and these become relevant only when their common humanity has been justly recognized.

[17]"The essential fallacy of the fixed poverty line is that it fails to recognize the relative nature of 'needs.' The poor will not be satisfied with a given level of living year after year when the levels of those around them are going up at the rate of about 3 percent per year. Old-timers may harken back to the 'good old days' when people were happy without electricity, flush toilets, automobiles, and television sets; but they must realize that once it becomes possible for all to have these 'luxuries,' they will be demanded and will quickly assume the status of 'needs.' " Herman P. Miller, *Rich Man, Poor Man* (New York: Thomas Y. Crowell, 1971), p. 120. See Bernard Gendron, "Capitalism and Poverty," in James Rachels, *Moral Problems,* p. 243ff.

[18]John Rawls, *A Theory of Justice,* p. 75.

The present distribution of wealth and income in the United States country is unjust. In 1978, the personal distribution of total income by families was: lowest fifth, 5.2 percent; second fifth, 11.6 percent; third fifth, 17.5 percent; fourth fifth, 24.1 percent; highest fifth, 41.5 percent. In other words, 40 percent of the American families received 65.6 percent of the income. In the same year, 11.4 percent of all families had income below the poverty level.[19] "According to one study, 'About 1.6 percent of America's adult population owns 82.4 percent of the publicly held shares in the nation's corporations.' In addition, Marxist critic Felix Greene maintains that the same 1.6 percent of the population in the United States owns 32 percent of the personally owned wealth, and at the lower end of the scale 50 percent of the adult population owns only 8.3 percent of the nation's wealth and has assets averaging only $1,800."[20]

This theory and the one outlined in the previous section are obviously "deontological" rather than utilitarian ("consequentialist"), although it is argued that they do not fly in the face of utilitarian concerns.[21] The issue between the theories is the point where characteristics other than humanity become relevant. This theory draws the line through a point much higher than a theory that calls for the basic necessities of life. Both seek to "level up" all members of a society, but ours believes that people, just because they are people, have a just claim to a relatively higher standard of living in a society that has ample resources. If it were possible to place these other "relevant" characteristics (talent, effort, productiveness) within the power of individuals to possess or exhibit, we would allow them a greater claim. But since it is not, they are resorted to only after society has provided generously for all its members. The claims based upon them are so dubious that the claim of common humanity must not only come first but loom more largely. This claim is based upon individuals' presence in a society where talents (and deficiencies) are part of the common pool. To recognize that claim in an equal manner is fair, and that is what justice requires.

Summary of the Issues

Both theories of distributive justice focus on the rights of individuals rather than the greatness of the state or the greatest happiness of the greatest number. They are thus deontological rather than utilitarian.

[19]U.S. Bureau of the Census. See *World Almanac and Book of Facts* (New York: Newspaper Enterprise Association, 1981), p. 133. For interesting statistics on "rich," "affluent," "upper-middle-class," "middle-class," "lower-middle-class," "poor," and "starving" families, see Sylvia Porter, "Rich Man, Poor Man, Beggar Man: Where Do You Stand?" *St. Louis Globe-Democrat,* March 12, 1981, p. 1B.

[20]Gerald F. Cavanagh, *American Business Values in Transition* (Englewood Cliffs, N.J.: Prentice-Hall, 1976), p. 109.

[21]For plausible utilitarian theories of distributive justice, the reader is referred to the writings of J. J. C. Smart and R. M. Hare. Two short essays appear in Arthur and Shaw, *Justice and Economic Distribution.*

The first theory emphasizes the rights to life, liberty, property, and the pursuit of happiness. What society owes to each individual, then, is, first of all, the basic necessities of life or a minimal standard of living. What one receives beyond this should be apportioned to one's merit. The exercise and display of merit requires freedom to act. The reward of merit requires protection for the property one has attained. The opportunity to exhibit merit requires accessibility to education and jobs.

The second theory approaches the problem quite differently. What society owes to each of its members depends on the amount of physical resources it possesses. An opulent society owes more to its members than a marginal one, just as a well-stocked lifeboat can divide its goods in much larger equal portions than can a poorly stocked one. Since there are good reasons for suspecting that merit and fairness are quite different concepts, this theory emphasizes equality at the expense of merit. It is only after a high standard of living is achieved for all that the principle of merit can be allowed to operate. The objective in the United States should be a high rather than a minimal standard of living.

Both approaches recognize the difficulty of determining the social conditions under which merit can truly be rewarded, and neither relies on a nondemocratic government to establish these conditions. The first theory believes that an economic system of free enterprise will roughly and in most respects justly reward merit. The second theory points out the conflicts in such a society between genuine merit and reward. It moves, therefore, to the left and finds "welfare state" and socialistic measures appropriate not only for raising the minimum standard of living but for rewarding merit.

Although both theories are based on concepts of rights and fairness, they deny that great utilitarian sacrifices are implied. Proponents of the first theory believe they can show that the greatest happiness of the greatest number is admirably served in a free enterprise system, where guarantees are minimal, while proponents of the second theory are equally confident that the utilitarian goal is more perfectly achieved in a regulated economy where guarantees are great.

Discussion Questions

1. Do you agree that a theory of distributive justice cannot be based on utilitarianism? Why?
2. Do you think that distributive justice in personal relations is quite a different matter from distributive justice as dispensed by society or the state? Explain.
3. Do you think that a person who refuses to work is entitled to food, clothing, shelter, and health care? Any more than that? Why?
4. Do you think that the kind of society described in the second essay would stifle initiative and thus have grave utilitarian consequences? Explain.
5. Do you think that a theory of justice can afford to ignore utilitarianism? Why?
6. Do you believe that a just society which possesses the means is required to offer free education at all levels? Why?
7. Do you think that our society, where health care is often unavailable for the poor, is, in that respect, just? Why?

8. Which do you believe is the more important touchstone of distributive justice —equality or merit?
9. Do you think that Plato's theory of justice has been too hastily dismissed in the essays above? Why?
10. Is it possible for a society that contains less total happiness than some other society to be more just than that other? Explain.
11. Is the lifeboat analogy a good one for speculating on distributive justice? Where do you think it breaks down? How do you think it could be extended?
12. Do you think that the people who oppose the Equal Rights Amendment are violating the principles of distributive justice?
13. Would you agree with Rawls's extension of equality in his theory of justice? Explain.
14. If it is assumed that a totalitarian regime could truly evaluate and reward merit, would you regard the state that it controls as having perfect distributive justice? Why? Would you choose such a state? Why?
15. Would you regard a perfect utopia in which everyone possessed all he or she needed as a just society? Why?
16. Do you think that a first-rate poet should be rewarded more than a first-rate plumber? Why?
17. What is your opinion of the Marxist slogan "From each according to his ability, to each according to his need"?
18. Do you agree with the social Darwinists that the incompetent should be permitted to perish? Why?
19. Are you drawn more to the ideas of Friedman or those of Galbraith? Why?
20. Do you think that our society has gone too far in "leveling up" and should now begin to "level down"? Why?
21. How would you assess the "equality of opportunity" in the United States?
22. How would you assess the "equality of opportunity" in the Soviet Union?
23. Do you think that distributive justice is more perfectly achieved in the Soviet Union than in the United States? What about Sweden?
24. Do you agree with those who say that the problem of distributive justice is in theory insoluble? Why?
25. How would you distribute goods in a society with scarce resources? In a society with marginal resources?

For Further Reading

Aristotle. *Nicomachean Ethics.* Book 5. Many editions.

John Arthur and William H. Shaw, eds. *Justice and Economic Distribution.* Englewood Cliffs, N.J.: Prentice-Hall, 1978.

Norman E. Bowie and Robert L. Simon. *The Individual and the Political Order: An Introduction to Social and Political Philosophy.* Englewood Cliffs, N.J.: Prentice-Hall, 1977. Chapter 7.

Richard Brandt, ed. *Social Justice.* Englewood Cliffs, N.J.: Prentice-Hall, 1962.

David Braybrooke. *Three Tests for Democracy: Personal Rights, Human Welfare, Collective Preference.* New York: Random House, 1968.

James C. Dick. "How to Justify a Distribution of Earnings." *Philosophy and Public Affairs* 4 (1975):248–272.

Milton Friedman. *Capitalism and Freedom.* Chicago: University of Chicago Press, 1962.
John Kenneth Galbraith. *The Affluent Society.* Boston: Houghton Mifflin Co., 1958.
John Kenneth Galbraith. *Economics and the Public Purpose.* Boston: Houghton Mifflin Co., 1973.
John Kenneth Galbraith. *The New Industrial State.* Boston: Houghton Mifflin Co., 1967.
Michael Harrington. *Toward a Democratic Left.* Baltimore: Penguin Books, 1968.
Howard E. Kiefer and Milton K. Munitz, eds. *Ethics and Social Justice.* Albany: State University of New York Press, 1968.
Russell Kent and David Miller. "Understanding Justice." *Political Theory* 2 (1974):3–31.
Karl Marx. *Critique of the Gotha Programme.* New York: International Publishers, 1938.
Onora Nell. "Lifeboat Earth." *Philosophy and Public Affairs* 4 (1975):273–292.
Robert Nozick. *Anarchy, State and Utopia.* New York: Basic Books, 1974.
James Rachels. *Moral Problems.* 3rd ed. New York: Harper & Row, 1979. Part 3.
John Rawls. *A Theory of Justice.* Cambridge: Harvard University Press, 1971.
Nicholas Rescher. *Distributive Justice.* Indianapolis: Bobbs Merrill, 1966.
Peter Singer. "Famine, Affluence, and Morality." *Philosophy and Public Affairs* 1 (1972): 222–243.
Karsten J. Struhl and Paula Rothenberg Struhl, eds. *Ethics in Perspective.* New York: Random House, 1975. Part 2, section 7.

COMPENSATORY JUSTICE

Preferential Hiring and Admission Are Legitimate Means for Rectifying Past Injustice

It would seem obvious that discrimination according to race or sex, when these qualities are irrelevant to the matter at hand, is unjust. Everyone is entitled to be judged on the basis of ability when being evaluated for a job, a promotion, or a place in an educational institution. This indisputable moral principle was partly enacted into federal legislation with the passage of the Equal Pay Act of 1963 and the Civil Rights Act of 1964. The former prohibits companies from paying women less than men for substantially the same work. Title VI of the latter prohibits discrimination on the grounds of race, color, or national origin in any program or activity receiving federal assistance. Title VII prohibits discrimination in employment on grounds of sex, race, color, religion, or national origin. The Equal Employment Opportunity Commission was set up to administer these provisions. Various state laws, before and after 1963, prohibited certain kinds of discrimination in their jurisdictions. Beginning in 1965, Executive Orders 11246, 11375, and others forbade the federal government or any contractor (including universities) with which it deals to discriminate against minority or female workers. Educational institutions were not covered by Title VII, but amendments in 1972 brought their employment practices into the coverage. Title IX of the Education Amendment Act (1972) states: "No person in the United States shall, on the basis of sex, be excluded from participation in, be denied the benefits of, or be subject to discrimination under any educational program or activity receiving Federal financial assistance." These and other federal and state enactments and orders have gone a long way to supplement and enforce the "equal protection" clause of the Fourteenth Amendment and the "due process" clause of the Fifth.

Justifying Affirmative Action But all this is not enough. Even if these measures did eliminate discrimination in all companies and schools in the United States (and they did not), something more would have to be done. The victims of the past must be given special consideration; injustice must be redressed. The action of the government in encouraging the establishment of "affirmative action" programs is a correct response to a long-standing injustice and should be supported by all people who believe in fair play. Victims of negative discrimination must now become the beneficiaries of positive discrimination. Only "invidious" discrimination, where some groups are excluded, is wrong; where it brings them together, it is benign. Despite "equal opportunity," minorites and women are still grossly underrepresented in skilled and professional jobs.[22]

Affirmative action programs are quite in the spirit of equality legislation and executive orders. Where an unjust situation has been created by past discrimination, means must be made available to correct it. A great many court opinions have declared that affirmative action (first required in Executive Order 11246) is a natural extension of the movement to stop discrimination. As one judge stated:

> It is by now well understood, however, that our society cannot be completely color-blind in the short term if we are to have a color-blind society in the long term. After centuries of viewing through colored lenses, eyes do not quickly adjust when the lenses are removed. Discrimination has a way of perpetuating itself, albeit unintentionally, because the resulting inequalities make new opportunities less accessible. Preferential treatment is one partial prescription to remedy our society's most intransigent and deeply rooted inequalities.[23]

The result for certain groups (minority races and females) of systematic and long-standing discrimination is that their members are badly prepared for open competition for jobs and admission to institutions of higher learning. They tend to be less well educated and trained. Their physical health may not in general be as good as that of members of more favored groups. They may be less disciplined in their work habits. They are less confident and less ambitious. Black men are encouraged to be athletes, not brain surgeons; women are encouraged to be nurses (or housewives), not mathematicians. Many of them (minorities and women) neither expect equal treatment nor are prepared to demand it. They have grown up in homes where "failure" is expected. Even standardized tests militate against

[22]See O'Neil, "The Case for Preferential Admissions," in Gross, *Reverse Discrimination,* pp. 66–72.
[23]*Associated General Contractors of Massachusetts, Inc.* v. *Altshuler* (1973). Justice Mathew Tobriner of the California Supreme Court, the long dissenter in the Bakke case, quoted from this opinion.

ethnic groups whose languages are not Standard English and whose experience of the dominant Anglo-white culture is limited. To make them compete equally with others would do little to alleviate the injustice of their present situation. It would preserve injustice in the name of "justice." As Justice Tobriner said in his dissent in the Bakke case: "Two centuries of slavery and racial discrimination have left our nation an awful legacy, a largely separated society in which wealth, educational resources, employment opportunities—indeed all of society's benefits —remain largely the preserve of the white-Anglo majority. Until recently, most attempts to overcome the effects of this heritage of racial discrimination have proven unavailing. In the past decade, however, the implementation of numerous 'affirmative action' programs . . . have resulted in at least some degree of integration in many of our institutions."[24]

Implementing Affirmative Action There are several ways in which affirmative action programs can deal with this "awful legacy." One is to state that where applicants are "equally" qualified, the choice should incline toward minorities and women. This does not go far enough, for the depressed group on average will be *less* qualified. And to give them the benefits of "ties" is simply to recognize the unusual applicant who has risen above his or her comrades. A second way is to state that where applicants are at least minimally qualified, the choice is to incline toward minorities and women. This is better, but it requires a level of preparation that is still beyond the ability of many members of disadvantaged groups. Can we go further than this and require companies and universities to choose people who are *unqualified*? Yes and no. The third way is to state that where the disadvantaged *can* by special training and remedial programs be brought to the level of being qualified, some of them should be selected over applicants that are already qualified. Individuals who are products of our unjust society will be accepted if and only if there is reasonable expectation of their ultimate success.

Such an outlook is not one of "discrimination in reverse." We are not discriminating in favor of minorities and women simply because they are minorities and women. These characteristics are no more relevant today than they were when we discriminated *against* them. Minorities and women have an *additional* characteristic, one that has been fastened on them by social practices of the past. This characteristic *is* relevant, and it is simply this: they have been placed at a disadvantageous position. It is this condition that affirmative action seeks to rectify. It is unfair for society to judge people "equally" when one of the negative traits has been fostered in some of them by society itself. The relevant characteristic of being disadvantaged must be perceived as important enough to override or counteract in some degree the relevant characteristic of relative qualification. That someone is a minority person or a woman really has nothing at all, *in itself,* to do with the matter! Had these people not been discriminated against in the past, they would neither demand nor need special consideration today.

[24]553 P. 2d 1152 (Calif. 1976).

Where the burden of proof for discrimination was on the government according to Title VII, the affirmative action movement generated by Executive Order 11246 places the burden on the institutions to show that underrepresentation is not a result of discrimination; and if they cannot do so, they have to show how they intend to deal with the situation. "When a society has committed past injustices or when historically disadvantaged groups exist side by side with more advantaged groups, it simply is not possible to achieve equality and fairness by applying neutral principles."[25]

Affirmative action programs do more than state how institutions will choose from among applicants. They describe how applicants are to be sought from injured groups, how the news of opportunity is to be brought to them, how they are to be recruited. They contain plans for a gradual movement toward representation of minorities and women in the work force or admission list that roughly corresponds to their presence in the population.

Quotas and Goals The affirmative action program we are defending does not call for the setting up of *quotas.* This is a bad word, because it reminds us of the days when quotas were restrictive: they were used to keep minority representation *down.* The intention now is just the opposite. Indeed, to establish positive quotas for underrepresented groups is in effect to establish restrictive quotas for all others (since the places are finite), which would be to repeat the evil of unjust hiring and admission policies of the past. Moreover, it is unreasonable to expect an institution to be able to state the degree to which it will fill its places with minority groups and women. It would be even more unreasonable to impose the same quota system on "similar" institutions. There are too many variables: the number of applications, the breakdown of the applications in terms of group membership and in terms of relative qualification, the facilities (actual and possible) of the institution for remedial work, the changing demands of the market for the various occupations and professions, and so forth. It is not unreasonable, however, to require that certain tentative and flexible *goals* be set up and that evidence be supplied that steps have been taken to realize or even surpass these goals. "We ask," said J. Stanley Pottinger (head of the Office of Civil Rights of the Department of Health, Education, and Welfare) in 1972, "for something more than the mere promise of good behavior."[26] Only if the institution could not show real effort and adherence to fair procedures would it be in trouble.[27]

[25]Howard A. Glickstein, correspondence. See Gross, *Reverse Discrimination,* p. 29.

[26]Pottinger goes on to specify what is asked of universities: "Universities are required to commit themselves to defined, specific steps that will bring the university into contact with qualified women and minorities and that will ensure that in the selection process they will be judged fairly on the basis of their capabilities. Universities are also required to make an honest prediction of what these efforts are likely to yield over a given period of time, assuming that the availability of women and minorities is accurately approximated, and assuming that the procedures for recruitment and selection are actually followed." Pottinger, "The Drive Toward Equality." See Gross, *Reverse Discrimination,* p. 44.

[27]This "trouble" could consist of forced instatement, back pay, fines, and/or loss of federal contracts and assistance.

The purpose of affirmative action programs is to undo the injustice of the past. As a result of the past, groups are not in an equal position. Something drastic must be done to enable all people to compete on equal terms for the good things of life. Because we have pushed some people down, we now have to pull them up. The justification of affirmative action lies in a legitimate claim for compensation. It is inspired not by a utilitarian concern for a happy society but by the duty to right an entrenched and long-standing wrong.

There should be no qualms about the constitutionality or legality of these programs. The Fourteenth Amendment, the Civil Rights Act, and other recent pieces of legislation forbid discrimination. Affirmative action simply attacks it more vigorously and tries to achieve real equality of opportunity by facing head-on the social realities created by past discrimination.

Problems It is true that even a pervasive and well-thought-out system of affirmative action has its problems. Two are especially obvious and troublesome. The first seems to be a case of injustice itself: Many white males will be excluded to make way for those for whom affirmative action has been devised. Through no fault of their own, they have lost out to individuals often less qualified than themselves. *They* have played no part in the injustice of the past, yet they have to pay the price of rectification. The very ones who perhaps have contributed to the injustice are exempt from paying the price, for they already have the jobs, degrees, security, and tenure. The bitterness of a Marco DeFunis, Allan Bakke, and Brian Weber can easily be understood. The young white male who reads this may well lose out to a less-qualified Chicano who applies to the same medical school. Even the white male who gets a job may lose it, for, in the spirit of affirmative action and to protect minorities against the "last hired, first fired" principle, the claims of seniority are sometimes qualifed when layoffs have to be made.

In answer, we can only point out that in the real world lesser injustices often must be done to remedy great ones. It is, in a sense, unjust to draft a person, but to do so presumably serves the end of preventing the greater injustice of being taken over by another power. It is, in a sense, unjust to deprive individuals of their earnings by taxing them to support public schools; but to deny children a free education would be a graver injustice. There are few if any beneficial social programs that do not hurt someone—often grievously. We do not have the luxury of choosing between relative goods; we must choose between relative evils and promote the least evil. And in this case, temporary evil for some (young white males) is preferable to continued and permanent evil for others (black females). It may also be observed that affirmative action seeks to get at only *some* of the social disadvantages that minorities and women suffer. The white male (collectively) will continue to enjoy other advantages (e.g., his control of the media, his disproportionate presence in positions of political power, his greater wealth, his past influence in institutions and culture that set the values and mores of the present). And these may well balance the disadvantageous position some individuals will find themselves in when applying for jobs and admission. They are still part of the "establishment."

As stated above, the condition of injustice is intended to be temporary. When society has become accustomed to selecting oppressed people for its better jobs and schools, when oppressed people have raised their standard of living and general educational level, when they can easily find "role models" in prestigious positions, when their expectations and confidence have risen to the point that they can aspire to all the things that white males do, there will no longer be a need for affirmative action. Individuals will freely compete, for no great group will have a millstone around its collective neck. The purpose of affirmative action is to remove the need for affirmative action. When the day comes that affirmative action is no longer necessary, the white male will no longer have to pay a special price. But he may find (and this is the bad news) that his dominant role in all departments of society has been markedly reduced.

The second obvious and troublesome problem is concerned with the selection itself of the "oppressed" classes. Typically, they are blacks, Indians, Chicanos, and women. Why these groups and no others? Is it because they are the most oppressed or because they are easily identified and have political "clout"? What about the rural poor of Appalachia? What about the children of miners in the coal fields? What about Puerto Ricans and Orientals? What about the children of sharecroppers? There are many groups that have been victimized by social injustice. Isn't it arbitrary to select some for preferential treatment while excluding others? The answer here cannot be completely satisfactory. But we can point out that there is a very high correlation between injustice and the groups usually selected. Admittedly, not all blacks are disadvantaged and not all disadvantaged people belong to racial minorities and the female sex. But a great deal can be done against social injustice in general by attacking it on behalf of these selected groups. Certainly blacks are more numerous than Bulgarians and more discriminated against than Jews and the Irish. As recipients of preferential discrimination, they are extensive and obvious targets. Perhaps more groups should be added to those that affirmative action has typically been concerned with. But the group approach, admittedly imperfect, is a sound one. There simply is not the time or bureaucratic apparatus available to administer compensatory justice in an individual case-by-case way.

It is no effective criticism of a plan for reducing injustice to show that the plan is imperfect or that it will not eliminate *all* injustice. Affirmative action, if carried out conscientiously and intelligently, will go a long way in rectifying a very bad situation. Until a better plan comes along, it deserves our support as individuals and enforcement (within the limits of constitutional law) by our government officials.

Preferential Hiring and Admission Are Illegitimate Means for Rectifying Past Injustice

Executive orders have directed universities that receive federal funds to devise affirmative action programs aimed at increasing the percentage of minority groups and women in their admissions. These orders have also directed employers with fifty or more employees and federal contracts in excess of $50,000 to set "goals and timetables" for bringing minority persons and women in their work force up to their percentage in the available labor pool. Whether these affirmative action programs are legal or even constitutional is a question that is still unresolved. A host of judicial decisions at all levels has been rendered.

The Bakke Case One important U.S. Supreme Court decision was made in the case of *The University of California* v. *Allan Bakke* (June 1978). Bakke had applied for admission to the medical school of the University of California at Davis. No nonminority applicant was considered whose grade-point average was below 2.5. Bakke's average was 3.5. The university, in its affirmative action program, had reserved sixteen places in the entering class of 100 for disadvantaged minorities (blacks, Chicanos, Indians, Asian-Americans). Although Bakke's average and test scores were higher than those of most of the sixteen admitted (some averages were as low as 2.1), he was denied admission. In his suit he claimed injury on the basis of the "equal protection under the law" clause of the Fourteenth Amendment and Title VI of the Civil Rights Act of 1964. When the California Supreme Court found in his favor, it stated that "the lofty purpose" of that clause "is incompatible with the premise that some races may be afforded a higher degree of protection against unequal treatment than others."

The U.S. Supreme Court also found in Bakke's favor. Four justices believed that the quota system at Davis was unacceptable and that Bakke should be admitted. These four also declared that the issue of race was irrelevant in admissions decisions. Four others declared that the race of an applicant could legitimately be taken into account in admissions decisions. Justice Lewis F. Powell added his vote to the first four, so by a 5–4 vote Bakke was vindicated and the quota system struck down. But he voted with the other four justices in holding that race is a relevant factor, so this also carried by a 5–4 vote. The decision seriously weakens affirmative action but does not destroy it.

On the first issue, the five justices cited the Civil Rights Act of 1964, while Justice Powell cited the Fourteenth Amendment as well. He said in his opinion: The University of California "urges us to accept for the first time a more restrictive view of the Equal Protection Clause and hold that discrimination against members of the white 'majority' cannot be suspect if its purpose can be characterized as 'benign.' . . . These individuals are likely to find little comfort in the notion that the deprivation they are asked to endure is merely the price of membership in the dominant majority and that its imposition is inspired by the supposedly benign purpose of aiding others. . . . The white 'majority' itself is composed of various minority groups, most of which can lay claim to a history of prior discrimination at the hands of the state and private individuals. Not all of these groups can receive preferential treatment and corresponding judicial tolerance of distinctions drawn in race and nationality, for then the only 'majority' left would be a new minority of White Anglo-Saxon Protestants."

Powell rejected three of the four arguments put forward by the university to justify its policy: (1) to reduce the shortage of minority doctors, (2) to counter the effects of discrimination by society, (3) to increase the number of doctors in areas that are underserved. He said: "Preferring members of any one group for no other reason than race or ethnic origin is discrimination for its own sake. This the Constitution forbids." The fourth argument, however, he found unobjectionable: to achieve a student body that is ethnically diverse. He believes that action for this purpose is protected by the First Amendment. When factors for admission are examined, ethnic membership, he believes, can be a plus. Here he was in agreement on the second issue with the other four justices that race can be considered a relevant factor. But Powell adds that this "does not insulate the individual [applicant] from comparison with all other candidates for available seats."

The Weber Case About a year later the case of Brian Weber was considered by the U.S. Supreme Court. In 1974, Weber, a white laboratory technician at a Kaiser Aluminum & Chemical Corp. plant, sought to get into one of the company's training programs that would prepare him for a much better job in the company. But Kaiser had an affirmative action program. At the time it was instituted, less than 2 percent of 273 skilled craftsmen at the plant were black, although 39 percent of the local work force were black. The program called for two lists, one of minority workers and one of white. Qualified applicants for training programs were to be chosen alternatively from the lists in order of seniority until the percentage of the skilled minority workers roughly corresponded to their presence in the nearby population. When Weber was denied admission, he sued the company and the United Steelworkers of America. He argued that he was senior to some blacks who had been chosen, and he cited Title VII of the Civil Rights Act.[28] A federal district court and the Fifth Circuit Court of Appeals agreed. When the case (*United Steelworkers of America* v. *Weber*) reached the U.S. Supreme Court in 1979, Weber lost, 5–2.[29]

[28]Section 703(a) states that it is unlawful for an employer "(1) to fail or refuse to hire or discharge any individual or otherwise to discriminate against any individual with respect to his compensation, terms, conditions, or privileges of employment, because of such individual's race, color, religion, sex, or national origin; or, (2) to limit, segregate, or classify his employees or applicants for employment in any way which would deprive any individual of employment opportunities or otherwise adversely affect his status as an employee, because of such individual's race, color, religion, sex, or national origin."

[29]Four of these five justices (Brennan, Blackmun, Marshall, and White) had voted in *Bakke* to uphold the constitutionality of the Davis plan. The fifth, Justice Stewart, had voted against the Davis plan, but not on the basis of its constitutionality. Justices Powell and Stevens did not take part in the *Weber* case.

Justice William Brennan in his majority opinion argued that affirmative action was in the spirit of the Civil Rights Act. But Chief Justice Warren Burger, in a very forceful dissent, pointed out that during the eighty-three days of debate on this bill in Congress, its proponents had argued "tirelessly" that the bill would not be used to require quotas or to *justify* them.

Questionable Legality Supreme Court opinions neither establish nor undermine the morality of a course of social action. But these two cases and others certainly demonstrate the questionable legality of affirmative action programs. It does indeed appear that some affirmative action programs may be at odds with civil rights legislation.[30] *Weber* did not set aside the *Bakke* decision. An institution must be careful in formulating its program in order to seem to adhere both to the law and to various demands from the executive department of this nation's government. Even before the *Bakke* and *Weber* cases, Thomas Sowell commented on the bewildering system of federal enforcement: "EEOC is only one of many federal agencies administering the Civil Rights Act in general or the 'affirmative action' programs in particular. There are overlapping jurisdictions of the Labor Department, the Department of Health, Education and Welfare (HEW), the Justice Department, the EEOC, and the federal courts. There are also regional offices of all these agencies, which vary significantly in their respective practices. Moreover, when one federal agency approves—or requires—a given practice, following such an approved course of action in no way protects an employer from being sued, on the grounds of following that very same course of action, by another federal agency or by private individuals. Indeed, federal agencies have sued one another under this Act."[31]

The expression *affirmative action* first appeared in Executive Order 11246, but its purpose was to militate against discrimination, not to foster reverse discrimination.[32] Executive Order 11375 (1967) repeated the term. It was in Order No. 4

[30]Section 703(j) of Title VII of the Civil Rights Act of 1964 states: "Nothing in this title shall be interpreted to require any employer . . . to grant preferential treatment to any individual or to any group because of race, color, religion, sex or national origin of such individual or group on account of any imbalance which may exist with respect to the total number or percentage of persons of any race, color, religion, sex, or national origin employed by any employer." Justice Brennan argued in the *Weber* case that while Section 703(j) of Title VII does not *require* affirmative action programs, it does not *forbid* them—i.e., it permits them. (Kaiser's was voluntarily created.) Opponents, however, could argue that in specifically *not* requiring such programs, the law was a declaration by Congress that they were inappropriate means for carrying out the purpose of achieving equal opportunity in employment.

[31]Thomas Sowell, " 'Affirmative Action' Reconsidered," in Gross, *Reverse Discrimination,* p. 117.

[32]The first two points of that order are: "(1) The contractor will not discriminate against any employee or applicant for employment because of race, color, religion, sex, or national origin. The contractor will take affirmative action to ensure that applicants are employed, and that employees are treated during employment, without regard to their race, color, religion, sex, or national origin. Such action shall include, but not be limited to, the following: employment, upgrading, demotion, or transfer; recruitment or recruitment advertising; layoff or termination; rates of pay or other forms of compensation, and selection for training, including apprenticeship. The contractor agrees to post in conspicuous

of the Department of Labor a few months later that employers were instructed to provide "goals and timetables."[33] It was stated in *Time* that the *Weber* ruling "was a strong endorsement of affirmative action programs, one that will both protect them from legal assault and spur their expansion."[34] But it must be admitted that it is a delicate matter to establish goals and timetables without establishing the forbidden quotas. An earlier decision had made a nice distinction: "While quotas merely to attain racial balance in employment are forbidden by the Civil Rights Act of 1964, quotas to correct past discriminatory practices are not."[35] As Michael Fontham, Weber's attorney, said: "Inch by inch, executive orders have, in effect, forced companies to impose quotas."[36]

The *Weber* decision said nothing about women or other minorities. *Time* observed: "Even some white ethnic groups that feel left out in the scramble for economic opportunity, such as Poles, Italians, Ukrainians, and Czechs, may interpret *Weber* as a challenge they cannot afford to ignore."[37] A Polish leader, Leonard Palentynowicz, immediately took up the challenge: "If America's job opportunities and money are to be parceled out to groups, we are a definable group, and we want our share."[38] Justice Powell in the *Bakke* case had said: "There is no principled basis for deciding which groups would merit 'heightened judicial solicitude' and which would not."

Many more judicial decisions will have to be made before the legal and constitutional parameters of affirmative action programs can be stated with any confidence. And what may hold for 1985 may not hold in 1990.[39] And in the meantime we will continue to see letters to disappointed white male applicants on stationery imprinted with the words "We are an equal opportunity employer."

The role of the government in our society should be that of enforcing the constitutional guarantee of equal treatment under the law. The Civil Rights Act of 1964 and the proposed Equal Rights Amendment are excellent means for doing this. The government should ensure that no individual loses out in competition

---

places, available to employees and applicants for employment, notices to be provided by the contracting officer setting forth the provisions of this nondiscrimination clause. (2) The contractor will, in all solicitations or advertisements for employees placed by or on behalf of the contractor, state that all qualified applicants will receive consideration for employment without regard to race, color, religion, sex, or national origin."

[33]By 1971, as a result of a delegation of authority from Labor to HEW, "goals and timetables" were applied to universities.

[34]*Time,* July 9, 1979, p. 48.

[35]*United States* v. *Wood, Wire and Metal Lathers International Union No. 46.*

[36]Quoted in *Newsweek,* July 10, 1979.

[37]*Time,* July 9, 1979, p. 49.

[38]Quoted in ibid.

[39]The majority opinion in the *Weber* case "is carefully limited in various ways. It emphasizes, for example, that the Kaiser plan was limited to securing rather than also maintaining a racial balance, and though that distinction is irrelevant as a matter of moral principle, it might be used to limit the impact of the decision for the future. . . . For all its careful limitations, the case marks another step in the Court's efforts to develop a new conception of what equality requires in the search for racial justice." Dworkin, "How to Read the Civil Rights Act," p. 43.

for a job or admission because he or she possesses a characteristic (sex, sexual preference, race, age, religion, etc.) that is irrelevant to how well the person will do as a worker or a student. As Justice William O. Douglas said in dissenting from the Court's decision not to hear the *DeFunis* case:

> The Equal Protection Clause commands the elimination of racial barriers, not their creation in order to satisfy our theory as to how society ought to be organized. The purpose of the University of Washington cannot be to produce Black lawyers for Blacks, Polish lawyers for Poles, Jewish lawyers for Jews, Irish lawyers for the Irish. It should produce good lawyers for Americans. . . . All races can compete fairly at all professional levels. So far as race is concerned, any state-sponsored preference to one race over another in that competition is in my view "invidious" and violative of the Equal Protection Clause.[40]

A related injustice is the salaries paid to minorities and women doing the same job as white males and the promotions accorded them. The Equal Pay Act and other legal provisions can deal with this. Enforcing the Constitution, passing laws, and issuing executive orders can indeed put a halt to these kinds of injustice, but they cannot undo the injustices of the past. Nothing can. But, after the passage of time in which discrimination has not been permitted to exist, the injustice will have disappeared.

Reverse Discrimination Even the proponents of affirmative action admit that the young white male pays the greatest price. Consistency here would seem to indicate that other white males share the burden. Doctors, lawyers, management people, tenured professors, and so on should thus resign to make way for minorities and women. After all, they are more likely to have perpetrated in the past than the young! But directives from Washington explicitly deny the need for this, and I know of no case in which an established white male volunteered to step aside to speed up the cause of compensatory justice.

"The belief that discrimination can be administered to the body politic in judicious doses in order to create nondiscrimination," writes Miro M. Todorovich, "is akin to the medical wisdom of curing an alcoholic with whiskey. Discrimination is addictive."[41] Not only do the favored groups continue to expect it, but other groups demand it. People no longer want justice; they want *preference.* Hostility between groups grows, and the very means chosen to eliminate an evil exacerbates it. There is rivalry even among the chosen groups. EEOC has been charged by women with being too indulgent toward Chicanos, and by

[40]416 U.S. (1974). The *DeFunis* case, a forerunner of *Bakke,* was declared moot (5–4) on the grounds that DeFunis would soon be graduating from University of Washington Law School, to which he had at first been denied admission. A lower court had found for DeFunis, but the supreme court of Washington overruled it. See *DeFunis* v. *Edegaard.*

[41]Miro M. Todorovich, correspondence. See Gross, *Reverse Discrimination,* p. 37.

Chicanos with being too indulgent toward blacks. Some middle-class women (who are not so badly disadvantaged) resent the preference shown minorities and are willing to take their chances without affirmative action. Many Jews, no longer as discriminated against as formerly,[42] have also opposed affirmative action. The growing split between the Jewish and black communities is particularly distressing in view of their past cooperation in working for civil rights.

Todorovich points to a logical difficulty in reverse discrimination: "We object to discrimination against a class of people because it unjustly hurts individuals of that class. If now we argue that it is all right to discriminate against members of other classes in order to compensate the first group, we shall have destroyed the basis of our objection to the very discrimination we sought thereby to eliminate."[43] But this cloaks an even more serious disharmony, one that was familiar to both John Dewey and Mohandas Gandhi: that between the means and the end. Is the one appropriate to the other? Does the one destroy the other while appearing to promote it? Can we honor and preserve the integrity of an end if we violate its very spirit in seeking it? Will we even know what it is after a period of ignoring it? Can people learn to ignore irrelevant factors by emphasizing them?

The unfortunate effect of many affirmative action programs is, as Justice Douglas said, to place "a stamp of inferiority" on certain groups, implying that their members cannot "make it on their individual merit." Many people have disagreed with Douglas, arguing that if preferential treatment were a stigma, blacks would avoid it, oppose it, and denounce it—and they do not.[44] Douglas, however, may be right. A stigma does not have to be *experienced* as a stigma in order to be one. And of the blacks who do experience it as such, many are willing to "swallow their pride" because there is something important to be gained for themselves and other blacks. But do minorities and women *need* preferential treatment? The fact is that all minority groups and women made great strides in the sixties—*before* the day of "goals and timetables." Blacks in particular "have pulled themselves up—from further down, against stronger opposition [than that encountered by other minorities]—and show every indication of continuing to advance."[45]

Despite the stigma of appearing to need preferential "justice," some Anglo-whites have *claimed* ethnic membership (perhaps from a grandparent!) in order to qualify for preferential treatment in order to get a job, to hold a job (when layoffs are in prospect), or, in the case of teachers, to avoid being transferred to a different school when desegregation is being carried out. We are all being forced to *think ethnically,* when we had just about progressed to the point of considering individuals on their own merit. Even small children, as Meg Greenfield reported, have to think ethnically in order to find out whether they will be able to get into

[42]Yale Law School did not drop its Jewish quotas until the 1950s.

[43]Ibid., p. 38.

[44]See James W. Nickel, "Preferential Policies in Hiring and Admissions," in Gross, *Reverse Discrimination,* p. 344.

[45]Sowell, " 'Affirmative Action' Reconsidered," in *Gross,* p. 130.

a certain course at school.[46] "And in Boston, teachers are required to take a daily census of their students, leading to more race consciousness in the Boston public schools than ever before."[47]

Positive Steps The truth in the arguments on behalf of preferential discrimination is that injustice must be redressed, that people who have been injured by society should receive compensation. How *can* we counteract the effects of past discrimination?

In the first place, we should rid ourselves of the group approach. To try to identify victims by racial and sexual groups is at once to do too much and not enough. Not all individuals in a given group have been injured, and no selected list of groups will include all individuals who have been injured. Since injury is an individual matter, injustice cannot be identified with group membership. Affirmative action programs necessarily deal with groups, and they are thus inappropriate instruments for redressing injustice. James W. Nickel deals with this matter in an interesting way. He grants that there may be much correlation between some groups and injury, but adds the consideration of family income in order not to be "overinclusive." But in order to avoid being "underinclusive," he suggests that the list of groups be longer than it typically is and that the relevance of other characteristics be taken into account. This approach goes a long way toward the individual treatment that claims for preferences are entitled to. It may be made administratively workable, Nickel believes, through such an application form as this:

> Preference will be awarded to persons who have a family income of less than *(specify amount)* dollars per year, *and* who are members of any of the following groups *(list groups).* Persons who do not qualify in accordance with the above criterion but who believe that they have the characteristics which justify preferences such as *(list relevant characteristics)* may apply for preference by presenting evidence for their claim on forms available from the admissions (or personnel) officer.[48]

But this is not yet enough. Affirmative action programs would have as their objective *remediation* instead of *placement* in jobs or academic and professional programs. Companies and universities may voluntarily do a great many things. They could mount remedial programs for individuals who, by reason of their earlier life and background, are judged to be disadvantaged. "Qualification" would consist of ability to profit from remedial work, not ability to do a job or pass courses in professional schools. If standardized tests are used, they would measure intelligence and aptitude; those standardized tests (PACE, MCAT, LSAT, GRE, etc.) which measure facility with the English language and familiarity with the dominant culture would come later. After the programs have been

[46] See Meg Greenfield, "Teaching Kids the New Discrimination," *Newsweek,* July 4, 1977.
[47] Leiser, *Liberty, Justice, and Morals,* p. 337. See Albert Shanker, *New York Times,* October 9, 1977, p. E7.
[48] See Nickel, "Preferential Policies in Hiring and Admissions," in Gross, pp. 344–347.

completed, individuals will compete for real jobs and places under the protection of antidiscriminatory laws. Many of the directives of Executive Order 11246 *are* nondiscriminatory. They should be retained. Even the industrial training course that Brian Weber sought admission to should have been open to the most qualified employees. Disadvantaged employees who could not win out should have been offered a preliminary kind of help that would have removed them from their position of disadvantage. Individuals, in short, should compete; but they should compete only after they have been *trained* to compete. Admission to programs would be based on individual injury; admission to jobs and places would be based on competence. Past injustice is the basis of the first; relative qualification is the second. The institution of such programs would be a very meritorious thing for companies and universities to do, and government funds should be provided to aid those that elect to do it.[49]

The redressing of past unjust discrimination should indeed have a high priority for all political jurisdictions. In addition to encouraging private institutions to offer programs, government very well may mount programs of its own. These programs have an objective that goes beyond redressing cases of racial and sexual discrimination. Their objective is the fundamental one of any free society: furthering the right of equal opportunity.

This approach based upon identifying injured individuals and assisting them through special programs (private and public) is far different from the kind of affirmative action championed by certain bureaucrats in Washington. The individuals are promised nothing but a chance to become competitive. The advantages they are accorded in training programs are based on their disadvantaged social condition. In the competition for jobs and professional schools, the only advantage they will have will consist of what they can demonstrate that they can *do.* Most affirmative action programs, if they hew to their "goals and timetables," perforce choose the less qualified. This is unfair not only to the candidates who are more qualified, but to consumers in society in general who one day will employ the services of a doctor, lawyer, dentist, schoolteacher, accountant, carpenter, plumber, or electrician.[50] The presence of teachers, doctors, and lawyers in the ghetto is a laudable objective, and so are role models in the universities and elsewhere. But it is more important that these people be competent than that they be black, female, or Samoan. Individuals should be certified and emulated for what they are and what they do rather than on the basis of ethnic or sexual irrelevancies.

When affirmative action plans became compulsory for universities that wanted to continue receiving federal contracts, an unseemly and piratic hunt began for

[49]One very serious handicap of many individuals is lack of money for entrance fees and tuition charges, as well as transportation. Much more money should be made available to individuals in the form of scholarships (or tuition waivers), whether they are doing remedial work, college work, or professional training.

[50]There are not very many whites playing centerfield, but we don't call for "affirmative action" in professional sports. If we won't settle for less than the best in sports, we should not do so in other areas either.

black and female instructors (and especially black women). But there simply were not enough such qualified people available to meet the "goals" of all the schools, so a coast-to-coast game of musical chairs was played. Blacks and women simply did not (and do not now) possess doctoral degrees in proportion to their population. The problem is one of supply, and affirmative action does not solve it. What may solve it is the old-fashioned idea of equal opportunity. This is not to say that universities had been innocent of discriminatory hiring.[51] But the cure for it is affirmative action to hire on merit, not affirmative action to lure minority personnel (at higher salaries) from other institutions or to settle for the less-than-qualified.

Among the groups identified in some affirmative action programs as entitled to preferential discrimination is that of the Vietnam War veterans. There is good reason to regard these veterans as victims of past discrimination. Most of them were drafted because they were not in college or enlisted because they could not get a decent job. They served in a war that was supported neither by the physical resources nor the spiritual blessings of their country. They were sent unprepared to an area of the world where drugs are easily available. Many returned crippled in body and mind. Some employers are awarded "plusses" of various kinds for employing them. They are given extra points on certain civil service examinations and special consideration in admission to some professional schools. In some situations, then, they are placed in advantageous position over *other* injured groups. All this is confusing and unsatisfactory. The federal government should, instead of *raising* them above others in the competition for jobs and places, extend to them the means to get into a *competitive* position with others. This kind of benefit is appropriate both to their injury and to the principles of equal opportunity, equal protection of the law, and the Civil Rights Act. It would consist of extensive medical care, psychological counseling, and generous allotments for education and training (as well as support for veteran and family while it is going on). The veteran with this kind of support will be able to compete.

What can be done for veterans can be done (perhaps to a somewhat lesser degree) for all groups for which injury can be claimed. And it should be done for all individuals, whatever their group, whose background places them at a disadvantage in the competitive struggle. It is the better part of justice to place individuals in a position where they may win on their own merits than to jump them ahead of others. Special programs for the disadvantaged rectify past injustice. Reverse discrimination simply compounds it.

Conclusion James W. Nickel makes a useful classification of justifications for "preferential policies." Their goals may be: (1) Compensatory justice—"counterbalancing benefits" for "those individuals who have been wrongfully injured,"

[51]They had not. And they had also been guilty of paying less money to minorities and women once they hired them, and also of failing to promote these people equitably. For an account of the underutilization of women in the higher ranks, see F. K. Barasch, "HEW, the University, and Women," in Gross, *Reverse Discrimination,* p. 54ff.

who have borne "unfair burdens in the past." (2) Distributive justice—eliminating those "inequalities in our society" (such as wealth, station, security) "that cannot be justified." (3) Utility—promoting benefits for society in general that outweigh their cost. As Nickel points out, some advocates of affirmative action appeal to more than one of these justifications, although the specific form that affirmative action will take is materially affected by which justification one is forced to choose.[52]

Where does the form of affirmative action fall which was sketched above? Clearly in the first category. It seeks to right the wrong experienced by individuals who have been injured through the accident of birth and early background. Where, as the result of unfortunate background, they are denied equality of opportunity, preferential treatment to restore this position of equality is owed them. It does make somewhat more concrete what these "benefits" and "injuries" are relative to: equal opportunity. This is not arguing from a theory of distributive justice, for most such theories require more than merely equality of opportunity, and some do not require even that. It may well be compatible with some theories of distributive justice, but it can be argued for independently of any such theory. This program is concerned only with eliminating conditions that would be regarded as handicaps in any conceivable society. The program is not based upon utility, but on a demand that any individual can legitimately make. It would be hoped that it would promote a happy, peaceful, and prosperous society, but this is not its justification. One can imagine a society containing a great many people who enjoy a great deal of happiness. But if its goods are improperly distributed, it is not just. And if its members who have been disadvantaged are not properly compensated, it also is not just.

Summary of the Issues

Both sides support the constitutional guarantees of equal protection under the law and applaud legislation on the national and local levels that prohibits racial and sexual discrimination in employing, promoting, and paying workers and in admitting people to educational programs. They also agree that injustice in the past has been perpetrated on certain identifiable groups and that affirmative action should be taken to correct a bad situation and to compensate people for the disadvantageous position they find themselves in. In short, they both oppose discrimination and demand compensatory justice.

One side, however, holds that until the "awful legacy" of the past is destroyed, appointments must be made on a *preferential* basis rather than on an objective weighing of ability or competence. It is unfair to judge candidates equally when some bear negative traits fostered on them by an unjust society. To right the wrongs entails choosing the less qualified and sometimes the unqualified. Nor is it enough to *seek* minority candidates. Businesses and schools should set up numerical goals and try to meet them.

[52]See Nickel, "Preferential Policies in Hiring and Admissions," in Gross, pp. 326–334.

The other side calls this "reverse discrimination," for it repeats an acknowledged evil from the past: People are still judged on the basis of their race and sex, and the white Anglo-Saxon male is placed in a position, through no fault of his own, of distinct disadvantage. Discrimination is a singularly inappropriate means for eliminating discrimination. Although we are told that this is only an interim measure, it needlessly repeats an error of the past. Moreover, most affirmative action programs arbitrarily choose two or three obvious groups for preferential treatment while ignoring others that have also been unjustly treated.

In partial agreement with the first side but in opposition to its policy of appointing the less qualified for purpose of attaining numerical goals set forth for blacks, Hispanics, and women, the second side offers an affirmative action program that would recognize *all* disadvantaged groups and would undertake remedial programs to counteract the results of that disadvantage. *Then* let individuals compete for appointments on the basis of merit.

Legislation on equal opportunity and affirmative action is so extensive and the constitutional issues so complex that a perfectly consistent legal and constitutional position has not yet emerged. The courts have, however, made some useful distinctions and provided valuable arguments on both sides of the issues.

Both sides offer consequentialist arguments for their respective affirmative action positions. While justice requires compensation, there are better and worse ways of providing it. One side takes a positive and aggressive stance in bringing "minorities" into the mainstream and wants to tip the scales in one direction (after they have been tipped the other way for so long) in order finally to right them. That the Anglo male must suffer awhile is unfortunate, but the cause is worthy—and he still retains some of his advantages! Preferential hiring and appointing are not only quick and effective means, but they demonstrate in a dramatic way the opportunities open to disadvantaged groups. The other side points out the harmful consequences of the preferential approach: It encourages people to think ethnically (or sexually); it exacerbates the tension between groups as each clamors for preferential status; it places stigmas on certain groups; it depresses the level of performance in positions where competence is ignored; it weakens respect and understanding for the principle of nondiscrimination.

Discussion Questions

1. Do you think that Weber was constitutionally treated by the Supreme Court? Why?
2. Do you think that Weber was treated morally by his employer? Why?
3. Do you think that Bakke was constitutionally treated by the University of California at Davis? Why?
4. Do you think that Bakke was treated morally by the University of California at Davis? Why?
5. Do you think that affirmative action has helped or harmed relations between the races? Why? Relations between the sexes? Why?

6. Do you think that the difference between "numerical goals" and "quotas" is a viable distinction? Explain.
7. Do you think that despite affirmative action programs, blacks, Hispanics, and women are discriminated against in hiring and promotions? What about admission to universities? Explain.
8. Would you (as a white) resent being passed over in favor of a less qualified black? Why?
9. Would you (as a black) feel guilty in having been chosen over a better qualified white? Why?
10. Do you think that Nickel's plan for compensating *all* disadvantaged groups is feasible? Explain.
11. Do you agree that *remediation* should take precedence over *preferential appointment*? Why?
12. If we can assume that nondiscrimination is right and proper, should it be practiced quite apart from its consequences? Explain.
13. If we can assume that discrimination is wrong, should it be attacked in a way heedless of other consequences? Explain.
14. Is it, in your opinion, fair for the present generation to have to pay for the sins of past generations? Explain.
15. Do you think that preferential treatment is counter to the Fourteenth Amendment? To the Civil Rights Act of 1964? Explain.
16. Do you think that discrimination in the past has *really* rendered some groups unable to compete in the present? If so, how?
17. Do you think that the distinction between legitimate discrimination, which seeks to bring groups together, and invidious discrimination, which seeks to exclude some groups, is a viable one? Explain.
18. Do you think that it is a realistic and worthwhile goal for minorities to be represented in all jobs, professions, and schools in rough proportion to their presence in the population? Why?

For Further Reading

Michael D. Bayles. "Compensatory Reverse Discrimination in Hiring." *Social Theory and Practice* 2 (1973):201ff.

William T. Blackstone. "Reverse Discrimination and Compensatory Justice." *Social Theory and Practice* 3 (1975):253–288.

Norman E. Bowie and Robert L. Simon. *The Individual and the Political Order: An Introduction to Social and Political Philosophy.* Englewood Cliffs, N.J.: Prentice-Hall, 1977. Chapter 9.

Ronald Dworkin, "The Bakke Decision: Did It Decide Anything?" *New York Review of Books,* August 17, 1978.

Ronald Dworkin. "How to Read the Civil Rights Act." *New York Review of Books,* December 20, 1979.

Ronald Dworkin, "Why Bakke Has No Case." *New York Review of Books,* November 10, 1977.

Gertrude Ezorsky. "It's Mine." *Philosophy and Public Affairs* 3 (1974):321–330.

Joel Feinberg. "Noncomparative Justice." *Philosophical Review* 83 (1974):297–338.

Marlene G. Fried. "In Defense of Preferential Hiring." *Philosophical Forum* 5 (1973): 309–319.

Nathan Glazer. *Affirmative Discrimination: Ethnic Inequality and Public Policy.* New York: Basic Books, 1975.

Alan H. Goldman. "Affirmative Action." *Philosophy and Public Affairs* 5 (1976):178–195.

Alan H. Goldman. "Limits to the Justification of Reverse Discrimination." *Social Theory and Practice* 3 (1975):289–306.

Barry R. Gross. "Is Turnabout Fair Play?" *Journal of Critical Analysis* 5 (1975):126ff.

Barry R. Gross. ed. *Reverse Discrimination.* Buffalo: Prometheus Books, 1977.

Burton M. Leiser. *Liberty, Justice, and Morals.* 2nd ed. New York: Macmillan Publishing Co., 1979. Chapter 11.

Michael Martin. "Pedagogical Arguments for Preferential Hiring and Tenuring of Women Teachers in the University." *Philosophical Forum* 5 (1973):325–333.

Thomas Nagel. "Equal Treatment and Compensatory Discrimination." *Philosophy and Public Affairs* 2 (1973):348–363.

Lisa Newton. "Reverse Discrimination as Unjustified." *Ethics* 83 (1973):308-312.

James W. Nickel. "Classifications by Race in Compensatory Programs." *Ethics* 84 (1974): 146–150.

James W. Nickel. "Discrimination and Morally Relevant Characteristics." *Analysis* 32 (1972):113–114.

Robert M. O'Neil. *Discriminating against Discrimination: Preferential Admission in the DeFunis Case.* Bloomington: Indiana University Press, 1975.

George Sher. "Justifying Reverse Discrimination in Employment." *Philosophy and Public Affairs* 3 (1974):159–170.

Roger A. Shiner. "Individuals, Groups, and Inverse Discrimination." *Analysis* 33 (1973): 185–187.

Robert Simon. "Preferential Hiring: A Reply to Judith Jarvis Thompson." *Philosophy and Public Affairs* 3 (1974):312–320.

Allan P. Sindler. *Bakke, DeFunis, and Minority Admissions.* New York: Longman, 1978.

Paul W. Taylor. "Reverse Discrimination and Compensatory Justice." *Analysis* 33 (1973): 177–182.

Judith Jarvis Thompson. "Preferential Hiring." *Philosophy and Public Affairs* 2 (1973): 364–384.

Mary Vetterling. "Some Common Sense Notes on Preferential Hiring." *Philosophical Forum* 5 (1973):320–324.

Richard Wasserstrom. "The University and the Case for Preferential Treatment." *Philosophical Quarterly* 13 (1976):165–170.

THE JUSTICE OF PUNISHMENT

The Only Moral Basis for Punishment Is Deterrence

Retribution It has long been believed that punishment, by individuals or by the state, is justified by the fact that an offense committed by an individual against the rights of others *merits* retaliation. These others affirm their rights by punishing those who violate them. Although this punishment should not be malicious or vindictive, it is required in order to balance the scales. To fail to punish an offender is, in effect, to abandon those moral ideals that society and its laws should uphold. Punishment, it is held, is not so much an act of vengeance as it is an expression by society that certain misuses of human freedom cannot be countenanced. It is an act of *retribution.* The severity of the offense must be countered by corresponding severity of punishment.

The philosopher most associated with this point of view is Immanuel Kant. The exercise of my freedom, he argued, is limited by the rights of others. When I violate their rights, I deserve to be punished—whether the punishment does me (or anyone else) any good or not. I have earned a punishment that it is the duty of society to provide, for it has taken a stand on behalf of certain rights and cannot forsake them. "If legal justice perishes," says Kant, "then it is no longer worth while for men to remain on this earth."[53] Two pages later Kant defines justice as "the aggregate of those conditions under which the will of one person can be conjoined with the will of another in accordance with a universal law." Just as moral laws and moral rights are universal in scope and hold irrespective of utilitarian consequences, so too does the propriety of punishment.[54] There is the moral imperative to punish wrongdoing, just as there is the moral imperative to tell the truth. While we cannot create a world in which virtue and happiness are perfectly conjoined, we can and must deprive evildoers of happiness. They must not be allowed to profit from their deeds. This would be unfair to the innocent.

Laws and the penal system are means that society has chosen to vindicate its commitment to the basic rights of individuals. Criminal justice consists of making the offender pay the appropriate price. Examples for Kant are death for murderers and castration for rapists.

This retributivist theory of punishment is fundamentally wrong-headed. The kind of punishment it recommends, even if it is not dispensed in a spirit of revenge, can at best be only an empty gesture, a symbolic act. It is literally pointless. Offenders are made to pay their "debt to society," but what in fact do they pay but their suffering? And how does this benefit society? Does their suffering restore the money to those they have robbed or life to those they have killed? What benefits accrue to *anyone* when society "rights" a wrong? Kant may be correct in saying that there are legitimate limits to the way one exercises one's freedom and that society has a duty to protect all its members from encroachment, but punishment per se neither preserves freedom nor protects rights. To extract a "tooth for a tooth" may constitute a categorical imperative that is intuitively certain for Kant, but that does not mean that it is for the rest of us. We want to know *why* this is a good thing. We want to know what *benefits,* if any, punishment can be expected to produce.

[53]Kant, *The Metaphysical Elements of Justice* (trans. John Ladd), p. 100.

[54]Kant recognized that legal statutes may not always be in accordance with genuine moral rights, but he believed that we owe them obedience while trying to change them.

Certain other criticisms can be made of the retributive theory.[55] (1) It is impossible to determine on objective grounds the degree of guilt and culpability in an offense and its corresponding degree of punishment. (2) If immoral action requires punishment, it would be required also for deeds in which no one but the agent is harmed. (3) Since punishment for all instances of the same crime is to be the same, a first-offender would have to receive the same penalty as a habitual criminal. (4) If the principle that we should balance virtue and happiness, as well as evil and unhappiness, is sound, we would be tempted to excuse a criminal who has already suffered a lot. (5) There may be cases in which it would be wise not to punish at all; retributivists deny this possibility. (6) Under such a rigid system no concern can be taken for the innocent family of the offender who may be injured by the punishment. (7) If the legal system does not impose a proper punishment, individuals may feel it is "up to them" to do it. (8) There might be cases in which it is wrong to punish violations of laws—when a law, for example, is unjust. Retributivists deny this possibility. (9) Offenders might argue that it is not wrong to commit a crime—say, kill someone—if they are willing to pay the price.

Deterrence The alternate approach to punishment is to ask: *What good can it serve?* This approach looks forward to beneficial consequences instead of backward to guilt. It is empirical and experimental instead of a priori and dogmatic. Since the basis for punishment is the belief that harming others is wrong, its only justification can be that it tends to reduce the incidence of such acts. The harm actually done cannot be eliminated, except in those few cases where stolen property is returned or illegal occupation is terminated, but the frequency of this kind of thing can be reduced. Genuine redress for the victim cannot usually be obtained, but punishment can prevent there being more victims. Punishment cannot "right the universe," but it can have an effect on future actions in society. This alternate approach is that of *deterring* people from committing offenses.

Deterrence operates in three ways: (1) When individuals realize that society intends to punish people for a certain action, they may decide not to perform that action. (2) When individuals are confined or executed for a certain action, they are unable for the duration of that punishment to do that action. (3) When individuals have experienced a punishment, they will, having "learned their lesson," be less likely to repeat their offenses.

Jeremy Bentham is the philosopher who first made this utilitarian approach to punishment plausible. He held that punishment, which is always some form of pain, is in itself an evil; it can thus justifiably be inflicted only in order to prevent a great evil or produce a greater good. Since people are not oblivious to the prospect or experience of evil, they can be constrained to obey the law by means of the threat and experience of punishment. The "expense" (in both the literal

[55] See the excellent discussions in Bowie and Simon, *The Individual and the Social Order,* pp. 224–231, and Golding, *Philosophy of Law,* chap. 5.

and the figurative sense) of punishment as borne by its recipient and dispenser must be kept as low as is consistent with its function to deter.

Bentham specified four cases in which punishment should not be inflicted:[56] (1) Where it is *groundless.* Acts that do not harm others or are done with their consent are in this category—also acts for which "adequate compensation" has been made. This consideration would exempt intoxication, sexual acts between consenting adults, and compensated injury from punishment. (2) Where it is *inefficacious.* Examples here are actions that were not crimes when committed, cases where the penal provisions were not conveyed to the agent, and cases where, for reason of infancy, insanity, or intoxication, the law could produce no effect on the agent. Bentham would probably regard the American experience with prohibition in the twenties as a case of punishment being inefficacious in halting the "mischief" of the sale and distribution of alcoholic beverages. (3) Where it is *unprofitable* (too expensive). Many factors have to be weighed to determine profitability: the sense of coercion the individual feels in the presence of a law with stiff punishment, the sense of apprehension suffered by the offender as well as the actual punishment, the pain experienced by the family and friends of the offender, the displeasure of other people and foreign powers, the expenses that would have to be borne by society in carrying out the punishment, and so forth. A ten-year prison sentence for illegal parking would indeed deter, but would be more than is necessary and thus "unprofitable." It is in the spirit of Bentham also to add that class of actions which are so pervasive that the cost to the community in enforcement and custodial care would exceed the mischief of the actions themselves. Marijuana smoking might be an example. The strategy of demonstrators who defy orders to desist is often based on the belief that the police will find it too "expensive" to lock them *all* up. (4) Where it is *needless.* There may be other means at hand that will deal more easily with the mischief: education, instruction, persuasion. One can deter the reading (if not the writing) of "pernicious principles" by the threat of legal punishment, but "the pen is the proper weapon to combat error with, not the sword."[57]

In a chapter entitled "Of the Proportion between Punishments and Offenses," Bentham states several rules: (1) "The value [amount] of the punishment must not be less in any case than which is sufficient to outweigh that of the profit of the offense."[58] (2) "The greater the mischief of the offense, the greater is the expense, which it may be worth while to be at, in the way of punishment."[59] (3) "Where two offenses come in competition, the punishment for the greater offense must be sufficient to induce a man to prefer the less."[60] Armed robbery, then, should have a greater punishment than unarmed robbery. (4) "The punishment

[56]See Bentham, *An Introduction to the Principles of Morals and Legislation,* chap. 13 ("Cases Unmet for Punishment").

[57]Ibid., p. 177.

[58]Ibid., p. 179.

[59]Ibid., p. 181.

[60]Ibid.

should be adjusted in such manner to each particular offense, that for every part of the mischief there may be a motive to restrain the offender from giving birth to it."[61] Theft of a small amount of money should have a milder punishment than of a large amount. Murder, since it often occurs after rape, should have a more severe punishment than rape. (7) "To enable the value of the punishment to outweigh that of the profit of the expense, it must be increased, in point of magnitude, in proportion as it falls short in point of certainty."[62] Hard-to-detect crimes will have a greater penalty. (9) "Where the act is conclusively indicative of a habit, such an increase must be given to the punishment as may enable it to outweigh the profit not only of the individual offense, but of such other like offenses as are likely to have been committed with impunity by the same offender."[63] A third offense will be dealt with more severely than a first offense.

Bentham says: "Men calculate, some with less exactness, indeed, some with more: but all men calculate. I would not say, that even a madman does not calculate."[64] So Bentham would have the state calculate also, so that people may be constrained from acting against the public interest. Although his concern in the chapters cited is with the "political sanction," he does point out that use of the other sanctions, especially the moral one, may produce the same effect.

Objections to the Deterrence Theory There are two common objections to this utilitarian theory of deterrent punishment. They are both rather easily answered.

The first is to emphasize the individual nature of the offensive act and its punishment. The critic argues that there may be good utilitarian grounds for punishing an innocent person. To do so might prevent rioting in the community and provide a useful deterrent for other people who are contemplating a deed similar to the one professedly punished. This is merely a conspicuous example of the kind of thing utilitarian justice permits. Any particular offender would have to be judged on the basis of the consequences of a severe or mild punishment, or none at all. The results for his family and friends would have to be taken into account as well as the general responses of society. Where "crimes" could be shown to benefit society, they would have to be excused (nay, praised!). Even some acts of private vengeance (e.g., hunting down and shooting a mugger) could be viewed as deterrent. In the realm where the "moral sanction" operates, similar judgments on punishment could be made that affront our sense of justice.[65]

One answer to this objection is to interpret utilitarian deterrence in terms of *rule* utilitarianism. To punish an innocent person is in violation of a rule that has

[61]Ibid.

[62]Ibid., p. 184.

[63]Ibid.

[64]Ibid., p. 186.

[65]For example, a man who breaks a promise to a friend that he will educate his son would not be condemned if he could show that he spent the money to educate his *own* son instead, because the latter showed promise of becoming a great surgeon.

powerful utilitarian backing. It should thus be upheld in particular cases whatever the extenuating circumstances. The objection could also be met by an interpretation in terms of *act* utilitarianism. Even when punishing *this* particular innocent person would serve a limited utilitarian purpose, it would reduce respect for the general principle that innocent people are exempt from punishment. An act of punishing the innocent tends to weaken a general principle the recognition of which leads to lawful conduct. Confidence in the belief that the innocent are safe must not be reduced by making exceptions. The habit of adhering to this general principle must not be weakened by making exceptions. The utility in the particular case is always less than the evil of bringing a general principle into disrepute.

On the positive side, the same reasoning applies. The person who has committed a crime should be punished—even though, in this particular case, it may not do much good. Consistent adherence to general rules has an enormous deterrent effect. We all know that we are safe if we obey the law and that we will be punished if we disobey. To weaken the rule that the law represents would be to say to all that the apparatus of justice operates capriciously, and that it hardly matters what we do.

Decisions in courtrooms would indeed be made in the light of individual circumstances, but they would be within the parameters specified by law. Each case would not be a new and unprecedented one where all the consequences would have to be charted. Most consequences are taken into account before the laws are enacted. Laws are simply rules adopted for the happiness of society on the basis or experience of what *does* serve this happiness.

As Mill said:

> Mankind have been learning by experience the tendencies of actions; on which experience all the prudence, as well as all the morality, of life are dependent. People talk as if the commencement of this course of experience had hitherto been put off, as if at the moment when some man feels tempted to meddle with the property or life of another, he had to begin considering for the first time whether murder and theft are injurious to human happiness. . . . There is no difficulty in proving any ethical standard whatever to work ill if we suppose universal idiocy to be conjoined with it. . . . It is a strange notion that the acknowledgment of a first principle is inconsistent with the admission of secondary ones.[66]

Just as there are "secondary principles" by which the individual decides his private action, so too there are "secondary principles" by which the state can make its laws and issue its punishments. There can be no greater deterrent than the expectation by citizens that laws will be enforced. Punishment according to rules thus has two justifications: (1) Each rule has been shown to deter. (2) The consistent application of a *system* of rules deters. The individual knows *what* punishment is to be expected and *that* it will be inflicted.

[66] *Utilitarianism,* pp. 24–25.

The second objection consists of asking whether punishment works, whether it does indeed deter. This is a strange objection. It may be made by someone who is a utilitarian and is looking for something *else* that, unlike punishment, *does* work or deter. Or it may be made by a retributivist who is not concerned with workability or deterrence in the first place. Whatever the source, the objection consists in emphasizing the many cases where punishment had not deterred crime. Murders continue to occur, the prisons are full, the rate of recidivism is high, and so on. For centuries societies have punished crime, but the criminal is always with us.

The answer to the objection consists, first of all, in admitting that punishment does not always deter. There will always be individuals who think they can avoid detection. There will always be individuals who, in the heat of passion, will not think at all. And there occasionally are individuals who cold-bloodedly are determined to do the deed *whatever* the consequences.[67] But the threat and experience of punishment for most people most of the time do *tend* to curb socially destructive actions. Among the great majority of law-abiding citizens, there are people for whom punishment has evidently worked. Would anyone want to experiment and suspend the system of punishment for just one month? In our own experience, we have refrained from illegal parking and excessive speed when we knew that police were in the vicinity. It is a fact that crime increases when there is a breakdown of law enforcement (e.g., the riots in Watts in 1965 and in Newark and Detroit in 1967, and the police strike in Montreal in 1969). During power failures there is usually an increase of crime (e.g., New York, July 1977). Studies have shown that shoplifting is reduced by the presence of wide-angle mirrors, that housebreaking is reduced by the conspicuous presence of alarm systems, that embezzlement is reduced by strict and frequent accounting checks, that hijacking is reduced by electronic searching devices, that pilfering from libraries is reduced by checkout stations, and so on. While punishment is not a perfect deterrence, it is a very effective one.

It could be even more effective. Detection could be improved—by means of better training and better personnel. Prosecution could be more effective—through eliminating dishonest and incompetent officials. Punishment could be more "certain" and "proximate"—by reforming ("streamlining") judicial procedures. While granting all the legitimate "rights" of the accused (to having their "rights" read to them at the time of arrest, to counsel at all stages from interrogation, preliminary hearing, and arraignment to the trial itself, to examine evidence against them before the trial begins, to cross-examine witnesses, to be tried by a jury of their peers, as well as protection against arbitrary search and seizure, extorted "confessions," admission of evidence illegally obtained, and self-incrimi-

[67]People who have no concern for themselves cannot be deterred. Disinterested actions may be malicious, as well as altruistic. See David Hume's discussion of "disinterested vengeance" (*Enquiry Concerning the Principles of Morals,* Appendix 2). See also chapter 9, second section, of the present volume.

nation), we should not interpret them so strictly that the accused may go scot-free for a crime that they were truly guilty of (and perhaps have even confessed to). We cannot tie the hands of our enforcement officials and expect them to get the full deterrence effect of our laws. And society should not have to pay for a minor violation by an official by having a murderer released in its midst. Too many offenders "get off" because of technicalities, appeals, and plea-bargaining. Some prisoners are paroled too soon. There may be need for changes in the amount of punishment meted out.[68] In view of all the abuses in our present systems of justice, it is perhaps amazing that deterrence operates at all. The answer, then, to the objection based on efficacy lies not in abandoning the deterrence principle of punishment, but in improving the system that applies it. This is precisely what Bentham was trying to do in 1790.

Rehabilitation We should, in conclusion, examine a position hinted at above. Is there another utilitarian approach that will "work" which is not based upon the principle of deterrence in the narrow sense? Some people have argued that punishment should never be applied against lawbreakers. Instead, they should be *treated* so that they will never be moved to commit the crime again. The best way of reducing crime is to *rehabilitate* offenders rather than punish them. It is indeed strange that we are willing to treat cases of obvious physical disease but prefer punishment for people who have obvious moral afflictions.[69]

This immediately recommends itself to us as a humane and constructive approach. It deals effectively with the case of emotionally disturbed individuals who are unable to anticipate punishment realistically or are so obsessed that they press forward nonetheless. The approach gets at people who temperamentally are resistant to the machinations of a system of deterrence. There are a great many crimes that we feel could only have been committed by an insane person, and a great many more that would seem to have their source in a sick or disturbed personality. Often a person is "disturbed" as a result of a poor early environment and a sense of hopelessness in improving his or her situation. It may be futile to deal with such people as if they were rational and calculating individuals.[70] It would also be unfair, for, in a sense, their actions are beyond their control. Therapy would serve them and society as a whole much better than would prison sentences.

The spirit of this approach is kindred to the deterrence approach: society takes proper and deliberate action to prevent the occurrence of crime. In the broad

[68]Burton M. Leiser reports that in England, when a new highway safety act that imposed much higher punishments for drunken driving was enacted, these were the results in the first twelve months: 1,152 fewer fatalities and 11,000 fewer injuries. See *Liberty, Justice, and Morals,* p. 210.

[69]Samuel Butler, in his novel *Erewhon,* asks us to imagine a society that issues moderate fines for simple colds and large ones for pneumonia, while confining lawbreakers to institutions where they receive skilled medical attention. This makes just as much sense as our practice.

[70]A recent experiment has been to try to shock juvenile offenders by bringing them to prisons and subjecting them to horror stories told by inmates. How deterrent this has been for potential criminals has yet to be determined.

sense of the word, rehabilitation is itself a kind of *deterrence.* Rather than frighten people (the word *deter* is derived from the Latin *terrere,* "to frighten"), however, the authorities *heal* them. The aim of both is the same: reduce their tendency to break the law.

There are certain rather obvious limitations to the approach: (1) Punishment would have to be retained for some crimes (e.g., speeding, embezzlement), for their commission cannot always plausibly be traced to a damaged psyche. In any case, it is difficult to draw the line between the deliberate criminal and the "driven" one. (2) The social expenditures for the comprehensive and systematic treatment of neurotic (or even psychotic) lawbreakers would have to be very great indeed. Until the public is willing to spend much more than it does now, the function of even the most humane penal institutions will have to be more custodial than therapeutic. (3) The success rate of penal institutions and mental health agencies is even more discouraging than that of the system of deterrence (in the narrow sense). Fatal errors are often made with respect to the criminally insane, and very few wardens can guarantee that real rehabilitation has taken place with respect to their charges (in those institutions where it is offered). Successful treatment of personality disorders is very difficult and very time-consuming. Even under the best of conditions it often eludes us.

A person who is confined may be subjected to the requirements of both senses of deterrence. He or she is both inflicted with punishment and blessed with rehabilitation. It would be hoped that the two would provide reciprocating support. But in fact, what may result is that each proves inimical to the other. The "treatment" may be so pleasant that no sense of punishment is felt; if the treatment is not successful, no deterrence will have been achieved. The confinement itself or the conditions of confinement may be so resented that the prisoner only "goes through the motions" of rehabilitation; if any deterrence at all is achieved, it would have to result from a resolve never to get into such a terrible place again ("reform"). So far as the prisoner is concerned, both deterrence (in the narrow sense) and rehabilitation are problematical. If we can get the best of both worlds, fine. But if we cannot get both, we should be sure to get *one* of them. What must be avoided is the kind of "punishment" that neither reforms nor rehabilitates.

Still, with all its limitations and problems, the idea of rehabilitation is an attractive one, perhaps one that can be made even more useful through research in sociology and psychology.[71] To the degree that it is possible scientifically and feasible economically, rehabilitation should be provided by society for those offenders who need it. At the very least, where treatment is impossible, prisoners should be provided with enough education and training to take a job when released. All this is quite in the spirit of utilitarianism, for the objective is *good results.* It also falls within the general concept of deterrence, for the objective is *prevention of crime.*

[71]There is a common saying, "tout comprehendre, c'est tout pardonner." Actually, we can already forgive. But if we understood, we could do much more: prevent the evil act in the first place.

Deterrence Is Not the Only Moral Basis for Punishment

It is admitted at the outset that deterrence is a proper basis for punishment. But unless it is carried out in a very careful way, it will lead to serious injustices. Punishment can be carried out justly only when utilitarian deterrence is qualified by certain insights provided us by the theory of retribution.

Limitations of the Deterrence Principle First of all, the attempt to protect the right of an innocent person from being "punished" by appealing to the utility of general rules is unacceptable. This right must have a higher standing than that of a derivative rule. For if it is simply that, a particular case of punishing an innocent person would sometimes be justified. One can imagine a situation in which the execution of a prisoner would indeed deter some revolutionists from performing some really violent acts. The prisoner has no friends or relatives, and his loss will not be mourned. The evidence against him is strong, and no one knows that he is innocent except the judge. No one else will find out (the rule will thus not be weakened), for the judge will keep silent in order to avoid disgrace. All the utilitarian reasons are present for setting aside the rule; it is, after all, *not* the basic principle. Yet a fair-minded person would have to oppose doing so. The right of the innocent is an unassailable one.[72]

Related to this point is the case of punishing a person who seems to be intent on committing a crime. There may be good reasons to place him or her in "preventive detention," but most retributivists would insist that a crime be committed before any kind of punishment can be just.

Second, it must be observed that the degree of punishment meted out to a *guilty* person should be determined not simply by its tendency to deter. A life sentence for failing to report all earnings on the income-tax form may indeed deter most people. The suffering of those few who are convicted is outweighed by all the good it does, and it has served its intended purpose; but the law would seem to have erred on the side of severity. At the other extreme, we might consider the case of a man who is guilty of a series of heinous crimes, including kidnapping, torture, rape, and murder. There would seem to be nothing to be gained by locking him up forever, for that would not bring his victim back to life. The criminal himself has "learned his lesson" and is so horrified by his own deeds that he will not repeat them. As far as deterring others is concerned, who but the most wretched person would do such things in the first place? For those who would torture and rape, deterrence does not work; for those who would not, deterrence is unnecessary. Despite these considerations, however, putting the man on probation for one year

[72]Rule utilitarianism can perhaps establish such a rule, but it brings in the a priori principle of universality, which Bentham and Mill professed not to need. Why should an act that *everyone* does have a higher ethical status than one that only *some* do? Although there are utilitarian reasons for supporting a general rule, there are also utilitarian reasons occasionally to violate it.

(with regular visits to his psychiatrist) would seem to err on the side of mildness.

The recent popularity of compulsory sentencing systems represents an attempt to require courts to apply specific rules rather than to examine particular circumstances. Such systems may be based on deterrence (citizens can be certain that they will receive the prescribed punishment if they are convicted of the crime) or retribution (a particular class of crimes merits a prescribed punishment in every case), but they often lead to results that seem unjust. William Rummel, a small-time crook in Texas, received a life sentence after being convicted of his third felony in nine years. His petty crimes netted him a total of $230. Whether the Texas "habitual criminal" law with compulsory sentencing is inspired by thoughts of deterrence or retribution, it does seem to have operated unfairly in the case of Rummel. His punishment was out of proportion to his crime.[73]

Third, it should be pointed out that the deterrence theory makes no distinction in the *quality* of the punishment. In a case of premeditated murder, the verdict may be execution. This is not necessarily a more severe punishment than life in prison (with no parole), but it is a quality of punishment that some believe is improper for *any* crime (not all retributivists agree with Kant). On utilitarian grounds it could (we will assume) easily be shown just. The murderer has sworn to exterminate the remaining members of the family he or she is feuding with, and execution will do much to deter others from continuing the feud. The state will be spared the expense of supporting the murderer in prison for forty years —where he or she would be an inveterate troublemaker anyway. In a case like this, all the arguments against capital punishment would be rejected out of hand: the moral imperative never to take a human life except in self-defense, the duty to provide an individual with an opportunity to reform (and perhaps redress the wrong done in a more effective way than by being executed), the need to entertain the possibility that the individual may have been insane at the time of committing the crime, the need to entertain the possibility that he or she may in fact have been innocent, and so forth. Whether capital punishment is ever justified is a profound question and one that deserves examination of retributist arguments as well as utilitarian ones.

Capital punishment is often called "cruel and unusual." It is not necessarily cruel, for many convicted criminals have begged for it over life imprisonment. And it is certainly, in the experience of civilized societies, not unusual. There are, however, some punishments that are cruel and unusual, and they can all be justified on utilitarian grounds. We will not horrify the reader with descriptions of the sort of punishments involving torture, public spectacles, and dismemberment that could be handed out to convicted prisoners. In modern times they have

[73]The Supreme Court upheld the decision (5–4). "In my view," wrote Justice Powell in dissent, "objective criteria clearly establish that a mandatory life sentence for defrauding persons of about $230 crosses any rationally drawn line separating punishment that lawfully may be imposed from that which is proscribed by the [Constitution]." See "Strict Views of the Law," *Newsweek*, March 31, 1980, p. 49.

become "unusual," except in certain benighted societies where respect for human dignity is not a recognized value. In all societies, they are "cruel." Not even the utilitarians recommend them, even though they may deter more effectively than prison sentences in institutions walled off from public view. But retributivists can oppose them because they feel that a human being, whatever his or her crimes, is still a human being. They have the ethical conviction that punishment should be inflicted with sorrow and sympathy, that even the evildoer has a right to experience punishment with dignity. The stereotype of the retributivist angrily and vindictively wreaking vengeance on the evildoer is erroneous. This is not in the spirit of true retribution. Fortunately, the utilitarians, in eschewing such qualities of punishment also, are *better* than their theory.

In the fourth place, the utilitarian theory of punishment would condone making an example of an offender. Some "utilitarians" do favor mutilation as a punishment. E. Winslow Chapman, police director in Memphis, which led the nation in per-capita rapes in 1980, holds that rapists should be castrated. His reasons are deterrent rather than, as was the case with Kant, retributivist. "The possible consequence of castration would dissuade 90 to 95 percent of rapists," Chapman said. "If maybe we can castrate rapists one or two times . . . that crime would go down the drain. I'm convinced of that." Chapman, a member of Reagan's National Advisory Task Force on Law Enforcement, reports that the local reception of his proposal was "almost totally positive."[74]

There is a fine line between punishing to deter and using an offender as a means to keep others in check. This line is not always observed. When society is deeply incensed about a particular crime or is fearful during a particular crime wave, it may demand a victim. Even if the evidence against the victim is good and the punishment just, the trial and publicity may have the character of "making an example" rather than of seeking once again to deter. This is wrong, as Kant would tell us, for it is a case of treating a person as a means rather than an end. It is to use a person in order to achieve a social good. Voltaire, in commenting on a case of an inept British admiral, said that the king had him shot *"pour encourager les autrui"*—to encourage the others. Perhaps the theory of deterrence can never get entirely clear of the mandate of the "second formulation of the categorical imperative," but it can use the act of the offender and its normal punishment as a means for deterrence without destroying the entire person. The person is not used as a means *only*. And it will not make the mistake of choosing to punish a few people severely (for greater deterrent effect) instead of many people moderately.

In the fifth place, advocates of deterrence are often so zealous for conviction that they are impatient with the complex set of rights of the accused that constitute due process. It is indeed true that if we are willing to overlook errors of officials and technical violations in judicial procedures, conviction rates would go up. And if we permitted police to search and detain anyone on the street who

[74]See *St. Louis Globe-Democrat,* February 3, 1981.

looked suspicious, the streets would be safer. And if we permitted police to enter homes without warrants, there would be more convictions.[75] But, as Burton M. Leiser writes: "Some of the world's most orderly societies and some of its safest streets and parks are to be found in precisely those totalitarian countries where guarantees of individual liberties are the weakest. Safety in the streets and security at home can be bought, for a time, by a citizenry that is prepared to forfeit certain rights and liberties that were considered to be fundamental during the development of the Western democracies. That price, however, is too high."[76] The most well-known protection that a suspect has is to be made aware of his or her rights with respect to interrogation. This was secured by the famous *Miranda* decision in 1966, although the interpretation of this right is still being debated.[77]

Finally, let us consider the question of whether all crimes should be punished. Where no good can come from the punishment, the utilitarian decision would be to dispense with it. Some retributivists would argue that this is wrong. Offenders must be punished because they are offenders, whether real deterrence is achieved or not. A related situation is one in which an individual violates an unjust law. A case could be made, however, that despite the utilitarian value of punishing all lawbreakers, a deeper appreciation of the moral aspects of the case would suggest that the individual not be punished because the law should not have existed in the first place. In violating a statute out of respect for a higher law, the individual has not *earned* punishment. According to one retributivist point of view, then, deterrence sometimes errs in not inflicting a punishment and sometimes errs in inflicting a punishment. The key to the distinction lies in the moral validity of the law itself.

Rehabilitation Let us, in conclusion, look at the rehabilitation theory with which utilitarians sometimes supplement (or broaden) their theory of deterrence. In this area, at least as much care must be taken as in the area of pure deterrence.

Perhaps the first thing to be noted is that while the approach may be a theory of "no punishment" in the strict sense, it does come very close to "punishment": the individual is detained against his or her wishes and might have to undergo some very unpleasant treatment.

It has long been recognized that offenders should not be held responsible for their crimes if they were insane at the time the act was done. The problem is what

[75]In 1980 the Supreme Court in effect invalidated the laws of twenty-three states that exempted police from acquiring warrants in routine felony arrests. The Court permitted exceptions in such cases where police are in hot pursuit of a suspect or it is likely that the suspect will flee. See "The Court Guards the Door," *Newsweek,* April 28, 1980, p. 81.

[76]Leiser, p. 194.

[77]The "Miranda warning" given by the FBI is: "Before we ask you any questions, you must understand your rights. You have the right to remain silent. Anything you say can be used against you in court. You have the right to talk to a lawyer for advice before we ask you any questions and to have a lawyer with you during questioning. If you cannot afford a lawyer, one will be appointed for you before any questioning if you wish. If you decide to answer questions now without a lawyer present, you will still have the right to stop answering at any time."

constitutes insanity. The United States had adopted the criterion set down in the famous *M'Naghton* case in Britain: "To establish a defence on the ground of insanity, it must be clearly proved that, at the time of the committing of the act, the party accused was labouring under such a defect of reason, from disease of the mind, as not to know the nature and quality of the act he was doing, or, if he did know it, that he did not know he was doing what was wrong."[78] This criterion of "knowing right from wrong" was long thought to be too narrow and was supplemented by the "irresistible impulse" test of 1929: "This impulse must be such as to override the reason and judgment and obliterate the sense of right and wrong to the extent that the accused is deprived of the power to choose between right and wrong."[79] The accused may know right from wrong, but he or she is *impelled* to do wrong. The criterion was broadened even more in the case of *Durham* v. *United States.* Judge Bazelon of the U.S. Appeals Court gave us the "Durham rule" when he wrote:

> We find that as an exclusive criterion the right-wrong test is inadequate in that (a) it does not take sufficient account of psychic realities and scientific knowledge, and (b) it is based upon one symptom and so cannot validly be applied in all circumstances. We find that the "irresistible impulse" test is also inadequate in that it gives no recognition to mental illness characterized by brooding and reflection and so relegates acts caused by such illness to the application of the inadequate right-wrong test. We conclude that a broader test should be adopted. . . . It is simply that an accused is not criminally responsible if his unlawful act was the product of mental disease or mental defect.[80]

Bazelon went on to describe mental disease as something that can improve or deteriorate, and mental defect as something that is congenital or the effect of injury of disease (in either case, permanent). He concludes his opinion this way: "The legal and moral traditions of the western world require that those who, of their own free will and with evil intent . . . commit acts which violate the law, shall be criminally responsible for those acts. Our traditions also require that where such acts stem from and are the product of mental disease or defect as those terms are used herein, moral blame shall not attach, and hence there will not be criminal responsibility."[81]

Here we have a matter on which both Bentham and the retributivists have reached virtual agreement, but for different reasons.

But there are serious problems. How sick does one have to be and who certifies it? To what extent does *anyone* have "free will"? Many people are poorly adjusted because of the environment in which they have been reared. Juvenile delinquents

[78] 8 Eng. Rep. 718, 722 (1843).
[79] *Smith* v. *United States* (1929).
[80] *Durham* v. *United States* (1954).
[81] Ibid.

are indeed "crazy, mixed-up kids." How far down do we go in the scale of mental illness before we find a person "not guilty" and remand him or her for treatment or rehabilitation instead of meting out a more conventional punishment? What about individuals (often highly placed in business and politics) who commit "white-collar" crimes? Are they sick also? Have they been victims of a disadvantaged youth or racial discrimination? Is it possible to draw the line between actions coolly and rationally selected and those that result from a personality defect of some kind?

One extreme answer is represented by those who would eliminate punishment entirely and blame society for violations of the law. These people would *treat* all "criminals" (confining those who are dangerous) while working to reform society. This has certain obvious dangers: (1) The individual is deeply in the clutches of society. It can reshape him (in theory) to whatever form it conceives a healthy and adjusted personality should have. The individual has no protection against indoctrination and "brainwashing." (2) Society can confine a troubled person as long as it likes—indefinitely—until it believes that he or she has "recovered." (3) The tendency to excuse all crimes as acts beyond the agent's control has the effect of destroying all sense of human responsibility. "A society that does not presume that most of its adult members are sane, intelligent, and in control of themselves in effect reduces them to second-class citizenship. It takes away their self-respect as moral agents—as persons who can in sincerity be told that they have done something wrong—and our respect for them as moral agents."[82] Modern psychiatric treatment is based on the principle that the patient should be induced to accept responsibility for his actions—both past and future. Many of the "criminally insane" have admitted that they knew what they were doing, as well as some of the consequences.[83]

If Dr. Karl Menninger can be taken as a representative of this extreme view,[84] Dr. Thomas Szasz (also a psychiatrist) can be taken as representative of the other extreme. Szasz would accept "mental illness" as a case of brain disease, but not simply difficulty in adjusting to society and its demands. Where there is brain damage or neurological defects (physicochemical conditions), the individual is not liable. But much that we *call* mental illness is not illness at all in any legitimate sense: it is an expression of the person's struggle with the problem of how to live. Neurosis is not a disease, and most of us have it (or *are* it) in some way or other.[85] George Santayana used the expression "normal madness." This should not deprive us of equal protection of the law, nor should it excuse us from violating it. Where individuals can improve their condition by consultation with

[82]Golding, *Philosophy of Law,* p. 105.
[83]"Freedom and Determinism" is the title of the third section of chapter 9.
[84]See Karl Menninger, *The Crime of Punishment.*
[85]See Szasz, *Law, Liberty, and Psychiatry.*

a psychiatrist, they should do so, but unless they have structural physical damage, they must be held responsible for their actions.[86]

It is not the intention here to derogate those well-meaning attempts to treat the troubled and the insane, to rehabilitate the underprivileged and the maladjusted, for these are positive steps in improving the quality of life both for individuals and for those around them. Utilitarianism is a valuable social outlook, and so is deterrence in both its narrow and broad senses. But here as elsewhere, certain fundamental insights from the retributivist side are worth pondering.

Summary of the Issues

Both sides reject the retributivist theory of punishment, for it requires acts that we intuitively recognize as wrong and deprives punishment of all points except that of making a symbolic gesture.

Both sides uphold the theory of deterrence, although the second side would qualify it in important ways derived from deontological thinking.

Deterrence operates by preventing an individual from doing a criminal action in the first place and by restraining an offender from repeating a crime. In its pure form it is utilitarian: punishment must serve the purpose of producing good results and preventing bad results. When punishment is groundless, inefficacious, unprofitable, or needless, it should not be inflicted. Several rules concerning the proportion between punishments and offenses can be derived from the principle of utility. That punishment or the threat thereof does not always work should not conceal the fact that it often does. Individuals do tend to act in accordance with their own interests.

The qualifications that should be made to the theory of deterrence are based on considerations that are not to be found in classical utilitarianism. Among them are the following: (1) The *innocent* have a right not to be punished, no matter how justified on utilitarian grounds such punishment may be. (2) The *appropriateness* of the punishment is not always derivable from the principle of utility. Severe punishment for a small crime and lenient punishment for a big crime may be quite utilitarian. (3) The *quality* of the punishment should be determined on grounds

[86]Dr. Robert A. deVito, formerly director of the Illinois Department of Mental Health and Developmental Disabilities and now chairman of the Department of Psychiatry at Loyola University Medical Center in Chicago, favors eliminating the "not guilty by reason of insanity" (NGRI) plea entirely. These two options, however, would be available: "culpable and mentally disabled" (CMD) and "mentally disabled, neither culpable nor innocent" (NCNI). The first places at least partial responsibility on offenders. They serve the remainder of their sentence after treatment and then are mandated for outpatient therapy. The second does not exonerate offenders and remands them for treatment under court control. In both cases, offenders would be confined under medium or maximum security rather than placed with nondangerous patients in minimal security psychiatric units. See "Should Insanity Plea Be Stricken from Law?" *St. Louis Globe-Democrat,* November 12, 1980, Illinois Section I, p. 1.

in addition to the utilitarian one. Barbarian, cruel, and unusual punishments could all pass the test of utility. (4) *Making an example* of an offender would seem to be a case of using humanity as a means, although the utilitarian could often approve it. (5) In their concern for swift and sure conviction, utilitarians sometimes ignore the right of the accused to judicial due process. (6) Utilitarians would sometimes dispense with punishment for violation of valid laws (which is wrong) and would sometimes inflict punishment for violation of invalid laws (which is wrong).

There is a third way to deal with lawbreakers: rehabilitation. Since this aims at good results and is thus utilitarian, it is often accepted as a humane alternative by adherents of the deterrence theory. Indeed, if we stretch the term *deterrence,* rehabilitation is a form of deterrence, since it seeks to prevent a repetition of criminal behavior. This is conceded to be an expensive and risky way to deal with crime, but it may be resorted to when conventional deterrence is not expected to work by itself.

Those who are most critical of deterrence tend to be critical of rehabilitation also. While granting that people who are insane when committing a crime should not be held responsible for it, they caution against blaming *all* crimes on psyches damaged by society. This is a dangerous view, for in application it tends to excuse all crimes as beyond the agent's control and thus is destructive to the sense of human responsibility. Moreover, it suggests that society has the right to detain everyone for as long as it takes to produce a "healthy and adjusted personality." Only offenders who were clearly insane when they committed the crime should be excused and remanded for treatment. The others, whether successfully deterred or not, should be subjected to conventional punishment.

Discussion Questions

1. Do you think that a psychopathic killer should be made to pay for his or her crime after being cured? Why?
2. Do you think that an insane person should be made to stand trial? Why? What about after the person has been certified sane?
3. Do you think that the "innocent for reason of insanity" plea is overused in criminal cases? Why?
4. Is Kant correct in saying that payment should be extracted for crimes whether it does any good or not?
5. Do you think that the line between sanity and insanity is as unmistakable as Bazelon seems to assume? Why? Are the ideas of Szasz more acceptable here?
6. If only free acts are punishable and if human freedom means that one cannot be counted on to respond to punishment, what happens to the doctrine of deterrence?
7. Do you think that deterrence could be made to operate more effectively if we were not so concerned to respect the rights of the accused to due process? Why?
8. Can you think of ways to make judicial procedures more expeditious without sacrificing the rights of the accused?

9. Does deterrence ever operate in your own life to prevent crime on your part? Explain.
10. Do you think it is ever right to punish innocent people for the deterrent effect on others? Why?
11. Do you think that something of Kant's sense of letting the punishment fit the crime should be preserved in an approach to punishment that is fundamentally deterrent? Why?
12. Are you uncomfortable with a theory of punishment that tries to utilize elements of both deterrence and retributivist theories? Explain. Could you defend either one of them as adequate in itself? Explain.
13. Do you think that the deterrence theory unavoidably "makes examples" of criminals? Is this right? Why?
14. Would justice be better served if we made public spectacles of criminal punishment as was done in earlier times? Why?
15. Do you think that capital punishment is an effective deterrent? Why? If it were, would you favor it? Why?
16. Why is it impossible categorically to forbid punishing the innocent on a theory of act utilitarianism? Or is it?
17. Rule utilitarianism could contain the rule "Never punish the innocent." But is this really utilitarianism? Explain.
18. Do you agree with Bentham that punishment should never be inflicted when it is inefficacious or unprofitable? Explain.
19. Do you agree with Bentham that punishment should never be inflicted for "victimless crimes"? Why?
20. Try to refute one of the nine specific objections to the retributive theory.
21. What do you think should be the punishment for a sane murderer? Explain. Can a sane person commit murder?
22. Do you think that second-offenders should receive a stiffer sentence than first-offenders? Why?
23. Do you think we have a prima facie duty to deprive an evildoer of happiness?
24. If legal procedures fail to bring a criminal to justice, under what circumstances, if any, should the individual take matters into his or her own hands?
25. What bearing does the fact of recidivism have on the theory of deterrence? Of rehabilitation?

For Further Reading

Raziel Abelson and Marie-Louise Friquegnon, eds. *Ethics for Modern Life*. St. Martin's Press, 1975. Chapter 7.

Johannes Andenas. *Punishment and Deterrence.* Ann Arbor: University of Michigan Press, 1974.

Jeremy Bentham. *An Introduction to the Principles of Morals and Legislation.* New York: Hafner Publishing Co., 1948.

Norman E. Bowie and Robert L. Simon. *The Individual and the Political Order: An Introduction to Social and Political Philosophy.* Englewood Cliffs, N.J.: Prentice-Hall, 1977. Chapter 8.

T. S. Champlin. "Punishment without Offense." *American Philosophical Quarterly* 13 (1976):85–87.

Gertrude Ezorsky, ed. *Philosophical Perspectives on Punishment.* Albany: State University of New York Press, 1972.

Herbert Fingarette. "Punishment and Suffering." *Proceedings and Addresses, American Philosophical Association* 50 (1975):504ff.

Rudolph J. Gerber and Patrick D. McAnany, eds. *Contemporary Punishment: Views, Explanations and Justifications.* Notre Dame: University of Notre Dame Press, 1972.

Martin P. Golding. *Philosophy of Law.* Englewood Cliffs, N.J.: Prentice-Hall, 1975.

Milton Goldinger, ed. *Punishment and Human Rights.* Cambridge, Mass.: Schenkman, 1974.

Hyman Gross. *A Theory of Criminal Justice.* New York: Oxford University Press, 1979.

H. L. A. Hart. *Punishment and Responsibility: Essays in the Philosophy of Law.* New York: Oxford University Press, 1968.

Donald W. Harward. "The Bitter Pill of Punishment: Retribution." *Journal of Value Inquiry* 10 (1976):199–204.

Ted Honderich. *Punishment: The Supposed Justifications.* Baltimore: Penguin Books, 1969.

Laurence D. Houlgate. "Excuses and the Criminal Law." *Southern Journal of Philosophy* 13 (1975):187ff.

Immanuel Kant. *The Metaphysical Elements of Justice.* Translated by John Ladd. Indianapolis: Bobbs-Merrill Co., 1965.

Burton M. Leiser. *Liberty, Justice, and Morals.* 2nd ed. New York: Macmillan Publishing Co., 1979. Part 2.

William Lyons. "Deterrence Theory and Punishment of the Innocent." *Ethics* 84 (1974): 346–348.

Edward H. Madden et al. *Philosophical Perspectives on Punishment.* Springfield, Ill.: Charles C Thomas, 1968.

Karl Menninger. *The Crime of Punishment.* New York: Viking Compass Book, 1972.

Herbert Morris. *On Guilt and Innocence: Essays in Legal Philosophy and Moral Pathology.* Berkeley: University of California Press, 1976.

Jeffrie G. Murphy, ed. *Punishment and Rehabilitation.* Belmont, Calif.: Wadsworth Publishing Co., 1973.

Jan Narveson. "Three Analysis Retributivists." *Analysis* 34 (1974):185–193.

Aryeh Neier. *Crime and Punishment: A Radical Solution.* New York: Stein and Day, 1978.

E. M. Opton, Jr. "Psychiatric Violence against Prisoners; When Therapy Is Punishment." *Mississippi Law Journal* 45 (1974):605ff.

Chana K. Poupko. "The Religious Basis of the Retributive Approach to Punishment." *The Thomist* 39 (1975):528–541.

James Rachels, ed. *Moral Problems.* 3rd ed. New York: Harper & Row, 1979. Part 4.

Thomas Szasz. *Law, Liberty, and Psychiatry: An Inquiry into the Social Uses of Mental Health Practices.* New York: Macmillan Co., 1963.

Thomas Szasz. *Psychiatric Justice.* New York: Macmillan Co., 1965.

D. Thompson. "The Means of Dealing with Criminals." *Philosophy of the Social Sciences* 5 (1975):1ff.

Ernest van den Haag. *Punishing Criminals: Concerning a Very Old and Painful Question.* New York: Basic Books, 1975.

Andrew von Hirsch. *Doing Justice: The Choice of Punishments.* New York: McGraw-Hill Book Co., 1976.

Andrew von Hirsch. "Giving Criminals Their Just Deserts." *Civil Liberties Review* 3 (1976):23ff.

Robert N. Wennberg. "Act Utilitarianism, Deterrence, and the Punishment of the Innocent." *The Personalist* 56 (1975):178–194.

Alan Wertheimer. "Should Punishment Fit the Crime?" *Social Theory and Practice* 3 (1975):403–423.

Glanville L. Williams. *The Mental Element in Crime.* London: Oxford University Press, 1965.

Barbara Wooton et al. *Social Science and Social Pathology.* New York: Macmillan Co., 1959.

Chapter 7

LIBERTY

This chapter is concerned with various kinds of freedom. Everyone is favorably disposed toward freedom, and it would seem as ridiculous to attack it as to attack motherhood or apple pie. Yet there would seem to be limits to freedom. One would not excuse bombing the university gymnasium or printing scurrilous lies about the athletics director on the grounds that these actions were simply expressions of freedom. We need to know what these limits are.

One aspect of freedom concerns the morality of the individual. What, ethically, is one free to do and what, ethically, is one not free to do? The answer to these questions constitute a true ethical theory. One exercises his freedom properly when one does what is right; one exercises it improperly when one does what is wrong. We are not dealing with this comprehensive problem here. *That* is the problem of chapter 1.

We will, however, discuss in the third section of this chapter the individual's use of freedom in a special case: when it runs counter to the law. Under what circumstances, if any, can the individual legitimately disobey the law? Some people argue that civil disobedience in a democracy is always wrong; others argue that it is not always wrong. Which side is correct?

Freedom is sometimes discussed in political theory as the freedom to count as one, equally with others, in democratic processes. One is free if one has not been disenfranchised or denied the full rights of citizenship. We will not be concerned with this kind of freedom either.

Still another sense of freedom is that which is counter to determinism. One is said to be free if one's actions spring from within the self rather than being constrained by exceptionless natural law. This sense of freedom will be discussed in the third section of chapter 9.

The sense of freedom that we will be concerned with in this chapter is the freedom of expression and action. Our concern, however, will be with the limits (if any) that *society* can place on the individual's exercise of these freedoms. In talking about society, we will be concerned both with its laws and public opinion, but primarily with the laws. We will assume that freedom to express ourselves in words and actions is a good thing and ask what constraints (if any) can legitimately be placed on it.

What are the limits of free expression of opinion, of political propaganda, of secret information, of artistic ideas (including pornography)? According to what principle are these limits imposed? Is the principle sound? Are its applications sound? These questions will be discussed in the first section.

What are the limits of freedom of action? Should morals be legislated? Should prostitution, euthanasia, drug usage, gambling, and nude bathing be prohibited by law? According to what principle? Is the principle sound? Are its applications sound? Is the interference by society on individual freedom a case of misguided and demeaning paternalism or is it a case of legitimate concern for public order and the general welfare? These questions will be discussed in the second section.

The first two sections thus try to answer this question: When is it proper for society to restrict individual freedom? The focus shifts in the third section from society to the individual. Here we will try to answer a quite different question: When is it proper for the individual to disobey the laws of society?

FREEDOM OF EXPRESSION

Neither the People nor Their Government Should Place Significant Obstacles in the Way of Free Expression by Individuals

The Value of Freedom The importance of freedom has long been recognized in the Western world. It has been set forth as a natural and inalienable right by some and defended as possessive and productive of great value by others.

John Stuart Mill, following the latter course, argues that freedom is an immediate good to those who experience it: When people are restrained by law and custom, they are deprived of "one of the principle ingredients of human happiness."[1] "All restraint, *qua* restraint, is an evil."[2] Writing about *On Liberty* in his autobiography, Mill calls the book a "kind of philosophic textbook of a single truth": "the importance to man and society, of a large variety in types of character, and of giving full freedom to human nature to expand itself in innumerable and conflicting directions."[3] He also argues that people in general benefit in a society that upholds freedom: "Mankind are greater gainers by suffering each to live as seems good to themselves, than by compelling each to live as seems good to the rest."[4] His concern for liberty is shown in the title of another important

[1]Mill, *On Liberty,* III, p. 181.
[2]Ibid., V, p. 219.
[3]Mill, *Autobiography* (New York: Henry Holt and Co., n.d.), p. 253.
[4]*On Liberty,* I, p. 137.

work, *The Subjection of Women.* In masterful style he shows how the emancipation of women will benefit women, men, children, and society itself. Near the end of the book he comes back to the "most direct benefit of all": "the unspeakable gain in private happiness to the liberated half of the species; the difference to them between a life of subjection to the will of others, and a life of rational freedom. After the primary necessities of food and raiment, freedom is the first and strongest want of human nature."[5] He again refers to a sense of freedom as "an element of happiness," and asks his male reader to recall how he felt "on emerging from boyhood," when he could discard the tutelage and control of others and take on the responsibilities of manhood. "Did he not feel twice as much alive, twice as much a human being, as before?"[6] One more quotation. "If a person possesses any tolerable amount of common sense and experience, his own mode of laying out his existence is the best, not because it is the best in itself, but because it is his own mode."[7]

How, in the view of Mill and others, freedom contributes to the general welfare will be set forth below, in this section and the next. But it seemed advisable to stress its immediate value first. The ideal of free individuals, choosing their own actions in a rational, humane, and responsible way, contemplating their own nature and perfecting it, is never far from Mill's mind.

Mill does, however, recognize that there are limits to freedom. These are set forth in his famous "harm principle." "The only purpose for which power can be rightly exercised over any member of a civilized community against his will, is to prevent harm to others. His own good, either physical or moral, is not a sufficient warrant."[8] Liberty is so important that it can legitimately be restricted only when its exercise harms others—who have rights of their own.[9] In discussing various expressions of liberty, we will examine both their utilitarian tendency to produce good for the self and others and their consistency with the harm principle. Where an expression of freedom meets both "requirements," it is surely a desirable thing. Where it only meets the second, it may be a bad or indifferent thing, but it would be wrong for people or the government to prohibit it. Two very important things are at stake here: the value (intrinsic and extrinsic) of freedom and the right of others not to be harmed. Where they conflict, the first must give way to the second.

In this section we will be concerned with freedom of expression in four of its forms: (1) expression of opinion, (2) expression of political propaganda aiming at action, (3) expression of facts that should be kept secret, and (4) artistic expression. Mill's essay is most concerned with the first.

[5]Mill, *The Subjection of Women* (Cambridge: M.I.T. Press, 1970), IV, p. 95.
[6]Ibid., p. 97.
[7]*On Liberty,* III, p. 192.
[8]Ibid., I, p. 135.
[9]Whether this recognition of the "rights" of others is utilitarian or not, is debatable. It does, however, seem to be a point on which Mill, a professed utilitarian, and deontologists can agree.

Expression of Opinion Mill's advocacy of freedom in the expression of scientific, philosophical, religious, or political beliefs would appear to be unqualified.[10] We will not, therefore, expect the principle of harm to come into play. His argument for freedom of expression of opinion is a classic of liberal thought. The new opinion may be true, it may be false, it may be partly true and partly false. In all cases, society penalizes itself in suppressing it.

If it is true, society denies itself the opportunity of correcting error, thus stifling intellectual progress. We cannot assume infallibility and declare that a particular new opinion cannot possibly be true. Societies and whole ages have been mistaken before. Our reliance on particular opinions is often the accidental result of the time and place in which we happen to have been born. Realization of this does not mean that we cannot confidently hold any views at all, but "there is the greatest difference between presuming an opinion to be true, because, with every opportunity for contesting it, it has not been refuted, and assuming its truth for the purpose of not permitting its refutation."[11] "The beliefs which we have most warrant for, have no safeguard to rest on, but a standing invitation to the whole world to prove them unfounded."[12] We must keep our minds open to the possibility that we may be wrong, otherwise we will make the same mistakes that other ages have made. Roman emperors tried to extirpate Christianity, the Church silenced Galileo, the American states suppressed the theory of evolution (not Mill's example)—all with the best of intentions. But no age, no society, and no individual are infallible.[13]

There is a common saying that truth will always win out in the end. This not only reflects an ungrateful attitude toward those authors of "splendid benefits" whom we persecute, but is false as well. The acceptance of many true ideas has been delayed by persecution, and some (no one knows how many) have been lost indefinitely—perhaps forever. There is no assurance that original thought will always be conjoined with effective and aggressive advocacy. "Men are not more zealous for truth than they often are for error, and a sufficient application of legal or even social penalties will generally succeed in stopping the propagation of either."[14]

[10]The appropriate region of human liberty "comprises, first the inward domain of consciousness; demanding liberty of conscience, in the most comprehensive sense; liberty of thought and feeling; absolute freedom of opinion and sentiment on all subjects, practical or speculative, scientific, moral, or theological. The liberty of expressing and publishing opinions may seem to fall under a different principle, since it belongs to that part of the conduct of an individual which concerns other people; but, being almost of as much importance as the liberty of thought itself, and resting in great part on the same reasons, is practically inseparable from it." *On Liberty,* I, pp. 137–138.

[11]Ibid., II, p. 144.

[12]Ibid., p. 146.

[13]Mill is here reflecting the attitude of Oliver Cromwell, who, impatient with his major-generals, swore the mighty oath: "I beseech you, by the bowels of Christ, bethink yourself that you might be mistaken!"

[14]*On Liberty,* II, p. 153.

If the new opinion is false, there are also compelling reasons for permitting its expression. The opinions of society must be subjected to challenges if they are not to be adhered to blindly, passively, and dogmatically. An opinion based on thought and knowledge of the alternatives is preferable to one based on "dull and torpid assent." A partisan must know his enemy. "He who knows only his own side of the case, knows little of that."[15]

In a great many cases, the new opinion (as well as the accepted opinion) is *partly true and partly false.* If both are one-sided (exaggerated, distorted), society profits from hearing both. Mill, for example, could see value in both Bentham and Coleridge, the party of progress and the party of order, rationalism and romanticism, hedonism and Christianity. When, indeed, do we ever possess the *whole* truth on any important issue?

The First Amendment to the United States Constitution protects free expression from federal action: "Congress shall make no law . . . abridging the freedom of speech, or of the press. . . ." The Fourteenth Amendment is commonly believed similarly to restrict the states. As Mill recognized, it is not only despotic governments but also democratic ones that must be kept in their place. "If all persons minus one, were of one opinion, and only one person were of the contrary opinion, mankind would be no more justified in silencing that one person, than he, if he had the power, would be justified in silencing mankind."[16] The right of free expression is a *moral* right, whatever the form of government and whether or not it chooses to recognize it.[17]

This right is subject to infringement by individuals and groups, as well as by governments. The following are immoral actions because they violate the right of free expression of ideas: (1) An individual shouts down a speaker at a meeting. The conduct of some students at Yale University when Professor William Shockley tried to present his part of a scheduled debate on race and the genetic basis of intelligence is an example. Shockley was not permitted to speak.[18] (2) An organization applies pressure against another organization that wants to sponsor a controversial speaker. This pressure takes the form of threats to disrupt the meeting, blacklist the individuals who attend, physically prevent the arrival of the speaker, damage the property of the leaders, or physically harm the leaders. All of these forms were employed in the South against civil rights groups during the voting registration drive a few years ago. (3) Groups or individuals seek to

[15]Ibid., p. 161.

[16]Ibid., p. 142.

[17]Despite the fact that the Constitution restricts the actions of government to its *delegated* powers, Jefferson and others were not satisfied. In addition, they wanted specific protection of certain rights.

[18]Several earlier attempts by organizations to bring Shockley to the campus had failed because of the pressure brought by concerned groups and individuals. The university administration itself had criticized the organization that wanted to sponsor him. An earlier invitation to George Wallace had been withdrawn because his appearance seemed likely to cause violence. See Report of the Committee on Freedom of Expression at Yale University (*Bulletin* of the American Association of University Professors [Winter 1976]) and Leiser, *Liberty, Justice, and Morals,* pp. 135–139.

intimidate those who traffic in unpopular ideas by actually damaging their property or harming their person. (4) An organization seeks to mount a boycott of the products of a company that has become identified with an unpopular point of view or whose officials have become so identified. Homosexual groups opposed the view of Anita Bryant by boycotting Florida oranges. (5) An organization seeks to intimidate stores and media that purvey "dangerous ideas." The John Birch Society held "card parties" that consisted of leaving cards on the shelves of bookstores that sold left-wing materials: "Always Buy Your Communist Products at. . . ." It also instructed its membership to protest to popular magazines whenever they published anything "un-American." It has conducted organized protests against television networks (and sponsors) who beam out questionable materials. (6) Organizations try to block the showing of material on television that it considers false and offensive. Early in 1980 all three major networks were pressured by groups to change their programming. NBC was forced by a coalition of blacks to postpone showing a miniseries called "Beulah Land," set in the pre–Civil War South. CBS was pressured by Jewish groups not to show "Playing for Time," a movie starring Vanessa Redgrave (a supporter of the PLO) as a concentration camp survivor. ABC is being pressured by a group of Sioux Indians who believe that its projected miniseries "Hanta Yo" is insulting. The "Moral Majority" (so-called) threatens to boycott sponsors of programs that do not reflect its own ethical values. (7) Organizations employ pressure to prevent theaters from showing movies that are judged undesirable. Residents of the Bronx tried to get Paul Newman's 1981 movie *Fort Apache, the Bronx* banned from theaters because it was thought to be racist. They have the right to organize a boycott against viewing the movie, but not against the theater that decides to exhibit it. (8) A citizens' group applies pressure against the library board because it feels that some of the books on the shelves are "unsuitable," or against the school board because some of the textbooks are "unsuitable." The key word here is *pressure*. Pickets, overblown rhetoric, and job threats are quite different from disagreement, argumentation, and public discussion. (9) Officials of a university discharge a professor or withhold promotion and raises because he or she holds unpopular views. This list is by no means exhaustive.

There is a very significant difference between opposing an opinion by arguing against it and seeking to prevent the opinion from being heard. And there is a significant difference also between ignoring the expression of an opinion and organizing a boycott against those identified with it. It is acceptable to view an opinion and its adherents with contempt, but it is not acceptable to intimidate the adherents and those who might come to agree with them. It is one thing to criticize the choice of books in a school or library (after all, the list in either case must be selective), but something else to stampede the populace to demand the removal of "offensive" titles. The dictum from the age of the Enlightenment (mistakenly attributed to Voltaire) still stands: "I disagree with what you say, but defend to the death your right to say it." Truth has the best chance of prevailing when all points of view have an equal chance of being heard. No individual or group is justified in telling the rest of us what we can hear and read, or say and write.

Expression of Political Propaganda There is another form of free expression that should be protected against interference. That is the expression of partisan political views that are calculated to produce action. Some people will accept free expression when its purpose is (or may be) the setting forth of truth, but will deny it when its purpose or effect seems to be inimical to the security of the nation. It is one thing, it is argued, to compete freely in the marketplace of ideas, but something quite different to propagandize on behalf of actions that will harm society itself. On the basis of this distinction, American legislators and officials have abridged the freedom of anarchists, Communists, and other radical groups to distribute their materials and to express their ideas.

The distinction between expression and incitement is difficult to make. Just about any point of view may be said to have consequences in action, and it may be regarded as "harmful" by some group or another. While one may grant that there are limits to free expression, it would appear that the suspected harm should be likely and substantial before the abridgment can be justified. It is precisely because of the difficulty of assessing likelihood and substantiality that so much disagreement exists on the scope of permitted activist literature and speech.

Supreme Court justices have tried to state the principle. Justice Oliver Wendell Holmes, Jr., in a dissenting opinion wrote: "I think we should be eternally vigilant against attempts to check the expression of opinions that we loathe and believe to be fraught with death, unless they so imminently threaten immediate interference with the lawful and pressing purposes of the law that an immediate check is required to save the country."[19] In the same year he enunciated the famous "clear and present danger" dictum: "The question in every case is whether the words are used in such circumstances and are of such a nature as to create a clear and present danger that they will bring about the substantive evils that Congress has a right to prevent. It is a question of proximity and degree."[20] Yet in this case Holmes was writing the *majority* opinion for the Court in upholding the conviction under the Espionage Act of 1917 of people who had printed and mailed documents opposing the war, distributing them to military recruits with the advice to "assert your rights," "do not submit to intimidation."

A generation later the United States was in another "war," this one "cold" and against Russia. This time it was the constitutionality of the Smith Act that was at issue. The Smith Act prohibited advocating and teaching the duty and necessity of overthrowing the government by force and violence. In the *Dennis* case (1951), the Supreme Court upheld the conviction of the eleven Communist Party leaders under the Smith Act. Chief Justice Fred Vinson wrote the majority opinion, joined by justices Reed, Burton, and Minton. Justices Robert Jackson and Felix

[19] *Abrams* v. *United States,* 250 U.S. 616, 624 (1919).
[20] *Schenk* v. *United States,* 249 U.S. 47 (1919).

Frankfurter wrote concurring opinions. Justices William O. Douglas and Hugo Black wrote dissenting opinions.[21]

Douglas conceded that the freedom to speak is not absolute. If evidence had been introduced indicating that Dennis and the others were "teaching the techniques of sabotage, the assassination of the President, the filching of documents from public files, the planting of bombs, the art of street warfare, and the like," they would deserve no protection. There is already a statute prohibiting seditious conspiracy. But the Smith Act seeks to get at something quite different: "conspiracy to form a party and groups and assemblies of people who teach and advocate the overthrow of our Government by force or violence and with a conspiracy to advocate and teach its overthrow by force and violence." It is concerned more with speech and its intentions than with seditious acts. The accused distributed books by Lenin and Stalin and argued that they be believed and acted upon. But this use of speech did not in fact constitute a "clear and present danger." "There must be some immediate injury to society that is likely if speech is allowed." Douglas quoted former Justice Brandeis with approval:

> Fear of serious injury cannot alone justify suppression of free speech and assembly. Men feared witches and burnt women. It is the function of speech to free men from the bondage of irrational fears. To justify suppression of free speech there must be reasonable ground to fear that serious evil will result if free speech is practiced. There must be reasonable ground to believe that the danger apprehended is imminent. There must be reasonable ground to believe that the evil to be prevented is a serious one.[22]

Douglas himself saw "no extreme case of peril" from the speech of the accused Communists. As a political party, the Communists are "of little significance." Communism may be a threat in other countries, but not in ours. "The First Amendment makes confidence in the common sense of our people and in the maturity of their judgment the great postulate of our democracy. Its philosophy is that violence is rarely, if ever, stopped by denying civil liberties to those advocating resort to force."

Justice Black in his dissenting opinion pointed out that the petitioners had not been charged with any "nonverbal acts" at all, nor even of employing speech to incite the overthrow of the government. He called the Smith Act "a virulent form of prior censorship of speech and press." He concluded prophetically: "Public opinion being what it now is, few will protest the conviction of these Communist petitioners. There is hope, however, that in calmer times, when present pressures, passions and fears subside, this or some later court will restore the First Amendment liberties to the high preferred place where they belong in a free society."

Whether his hope was borne out is questionable. A few years later the Court, with new personnel, drastically limited the power of the Smith Act, creating a

[21] *Dennis et al.* v. *United States*, 341 U.S. 494 (1951).

[22] See *Whitney* v. *California*, 274 U.S. 357 (1927).

line between *actual* advocacy and merely *theoretical* advocacy.[23] And in 1961 the Court ruled that simply being a *member* of an organization committed to the overthrow of the government was not a criminal offense.[24] But the Court was not especially courageous in protecting individuals during the McCarthy era against the harassment of notorious congressional committees.

Expression of Secret Information Some forms of expression have been considered dangerous to society not because they provoke or incite, but because they reveal facts the knowing of which is counter to our national security. Should newspapers be permitted to publish the text of classified materials? Should former CIA members be permitted to write books about "the company"? Some things, it is felt, are better left secret.

The issue of free expression is a live one today. The Supreme Court wisely upheld the right of newspapers to publish the "Pentagon Papers," although these were classified documents and had been obtained illegally by Daniel Ellsberg, a former employee of the Defense Department. The claim based on "national security" was not deemed important enough to infringe freedom of the press. Former CIA agents evidently are free to write books in criticism of their former employers. We may deplore the breaking of the law by Ellsberg and the breaking of promises by the agents, but their offenses do not cancel the right of the press to publish their material.

The fact is that the government and its agencies can "get away" with the most nefarious and odious actions simply by classifying documents relating to them and/or claiming "national security." Not only the Watergate crimes, but several far more serious ones committed by the FBI and CIA are hidden from the public eye by these devices. To take just one example from the "horror file": David Wise describes "Sub-Project Number 3" of the CIA:

> On Bedford Street in Greenwich Village, New York, and on Chestnut Street on Telegraph Hill in San Francisco, C.I.A. agents secretly rented what were known as "safe houses," or apartments. These were maintained in order to experiment with drugs on unsuspecting or, as the intelligence community likes to call them, "unwitting" persons. Men were lured to these "safe houses" by prostitutes. There they were drugged with LSD, their conversations were tape-recorded, and their actions were observed through one-way mirror windows.[25]

The documents pertaining to this operation were, of course, classified. This is understandable. Many less questionable activities of governmental agencies are

[23]See *Yates* v. *United States*, 354 U.S. 298 (1957).
[24]See *Scales* v. *United States*, 367 U.S. 203 (1961).
[25]David Wise, "A Secretive Security," in Bartlett, *The First Amendment in a Free Society*, pp. 81–82.

legitimately screened from public view. National security does require that state secrets remain secret.

But officials often appeal to "national security" in order simply to avoid political embarrassment. As the columnist Jack Anderson says: "Given our democratic traditions, [the people in power] cannot properly censor the news—so they classify it, using the cloak of official security to hide their embarrassments."[26] "The abuses of what we call our classification system, our system of official secrecy, are well-known by now."[27] In 1976, 4.5 million documents in the executive branch alone were classified. The Defense Department alone has a million cubic feet of classified documents, according to the Pentagon's chief classifier. David Wise reports several ludicrous cases of classified documents: in World War II information about the bow and arrow (a "silent, flashless weapon"), the fact that monkeys were sent into outer space (although they were on display in a zoo with a plaque recounting their exploits), and a "contingency plan" from 1912. In view of the serious and ludicrous abuses of the classification system, individuals may be forgiven for disclosing certain information to the public even if some "laws" are broken. The classification system was designed to protect, not crimes or political position, but national security. Where national security is not violated, the First Amendment, together with the public's need to know, must take precedence. The alternative to a free press is manipulated news. American presidents are adept at doing this. They can select what will be announced and what will be concealed.[28]

Anderson does not deny that investigative reporters must themselves take into account the nation's security. But they may take a different view of it than the administration. Perhaps if the *New York Times* had printed what it knew in advance of the Bay of Pigs invasion, that fiasco might not have occurred. Perhaps Anderson's exposure of the Iranian invasion plan prevented another fiasco. Perhaps Anderson's report of Nixon's dangerous military maneuvers in support of Pakistan during its war with India averted a catastrophe. Anderson did not hesitate to expose the Tonkin Bay "menace," the plans to bomb North Vietnam and mine Haiphong harbor, and Kissinger's complicity with the Shah of Iran in raising oil prices—all to no avail. After the Bay of Pigs invasion, President Kennedy asked newspapers not to stop with the question "Is it news?" They should also ask, "Is it in the interest of national security?" This works both ways. Newspapers may have a sounder view of what this is than Washington officials. Some have defended Philip Agee's exposure of CIA secrets as contributing to national security, for reduction of its clandestine activities serves the cause of peace!

[26]Jack Anderson, "Why I Tell Secrets," *Parade*, November 30, 1980, p. 22.

[27]Wise, p. 83.

[28]As Anderson points out, when it is in their interest they can announce (or cause to be leaked) the most secret of classified materials. Carter, he says, did this with respect to the "stealth bomber" for political reasons. During the 1980 campaign he had been charged with letting defenses lag. See Anderson, "Why I Tell Secrets."

Artistic Expression: Court Cases The expression of artistic works has been an issue in the United States since the Puritans landed at Plymouth. Just as we can look backward in shame to the abridgment of free expression of opinion in moments of panic, we can look back in shame to the repression of artistic expressions. A great many books were deemed to fall outside the pale of the First Amendment because they were offensive to public morals. Among the books that have been attacked successfully in the courts by guardians of public morals are such contemporary novels as James Joyce's *Ulysses,* D. H. Lawrence's *Lady Chatterly's Lover,* William Faulkner's *Sanctuary,* Henry Miller's *Tropic of Cancer* and *Tropic of Capricorn,* and Ernest Hemingway's *The Sun Also Rises;* and classical works such as Aristophanes' *Lysistrata,* Ovid's *The Art of Love,* and *The Arabian Nights.* Somewhere in between we find works by Boccaccio, Balzac, Defoe, Flaubert, and Rabelais.

These targets of a generation ago are very tame by today's standards. The issue today is whether hard-core pornography in movies and books deserves the protection of the First Amendment. Pornography depicts people as graphically as possible in various kinds of sexual activity ("straight" and "perverse") with the sole aim of arousing sexual feeling on the part of its viewers or readers.

The courts have been wrestling with the issue for some time, and it is difficult to state just what the parameters of legal pornography are today. One of the problems is to define in a specific and enforceable way exactly what *pornography* and its assumed synonym, *obscenity,* mean. A very early definition was provided in the *Hicklin* case: "The test of obscenity is . . . whether the tendency of the matter charged as obscenity is to deprave and corrupt those whose minds are open to such immoral influences, and into whose hands a publication of this sort may fall." The American Law Institute proposed this definition: "A thing is obscene if, considered as a whole, its predominant appeal is to prurient interest, i.e., a shameful or morbid interest in nudity, sex or excretion, and if it goes substantially beyond customary limits of candor in description or representation of such matters."[29] In the case of *Roth* v. *United States* (1957), it was affirmed that obscene material had no protection under the First Amendment. Justice Brennan wrote that obscenity is not a case of expressing ideas and "is utterly without redeeming social importance." Justice Harlan held that obscene works consist of "debasing portrayals of sex" in a "patently offensive way." Justice Stewart admitted that he could not define "hard-core pornography" but claimed: "I know it when I see it." The case of *Ginsberg* v. *New York* (1968) also upheld the right of government (in this case, the state of New York) to ban pornography. Though the state could not produce conclusive evidence of a connection between obscene material and antisocial behavior, Justice Brennan said: "We do not demand of legislatures 'scientifically certain criteria of legislation.' " This case is not to be confused with the earlier *Ginzburg* v. *United States* (1966), which upheld the conviction of the

[29]See Leiser, *Liberty, Justice, and Morals*, p. 169. This section is indebted to chapter 5 ("Obscenity and Pornography") of Leiser's book.

petitioner for printing and circulating obscene materials. It was in this case that Justice Hugo Black in a dissenting opinion argued that "obscenity" is indefinable and that it is unjust to pass laws that people cannot understand.[30]

Two important cases were decided together in 1973: *Miller* v. *California* and *Paris Adult Theatre I* v. *Slaton*.[31] Chief Justice Warren E. Burger wrote the majority opinions in which the *Roth* decision was upheld. He declared that "the States have a legitimate interest in regulating commerce in obscene material and in regulating exhibition of obscene material in places of public accommodation, including so-called 'adult' theaters from which minors are excluded." He also dropped the word *utterly* from the expression "utterly without redeeming social value," declaring that the work must be judged as a whole. Anything is obscene that "taken as a whole" appeals to "the prurient interest," "lacks serious literary, artistic, political, or scientific value," and depicts sexual conduct "in a patently offensive way." He also said that each state could apply its own "contemporary community standards" to the question of pornography.

There were two notable dissents in these cases. Justice Douglas (in the *Miller* case) lamented that people could be sent to prison for violating standards they did not understand. He also argued that it was unconstitutional to try to regulate personal taste. In any case, it would be impossible to stamp out all the various forms of "garbage" found in theaters, the media, and political campaigns. Justice Brennan (in the *Adult Theatre* case) made several good points: (1) "Obscenity" cannot be defined specifically and clearly enough to provide fair notice to citizens. (2) There is no good evidence that "exposure to obscene materials" leads "to deviant sexual behavior or crimes of sexual violence." (3) If the basis for repression is that obscene material corrupts and debases the mind, it would follow that a state could prescribe what we *must* read and view. (4) Previous decisions had upheld the right of individuals to indulge their tastes in private, while at the same time recognizing the right of the state to protect the interests of children and nonconsenting adults. These principles may be applied to the use of obscene materials and the manner in which they are distributed. (5) In view of the danger to legitimate free expression, attempts to prohibit the distribution of obscene material are in violation of the First and Fourteenth Amendments.

Pornography and the Harm Principle No argument for censorship is sufficient to set aside the right of individuals freely to express themselves artistically. None shows that such expression, even pornography, falls under the harm principle expressed by Mill.

One argument appeals to the giving of *offense* to others. This can be met by government regulations on the display and advertising of obscene materials. They should not be thrust before the eyes of the public. They should be such as to be easily avoided by those who would find them offensive. If one does not like dirty

[30]The Police Board of Censorship of Chicago once held the Disney movie *The Vanishing Prairie* to be obscene because it depicted a buffalo giving birth.

[31]*Miller* v. *California* 413 U.S. 15 (1973) and *Paris Adult Theatre I* v. *Slaton* 413 U.S. 49 (1973).

books, one simply won't read them; if one doesn't like dirty movies, one simply declines to view them. It's easy enough to determine the tone of these materials without exposing oneself to them. "Enjoyment" of obscene materials should be in private (in homes or buildings closed to children) and would be on the same level as other private actions. If a community fears that the presence of Triple-X theaters and bookstores lowers the value or attractiveness of certain commercial or residential areas, they can be restricted to designated areas.

Another argument appeals to the *corruption of the morals* of those who use obscene materials. This is a dubious assumption and also a very vague one. Where is the evidence that this is so? *In what way* does exposure corrupt morality? Even if one admits that immoral people are found in X-rated movie houses, is it not possible that they would have been immoral even if they had never set foot in such a place? But the chief difficulty with this argument is that it is paternalistic. It assumes that the state has the duty to shield adults from harmful influences (which cannot be done in any case) and to condition them somehow to grow in grace and purity. That individuals may be harmed by pornography is not nearly so certain as that their dignity as free beings is insulted by the state's dictating to them what they may read or view. Their development as moral beings is *their* business and no one else's. The purveyors of smut are no doubt low types, but they too have made their choice, and that should be the end of it.

The third argument is perhaps the best: Pornography should be prohibited because it *produces violent and antisocial behavior* on the part of those who patronize it. This is a definite harm, and it would be recognized as such by Mill and recognized as a "clear and present danger" by legalists. If these are the effects of pornography to any substantial degree, its distribution should be stopped by law. The most thorough and extensive attempt to determine the effect of pornography was the study conducted by the Commission on Obscenity and Pornography, established and handsomely funded by Congress in 1967. The commission submitted its final report to the president and Congress in 1970. One of its most important findings was no finding at all. "Empirical research designed to clarify the question has found no evidence to date that exposure to explicit sexual materials plays a significant role in the causation of delinquent or criminal behavior among youth or adults. The commission cannot conclude that exposure to erotic materials is a factor in the causation of sex crime or sex delinquency."[32] It could not even find a statistical correlation between crimes of sex and exposure to explicit sexual materials. To the dismay of the president who had appointed them, the members of the commission recommended that all laws prohibiting the sale, distribution, and exhibition of obscene materials to consenting adults be repealed.[33]

[32] *Report of the Commission on Obscenity and Pornography,* p. 32.

[33] President Nixon agreed with Billy Graham that the report was "one of the worst, almost diabolical reports ever made by a Presidential Commission" (*New York Times,* October 14. 1970, p. 30). It was denounced and rejected in the Senate, 60–5. The five in the minority were senators Case, Javits, McGovern, Mondale, and Young.

The People and Their Government Should Place Significant Obstacles in the Way of Free Expression by Individuals

Liberty is a beguiling ideal, but it can be, as John Ruskin called it, "a treacherous phantom." Daniel Webster said, "Liberty exists in proportion to wholesome restraint."[34] Madame Roland is supposed to have said just before she was executed during the French Revolution, "O Liberty, what crimes are done in thy name!"

Obviously Justifiable Restrictions on Free Expression Zealous adherents of liberty often overlook its most obvious restrictions. Defamation of character or reputation by false written work (libel) or spoken word (slander) is an improper use of free expression, for it violates an important right of others and is thus harmful to them. The law recognizes this.[35] Even when the charges against others are true, it may be wrong to make them. Even individuals whose character is not beyond reproach have a right to privacy unless the public disclosure of their flaws serves the public interest in some way. That a respected faculty member plays a lot of poker (and badly) would not seem to be a matter the public needs to know about. Some states protect the individual from verbal attacks that are true. And it does not always have to be an "attack" in the strict sense: it may be an invasion of privacy. Oliver Sipple, the ex-Marine who in effect saved the life of President Ford by jostling the arm of gunwoman Sara Jane Moore, sued several California newspapers for invasion of privacy. They had reported that Sipple was a homosexual, and not of the "closet" variety. But his family in Ohio did not know this. When they read about it in the newspapers, they disowned him. A champion body surfer, Michael Virgil, sued *Sports Illustrated* for reporting that he ate spiders, extinguished lighted cigarettes in his mouth, and performed other eccentric acts to impress women. He lost. But the right to privacy is an important one that courts should protect, and some news reporters are worried. Printing gossip, even when true, has limits. Floyd Abrams reported: "At an American Bar Association meeting of a committee on free speech and free press held [in 1977], all the lawyers present agreed that the expansion of privacy law posed more of a threat to the press than any other."[36] Some states permit the destruction of certain court records after a stated period for certain misdemeanors; others prohibit "the release of information about arrests that do not result in conviction."[37] A com-

[34]Speech at the Charleston Bar Dinner, May 10, 1847.

[35]Perhaps the law does not go far enough. "Eyewitness News," KABC-TV, has been very critical of the Los Angeles Police Department. Some of its sensational reports have been erroneous. In 1980 three members of the force filed a class-action lawsuit against the station for conspiring to defame the 4,500-officer department. Unfortunately, most libel-slander laws hold that *large groups* cannot be defamed!

[36]Floyd Abrams, "The Press, Privacy and the Constitution," in Bartlett, *The First Amendment in a Free Society*, p. 50.

[37]Ibid., p. 61.

pletely innocent person may also be harmed by public disclosure.[38] Reporters (and their lawyers), of course, plead that items that are "newsworthy" should not be barred, and that they are protecting the "right to know" of the public. But there is a line beyond which these notable aims cannot legitimately be pushed.[39] And reporters are not always the most objective judges.

It is believed (and reflected in our laws) that public figures should not be protected against libel and slander to the same degree as others, for their character and deeds are more often connected with matters of public importance. In fact, public disclosure is thought to be so important that the charge does not have to be true to be permitted expression. But even here there is a restriction: the charges must have been made in the belief that they were true and on the basis of some evidence. Malicious and reckless charges, even against public figures, are not afforded the protection of the right of free expression.[40]

Free speech cannot be extended to the point of passing off someone else's work as one's own. This is plagiarism. The right of free expression also does not cover appropriating the substance of someone else's work even when credit is given. This violates copyright laws. One cannot, either in the print or wire media, appropriate someone else's "act"—whether it be a book, article, or a live performance in a theater or an athletic field—without permission.

Other reasonable restrictions on free expression of ideas are as follows: (1) Speaking in a way that is "out of order" at a formal meeting. (2) Divulging "privileged information" acquired as a doctor, lawyer, or priest. (3) Revealing information that as an employee of the government or a business one has pledged to keep secret. (4) Publishing information that one has no right to have in the first place—such as that obtained by eavesdropping and opening others' mail. (5) Divulging information received in letters of recommendation. (6) Making false claims on behalf of the products in the business world. Public opinion and/or law are justified in seeking to restrict these and similar forms of free expression.

[38]A woman in Missouri has sued two newspapers and the city of Columbia. Since her name was printed in an account of an attack on her by a man (who was not captured), she has, she says, been threatened by the attacker—in person and by phone. The message is always the same: "I'm going to kill you." Police in Columbia say they use names of victims in their public reports, except in cases of sexual assault.

[39]The right to privacy may also be violated in "artistic" accounts of notorious criminals or their victims if permission of the principals is not obtained. The play *Desperate Hours* and the novel *In Cold Blood* are possible examples. Norman Mailer's novelized account of the murderer recently executed in Utah may be another (*The Executioner's Song*).

[40]In the state legislature of Wisconsin, Representative William Rogers accused Robert S. Gallagher, editor of the *Green Bay Press-Gazette*, of being a "headhunter . . . drunk with the power of the press." Gallagher had presumably hounded Judge James W. Byers to his death by a series of unsupported charges in his newspaper. In the heated exchange between editor and representatives, the former appealed to the right of a free press; the latter protected themselves with "legislative immunity." See "An Exposé Carried Too Far?" in *Newsweek*, April 14, 1980, pp. 53–54.

"Censorship" One of the most highly charged words in our vocabulary is *censorship.* When we hear it we think of a despot dictating to helpless subjects what they may read. The image of a brutal tyrant stifling all freedom of thought is abhorrent to the liberal mind, and rightly so. The word lends itself to what logicians call the "persuasive definition fallacy." A word (e.g., *censorship*) is given a new meaning (which, if openly done, is not reprehensible), but the negative emotive force of that word deriving from its *old* meaning is carried over to the new. The fallacy represents a dishonest attempt to have one's cake and eat it too. *Censorship* is taken in a sense that makes it applicable to a great many activities that, strictly speaking, are not denoted by the word. But the old emotive force is exploited in order to condemn these activities.

When, for example, parents are properly concerned with the nature of the texts that their children are assigned to read in school, they are not practicing censorship in the ordinary sense. As members of a school district, they have a legitimate right to influence educational goals and means. If they try to do this in an orderly and thoughtful way, they should not be charged with "pressuring" officials, and certainly not with censoring reading material. If a school district resolutely avoided Shakespeare or Euclidean geometry, citizens would rightly be concerned. If the district refused to place books by lefthanded authors on its reading lists, citizens would be entitled to ask some questions. Not all subjects can be covered, and not all authors can be included. There must be selection and discrimination. Their input into the decision-making process is an acceptable aspect of good citizenship. Similarly, citizens who support a library district have a right to say how their tax dollars will be spent. The library cannot buy *all* the books that roll from our presses. If, for example, the acquisitions librarian makes a practice of buying nothing but books on French history, some questions ought to be asked. Bureaucrats are not infallible, and professionals do not like to be challenged by laymen. But they are their employees and are subject, directly or indirectly, to their control.

The media are private institutions but have a great deal of public responsibility. They too can be called to account by the society they serve. Citizens may criticize a network for presenting works of poor artistic quality, programs that are insulting or offensive to particular groups, movies that are violent or salacious, news broadcasts that are biased or one-sided, and commercials that are in poor taste. These protests are not attempts at censorship, but simply attempts to raise the quality (as evaluated by the viewers) of programing. Viewers are not simply consumers of the broadcasts that come into their homes; they also have a proprietary interest in the use of the airwaves. On both grounds they are justified in expressing their opinions. They can, of course, turn off their sets (call it "boycott" if you will), but their rights are really greater than that which can be summarized in the expression "Take it or leave it." If they organize to boycott the products produced by sponsors of sleazy television shows, they are within their rights. The Coalition for Better Television, for example, is trying to improve the quality of programing; it is not conspiring to dismantle the First Amendment.[41] Newspapers are in a similar situation—especially those which are the only ones in their town. Readers have a right to balanced news coverage, clear distinctions between editorial opinion and reported fact, and feature articles that are in good taste. They have a right to question editorial policy and to protest unfair or libelous news items. Freedom of expression is a two-way street. Someone who accuses critics of "censorship" is trying to deprive them of *their* freedom of expression.

Instances of scheduled speakers being shouted down on such campuses as Yale are indeed reprehensible. They had a right to be heard by those who invited them and those who come to the meeting for that purpose. Although we can perhaps understand the anger and indignation felt by hecklers toward a racist, charlatan, or fascist, this does not excuse their failure to respect the freedom of others. But something can be said on behalf of officials and students at universities who question some of the choices made by student organizations. Too often they choose the notorious, the glamorous, or the controversial speaker, the one who is in the public eye, rather than the sober but qualified person who is not so spectacular. Popular visitors to campuses in recent years have been Dick Gregory, Jane Fonda, Bella Abzug, Abbie Hoffman, Muhammed Ali, Daniel Schorr, George Wallace, Jack Anderson, Imamu Baraka (LeRoi Jones), and Ralph Nader. One might argue that people like William Shockley should not have been offered a platform in the first place because they are racists and/or scientific charlatans. Shockley's presence on the campus was an affront not only to blacks but to objective scholarship as well. A university, presumably engaged in the pursuit of truth, is not the proper place for serious consideration of crackpot ideas. It should not accord them a dignity they do not deserve. We may attend a meeting where an extremist (say, an American Nazi, a Black Panther just out of prison, or a radical feminist) is scheduled to speak, out of curiosity, for we have seen their pictures in the paper, but we should not expect to hear a rational presentation; no great damage would be done if they were not able to get their message across. This is *not* the kind of free speech that Voltaire would have fought to the death for!

Incitement There is one other great class of exceptions to free expression. It is recognized by Mill himself:

> Even opinions lose their immunity, when the circumstances in which they are expressed are such as to constitute their expression a positive instigation to some mischievous act. An opinion that corn-dealers are starvers of the poor, or that private property is robbery, ought to be unmolested when simply circulated through the press, but may justly incur punishment when delivered orally to an excited mob

[41]See the excellent column by George F. Will, "Call to Boycott Sponsors of Sleazy TV Shows," *St. Louis Globe-Democrat*, February 9, 1981.

assembled before the house of a corn-dealer, or when handed about among the same mob in the form of a placard.[42]

When someone uses words to *incite* others to action that is harmful, he or she is not excused on grounds of exercising free speech. Perhaps we should not even call it a case of expression of an opinion, for the words are not used to set forth a point of view so much as to provoke an action. The prankster who shouts "Fire!" in a crowded theater is not expressing an opinion about conditions in the building, but is employing a word as a stimulus for a desired response. The demagogue who exhorts the mob to break into the jail has no justification based on the right of free speech. Nor do the rabble-rousers who, while keeping their own hands clean, incite others to riot, to break up meetings, to "trash" buildings, to tie up traffic, and to assault police officers. Those who foment crimes must bear some of the guilt themselves.

This brings us to the question of the limits that may exist in the use of persuasive political propaganda, or expressing ideas for activist purposes.

There is not proper appreciation in some quarters of the harm to national security that may flow from unbridled freedom of political expression. The opinions expressed in and about the *Dennis* case during the fifties are worth looking at today. Chief Justice Vinson declared that the "conspiracy to organize the Communist Party and to teach and advocate the overthrow of the Government of the United States by force and violence created a 'clear and present danger,' " whether or not it had a chance of succeeding. The attempt itself could be damaging "physically and politically" to a nation. "If Government is aware that a group aiming at its overthrow is attempting to indoctrinate its members and to commit them to a course whereby they will strike when the leaders feel the circumstances permit, action by the Government is required." Justice Jackson pointed out that Communists have "no scruples against sabotage, terrorism, assassination, or mob disorder." "Force or violence, as they resort to it, may never be necessary, because infiltration and deception may be enough." Citing the strategy of the Communist takeover in Czechoslovakia, Jackson rejected the application of the "clear and present danger" dictum. In the case of Communism, this requires the Court to be a prophet. If it were applied in the present case, it would mean that "the Communist plotting is protected during its period of incubation; its preliminary stages of organization and preparation are immune from the law; the Government can move only after imminent action is manifest, when it would, of course, be too late." The true ground for conviction is that since insurrection is a crime, *incitement* or *conspiracy* to do a crime may be also. The First Amendment does not protect expression directed toward criminal action. "No overt act is or need be required."

[42] *On Liberty,* III, p. 180.

It is a form of fanaticism to uphold the freedom of expression on behalf of those who would destroy it. As Sidney Hook said, "No right is absolute when it endangers rights of equal or greater validity."[43] When ideas compete in an open market, truth may be expected to prevail among reasonable people; and if it does not, they deserve their fate. "What the liberal fears is the systematic corruption of the free market of ideas by activities which make intelligent choice impossible. In short, what he fears is not heresy by conspiracy."[44] Some forms of political activism, such as Communism, operate against the rules. They operate secretly and through fronts. Communists seek positions of influence in unions, schools, and religions for the express purpose of destroying "bourgeois democracy." As Roger Baldwin, former head of the American Civil Liberties Union, said, "A superior loyalty to a foreign Government disqualifies a citizen for service to his own." Communist arguments are not arguments at all, but political propaganda to derogate America and to win adherents to a movement that is pledged to destroy it. This propaganda can be tolerated when that movement is relatively powerless, but when it approaches the position of threatening the security of this country, it should be curbed.

It is a matter of common knowledge that freedom of expression does not exist in the Soviet Union and all the other Communist countries. It is not argued here that we should deprive Communists in this country of their rights because they do not respect these rights when they are in control. Two wrongs, in this case, do not make a right. What is argued is that if we cherish our freedoms, we must be willing to take strong action against those (of whatever persuasion) who conspire against them—at that point when they constitute a substantial threat. We should be willing to accept inconvenience, insults, and lies, but when the harm takes the form of breaching our security or threatening the very existence of the nation, we cannot permit the conspiracy to escape under the shield of the First Amendment.

Security Similarly we should not permit individuals to distribute and publish classified materials under cover of protection of the First Amendment. Any nation, no matter how liberal, has state secrets to protect. Just as we punish foreign agents who commit espionage, so too should we punish our own citizens who, in the name of freedom, proclaim to the world those very facts which it is in the national interest to conceal. Just as citizens are protected against speech about their private lives, so too are government officials to be protected against public disclosure of some of the actions they perform in the line of duty. The public has the "right to know" many things about the conduct of a democratic government, but not all. Can the president effectively conduct delicate diplomacy if his list of options, "fall-back" positions, and points that he is willing to compro-

[43]Hook, *Heresy, Yes—Conspiracy, No,* p. 20.
[44]Ibid., p. 21.

mise are displayed on the pages of newspapers?[45] Can a congressional committee acquire the information it needs if the identities of its sources are proclaimed in newsletters? Can the FBI deal with interstate crime if the faces of its undercover agents are displayed on TV screens? Can the Department of Defense protect the country from attack if the location and nature of its missile bases are matters of common knowledge? That a recent administration has falsely appealed to "national security" to justify its nefarious actions does not mean that considerations of national security are always irrelevant. That the CIA does not have an unblemished record does not mean that it must cease being a secret organization. The fact is that unfriendly critics of America, individuals with political or personal grudges, and reporters who want to write sensational stories often wrap themselves in the mantle of freedom in order to forestall criticism and escape punishment. What they have done is to prostitute a noble ideal in service to ignoble purposes.

Pornography: Court Opinion Let us now turn to the question of pornography. Here we have another harmful activity seeking the protection of our most noble freedom. It is supposed to be a form of "artistic expression." Obscene literature is "that literature which presents, graphically and in detail, a degrading picture of human life and invites the reader or viewer, not to contemplate the picture, but to wallow in it."[46] Obscene pictures and movies present the spectacle directly. Majority opinions in recent Supreme Court decisions upholding the constitutionality of antipornography laws have recognized that such works are harmful and do not deserve the protection of the First and Fourteenth Amendments.

Chief Justice Warren E. Burger wrote the majority opinion in *Paris Adult Theatre I* v. *Slaton*, a case that upheld the right of the state of Georgia to regulate obscene material. Even if we assume that "it is feasible to enforce effective safeguards against exposure to juveniles and to the passerby," there are other dangers to the state in commercialized obscenity. Burger seems to recognize three such dangers: (1) to the "quality of life and the total community environment, the tone of commerce in the great city centers," (2) to the maintenance of a decent society, and (3) to the public safety.

[45]In August 1980 Jack Anderson wrote about "a startling, top-secret plan to invade Iran with a powerful military force." The purpose of the plan was not only to rescue the hostages and punish their captors, but also to ensure reelection for Carter. Anderson boasted that the documents seen by his associate were "so secret that the code word to classify them is itself classified." The *St. Louis Globe-Democrat* published the column on the front page, but did so only because the contents of the story had already leaked out. The *Globe-Democrat* stated: "It is the voluntary policy of The Globe-Democrat, and most members of the media in America, not to print information about a sensitive national security matter prior to public action by the government. Such a policy was rarely, if ever, violated during both world wars, Korea, and Vietnam." *St. Louis Globe-Democrat*, August 18, 1980, p. 1A.

[46]Clor, *Obscenity and Public Morality: Censorship in a Liberal Society*, p. 234.

With respect to the first danger, Burger grants the right of individuals to perform indecent actions in the privacy of their own home and to read or view whatever materials they wish, but he denies the right of the pornography dealers to distribute their wares in public and their clients to consume them in public (even when done discreetly). This kind of thing cannot fail to impinge on the privacy of *others*. "The idea of a 'privacy' right and a place of public accommodation are . . . mutually exclusive." It is accepted that societies can "impose regulations to protect both public health and the appearance of public places." We do not consign the problem of garbage and sewage disposal to individual choice. Control of smut is a comparable problem. No real question of free expression comes up, for obscene material "lacks any serious literary, artistic, political, or scientific value as communication."

With respect to the second concern, Burger believes that the states have a right to employ legislation in seeking to maintain a decent society. They have passed many laws in the area of commerce designed "to protect the weak, the uninformed, the unsuspecting, and the gullible from the exercise of their own volition." If they wanted to shift to a different policy ("laissez-faire") for obscenity, they could do so. Nothing in the Constitution *compels* them to pursue the policy of consumer protection. But many states and municipalities believe that standards of decency can be upheld by attacking pornography. We do believe, says Burger, that "good books, plays, and art lift the spirit, improve the mind, enrich the human personality and develop character." It is not unreasonable to suppose that matter opposite in tone will have contrary effects. "The sum of experience . . . affords an ample basis for legislation to conclude that a sensitive, key relationship of human existence, central to family life, community welfare, and the development of human personality, can be debased and distorted by crass commercial exploitation of sex."

With respect to the third concern, Burger cites the minority report of the Commission on Obscenity and Pornography, which holds that there is at least an arguable correlation between consumption of obscene materials and crime. "Although there is no conclusive proof of a connection between antisocial behavior and obscene material, the legislature of Georgia could quite reasonably determine that such a connection does or might exist."

There is much in the minority report of the commission that should be taken seriously. For example: (1) One study found "a definite correlation between juvenile exposure to pornography and precocious heterosexual and deviant sexual behavior." (2) Another study found that the group of convicts most provoked to masturbation by pornographic materials were the rapists. Apparently masturbation was not a catharsis sufficient to keep them from performing sex crimes. (3) The same study reported that 80 percent of the convicts wanted to try actions they had seen in obscene movies, and about 40 percent of these actually did so. (4) The study also reported that 39 percent of sex offenders admitted that "pornography had something to do with their committing the offense" for which they were convicted.[47]

Pornography and the Harm Principle Susan Brownmiller, for one, believes the law enforcement people who report that pornography has a causal relation to sex crimes. We certainly believe that violence and racial attacks on television have causal effects, so why deny it for pornography? "One does not need scientific methodology in order to conclude that the anti-female propaganda that permeates our nation's cultural output promotes a climate in which acts of sexual hostility directed against women are not only tolerated but ideologically encouraged." Brownmiller asks us to imagine "the bookstores and movie theaters lining Forty-second Street in New York City [being] devoted not to the humiliation of women by rape and torture, as they currently are, but to a systematized, commercially successful propaganda machine depicting the sadistic pleasures of gassing Jews or lynching blacks." *Then* the liberals might want to take some action, for free expression has gone too far![48]

If one views pornography as a case of expression of ideas, its commercial form would have to be curbed on the basis of Mill's harm principle. The harm it produces are (1) lowering the tone of the life of commerce and the areas in which it takes place, (2) providing offense to the general population who cannot possibly avoid its advertising and marquees, (3) corrupting the morality of those on whom it is foisted, and (4) causing antisocial and violent actions against society. These are substantial and vastly outweigh the loss of freedom.

What, precisely, are the moral values that pornography is calculated to corrupt? In addition to its probable tendency to produce acts of rape, of cruelty, of perversion, and of precocious sexual activity, it portrays sexual activity in a thoroughly dehumanized way. Its emphasis is on physical coupling, where affection and mutual respect are utterly lacking. It portrays pleasure, perhaps, but not joy. It presents sex as mechanical, with no subtlety or poetry. Young people derive a distorted view of the sexual relation and an unrealistic notion of what it is and what it can be. Their expectations are at once too great (circuses, orgies, superhuman performances) and too low (friction and orgasm). Older people, perhaps married, experience discontent with their mates, who can offer them only "straight" sex, and they undervalue the spiritual and enriching relations they have or might have. If one's spouse is not a sexual athlete and favored with stunning physical dimensions, one feels cheated.

Those who create and distribute pornographic pictures and movies are also guilty of treating people as means rather than ends. They hire their models and

[47]See *Report of the Commission on Obscenity and Pornography*, part 4, and Leiser, *Liberty, Justice, and Morals*, pp. 179–180.

[48]Susan Brownmiller, *Against Our Will: Men, Women, and Rape* (New York: Simon & Schuster, 1975), pp. 395–396.

actors to perform depraved poses and actions simply for the sake of making a profit. Many of these people are vagrants, mental defectives, and drug addicts who need a "fast buck." It is difficult to imagine how they can preserve a shred of dignity and self-respect. Not only are young adults exploited, but children also. "Kiddie porn" is probably the most horrifying aspect of this sorry trade in flesh.

Although our concern here is with the turpitude of the peddlers of smut, we cannot avoid noting that their clients are also guilty of violating the humanity-as-ends principle of Kant. For by their demand for the product, they encourage its production. A middle-aged man would be saddened should he happen to see his daughter on a Triple-X screen. He should be saddened to see *any* daughter in that situation.

The real harm that pornography does is to cater to the lowest taste of the public, to whet that taste and to confirm it. The classical philosophers would see what is going on. Epicurus, who could recognize "unnatural desires," warned that they had to be checked before they enslaved the human personality. The Stoics, who emphasized reason over passion, would hold that the addict of pornography and the sexual life it portrays had lost all self-control. Plato in his eloquent description of the "despotic man" called the person who is subject to a "master passion" the most wretched and miserable of all. "Like a swarm buzzing round this creature, the other desires come laden with incense and perfumes, garlands and wine, feeding its growth to the full in the pleasures of a dissolute life, until they have implanted the sting of a longing that cannot be satisfied."[49] Usurpation by a base passion, whether it be for drugs or obscenity, reduces the rest of man's nature to helplessness.

In view of all the harm that pornography does, it is foolish to defend it on the ground of free artistic expression—even if it were conceded that it *is* artistic expression.

Summary of the Issues

Whether we hold that freedom is a natural right or that it is an intrinsic good that is also often an extrinsic good as well, we will concede that there are limits to the exercise of freedom and that society should enforce these limits. What these limits are can be derived from the harm principle. At what point does free expression by the individual begin to constitute a definite harm to others?

Expression of opinion. One side argues that there are no limits here. Free expression of opinion never harms society; on the contrary, society harms itself when it seeks to suppress it. It must therefore be protected against the incursions of all governments (even democratic ones) and from infringement by groups and individuals. The other side points out some rather obvious limitations: libel,

[49]Plato, *Republic* IX.

slander, invasion of privacy, plagiarism, and many others in which harm to other people can be shown. It also exposes the rhetoric of "censorship." To challenge the choices of libraries, school boards, and the mass media is not to infringe their freedom of expression but to criticize the choices they make.

Expression of political propaganda. This is partisan and designed to produce action. One side takes a strict interpretation of harm and requires that the material constitute a real danger to the nation before it can be suppressed. There should be more concern for overt action than advocacy, for actual plots to commit acts of sedition than conspiracies with long-range goals. The other side is more willing to declare that harm has been done, and points out that even Mill opposed *incitement* to evil or criminal action. Rabble-rousers and fomentors of crime deserve no protection. We do not have to wait until sedition and other crimes succeed before taking action. "Heresy," insults, lies, and inconveniences may all be tolerated, but conspiracies that threaten the existence of our nation and its values (including freedom itself) are harms that should not be tolerated.

Expression of Secret Information. One side argues that the harm in protecting the government's tendency to conceal what it is doing is greater than the harm of revelation. The people must know what is going on and be very suspicious of claims based on "national security." The other side points out that the government cannot function effectively, domestically and internationally, if all its actions, plans, and options become matters of public knowledge. The "right to know" is pushed by sensation-seekers to a point where the national interest is sometimes significantly harmed.

"Artistic" expression (pornography). Is it legal to ban pornography? One side gives a negative answer to the question. The arguments of justices Brennan and Douglas are valuable. The other side gives a positive answer. The arguments of Justice Burger are valuable. Is it moral to ban pornography? One side gives a negative answer, for pornography does not constitute a real harm. The other side gives an affirmative answer, for pornography does constitute a real harm. Among the debated points are: (1) The offensiveness of pornography to those who do not patronize it, (2) the tendency of pornography to corrupt the morals of those who are exposed to it, (3) the tendency of pornography to produce violent and antisocial behavior, (4) the tendency of pornographic establishments to ruin neighborhoods. Most people who believe that it is legal to ban pornography also believe that it is right to do so; and most people who believe that it is illegal to ban pornography also believe that it is wrong to do so. The same considerations may be relevant to both the legal and the moral questions, for the government (especially on the state and local levels) has some responsibility for fostering a decent society. The issue throughout is whether pornography should be banned, not whether pornography possesses any value in itself.

Discussion Questions

1. Is freedom of expression a natural right or a utilitarian right? Explain.
2. What are the limits, if any, of the freedom of expression of opinion by teachers in the classroom? Explain.
3. Would you defend the right of a Nazi to distribute anti-Semitic tracts in the mail? Why?
4. If you were in the audience when a speaker was giving a speech on the genetic inferiority of blacks, what would you do? Why?
5. Do you think that the school newspaper has the right to print true accounts of your sexual life? Why?
6. Do you believe that a magazine that printed an account, false but believed by the editor to be true, of the financial shenanigans of a public figure should be sued? Why?
7. Do you believe that the truth will eventually prevail? If so, would it follow that society is excused when it bars the expression of a certain opinion? Why?
8. Mill argues that even the expression of false opinions is useful to society. Why? Do you agree?
9. Where do you stand on the *Dennis* decision? Why?
10. Do you think that if something is a crime, then incitement to do that act is also a crime? Why?
11. Do you think that incitement is really a case of freedom of expression or do you think it could more properly be discussed in the section on freedom of action? Why? Can you make a viable distinction between *incitement* and *advocacy*?
12. Can you think of any groups that are so dangerous to our society today that their freedom of expression should be curtailed? Explain.
13. How far do you think citizens should be permitted to go in revealing state secrets? What criteria have you used in arriving at your answer?
14. Someone who reveals our state secrets to a foreign nation is guilty of *espionage.* Is there any significant difference when a citizen reveals state secrets to the public? Explain.
15. Do you think that the efforts of states to ban pornography is in violation of the First and Fourteenth Amendments? Why?
16. If we can assume it is constitutional for states and municipalities to pass legislation to ban pornography, do you think that such legislation is morally justified on the basis of the harm principle? Why?
17. If you think it is wrong to ban pornography, would you favor restrictions on how and where it may be distributed or displayed? Explain.
18. Do you think that the use of and access to pornography is the individual's own business and should not be interfered with by anyone? Why?
19. Do you think that pornography corrupts the morals of those who patronize it? Why?
20. Do you agree with the report of the President's Commission on Obscenity and Pornography (1970) or with the politicians, preachers, and police personnel who have attacked it? Why?
21. If no one can be sure of the nature and extent of the effects of pornography, what bearing, if any, does that have on the question whether it should be banned? Explain.

22. Do you think that *pornography* or *obscenity* can be defined in a way that would make it usable in legislation? If so, how? If not, would it follow that no laws should be made with respect to it? Why?
23. We have throughout assumed that the "harm principle" is the only principle that can limit freedom. Is this correct—or is there a better principle?

For Further Reading

Paul C. Bartholomew. *Significant Decisions of the Supreme Court.* Washington: American Enterprise Institute for Public Policy Research, annual publication.

Jonathan Bartlett, ed. *The First Amendment in a Free Society.* New York: H. W. Wilson Co., 1979.

Tom L. Beauchamp, ed. *Ethics and Public Policy.* Englewood Cliffs, N.J.: Prentice-Hall, 1975. Chapter 5.

David S. Bogen. "The Supreme Court's Interpretation of the Guarantee of Free Speech." *Maryland Law Review*, 35 (1976):555ff.

Haig A. Bosmajian. *The Language of Oppression,* Washington: Public Affairs Press, 1974.

Paul S. Boyer. *Purity in Print.* New York: Charles Scribner's Sons, 1968.

Nicholas Capaldi, ed. *Clear and Present Danger: The Free Speech Controversy.* New York: Pegasus, 1969.

Harry M. Clor. *Obscenity and Public Morality: Censorship in a Liberal Society.* Chicago: University of Chicago Press, 1969.

Henry S. Commager. *Freedom, Loyalty, Dissent.* New York: Oxford University Press, 1954.

J. Elwood Daily. *The Anatomy of Censorship.* New York: M. Dekker, 1973.

Thomas I. Emerson. *The System of Freedom of Expression.* New York: Random House, 1970.

Albert Gerber. *Sex, Pornography, and the Law.* 2nd ed. New York: Ballantine Books, 1964.

Harry K. Girvetz, ed. *Contemporary Moral Issues.* 2nd ed. Belmont, Calif.: Wadsworth Publishing Co., 1968. Part 1.

David Holbrook, ed. *The Case against Pornography.* LaSalle, Ill.: Library Press, 1972.

Sidney Hook. *Heresy, Yes—Conspiracy, No.* Westport, Conn.: Greenwood Press, 1973.

Edwin P. Hoyt and Olga G. Hoyt. *Censorship in America.* New York: Seabury Press, 1970.

Douglas A. Hughes, ed. *Perspectives in Pornography.* New York: St. Martin's Press, 1970.

Philip B. Kurland, ed. *Free Speech and Associations: The Supreme Court and the First Amendment.* Chicago: University of Chicago Press, 1975.

Burton M. Leiser. *Liberty, Justice, and Morality.* 2nd ed. New York: MacMillan Publishing Co., 1979. Chapters 4–5.

Robert A. Liston. *The Right to Know: Censorship in America.* New York: Franklin Watts, 1973.

I. A. MacDonald. "The 'Offense Principle' as a Justification for Censorship." *Philosophical Papers* 5 (1976):67ff.

Alexander Meiklejohn. *Political Freedom: The Constitutional Powers of the People.* New York: Oxford University Press, 1965.

John Stuart Mill. *On Liberty.* Many editions. Parts I–II.

Richard S. Randall. *Censorship of the Movies: The Social and Political Control of a Mass Medium.* Madison: University of Wisconsin Press, 1968.

The Report of the Commission on Obscenity and Pornography. New York: Bantam Books, 1970.

Frederick F. Schauer. *The Law of Obscenity.* Washington: Bureau of National Affairs, 1976.

Joseph Tussman. *Government and the Mind.* New York: Oxford University Press, 1977.

FREEDOM OF ACTION

Neither the People nor Their Government Should Place Significant Obstacles in the Way of Free Action by Individuals

The Value of Freedom of Action Clearly, when an action by an individual threatens to harm others, that individual should be restrained. Individual freedom has a limit, and Mill has stated it.

But this "harm principle" should be applied very carefully, for what is at stake is a very important right or value. The importance of freedom itself as a component of happiness was discussed in the previous chapter. Here we will recapitulate some of Mill's arguments for the view that individuals and society benefit when people are permitted to act in ways chosen by themselves.

The individual benefits because in an atmosphere of freedom he or she has to rely on his or her own mental and moral faculties. These are strengthened by being used. If one slavishly follows custom or public opinion, or if one must hold to a course prescribed by law, one's active capacities atrophy. Mill believes that human nature has many different springs and impulses. It is not finished and definite. The character that one is to emerge with is something one must fashion for oneself. Unless a man or woman exercises free choice, he or she is doomed to copy models set forth by public opinion. "Human nature is not a machine to be built after a model, and set to do exactly the work prescribed for it, but a tree, which requires to grow and develop itself on all sides, according to the tendency of the inward forces which make it a living thing."[50]

Mill is restating the Greek ideal of self-realization—but with a difference. Self-realization consists, not in achieving an essential pattern that corresponds to some ideal of "humanity," but in each particular self deciding what his or her own self is to be. Mill's view is thus much closer to the existentialist thesis that the individual has a "constantly renewed obligation to remake the Self."[51] If there is a human essence for Mill, it is that of the individual employing whatever mental

[50] *On Liberty*, III, p. 184.

[51] Jean-Paul Sartre, *Being and Nothingness*, trans. Hazel E. Barnes, (New York: Philosophical Library, 1956), p. 35.

and moral sensibilities he possesses in order to form whatever character he chooses for himself. In this lies the ultimate dignity of the individual.

Unlike the existentialists, Mill believes that human freedom *can* be stifled by society and government.

> In our times, from the highest class of society down to the lowest, every one lives as under the eye of a hostile and dreaded censorship. Not only in what concerns others, but in what concerns only themselves, the individual, or the family, do not ask themselves—what do I prefer? or, what would suit my character and disposition? or, what would allow the best and highest in me to have fair play, and enable it to grow and thrive? They ask themselves, what is suitable to my position? what is usually done by persons of my station and pecuniary circumstances? or (worse still) what is usually done by persons of a station and circumstances superior to mine? I do not mean that they choose what is customary, in preference to what suits their own inclination. It does not occur to them to have any inclination, except for what is customary. Thus the mind itself is bowed to the yoke; even in what people do for pleasure, conformity is the first thing thought of; they live in crowds; they exercise choice only among things commonly done: peculiarity of taste, eccentricity of conduct, are shunned equally with crimes: until by dint of not following their own nature, they have no nature to follow: their human capacities are withered and starved: they become incapable of any strong wishes or native pleasures, and are generally without either opinions or feelings of home growth, or properly their own. Now is this, or is it not, the desirable condition of human nature?[52]

Here Mill is much closer to Alexis de Tocqueville and Friedrich Nietzsche. De Tocqueville, who could perhaps muster two cheers for democracy, wrote: "When I survey this countless multitude of beings, shaped in each other's likeness, amidst whom nothing rises and nothing falls, the sight of such universal uniformity saddens and chills me, and I am tempted to regret that state of society which has ceased to be."[53] Nietzsche wrote: "By my love and hope, I conjure thee: Maintain holy thy highest hope. Cast not away the hero from thy soul." "And be on thy guard against the good and the just! They would fain crucify those who devise their own virtue—they hate the lonesome ones."[54] These ideas were applied to contemporary American life in the influential book *The Lonely Crowd* (by David Riesman and others), in which the distinction was made between "other-directed" and "inner-directed" persons. Over a century ago Mill wondered whether individuality could withstand the forces making common life more and more standard.[55] Since his time, with the development of mass communication, mass education, and mass production of commodities, individualism has been placed in mortal danger.

[52]*On Liberty,* III, pp. 185–186.

[53]Alexis de Tocqueville, *Democracy in America*, ed. Richard D. Heffner (New York: Mentor Books, 1956), p. 315.

[54]Friedrich Nietzsche, *Thus Spake Zarathustra* (trans. Thomas Common), I-17.

[55]In the United States, Ralph Waldo Emerson had the same fears.

The consequences of freedom are also beneficial to society in general. Progress depends on new ideas. We need people who will commence new practices, experiment in styles of living, "set examples of more enlightened conduct." We should cherish those who are willing to be different. "The despotism of custom is every where the standing hindrance to human advancement. . . . That so few now dare to be eccentric, marks the chief danger of the time."[56] As a horrible example of a society that has been stationary for centuries, Mill cites China. The Chinese "have succeeded beyond all hope in what English philanthropists are so industriously working at—in making people all alike, all governing their thoughts and conduct by the same maxims and rules; and these are the fruits."[57] Evidently, the Chinese have replaced one form of uniformity with another.

Legislating Morals Because Mill claimed to be a utilitarian (not always consistently), it is tempting to say that his theory implies that all immoral action should be legislated against.[58] Since all immoral actions produce harm according to the utilitarian criterion of rightness and liberty may be abridged when harm is done, the individual should not be permitted to be immoral. This obviously misses two crucial ideas: (1) Where the harm of an immoral act comes down only on the head of the agent (and his willing partner), society has no interest in the matter. (2) Since freedom itself possesses great value, the harm that its abridgment produces must be exceeded in likelihood, scope, and intensity by the consequences on others of the action itself. The harm principle may (or may not) be consistent with utilitarianism; it is not simply a restatement of the utilitarian thesis. The "harm" that Mill had in mind was not simply bad consequences for others, but substantial injury to their "rights."

In espousing a philosophy of freedom, we are not maintaining that anything that a person chooses to do is moral. We are maintaining that a man or woman should be permitted to do what he or she *chooses* to do. What is chosen may or may not be moral. It is hoped that it will be moral—or at least not immoral. Which it is must be judged on its own merit, and people may well disagree in their verdicts. But society should permit individuals to do as they please, for better or for worse, so long as their actions do not harm others. Each of us should grant the same freedom to others that we demand for ourself.

Since most of us have some interest in the moral quality of others' actions, it is tempting to try to legislate morality. If contraception is wrong, pass a law against it. If honoring parents is right, apply great public pressure on its behalf. If going to church is moral, build compulsory church attendance into the Constitution. We can, however, look back in history at coercion that clearly seems benighted: laws against painless childbirth, sexual relations between consenting adults, swearing, drinking, consumption of certain foods, card playing, dancing,

[56]*On Liberty*, III, pp. 194, 192.

[57]Ibid., p. 196.

[58]See, for example, A. R. Louch, "Sins and Crimes," in Wasserstrom, *Morality and the Law*, p. 73ff.

and the like. We realize that these attempts to control behavior were ill-advised, to say the least.

The loss of freedom is a serious evil consequence of the attempt to enforce morals. To this may be added other undesirable consequences: (1) The resources of law enforcement will be employed to deal with morals cases instead of used against clearly harmful acts such as murder, rape, robbery, governmental corruption, and white-collar crime.[59] (2) Because of the difficulty of detecting and getting convictions for some "crimes of morality," law enforcement officials may be tempted to go after the easier ones or the ones that most affront them. (3) The opportunity for blackmail and extortion is increased. The threat of exposure is often feared more than the legal penalty for the offense: the arrest announces the "sin" to all the world.

Those who would enforce morals by legislation claim that morality is essential to the survival of society and refuse to distinguish private morality from public morality. Society is harmed when its standards are violated. Toleration of clearly immoral acts is an invitation to moral anarchy in the same way that toleration of subversive acts is an invitation to political anarchy. How should we answer this argument? Even if we grant what is not true, namely that society's conceptions of what is moral are true and correct in all respects, it does not follow that toleration of some classes of violations will encourage people to commit them, or to perform other acts of immorality (now that the bars are down), and finally will lead to unbridled moral licentiousness. "We have ample evidence for believing that people will not abandon morality, will not think any better of murder, cruelty, and dishonesty, merely because some private sexual practice which they abominate is not punished by law."[60] Danger to the moral fabric of society is much too dubious a form of harm to cite in limiting freedom. It is also too vague and comprehensive. If harm is to be any kind of criterion at all for limiting the law, it must be applied to the specific consequences of the action itself. Sin and crime are two different phenomena. Sometimes the former may be deemed a crime (e.g., killing, stealing, lying on oath); sometimes it may not.

Influencing Morals Opposing social actions against immoral actions that do not harm others does not imply that we should be *oblivious* to the morality of others. We would not want to advocate as an ideal that of the philosophic sages or religious saints who get their own house in order and, secure in their blessedness, let the rest of humanity go to hell. We may argue with people and seek to persuade them to give up their wicked ways. We may write eloquent treatises on "the good life." We may form organizations and proselytize members. We may educate our children and try to set a good example. We may refuse to associate with people whose conduct is offensive.

[59]The police in St. Louis, a city with a high incidence of violent crime, have dressed some of their policewomen as prostitutes and have assigned them the job of walking the streets. When a man accosts them and makes a deal, he is arrested.

[60]H. L. A. Hart, "Immorality and Treason," in Wasserstrom, *Morality and the Law*, p. 53.

There is sometimes a fine line between pressuring people and persuading them, between coercing people through public opinion and educating them, between brainwashing and proselytizing, between indoctrinating and training. We step over that line when we fail to treat others as autonomous and dignified subjects, when we try to condition them instead of simply instructing them. The following would seem to be on the right side of the line: (1) A teacher states her own view on a controversial issue, but lets the students know the other side and come to their own conclusion. (2) A preacher explains and demonstrates the comforts of a trust in God. (3) A person tells his friend that he can no longer condone a certain kind of action. (4) A group of people pledges not to buy the products of a company that it believes to have acted unjustly. The following would seem to be on the wrong side of the line: (1) The teacher who uses his prestige and power to bring the student around to his own "enlightened" viewpoint. (2) The religious zealot who capitalizes on fear, poverty, misery, and ignorance to gain control of a person's life. (3) A person who treats others badly because they have long hair or wear outlandish clothes. (4) An organization that uses lies, character assassination, and emotional appeals against people who have different moral points of view.

There are other actions that should be free from public pressure: those that, while not obviously immoral, are undesirable in some other way. Such actions may be dangerous or harmful to the agent or offensive to others. There is a tendency in some quarters, often with the best of motives, to control these actions also, even when no substantial harm to others can be shown. Here again, segments of society may attempt to influence behavior in these areas but are unjustified in exerting pressure.

Prostitution Let us now return the question of *legal* enforcement of desirable behavior. Here we will be more specific and will discuss prostitution and euthanasia (actions thought by many people to be immoral), failure to use seat belts and crash helmets (thought by many people to be dangerous), drug usage and gambling (thought by many people to be harmful to the self), and nude bathing (thought by many people to be offensive). Whether these actions are in fact ndesirable is beside the point. The issue here is not whether they are ethical or prudential forms of conduct but whether government is justified in prohibiting them. Do they violate the harm principle?

Prostitution would appear to be a practice that produces harm for others. The prostitute is likely to harm her client by infecting him with venereal disease. And the client harms the prostitute by treating her as a piece of merchandise. But the prostitute-client relationship is one freely entered into by both parties. The man is willing to risk infection (and so is the woman). The woman has freely decided to sell her body, and she is not being "used" any more than she is "using" her client to build up her bankroll. If exploitation is taking place, it does so on a two-way street. It is difficult to see how anyone else is directly and substantially harmed by a business transaction between two adults, sordid as that transaction may be. Let the buyer and the seller beware.

It is true that "undesirable elements" may work their way into "the lively commerce" and do all kinds of things that may harm the public: run dope, impress young girls into service, spread disease, use the business as an adjunct to organized crime, rob or blackmail clients. These things, however, are not unique to prostitution. They may occur in any industry. Prostitutes, clients, and the public at large are entitled to the protection that people involved in or affected by any other business are entitled to. Taxi companies are not permitted to traffic in drugs. The military services are not permitted to shanghai underaged people. Food handlers are subject to periodic health checks. Loan companies are required to sever connections with organized crime. Hotels are not permitted to rob or blackmail guests. The reason, perhaps, that "undesirable elements" are attracted to prostitution is because it falls outside the normal pale. When prostitution is illegal, only those who are willing to break the law are willing to take a "piece of the action."

It is also true that young women "ruin their lives" by entering the profession. There are other ways that they can legally do this (e.g., by marrying a sadist or drinking to excess or taking a job in an unsafe coal mine), but the choice is theirs. A system of laws that would succeed in closing off all roads to perdition would be a very oppressive one indeed. The client, too, makes a poor choice. He could more beneficially spend his money on good books, a new coat for his wife, or a bike for his child. But here again, there is nothing unique in his decision to spend his money foolishly. Golf can be an expensive item too, and the exercise gained is often less than that obtained in a boudoir. But the crucial point is that the harm that both prostitute and client produce is their own, and is thus not subject to the harm principle.[61]

The harm done to others by prostitution is neither direct nor substantial, and it is not uniquely and necessarily linked with prostitution. Prostitution, therefore, does not qualify under the harm principle. If it is believed to be immoral, it should be attacked with education and exhortation instead of with laws.

Euthanasia: Voluntary and Nonvoluntary *Euthanasia* is derived from two Greek words: *eu* and *thanatos*. The first means "good" or "easy"; the second means "death." In our day, the concept of "mercy" or "granting" has been added, so the term now means "granting to others a good or easy death" or "mercy killing." Quite apart from the morality of an individual taking his or her own life or a person assisting someone who seeks for an easy death, we must ask whether government is justified in prohibiting these actions.

When individuals who are of sound mind seek their own death, they are exercising their freedom to dispose of what is indisputably their own. If they can do so through their own efforts or with the aid of a confederate, they should be permitted to do so. The confederate, who respected the other's wishes, should in

[61]One might argue that the client harms the prostitute, and the prostitute harms the client, so others *are* involved. But the harm principle does not apply when the other is a *willing partner* of an action.

no way be accountable to the law. This holds not only for the easy cases of individuals who face a lingering period of painful or sedated suffering before the inevitable finally occurs, but for other cases as well: the individual who faces an indefinite future of physical disablement that seems to be bleak, joyless, and hopeless; the individual whose prospects seem to be unrelieved misery (e.g., the person sentenced to life imprisonment); the individual who, if he or she continued to live, would be disgraced and dishonored (e.g., the person about to be exposed as a traitor). These do not exhaust the possibilities. We may want to expostulate with such people and offer help and encouragement, but their decision, whether moral or immoral, is their own. We may, for ethical reasons of our own, decline to assist them, but we have no right to punish those who do.[62]

Although it is difficult to imagine an action (or inaction) that does not harm someone somewhere somehow sometime, the consequences of euthanasia are not the kind that the harm principle is designed to prevent. The individual's loved ones will suffer, but their pain is usually a result of the whole tragic situation rather than its outcome. Just as many of the loved ones will be thankful that the sick person's ordeal is over. Children may lose a parent, adults may lose spouses, and parents may lose children. But it is difficult to specify and defend "rights" that the individual owed them which are violated by the individual's death. An individual who is determined (for whatever reason) to die will be very little use to others in any case.

Glanville Williams states two values promoted by voluntary euthanasia: It is cruel to allow a human being to linger for months in the last states of agony, weakness, and decay and to refuse the demand for merciful release. There is also a second cruelty involved—perhaps not quite so compelling, but still worth consideration: the agony of the relatives in seeing their loved one in such a desperate plight. Criminal law should not be invoked to repress conduct unless this is demonstrably necessary on social grounds. What social interest is there in preventing the sufferer from choosing to accelerate death by a few months? What positive value does this life still possess for the patient or for society that he or she should be forced by law to retain it? The patient has the freedom to die, and the family, friends, and doctor have the freedom to cooperate with the patient in carrying out his wishes. It is the doctor's responsibility to do everything possible to prolong worthwhile life, or, in the last resort, to ease the patient's passage. If the doctor honestly and sincerely believes that the best service that can be performed for a suffering patient is to accede to the request for euthanasia, it is a grave thing that the law should forbid the doctor to do so.[63]

The case of persons who are not in a position to make a decision is somewhat different. If, as the result of an accident or sudden illness, a person is in a coma

[62]EXIT, a British organization that espouses "the right to die with dignity," published a manual in 1980 called *A Guide to Self-Deliverance*. General Secretary Nicholas Reed says that since it is illegal for doctors to practice euthanasia, the only alternative for the terminally ill who don't want to live is "to do it yourself." See *Newsweek*, April 7, 1980, p. 77.

[63]Glanville Williams, "Euthanasia Legislation: A Rejoinder to Nonreligious Objections," in Mappes and Zembaty, *Social Ethics: Morality and Social Policy*, p. 56.

or otherwise not of sound mind, we cannot directly assess his or her wishes. But if the family, on the basis of indubitable medical information, knows that recovery is impossible or that the only hope of survival would be life as a "vegetable," and wishes to direct the hospital to terminate all life-support systems, it should be permitted to do so. Neither family, doctors, nor hospital should be restricted by law in assisting in the death of a person who has no chance of human survival. Whether family or medical officials should take this step is a matter of their moral choice. It should not be interfered with by law. They are not *harming* the unfortunate one; they are helping him or her.

We have now entered a very delicate area. While it is obvious that the law cannot permit nonvoluntary euthanasia in those cases where the family and consulting doctors oppose it, it should permit it in those cases where the family and physicians approve it. Government regulation is necessary to draw the line between cases where euthanasia is prohibited and cases where the family and physicians are free to carry it out according to the dictates of their own conscience. Nonvoluntary euthanasia, presumably, would be prohibited if it is on the grounds of race, insanity, or senility, but permitted on grounds of painful or vegetablelike existence where there is no hope for recovery. Difficult cases would be those involving deformed or defective births.

One argument against nonvoluntary euthanasia is the "wedge" or "slippery slope" argument: wherever we draw the line, pressure will build up to extend it to still more cases until society is killing anyone who seems to be a burden or who falls short of an arbitrary norm for effectiveness. The answer to this argument is that we should do what we think is right. We draw the line and adhere to it because it reflects our moral judgment. If we move (or retain) the line, that too will reflect our best moral judgment. As C. M. Cornford put it, the argument amounts to saying that you should not act justly today for fear that you may not act justly tomorrow. Related to this argument is the one based on fear that we will lose sight of the sanctity of life. This is also wrong-headed. Euthanasia is itself based on respect for the sanctity of life. The view is that life should not be prolonged when it has deteriorated to a point of ceaseless pain, sedated or comatose oblivion, or vegetablelike existence. It is to spare life of these degrading conditons that euthanasia is recommended.

Many victims are not in a position to make a calm and deliberate choice. They may be in great pain, under heavy sedation, or in a coma. In the Karen Quinlan tragedy, no one could ascertain her wishes in the matter. Her parents had recalled, however, that she had expressed a wish before her accident that she would never have to suffer a lingering and painful death.

An individual should have the right "to execute a document directing that he shall have the right to death with dignity, and that his life not be prolonged beyond the point of meaningful existence,"[64] and have its provisions carried out in the hospital. One formulation of such a "living will" is this:

[64]This expression is from the language of the Sackett bill, which was defeated in the Florida legislature in 1971.

> If at any time I should have an incurable injury, disease, or illness certified to be a terminal condition by two physicians, and where the application of life-sustaining procedures would serve only to artificially prolong the moment of my death, and where my physician determines that my death is imminent whether or not life-sustaining procedures are utilized, I direct that such procedures be withheld or withdrawn, and that I be permitted to die naturally.[65]

A patient who has not made such a will but is of sound mind should be able to *request* such treatment (voluntary euthanasia): and if he or she is not of sound mind, loved ones and doctors should be able to grant it (nonvoluntary euthanasia).

Euthanasia: Passive and Active One issue in the euthanasia controversy centers on the distinction between *passive* and *active* euthanasia. Some people favor the former only; others favor the latter as well. The family of Karen Quinlan, the young woman who had been in a coma for a long time and whose future was hopeless, pleaded with authorities to permit the disconnection of the respirator that kept her alive. This was a plea for passive euthanasia. The superior court of New Jersey was not willing to make a distinction between passive and active euthanasia, holding that to discontinue life-support systems would be homicide. "There is no constitutional right to die that can be asserted by a parent for his incompetent adult child."[66] This decision was overruled by the Supreme Court of New Jersey. Justice C. J. Hughes did make the distinction between abandoning extraordinary means of life support (passive) and homicide (active), and permitted the respirator to be turned off. Although the doctor who first attended Quinlan is an exception, most doctors accept passive euthanasia while rejecting the active form that consists of a deliberate and positive action designed to end life (e.g., a lethal injection of a drug).[67]

Pope John Paul II issued a document in 1980 permitting passive euthanasia, both voluntary and nonvoluntary. "When inevitable death is imminent," patients may refuse "forms of treatment that would only secure a precarious and burdensome prolongation of life." Not only the hardship of the patients should be considered, but that of their families as well. Another utilitarian note was struck

[65]See Paul Ramsey, *Ethics at the Edges of Life* (New Haven, Yale University Press, 1977), p. 324.
[66]Justice Robert Muir, Jr., "Opinion in the Matter of Karen Quinlan," Superior Court of New Jersey, Chancery Division, Morris County, November 10, 1975.
[67]The House of Delegates of the American Medical Association endorsed this statement: "The intentional termination of the life of one human being by another—mercy killing—is contrary to that for which the medical profession stands and is contrary to the policy of the American Medical Association. The cessation of the employment of extraordinary means to prolong the life of the body when there is irrefutable evidence that biological death is imminent is the decision of the patient and/or his immediate family. The advice and judgment of the physician should be freely available to the patient and/or his immediate family." December 4, 1973. In 1972, Dr. Walter Sackett, leader of the euthanasia movement in Florida, said: "I have let hundreds of people die." See O. Ruth Russell, *Freedom to Die,* p. 178.

when the Vatican directed that "the treatment to be used, its degree of complexity or risk, its cost and the possibilities of using it" be assessed and compared with the results that could reasonably be expected. "The Vatican's statement gives to individual doctors and institutions moral support for acting in the best interest of the patient," says a Jesuit theologian of Georgetown University. "It says that the decision mechanism lies with the patient, family and physician and that in cases where the patient is incompetent, like Karen Ann Quinlan, you don't have to justify dying to a court."[68]

This freedom to *permit* to die does not go far enough. *Active* euthanasia, which is universally prohibited, has much to recommend it in cases where the future of the patient is hopeless. It is a quicker and thus more humane cessation of life than the lingering suffering that passive euthanasia makes possible.[69] Victims may beg for a merciful end, and their families may support them, but that merciful injection is denied them. Frederick Stenn, a dying physician, wrote to a medical journal, pleading for active euthanasia: "Man chooses how to live. Let him choose when to depart, where and under what circumstances the harsh winds that blow over the terminus of life must be subdued. . . . As one who has had a long, full, rich life . . . whose days are limited by a rapidly growing, highly malignant sarcoma of the peritoneum, whose hours, days and nights are raked by intractable pain, discomfort and insomnia, whose mind is often beclouded and disoriented by soporific drugs, and whose body is assaulted by needles and tubes that can have little effect on the prognosis, I urge medical, legal, religious, and social support for a program of voluntary euthanasia with dignity."[70] Dean W. R. Inge said: "It seems anomalous that a man may be punished for cruelty if he does not put a horse or a dog out of its misery but is liable to be hanged for murder if he helps a cancer patient to an overdose of morphine." The moral difference between *withholding* the means for life and *taking* life is a difficult one to see in these situations.

Euthanasia: Legislation The attempts of state lawmakers to legalize various forms of euthanasia have generally failed. A "Right to Die with Dignity" bill in Wisconsin (1971) did not get out of committee. A "Death with Dignity" bill in Washington (1973) permitting passive and voluntary euthanasia did not get out of committee. Bills in Massachusetts and Delaware (1973) to legalize the "living will" were voted down. In Maryland and California (1974) attempts to permit passive euthanasia also failed. In Idaho, Oregon, and Montana attempts to permit active euthanasia failed in the early seventies. The Sackett bill was defeated in the Florida legislature in 1971. California became the first state to permit voluntary

[68]See "To Live and Let Die," *Newsweek*, July 7, 1980, p. 58.

[69]Karen Quinlan did *not* die when the respirator was disconnected. Six years after the court decision she is still biologically alive—and still comatose.

[70]See Daniel Q. Haney, "Dying Doctor Pleads for Euthanasia for Terminally Ill," *St. Louis Globe-Democrat*, October 9, 1980, p. 2A.

passive euthanasia (October 1976). The Natural Death Act provided that terminally ill people who had given prior authorization ("living will") could be permitted to die. Texas and New Mexico have passed similar bills. Arkansas permits nonvoluntary (passive) euthanasia for a child or incompetent adult with the permission of parent, spouse, child, or guardian. Legislation is pending in most of the states, but most of it deals with passive euthanasia only.

It is hoped that this trend continues. Individuals should be permitted to practice nonvoluntary and active euthanasia in accordance with requirements set by the law to protect the interests of the individual whose survival is in question. It is sometimes in the individual's best interests to die.

Seat Belts and Crash Helmets Should it be against the law to drive without seat belts or cycle without crash helmets? Those who answer in the affirmative display a paternalist attitude utterly at odds with the right to free action. If people are imprudent enough to take these risks, they should be permitted to do so. If danger is part of the life style they have chosen, the government should not interfere.

What harm do they produce for others? They do not *cause* accidents, as do drivers who choose not to wear their needed and required spectacles. They might become a burden to their families or to the insurance companies because of their decision, but so too might anyone who engages in *any* dangerous activity: the mountain climber, the scuba diver, the parachutist, the automobile racer, the hockey player, and the intrepid adventurer who sails a small boat around the world. It is difficult to know where to draw the line between dangerous actions that are permissible and those that are not. It is thus better not to draw the line at all. That some individuals will by their imprudence become burdens on others and society in general is a fact of life. Not all the laws in the world will prevent it—unless we keep adventurous souls locked up except when accompanied by a government guardian of some kind. In the case of dangerous acts, as in the others, we have to weigh the loss of freedom against the beneficial consequences of legislation, and conclude that the latter does not compensate for the former.

Drug Usage Should it be against the law to use (without prescription) such drugs as heroin, cocaine, amphetamines, "angel dust," LSD, and the like? There is no question that these harm the users terribly. But the issue is whether the use of them by some causes enough harm to others to warrant police protection. This is a very hard case.

There are parallels between drug and alcohol consumption. In both, the individual can become unfit for normal existence. If we respect the freedom of drinkers thus to destroy themselves, we should accord the same freedom to drug users. Sooner or later, the drug user will be an addict, a condition or illness like alcoholism, which can be healed only by the most strenuous acts of will. The steps that lead to alcoholism are not crimes, so those that lead to drug addiction should not be either. The decision to "experiment" with drugs and alcohol is a free choice.

The great difference between drug and alcohol usage is that the latter can be controlled by the individual somewhat more easily than the former can. Alcohol can be consumed by some people in moderation and may even contribute to their well-being. But drugs are harmful in themselves, in whatever quantity, and can be handled moderately by few, if any, users. Drugs are dangerous substances, and their manufacture should be strictly regulated by the government, and their distribution (except through a doctor's prescription) should be absolutely forbidden by law. And there should be severe and quick punishment for drug dealers. That people can make money by purveying commodities whose only use is destructive of the human personality is a horrible state of affairs. Nothing would benefit the national health more than a successful campaign to rid the country, its streets and schools, of drugs. The function of government is to end the *flow* of drugs, not their *use*. Success in the former would do much to prevent the latter.

Drug usage does produce harm for others: grievous pain for loved ones, expense in maintaining public health service, crime, and so on. But it is difficult to see how laws against users would reduce this harm more effectively than laws against distributors. If drugs are available, there will always be people foolish enough to "try" them and to feed their habit once it is formed. If in the face of all the warnings and education they have been subject to, people choose to use a destructive substance, that is their right. Concentration on the *distribution* of drugs rather than the *usage* of drugs is a way to counteract the harmful social effects of drugs while continuing to respect the freedom of individuals to destroy themselves. Those who succumb to drugs are foolish, weak, and pitiable; those who purvey drugs for a profit are enemies of the state. The former should be treated, the latter sent to prison. The harm produced by usage is confined mostly to *oneself;* the harm produced by dealing is a certain and substantial harm to *others.*

Gambling What about gambling? It is often very harmful to the compulsive gambler, and chapters of Gamblers Anonymous meet and hear tales just as horrifying as those recounted at meetings of Alcoholics Anonymous. But, again, the issue is not that of the harm visited upon the gambler but that which results for others.

When gamblers bet and lose, their families suffer. And when they win, they're "hot" and continue to bet until they lose—and the families suffer. Gamblers do not like to work, for they expect to pick a winning horse or hit their number. Compulsive gamblers are not much use to their loved ones or to society in general. They may be on welfare and spend their money at the track. Their children may not get new shoes because they blow their money on a "sure thing."

But once again, society should be able to tolerate such ne'er-do-wells. Although the government takes a lot of our money in taxation, we still recognize the "right" of individuals to spend what is left as they see fit. Some people make poor investments. Others buy frivolous products. Others run up ridiculous charge accounts. But how they spend their money is so closely related to the life style they choose that to restrict the former is in effect to restrict the latter. Gambling may make people ignore their family obligations, but there are many other kinds of behavior that do the same thing. Law cannot create good citizens and model parents and spouses. If individuals clearly inflict physical injury, consistently and flagrantly fail to support their dependents, or violate the legal rights of others, there are already remedies for these harms. No special legislation is required for gamblers.

There are several anomalies in, and misunderstandings about, the practice of gambling. The professional gamblers who make book or operate casinos or run racetracks or sell numbers are really not gamblers at all. They are business entrepreneurs who have all the probabilities working in their favor, virtually guaranteeing them a profit. Some of these operators are protected by law; some are not. Jurisdictions often permit such operations because of the tax revenue derived. The "harm," presumably, is outweighed by the good the state can do with the money. It would seem that all forms of gambling should be tolerated if some are—so long as the operation is run honestly. With the "edge" claimed by the professionals (it is built into their system), there is really no need for them to cheat to make a profit. If individual bettors are foolish enough to deal with such operations, where the odds are against them across the board, they should be permitted to do so. What they are buying, perhaps, is excitement.

States not only permit some forms of gambling while prohibiting others, but occasionally go into the gambling business themselves. The lotteries are the most vicious form of all. Not only is the return for the bettors very low (much lower than on the gambling dollar spent in the casinos of Las Vegas), but there is no excitement as is derived from the running of horses, the spinning roulette wheel, or the draw to the inside straight. There is simply a number (abstract and lifeless), which may or may not denote a fortune. The "instant lotteries" in which the buyer knows immediately if he or she has won appeals to the person who wants or needs to make a quick killing. It is not surprising that most of the big winners in lotteries are poor and ignorant people. It is precisely such people who waste their money on such schemes as state lotteries. A better case could be made for the state itself to get out of the gambling business than for it to prohibit organized gambling.[71]

[71]The proposal in the spring of 1980 that the state of New York get into the numbers game was greeted with parades and demonstrations in the city by the illegal operators it would replace. A Harlem community leader chanted, "The numbers are for the people! One and inseparable!" A placard read, "The government takes this, the government takes that. The numbers remain with the people!" One partisan of "free enterprise" pointed out that the numbers operation employs thousands and is the fifth largest industry in New York City. The state is now muscling in! Is this another case where the official, who should regulate and monitor, is now "running with the ball"?

What is really unconscionable is the prohibition of gambling among private individuals—which is the case in many jurisdictions that permit organized gambling and state lotteries. The only time gamblers get a fair shake is when they are playing in a game (or lottery or pool) where all the money *stays in the game*. Nothing comes off the top for the professional or the state. In a poker game in Las Vegas, 10 to 15 percent comes out of each pot; in a poker game in someone's rec room, nothing comes out. In a craps game a casino will pay 6 to 1 for a "hard ten"; in a dice game in an alley you can get 8 to 1 (which represents the true odds). At the track, much of the money bet goes to the operator and the state; in an office pool, it all stays downtown.

Finally, we observe that the stereotype of the compulsive gambler should not be extended to apply to those who occasionally like to engage in a game of chance. That the former (a minority) may cause harm to others, does not justify the state in prohibiting the rest of us from gambling—or restricting our gambling to those forms that produce revenue for the state. The person who enjoys a poker game at home, the senior citizen who enjoys a game of bingo, and the couple who enjoy an evening at the track are exercising their freedom in legitimate, if not edifying, ways. The state should not interfere.

Paternalism Gerald Dworkin makes an interesting distinction between "pure" and "impure" paternalism. Pure paternalism consists in making laws against actions that would harm the agent. Impure paternalism consists in making laws against the actions of some that would leave the way open for others to be harmed. In the first case, the liberty of the persons whose benefit is intended is restricted. In the second case, the liberty of persons other than those whose benefit is intended is restricted. Examples of pure paternalism are legislation requiring seat belts, crash helmets, blood transfusions, and legislation against dueling, gambling using drugs, committing suicide, and swimming in areas without lifeguards. Examples of impure paternalism are forbidding the manufacture and distribution of cigarettes and drugs and the operation of gambling establishments and houses of prostitution. In the latter, while the liberty of some is restricted in order to prevent harm to others, it is not quite the same thing as, say, legislation against impure food or pollution of the air, for customers of the cigarette, drug, gambling, and prostitution proprietors can easily avoid the harmful "products" (they have free choice in the matter), while people who eat and breathe could not easily avoid the other products. "It may be that impure paternalism requires arguments or reasons of a stronger kind in order to be justified, since there are persons who are losing a portion of their liberty and they do not even have the solace of having it be done 'in their own interest.' "[72] It may be added that the customers are losing some freedom also, if there are no drug dealers or gambling operators that they can patronize.

[72]Gerald Dworkin, "Paternalism," Wasserstrom, *Morality and the Law*, p. 111.

Both kinds of paternalism are generally wrong, for they restrict freedom. But drug dealing is in a special category. While it is true that users or potential users may decline to buy the drugs, the harm that they would do themselves is so great that the drug dealer should be restricted from contributing to it. And the person already hooked on drugs really has very little choice in the matter—hardly more than those who have to breathe dirty air. If users want to concoct their own poisonous substances, let them do it, but do not permit others to profit in the trade. In this case, it is easier to defend "impure" paternalism than the "pure" variety.

Nude Bathing Finally, let us consider nude bathing. Such actions are supposed to belong to the class of actions that are "offensive." Indecent exposure, either stationary ("flashing") or moving ("streaking"), also belongs in this category. "Disgusting" actions such as public defecating and copulating may also be added. Should the state enforce a code of inoffensive behavior?

What may be offensive to some is often not offensive to others. Lurid posters depicting sexual acrobatics may offend some, but will be sought out by others. Public nudity will offend some, while others will form societies and pay dues in order to be a part of it. Some cannot witness defecation and copulation without a feeling of revulsion, while others can. Some find rock music and disco dancing offensive; others love them. The solution, then, to the problem of freedom to do "offensive" acts is simply to require that actions that seem likely to offend people be done in private. Nude bathing will be permitted in designated areas only. Raucous music will be permitted, but not to the extent that it will reach sensitive ears. People may flash, streak, defecate, and copulate to their heart's content, but not on a public sidewalk. When this principle is observed, other people will not be offended. They can easily avoid viewing the offensive act.[73]

The principle does not quite solve all the problems. There are a great many acts that some people would find offensive, and it does not appear feasible to shield them off from public view. The following actions would be offensive to some people: long hair or beards, interracial dating, the exhibition of certain advertisements, telephone soliciting, the display of bumper stickers, and people sleeping in the park. It cannot, however, be claimed that the harm felt by offended persons is extensive enough or acute enough to warrant legislation. This writer has an abiding antipathy toward leisure suits but would not dream of outlawing the wearing of them. We will simply have to tolerate these actions in the interest of

[73]A more difficult case of offensiveness was involved in the decision of the American Nazi organization to parade through the streets of Skokie, Illinois (after having been denied permission to hold a rally in a Chicago park). This was clearly offensive to the many Jews of Skokie (some of whom were concentration camp survivors). And while viewing the parade (or most of it) could be avoided, it could not "easily" be avoided. The American Civil Liberties Union defended the freedom of the Nazis to march. For pro and con arguments in this case, see Jonathan Bartlett, ed., *The First Amendment in a Free Society* (New York: H. W. Wilson Co., 1979), chap. 4.

freedom and in recognition of the right to be eccentric, for the harm they do us is either mild or chargeable to our *own* eccentricity.

It may be that we have dealt too flippantly with the offense form of the harm principle. It may be the last refuge of morals enforcers. If they can be induced to admit that no great concrete harm is produced for others by certain types of immoral action, and that society will not dissolve if its moral code is not protected by law, they may still maintain that some immoral acts are *offensive,* whether done in private or not. What offends them is not simply encounters with nude bathers, solicitations by a prostitute, the sight of lurid billboards, or confrontation with fornication, all of which they can rather easily avoid, but the realization that the society *tolerates* nudity, prostitution, pornography, and fornication. These things are offensive by virtue of their *existence,* whether viewed or not. They can be avoided but not ignored. There is not much that has to be said on this. "Offense" has now been converted from shock at direct confrontation to something like the reaction of the "moral sense." To say that anything that is offensive in *this* sense is harmful is to identify immorality with harm, and the proposition "Immorality ought to be legislated against" becomes a tautology. This takes us so far down the road of democratic tyranny as to warrant no further discussion.

The People and Their Government Should Place Significant Obstacles in the Way of Free Action by Individuals

The One-Sidedness of Libertarianism Mill makes a very strong case for a society of freely acting individuals, and no one can deny its partial truth. A sense of freedom is pleasurable for the agent, and social progress requires the existence of individuals who dare to be different. But all this is one-sided. There is another side to the issue that is at least as important. To ignore it is to court anarchy.

An emphasis on freedom is an invitation to ignore duties to others and to society itself. Individuals, avid to "do their own thing," see themselves as the source of all value and refuse to limit their voracious desires by any standard outside themselves. Impatient with restrictions imposed by public opinion and law, they tend to dispense with the restrictions of morality itself.

The philosophy of freedom was proclaimed by the French *philosophes* of the eighteenth century. Their contempt for history was notorious. They had no respect for human achievements in the past and suspected that most of the institutions of their day were founded on nothing more than force and superstition. Voltaire said of the Church, "*Ecrasez l'infâme!*" (Crush the infamous thing!). And D'Alembert said that the record of all past events should be blotted out. So adept were they in criticizing what they had inherited, in questioning everything that was established, that they often threw the baby out with the bath water. They did not look deeply enough into society's "prejudices" to see that some of them contained important truth. Bentham and his followers in Britain accepted this philosophy of freedom. They were so concerned about progress that they had no proper regard for conserving the values of the past. They valued change and ignored order. They preferred the insights of their own generation to the accumulated insights of the ages.

If progress is important (and it is), it is just as incumbent upon us to save what is good from the past as to discover new goods for the future. Edmund Burke, the great conservative, wrote: "People will not look forward to posterity, who never look backward to their ancestors. Besides, the people of England well know, that the idea of inheritance furnishes a sure principle of conservation, and a sure principle of transmission; without at all excluding a principle of improvement. It leaves acquisition free; but it secures what it acquires. . . . In what we improve we are never wholly new; in what we retain we are never wholly obsolete."[74]

Individualism in a society can go too far. There can be too much "eccentricity" and aberrant behavior. Society is, or can be, more than an aggregate of individuals. If it is only this, it is doubtful that we can even call it a society. A society consists of people with common interests, concerns, and loyalties. It is a *community,* a *commonwealth.* Its members are solicitous of one another, realizing that the effects of their actions pervade the whole society. Its members do not see themselves as separate atoms whirling around in a vacuum or supposed areas of "private space." It is the function of public opinion and law to prevent antisocial behavior, just as parents attempt to socialize their children. Society must achieve at least a moderate amount of unity, of a sense of devotion to a common enterprise.

The *philosophes* knew very well the deficiencies of the governments of their day and their predecessors. The notion of a "do-nothing" government attracted the political thinkers of the eighteenth and nineteenth centuries. Thomas Jefferson could say that the government is best which governs least, and the Benthamites would say that "governments can do no better than to do nothing." The anarchists took the next logical step and called for the elimination of government altogether. Burke's old foe, Thomas Paine, started talking about the "rights of man" and ended in anarchism. Crane Brinton assures us that "the debate between Burke and Paine, whose famous *Rights of Man* was a pamphlet in reply to Burke's *Reflections on the French Revolution*, has been decided in favor of Burke as clearly as the debate over the relation between the motions of sun and earth has been decided in favor of Copernicus."[75]

We may be forgiven for having a higher notion of government than that practiced by Bourbon kings, Russian czars, and English gentry. Government when democratic does not have to be the tool of "sinister interests." We believe that government can do many positive things on behalf of the community and

[74]Edmund Burke, *Reflections on the Revolution in France*. See *Reflections on the Revolution in France (Edmund Burke) and The Rights of Man (Thomas Paine)* (Garden City, N.Y.: Dolphin Books, 1961), pp. 45–46.

[75]See Peter Viereck, *Conservatism Revisited* (New York: Collier Books, 1962), p. 84.

its shared interests. It can regulate the conditions of work, thus softening the ravages of a laissez-faire economy. It can look out for the indigent and the weak. It can sponsor a comprehensive system of public education. It can harness the skills and energies of a people in ambitious projects of public works (e.g., TVA), exploration (e.g., placing a person on the moon), and scientific research (e.g., grants to scientists).

John Stuart Mill, the great apostle of freedom and individualism, could probably accept much of the above. We have only to read his essay on Coleridge[76] and certain sections of *Considerations on Representative Government*[77] to realize that his essay on liberty does not tell Mill's whole story. Even passages in later editions of *Principles of Political Economy* testify that *On Liberty* overstates the case. Those of us who read only *On Liberty* derive a distorted opinion of Mill's social philosophy.

Devlin and Public Morality It is doubtful, however, that Mill would grant to government the right to try to control in any direct way the moral tone of the society it serves. The Englishman Patrick Devlin argued in an influential book that society *does* have this right.

Lord Devlin first establishes the thesis that society has the right to pass judgment on matters of morality. That there is a public morality is acknowledged even by those who would not make it legally binding on individuals (e.g., the Wolfenden Committee). Although some individuals might believe that homosexuality, prostitution, and bigamy are acceptable ("private morality"), society in general condemns them. Monogamy, for example, became part of the structure of society because it is Christian, "but remains there because it is built into the house in which we live and could not be removed without bringing it down."[78] Even non-Christians, if they are to live in our society, must accept it.

> Society means a community of ideas; without shared ideas on politics, morals, and ethics no society can exist. Each one of us has ideas about what is good and what is evil; they cannot be kept private from the society in which we live. If men and women try to create a society in which there is no fundamental agreement about good

[76]See, for example, his discussion of the prerequisites for a "permanent political society": a system of education, "one main and incessant ingredient" of which is restraint and discipline, a feeling of allegiance or loyalty, and "a strong and active principle of cohesion among the members of the same community or state." The *philosophes,* he said, "threw away the shell, without preserving the kernel; and, attempting to new-model society without the binding forces which hold society together, met with such success as might have been anticipated." Does it follow that a free government "cannot exercise a free agency of its own?—that it cannot beneficially employ its powers, its means of information, and its pecuniary resources (so far surpassing those of any other association or of any individual), in promoting the public welfare by a thousand means which individuals would never think of, would have no sufficient motives to attempt, or no sufficient powers to accomplish?" Mill, *Coleridge,* in *The Six Great Humanistic Essays of John Stuart Mill*, pp. 89–91, 94, 114–115.

[77]See especially chap. 2.

[78]Devlin, *The Enforcement of Morals*, p. 9.

and evil they will fail; if, having based it on common agreement, the agreement goes, the society will disintegrate. For society is not something that is kept together physically; it is held by the invisible bonds of common thought. If the bonds were too far relaxed the members would drift apart. A common morality is part of the bondage. The bondage is part of the price of society; and mankind, which needs society, must pay the price.[79]

The next question that Devlin raises is whether society has the right to enforce public morality by law. It surely has a prima facie right to do so, for if a recognized morality is essential to the existence of a society, it has the right to safeguard it. Even the Wolfenden Committee believes that the young should be protected against exploitation and corruption. It admits that exploitation is also involved in prostitution and other immoral acts between consenting adults. It cannot, however, draw the line that separates warranted from unwarranted interference. It is really impossible, says Devlin, to draw a line between permissible and impermissible legislation against immorality. We must prevent the disintegration of society from within, just as we do from without, and we are entitled to choose appropriate means. "The suppression of vice is as much the law's business as the suppression of subversive activities; it is no more possible to define a sphere of private morality than it is to define one of private subversive activity."[80]

How do we establish the tenets of public morality? Not by taking polls. Instead, we rely on the standard of "the reasonable man," "the right-minded man." His reasonable views are derived not from theological or philosophical meditation, but from the continuous sharing in the experience of society. What the right-minded person holds is a conception of "practical morality" grounded in "common sense."

Devlin does not maintain that the individual must "surrender to the judgement of society the whole conduct of his life."[81] There must be give and take, an attempt to reconcile counteracting claims, each of which has some merit on its side. The solution does not lie in the impossible aim of carving out separate areas of private and public morality. "There must be toleration of the maximum individual freedom that is consistent with the integrity of society."[82] This principle is different also from the one that we should restrict the few for the convenience of the many.

The principle may be applied in the light of three rules. (1) One indicator of the limit of toleration is the *feeling of reprobation* experienced by society. Is the feeling of disgust real and deeply felt? If society genuinely abhors cruelty to animals, homosexuality, and prostitution, it has the right to eradicate them. "Not

[79]Ibid., p. 10.
[80]Ibid., pp. 13–14.
[81]Ibid., p. 15.
[82]Ibid., p. 16.

everything is to be tolerated. No society can do without intolerance, indignation, and disgust; they are the forces behind the moral law" and they must be present before individuals can be deprived of free choice.[83] (2) *Changes in laws enforcing morality* should not be quickly made. This is because, while the social morality may not change much over the course of time, society's tolerance of immorality does shift. If, in a permissive period, we weaken the law, we seem to support immorality. If in an "intolerant" period we pass a law, it may lack the strong support needed when society's sense of indignation has abated. (3) *Privacy should be respected*. The police should never have a general right to search. One's home is one's castle. This is not an absolute rule, but it is something to be taken into account. An action that does not flout common decency is not to be feared as much as one done openly with disregard of society's sensibilities.

If Devlin is right, the harm that immoral action produces in the form of destroying the quality of the life of society itself should be added to the more concrete harms acknowledged to result from such immoral actions as prostitution and other sexual transgressions.[84]

Euthanasia The lengths to which libertarians can go is indicated by their support of euthanasia—an act that clearly harms the victims, whether he or she knows it or not. Involuntary euthanasia, whether active or passive, places too much reliance on the "loved ones." They may have a lot to gain by the death—easing a burden, decreasing costs, or coming into an inheritance, for example. Even when these considerations are not relevant, a misguided sympathy for the suffering of the victim may bring about an impulsive decision. No one knows for sure that a condition is hopeless. Medical conditions that were hopeless yesterday are treatable today. The ailing person must be given every opportunity to recover. This consideration bears on voluntary euthanasia also. While we cannot always prevent individuals from committing suicide (and laws against it have no deterrent effect), laws against *aiding* them should be supported. Instead, we should do everything we can to prolong their lives and to enlist their support in this aim. What significance can their "choice" to die have? If it was made before their illness or injury, they may want to change it when they are wrestling with death. If it is made in the hospital, it may be dictated by pain or poor judgment or simply the wish not to be a drain on the emotions or finances of loved ones. Here too, they may change their minds from day to day.

There is one good point made by some of the pro-euthanasia people, and that is that there is no real difference between withholding the means of life and killing. The conclusion that we should draw from the difficulty of making the distinction

[83]Ibid., p. 17.

[84]The specific harms produced by commercialized prostitution and pornography are recognized in the *Model Penal Code of the American Law Institute* (1962). See *Columbia Law Review* 63 (1963): 669ff and Louis B. Schwartz, "Moral Offenses and the Model Penal Code," in Wasserstrom, *Morality and the Law,* p. 87ff.

is that the law should prohibit *both* active and passive euthanasia. If it permits the one (passive), it encourages doctors surreptitiously to perform the other. Doctors know that inaction is a form of action; and if lethal instances of the former are permitted, it is not a great step to perform the lethal acts *actively.*

The best argument against euthanasia is the one based on rule utilitarianism. Adherence to a rule that life should be respected and upheld in all cases (except in self-defense and just war) has great utility for society. Act utilitarianism may also be used against euthanasia. To make exceptions to a general rule that protects the life of innocent people would weaken the sentiment that gives the rule its efficacy: respect for human life. We may strictly limit euthanasia, but to permit it at all (even conceding some utility) will, since we will have compromised the respect-for-life principle, make it easier to extend euthanasia to defective children and hopelessly senile adults. Every weakening of the respect-for-life principle makes it easier to weaken it still more at a later time.[85] This comes to be, therefore, a substantial social harm. The law must consistently take its stand on the side of life. It must provide no excuse for people to reduce their respect for life. If people must die, let it be a natural death in the true sense: one that occurs in the face of all medical attempts to prevent it.

The Harm Principle In all the other cases cited by the libertarian we find a great reluctance to accept any harm that is not direct and substantial. There is no reason that society should protect itself *only* from direct and substantial harm. Why should individuals be protected in performing *any* harmful action? The harm principle should be applied not strictly, but *whenever* the public welfare is endangered. The area of individual freedom will still be an extensive one if restricted to actions that are not harmful *at all.* The public has a right to protect itself against nuisances like drug addiction and gambling. If these activities are a drain on public resources, they should be curbed. In doing this, society does not blight any individual's life or arrest anyone's self-development. The attempt in the case of drug usage to distinguish drug *consumption* from drug *peddling* is disingenuous and is similar to the former practice of arresting prostitutes and letting their clients go free. Both the buyer and the seller are parties to the same transaction. If the presence of people ruined by drugs and committing crimes in order to acquire drugs is a public problem (and it is), then anyone who contributes to the problem (buyer and seller) should be restrained. The libertarian argues that

[85]This danger is implicit in the program of Dr. Sackett. "He spoke specifically about the 1,500 severely mentally and physically retarded residents of two institutions in Florida, 'some with heads as big as buckets, some small as oranges, grotesque and drawn up in contracture.' Thirty to forty years ago such severely defective children usually died at an early age, but now they can be kept alive until they are 50 or 60. Dr. Sackett stated that it will cost the state of Florida five billion dollars to care for that number of helpless defectives over the next 50 years; on the national level it will cost roughly 100 billion dollars to care for them. He thought that money might better be spent saving the lives of those who could benefit from medical care rather than on those so severely retarded that they are 'bedridden, diapered, tube-fed and completely unaware.'" Russell, *Freedom to Die,* pp. 178–179.

if we restrain the seller, the buyer will have no one to turn to. But one could argue it the other way too: Restraining the buyer would deprive the seller of a market. Surely it makes more sense to place legal disabilities on *both*.

Before we leave this subject, we should question the validity of the harm principle itself. Is there not, after all, a place for public concern for the welfare of individuals? This is called paternalism, and *paternalism* is a dirty word. But why should this be so? The protective concern of an older and more experienced person for the young and inexperienced is a noble thing. The state with its traditions, resources, and enlightened leadership may function in a way not too different from that of an older counselor. It may, in a gentle or severe way, protect its people from moral corruption, drug addiction, compulsive gambling, and dangerous and debilitating practices. It does protect us from impure food, inform us about cancer research, and insist on certain safety precautions in industry. It tells us what we may study in the schools. Many people look to the state for guidance. We are in willing tutelage when we see the benefits. If the state conducts experiments on automobile accidents and then orders us to wear seat belts, we should gratefully obey. The case for mandatory helmets for motorcyclists is also very strong.[86] Some people, who would like to give up smoking, even wish that the state would make the sale of cigarettes illegal![87] There is a limit to political paternalism, of course, but when it protects us from ourself, it is a benign and welcome practice.

John Stuart Mill, because of the value he places on freedom, denies the propriety of virtually all paternalistic acts. But he does make exceptions. One obvious one is on the freedom to sell oneself into slavery.[88] This freedom he denies—quite paternalistically—because of the harm to the person himself. The harm consists in loss of future freedom. In his *Principles of Political Economy* he admits of exceptions to the principle that people take a "juster and more intelligent views of their own interest" than that which their government can do. One exception is in the field of education.[89] Another is the case of entering into irrevocable contracts without sufficient knowledge of the future.[90] Another is the case of the person who favors the aims of certain collective action that can be achieved only

[86]The fatality rate for motorcyclists is seven times that for automobile occupants. Between 1977 and 1979, twenty-eight states either repealed or weakened their laws requiring helmet use. The result was a 40 percent jump in fatalities. Joan Claybrook of the National Highway Traffic Safety Administration said, "This has been a horrible social science experiment." See Jane E. Brody, "Repeal of Helmet Law Proves Deadly to Cyclists," *Edwardsville Intelligencer,* July 21, 1980, p. 7.

[87]Did not Odysseus instruct his men to tie him firmly to the mast so that he would not misuse his freedom later when the sirens beckoned?

[88]Mill, *On Liberty,* V, p. 227.

[89]"The uncultivated cannot be competent judges of cultivation." See Mill, *Principles of Political Economy,* ed. W. J. Ashley (London: Longmans, Green, and Co., 1909), book 5, chap. 11, sec. 8, pp. 953–956.

[90]"The practical maxim of leaving contracts free is not applicable without great limitations in case of engagements in perpetuity." Such contracts occur in business—and in matrimony. See ibid., sec. 10, p. 960.

if the group acts in concert but who, without legislation, might be tempted to act in opposition to it (e.g., the nine-hour day).[91]

As a matter of fact, individuals often do not take an intelligent view of their own interests. Some are children, and should be protected. Some are *like* children, and should be protected. We should save money for our old age, but if Social Security (or some kind of retirement system) did not require us to, many of us would not. We are often ill-informed. We sometimes act impulsively or in a state of great emotion. We may want to commit suicide today, but may see things differently tomorrow. Sometimes we are insane and would do ourselves great harm unless we were committed and restored to mental health.[92] Gerald Dworkin suggests "that we would be most likely to consent to paternalism in those instances in which it preserves and enhances for the individual his ability to rationally consider and carry out his own decisions."[93] This is quite in the spirit of Mill. Dworkin makes out a very good case for a great many paternalistic acts —including the famous seat-belt example.

In summary, we have argued that society should take a broad interpretation of "harm" when the actions of individuals tend to harm others, but this is not the only principle. Society also has the duty to protect individuals from the follies of their own actions. How far society goes in restricting human freedom is determined by society's own conception of the nature of a good society.

Summary of the Issues

No one can deny the value of freedom in itself and as a means for developing one's own nature and contributing to the progress of society. One side, however, emphasizes it and calls for eccentricity. It opposes prohibiting evil acts ("legislating morality") even though these actions may produce harmful consequences. Except when the harm is substantial, unmistakable, and to *others,* the harm prevented does not compensate for the loss of freedom. There is no reason to believe that individuals require a public stand against "immorality" in order to act according to their own moral standards: They can distinguish between "legal" and "moral." The other side holds that libertarianism is one-sided. Progress requires preservation of the values from the past as well as discovery of new goods for the future. Too much eccentricity can be a bad thing in itself and socially disruptive. Society not only should pass judgment on morality but should enforce

[91]"The interference of the law is required, not to overrule the judgment of individuals respecting their own interest, but to give effect to that judgment: they being unable to give effect to it except by concert, which concert cannot be effectual unless it receives validity and sanction from the law." See ibid., sec. 12, pp. 963–966.

[92]Mill specifically excludes lunatics, idiots, and children from his bar against paternalism, but pointedly does *not* exclude women! See ibid., sec. 9, pp. 956–959.

[93]Gerald Dworkin, "Paternalism," in Wasserstrom, *Morality and the Law,* p. 125. This paragraph and the preceding one are indebted to Dworkin's excellent article.

that aspect of it that is essential to its existence. Laws should reflect the moral values of society in order that it not disintegrate from within. While society will not, of course, regulate all actions, it must preserve its collective moral integrity.

A parallel difference of opinion is present on the question of influencing morals through nonlegal means. One side will accept argument, persuasion, and training (of children); the other side will accept public pressure and indoctrination. The main concern in the debate, however, is with legal sanctions. But in both cases, the issue is whether society should take a stand in order to prevent moral chaos and disorder.

Four kinds of undesirable actions are considered. The question is whether the harm they cause to others is of the type of warrant prohibition.

1. Actions that may be assumed to be immoral. In the case of prostitution, one side argues that the harm to others is neither direct nor substantial, and it is not uniquely linked with prostitution. The other side could dispute this. In the case of euthanasia, one side argues that neither voluntary, nonvoluntary, passive, nor active euthanasia (in many cases) is productive of harm for others in sufficient degree to warrant its prohibition. Individuals must be permitted to follow their own moral beliefs in deciding whether to perform or assist in acts of euthanasia. There may be legal guidelines for nonvoluntary euthanasia, but a large scope of discretion must be preserved for individual choice. The other side holds that involuntary euthanasia (whether active or passive) produces great harm, and so does assistance in voluntary euthanasia. Just as serious as the harm to the victim is the harm to society in general when the principle of respect for life is compromised.

2. Actions that are dangerous. One side argues that they should be prohibited only if they pose a definite and likely threat to others. The other side tries to show that they often do.

3. Actions that are clearly harmful to oneself. One side would prohibit drug use and gambling only if they can be shown to be directly and substantially harmful to others—and they usually cannot. The other side stresses the harm to others. Drug *dealers* would be barred by the libertarian, for they are purveying products clearly harmful *to others.*

4. Actions that are offensive. One side, again, would prohibit offensive acts (such as nude bathing) only when they really bother others *and* when they cannot easily be avoided. The other side will emphasize the degree of offensiveness and the difficulty of avoiding it.

The antilibertarian position is at a disadvantage in many of these arguments, especially the second and third. Though its proponents will argue about the degree and scope of harm to others, they are in some cases opposed to the paramount importance of the harm principle. Instead, they would rely on paternalism. For the libertarian, paternalism is appropriate only for children and the mentally disabled; but their opponents believe that paternalism represents a noble sentiment and is a benign and legitimate province of government.

Discussion Questions

1. Is Mill saying in effect that one has the right to be immoral? If so, isn't this paradoxical? If not, what *is* he saying?
2. Do you believe that prostitution should be legalized? Why?
3. Where prostitution is illegal, do you think the client ought to be arrested along with the prostitute? Why?
4. Do you think the line between moral training and indoctrination can be drawn? Explain.
5. Under what conditions, if any, would you permit a person to perform an act of nonvoluntary euthanasia?
6. Do you think it is reasonable to permit passive euthanasia while prohibiting active euthanasia? Why?
7. In some countries, it is mandatory to wear seat belts in cars. Would you favor such a law in the United States? Why?
8. How would you distinguish Mill's humanism from that of theories of self-realization? Which is more defensible? Why?
9. Is it wise, in your opinion, to require that offensive action be both very offensive *and* not easily avoidable in order to be prohibited? Why? Give examples.
10. Do you think that the harm principle is too vague to do the job it is asked to do? Can you think of any alternative?
11. Do you think that a libertarian society would be a licentious one? Why?
12. Do you think that a society that did not reflect its basic moral values in its laws would lose its unity and identity? Why?
13. Are there, in your opinion, any "victimless crimes" in this country? If so, should they be declared no longer crimes? Why?
14. Do you agree with the contention that drug users should not be punished by law, but that drug dealers should be severely punished? Why?
15. Would you defend the right of individuals to gamble but prohibit the existence of professional gamblers? Why? What if the professionals are dishonest?
16. What justification, if any, does the state have if it forbids professional gambling but operates a lottery?
17. Should homosexual relations between consenting adults be prohibited by law? Why?
18. Should live sex shows be prohibited by law? Why?
19. What is your attitude toward nude bathing on public beaches? Explain.
20. Do you think that it would be consistent to legalize prostitution when adults are involved, but to ban it when children are involved? Why?
21. What is your view of paternalism by statute?
22. What is your view of paternalism by public opinion?
23. What is the legal situation of living wills in your state? Do you think it should be changed? Why?

24. Do you think that a pro-euthanasia position places one on a "slippery slope"? Explain.
25. Do you think that the Moral Majority is trying to legislate morality?
26. What bearing does the fact of ethical disagreement have on the question of legislating morality? Do you think that this consideration is carried too far by libertarians? Explain.

For Further Reading

Paul C. Bartholomew. *Significant Decisions of the Supreme Court.* Washington: American Enterprise Institute for Public Policy Research, annual publication.

John W. Chapman and Pennock J. Roland, eds. *The Limits of Law* (*Nomos* XV). New York: Lieber-Atherton, 1974.

David A. Conway. "Law, Liberty, and Indecency." *Philosophy* 49 (1974):135ff.

Patrick Devlin. *The Enforcement of Morals.* London: Oxford University Press, 1969.

A. B. Downing, ed. *Euthanasia and the Right to Death: The Case for Voluntary Euthanasia.* New York: Humanities Press, 1969.

J. C. Dybilowski. "Lord Devlin's Morality and Its Enforcement." *Proceedings of the Aristotelian Society* 75 (1974–1975):89ff.

Jonathan Gould and Lord Craigmyle, eds. *Your Death Warrant?* New York: Arlington House, 1971.

H. L. A. Hart. *Law, Liberty and Morality.* Stanford, Calif.: Stanford University Press, 1963.

Paul Kurtz. *Moral Problems in Contemporary Society.* 2nd ed. Buffalo: Prometheus Books, 1973. Chapter 3.

Burton M. Leiser *Liberty, Justice, and Morality.* 2nd ed. New York: Macmillan Publishing Co., 1979. Chapters 1–3.

Marya Mannes. *Last Rights.* New York: William Morrow and Co., 1973.

Thomas A. Mappes and Jane S. Zembaty, eds. *Social Ethics: Morality and Social Policy.* New York: McGraw-Hill Book Co., 1977. Chapters 2, 7.

Donald Meiklejohn. *Freedom and the Public: Public and Private Morality in America.* New York: Oxford University Press, 1965.

John Stuart Mill. *On Liberty.* Many editions. Parts III–V.

B. Mitchell. *Law, Morality and Religion in a Secular Society* London: Oxford University Press, 1967.

Peter Radcliff, ed. *Limits of Liberty.* Belmont, Calif., Wadsworth Publishing Co., 1966.

David Riesman et al. *The Lonely Crowd.* New York: Doubleday Anchor Books, 1954.

Wade L. Robison and Michael S. Pritchard, eds. *Medical Responsibility: Paternalism, Informed Consent, and Euthanasia.* Clifton, N.J.: The Humana Press, 1979.

O. Ruth Russell. *Freedom to Die.* New York: Dell Publishing Co., 1976.

Norman St. John-Stevas. *Life, Death and the Law.* Bloomington: Indiana University Press, 1961.

Edwin M. Schur. *Crimes without Victims.* Englewood Cliffs, N.J.: Prentice-Hall, 1965.

Alexis de Tocqueville. *Democracy in America.* Many editions.

Richard Wasserstrom, ed. *Morality and the Law.* Belmont, Calif.: Wadsworth Publishing Co., 1971.

Glanville Williams. *The Sanctity of Life and the Criminal Law.* New York: Alfred A. Knopf, 1957.
"Wolfenden Report." *Report of the Committee on Homosexual Offenses and Prostitution.* New York: Stein and Day, 1963.

CIVIL DISOBEDIENCE

Civil Disobedience in a Democracy Is Always Wrong

Disobeying a law is, of course, illegal. The issue is whether it may sometimes be moral.

Dissent and Disobedience Socrates, according to Plato's account in *Crito,* argued that we have a moral duty to obey the state. The state has provided us with security, nourishment, education, "and a share in all the good things at [its] disposal." There is an implicit contract between the individual and the state: in return for benefits, the individual owes obedience.

Individuals are not helpless pawns in a democratic state. They can work to change laws and policies they believe to be unjust. Legal procedures and channels are open to them. As voters they possess political rights equal to those of everyone else. They cannot expect their view of what the laws should be always to prevail. Fairness requires that they accept majority rule while working to alter its perception of justice. Modern democracies protect the rights of free speech, free press, and free assembly. Supreme Court Justice Abe Fortas states:

> The protestor has the full scope of First Amendment rights. He is entitled to the full protection of the state and the courts in the exercise of speech and symbolic speech, however hostile. . . . Our scheme of law affords great latitude for dissent and opposition. It compels wide toleration not only for their expression but also for the organization of people and forces to bring about the acceptance of the dissenter's claim. Both our institutions and the characteristics of our national behavior make it possible for opposition to be translated into policy, for dissent to prevail.[94]

There are, in a democracy, alternatives to disobedience.

There is still another recourse open to individuals who feel that the laws of their state are unjust, and Socrates recognizes it: They may leave the state. If they feel that the "contract" is not in their interest because they are required to be a part of an immoral enterprise or because the state has not kept its part of the bargain, they can emigrate. This view is the forerunner of the contemporary slogan "America—love it or leave it."

In recent years, civil disobedience has become very popular among activists, and even defended by philosophers who should know better. Their objective has

[94]Fortas, *Concerning Dissent and Civil Disobedience,* pp. 47, 61.

been to protest against political policies or laws that they regard as unjust. They violate the "unjust" law itself and, in order to create dramatic publicity, other laws as well. After World War II, the atmospheric testing of nuclear weapons was a popular target. Then civil rights leaders protested voting laws and segregation in the South. The Vietnam War sparked action against the war itself and the draft law as well. Universities that were believed to support the war or discrimination also experienced the anger of the activists. Distributive injustice in the ghettos was another "policy" that inspired civil disobedience. Today, the issues that inspire most civil disobedience are the construction and operation of nuclear power plants and abortion clinics.

Civil disobedients have refused to be drafted, have burned draft cards, and have broken into government buildings to destroy records. They have conducted sit-ins, talk-ins, and be-ins. They have occupied university and government offices. They have disrupted meetings, traffic, and the conduct of business. They have demonstrated in defiance of laws designed to protect the public safety and the rights of others. They have "trashed" premises and destroyed property. They have burned buildings and have contributed to the bodily injury of many and the death of some. So earnest have they been in their moral convictions that they have utterly ignored the moral value of law and order itself. So desperate have they been to achieve their aim that they viewed with contempt the legal political channels open to them.

We may agree with many of the aims of the civil disobedients, but must deplore their methods. The rest of society has convictions also, and they deserve respect. The outraged minority arbitrarily discounts *others'* views and employs direct action to make their own views the dominant ones. They want new laws but weaken the very legal system that would administer them once they were successful. They alienate law-abiding people who might support them if their methods were not so radical. They give their causes (occasionally noble ones) a bad name, as they become identified in the public mind with anarchism.

Moral Justifications One argument of the civil disobedient is based on the London Agreement of 1945, which established the International Military Tribunal to conduct the trials at Nuremberg. The agreement stated that the fact that an individual acted on orders does not free him or her of responsibility for crimes against peace, crimes of war, and crimes against humanity. Just as Germans should have refused on moral grounds to participate in Nazi atrocities, so too Americans should refuse on moral grounds to participate in immoral national programs; and just as the Germans should have illegally stopped the crimes, so too should Americans. This is a poor argument. In the first place, the analogy is a bad one. None of the "crimes" that the United States may have committed are as indisputably monstrous as those committed by Nazi Germany. Moreover, the Nuremberg tribunal did not try to punish *all* the people involved in the crimes. It sought the leaders, the instigators, the driving forces. The people who were actually convicted had substantial freedom of choice. They were not bureaucrats or soldiers in the lower echelons, but were dedicated leaders who conceived and created plans and enthusiastically carried them out. Those many Germans who obeyed (perhaps reluctantly) and followed orders because they were the "law of the land" were not prosecuted.

In the case of America, individuals who believe that capital punishment or abortion is immoral cannot be blamed if the government, which their tax money supports, conducts or condones such actions. Nor can the rank and file who answer the draft call be blamed if the commander in chief employs the armed forces in ways that the draftees think are immoral. Many of us cannot condone the support given to the Shah of Iran or the bombing of Cambodia, but we know that officials are fallible and we do not try to pull down the government whenever this fallibility is demonstrated. We value law and government policy because of the good things they accomplish, and when they err we use the channels available to change them.

One moral justification that the civil disobedient occasionally relies on is the principle that people who are willing to pay the penalty for violating a law are morally justified in violating it. They have not sought to escape or to argue contentiously in court, so their hands are clean. If this makes sense at all, it does so only on a retributive theory of punishment: the society has redressed the wrong by punishing the wrongdoer, and true balance in society has been restored. That this approach is wrong-headed may be seen in such cases as these: the murderer has not justified murder by being executed; the rapist has not restored the sanity of his victim by serving a fifteen-year sentence; vandals can never "pay for" the masterpiece they have destroyed. Whatever else it may do, punishment does not wipe the slate clean.

Possible Exceptions There are two cases that would seem to be exceptions to our thesis that civil disobedience is always wrong.

The first has to do with the matter of conscientious objection to serving in the armed services. Draft acts since 1864 have exempted from combat any person who was conscientiously opposed to war in any form by reason of "religious training and belief." Such a person will be assigned a noncombat job; and if he is conscientiously opposed to military service in any form, he will be assigned "work of national importance under civilian direction." As originally construed, the draft law in operation during the Vietnam War could not grant C.O. status to a person whose opposition to war was based simply on moral convictions. In the *Seeger* case of 1965, the Supreme Court let stand the law's stipulation that exemption could not be granted on the basis of "essentially political, sociological, of philosophical views or a merely personal code," but did declare that people who held a profound "belief that is sincere and meaningful" and that occupied "a place in the life of its possessor parallel to that filled by the orthodox belief in God of one who clearly qualifies for the exemption" could themselves be exempted. This was a great step forward, although no relief was offered to those who were selective as to which wars they conscientiously opposed. Despite the draft law, then, people otherwise eligible for military service could be excused on moral grounds. This was not a case of civil disobedience; they did not have to *disobey the law*. They had only to qualify for exemptions provided by the law itself.

The second possible exception has to do with the testing of laws that are believed to be invalid because they conflict, not with moral law, but with higher levels of human law. Individuals may disobey these laws—in nonviolent and peaceful ways—until they are upheld or invalidated by courts of a higher jurisdiction. The movement led by Martin Luther King, Jr., was clearly of this kind. He and his followers openly disobeyed invalid laws and, despite having to spend some time in jail, were ultimately vindicated. Abe Fortas offers three other examples: John Milton refused to seek permission for official censors to publish a book, believing that the law requiring it violated basic English rights. Vivian Kellems refused to pay withholding taxes, believing that the law requiring it conflicted with the Bill of Rights. A young man refused to report for induction, believing that the draft law was unconstitutional since the United States was not officially at war. But when the Supreme Court speaks, that should be the end of the matter. If the law is struck down, the petitioners were right in regarding it as invalid, and in the strict sense were not civil disobedients at all. If the Court upholds the law (or refuses to consider its constitutionality), the petitioners were wrong and, realizing this, will employ other methods to try to change it.

Conclusion Thomas Hobbes, who had seen a great deal of disobedience in his long life, had great respect for the law and the system of peace and order that it upheld. So great was his respect that he taught obedience to the sovereign whether it was democratic or not. He recounted the Old Testament story of Naaman, who was forced by his king to bow down to false gods. Naaman did well to obey. The infidelity attached not to him but to the king.

> When the civil sovereign is an infidel, every one of his own subjects that resisteth him, sinneth against the laws of God (for such are the laws of nature), and rejecteth the counsel of the apostles, that admonishes all Christians to obey their princes, and all children and servants to obey their parents and masters in all things. And for their *faith,* it is internal and invisible; they have the license that Naaman had, and need not put themselves into danger for it. But if they do, they ought to expect their reward in heaven, and not complain of their lawful sovereign; much less make war upon him.[95]

This will seem extreme to many of us. But Hobbes does bring out the principle that one may obey the state in even its unjust programs without incurring guilt. In obeying, one meets the moral requirement of keeping the peace; in withholding spiritual assent, one maintains one's moral integrity.

[95]Thomas Hobbes, *Leviathan,* ed. Michael Oakeshott (New York: Crowell-Collier, 1962), III, 43, p. 436.

Civil Disobedience in a Democracy Is Not Always Wrong

Selective Disobedience Margaret Sanger (1883–1965) disobeyed the Comstock Laws of 1873, which prohibited using the mails to distribute birth control information. She violated state laws against the use and sale of contraceptives. She challenged municipal laws against the establishment of birth control clinics. She was arrested several times and was imprisoned. She never agreed to stop her disobedience of the laws in return for freedom or a lighter sentence. Having "witnessed the destructive burdens of unchecked reproduction among the poor and underprivileged,"[96] she felt that her cause was just and her disobedience of the law moral.

Civil disobedients are not opposed to law or public policy as such. They are not anarchists. They select a particular law or policy that is intolerably unjust, defy it, and leave the rest of the structure standing. Not even Thoreau withheld *all* his taxes. Those laws that supported the extension of slavery were bad; those that supported highway construction were not. Civil disobedients, knowing that perfect justice is impossible, will accept some injustices in a democratic state. But they will rise up against others that are especially serious and grievous. Only if policies and laws in general are viewed as unjust would anarchism be seen as a preferable alternative.

Civil disobedience is not an act of revolution. It does not aim at destroying the government. It does not employ violent means. It aims at getting a policy or a law changed by refusing to support that policy or obey that law. The experience of Socrates is often misinterpreted. He did *not* agree to give up his questioning and speculation. If he had, he would not have been executed. He was, and remained, a civil disobedient.

The Requirements of Genuine Civil Disobedience Norman Bowie and Robert Simon make a good case for viewing civil disobedience as a *support* for democratic institutions.[97] Citizens employ it in order to make a moral appeal to others for support in getting grievances redressed. They hope that disobedience will provoke a public discussion that will induce the government to reexamine its policies and change them. If the purpose of government is to promote justice, the disobedient performs a valuable function by arousing support for the correction of an injustice.

It is for this reason that the philosophy of civil disobedience requires, first of all, that the act be *done in public.* Secret disobedience would have no effect on public opinion. It would simply be an act of injury to the state. This would be acceptable in a tyranny but not in a democratic state. The reason disobedients

[96]Sheila Ruth, *Issues in Feminism* (Boston: Houghton Mifflin Co., 1980), p. 506.
[97]See Bowie and Simon, *The Individual and the Political Order,* p. 239ff.

act openly is that they *expect* to get support. They believe that "the principles [they invoke] are principles" that "are generally acknowledged."[98] Moral conviction is present, but they do not present themselves as moral innovators who are going to change things around or as conscientious members of a particular group seeking special dispensation (such as Quakers who refuse to serve in the armed services). Their actions are also different, to use Marshall Cohen's examples, from those of the young man who surreptitiously evades the draft and the doctor who secretly performs an illegal abortion.

Second, the act must be *nonviolent.* Martin Luther King, Jr., following the teaching and example of Mohandas Gandhi, would in the spirit of respect for life avoid physical injuries to others. This humanitarian interest serves certain strategic interests as well. Violent means would alarm much of the public the disobedients hope to win over. The disobedients would be seen as revolutionists and distrusted. The conduct of the Weathermen and other violent groups a decade or so ago went beyond civil disobedience. Bombing, arson, beatings, and rock-throwing not only injure people but arouse the righteous indignation of the "silent majority." Nonviolent resistance is based on the principle that disobedients are willing to endure more suffering than they inflict, that they will be the patient and innocent recipients of all the evil the state can impose. Violence alarms the authorities and brings about counteraction that the disobedients are unable to resist. When Governor Rhodes sent the National Guard to the campus of Kent State University in the spring of 1970, he stated that the organized radicals were "worse than the Brown Shirts and the Communist element and also the night-riders and vigilantes. They are the worst type of people that we harbor in America." Violence on the part of disobedients provokes greater violence from the state (as it did in Chicago in 1968 and on the Kent State campus). This in turn can provoke increased violence from the protesters, and the result is civil war—or at least guerrilla warfare. At this point, the moral issue is lost. Civil disobedience must be viewed by others as an *appeal,* not an attack.[99]

Exactly what "violence" is to mean is a matter of disagreement among advocates of civil disobedience. If it means that we should not inflict bodily harm at all, an act of self-immolation would be wrong—even if, in a given situation, it brought some people to their senses. If it means that we should not cause physical damage to things, destruction of property would always be wrong. Cohen suggests that this might be a mistake, "for the violation of symbolically important

[98]Cohen, "Civil Disobedience in a Constitutional Democracy." See Beauchamp, *Ethics and Public Policy,* p. 146.

[99]Martin Luther King, Jr., said it well: "Violence as a way of achieving racial justice is both impractical and immoral. It is impractical because it is a descending spiral ending in destruction for all. The old law of an eye for an eye leaves everybody blind. It is immoral because it seeks to humiliate the opponent rather than win his understanding; it seeks to annihilate rather than convert. Violence is immoral because it thrives on hatred rather than love. It destroys community and makes brotherhood impossible. It leaves society in monologue rather than dialogue. Violence ends by defeating itself. It creates bitterness in the survivors and brutality in the destroyers." *Stride toward Freedom,* p. 213.

property may be a dramatic, and not very dangerous way of lodging effective protests, and the razing of the slums had been understood as a cry of despair as often as it has been perceived as a declaration of war."[100] The view held here is that civil disobedience should not endanger the safety of other people and that destruction of property is justified only in extreme cases and only when it may be expected to have beneficial results.

The third element in legitimate civil disobedience is that disobedients should be willing to *take their punishment* for violating the law. They recognize the legal right of the state to enforce its laws. They claim no immunity. They do not say that this willingness *excuses* their action, for they need no excuse; or that they and the state are now "even," for they still believe that the state is acting unjustly in not changing its law or policy. They demonstrate that they are so convinced of the rightness of their cause that they are willing to suffer for it. Civil disobedients may win sympathy and support from the public when it is seen that the injustice they protest is serious enough to inspire the willingness to undergo extensive pain.

Finally, legitimate civil disobedience must *confine itself to actions against the law or policy that is being protested.* The concept of civil disobedience does not justify wholesale defiance of all laws or of laws that are only remotely connected with the issue in question. The case of Margaret Sanger is relatively simple. The law said not to distribute contraceptives. She did. The American policy of fighting a war in Vietnam was not itself a law, so could not itself be violated. In this case "indirect disobedience" is necessary. The building of nuclear power plants is also something that does not lend itself to direct disobedience. Sit-ins, marches, demonstrations, and acts of disruption must be resorted to—if the policy in question is considered wrong. These techniques are often deemed illegal, and court injunctions are obtained to stop them. Refusing to report for induction was the violation of the selective service law (which was considered by many to be unjust) and was also an act of civil disobedience against the war that it served. The refusal of a soldier to fight in Vietnam was an act of civil disobedience against the war policy, if he did so openly and accepted his punishment.[101] There are many injustices, however, that are not perpetrated through easily identified laws, and to require that *only* the law that is unjust should be disobeyed would tie the hands of civil disobedients. Moreover, the injustice may consist of an *absence* of a law (e.g., of equal opportunity in jobs or of safe nuclear waste disposal), and there is no way to violate a nonlaw. Even when there is a specific law that is unjust, civil disobedients may, as part of their strategy, violate other laws, when, by doing so, they publicize the injustice in question. Draft-card burning is an example. Laws against trespass, disruption, and certain kinds of demonstrations and assemblies can also be cited. Cases of disobedience should be *related* to the law or policy

[100]Cohen, p. 150.

[101]If, however, the soldier deserted and fled to Canada, it was not.

being attacked; they should be selected for their usefulness in drawing attention to a specific law or policy.[102]

Fortas Former Supreme Court justice Abe Fortas has suggested that testing the validity of a law is a genuine form of civil disobedience. Perhaps it is. Many of those who participated in the civil rights movement in the late fifties and early sixties believed they were practicing civil disobedience. Perhaps it is not. A law-tester is not quite the same thing as a lawbreaker. If the individuals are vindicated by congressional action or federal court decisions (as the civil rights people were), then it turns out that they were not lawbreakers at all. If protesters are not vindicated (as was the case of those who argued that the Vietnam War and the draft law were unconstitutional) and then desist in their efforts, they are more properly called "unsuccessful law-testers" than lawbreakers.[103] Unlike civil disobedients, they never intended to violate a *law* (in the strict sense of that word).

But the real mistake in Fortas's view, according to Cohen, is the assumption that once the federal courts (especially the Supreme Court) speak on an issue, it is settled once and for all. This is not so, for there may still be a need for civil disobedience. What is protested now is the Constitution itself or a particular interpretation of it. If the Constitution did not protect free speech or did not possess an equal rights amendment, it may be thought to support injustice, and civil disobedience could be embarked on in an attempt to change it. If an interpretation of the Constitution is deemed unsatisfactory, civil disobedience may be embarked on to bring about a reconsideration. The Supreme Court is not entirely isolated from public opinion. And its personnel does change. The Court has, as we all know, reversed previous decisions. In *Brown* v. *Board of Education* it stated that a previous dictum on "separate but equal" educational facilities for the races was erroneous. In *West Virginia State Board of Education* v. *Barnette* it reversed the ruling of a few years ago that members of the Jehovah's Witnesses religion could be required to salute the flag. Some cases of constitutionality the Supreme Court *declines* to consider. The Court never did issue an opinion on the constitutionality of the Vietnam "war," the draft, or the Tonkin Bay resolution (1964)—to the dismay of justices Stewart and Douglas. "If the case for civil disobedience is strengthened when there is reason to believe that the courts are in error it is strengthened still more when there is reason to believe that the courts will refuse to adjudicate the issues at all."[104]

[102]The activists at Kent State in 1970 probably went too far in protesting the escalation of the Vietnam War: "trashing" and intimidating business establishments, burning the ROTC building, attacking the National Guard with rocks, tear gas, and obscenities, etc. The Scranton Commission, which conceded that "the actions of some students were violent and criminal and those of some others were dangerous, reckless and irresponsible," nevertheless declared: "The indiscriminate firing of rifles into a crowd of students and the deaths that followed were unnecessary, unwarranted, and unexcusable."
[103]See Bowie and Simon, p. 233.
[104]Cohen, p. 154.

Tolerating Civil Disobedience If civil disobedience is often a case of good citizenship, it can be argued that it should enjoy some toleration in a just society.[105] We may grant that government has the right to punish lawbreakers, but it does not follow that it should always *exercise* that right. Civil disobedients differ from ordinary lawbreakers. There is real doubt in some cases that the law they break is a *valid* one. Even when it is valid, they break it for moral purposes rather than for gain, and they do not try to escape punishment for doing so. If, however, the expectation of "getting away with it" is present, they do not deserve much consideration. When the deterrence aspect of punishment for lawbreaking in general would be seriously weakened, it would of course be wrong to withhold punishment. Discretion is needed. But when society can *afford* to forgive principled seekers after justice, it should do so. Pardon or commutation for convicted disobedients can often be justified—especially for those who opposed policies (e.g., the war) that seem in retrospect to be wrong.

The issue of amnesty for draft dodgers and deserters is a difficult one—simply because we cannot judge their motives. They were not civil disobedients in the style described above, but many of them acted on moral grounds. The issue is also complicated by the constitutional ambiguities involved. Was the war legal? Was the draft, since it discriminated against the poor, the black, and the uneducated, legal? Was it fair to deny conscientious objector status to those who could maintain that they were morally opposed not to war in general but to the Vietnam War? In view of these problems and others, and despite the fact that some of those who stayed out (or got out) of the armed services were deadbeats and cowards, many people have argued for unconditional amnesty.[106] President Carter did grant limited amnesty.

Conclusion Since much of the early philosophic analysis of the concept of civil disobedience was done by the philosopher John Rawls, it is fitting to close this essay with two quotations from his work:

> While civil disobedience should be recognized, I think as a form of political action within the limits of fidelity to the rule of law, at the same time it is a rather desperate act just within these limits, and therefore it should, in general, be undertaken as a last resort when standard democratic processes have failed. In this sense it is not a normal political action. When it is justified there has been a serious breakdown; not only is there grave injustice in the law but a refusal more or less deliberate to correct it.
>
> Legitimate civil disobedience properly exercised is a stabilizing device in a constitutional regime, tending to make it more firmly just.[107]

[105]See Bowie and Simon, pp. 243ff.

[106]See Ronald Dworkin, "On Not Prosecuting Civil Disobedience," *New York Review of Books,* June 6, 1968.

[107]John Rawls, "The Justification of Civil Disobedience." See Beauchamp, pp. 139–140, 141.

Summary of the Issues

Civil disobedience is an illegal way of seeking justice. The question is whether it is also an immoral way.

One side argues that in a democracy each of us is a voter with as much power as anyone else. We cannot expect our convictions always to be in the majority. There are channels open to us for seeking change. We are protected in our right to speak, write, and assemble. We may dissent, but we may not disobey. The other side argues that we may conscientiously disobey those laws and protest illegally against those policies that are an affront to our sense of justice. We may endure some bad laws, but on serious issues we may, as a last resort, choose disobedience. We are then merely seeking to publicize and change a selected law or policy that is morally intolerable.

The Nuremberg trials are viewed differently by the two sides. The supporter of civil disobedience sees them as the recognition of the principle that one ought to disobey bad laws and directives for reason of human decency. The other side, however, points out that the Nuremberg trials sought only to punish the leaders and creators of a monstrous regime. Those in the rank and file who simply carried out orders were spared. The individual is never to be blamed for obeying a sovereign ruler.

Conscientious objection is not really civil disobedience when status is granted on the basis of laws already in place. If these laws are thought to be inadequate (e.g., they do not recognize selective opposition to war), then civil disobedience is possible. One side would regard this as illegitimate; the other side would not. Disobeying a law that is thought to be in violation of a higher law may be viewed as testing the law rather than civil disobedience. If the Supreme Court speaks, there should, according to one side, be no more disobedience. According to the other side, good reasons to disobey may still be present.

Civil disobedience is believed to be most effective and most consistent with the disobedient's moral integrity when the act (1) is done in public, (2) is nonviolent —i.e., does not injure others or (except in special circumstances) damage property, (3) is something for which the disobedient is willing to take punishment, and (4) confines itself to the law or policy being protested. This last does not mean that disobedients must violate only the law in question, for they may be protesting a policy that is not set forth in laws. In any case, their actions must be clearly related to what they are protesting against and may involve the violation of laws against trespass, disruption, and the like. The opponents of disobedience may admit the effectiveness of a carefully thought-out program of protest, but they cannot condone its morality when laws are violated.

On whether civil disobedience can sometimes be tolerated, one side obviously answers in the negative. Punishment must be meted out. The other side argues that although government has the right to punish, this does not mean that it should exercise that right—particularly when the disobedient is acting on principle and not, as a common criminal, for private gain. This side will thus be more likely to favor pardon, amnesty, and commutation.

Discussion Questions

1. Some civil disobedients are quite vague on how far they can go in breaking laws in addition to the one that is being protested. Can you help them out?
2. "America—love it or leave it." What do you think of this slogan?
3. What is the utilitarian element in civil disobedience? What is the deontological element?
4. Would you arrest protesters at abortion clinics who illegally trespass and disrupt? Why? Would you prosecute them? Why?
5. Can you think of an unjust law or policy in this country today that would justify civil disobedience? Explain.
6. Do you view Socrates as a civil disobedient or a defender of state power? Explain.
7. Compare and distinguish these actions against the state: civil disobedience, revolution, anarchistic destruction.
8. What do *you* think is the lesson of Nuremberg?
9. Do you think it is ever proper to engage in civil disobedience with respect to a clear Supreme Court decision? Explain.
10. Do you think that civil disobedience is more defensible in a nondemocratic state than in a democratic one? Why?
11. What do you think of the Hobbes quotation about Naaman?
12. Can you think of a cause for civil disobedience so important that substantial destruction of property would be acceptable? Explain.
13. Can you think of a cause for civil disobedience so important that violence against persons would be acceptable? Explain.
14. To what extent would you favor pardon or amnesty for disobedients during the sixties and seventies?
15. To say that civil disobedience is not always wrong does not mean that it is never wrong. Can you imagine a case of civil disobedience that *is* wrong? Explain.
16. To say that civil disobedience is not always wrong does not mean that it is sometimes *obligatory*. Can you imagine a case of civil disobedience that *is* obligatory? Explain.
17. In a particular situation, is it possible to have both the prima facie duty to obey the law and the prima facie duty to disobey the law? Explain.
18. General Grant stated in his inaugural address of 1869: "I know no method to secure the repeal of bad or obnoxious laws so effective as their stringent execution." Comment.
19. Can you find any scriptural basis for civil disobedience in the New Testament?

For Further Reading

American Academy of Political and Social Science. *Protest in the Sixties*. Philadelphia: American Academy of Political and Social Sciences, 1969.

Tom L. Beauchamp, ed. *Ethics and Public Policy.* Englewood Cliffs, N.J.: Prentice-Hall, 1975. Chapter 3.

H. A. Bedau, ed. *Civil Disobedience: Theory and Practice*. New York: Pegasus, 1969.

D. V. Bell. *Resistance and Revolution.* Boston: Houghton Mifflin, 1973.

Norman E. Bowie and Robert L. Simon. *The Individual and the Political Order*. Englewood Cliffs, N.J.: Prentice-Hall, 1977. Chapter 8.

James F. Childress. "Nonviolent Resistance: Trust and Risk Taking." *Journal of Religion and Ethics* 1 (1973):87ff.

Carl Cohen. *Civil Disobedience.* New York: Columbia University Press, 1971.

Marshall Cohen. "Liberalism and Disobedience." *Philosophy and Public Affairs* 1 (1972): 283–314.

Daniel M. Farrell. "Paying the Penalty: Justifiable Civil Disobedience and the Problem of Punishment." *Philosophy and Public Affairs* 6 (1977):165ff.

James Finn. *Protest: Pacifism and Politics: Some Passionate Views on War and Nonviolence.* New York: Random House, 1968.

Abe Fortas. *Concerning Dissent and Civil Obedience.* New York: Signet Books, 1968.

Mohandas Gandhi. *Gandhi on Non-Violence.* New York: New Directions, 1966.

Alan Gewirth. "Reason and Conscience: The Claims of the Selective Conscientious Objector." Virginia Held et al., eds. *Philosophy, Morality and International Affairs.* New York: Oxford University Press, 1974.

Harry K. Girvetz, ed. *Contemporary Moral Issues.* 2nd ed. Belmont, Calif.: Wadsworth Publishing Co. 1968. Part 1.

Robert T. Hall. *The Morality of Civil Disobedience.* New York: Harper Torchbooks, 1971.

A. P. Hare and H. H. Blumberg, eds. *Non-Violent Direct Action*. New York: World Publishing Co., 1968.

Gene G. James. "The Orthodox Theory of Civil Disobedience." *Social Theory and Practice* 2 (1973):475ff.

Gene G. James. "Socrates on Civil Disobedience and Rebellion." *Southern Journal of Philosophy* 11 (1973):119ff.

Mortimer R. Kadish and Sanford R. Kadish. *Discretion to Disobey: A Study of Lawful Departures from Legal Rules.* Stanford, Calif.: Stanford University Press, 1973.

Morton A. Kaplan. *Dissent and the State in Peace and War*. New York: Dunellen, 1970.

Menachem Marc Kellner. "Democracy and Civil Disobedience." *Journal of Politics* 37 (1975):899ff.

Morris Kenton. "The Morality of Civil Disobedience." *Texas Law Review* 43 (1965).

Martin Luther King, Jr. *Stride toward Freedom.* New York: Harper & Row, 1958.

Martin Luther King, Jr. *Why We Can't Wait.* New York: New American Library, 1964.

Burton M. Lieser. *Liberty, Justice, and Morality.* 2nd ed. New York: Macmillan Publishing Co., 1979. Chapter 12.

John Moreall. "The Justifiability of Violent Civil Disobedience." *Canadian Journal of Philosophy* 6 (1976):35ff.

Samuel Eliot Morison et al. *Dissent in Three American Wars.* Cambridge: Harvard University Press, 1970.

Milton Munitz et al., eds. *Ethics and Social Disobedience.* New York: New York University Press, 1968.

Jeffrie G. Murphy, ed. *Civil Disobedience and the Law.* Belmont, Calif., Wadsworth Publishing Co., 1971.

Robert Schwarz. "Disobeying the Law: A Critique of a Critique." *Journal of Social Philosophy* 4 (1973):11ff.

Samuel I. Shuman, ed. *Law and Disorder: The Legitimation of Direct Action as an Instrument of Social Policy.* Detroit: Wayne State University Press, 1971.

Mulford Q. Sibley. *The Obligation to Disobey.* New York: Council on Religion and International Affairs, 1970.

Peter Singer. *Democracy and Disobedience.* Oxford: Clarendon Press, 1973.

U.S. National Advisory Commission on Civil Disorders. *Report.* New York: Bantam Books, 1968.

U.S. National Commission on the Causes and Prevention of Violence. *The Final Report.* New York: Bantam Books, 1970.

U.S. National Commision on the Causes and Prevention of Violence. *Rights in Conflict.* New York: Bantam Books, 1968.

Ernest Van den Haag. *Political Violence & Civil Disobedience.* New York: Harper & Row, 1972.

A. D. Woozley. "Civil Disobedience and Punishment." *Ethics* 86 (1976):323ff.

Howard Zinn. *Disobedience and Democracy: Nine Fallacies on Law and Order*. New York: Random House, 1968.

Chapter 8

WAR AND PEACE

Having applied ethical concepts to personal problems and to social problems, we are now ready to apply them on a worldwide scale.

The three problems selected for this chapter are not very closely related to one another, and they certainly do not exhaust the subject of global ethics. They are all important, however, and they are all timely.

The first problem is the practical one of preventing war. We assume that war is bad and try to find an effective means to prevent it. If war came, we would probably react to it in different ways, but we would agree that we should do what we can to prevent it from occurring in the first place. In view of the fact that war is such a monumental evil, it is tragic that there are so few realistic ways to avert it. The two most plausible ones are world federalism and nuclear deterrence. One requires a surrender of national sovereignty; the other requires heavy spending and living in the constant shadow of the thermonuclear bomb. Which "solution" is better? And where does arms limitation fit into the picture?

The second problem is that of proper response to the draft. Are young people obligated to submit or do they have the right to refuse? This topic gets us into various theories of pacifism, the "just war," and the reasons for trusting our government leaders. Young Americans have had to come to terms with the draft on several occasions since 1940, and it looks as if they will have to again. Readers may want to jot down their view of the matter right now and see whether it changes after reading the essays about it.

The third problem seems to be quite a simple one. We know that we in the United States are very fortunate in having plenty of food to eat. Indeed, we eat more meat than is healthful and we waste enough food to feed millions annually. Do we have any obligation to share our bounty with others? Or should food aid be employed only to advance our own interests as a nation? Good arguments have been advanced on both sides. The issue is not quite so clear-cut as it might appear. There are political, economic, and social factors that bring *self-interest* close to neocolonialism and that make the *humanitarian ideal* difficult to carry out effectively. Combining the two approaches, as Public Law 480 tries to do, brings both sets of difficulties down on us.

We started with sex, which dealt with individual decisions. We end with the world, which deals with national decisions. But the ultimate decision still lies with the individual. Will *you* support world government or deterrence or something else? Do *you* think war is just and will *you* submit to induction? Will *you* support food aid, and in what degree, in what form, and for what purpose? And will you, in each case, arrive at your conclusions in the light of true facts, accurate ethical judgments, and sound argument?

PREVENTION OF WAR

The Best Means for Fostering Peace Is a System of Enforced World Law

Atomic Warfare The greatest problem facing the world today is that of preventing war. We have entered the atomic age and will remain in the atomic age until some even more powerful forces are discovered—or until civilization is so destroyed that atomic technology itself is buried in the rubble. War, always a tragic and wasteful enterprise, is today a threat to our very existence.

Let us be clear on the destructiveness of nuclear weapons. The biggest conventional bombs used in World War II ("blockbusters") contained about one ton of TNT. Atomic bombs were first measured in terms of kilotons (thousands of tons). The bombs dropped on Japan in 1945 were based on the principle of releasing energy through the splitting of heavy atoms (fission). The Nagasaki bomb had a force of 20 kilotons, or the equivalent of 20,000 tons of TNT. By today's standards, these are primitive. Bombs are now made to release energy by combining light atoms (fusion) and are measured in megatons (millions of tons). "A one megaton bomb would destroy brick structures out to a distance of 3½ miles; it would ignite most fabrics and paper out to 6 miles; it would cause second-degree burns out to 11 miles."[1] The process of fission is now merely a trigger or means by which enough heat is generated in order for the fusion to begin. The new weapons were first called hydrogen bombs, but are now called thermonuclear. The first thermonuclear bomb exploded by the United States (November 1, 1952) had a force of 20 megatons. In 1961 the Soviet Union exploded a bomb with the force of 58 megatons—equivalent to 58 million tons of TNT.

It has been estimated that the United States has a total megatonage in excess of 35,000. This is equivalent to about 10 tons of TNT for every person in the world. When we add the stockpile of the Soviet Union and other nuclear nations,

[1]Ziegler, *War, Peace, and International Politics,* p. 66. A one-megaton bomb dropped on New York would kill one million people within eleven seconds, many of them vaporized. A total of 2.25 million would die and another 3.6 million would be seriously injured with "crushing injuries, ruptured lungs and ruptured internal organs," according to Professor H. Jack Geiger. See "Nuclear War Probably Will Break Out within 20 Years, Scientists Predict," *St. Louis Post-Dispatch,* September 28, 1980, p. 12A.

we must realize that the world is indeed sitting on a powder keg. Can this destructive power be delivered? Unfortunately, much of it can. Aircraft can carry bombs, underground silos can launch intercontinental missiles, and submarines can launch ballistic missiles. They cannot all be stopped. Defensive techniques have not kept pace with offensive techniques. If only 10 percent of the nuclear warheads possessed by a major power reached their targets, the results for the attacked nation would be devastating. It is generally admitted, however, that neither the United States nor the Soviet Union has the means to destroy the ability of the other to retaliate against a preemptive first strike. Both lack "first-strike capability." The planes in the air and the launchers under the ground and the sea would still be able to retaliate even after a surprise first attack in a way that would destroy the enemy's major cities. This has been called "assured-destruction capability," and both major nations possess it. All this could take place in a matter of hours.[2] One day of atomic bombing would far surpass the destruction "achieved" in five years of World War II bombing.

The Deterrence Theory The fact that all countries are vulnerable, to both massive first and retaliatory strikes, is believed by some to be reassuring. Since to start an atomic war would result in "unacceptable" damage visited on the territory of the aggressor, no one would be foolish enough to start one. A "balance of terror" exists; each side is deterred from nuclear aggression. The old slogan "*Si vis pacem, para bellum*" (If you want peace, prepare for war) still applies.

But does it? There are several rather obvious difficulties in the theory of mutual deterrence.

1. The situation does not remain the same. Since prudence dictates that the enemy's forces be overestimated (that is, not underestimated), each power amasses more and better weapons to retain parity. An arms race thus takes place, not simply to get ahead, but to stay even. For all practical purposes, there can be no "balance" when neither side knows when true parity exists.

In actual fact, nuclear powers tend to seek superiority in quantity and quality. The greater quality they possess in terms of accuracy and resistance to defensive weapons, the more warheads will be delivered on target. It is said that strategic bombers can now be built whose presence cannot be picked up by radar. The attacking weapons are also improved with the aim of destroying the capacity of the enemy to retaliate. If ballistic missiles can be developed that can seek out and destroy the enemy's launching systems (in the ground or the sea) and destroy its planes in the air, the threat of a retaliatory strike can be all but eliminated. Stationary launching systems are already regarded as vulnerable by some, and the call has gone out for movable sites. Missiles that could destroy ballistic missiles in the air would have the same effect of reducing fear of retaliation. Where, then, is the deterrence? Possession of the means to immobilize the enemy's retaliatory

[2]ICBMs need about half an hour for the trip between the Soviet Union and the United States.

capability places the side that is willing to make the first strike in a decided position of advantage.

Although neither side has "first-strike capability" today, one side may have it tomorrow—or may *think* it has it, or think the other side has it. Duty-bound to protect their own country, officials may believe that they are obliged to attack when the situation is perceived to be in their enemy's favor if they do not. Calculations must be made every day, as the situation changes. It is suicidal to rely on a "balance" that continually changes and in ways that no power can be certain of.

Some experts, for example, doubt that Soviet missiles could destroy enough of the stationary Minuteman silos to prevent significant retaliation (from the ground as well as sea and air), while others believe that not even the MX system with its 200 tracks would be invulnerable. The Soviets might build enough warheads to knock out all 4,600 shelters. How accurate are the Trident missiles being fitted onto our submarines? And how many of the B-52s will get through? There is wide difference of opinion on what our weapons can do and the direction that improvement should take, as well as on what the enemy's weapons can do.

2. Horrifying scenarios can be imagined. Perhaps deterrence is already obsolete. The Soviets might think that the American pledge to respond massively to an attack is a bluff. What *would* the United States do if the Soviet Union attacked our missile bases and held back enough missiles of its own to destroy our cities? The United States would be in a dilemma. We either surrender or launch a massive attack against Soviet cities—which results in destruction of our own. Carter's Presidential Directive 59 called for study of a strategy involving a *measured* response—short of population destruction—in order to spare our own cities. "Critics argue that the very ability to spar in that way makes a once unthinkable nuclear holocaust dangerously thinkable."[3] The deterrence theory calls for certain, immediate, and unacceptable retaliation. *This* kind of strategy is not deterrence at all, but an attempt to find a compromise between surrender and suicide, to conduct a "limited" nuclear war in the hope that the other side will do so also. If various scenarios can be imagined, what we have working is not "mutual assured destruction" (MAD), but old-fashioned hypothetical reasoning. And who really knows who will do what to whom in this or that situation?

3. National leadership cannot be depended upon. A wise and careful chief executive will indeed refrain from resorting to nuclear attack whatever the provocation. But even such a person may not be fully rational in all moments. Working under formidable pressures, perhaps involved in an acute international crisis, the chief executive may have a momentary lapse. This is all that it takes to plunge the world into a nuclear holocaust. Or the chief executive may be unstable to start with—an adventurer or paranoid. Even if we are confident of the leadership of

[3] *Newsweek,* October 27, 1980, p. 51.

the United States and the Soviet Union, what of the other countries that have nuclear capability (Britain, France, China, India) and those who soon will join the "club"?[4] A third power could launch an attack in order to provoke the two great powers into mutual destruction. *Any* nuclear attack on the United States or the Soviet Union would be perceived as coming from the other, and retaliation would be immediate. It is also possible for unauthorized persons below the top level to instigate nuclear war. That there are devices for preventing this does not rule out the possibility that these devices could be subverted.

4. Accidents occur. Strategic bombers carrying thermonuclear bombs have crashed, and submarines carrying Polaris missiles have malfunctioned. Murphy's Law operates.[5] Khrushchev admitted that an intercontinental ballistic missile had accidently been fired by Russia in the direction of Alaska and had to be destroyed. The explosion of an armed Titan II missile in Arkansas (September 1980) raises the question of what would have happened had the explosion launched the missile. A flight of geese was picked up by an American warning system and was interpreted for a time as a Soviet attack.[6] The "hot line" is helpful when an accident occurs, but it is not an infallible device for preventing a reaction that could touch off a nuclear war. "There is no guarantee that what is coming over the Hot Line is true. Certainly any plans for a first strike would include use of the Hot Line to lull the other side into believing it was only a test of a salvo of missiles."[7]

5. Nuclear deterrence does not stop conventional warfare. The hope shared by many people after Hiroshima that the atomic bomb had made warfare obsolete certainly has been dashed by the events of the last thirty-five years. A partial listing of postbomb wars: Korea (1950–1953), India-Pakistan (1971), Turkey-Cypress (1974–1975), Vietnam (1959–1975), Israel-Arab nations (1948, 1956, 1967, 1973), Angola (1975), Congo (1960), U.S.S.R.-Hungary (1956), U.S.S.R.-Czechoslovakia (1968), United States-Dominican Republic (1965), U.S.S.R.-Afghanistan (1979–1980), Iran-Iraq (1980–).[8] *Modern* conventional warfare is quite different from that pursued in 1939–1945. New weapons have been

[4]"At least twenty-five additional states have the technological base and the economic capability to develop atomic weapons and in some cases to deploy fairly large-size force." Rosen and Jones, *The Logic of International Relations,* p. 255.

[5]See Bill Wickersham, "Murphy's Law and Nuclear Disarmament," *Prioritas* (October 1976), pp. 9–14.

[6]Charles Osgood recounts a harrowing experience in 1960 when warning signals gave every indication of a multimissile attack from the U.S.S.R. American forces went on war alert and retaliatory systems all over the world stood by to receive the order to attack. Restraint was exercised by American and Canadian officials only because Khrushchev (an unlikely Soviet sacrifice) happened to be in New York at the time. The explanation turned out to be this: The radar installation in Greenland was bouncing signals off the rim of the rising moon. See Osgood, *An Alternative to War or Surrender,* pp. 47–48.

[7]Ziegler, p. 234.

[8]Sixty-five wars have been identified between 1945 and July 1976. See Rosen and Jones, p. 204.

developed, and still others are on the horizon. We have witnessed the lethal effects of napalm, fire bombs, fragmentation bombs, and "smart" weapons. "The biggest difference in new weapons is in the accuracy of projectiles which has been made possible by radar, television, heat seeking devices, infra-red devices, laser beams, radio control, and tiny computers. . . . The arms race that has focused almost exclusively on nuclear weapons will consequently shift more and more to the development of ever more sophisticated 'conventional' weapons."[9] The wars of the future, even if nuclear weaponry is not used, will be quite devastating enough. Do we have to wait until a balance of terror builds up in conventional warfare? In the meantime, of course, a great deal of conventional warfare has taken place involving superpowers. Deterrence has perhaps prevented the Soviet Union from attacking the United States, but the Soviets have been aggressive in other parts of the world. The United States has not attacked the Soviet Union, but it has conducted military actions in other parts of the world. Some adherents of the deterrence theory even claim that these two powers could engage in a conventional war with one another!

6. Conventional warfare may escalate into nuclear warfare. Wars since 1945 have been "contained"—that is, they have not led to direct combat between the two major powers. And they did not utilize nuclear weapons. The world was fortunate. The danger is that some war somewhere (and wars are always going on) will lead to one or both of these results. At what point will a nuclear power believe that its interests require the employment of the bomb? Many Americans wanted to use it in the Vietnam War. The situation is complicated by the fact that nuclear powers are involved in various pacts and alliances. The United States, for example, is obligated to protect Western Europe. A conventional war between the two great powers could escalate to the point where one of them feels compelled to resort to the bomb. Some countries are developing "miniaturized" atomic weapons for tactical use. NATO and Warsaw Pact nations already have tactical nuclear weapons. If hostilities break out, the step to full-scale strategic use may be perceived to be not so great. The United States is regarded as the "nuclear umbrella" for Western Europe.

It was not the original intention of the major powers in World War II to bomb to destruction entire civilian population centers, but they finally did so. It was not the original intention of the United States to use napalm in Vietnam, but it did so. It is very difficult to keep wars in bounds, in terms of participants and weaponry, and probably impossible in the long run. Nuclear deterrence will not work when a country has gradually moved to a point in hostilities where its fundamental interests seem to be at stake. The time will come when it is forced to rely on its "best shot."

[9]Ronald J. Glossop, "Confronting the War Problem," chap. 13-G ("Modern Conventional Weaponry"), unpublished manuscript. Southern Illinois University at Edwardsville, 1980.

The fact is that nuclear deterrence has *not* prevented war. The best that can be said for it is that it has *up to this point* prevented *nuclear* war. Millions of people, soldiers and civilians, have perished nonetheless. And this may only be a prelude for the even vaster destruction that lies in wait for us unless we can devise a system that will prevent a grass fire from enveloping the whole forest.

Nuclear deterrence is not the only means that has been suggested for preventing war. Let us look at some others.

The Balance of Power Theory Traditionally, the theory of *balance of power* has meant preventing or controlling war by the formation of alliances against states that become too strong or too aggressive. Alliances shift in such a way as to prevent any state or coalition of states from achieving a position of dominance. This international policy is supposed to have worked well in the eighteenth and nineteenth centuries (the Napoleonic Wars being an exception) in preventing wars and mitigating their effects. The former was accomplished by making clear that war would be costly to the aggressor. The latter was accomplished by preventing one side from achieving "total victory." Even if one's enemy was vanquished, restraint was in order, for today's enemy may be tomorrow's ally. A state sought security by making alliances, not by building up its arms and threatening "massive retaliation." If we grant that the system worked in the past (and this is debatable), does it have any relevance for the present?

Now that the United States and the Soviet Union are not the only superpowers in the world, the answer would seem to be in the affirmative. China has nuclear weapons and has been accepted in the United Nations. Western Europe has forged an identity of its own and has great military power (including nuclear). Japan has great industrial resources and could build the bomb if it wished to. Richard Nixon, when president, stated:

> We must remember the only time in the history of the world that we have had any extended period of peace is when there has been a balance of power. . . . I think it will be a safer world and a better world if we have a strong, healthy United States, Europe, Soviet Union, China, Japan, each balancing the other, not playing one against the other, an even balance.[10]

To these might be added such entities as India, Canada, and the OPEC nations, all of which could be useful allies in the shifting combinations for restraining aggressors.

However, the system will not work. In the first place, the states are still much too unequal. Neither the United States nor the Soviet Union could be restrained by the collective might of the rest. In the second place, a major power is not benefited by adding an ally if it already has enough nuclear bombs to destroy the

[10]See *Time,* January 3, 1972, p. 15.

world. In the third place, there is reason to believe that the enmity between some states is too great to make an alliance possible. In the fourth place, a war involving the great powers could not be expected to halt with limited gains and to spare the "aggressor." It is hard to exercise restraint while the enemy still possesses nuclear power. In the fifth place, it is doubtful that the United States, after its experience in Korea and Vietnam, would be willing to fight another limited war. Nor would the Soviet Union, if its foe were the United States. In the sixth place, the system ignores the interests of a great many lesser states, some of which will have nuclear arms. We cannot deal with them as cavalierly as in the past. Finally, and most important, aggression today can occur much more quickly and unexpectedly than it could in the past. A state need not give advance warning before air-lifting its troops (or releasing its missiles). So there is no opportunity for making the right alliances and applying diplomatic pressure.[11]

The Theory of Collective Security The theory of *collective security* is like the preceding one in that it threatens the aggressor with collective action. The purpose of a collective security system, however, is to protect the member states *from one another.* Participants in collective security have agreed that if any of its members attack, *all the others* will retaliate. Each has renounced force except when one of its number has resorted to force. There are no alliances until the peace is broken; then everyone else automatically becomes part of a coalition against the peacebreaker.[12] The system works best when all (or most) states are members and when there is some kind of organization that can declare that a violation has taken place and can coordinate defensive efforts. If very little sovereignty was given up by the several states in the balance-of-power system, a great deal is given up in a collective security system. Each state is *mandated* to act when aggression has been identified.

The prerequisites for collective security presumably were met when the League of Nations was formed after World War I. Article 16 of the Covenant clearly states the principle of collective security: "Should any Member of the League resort to war in disregard of its convenants . . . it shall, *ipso facto,* be deemed to have committed an act of war against other Members of the League." Economic sanctions would be applied first, then (if necessary) military sanctions.

The history of the League is familiar to most of us. Japanese aggression in Manchuria in 1931 was the first test. Although the League finally condemned Japan in 1933, it held that Article 16 did not apply since Japan had not declared war! In any case, strong action in the Pacific was unfeasible because the Soviet Union had internal problems and chose appeasement, Britain felt that its real interests lay in Europe, and the United States was not even a member. The Bolivian-Paraguay War (1932–1934) was ended more as a result of the action of

[11]See Ziegler, pp. 171–186.

[12]NATO, the Warsaw Pact, and other organizations today are simply defensive alliances. They exist to protect its members from *non*members, not *other* members.

the United States than of the League. The invasion of Abyssinia by Italy in 1935 was a clear case of aggression, but all the League would do was to apply partial economic sanctions. It lifted the sanctions in 1936 and later recognized Italian control over Abyssinia!

The reasons for the failure of the League are reasons for the failure of any system of collective security: (1) The tendency of member states to think first of their own security. Britain and France were more concerned about the growing power of Germany than about what Japan and Italy were doing. In fact, Italy was a potential partner in the balance-of-power game against Germany. (2) The tendency of smaller states to be more fearful of great powers on their border (e.g., Albania with respect to Italy) than of the League. (3) The unwillingness of some partners to respect a declaration of an embargo when it is not profitable. (4) the nonmembership of such giants as the United States. (5) The difficulty of defining "aggression." This, of course, is still a problem. Who was the aggressor in the Middle East in 1967? Egypt, which closed off Israel's trade with Asia, or Israel, which then attacked Egypt? Was Russia an aggressor when its troops invaded Hungary in 1956 and Afghanistan late in 1979, or was it simply helping a friendly government put down an insurrection? Was the United States an aggressor when it sent troops to the Dominican Republic in 1965 and to South Vietnam?

In joining the League of Nations, the states had not really given up the measure of sovereignty required. This is the problem that all collective security systems face. The state will continue to serve its own short-range interests: to follow the policy of economic profit, to help its traditional allies and harm its traditional foes, and to scrutinize closely the balance of power in regions where it has an interest. These policies are all but inevitable for strong and weak state alike, when they cannot trust the resoluteness of the international organization they have joined. How many ICBMs does *it* control?

The United Nations Established after World War II, the United Nations did include all the major powers, and with the addition of mainland China (1971) and the dozens of new states, it can claim to be a world body. The power to deal with war is vested in the Security Council consisting of five permanent members (United Kingdom, United States, Soviet Union, France, and China) and ten nonpermanent members. Article 39 of the charter states that the Council "shall determine the existence of any threat to the peace, breach of the peace, or act of aggression and shall make recommendations, or decide what measures shall be taken . . . to maintain or restore international peace and security." Article 41 gives the Council authority to apply nonviolent sanctions against aggressors. Article 42 permits it to call for military action. Article 43 requires the member states to supply military forces for such action. Article 51 permits "individual or collective self-defense . . . until the Security Council has taken the measures necessary to maintain international peace and security."

Nine votes are needed for Security Council action, but these must include the concurrence of all five permanent members. The charter thus recognizes the sovereignty of some states, while denying it for others. This is supposed to be realistic. It recognizes that a decision to act against the major powers either would not be carried out or would precipitate a major war. It was hoped that the coalition that had won World War II would continue to stand together to maintain the peace.

The failure of the United Nations to keep the peace is even more conspicuous than that of the League of Nations and that of nuclear deterrence. Nuclear deterrence has at least prevented nuclear war. It would be difficult to show that the UN has prevented *any* war. The Security Council legitimized the action of the United States in meeting the aggression of North Korea in 1950, but this was possible only because the Soviet Union was not present to cast its veto.[13] Articles 42 and 43 have never been employed. The token forces that joined the United States in Korea were volunteered by individual states acting on their own. With respect to Article 51, David W. Ziegler writes: "The UN does not even go so far as to outlaw all war. . . . The difficulty of determining when an action is self-defense makes the qualification of this article next to useless."[14] Who was acting in self-defense in the war between India and Pakistan in 1971? The escalation of violence had been so gradual that each could make a plausible claim to self-defense. This issue was not even placed on the agenda of the Security Council.

Not only has the Security Council been unable to take action in hostilities involving the interests of the major powers, but it has been ineffectual in matters in which these interests are not even threatened. The war in Nigeria (1967–1969), which took about two million lives, posed an impossible problem for the UN simply because the principle of secessionism was involved and too many countries found that to be too sensitive.

About the only contribution the UN has made to the cause of peace is through its "peacekeeping" missions. These have had some success in supervising periods of truce between warring groups: the Suez war (1956), the Congo war (1960), the Cyprus war (1964), the Middle East war (1973). The peacekeeping forces are made up by soldiers from the lesser powers. They do not *make* peace but interpose themselves between warring groups when a stalemate has occurred. They keep the peace so that diplomacy may take place.

The Secretariat under the leadership of men like Dag Hammarskjold, U Thant, Ralph Bunche, and Kurt Waldheim has sought with minimal success to mediate conflicts, achieve truces, and conduct fact-finding inspections. But these efforts, like the peacekeeping one, are more in the nature of "third party" functions by neutrals than official action by a prestigious world organization. The diligent efforts of Secretary-General Waldheim in 1980 did not result in the release of the American hostages by Iran.

[13]The Soviet Union had walked out in protest of the decision to exclude mainland China from the UN.

[14]Ziegler, p. 300.

As for the General Assembly, that is primarily a debating society. Declarations are made by majority vote of member nations, but they do not carry any weight. Decisions made by the Security Council are binding; resolutions made by the General Assembly are not. Perhaps the Assembly provides a safety valve of a kind. The United States and the Soviet Union can attack one another in the Assembly in lieu of military action and hope to convince the other nations of the soundness of their views. But it is the Third World or "developing" countries that have the most votes and delight in using them to embarrass both great powers.

International Law Most nations most of the time feel obligated to obey certain laws that are supposed to govern relations between them. Where do these laws come from? (1) The most obvious source is the treaty or international convention. Those that are ratified by several nations are thought to have the status of international law.[15] The Convention on the High Seas (Geneva, 1958) stated worldwide sailing and fishing rights (although the participating nations could not agree on the point where "territorial waters" ended). The Convention on War (Geneva, 1929) prescribed rules for treatment of prisoners of war. The Geneva Protocol of 1925 outlawed use of poisonous gases in warfare. The London Convention of 1936 regulated submarine warfare. More recent examples are the Partial Test Ban Treaty of 1963, the Non-Proliferation Treaty of 1968, the Seabed Treaty of 1971, and the Biological Weapons Treaty of 1972. Many agreements have been made by nations springing from mutual respect for sovereignty: border inspections, treatment of diplomatic corps, protection of diplomatic communication, and others. (2) Customary usage is another source of international law. This seems to be based on an intuitive conception of what national sovereignty is and how it should be respected, as well as of natural laws of a humanitarian or moral nature. Many of these insights into what is proper in relations between nations and people of different nationality have now been made explicit in written form, but they compelled obedience even before official ratification. The rights of civilians during a war, the right of a captive not to be enslaved, and the immunity of an individual carrying a white flag did not require formal treaties in order to be respected. (3) Interpretations made of written and unwritten law by courts are another source. Generally, these interpretations are made by international judicial bodies (standing international tribunals and panels established to deal with special problems), but opinions of national courts are sometimes relevant and important.

A new development of international law since the end of World War II has been to apply it to *individuals.* Individual *rights* are protected by such pronounce-

[15]Bilateral treaties also create international law in a sense, but the obligation to obey them rests only with the parties involved. One can perhaps say that international law in the broad sense requires adhering to agreements freely entered into.

ments as thc Universal Declaration of Human Rights, the International Covenant on Economic, Social, and Cultural Rights, the International Covenant on Civil and Political Rights, and the Protocol to the last. Individual *actions* are forbidden by international conventions dealing with hijacking, the taking of hostages, and terrorism. The Nuremberg tribunal held certain individuals responsible for crimes against peace, humanity, and the rules of war.

How are alleged violations of international law adjudicated? We think immediately of a world court. The "World Court" was set up in 1920 by the League of Nations, and it became the International Court of Justice in 1946 under the United Nations. This court is the highest international tribunal and is intended to adjudicate all disagreements brought to it by member states. It has not been very busy. In its first twenty-five years, it "was given only 56 cases. Of these, 14 were only requests for advisory opinions. Of the remaining 42 cases, only 13 were decided; the rest were withdrawn, discontinued, settled outside court, or left pending."[16] A visitor from Mars would mistakenly infer that the nations of this planet are very law-abiding.

Adjudication, of course, is not the same thing as enforcement. Since the court has no police or military detachments, it can only pronounce on the justice of the case. Whether physical or economic sanctions are carried out against the offender is up to individual nations themselves—or, theoretically, the Security Council of the UN. The taking of the American hostages in Iran in 1979 was clearly a violation of long-established and respected international law and was judged to be so by the court, but its advisory opinion did not secure the release of the hostages.

Without means for international enforcement, international law is interpreted and responded to pretty much in the way that sovereign states see fit to do so. The Nuremberg trials were a form of enforcement. It was not, however, a world body that enforced the "law," but a group of triumphant nations. This kind of "enforcement" (against individuals and states) has always been with us. Just as states may choose to enforce "law," they can choose to violate it also. Hitler called the treaty protecting Belgium "just a piece of paper." Germany disobeyed the law on submarine warfare in World War II because neutral ships were carrying supplies to its enemies. All sides since the start of World War II have violated rules protecting civilians, for it was in their national interest to do so. An early protocol on the use of poison gas was violated in World War I. The principle of *rebus sic standibus* ("if things remain the same") may be invoked to avoid the law—as Germany did in repudiating the Versailles Treaty. Since 1963, the United States and the Soviet Union have abided by their agreement not to test nuclear weapons in space—but things may change. Nations that have not signed agreements often do not feel bound by them. Japan had not signed the Geneva Convention of 1929 and violated the "law" concerning treatment of prisoners in World

[16]Ziegler, p. 291. The court will not render a decision on a case unless both parties agree in advance to accept the decision.

War II. Many nations have not signed the Non-Proliferation Treaty and thus are free to build nuclear weapons.[17] Another problem is that the bewildering array of new states refused to accept as law agreements made in their area by former colonial rulers. Finally, we may note the "neorealistic" interpretation that gives the force of law to unilateral pronouncements such as the Monroe Doctrine and the Truman Doctrine. A state "will show the reliability of formal agreements and justify its behavior on the claim that its value objectives are superior to those of its adversary, that its foreign policies more nearly approximate the goals of human dignity than do those of someone else."[18]

In view of the zealously guarded sovereignty of the individual state, it might seem that international law is useless, even meaningless. But adherence to it is surprisingly general. Arms have been kept out of Antarctica, outer space, and the sea bed. Diplomats (with one conspicuous exception) have been unmolested. Poison gas and germ warfare were not employed in World War II. Prisoners of war were, for the most part, treated properly in Western Europe in World War II. International law is violated, but not lightly. A nation's reputation will suffer. It will be thought to be predatory or untrustworthy. It will be attacked in the General Assembly. And it may provoke retaliation in the form of embargoes, seizure of assets, or even war—not from an official and international body, but from other sovereign states.[19]

The unhappy conclusion, however, is that international law does not prevent war. It may even be invoked to initiate a war! Before international law can be an effective means to peace, it must become world law, and it must possess the means for enforcement.

A Plan for International Order We have examined several methods for preventing and ending war and found them all inadequate. If thermonuclear destruction is to be avoided, something else must be tried. But the purpose of showing that none of the available methods is adequate for ensuring peace on earth is not simply to clear the way for some other method (or desperate alternative), but to derive from these unsatisfactory methods some clues for formulating a method that will work. Such a method will avoid the features that have made the others fail and will include the features that gave them the limited success they had. A system of *world government* does both these things and thus can be recommended not simply as a *different* method but an efficacious one as well.

[17]Even those who have signed can get out by invoking Article X.

[18]Rosen and Jones, p. 320.

[19]Ronald J. Glossop argues plausibly that the oil-hungry nations did not employ military action to take over the oil fields in the Near East when the Arab countries quadrupled prices (in a period of one year) out of a sense of respect for a moral principle. "A take-over by military force would have amounted to outright international theft. It would have made a mockery of international law. It would have reduced international relations completely to the rule of force, a notion which has been steadfastly resisted in liberal Western philosophy." See Glossop, chap. 12-H.

Grenville Clark, a leading lawyer and presidential adviser, has set forth a plan for world government in several publications.[20] His purpose is to achieve a federal union of global scope that is capable of keeping peace in much the same way that individual nations now keep peace within their borders. He believes that "the world is far more likely to make progress toward genuine peace, as distinguished from a precarious armed truce, when a *detailed* plan adequate to the purpose is available, so that the structure and functions of the requisite world institutions may be fully discussed on a world-wide basis."[21]

The basis for the new policy is the United Nations, but Clark would revise its charter in such a way as to provide effective legislative, judicial, and executive branches. The sovereignty of a member state in running its own internal affairs would be protected, but its sovereignty as a warmaker would be seriously restricted. The aim is the limited but very important one of maintaining world order through a strengthened world body.

Fundamental law would be set forth in the "constitution" or revised charter. Basic rights and duties would be clearly defined. Member states "would know in advance within close limits what obligations they would assume by acceptance of the new world system, and only a restricted field of discretion would be left to the legislative branch of the world authority."[22] Both fundamental and enacted law would be interpreted, applied, and enforced by world tribunals and executives.

Among the fundamental "constitutional" laws would be the following: prohibition of the use of force by any state against any other (except in self-defense), complete disarmament of all states through specified stages and close inspections, creation of a world police force—the only military force in the world—adequately staffed to "forestall or suppress any violation of the world law against international violence." In the manner of Hobbes, Clark argues that no declaration of peaceful intention and promise to obey the charter can be relied on unless there exists an external power strong and resolute enough to punish violators. He suggests that the revised charter begin to operate after ratification by five-sixths of the world population, and including the twelve largest states. Membership would be permanent: no state could withdraw or be expelled.

The *General Assembly* would be limited to legislation directly related to enforcing the peace. It would not seek to regulate trade or interfere in domestic matters.[23] But since its responsibility in performing its stated function is great, the present system of representation would have to be changed. The larger states would not be content in a situation where they could constantly be outvoted in substantial matters by tiny states. On the other hand, the twelve largest states should not be permitted to dominate the other 117 (the number that existed in 1966 when Clark's proposal was published). So Clark suggests a formula of

[20]See Clark and Sohn, *World Peace through World Law.*

[21]Grenville Clark, "Introduction to World Peace through World Law," in Beitz and Herman, *Peace and War,* p. 163.

[22]Ibid., p. 165.

[23]It would be permitted, as it does now, to make recommendations, but these would be nonbinding.

weighted representation.[24] The selection of representatives will, in the early years, be by the national legislatures of the member states, but eventually will be from the member states' qualified voters.

The *Executive Council* would replace the Security Council and consist of seventeen representatives elected by the General Assembly and responsible to it. Special provisions would be made so that all nations at some time or another would be represented, although the four largest nations (China, India, U.S.A., and U.S.S.R.) would each be entitled to have representation at all times. Twelve votes will be required for decision. There would be no veto power, but on substantial matters these twelve votes would have to include a specified majority of the larger states represented on the Council.[25] The Council would control the World Peace Force, under the watchful eye of the Assembly. This peace force "would be recruited mainly, although not exclusively, from the smaller nations," and the Military Staff Committee that directs it would consist entirely of nationals of the smaller states.[26]

The *judicial branch* will consist of several bodies. The International Court of Justice will adjudicate disputes where legal principles are involved. The General Assembly may direct the submission of such disputes to that body when it feels that they endanger world peace. The court will have "compulsory jurisdiction to decide the case, even if one of the parties should refuse to come before the Court."[27] The court would also decide "constitutional" questions relating to the meaning of the charter or the propriety of laws passed by the Assembly. The World Equity Tribunal will settle disputes where legal principles are not so clearly involved. Its decisions are not legally binding *except* when in the opinion of a special majority of the General Assembly they are deemed to be essential for preserving the peace. The World Conciliation Board would respond to requests of states for impartial mediation and conciliation in situations dangerous to peace. If a voluntary settlement is not forthcoming, the case could be taken to one of the other bodies.

These judicial decisions must be *enforced.*

> In case of a serious violation of the revised Charter or any law or regulation enacted thereunder for which a national government is found to be directly or indirectly responsible, the General Assembly could order economic sanctions against the nation concerned. In extreme cases the Assembly (or the Executive Council in an emergency and subject to immediate review by the Assembly) would also have authority to order the United Nations Peace Force into action. Any such enforcement action would correspond to the above-mentioned action available for the enforcement of judgments of the International Court of Justice or of the recommendations of the World Equity Tribunal for the settlement of a dispute when the General Assembly has decided that a continuance of the dispute would be a "serious danger" to peace.[28]

[24]See ibid., p. 167.
[25]See ibid., p. 169.
[26]See ibid., pp. 172–173.
[27]Ibid., p. 174.
[28]Ibid., p. 176.

The support of these and other institutions of the new world government will cost money. Clark estimates an annual sum of $9 billion for the Peace Force alone. But this is far less than what the world is spending for armaments today. An interesting feature of Clark's plan is a program for the economic betterment of the underdeveloped nations, under the World Development Authority. The gross disparity between these nations and the rest of the world constitutes a serious danger to world stability and peace. So he recommends an annual sum of $25 billion for use in developing their capacity for a better life. The *total* bill for the federal world state would be about $36 billion per annum, which is far less than the amount the United States spends in the arms race.

Evaluation of the Plan The culmination of nationalism, as John Dewey asserts, "is the doctrine of national sovereignty." We may call it patriotism, unity, or manifest destiny, but "the doctrine of national sovereignty is simply the denial on the part of a political state of either legal or moral responsibility. It is a direct proclamation of the unlimited and unquestionable right of a political state to do what it wants to do in respect to other nations and to do as and when it pleases. It is a doctrine of international anarchy; and as a rule those who are most energetic in condemning anarchy as a domestic and internal principle are foremost in asserting anarchic irresponsibility in relations between nations."[29] The notion that governments in today's world can be "sovereign" in any real sense is a fiction in any case. They simply cannot protect their people from other states. This is obviously true for the weaker states; superpowers are also vulnerable to attacks from other superpowers; all may be innocent victims of nuclear war between others. A system of world government recognizes reality. If no state can stand alone, it must seek membership in a system that enables it to survive while permitting it to have a say in how the world order will function.

Clark's system preserves sovereignty in the domestic sphere, but eliminates it precisely in the area where it can threaten others. The system promises deterrence to aggression and institutionalizes a worldwide plan of collective security. It establishes a system of international law and enforces much of it. It offers the opportunity for diplomacy, adjudication, mediation, and conciliation, as well as debate and voluntary cooperation. Most important, it takes military weapons from individual states and places them in the hands of the United Nations. Clark's plan utilizes the best elements of all known means for keeping the peace, but shores up their weaknesses.

It is not without its dangers. Will the Peace Force always be used for its stated purposes? Can the member states be kept from secretly rearming or training domestic police for aggressive action? Will the General Assembly wisely exercise its powers to promote peace? Will the judicial bodies respect the law and make just decisions? But these dangers are less than the real evils the world endures

[29]Dewey, "Nationalism and Its Fruits" (1927). See his *Characters and Events* (New York: Henry Holt and Co., 1929), vol. 2, p. 802.

in constant war and preparation for war. And they are far less than the dangers we face from nuclear war.

How long can the world sit on the nuclear powder keg, one that is getting larger every year as nuclear powers increase their stockpiles and new nations join the "club," before it is touched off? The gamble pits certain monstrous evils against problematic ones of lesser intensity. It is a gamble we must take because we have so much to gain and so little to lose.

The ethical ramifications of the matter are clear. Most of us are opposed to war, but would engage in it as an act of self-defense. But not even self-defense will be necessary if the states are disarmed and an international force stands ready to put down aggression and enforce lawful settlements. The real ethical issue is not whether states or individuals should adopt a pacifistic attitude, but how they can work for world institutions that make war (in the normal sense of that word) unlikely or impossible. Rather than debate what this country should do in the event of an atomic attack on ourselves or our allies or a conventional attack in parts of the world where we believe we have a national interest, we should apply every effort to create a situation in which such decisions would not have to be made. What is at stake is the survival of the human race and its civilization. No individual or sovereign nation should be permitted ever to be in a position of having to consider actions that will contribute to the destruction of the human race and its civilization.[30]

The problem of preserving peace is the most serious and the most urgent problem that moral philosophy has to deal with. It demands our deepest thought and most persistent actions. Unless this problem is solved, all other problems must be approached in a spirit of unreal and provisional seriousness. A judgment on abortion seems almost frivolous when ICBMs are aimed at the great population centers of the world. A judgment on distributive justice is useless when our industrial plant faces total annihilation. A judgment on public-sector strikes is meaningless if public sectors cease to exist. And who will care about the propriety of extramarital sex when survivors are poking around in the ruins of a nuclear attack? As long as people live, they will be obliged to seek ethical solutions of "contemporary issues." The point is that the world would be so devastated after a nuclear holocaust that most of our hard-earned ethical convictions would no longer be applicable. Peace between nations must claim top priority.

Professor Ronald J. Glossop asks us to imagine a pair of astronauts in a space vehicle who get into an increasingly vigorous dispute on religion and politics. Red lights come on signaling trouble with oxygen supply, water supply, and waste disposal. Ground control directs them to stop arguing and to give full attention to the problems threatening their survival. If they do not abate their dispute (they don't have to agree), they can never attend to the other problems for which

[30]The recent exploration by American leaders of the possibility of striking military and political targets in case of nuclear attack instead of the cities is perhaps a recognition that such an action would be not only suicidal but murderous as well.

cooperative solution is possible. Quarreling states, like quarreling astronauts, ignore the problems that cry out for solution—on either an individual or a cooperative basis.[31] Conflict not only leads the participants to war but distracts them from recognition of other dangers. Lester Brown writes: "It is one of the great paradoxes of the late twentieth century that the really serious threats to man's future existence are receiving so little attention while leading powers fritter away their financial resources, scientific talent and the time of their leaders on ideological conflicts."[32] Barry Commoner says that "peace among men must precede peace with nature."[33]

The ethical problem is at least simplified by the fact that peace is an end that can be judged worthy by virtually everyone in the world. This is not to say that most people are pacifists. War will be accepted as a desperate resort by many who are quite aware of its horrors. But most people would hope that something could be done to eliminate war as a feasible expression of national policy. Far from viewing war in general as productive of value, they see it as productive of evil.[34] They see the problem of achieving peace as both important and legitimate. For most of us, this is the concrete problem *par excellence.* If it cannot be granted that the idea of world government is, at least in theory, a solution to it, we must ask for something else. But there is, as we have seen, nothing else available at this time. If it is granted that world government, at least in theory, is a solution, we must ask whether it is a practical one.

For many people, it is not. States will not, it is argued, divert themselves of nuclear weapons and trust their security to a world government. The answer to this is that states must do what their people demand, and a campaign of education can show them not only that the present course of international relations is suicidal (they already know that), but that it does not *have* to be. Political campaigns are conducted on the basis of which party can mount a better nuclear strike when they should be conducted on the basis of how the *need* for a nuclear strike can be avoided. Candidates for national political office should be judged on what they can do for peace rather than on how they can fight a war. They talk peace but have only deterrence to offer as a means for it.

The notion of national sovereignty, it is argued, is too ingrained. States will not scale down their "right" to do what they perceive to be in their best interests. The answer to this is that the notion of sovereignty is a late arrival on the world scene and does not always have to be with us. It was not a ruling concept in the days of the Pax Romana, and it had few adherents in the Middle Ages. As late as the eighteenth century each of the American colonies was willing to give up its "sovereignty" "in order to form a more perfect union" and "insure domestic tranquillity." The heyday of the concept of sovereignty was the nineteenth cen-

[31]See Glossop, chap. 1.

[32]Lester Brown, *World without Borders* (New York: Random House, 1972), p. 156.

[33]Barry Commoner, "Ecosystems Are Circular: Part II," *American Forests* (May 1974), p. 60.

[34]For a good exposition and criticism of views that war has biological, technological, psychological, sociological, and moral value, see Glossop, chap. 10 ("The Value of War in Society").

tury, and it culminated in World War I, which laid the basis of World War II. In our own century we have seen the concept compromised in actual political and economic organizations: the League of Nations, the United Nations, the European Economic Community, the North Atlantic Treaty Organization, the Warsaw Pact organization, the Organization of Petroleum Exporting Countries, the Central American Common Market, the Latin American Free Trade Association, the East African Common Market, and others. Nations have already shown their willingness to sacrifice individual prerogatives on behalf of defense and profits. It is not unlikely that they will be willing to sacrifice even more on behalf of genuine security.

The ideal of a world order guaranteeing peace qualifies as an object of faith in John Dewey's sense of the word. "I should describe this faith as the unification of the self through allegiance to inclusive ideal ends, which imagination presents to us and to which the human will responds as worthy of controlling our desires and choices."[35] The religious attitude can be harnessed in service to an end that is comprehensive and is conceived to be a solution to a besetting human problem. Inspired individuals all over the world can devote their best efforts to this end, working patiently and persistently, individually and collectively, for what is not an impossible goal in this life. They need not be doctrinaire followers of Clark's particular plan, but can revise their end as it draws near, just as they revise their means as conditions change. One thing only will remain constant: the search for peace through world union.

One organization that is actively working for "world peace through world law" is the World Federalists Association, with headquarters in Arlington, Virginia. Those who believe that peace is important and that world government is preferable to world anarchy should support this or similar organizations with their time, money, and energy. World War I gave us the League of Nations. World War II gave us the United Nations. Do we have to wait for World War III in order to establish an *effective* system of enforced world law?

The Best Means for Fostering Peace Is Nuclear Deterrence

Criticism of World Government The most obvious objection to enforced world law as a means for fostering peace is that it is not available at present. Before it could begin to operate, the commitment of most of the world powers (and all the major ones) is necessary. Even if we were willing to grant that in theory it is desirable and efficacious, we would have to face the fact that a system of world government is not in place today. When will it be in place? No one knows. Some of its proponents have been wildly optimistic. Grenville Clark offered a "reasoned prediction" in 1960 that by 1980 a "comprehensive plan" would have been

[35]John Dewey, *A Common Faith* (New Haven: Yale University Press, 1972), p. 33.

officially formulated and "submitted to all the nations for approval" and that by around 1985 it would have been ratified by the requisite states.[36] It is doubtful that Clark's plan (or any other) is any closer to being accepted today than when it was first conceived.

In the absence of a system of world government, considerations of national security (as well as international justice) require us to find more realistic methods for preventing and containing war. Before we turn to these other methods, however, we will look at the Clark plan from the point of view, not of practicality, but of theoretical soundness. Is it an idea that should command our devotion? Is it something we should work for, while we use other approaches in the interim between international "anarchy" and "world federalism"?

Inis L. Claude, Jr., takes issue with the view that world government is the theoretical solution. He thus disagrees with Gerhart Niemeyer and Hans Morgenthau:

> While the only certain guarantee against further international wars is the formation of a world state, global unity is not feasible at the present time.[37]

> The argument of the advocates of the world state is unanswerable: There can be no permanent international peace without a state coextensive with the confines of the political world.[38]

International anarchy is not as bad as is charged, and world federalism is not as good as is claimed.

The first point that Claude makes is to show that peace is not impossible *without* world government and that it is not guaranteed *with* world government. On behalf of the first, he cites the existence of friendly relations between a great many states. The world is not an entirely safe place, but it is not a Hobbesian jungle either—constant and universal war of every state against every other state. On behalf of the second, Claude points out that superstates do not always succeed in preventing violence and disorder in their realms. The danger to peace in a world state would consist of "civil war," in every way as destructive as international war. "Outcroppings of uncontrolled violence are a familiar phenomenon in human societies equipped with governmental mechanisms."[39] Spain, China, the United States, France, Latin America, the Soviet Union, and Nigeria provide obvious examples of serious outbreaks against legitimate sovereign power. Civil wars arise when the central authority is weak; they also occur in protest against one that is strong. While it may be conceded that government contributes in some cases to social order, "the tactic of creating a government is not tantamount to

[36]See Clark, p. 181.

[37]Gerhard Niemeyer, quoted in Inis L. Claude, Jr., "World Government," in Beitz and Herman, *Peace and War,* p. 189.

[38]Hans Morgenthau, quoted in ibid.

[39]Claude in Ibid., p. 192.

the waving of a magic wand which dispels the problem of disorderliness."[40] A world state, composed of many peoples, traditions, and interests, would be a standing invitation to rebellion. Sometimes people get along better when they are separate states than when they subsist as components of the same state—Norway and Sweden, for example.

Claude's second point is to question the notion of a *monopoly of power* presumably possessed by the world state. This monopoly is based upon an unrealistic appraisal of national states. As the history of revolution shows, states seldom have possessed such monopoly, and indeed, when the revolutions have succeeded, they are found to have *less* than the insurgents. Not even the state's organized military forces can be counted on to be loyal in all circumstances.[41] What binds nations together is a sense of national interest, not a national army or police force. The tradition of most states, including our own, is that of *preventing* all physical power from becoming a national monopoly. The international state would thus have to do what few national states have succeeded in doing—or wanted to do. Member states do retain their police forces, which could be substantial in power.

Would a monopoly of physical force be a good thing in a world state?[42] Would we perhaps have created a monster that would tyrannize us the way a Hobbesian sovereign can tyrannize a nation? Would "peace" be a price too high to pay? Certainly the power wielded by the world state would have to be very great to keep in check its disparate parts and factional interests. "In the absence of consensus, great amounts of power would be needed to institute and maintain a world government. But concentrating all this power in one place would create a temptation to seize it."[43]

Claude's third major point is to question the assumption that the greatest violators of peace would tend to be individuals and organizations rather than particular states. Rather too easily do Clark and others assume that sovereignty will diminish in the face of institutional arrangements designed to produce international officials responsible to "the world" rather than to their governments.[44] Even financial support is to bypass individual states. They "shy away from the problem of grappling with the reality of states."[45]

[40]Ibid., p. 194.

[41]"It is still a reasonable hunch that a Texan in the American forces who is certainly available to bomb Moscow is probably not available to bomb Houston." Ibid., p. 197.

[42]This paragraph is a digression from Claude's argument, but it deals with an issue he has raised: monopoly of power.

[43]Ziegler, p. 150.

[44]"At no point in the machinery of the system is provision made for governments of the states constituting the organization to be represented by spokesmen authorized to state their policies and positions, present their complaints, negotiate agreements, or accept commitments." Claude in Beitz and Herman, p. 202.

[45]Ibid., p. 203.

The basic analogy of the world approach is that between an individual state that keeps order and a world state that is expected to do the same. The differences between the two are often ignored by the world federalists, but careful attention to the similarities would also spare them some errors. A state may succeed in controlling lawless individuals in Kalamazoo, but criminal behavior is not its greatest problem. Its greatest problem is controlling groups and organizations that have special interests. If such control is to be successful, it will be through political adjustment, not force. "A successful political process, rather than effective legal process, is the dominant feature of government at its best."[46] When adjustment, accommodation, and compromise break down, *then* violence breaks out. "One of the lessons of government experience is that coercion can seldom be usefully invoked against significant collectivities which exhibit a determination to defend interests, as they conceive them, against the public authority."[47] If we must use the analogy, we should compare member states to domestic collectivities —against which violence is self-defeating. The analogy is not between lawbreakers in the world polity and lawbreakers on the streets of our cities.

In view of what John Dewey wrote in 1932 in opposing the use of sanctions by the League of Nations, it is doubtful that he could accept a plan for world government similar to Clark's. He held that "enforcement of peace" is a self-contradictory term. He viewed the League as a group of nations playing power politics and early opposed American participation.[48] "I do not see how world organization of and for peace can be brought into existence without the growth of harmony of interests and community of values along many different lines. I do not know of any single device which would bring it automatically into being."[49] The device of attacking "peacebreakers" certainly does not qualify. "To suppose that the use of combined coercive force is the means of promoting such an organization . . . is like supposing that individuals can be clubbed into loving each other."[50] Nor would the presence of coercive force be sufficient to keep a world state together once it was formed. The analogy between a world state and an actual state that preserves peace within its borders breaks down, for with respect to the latter, "there already exists a body of laws (common and statute) which determines the manner and the use of force. . . . Within each state where

[46]Ibid., p. 207.

[47]Ibid., p. 208.

[48]The Europeans "want us now for the same reason that they wanted us during the war—to add power to *their* policies. . . . The League is *not* honestly named. It is a League of governments pure and simple." Dewey, "Shall We Join the League?" (1923), *Characters and Events,* vol. 2, pp. 625, 627. "The notion that we can really be of help to Europe by joining in their affairs on terms that are set by their unhappy international and diplomatic heritage seems to me to be silly. We shall simply be drawn in, and our system assimilated to theirs." Dewey, "American Responsibility (1926)," *Characters and Events,* vol. 2, p. 693.

[49]John Dewey in *Are Sanctions Necessary to International Organization?* (1932), a discussion between Dewey and R. L. Buell. Dewey's contribution is printed in Joseph Ratner, ed., *Intelligence in the Modern World: John Dewey's Philosophy* (New York: Modern Library, 1939). See p. 586.

[50]Ibid., p. 585.

the laws run, there is substantial agreement as to important interests and values."[51] "If the population of New York State were practically unanimous in refusing to obey a federal law, it would not be the police which would be called out if it were decided to use coercion, but the army and navy. The result would be civil war, not the ordinary processes of courts and sheriffs."[52] American federalism worked not because force was exerted from the outside, but because it organized forces from the *inside.* "We do not enjoy common interests and amicable intercourse in this country because our fathers instituted a United States and armed it with executive force. The formation of the United States took place because of the community of interests and the amicable intercourse already existent."[53] One final quotation: "All proposals short of a league of nations whose object is not the negative one of looking after economic and social needs which are now at the mercy of chance and the voracity of isolated states, assume that war is the effect of bellicosity—which is exactly on the intellectual level of the famous idea that it is the dormitive power of opium which puts men to sleep."[54] The views of Dewey thus anticipate many of those of Claude.

Nuclear Deterrence If it is the case, for reasons of practicality or theory, that we cannot rely on world government to ensure peace, where can we turn? World law without sanctions is useless. Collective security died with the League of Nations. Balance-of-power politics is inapplicable in the atomic age. We must return to the ancient wisdom that the best way to work for peace is to prepare for war.

Perilous as it may be, a condition between nuclear powers where each can retaliate with results unacceptable to the other is the only condition that will prevent nuclear war. This strategy cannot be depended upon with certainty to work forever, but it is the only realistic one available now. And it has worked in the recent past. Despite the dozens of wars on our planet since the atomic age opened, several of which involved nuclear powers, none has become a nuclear war. Korea, for example, "was dramatic evidence that the capacity for violence can be consciously restrained even under the provocation that measures its military dead in tens of thousands and that fully preoccupied two of the largest countries in the world."[55] The retaliation feared here was not even nuclear! Vietnam and Afghanistan are more recent examples of *nuclear* deterrence: The Soviet Union opposed U.S. action, but did not attack; the United States opposed Soviet action, but did not attack.

The very consideration that causes us to fear nuclear attack is the same consideration that acts as a deterrent: *some of the missiles will get through.* This holds

[51]Ibid., pp. 588–589.

[52]Ibid., p. 590.

[53]Dewey, "Force, Violence and Law" (1916), *Characters and Events,* vol. 2, p. 640.

[54]Dewey, "Morals and the Conduct of States" (1918), *Characters and Events,* vol. 2, p. 648.

[55]Thomas C. Schelling, "The Diplomacy of Violence," in Beitz and Herman, p. 88.

for both the first strike and the expected retaliatory strike. Although the attacking power will have the advantage of surprise, it will be able neither to knock out all the launching sites of the attacked nation nor to intercept all its missiles. The United States has superior capability in strategic aircraft and missile-equipped submarines. And its stationary missile sites are buried deeply in the ground in concrete silos. A Soviet attack would be met by ruinous retaliation—on enemy population and industrial centers. This is the doctrine of "mutual assured destruction" (MAD).

Critics of the arms race have argued against the increase of nuclear power on grounds that the United States and the Soviet Union already have enough explosive power to destroy everyone in the world fifty times over. If deterrence has any validity, it is argued, each state can stand pat. Arms limitation should naturally and unilaterally occur. This view ignores four obvious considerations: (1) It is not the sheer megatonnage that is important. Ten "small" bombs will do more total damage to ten cities than one very large one that destroys just one city. Nation *A* could have twice the power of Nation *B* but only half its destructiveness. (2) The more missiles that are launched (other things being equal), the more will get through to their targets. (3) The more accurately missiles can be fired, the greater chance they will have of destroying the power of the attacked nation to retaliate. Thus a nation must engage in a *qualitative* race to protect its own launching pads and to be able to respond accurately to a first strike. The United States is now planning a mobile missile launching system (MX), the manufacture of cruise missiles released from aircraft, and more accurate missiles to be launched from Trident submarines. Also, the better the warning system is, the better chance there will be of firing ground-based missiles before they are hit by the attacking power. (4) Nations must be concerned with a third strike. The retaliatory strike must be massive enough or destructive enough to prevent an additional strike by the original attacker. Whether this is done by destroying all the attacker's cities or by "surgical" strikes against military and political targets (which is what American leaders are talking about today), the element of deterrence must be present. The issue between MAD and the new view is not on deterrence per se, but on which form of retaliation would be a more *effective* deterrence. It must be perceived by our enemy to be productive of results that are certain and unacceptable.

The need to maintain deterrent power is constant, but the factors that condition it change with time. Nuclear strategy is based upon quantitative and qualitative factors. The power to retaliate effectively depends upon the *amount* of tonnage a power has in its missiles and the *number* of the missiles it possesses, as well as the capability to *deliver* warheads effectively after a first strike has been experienced. What one power can do is a function of what the other power can do. If all of the missiles of a nation could be destroyed in a first strike, there would be no deterrence. If retaliatory missiles, planes, and submarines could be intercepted and destroyed by the attacking nation that is ready for them, there would be no deterrence. If the damage inflicted by a retaliatory nation is deemed not unacceptable, there is no deterrence. So each nuclear power must, for its own security, keep pace with the other in both stockpiles and technology. There can be no rest.

Arms Limitation Where will it end? It can only end when competitors in the arms race realize that each is secure from attack by the other and that further development of deterrent capability is superfluous. There must be a dawning realization that massive expenditure of national resources can never give one side any significant advantage over the other and that wisdom dictates an end to the race. If it is seen that neither party will drop from the race (and thus grant superiority to the other), the two sides may begin to take the steps that will freeze the military preparation of both. The race ends when the parties to it accept the principle that started it in the first place—deterrence—and are convinced that it has been achieved.

Americans who stress superiority and thus oppose arms limitation are perhaps victims of the delusion that American "know-how" will eventually enable them to resist any first strike and/or deliver a thoroughly disabling strike of their own. This is possible, but if this condition is achieved, we will have passed beyond deterrence. This view represents a wistful attempt to regain the upper hand that the United States possessed during the 1950s.[56] The trouble with this viewpoint is that the Soviets may achieve this strategic dominance before we do. There is no assurance that we can outthink them and outspend them. Russians who seek superiority and thus oppose arms limitation are perhaps victims of the delusion that their country, gigantic in size and actively dispersing population centers and building bomb shelters, will eventually be able to withstand any retaliatory strike.[57] Once again, deterrence is lost sight of. Extremists on both sides look for a great technological breakthrough—as the atomic bomb itself was in 1945.

It is the guess here that leadership on both sides is committed to deterrence and would be satisfied with an arms limitation plan and would support it. But there are political and strategic difficulties in coming to an agreement. Each side distrusts the other, is obsessed with security, and has ongoing programs it does not want to drop. Moreover, it is difficult to weigh and compare the various capabilities of each side. There is great variance in the two sets of strategic weapons. Each side wants to be sure that it has *at least* parity with the other.

Despite these difficulties, the United States and the Soviet Union achieved an important first stage in arms limitation in 1972. SALT I accepted Russian superiority in land-based missiles, modern submarines, and "throw weight." But at the same time, the United States retained the advantage in "arming points," for many of our land- and sea-based missiles could launch multiple warheads. Many of

[56]The most dramatic demonstration of nuclear superiority occurred during the Cuban missile crisis of 1962. Soviet armament, well under way in 1962, increased tremendously after this setback and shortly reached a point where neither side could claim superiority.

[57]China has openly boasted of its ability to survive a nuclear attack. The United States does not fear China, for it has not yet acquired the capability to launch an attack against us.

these warheads were MIRVs (each could be directed to separate targets). Our advantage in number of warheads was great. Also, our submarines could be more effective, for they operated from bases outside the United States. Also, our missiles, though less powerful, were more accurate. Several accurate explosions will do much more damage than one much more powerful. The Soviet missile, the SS-9, packing 25 megatons, will make a very big hole, but it would be much less destructive than one MIRV'd Minuteman missile containing three warheads of 200 kilotons each. Finally, the Americans have a substantial lead in strategic bombers.[58]

Although the agreement was to last for five years, both sides have adhered to it. SALT II was supposed to take the next step, but it has bogged down in political difficulties in the United States, largely as a result of Soviet aggression in various parts of the world. The delay has been unfortunate, for the Soviet Union has had the opportunity to close the technological gap before new restrictions could be imposed. At the same time, the United States has developed cruise missiles and other technological programs in an attempt to retain the gap. The American lead in warheads has increased since SALT I, while the Soviet Union has increased its lead in ICBMs and missile-launching submarines. All this is compatible with the SALT I agreement.

One agreement cannot stop this kind of competition. The journey to stable deterrence has many stages; we should not stop now. "Nobody pretended that [Salt I] was a comprehensive agreement. It was designed to freeze one part of the competition—sea- and land-based ballistic missile launchers—while negotiations took place on a more comprehensive, longer lasting treaty."[59]

One result of SALT I was the ABM Treaty of May 1972, which restricts each country to two antiballistic missile sites.[60] This is important, for if a really effective defensive system based on perfected ABMs could be constructed, the element of deterrence would be lost. "Arms control advocates argue that any weapon which makes it rational to go first in war is a bad one."[61]

SALT II The basic principles of SALT II, agreed upon by the United States and the Soviet Union in 1979 but not yet ratified in the Senate are these:

> A ceiling of 2400 on the aggregate number of strategic nuclear delivery vehicles, to be lowered to 2250 by 1982.

[58]In evaluating the matter of relative advantage, two other factors should be taken into account: (1) The United States has two allies possessing nuclear weapons (Britain and France); the Soviet Union has none. (2) The United States has tactical nuclear weapons in the hands of NATO forces in Europe. These could be used against the Soviet Union; the Soviet Union has no tactical weapons that can be used against American territory.

[59]"Pass the SALT: An Interview with Paul Warnke," p. 40.

[60]This was reduced to one site and 100 launchers by the ABM Treaty Protocol of 1976.

[61]Ziegler, p. 232.

A limit of 1320 on launchers of ballistic missiles equipped with multiple, independently targetable reentry vehicles (MIRV's) and on heavy bombers equipped for long-range cruise missiles.

A lid of 1200 on the number of MIRV'd ballistic missiles alone.

A ceiling of 820 on MIRV'd, land-based intercontinental ballistic missile (ICBM) launchers.

A prohibition against any increase in the number of reentry vehicles (RV's) carried by existing types of ICBM's. The number of warheads on existing type of ICBM's will be frozen at the maximum with which that missile has been tested. New types of ICBM's will be limited to 10 RV's and new types of SLBM's to 14.

A ban on the construction of additional fixed ICBM launchers and on any increase in the number of heavy ICBM launchers, defined as those larger than the Soviet SS-19 missile.

A restriction to one new type of ICBM during the lifetime of the Treaty.

A ban on certain new types of strategic offensive systems such as ballistic missiles on surface ships.

A ban on the development of the Soviet SS-16 missile for the Treaty's duration.

An exchange of data on the weapons systems that are limited by the Treaty.[62]

The Treaty would extend the verification procedures established in SALT I and would be in effect until 1986.

The attempt is to achieve basic parity in nuclear power. The Soviet Union would retain superior throw power, but the United States would retain superiority in warheads by a ratio of 1.6 to 1. The Soviets would have to dismantle several existing weapons. American development of the B-1 bomber and the Mobile MX missile system would not be barred. The United States would be expected to retain its superiority in strategic bombers, although the Soviet Union would be permitted (by a separate agreement) to build thirty "Backfire" bombers per year, with certain improvements prohibited.[63]

There are many other elements to take into account when pondering whether genuine parity has been achieved.[64] "The less chance there is of either side counting on any sort of decisive superiority, the more stable the strategic situation."[65] SALT II does afford deterrence for both sides, as well as a ceiling, in some sense, for military expenditures. And it does hold out hope for the future. Under

[62]Barbara G. Levi, "SALT II—The Terms of the Treaty," *Physics Today,* June 1979, p. 34.

[63]This bomber can reach the United States without refueling, although it could not return. Whether it is indeed a "strategic" weapon is thus debatable. The Soviet Union has promised not to seek to increase its range.

[64]For an excellent debate on SALT II between Wolfgang Panofsky (for) and Edward Teller (against), see *Physics Today,* June 1979, p. 32ff.

[65]"Pass the SALT," p. 41.

the Joint Statement of Principles, the powers commit themselves to pursue future discussion aimed at numerical and qualitative limitations.

In the political arena, the agreements are criticized from two sides. One views it as counter to American security. Senator Jackson is fond of the term "appeasement." Some still yearn for "strategic superiority." But this is a dream of the past, before Russia built its ICBMs. Strategic superiority can only mean that the side that possesses it can destroy the other side's retaliatory force—which is now impossible. "Superiority" works two ways, both destructive: (1) Nation *A* attacks Nation *B* because it is superior and need not fear unacceptable retaliation. (2) Nation *A* attacks Nation *B* because it (Nation *B*) is superior; *A* is fearful and can only survive if it launches a surprise first strike that will weaken its enemy. The other side criticizes SALT II for not going far enough: It does not decrease federal spending, but almost forces the United states to spend to the limits set in the treaty. Improvements in quality of missiles and delivery systems do not come cheaply. But the fact of the matter is that without SALT II, the cost of the arms race would indeed be astronomical.[66]

The Jesuit magazine *America* states: "The continuing waste of human and material resources in the face of desperate poverty and hunger remains the scandal of our age. The SALT II treaty will not, of itself, restore order to a crazy world. In fact, some new weapons systems may be put into production as a result of the treaty. Such decisions only perpetuate the treadmill of the arms race and are regrettable. Despite this, the treaty is still an important moment in a process that does seek to control the expanding technology of war by human decisions and in the light of human values. In this sense, it represents a small, significant, even indispensable, step toward sanity."[67]

SALT II is no panacea. There are other problems not even touched on. One is the whole field of "conventional" arms. Another is the question of tactical nuclear weapons in the arsenals of Warsaw Pact and NATO forces. Another is the possible deployment of strategic nuclear warheads in Western Europe. It is important that we ratify SALT II so we can proceed to III, IV, and so on.

If the destructiveness of nuclear warfare has forced the United States and Russia to enter arms control agreements in the nuclear field, the prospect of conventional war sparking a nuclear holocaust might lead to arms control in conventional weapons also. What is significant is that agreement has been reached to limit weaponry and even, in some cases, to reduce it. This is what we must build

[66]The military budget of the United States in 1978–1979 was $123.7 billion and in 1979–1980 about $126 billion. The actual outlay for 1979–1980 was $134 billion. "The fiscal 1981 budget calls for military outlays of $153.7 billion, more than $2,000 for every American family" (*The Defense Monitor,* Center for Defense Information, Washington, D.C., vol. 9, no. 7, 1980, p. 1). Projections for 1981 to 1985 come to a round $1 trillion. At present, about 40 percent of our taxes go for military expenditures—46 percent if we include veterans' benefits. The actual amount approved for 1980–1981 was $161 billion—more than Carter had requested. Over $1 billion was included for the MX system —which, if completed, will cost between $40 and $80 billion.

[67]Editorial, *America,* June 30, 1979, p. 524.

on. The concept of deterrence, a concept very real and important to both sides, could conceivably lead to something much better: bilateral disarmament.

Bilateral disarmament will not necessarily put an end to war, but it is a major step to peace. Each of the great powers has many countries aligned with it and subject to its influence, so they will be brought into the disarmament movement also. It will then be the task of the two great power blocs to restrain the aggression of the Third World countries. Limitations in sale and gifts of modern arms to the Third World countries would be very helpful, for most of them cannot manufacture them themselves. With the possible exception of China, it is difficult to imagine any such country standing against the diplomatic and economic pressures of the East and West blocs. All this is very speculative, of course. The point is that SALT II serves the cause of peace in two ways: (1) It preserves deterrence while placing limits on armaments. (2) It is a case of agreement between military giants that could lead to even more significant cases of agreement, thus reducing world tensions.

Soviet aggression in Afghanistan and elsewhere should not dissuade the American side. We punish ourselves at least as much if, in a spirit of spite, we reject SALT II in an attempt to punish the Soviet Union. Continuation of the arms race (once deterrence on both sides is achieved) benefits no one. Discontinuing it will save us some money, but it may do much more: It may lead to the kind of accord and demilitarization that will make deterrence unnecessary. This policy is really more in line with Dewey's thinking than the artificial creation of a global leviathan.

> Upon what shall those who desire a world organized for peace depend: upon force and the threat of force, or upon peaceful measures in the development of common interests and purposes? . . . To some it will seem unrealistic to put faith upon strictly moral agencies and influences. . . . We do not insist that good faith and moral pressure are *sure* to operate, that they are bound to be sufficient. But we do say that the measures which can be taken in their name are more promising roads to stable and enduring peace than is recourse to coercion, actual or veiled. . . . [Coercion] weakens the operation of good faith and public opinion which are admitted to be the ultimate reliance. . . . [There should be] increased use of all possible means of consultation, conference, mediation, arbitration, and all other possible agencies of peaceful settlement.[68]

Increased accord (treaties, conventions, protocols, and agreements of all kinds), together with growing respect for international law and trust among nations, could over a period of time come to constitute a sense of community that alone would make a world state feasible—but by then, a world state might not even be necessary.

At the start of the Vienna summit where SALT II was signed (June 1979), President Jimmy Carter said that good relations between the United States and

[68]Dewey, *Intelligence in the Modern World,* pp. 597–601.

the Soviet Union would preserve peace for the entire world. Soviet leader Leonid Brezhnev, with uncharacteristic piety, responded, "God will not forgive us if we fail."

Summary of the Issues

Both sides agree that the problem of war is the greatest problem facing us today. The problem is not the philosophical one of the morality of pacifism. Nor is it the one of trying to decide how or why or when we should fight. It is the practical problem of trying to achieve a situation in today's world such that we will not *have* to fight. Since the development of nuclear weapons, the problem of preventing war, always a grave and important one, has become one of unsurpassed importance and a matter of extraordinary urgency.

Both sides agree that the solution is not to be found in "balance of power" or "collective security" theories, nor is it to be found in the institutions of the United Nations and international law. While one side rejects these out of hand, the other side sees some elements in these approaches that could be utilized in an effective solution.

The two separate solutions that are put forth are *nuclear deterrence* and *world federalism.*

The side in favor of nuclear deterrence argues that the best way to work for peace is to prepare for war. Though this may be perilous, it is the only realistic option we have at the present time. Powers that might tempted to launch a first strike realize that they cannot destroy the power of the enemy to retaliate—massively and ruinously. Mutual assured destruction (MAD) will keep the peace. Despite the occurrence of many conventional wars in the past thirty years or so, deterrence has proved effective in preventing *nuclear* warfare.

The other side criticizes the deterrence theory by pointing out: (1) The situation does not remain the same. Each power, in order not to be behind, seeks to get ahead. Mutual deterrence produces, not a real balance, but nervous calculations instead—and a frantic arms race. (2) Various scenarios can be imagined with destructive consequences. (3) National leadership cannot be depended upon—on the part of major powers or the others. (4) Accidents can happen that can trigger nuclear war. (5) Nuclear deterrence has not prevented conventional war (sometimes even involving the major powers). (6) Conventional warfare can escalate into nuclear warfare.

The deterrence side admits that no power can stand pat when the others do not. We must continue to increase our deterrent power quantitatively and qualitatively, as well as our defensive capabilities. This not only heightens the terror but is very expensive. But unilateral disarmament would be suicidal. Deterrence does not, however, rule out the possibility of multilateral agreements to freeze or even reduce military preparedness. Indeed, this is what we should work for. Strategic domination is probably impossible; but even if it were not, there is no assurance that we would get there first, that we will make the big technological breakthrough. So instead of seeking strategic domination, which goes *beyond* the requirements of deterrence, we should strive for multilateral arms limitations. SALT I was a great step forward. That SALT II broke down was tragic. Talks should be renewed. When mutual deterrence has been achieved (and it has), neither power can reasonably expect more.

The side critical of deterrence has a solution of its own: achieve international order through a world government or a federal union of global scope. The plan of Clark is an excellent one. It starts with the UN but would revise its charter in a way that would set up a schedule of complete disarmament, prohibit the use of force by any state, and create a world police force that would be the only military force in the world. The function of the General Assembly, an Executive Council, and several judicial bodies is described, as well as the means of representation. While states preserve sovereignty over their internal affairs, they lose it in international affairs where peace may be at stake. No state is permitted to make war. International law and judicial decisions are enforced by the world police force. This is a practical solution to the war problem, and individuals, groups, and states should make earnest effort to utilize it.

The other side argues on the practical level that world federalism, even if sound in theory, is no closer to reality now than it was twenty-five years ago. Since we do not have it now, what do we do in the meantime? *Deter.* Many critics argue that it is not even theoretically sound: (1) Peace is not impossible *without* world government, and it is not guaranteed *with* world government. (2) A monopoly of power in a world state is not necessarily a good thing—even if it could be achieved. (3) There is not yet in the world a sense of community great enough to permit federalism to succeed in the same way it has succeeded in the United States. The plan would have us seek community through force. Community must come first—and there is a long way to go.

Discussion Questions

1. In the problems discussed in earlier chapters, there was no middle ground between the two sides. Do you think that on this problem a reasonable solution could be found by taking something from both sides? Explain.
2. Does deterrence necessarily imply that a state is *willing* to use its retaliatory power or simply that it must be *thought* to be willing? Explain. If the United States were suddenly attacked, would *you* give the order to destroy all the major population centers of the attacking country? Why?
3. Efforts are being made to strengthen nuclear defensive systems. What effect could great success in this area have on the theory of deterrence? Explain.
4. Efforts are being made to strengthen the attack capability so that the target country would be incapable of significant response. What effect would success here have on the theory of deterrence? What might be the reaction of a nation that realized that its enemy had achieved this capacity? Explain.
5. Do you think that "strategic superiority" and MAD are compatible concepts? Do you think that some who call for deterrence are really seeking superiority? Explain.

6. If you were a U.S. senator, would you have voted for SALT II? Why?
7. If you were the Soviet chief of state, would you have supported SALT II? Why?
8. Do you think that backing off from SALT II was a fitting punishment for Soviet aggression in Afghanistan? Why?
9. This problem of war has been approached in terms of Dewey's philosophy. Can you think of any other ethical theory that would be relevant here? Explain.
10. Do you think that a plan like Clark's is so utopian as not to warrant our attention? Why?
11. Someone said, "The U.S. already has enough nuclear bombs to destroy the world ten times over." Someone else retorted, "We already have enough ice-picks to kill everyone in the world." What is the significance of this exchange?
12. Would you be willing to see your country lay down its arms if all other countries did so also? Why?
13. Are the theoretical objections made to world federalism sound? Why?
14. What are the logical consequences with respect to the deterrence of hostile nations achieving third-strike, fourth-strike, fifth-strike capability? Explain.
15. The Reagan administration is committed to increasing military spending and decreasing social services. What is your opinion of such a policy?
16. If you agree in principle with world federalism, what (if anything) do you think you, as an individual, could do to advance the cause?
17. Some people argue that we are spending too much money on nuclear weapons and not enough on conventional weapons. Do you agree? Why?
18. If the United States and the Soviet Union were to go to war tomorrow, do you think that the concept of nuclear deterrence would operate to restrict them to conventional weapons? If not, who would resort to nuclear weapons first? Why?
19. Bertrand Russell favored threatening war against the Soviet Union to force it to take part in the internationalization of atomic energy when it *did not have the bomb.* But after the Soviets acquired the bomb, he favored unilateral disarmament! Does this make sense to you? Why?
20. If we could effectively destroy Soviet nuclear capacity by a surprise preemptive strike, do you think we should launch one? Why?

For Further Reading

Charles R. Beitz and Theodore Herman, eds. *Peace and War.* San Francisco: W. H. Freeman and Co., 1973. Chaps. 3, 5, 6, 7, 9.

Harold Brown. *Department of Defense Annual Report, Fiscal Year 1981.* Washington, 1981.

Grenville Clark and Louis B. Sohn. *World Peace through World Law.* 3rd ed. Cambridge: Harvard University Press, 1966.

John Cox. *Overkill: Weapons of the Nuclear Age.* New York: Thomas Y. Crowell, 1977.

Robert Ginsberg, ed. *The Critique of War: Contemporary Philosophical Explorations.* Chicago: Henry Regnery, 1969.

Stanley Hoffman. "Reflections on the Present Danger." *New York Review of Books* 27 (March 6, 1980):18–24.

Charles Osgood. *An Alternative to War or Surrender.* Urbana: University of Illinois Press, 1962.

Wolfgang Panofsky and Edward Teller. "Debate on SALT II." *Physics Today* 32 (June 1979):32–38.

"Pass the SALT: An Interview with Paul Warnke." *New York Review of Books* 26 (June 14, 1979):39–43.

Steven J. Rosen and Walter S. Jones. *The Logic of International Relations.* 2nd ed. Cambridge, Mass.: Winthrop Publishers, 1977.

Emma Rothschild. "Boom and Bust." *New York Review of Books* 27 (April 3, 1980): 31–34.

Frederick Schuman. *International Politics: Anarchy and Order in the World Society.* 7th ed. New York: McGraw-Hill, 1969.

Ruth Leger Sivard. *World Military and Social Expenditures: 1978.* Leesburg, Va.: WMSE Publications, 1978.

John Stoessinger. *Why Nations Go to War.* 2nd ed. New York: St. Martin's Press, 1978.

David W. Ziegler. *War, Peace, and International Politics.* Boston: Little, Brown and Co., 1977.

THE DRAFT

The Individual Has a Moral Obligation to Submit to Induction

Compulsory military service in the United States came to an end in 1973; registration was suspended in 1975. But in 1980 the president ordered a resumption of registration, and it is quite possible that Congress will soon be asked to reinstate the draft. Virtually all politicians favor in principle "volunteer" military forces, but a great many of them now believe that the volunteer forces are inadequate, quantitatively and qualitatively, for today's situation. Whether this is so or not, there is good reason to believe that the draft will be reinstated sooner or later. The moral problem is whether the individual is obligated to submit to induction. This is a problem, not only for the young people who are directly affected, but for those who may judge or counsel them.

Critique of Pacifism One reason offered for the view that one is *not* morally obligated to submit to induction is found in the philosophy of pacifism: War is wrong; to take part in a war is therefore wrong. If one does not intend to fight, one should refuse entry into the armed services and decline to support the war effort in any way. The basic principle of pacifism is that it is always wrong to employ violence, even in response to violence. Violence is such an immoral act that it can never be countenanced. Pacifists are so opposed to violence that they refuse to use it to defend themselves or anyone else. Being opposed to violence, pacifists will do everything they can to oppose it (persuasion, education, diplomacy, surrender) short of employing it themselves. They are apparently quite consistent in their nonviolent position. They refuse to act in a way that they condemn in others.

Pacifism, however, is an unsound ethical position. It is, as Jan Narveson argues, a self-contradictory theory.[69]

Why, we may ask, is violence wrong? The answer must be that it violates a right of the person who is the recipient of violence. Everyone possesses the right of not having violence done to him or her. It is because this is an important and almost unqualified right that violence is perceived, correctly, to be wrong. Now, if people *have* this right, it follows that they have a right to protect themselves and others when it is violated. Resistance is in order. "A right just *is* a status justifying preventive action.... One has a right to whatever may be necessary to prevent infringements of his right."[70] The very thing that makes violence so wrong in what makes resistance to it permissible.

How can we resist violence? In many cases, it can be resisted only by force. This force may itself take the form of violence. In order to protect the right not to be violently dealt with, we may have to resort to force ourselves. "The pacifist, of *all* people, is the one most concerned to insist that we do have some rights, namely, the right not to have violence done to us. This is logically implied in asserting it to be a duty on everyone's part to avoid violence. And this is why the pacifist's position is self-contradictory. In saying that violence is wrong, one is at the same time saying that people have a right to its prevention, by force if necessary. Whether and to what extent it may be necessary is a question of fact, but, since it is a question of fact only, the moral right to use force on some possible occasions is established."[71]

It might appear that the critics of pacifism are involved in a self-contradiction themselves. Do they not both condemn violence and rely on it? Do they not defend the right to be free of violence, then prepare to violate that right? Actually, there is no self-contradiction here. The party that has perpetrated violence has *forfeited* its right to be free of violence. We used the expression "almost unqualified right" above. There is at least one way that the right not to be violently dealt with can be restricted: violent action by the agent himself or herself.

There is another version of pacifism that does not go nearly so far as the one just discussed. A distinction is made between fighting for oneself and fighting for others. The second is permissible; the first is not. Although a few Christians take a universal stance against violence,[72] most would accept this distinction. One should turn one's own cheek, but not that of one's innocent neighbor. Jesus recognized the military as an honorable calling, and both Catholic and Protestant theology does also. Martin Luther wrote a pamphlet called "Whether Soldiers, Too, Can Be Saved," and concluded that they could. Augustine, like Jesus, would not harm another in order to save himself, but the danger to others makes a difference. Augustine "reasoned that the same unselfish love for others would this

[69]See Jan Narveson, "Pacifism: A Philosophical Analysis," in Rachels, *Moral Problems*. This article is derived from two articles by Narveson published in *Ethics* (vols. 75 and 78). Citations will be from the Rachels volume.

[70]Ibid., p. 419.

[71]Ibid., p. 421.

[72]For example, George Fox and some of his Quaker followers.

time demand that he sacrifice himself in defense of the innocent victims of unjust attack. He would fight and, if need be, die in their defense. On this occasion, resort to violence was to be seen . . . as a work of charity."[73] Thomas Aquinas offered certain conditions for a "just" war. The same kind of thinking that justifies punishment for civil offenders justifies war against external enemies: the duty to protect others. The executioner and the soldier are both necessary. That society must employ both is tragic, but not wicked.

Narveson criticizes this position also, arguing that "mere difference of person, as such, is of no moral importance."[74] If I have a right to defend others, I have a right to defend myself. If people do not have the right to defend themselves, they do not have the right to defend others. "The right of self-defense can be denied coherently only if the right of defense, in general, is denied."[75]

Narveson's criticism ignores the basic idea of Christian ethics: love. It is because of love that a difference of person is crucial on no other grounds than that it *is* a difference of person. Christians make no claims for themselves. They do not express their ethics in terms of *rights*—for themselves or for others. They are required simply to act on behalf of others with no concern for themselves. Christianity does not teach justice or equality. It teaches unbounded charity for others, regardless of their "rights" or merits. Even when Christians are required to do ill to some on behalf of others, they are enjoined to act always in a spirit of love. Luther's soldiers and hangmen kill in a spirit of love.

If Narveson is correct, then this theory of limited pacifism is misguided. If Luther and others are correct, then this theory of limited pacifism is not misguided. But in either case, limited pacifism provides no ethical justification for refusing military service, for if the one interpretation is correct, the theory is wrong-headed, and if the other interpretation is correct, the possibility is left open that individuals should come to the aid of their country.

The Effectiveness of War Another form of pacifism, although this stretches the term somewhat, is the position that war is ineffectual. Violence breeds more violence, and we are no better off after employing it than we were before. Although violence is seen as an evil in itself, it is its failure to produce the desirable ends at an acceptable price that is emphasized. It is a poor means. It is not a case of the end not justifying the means because the two are incommensurable (killing is always wrong) or because the two are incompatible in spirit (killing to stop killing); it is a case in which the means *in fact* has not produced the intended end or has done so at too great a price. This is a historical or empirical position. Where important moral ends can only be achieved by morally dubious means, they should be so promoted, provided that the values outweigh the evils. But war, as a means, does not in fact succeed in this way. The American anarchist Adin

[73]Ralph B. Potter, Jr., "The Moral Logic of War," in Beitz and Herman, *Peace and War,* p. 9.
[74]Narveson, p. 416.
[75]Ibid., p. 418.

Ballou, who is called a pacifist, expressed the disutility of war in this passage: "Take the worst possible view; resolve all the assailed and injured into the most passive non-resistants imaginable, and let the offenders have unlimited scope to commit all the robberies, cruelties and murders they pleased; would as many lives have been sacrificed, or as much real misery have been experienced by the human race, as have actually resulted from the general method of self-preservation, by personal conflict and resistance of injury with injury? He must be a bold man who affirms it."[76]

It is true that wars, to date, have not prevented wars; people still fight, hoping that each war will be the last. But has there been no war with a morally defensible outcome achieved at an acceptable cost? Has war as a means in fact never been justified by its desirable results? What we must do is to find not only a "just" war, but a just war that was also successful. If we do so, then this third form of pacifism is an unacceptable moral argument for resisting the draft.

The American Revolutionary War qualifies. A new state was formed with representative government and a bill of rights guaranteeing freedom of religion, speech, and assembly. A group of people escaped domination from an external power to assume control of their own destiny. The American Civil War, begun to prevent the spread of slavery, ended with the destruction of that hateful institution. The inhuman regime of Nazi German was terminated in World War II. The Korean War preserved the integrity of the nation of South Korea. The American war record is far from despicable.

In thinking utilitarianistically about war, we have to view the value of life as being very important, but not incommensurable with other values. To save a dozen innocent lives may require the loss of six innocent defenders. To relieve the misery and degradation of a whole generation may require the loss of thousands of innocent lives. Difficult choices must be made by individuals and officials, but the world is such that moral solutions are not always comfortable. The decision to drop the atomic bomb on Japanese cities was made in order to spare the hundreds of thousands of people who would have been killed had the war been prolonged. The decision to destroy the oppressive and stupid Bourbon regime was made by many of the French in full awareness that the cost would be great, but many of them preferred to "die on their feet rather than live on their knees." With respect to Communism, many Americans would rather be "dead than red." National movements of liberation are often inspired by ideals of human dignity and freedom. In judging wars, we must weigh not only life against life but also life against other values—those that make life worth living.

Quite often individuals who tend to pacifism will change their mind as the realization of what is at stake becomes clearer. Albert Einstein called himself an "absolute pacifist" in 1929, yet supported the United States in World War II and contributed to the development of the atomic bomb. A. A. Milne, a pacifist when

[76] Adin Ballou, "Christian Non-Resistance," in Lynd, *Nonviolence in America: A Documentary History,* p. 39.

he wrote the book *Peace with Honour* (1934), also changed his mind: in 1940 he published *War with Honour.* A peace-loving individual may feel that *in a particular case* violence is the only recourse. Martin Buber, in his letter to Gandhi, who in 1938 had advised the German Jews not to use violence against the Nazis, wrote: "An effective stand may be taken in the form of nonviolence against unfeeling human beings in the hope of gradually bringing them thereby to their senses; but a diabolic universal steam-roller cannot thus be withstood. . . . If there is no other way of preventing the evil destroying the good, I trust I shall use force and give myself up into God's hands."[77] Even Gandhi left open the use of force in his efforts for Indian independence. "Have I not repeatedly said that I would have India become free even by violence than that she should remain in bondage?"[78]

Sigmund Freud, no warmonger, was a realist when he wrote: "Our logic is at fault if we ignore the fact that right is founded on brute force and even today needs violence to maintain it."[79] The refusal "to examine the beneficial use of violence at once drives one to means that may be worse, to the acceptance of conditions that violent actions can alter, and to the surrender of values that violence can preserve."[80] Violence in itself is bad, but it may be an instrument, the last desperate remedy, for an end that is good.

The Just War If some wars are justified and some are not, how is one to tell the difference?

Many people have tried to state clearly and comprehensively the nature of the just war: the ancient Christian theologian Augustine, the medieval Catholic theologian Thomas Aquinas, and the contemporary Protestant theologian Paul Ramsey. Joseph C. McKenna has presented a plausible exposition and defense of the Scholastic position.[81] These accounts not only state how a war can be conducted justly, but the criteria for conducting it at all.

Richard L. Purtill argues that "Nation A is justified in waging war with Nation B if and only if these criteria are met:[82]

1. "Nation A has been attacked by Nation B or is going to the aid of Nation C, which has been attacked by Nation B." Although people may disagree on what constitutes aggression (or who attacked first), there is general agreement among nonpacifists that the party that strikes first is wrong.

2. "The war has been legally declared by the properly constituted authorities of Nation A." Again, there may be difference of opinion (e.g., does the Tonkin Bay resolution constitute an official declaration?), but both parties to the disagree-

[77]Martin Buber, "Letter to Mahatma Gandhi," in Mayer, *The Pacifist Conscience,* pp. 272, 281.
[78]*The Collected Works of Mahatma Gandhi,* vol. 23 (Delhi: Publications Division, Ministry of Information and Broadcasting, 1965), p. 30.
[79]Sigmund Freud, Letter to Albert Einstein, "Why War?" See Mayer, p. 243.
[80]Runkle, "Is Violence Always Wrong?," p. 376.
[81]See Joseph C. McKenna, "The Just War," *American Political Science Review* 54 (1960): 647–658.
[82]Richard L. Purtill, "On the Just War," in Beauchamp, *Ethics and Public Policy,* p. 190. This essay appeared as an article in *Social Theory and Practice* 1 (Spring 1971): 97–102.

ment regard the criterion as relevant. The criterion would exclude military action that is not openly sanctioned by the ruling power.

3. "The intentions of Nation A in waging the war are confined to repelling the attack by Nation B and establishing a peace, fair to all." The person who opposed the permanent conquest of North Korea or Israel's colonization of the Sinai appeals to this criterion. The demand for "unconditional surrender" is incompatible with this criterion.

4. "Nation A has a reasonable hope of success in repelling the attack and establishing a just peace." Critics of the Vietnam and Biafran wars have appealed to this criterion. Czechoslovakia's decision not to resist the Soviet invasion was sound, for resistance would have resulted in defeat and the pointless loss of many lives.

5. "Nation A cannot secure these ends without waging war; it has considered or tried all other means and wages war only as a last resort." Some might argue that the American invasion of the Dominican Republic was invalidated by this criterion and that the American war against Japan was not. "At any rate, no one seems anxious to admit that they employed war or used violence as other than a last resort."[83]

6. "The good done by Nation A waging war against Nation B can reasonably be expected to outweigh the evil done by waging war." It was consideration of this criterion that caused many people to move from a hawkish to a dovish position with respect to Vietnam and, in the face of mass misery in the Biafran war, to oppose that war also.

7. "Nation A does not use or anticipate using any means of waging war which are themselves immoral, e.g., the unavoidable killing of innocent persons." On the basis of this criterion, one may condemn the use of poison gas, germ warfare, antipersonnel weapons, and the bombing of population centers. Again, while there is disagreement on the application of the principle, there is agreement on the relevance of the principle itself. That the death of some innocent persons in a war *is* unavoidable does not in itself invalidate a war.

It is true that these criteria may be twisted or distorted by partisans to "justify" a great many unjust wars. "Plainly deceitful claims are often made that such criteria are met when in fact they are not, and passion and partiality often blind participants in a conflict to gross violations of such criteria." But it is not "impossible for reasonably impartial persons to discover whether in fact these criteria are satisfied in particular instances."[84]

These particular criteria give us the choice between two extremes: The "righteous cause" position, which would "justify" any war that seemed to advance national values (political, racial, economic, religious); and the pacifist position, which, refusing to choose the lesser of two evils, would not justify any war. "No

[83]Purtill in Beauchamp, p. 194.
[84]Ibid.

doubt it would be best if all conflicts ceased. But unless and until they do we are forced to take sides, and in taking sides are forced to use some standards."[85]

Can these criteria, which are similar in many ways to those of medieval philosophy, be applied to the present when nuclear weaponry has placed a new aspect on modern warfare? Yes. The last five criteria would bear heavily against nuclear warfare. Certainly if the result of a war would be the destruction of the human race, it would be unjust. But the criteria do not rule out conventional war or even nuclear war if it can be kept within limits.

It is by no means certain that wars in the atomic age will be atomic wars. None of the dozens that have occurred in the last thirty-five years has gone to this extreme. For humanitarian and prudential reasons, nations have not utilized all the power they had at their disposal. The danger of pacifism is that it is an all-or-none proposition. It "teaches people to make no distinction between the shedding of innocent blood and the shedding of any human blood. And in this way pacifism has corrupted enormous numbers of people who will not act according to its tenets. They become convinced that a number of things are wicked which are not; hence, seeing no way of avoiding 'wickedness,' they set no limits to it. How endlessly pacifists argue that all war must be *à outrance*! that those who wage war must go as far as technological advance permits in the destruction of the enemy's people."[86] Pacifism, unless exposed, contains a self-fulfilling prophecy.

What about civil war? The criteria are stated in terms of "nations," so they would seem to be inapplicable—unless we give *nation* a much broader meaning. Even so, it would be necessary to rephrase most of the criteria in order to use them to distinguish between justified and unjustified civil conflict. But it could be done. The first criterion, for example, could be stated in such a way as to distinguish between isolated acts of violence and brigandage perpetrated for private gain and a campaign led by recognized leaders for broader social ends. The defense of war and the criticism of pacifism can be made at least as easily for civil conflict as for international conflict. It is, of course, in the interest of tyrannical and repressive regimes to instill the sentiments of pacifism in its subject populations. They can inveigh against violence while seeking to preserve a monopoly in the means for violence. If it is true that some interstate wars are, in principle, just, so too are some intrastate wars.

Who Decides? Let us now return to the basic question: Are individuals morally obliged to submit to induction? It would appear that if the war for which the draft is instituted is just, individuals are obliged to submit, but if it is not, they have the right (and perhaps the duty) to resist. Although nonpacifists may agree on the criteria for a just war, they frequently disagree on how they are to be applied

[85]Ibid., p. 195.
[86]G. E. M. Anscombe, "War and Murder," in Rachels, *Moral Problems,* p. 402.

to actual situations. Thus individuals must make up their own minds and act accordingly. This answer, for reasons that are set forth below, is erroneous. Individuals should defer to the judgment of their government.[87]

1. It is often the case that registration or the draft is instituted at a time of national danger, when war itself does not exist. This was the case in 1980 as well as in the months before the American entry into World War II. It is unknown who will be the enemy or what type of war will be fought and where. A large military force or "ready reserve" may well be part of national preparedness when no war exists or is intended. If the government waited for overt hostilities before requiring compulsory military training, it might be too late. Since it is not known what uses the military forces will be put to, individuals are not in a position to judge whether they will be put to just uses. It is thus impossible for them to make moral judgments with respect to the draft—beyond the customary duty to obey the government.

2. Suppose the draft does occur in a time of war, as was the case when the United States was involved in Vietnam. Do individuals then have the right to refuse service? Or suppose that they are drafted during peacetime, then find themselves soldiers in an "unjust" war. Do they then have the right to desert? The answer to both questions is no. They may disagree with the foreign policy of the government, but should obey nevertheless. Why? In the first place, from a sense of gratitude: they owe their country loyalty and obedience. Circumstances are seldom such that they can be certain that their convictions are correct and those of their country are wrong. They should be willing to give it the benefit of the doubt. In the second place, they should recognize that the officials of their country are better informed than they are on the dangers facing the nation and the best way to restrain and deter aggressors. They are not privy to all the diplomatic and strategic factors that condition a wise decision. In the third place, they are citizens of a democratic state in which officials are elected to act on behalf of all. One is obligated in a democracy to bow to the will of the majority.

3. If individuals do succeed in establishing themselves as conscientious objectors, they will have to perform some kind of equivalent service. They thus contribute to the war or preparedness effort in any case. What they do to benefit society will free others to directly or indirectly serve military goals. Modern war enlists the efforts of everyone—from middle-aged taxpayers to riflemen in the front lines. The army itself is composed mainly of people who do not perform deeds of killing: cooks, medics, technicians, supplymen, signalmen, reconaissance personnel, and others. If individuals consent to helping the war effort, but draw back from pulling the trigger, their refusal to participate in actual combat would appear to be a matter not of ethics, but of taste. Conscientious objectors can only avoid assisting their country by fleeing from it. This would do little to stop the war that

[87]This obviously can hold only for interstate war. When the issue is whether individuals should take part in a civil war, they will have to consult their own consciences—although there may be a prima facie duty to remain loyal.

they oppose. It would be a case of deserting their country when it is not only in military danger but perhaps in moral disarray as well.

It does not follow from the injunction to submit to the draft that individuals should ignore the ethical implications of their country's foreign policy. As good citizens, they learn what they can about what is going on and make judgments about it. As responsible human beings, they should examine the ethical implications of all actions that affect other human beings. But the duty to obey the commands of their country must take precedence. They may feel in their hearts that their country is wrong, and they may speak out boldly, but they are not justified in defying the draft. Some wars, after all, are just. Even if this one is not, they can conscientiously serve in a bad cause while hoping that their leaders or the electorate will come to their senses.

No one holds an individual responsible for carrying out the orders of duly constituted authorities when they do not clearly violate international law. The Nuremberg tribunal punished the Axis leaders for their war crimes, because they knew the international law and violated it under orders or on their own. There is, of course, the possibility that the draftee will someday be ordered to do an especially heinous act that does little to advance the war: shoot prisoners, torture civilians, bomb hospitals, or bayonet babies. But these are only possibilities. Soldiers may have to disobey at some point in their military service in order to follow their conscience, and their right to so disobey is recognized by the military codes of virtually all nations.[88] But draftees do not have to face up to these problems. That there is the chance that they may as soldiers have to do something someday that is thoroughly revolting does not relieve them of the duty to become soldiers in the first instance. Agreeing to participate in a war is not the same thing as agreeing to perform whatever atrocities may be commanded. The alternative to pacifism is not willingness to preside over My Lai massacres.

The Individual Has the Right to Resist the Draft

Conscientiousness There can be no question about whether individuals have the moral right to follow their conscience. Not only do they have a right to do what they believe morality directs, but they *ought* to do it. This liberty may not fall among their political rights or even their "natural" rights, but it is mandated by their status as moral agents. The individual who believes that submitting to

[88]The American *Law of Land Warfare* (1956), for example, states: "The fact that the law of war has been violated pursuant to an order of a superior authority, whether military or civil, does not deprive the act in question of its character as a war crime, nor does it constitute a defense in the trial of an accused individual, unless he did not know and could not reasonably have been expected to know that the act ordered was unlawful. In all cases where the order is held not to constitute a defense to an allegation of war crime, the fact that the individual was acting pursuant to orders may be considered in mitigation of punishment."

induction violates moral law is obliged to resist. In Kantian terms, one can exemplify a good will only when one seeks to do those things which one ought to do.

This Kantian position is believed in some quarters to be circular or paradoxical. "One ought to do what one ought to do." But what ought one to do? "Obey the moral law." What is the moral law? "To develop a good will." What is the good will? "A will that is attuned to what is right because it is right." Or we might say: "An act is right when done because it is right." This formulation may be expanded to: "An act is right when done because it is done because it is right." There is no limit to the expansion. Another way to put it: "Your duty is to do what you believe to be your duty." This may be expanded *ad infinitum,* the first expansion being: "Your duty is to do what you believe to be what you believe to be is your duty."

These verbal puzzles can be eliminated quite easily on Kant's own terms. He does distinguish between moral law and motive. The former is objective and is known by reason. The latter is subjective and attaches to the will. A right act is in conformity to the moral law, but it can be done by a bad or indifferent person. The *doing* of it has no moral value. Only an act done from respect for the moral law has moral value—although the agent may be incorrect in what he or she believes the moral law requires. The goodness of the motive makes sense only when there is an objective moral law that the agent seeks to put into practice because it *is* an objective law. The will can only be good when it seeks to do those things which it ought. A good will is not invalidated by erroneous philosophizing; it *is* invalidated by failure to respect and seek the moral law. One's primary obligation is to carry out the moral law *as one sees it.* Conscientiousness consists of following one's conscience, although that conscience may be misinformed.

It may be difficult to know in individual cases whether one has seriously sought the moral law and made a decision out of respect for what one thinks one has found. But if one has done these things and found that military service is a violation of moral law, one has the right *and* the obligation to resist. Only the individual will know whether he or she has acted on moral principle rather than cowardice, greed, or particular inclinations. To act on moral conviction is itself a moral act.

Our main concern here, however, is not with motive (which would apply to all the ethical problems discussed in this book), but with moral principle. Is the belief that participation in the draft is wrong a justified conclusion of ethical thinking?

Pacifism Absolute pacifism is not an implausible theory for one who accepts Christianity. It is clear that universal love is central to Jesus' teaching and that acts of violence are manifestations of something else. Pacifists refuse to do harm to anyone. They do not look for justifications and reject any that are offered. They regard life as precious and will not take it under any circumstances. To refuse to kill is the very least that they can do in honoring the great commandments to love God (who has created life) and to love other human beings (who bear life). Whatever else they may be able to do for others, it is an absolute requirement that they not destroy them.

The absolute pacifist does not do violence on behalf of others. To question this not only suggests an easy excuse for people who want to work for good ends in violent ways, but is to countenance an immorality that no results can justify. Violence is a violation of God's law and a corruption of the agent's soul. The world is indeed a difficult and dangerous place. Individuals must not adopt the ways of the earthly city, but must preserve their souls for membership in the heavenly city. They will lament the sorrows and incursions that others (as well as they themselves) may have to bear, but they will not make the world worse by contributing in any way to death and violence. Their stance may not serve themselves or others very well in this world, but they perhaps have another world to think of. George Fox, the founder of the Society of Friends, wrote: "When Christ was on earth, He said His Kingdom was not of this world; if it had been, His servants would have fought; but it was not, therefore His servants did not fight."[89] A. A. Milne asked, "What matter if we are a conquered race, so long as we continue to serve God?"[90]

Such a pacifist rejects the notion of "fighting in the spirit of love." It is impossible to treat others *as* enemies without feeling that they *are* enemies. If we heed the injunction to love, we will not be able to kill the aggressor—even to save our life or that of others. The aggressor *also* is one of our "loved ones"! In case of war, the enemy troops are draftees or "volunteers"—as we ourselves would be. Most of them are no happier to be where they are than we would be. They are citizen-soldiers too, sent out by their government to do its dirty work. As Muhammed Ali said when he declined military service during the Vietnam War, "I ain't got nothing against them Congs!" The people we are asked to kill in warfare have no more claim to be hated than anyone else. Yet, if we love them, how can we kill them?

If there is anyone who deserves to be hated, it is the government officials and their civilian supporters who send enemy troops into combat.

> The men that worked for England
> They have their graves at home:
> And bees and birds of England
> About the cross can roam.
>
> But they that fought for England,
> Following a falling star,
> Alas, alas for England
> They have their graves afar.

[89] *The Journal of George Fox,* ed. Rufus M. Jones (New York: G. P. Putnam's Sons, Capricorn Books, 1963), p. 385.

[90] A. A. Milne, "Onward, Christian Soldiers," in Mayer, p. 266.

> And they that rule in England,
> In stately conclave met,
> Alas, alas for England
> They have no graves as yet.[91]

But even these require our forbearance and forgiveness, for they know not what they do.

Something else can be said on behalf of "pacifists" who oppose violence but who will defend their fellow citizens. Can this position be made the basis of a conscientious refusal to submit to the draft? Yes. If a young man or woman is to be drafted at a time when the nation is at peace, he or she does not *know* whether future military action will be offensive or defensive. He or she cannot then take the oath to fight whenever called upon. Or if the nation is indeed involved in a war, it may be the kind (Korea, Vietnam) where the protection of the draftee's fellow Americans cannot be the intention. He or she would, therefore, on the "protection only" criterion, have to conscientiously refuse induction. Some people may plausibly refuse to fight unless the enemy directly attacks this country or mounts an invasion against it.

The "protection of others" criterion, if applied liberally, could be used to justify a great many military actions, for it can often be argued that war will be protective of some people somewhere in the world. This takes us beyond pacifism and to the concept of a just war.

The Just War The criteria offered by Purtill admittedly are subject to controversy and various interpretations. Purtill is correct in saying that a great many people would accept them in principle. But that they may yield so many conflicting conclusions when applied to actual events makes their value highly questionable. It is quite possible to interpret these criteria in a rather pacifistic way.

The sixth criterion, for example, requires us to weigh the good accomplished by a war against its evils. Even if it could be assumed that a utilitarian calculus is available to perform the weighing (and this is a great deal to assume), one could argue that the immense harm produced by a modern war in terms of death and suffering would make such a war unthinkable. In a big war in the nuclear age, casualties would number in the millions. "There is simply too much horror to be subsumed under the medieval notion of proportionality."[92] What national advantage could outweigh this? Political concerns could not. "After all," asks Donald Wells, "is there really any doubt that men can live well under a variety of systems: capitalistic, communistic, monarchic, or democratic? It is equally obvious, I assume, that men may live poorly under any of these systems."[93] But, it may be asked, can we not defend the propriety of a small (limited, contained, conven-

[91] G. K. Chesterton, "Elegy in a Country Churchyard."
[92] Donald Wells, "How Much Can 'the Just War' Justify?" in Beauchamp, p. 184. Wells's article first appeared in *Journal of Philosophy* 66 (December 4, 1969): 23.
[93] Wells in Beauchamp, p. 185.

tional) war, in which the destruction would not be so great? This position calls for an even more dubious assumption: The warmakers know in advance the results of their actions. Officials cannot design and execute a war in the way a tailor fashions a suit of clothes! One thing leads to another. Individuals confronted with the draft can thus refuse to submit, not because they are opposed to all war, but because they believe that the current situation is such that the sixth criterion will surely be left unmet or is in grave danger of being unmet once a "limited" war has begun.

The seventh criterion fares no better. How are we to interpret "unavoidable killing" and "immoral means"? The first refers to civilians; the second to weapons. They go together. Even in the Vietnam War, where atomic weapons were not used, the weapons that were used brought death to hundreds of thousands of civilians. When nuclear weapons are used, the number will be in the millions. The idea of "surgical strikes" is a myth, just as "precision bombing" was a myth in World War II. What is deemed "unavoidable" changes with the strategic situation. In World War II, saturation bombing, rockets, and atomic bombs were placed on the list. If the United States goes to war against another nuclear power (or if such a power enters the war), nuclear bombing of population centers may well be deemed "unavoidable" by both sides.

The third criterion speaks of "good intentions." Intentions may be good, but they would have to be entertained in the presence of a great deal of ignorance or stupidity. How can intentions really be good if a war by the United States is launched in full awareness of the human misery it is certain to produce? The criterion is couched in terms of "repelling the attack of Nation B," but no limits are set on lengths to which a nation may go in protecting itself or its friends. Clearly, the best way to repel an attack is not, as Churchill would say, by fighting on the beaches, on the landing grounds, in the fields, in the streets, and in the hills, but by destroying the enemy's capability of attacking. This requires an attack of our own—against the aggressors' launching sites and eventually their cities (while they respond in kind). Escalation reaches a point where the original purposes are forgotten. Hatred has escalated also, and if there are any left to make a peace, "fairness" will be the furthest thing from their minds. Perhaps there was a time when good intentions and fair peace treaties were possible, but that time is past. Since this criterion is impossible to meet, except in cases where the vital interests of another great nuclear power are not threatened, individuals should refuse to be any part of a military effort. Even if they accept the theory of deterrence, they must know that American nuclear military power is adequately staffed by volunteers. To increase the military forces through the draft is to prepare for something more than deterrence.

The fifth criterion is perhaps the most troubling. War as a "last resort" can too easily be claimed by an ambitious nation. Japan tried peaceful methods in the South Pacific but had to resort to attacking Pearl Harbor. Germany asked for passage through Belgium, but finally had to invade that nation in World War I. No one can say at what point the leaders of one's nation will feel they have run out of peaceful alternatives. Individuals who believe that the horror of nuclear war is so great that it is now unthinkable, will want to do more than interpret this criterion strictly. They will want to say that war is no resort at all. They will argue, not that peaceful means for settling disputes should be tried *first,* but that they are the *only* means that should be tried. So long as war looms in the background as a "last resort," these disputes do not *have* to be settled peacefully.

Individuals may thus reject induction, not because they are conscientiously opposed to all war, past, present, and future, but because they believe that a war by the United States under the present conditions would in all likelihood be a case of unjust war—either in its inception or in its development. They see their presence in the military forces as contributing to such a war. True, an individual is only a tiny part of the machine, but it takes over *all* of that person. One cannot morally lend one's person to an enterprise that is doing, or is being trained to do, actions that one believes are wrong. Here the position is conscientious, but selectively conscientious: Nuclear war on the part of the United States in 1980 is wrong; limited war in the same circumstances is wrong because it may lead to nuclear war.

H. J. N. Hosburgh carefully examines the factors that are supposed to limit the disruptiveness of war and finds that none of them can be realistically expected to significantly limit the destructiveness of a modern war. Instead, the tendency is for war to become increasingly erosive of moral quality.

> Hatred, bitterness, and fear—all of which steadily increase throughout the period of hostilities—produce tremendous temptations to set aside . . . self-denying ordinances. And these temptations are aggravated by the systematic representation of the enemy as even more vicious than [the enemy] is. So one is pushed along the broad road that leads to mutual destruction, reprisals being followed by counterreprisals of even greater bloodiness, the whole process being a terrifying illustration of the self-validating power of that fear and hatred which transmutes enemies who are much like ourselves into absolute monsters. Again, savagery can be resorted to as a means of intimidating the enemy. Ruthlessness can also add to the effectiveness of a surprise assault. . . . And finally, any scruple is necessarily cramping from a military standpoint. As wars develop and military considerations become increasingly paramount even in the eyes of politicians, anything which places one at the slightest military disadvantage is bound to be set aside.[94]

Richard A. Wasserstrom, after carefully examining the place of moral considerations in assessing the practice of war and refusing to condemn war per se, comes to this conclusion:

> If wars were conducted, or were likely to be conducted, so as to produce only the occasional intentional killing of the innocent, that would be one thing. We could then say with some confidence that on this ground at least wars can hardly be condemned

[94] H. J. N. Hosburgh, "Critique of Armed Force as an Instrument of Justice," in Beitz and Herman, pp. 25–26.

> out of hand. Unfortunately, though, mankind no longer lives in such a world and, as a result, the argument from the death of the innocent has become increasingly more convincing. The intentional, or at least knowing killing of the innocent on a large scale became a practically necessary feature of war with the advent of air warfare. And the genuinely indiscriminate killing of very great numbers of innocent persons is the dominant legacy of the birth of thermonuclear weapons. At this state the argument from the death of the innocent moves appreciably closer to becoming a decisive objection to war. For even if we reject, as I have argued we should, both absolutist interpretations of the argument, the core of truth that remains is the insistence that in war, no less than elsewhere, the knowing killing of the innocent is an evil that throws up the heaviest of justificatory burdens. My own view is that in any major war that can or will be fought today, none of those considerations that can justify engaging in war will in fact come close to meeting this burden. But even if I am wrong, the argument from the death of the innocent does, I believe, make it clear both where the burden is and how unlikely it is today to suppose that it can be honestly discharged.[95]

I would simply want to add that today the class of "innocents" is virtually the entire populations of the belligerent countries. Civilians are innocent in a sense, but so too are the military personnel, for most of them have either volunteered to defend their country or have been conscripted as "citizen-soldiers." Neither citizens nor soldiers actively plot and carry out wars. Soldiers, who are misguided in their patriotism, arms workers, who are trying to earn a decent living, and other civilians who pay their taxes to support the war-preparedness effort, are all innocent in the sense that they are opposed to war. The loss of all is equally regrettable. Perhaps only the people who lead their nations into war are guilty.

From another point of view, all must share some guilt: soldiers who did not exercise their right to stay out of the armed services, arms workers who did not decide to take a less remunerative job, and the other civilians who did not refuse to pay their taxes—and who supported their hawkish political officials.

The views of people who defend war on the basis of a distinction between "war" and "murder"[96] assume that the line between "the guilty" and "the innocent" can clearly be drawn. This is just not so. Between children on the one side (clearly innocent) and heads of state on the other (clearly guilty) is that vast twilight range of partial guilt and innocence.

Aside, however, from the innocence or guilt of the populations of states, it seems clear that war at this time would be fatal to too many of them to justify any end their leaders may hold out to them.

The first criterion justifies war only in defense of one's own nation or some other. It may be conducted only against aggressors. Setting aside the difficult

[95]Richard A. Wasserstrom, "On the Morality of War," in Wasserstrom, *War and Morality,* pp. 100–101.

[96]G. E. M. Anscombe, for example.

problem of defining *aggression,* we may question the extent to which we have the right to defend others. Afghanistan, which is not an ally? West Germany, which is? This criterion is only one, and is not put forward as alone justifying war. The other criteria would have to be met also before the war could be declared just. In view of the difficulty of meeting the others, as shown above, it is quite possible that wars in defense of our friends would not necessarily be just.

What about war in defense of one's own nation? This is often put forward, not as a necessary condition for a just war, but as a sufficient one. Attack against the United States itself gives us the right of military response. One may argue that while we thus have the right of response, it is one that we should not exercise if this response consists of nuclear action or action that is likely to lead to nuclear action. It may well be the more moral action to surrender. Purtill is correct in saying that self-defense is not sufficient—the other criteria have to be taken into account. In view of the wholesale death and misery that would be expected (sixth and seventh criteria), the moral choice, even for a nation under attack, might well be that of surrender. If the war can be won only by releasing missiles aimed at the enemy's population centers, which would bring about similar nuclear destruction of our population centers, should we try to win it? A war of defense soon becomes a war of mutual destruction.

Obedience There are, then, several arguments that can be put forth against war. It can plausibly be maintained that military technology today is such that a nuclear war could not possibly meet the requirements of a just war, and that even conventional war should be eschewed because of the likelihood of its leading to nuclear war. Individuals who clearly recognize the present impossibility of a just war should, therefore, refuse to be a part of any enterprise (including military training) that is directed toward war. They will agree with Martin Luther King, Jr., who said: "The choice today is no longer between violence and nonviolence. It is either nonviolence or non-existence."[97] And with Bertrand Russell: "Shall we put an end to the human race; or shall mankind renounce war?"[98] This is not old-fashioned pacifism, but the conviction that war can *no longer* be justified by its results: war in the atomic age is simply unacceptable.

The arguments on the morality of war are perhaps nondecisive. Conscientious objectors may be told that military power will be used only in defense and that a country that refused to fight for its values does not deserve to retain them. They may be told that the military forces are to be armed with, and trained in the use of, conventional weapons. They may be told that their country plans to fight only limited wars, that every effort will be used to prevent escalation into a nuclear holocaust. They may be told that their country intends nothing but a "just" war and a "just" peace, and that it will always be concerned with the welfare of

[97]Martin Luther King, Jr., "Pilgrimage to Nonviolence," *Christian Century,* April 13, 1960.
[98]Bertand Russell, *Portraits from Memory and Other Essays* (New York: Simon & Schuster, 1956), p. 235.

civilians at home and abroad. They may be told to be good citizens and, in this controversial area, to abide by the decisions of their duly elected officials. They have the right to disagree, but not to disobey.

This is not an acceptable argument. Individuals cannot forfeit their moral autonomy by deferring to an external agency when they are convinced that it is wrong. Their "debt" to their country does not require them to cooperate in a monstrous evil. The greater diplomatic, strategic, and technical knowledge that government officials may have does not invalidate the moral conclusions that individuals can draw from their own general knowledge of the nature of modern warfare. That they live in a more or less democratic state does not obligate them to accept *all* the decisions of its leaders. They may accept most of the unfavorable decisions made by duly elected and appointed officials because they prize the system and realize that it does not exist solely to benefit themselves. But when it pursues a policy that runs counter to a basic and significant moral conviction, they have the right to decline to participate. When national leaders are tragically wrong, one has the right to disobey.

And national leaders *have* been wrong. Lyndon Johnson, a humane and popular leader, was wrong on Vietman. John F. Kennedy was mistaken on the "missile gap." Anthony Eden erred in the Suez crisis. Richard Nixon was wrong to order the bombing of Cambodia. Jimmy Carter was perhaps wrong in backing the mobile MX missile system, in having supported the Shah of Iran, and in using force in an attempt to free the hostages in Iran. Adolf Hitler was profoundly and morally wrong in virtually every major project he pursued. Leonid Brezhnev was wrong to order the invasion of Afghanistan. Even religious leaders have been wrong: Pope Pius XII, who held that the threat of Communism was grave enough to justify the use of atomic, chemical, and biological bombs, and who refused to accept conscientious objection on the part of German Catholics when NATO was being formed; Paul Ramsey, the Protestant theologian who assured the possible victims of a nuclear war that the preservation of civilization was worth the price.[99] The U.S. Senate has not (as of 1980) even approved the SALT II accords. "In August, 1958, the U.S. Senate voted 82 to 2 to deny government funds to any person or institution that proposes or actually conducts any study regarding the possible results of the surrender of the U.S. as an alternative to war."[100]

We do have the right to refuse to participate in immorality. It is true that the rank and file in the Axis nations were not blamed at Nuremberg for the atrocities of World War II and the events leading up to it. It was the "leaders" who had to pay the price, and there were many of them available to do it. But where do we draw the line? Were Hitler and Himmler guilty? Of course. What about the commandants of the concentration camps? Probably. What about the guards and the technicians who operated the ovens? What about the soldiers? The civilians who supported them? The guilt was not equal, but perhaps they *all* should bear

[99]See Wells, pp. 184, 183, 186.
[100]Ibid., p. 186.

some degree of guilt. Whether they were all guilty or not, they did have the *right* to disobey.

Since Nuremberg, obedience to orders is no excuse. To what may individuals appeal when they believe that improper actions are demanded of them? On legal grounds, they may invoke international law, but international law is not clear on the use of nuclear weapons—although a case against it may be plausibly made on the basis of accepted laws.[101] In actual fact, however, "the 'dictates of the public conscience' have seemingly surrendered to military expediency."[102] This leaves but one alternative: individual conscience. "There comes a point," said Sir Hartley Shawcross at Nuremberg, "where a man must refuse to answer to his leader, if he is also to answer to his conscience."[103] The armed services are equipped with nuclear weapons. Military personnel are trained to employ them. It is not just the commander in chief whose finger may be on the button. Any draftee's finger may be there. Morality may require that allegiance to humanity supersede allegiance to nation. "The weapon of indiscriminate mass destruction," wrote George T. Kennan, "goes further than anything the Christian ethic can properly accept."[104]

Disobedience often requires great courage, and one hesitates to condemn the individual who declines to exercise this right. Failure to do what is morally admirable is not necessarily immoral. But individuals who feel that their own moral convictions are at odds with those of their country's leaders act morally when they defy those leaders. They do not simply protest in their hearts and play the part of good citizens; they do not simply protest with words and grumble as they obey. They protest with their entire person and refuse to serve in the armed services. "Be men first," said Thoreau, "and subjects afterwards."[105]

If it should turn out that people cannot get conscientious objector status because they oppose contemporary war rather than war in general, or they oppose this particular dangerous war, they are justified in taking some form of civil disobedience. As argued in the previous chapter, this is more defensible morally than fleeing to Canada or deserting in the face of the enemy. Genuine civil disobedience, it may be recalled, consists of actions that are done *in public,* that are *nonviolent,* for which *punishment* is *accepted,* and that are *against only the law or policy that is being protested.* Civil disobedients, selective in their choice of immoral wars, are selective also in their resistance to government. They are not rebels against authority itself, but against that *one exercise* of authority that outrages their moral sensibilities.

[101]See Guenter Lewy, "Superior Orders, Nuclear Warfare, and the Dictates of Conscience," in Wasserstrom, *War and Morality,* pp. 126–129.
[102]Ibid., p. 129.
[103]Ibid., p. 132.
[104]Quoted in ibid., p. 133.
[105]Henry David Thoreau, "Civil Disobedience," *Walden and Other Writings* (New York: Modern Library, 1950), p. 637.

Summary of the Issues

One has the moral right to do whatever is moral. One must follow one's conscience. This is tautologous. But it is not tautologous to say that to act on erroneous moral conviction itself has moral value—not because it is erroneous, but because it is acted on as a matter of principle. The problem here, however, is to discover what the objective moral law does indeed require. Is an individual obliged to submit to induction?

One basis for an answer is the philosophy of pacifism. The side that would justify resistance to the draft argues that it is always wrong to do violence. Christian love can never condone violence, even when done on behalf of others. To repay violence with violence because violence is wrong is self-contradictory. The other side argues that persons have the right not to be treated violently, but they forfeit that right when they act violently themselves. We have a prima facie duty not to kill, but it is not an absolute duty.

A second version of pacifism is that violence is acceptable only when done to protect others. This is the usual Christian interpretation. One side argues that this kind of pacifism would not justify resistance to the draft, for military service may be regarded as protection against aggressors. The other side would justify refusal to be drafted, for the United States is not under threat of aggression.

A third version of "pacifism" is that war never succeeds, that violence breeds more violence to the ruination of all parties. This position is criticized by pointing to wars that have succeeded. The cost was great, but utilitarian thinking can show that more was gained than lost. Many pacifists have changed their minds when the values at stake became apparent.

This brings us to the concept of a just war. Those who insist on submission to the draft argue that this concept provides a realist alternative to the two extremes of warmongering and pacifism. War is not an all-or-nothing proposition. Criteria for a just war are presented and defended. The other side argues that the criteria are so vague as to be useless. Any prior view can find support in them. Although some people on this side might argue that objection to war should be *selective* rather than categorical, they argue that *any* war today would produce such colossal evil that it would almost certainly be unjust. The individual can rightly resolve to be no part of it.

Who is to decide whether a war is just or unjust? The individual must decide in any case. One side believes, however, that one should defer in one's judgment to one's government and serve whenever called. Several plausible arguments are presented for this principle of obedience. The other side rejects them all. The duty to obey is only prima facie. Individuals must act on the basis of where they think their real duty lies. Disobedience often requires great courage. While we may not condemn the individual who lacks it, we honor the individual more who has protested with his or her whole person than one who has simply protested with words. The road of civil disobedience is open to those who have the courage to walk it.

Discussion Questions

1. In what sense, if any, are you a pacifist? Explain.
2. Do you believe that utilitarian calculation can be employed to show that some wars are "successful"? Explain.
3. What deontological elements do you find in Purtill's criteria for a just war? What utilitarian elements?
4. Would you reserve conscientious objector status only for those who oppose *all* wars? Why?
5. What would be your opinion of people who submitted to the draft in peacetime, then deserted later when they found themselves in an "unjust" war?
6. Do you think that a war between the United States and the Soviet Union would necessarily be an unjust war? Why?
7. Do you think that a pacifist could consistently accept a noncombatant role in the armed services? In "alternative service" outside the military? In a war plant? On a farm? In a civilian hospital? In a toy factory? Explain.
8. Do you accept the distinction between what one has a *right* to do (optional) and what one has an *obligation* (not optional) to do? Why?
9. Would you rather be "dead than red"? Why?
10. What is your reaction to Narveson's refutation of pacifism?
11. Which interpretation of the pacifist teachings of Jesus is correct? That of George Fox or Martin Luther? Why?
12. How do *you* feel about America's war record?
13. Why did nonviolent resistance work in India under Gandhi but not in Germany for the Jews?
14. Do you think it is possible to formulate criteria for a just war? Why? Does the fact that individuals can distort or misuse a set of criteria mean that they are useless? Explain.
15. Do you believe that individuals should defer to the state in their actions (if not in their minds) when asked to serve in the military? Why?
16. In what sense, if any, do you believe that a nation at war can refrain from "unavoidable killing" and "immoral means"?
17. Were Americans justified in bombing population centers in Japan and Germany during World War II? Why?
18. Read and comment on Housman's poem "The Day of Battle" (*Shropshire Lad,* LVI).

For Further Reading

Tom L. Beauchamp, ed. *Ethics and Public Policy.* Englewood Cliffs, N.J.: Prentice-Hall, 1975. Chapter 4.

Charles R. Beitz and Theodore Herman, eds. *Peace and War.* San Francisco: W. H. Freeman and Co., 1973. Chapters 1 and 8.

J. Cameron. "It's Time to Bite the Bullet on the Draft." *Fortune* 101 (April 7, 1980): 52–54+.

"Controversy over Proposed Draft Registration." *Congressional Digest* 59 (April 1980): 99–128.

Staughton Lynd, ed. *Nonviolence in America: A Documentary History.* Indianapolis: Bobbs-Merrill Co., 1966.
Albert Marrin, ed. *War and the Christian Conscience.* Chicago: Henry Regnery Co., 1971.
Peter Mayer, ed. *The Pacifist Conscience.* Chicago: Henry Regnery Co., 1967.
James Rachels, ed. *Moral Problems.* 3rd ed. New York: Harper & Row, 1979. Part 5.
Gerald Runkle. "Is Violence Always Wrong?" *Journal of Politics* 38 (May 1976):367–389.
Richard A. Wasserstrom, ed. *War and Morality.* Belmont, Calif.: Wadsworth Publishing Co., 1970.

FOREIGN AID

American Food Aid Should Be Governed by the Principle of National Self-Interest

The Good State The United States is an affluent nation. It has a gross national product that greatly exceeds that of any nation in the world. It is blessed with land and climate that yield bountiful harvests. Many people in the world are starving, and many more suffer from malnutrition. It would appear that the United States has a moral obligation to assist the developing nations meet the basic needs of their people for food. Since we have so much and they have so little, should we not share our blessings?

The belief that we should is perhaps drawn from an analogy between states and individuals. When one is fortunately situated, a case could be made that one is morally bound to help other individuals who are in dire straits. How far one should go in this generosity is determined by the nature of the relations obtaining between oneself and the others, as well as by one's situation and theirs. Although it may be granted that most ethical theories would recognize the prima facie duty of a fortunate individual to aid the unfortunate ones, it does not follow that individual *states* bear similar ethical obligations to other states. States are not persons. To argue that the duty of the former corresponds to the duty of the latter is to commit the fallacy of argument from analogy.

A state is a group of people united under one government to pursue their joint interest. Governments exist to serve the governed. A government is responsible solely to the people that constitute the nation. Its only excuse for being is to carry out the common concerns of the society on which it rests. It should be judged on the basis of its faithfulness to national aims and its effectiveness in carrying them out. States are not moral or immoral; they are successful or unsuccessful. While as an individual one may be required to weaken or even sacrifice oneself, states cannot do the same. While individuals are subject to moral law, states are not. Although we speak of "international law," this is not an objective and binding set of norms, but a hodgepodge of principles agreed on by particular states for certain prudential reasons. Citizens who have given their "consent to government in some hypothetical sense have given their consent to a power that will look after their own social interests. They have not generated a "leviathan" that with other "leviathans" is to play a moral role on a global stage. A "just" state is one that has ordered the relations of its people in a just way, not one that seeks to satisfy the rights of other *states.*

A state is properly concerned with the flow of wealth within its own borders. It has the right to tax and to use this money in ways that will serve the cause of justice, prosperity, or anything else that advances the national interest. But it steps outside its proper function when it expends national wealth or resources to redress what seems to be international injustice. Only a world government could do this. Individuals who pay their taxes can demand that they be used for national purposes. When they see their tax money employed for charitable purposes entertained by their leaders, they are entitled to object. Individuals can be as charitable as they like (or as their moral codes require), but states by their nature are restricted to their own society. The one thing uniting all citizens is that they pay their taxes in order to support a good society—although they differ on what this may be. They do not pay their taxes to foster a good *world.* They are not citizens of a world; they are citizens of a state.

Some *organizations,* it is true, have aims that go beyond the interests of the organization itself. A charitable or service society may indeed utilize funds for broadly humanitarian interests. Its choice need not enjoy the support of each and every member. Such organizations are different from individuals, for they perform *collective* acts of generosity. They are also different from states, because membership and participation are *voluntary.* Individuals who object to the Hieronymus Society giving scholarships to left-handed dentists can *resign.* But citizens who object to their country giving aid to Lower Slobovia at the expense of their own society cannot so easily resign. Not only is membership in the charitable organization voluntary, but the decision to perform a specific act of charity is voluntary also (in a collective way). That such an act be voluntary would seem to be a requirement of genuine charity. Aid from one country to another would not qualify, unless we illegitimately view the donor country as an individual person or an organization in which membership is optional.

Apart from states, citizens can, as free individuals or members of voluntary organizations, respond to their own conceptions of obligatory or supererogatory humanitarianism to their hearts' content. But they are rightly indignant when their state pursues an aim beyond that of national self-interest.

Catastrophic and Chronic Need It would appear to be callous on the part of a state to refuse to come to the aid of a people in dire nutritional straits. Many commentators assume that an affluent nation should help out in a catastrophe brought about by weather, war, or some other unusual misfortune—even though it may not be obligated to carry out a regular program of aid to a developing country. For example:

> We must take care to distinguish between humanitarian aid during an acute, emergency situation and the chronic problem of poverty and hunger. It is difficult to believe that any thinking person would deny food and health aid during natural

disasters like those resulting from adverse weather conditions such as typhoons or epidemics.[106]

In addition to the argument given above about the state as performer of humanitarian action toward other states or peoples, two other points can be made against this view. First, the line between emergency and chronic situations is difficult to draw. Is the acute distress a nation faces a one-time thing or is it simply one of several low points in its history of inadequate agricultural production and/or weak purchasing power? When famine is inevitable (as it is, for example, in Africa's "hunger belt"), is the condition "catastrophic" or "chronic"? A nation may experience a series of food crises as a result of a system of food acquisition that is fundamentally unsound. Emergency aid in most cases fails to solve the problem; it merely provides a brief respite. Humanitarian response to acute need that does not get at the deeper cause merely confirms the distressed country in its dependence, while saving some lives that will perish in the next crisis if aid is not repeated. Second, the way is always left open for individuals voluntarily to contribute relief aid. Such individuals can express their humanitarianism according to their own conceptions of the requirements of morality. They do not have to depend on the state to act on their behalf in a cause believed to be moral.

The resources of the United States are limited. Even with the best of intentions, we could not solve the world food problem. There are too many starving and undernourished people on this planet.[107] In 1980 the UN World Food Council stated that twenty-six nations were facing "abnormal food shortages"—that is, famine.[108] Even if it were granted that we should provide aid, choices would have to be made regarding *who* would be helped and *what form* the help would take. Many principles have been suggested for answering these questions: We should help our friends, we should help those who most merit help, we should help those whose case is otherwise hopeless, we should help those who will benefit most, we should help those toward whom we have special obligations or commitments, we should help in a way that would promote self-sufficiency, we should direct our help toward the more desperate elements of the particular population, and so on.

Pursuing the false analogy between person and state, we might argue that some nations are our *friends* and should therefore be helped. States can be allies, but not friends. If we help our allies, it is for reason of self-interest, not ethics. If we

[106]James R. Simpson, "Humanism and Hunger," *Humanist,* March–April 1980, p. 42.

[107]In 1980 the State Department and the Council on Environmental Quality submitted a report to the president called "Global 2000." It predicted that the world's population would increase by 55 percent and reach 6.35 billion in 2000. Nearly all this growth will take place in the less developed countries. "The increasing demand for food threatens to dwarf the harvests of available arable land: while one hectare (2.4 acres) fed 2.6 people in the early 1970s, by the year 2000 it will have to support four. And the world's tillable soil will be menaced by erosion and the steady buildup of salt and alkali. Hundreds of millions of people will be hungry." See *Newsweek,* August 4, 1980, p. 38.

[108]Botswana, Djibouti, Ethiopia, Kenya, Somalia, Sudan, Uganda, Tanzania, Zambia, Cape Verde Islands, Chad, Gambia, Mali, Mauretania, Niger, Senegal, Upper Volta, Bangladesh, Burma, Indonesia, Philippines, Sri Lanka, Haiti, Grenada, Honduras, and Nicaragua.

have made a *commitment* to a foreign power, we should, in order to maintain credibility, honor that commitment, but this also is a matter of self-interest rather than ethics. If we are partly *responsible* for the plight of another state, that is, a contributory factor to its present condition, we might feel that we had a responsibility to assist it. This might be viewed as a matter of restitution. However, the United States does not have a history of colonialism (rapacious or other); and even if it did, the present generation should not feel guilt for what its ancestors may have done, nor do present sufferers in Third World countries (now free) have a claim for redress on behalf of *their* ancestors. In any case, contact with Western culture has already brought significant benefits to developing nations—not least of which is an extended life-expectancy.

The Deserving Poor Is it not the case, however, that some nations are in dire straits through no fault of their own? If so, these states would be the "deserving poor" and would seem to warrant aid from the more fortunate. This would follow only if they have not utilized to the full their capacity to help themselves. We may *pity* a state that refuses to help itself, but morality does not require us to help it. It would be a supererogatory act on the part of the assisting state, but not a required act. Such supererogatory acts are best left to private individuals. When benevolent actions on behalf of an undeserving state confirm that state in a position of dependence, they would lose whatever positive moral quality they are presumed to have. They remove the urgency for reform. Another unethical aspect of aid to the undeserving is that, in demanding and receiving aid as a matter of "right," the undeserving state is using the affluent nation and its people as means for its own goals. Even if developed nations have the resources for eliminating hunger, it would not follow that they are obligated to do so in every corner of the world. The most that can be claimed is that they have an obligation to assist those people who have made a reasonable effort to help themselves.

Some states would seem not to merit any aid at all:

1. Those that make no effort to control their growing populations. There are two obvious ways to deal with hunger: increase the supply of food and decrease the number of eaters. A nation that cannot do the former to a sufficient degree must do the latter. This is its responsibility. "Individual procreators [in Bangladesh], looking to their personal gain and 'security,' victimized their own children individually and their fellow countrymen collectively, as well as any foreign donors who send them food. . . . The onus of multiplying empty stomachs in the Sahel lies exactly where it belongs, on a callous progenitive populace."[109] Developing states that do not seek to control their population in a situation of limited resources are injuring their own people. "Present persons can be injured

[109]Joseph Fletcher, "Feeding the Hungry: An Ethical Appraisal," in Lucas and Ogletree, *Lifeboat Ethics,* p. 59.

by the production of more persons."[110] And those who help such states may be guilty of injuring future persons, for the demand for food at a later date may exceed the resources of this planet—or the willingness of affluent states to contribute. Overpopulation will be even greater, and there will be more people suffering and starving. "The injury of not feeding present persons may be outweighed by the very likely injury to even more future persons which would, all else being equal, result from feeding present persons. If one ought to choose to injure fewer persons rather than more persons, then the calculation of the impact of present policies on future persons must be considered. In short, the scope of moral concern must have a future-oriented dimension. . . ."[111] The failure of a poor nation to exercise birth control does not simply *excuse* us from helping it; it might *require* us to deny aid.

2. Those that spend excessive proportions of their GNP on military goods. "Third World leaders seem to be squandering their meager surpluses on guns instead of butter. . . . A powerful army, it is thought, is an indispensible attribute of nationhood. . . . In 1972, less developed countries spent almost two and a half times as much on military budgets as they received in foreign economic aid ($30 billion vs. $13 billion)."[112]

3. Those that economically oppress their own people. Unequal distribution of wealth is much greater in developing countries than in others. In Colombia, for example, the top 5 percent of the population receive 42 percent of the income, while in the United States the top 5 percent get only 16 percent. In India, another very needy country, the top 20 percent receive 65 percent of the income. In Mexico, the bottom 40 percent receive only 10 percent of the income. In most countries redistribution of wealth and land would rescue many from starvation. Even in Bangladesh, food production in most years is sufficient for the population —if the poor had funds to buy it. The income of the rich is often wasted on consumption of imported luxury goods rather than invested in economic development. Some, of course, is saved: Sizable amounts are "sent abroad to avoid taxes and possible confiscation. The 'Swiss banks' factor is said to have drained more than $3 billion out of Latin America alone in unauthorized outflows during the 1960's. Keeping this money at home for useful investment could have replaced about one-third of foreign aid."[113]

4. Those that are riddled by political corruption. Not all the taxes are collected. Officials avail themselves of public funds—legally and illegally. Prestige

[110] H. Tristram Engelhardt, Jr., "Individuals and Communities, Present and Future," in Lucas and Ogletree, p. 76.
[111] Ibid., p. 82.
[112] Rosen and Jones, *The Logic of International Relations,* pp. 132–133.
[113] Ibid., p. 136.

projects and objects (luxury cars, presidential palaces, ostentatious airports, etc.) are another form of waste through corruption.

5. Those that freely decide to grow agricultural products for export instead of for their own food needs. Some really strange cases can be cited of poor countries that have their land in cultivation of products that do not or cannot serve their own nutritional needs. Africa in general, for example, "is a net *exporter* of barley, beans, peanuts, fresh vegetables, and cattle (not to mention luxury crop exports such as coffee and cocoa), yet has a higher incidence of protein-calorie malnutrition than any other continent."[114] Land devoted to rubber, cotton, and flowers does little for local food consumption. Something is wrong with local leadership in Mexico, for example, which supplies the United States with much of its winter and early spring vegetables while its own people are badly nourished.

6. Those that let vast tracts of arable land lie idle because it is not profitable for their owners to cultivate them. Again, local leaders fail to utilize their own resources. Related to this is the failure to utilize the energies of their unemployed populations. Unfortunately, there is a lot of overlapping in these groups of undeserving states.

A good state (developed or developing) makes every effort to take care of its own people. If the developing nation is to be a good state, it must seek to take care of its own people. Where its best efforts fall short, it can appeal to outside agencies and perhaps make a moral claim for assistance. The burden of proof rests on the petitioning state: It must demonstrate that it has taken drastic steps to solve its own problems and will continue to do so. Perhaps, on this principle, very few states would be able to qualify as "deserving," and the level of morally required aid would be very low. The "moral argument" advanced by "do-gooders" would thus, in the last analysis, justify only a small part of what they are prepared to donate!

National Self-Interest There is, of course, a good reason for extensive American aid to other countries, and that reason is national self-interest. An open admission of this aim would have certain advantages: (1) It would dispel some of the hypocrisy of our national declarations and diminish our moralizing posture on the global scene. (2) It would permit a hard-headed examination and improvement of our aid programs, free of speculation about the requirements of international justice. (3) It would deter humanitarian gestures by American officials, many of which are to curry favor with humanitarian elements of the electorate at the expense of the nation as a whole. (4) It would put an end to imponderable arguments involving "need" and the "deserving poor." No one wants to criticize

[114]Frances Moore Lappé and Joseph Collins, *Food First: Beyond the Myth of Scarcity* (Boston: Houghton Mifflin Company, 1977), p. 15. Permission to quote given by Ballantine Books, a Division of Random House, Inc.

foreign aid in principle or eliminate it entirely. "Whatever happens in recipient countries can . . . be adduced to support maintenance or extension of aid. Progress is evidence of its efficacy and so an argument for its expansion; lack of progress is evidence that the dosage has been insufficient and must be increased. Some advocates argue that it would be inexpedient to deny aid to the speedy (those who advance); others, that it would be cruel to deny it to the needy (those that stagnate). Aid is thus like champagne: in success you deserve it, in failure you need it."[115]

Can the United States serve itself by serving others? Yes.

1. National prosperity. By facilitating the commercial sale of grain to other countries, the United States assists its own food producers. Their surplus finds a market. The government also is spared the expense of compensating farmers for land held out of production.[116] The United States is indeed the world's "breadbasket," possessing far more exportable grain than the total of all nations in the world.[117] Storage costs for both farmers and the government are reduced if the food can be shipped promptly to the recipient nation. Special trade concessions may be made. Even low-cost loans can be offered to encourage purchase. These profitable deals can be made with our "enemies" as well as our friends, with "developed" countries as well as "developing." Another benefit of increased export of American foodstuffs would be a reduction of balance-of-payment deficits. All areas of the world, with the exception of North America, Australia, and New Zealand, are dependent on imported grain.

Sales under Public Law 480 can also serve national prosperity. Even when the food is paid for in the recipient's currency and cannot leave the country, American farmers benefit, since they are paid by the American government. The foreign currency may be used to support other forms of aid, Fulbright scholars, and purchases for U.S. military installations and activities in the recipient nation.

Even food delivered gratis to the recipient nation benefits American food producers who sell it to the government. This is far better than a cash grant to the recipient country, for the money could be spent to buy food anywhere on the world market.

To the extent that sales (commercial or concessionary) and grants of food to developing countries assist them in achieving economic stability, the donor country tends to benefit in having a better market for its exports in general. Their prosperity could contribute to American prosperity. Food aid in all its forms (food, technical assistance, improved seeds and fertilizers, modern farming equipment) is a form of "pump-priming" that in time could be very profitable. Local

[115]Bauer and O'Sullivan, "Foreign Aid for What?," p. 41.

[116]In 1974 no "land-bank" payments were made to American farmers. In previous years more than 50 million acres were kept out of cultivation. In 1972 this amounted to the equivalent of 78 metric tons of grain. See Lester R. Brown, *By Bread Alone,* pp. 59–60.

[117]"North America today controls a larger share of the world's exportable surplus of grains than the Middle East does of current world oil exports." Ibid., p. 61.

currency obtained in concessional sales can be invested in the recipient nation for production of machinery, as well as irrigation and transportation facilities. If we give a poor nation food assistance today, it may buy our automobiles tomorrow. Even in the short run, trade concessions may be made by the recipient nation.

According to the United States Agency for International Development, "in fiscal year 1971, the economic assistance portion of the aid program financed purchases totaling $976 million from more than 4000 firms in all fifty states. In addition, U.S. companies and institutions benefited from $632 million in technical service contracts."[118]

2. Political advantage. Aid may build friendship, thus furthering our diplomatic aims. We not only promote our economic advantage in the other nation but also cement ties that will help us in such areas as treatment of nationals, access to scarce raw materials, and support in the United Nations. Where a regime needs food for its people in order to stay in power, bargains (tacit or explicit) can be struck that serve the interests of both parties. It may be granted that this is a pretty risky business. Recipient nations do not always love the donor, but they can be kept out of the Soviet bloc. The regimes we deal with may be ousted from power (e.g., the Shah of Iran) and a backlash may occur, but in many more cases the understanding achieved with one regime will carry over to the next (e.g., South Korea and Taiwan). The regime we deal with may be unsavory and stand very low with respect to such criteria as respect for human rights (e.g., Samoza in Nicaragua), but it is not our business to *choose* a national government, rather we must deal with it in a way that serves our national purposes.

Senator Hubert Humphrey saw the situation quite idealistically in 1959, stating in his testimony before the Senate Committee on Foreign Relations:

> We have been told repeatedly that this is a worldwide struggle between the forces of evil and the forces of decency. . . . We all know we are engaged in the struggle for men's minds, for their loyalties. There is a struggle between ways of life, a system of values. Our values are different from those of the totalitarians. If it is a worldwide struggle, it would seem to me we should want to mobilize all the resources we possibly can in order to win it. And in a world of want and hunger what is more powerful than food and fibre?

Two years before, he struck a realistic note:

> I have heard . . . that people may become dependent on us for food. I know that was not supposed to be good news. To me, that was good news, because before people can do anything they have got to eat. And if you are looking for a way to get people to lean on you and to be dependent on you, in terms of their cooperation with you, it seems to me that food dependence would be terrific.[119]

[118]Lappé and Collins, p. 357.
[119]Hubert Humphrey, quoted in ibid., pp. 337, 343.

Both these views are still right and proper.

3. Military and strategic advantage. The United States needs allies and it needs military bases. These may be developed countries, such as those in Western Europe, and developing countries, such as Turkey and the Philippines. Our deterrent capability is greatly enhanced by the fact that we have missile sites, refueling stations for our submarines, and military detachments beyond our borders. Strategically, we would be much better off if Cuba were our ally (or at least a neutral). It is no longer (if it ever was) feasible to create military partners or satellites by force. This failed to work in Indochina and mainland China. But it *is* feasible, as well as less costly in lives and money, to enhance our strategic concerns by means of intelligent aid programs. Perhaps Soviet dependence on American wheat (on the commercial market) is the best deterrence against an attack! And the Chinese wheat deal of 1980 will at least neutralize a powerful force in the Far East.

4. The cause of peace. It is to the interest of the United States, as it is to all countries, to maintain peace. One of the contributing causes of war is human suffering. This tends to inspire hostility between states as well as civil war. [120] When violence breaks out between states, the interests of the United States may be threatened. Not only is our supply of oil threatened, but that of other essential minerals.[121] This is so even when the warring states are our "enemies"—for example, Iran and Iraq. The civil war in South Vietnam was regarded as not in our interest, and the same can be said for the Cuban revolution that brought Castro to power. Political and economic instability may spark wars of both kinds. A "minor" war may become a major one; other countries are brought into it. Robert Heilbroner writes of the possibility of poor states, in their misery, taking desperate steps. " 'Wars of redistribution' may be the only way by which the poor nations can hope to remedy their condition." Nuclear weapons (already possessed by India) may "be used as an instrument to force the developed world to undertake a massive transfer of wealth to the poverty-stricken world."[122] It is for reasons like these that the term often used for the American food aid program, "Food for Peace," is not *all* rhetoric.

[120]"In the desert of northwestern Kenya, a Turkana warrior loaded his bandolier with cartridges in preparation for a cattle raid across the Ugandan border. His body was shrunken from hunger. He knew that he would eat in a day or two—and that he would have to kill someone for the privilege." *Newsweek,* August 25, 1980, p. 48.

[121]Of the thirty-six minerals listed by the U.S. government as "strategic" (i.e., essential to our industry and defense), twenty-three come in most part from other countries, many of which are "volatile and sometimes unfriendly." In 1980, Alexander Haig warned of a "resource war." See *Newsweek,* November 10, 1980, p. 98.

[122]Robert Heilbroner, *An Inquiry into the Human Prospect* (New York: W. W. Norton, 1974), p. 43.

Food Aid in the Past This view may sound like the "dollor diplomacy" of bygone days. There is an important difference, however. The policy defended here is not one in which the state is a tool used by private corporations to protect and advance their profits, but one in which the government employs food aid on behalf of broad and legitimate national interests. A better comparison would be to the Marshall Plan. This was the result of the Truman Doctrine stated in 1947: "It must be the policy of the United States to support free peoples who are resisting attempted subjugation by armed minorities or by outside pressure. . . . Our help should be primarily through economic and financial aid which is essential to economic stability and orderly processes." President Truman requested $400 million for Greece and Turkey to help their governments resist a Communist takeover. Later in the same year, Secretary of State George C. Marshall met with representatives of European countries to work out plans for reconstruction with American aid. In three years the sum of $22 billion was appropriated for this purpose. Western Europe was saved from Communism, and by 1950 the GNP of Marshall Plan countries had increased by 25 percent. This plan was supplemented by Point Four aid for "underdeveloped areas" in Asia, Africa, and Latin America.

Previous to these programs (and UNRRA in 1943), the United States had never expended significant sums for foreign aid, although there had been ample humanitarian grounds for doing so. Indeed, it was widely believed to be unconstitutional. Congress refused to appropriate money for food to relieve the great potato famine in Ireland (1845–1846), the great famine in Russia (1891), Belgian relief (1914), or the Russian famine of 1922. Private charity, however, responded: $1 million in six months for Ireland and $80 million for the Russians in 1922, for example. In the World War I era, the United States refused to cancel the war debts (Coolidge: "They hired the money, didn't they?") of its allies. In the months before its entry into World War II, the United States followed policies of "cash and carry" and "lend-lease" with the favored nations.

What was the difference? A sense of national self-interest. President Truman did appeal to humanity in his speech on behalf of Point Four: "Only by helping the least fortunate of its members to help themselves can the human family achieve the decent, satisfying life that is the right of all people." But in the same speech, after vividly describing the misery of starving people, he said: "Their poverty is a handicap and a threat to them *and to more prosperous areas.*"[123] The previous year the Soviet Union had invaded Czechoslovakia and that summer would explode an atomic bomb. The cold war had begun.

It is not claimed that action on behalf of national interests has always been successful. Aid has not always achieved recovery or prosperity for the recipient state, nor has it always produced democracy, friendship, or peace. And it would take some high-level accounting to show that the returns for American prosperity

[123]Inaugural Address, January 20, 1949. Emphasis added.

from aid exceed expenditures. But all these things together should be the *aim* of aid policy, for only self-interest can justify it.

Public Law 480 Public Law 480, the amendments to it, and the administration of it have sometimes served this end and sometimes have not. It was passed in 1954, making it "the policy of the United States to use [its] abundant productivity to combat hunger and malnutrition and to encourage economic development in the developing countries" through concessional sales and humanitarian grants.[124] Under Title I of this law, food is sold to governments under long-term loans at low interest rates. Before 1971, these loans were repaid in local currency which could not be spent by the United States outside the borders of the recipient county. Since 1971, most payments have had to be in convertible currencies or dollars. Under Title II, "most food is provided on a grant basis to governments, voluntary agencies and the U.N. World Food Programme (WFP). The commodities supplied are used in nutritional programs for vulnerable groups such as mothers, infants, and school children; in 'food for work' programs to build needed infrastructure such as irrigation and drainage facilities, schools, and roads; and in disaster-relief activities."[125] Awards can be increased or decreased in the light of the availability of American food, prevailing prices, and the needs of food sharing in the United States itself. In 1974–1975, for example, domestic food programs (child nutrition, special milk, food stamps) hit an all-time high, accounting for three-fourths of the Department of Agriculture budget, and the food shipments under PL 480 (both titles) were halved.

In order to reduce the amount of food supplied to *military* allies, Congress in 1975 amended the law to say that at least 70 percent under Title I had to go to the countries on the UN list of "most seriously affected countries." This was dictated by humanitarian concern and was ill-advised, for it reduced the flexibility and efficiency in food provision that the law was originally passed to provide. There was another factor that troubled many members of Congress: "allowing an international or non-U.S. government to establish the criteria used for setting food aid priorities."[126] So the restriction was dropped later in 1975. Another criterion imposed by Congress, in order to depoliticize what many believe should be a humanitarian program, is that there be a 75–25 split between poor and wealthy nations, with the distinction based on per-capita GNP. This is an unsatisfactory formula because per-capita GNP neither indicates the relative need for food among countries nor does it tell us anything about how income is distributed in a particular country. This defeats the humanitarian goals of those who espouse it. Some have proposed that effective birth control measures be made a criterion

[124]See Brown, *By Bread Alone,* p. 64.

[125]Ibid., pp. 65–66.

[126]See Daniel E. Shaughnessy, "The Political Uses of Food Aid: Are Criteria Necessary?" in Brown and Shue, *Food Policy,* p. 96.

for receiving aid—which insults the sovereignty of other nations. Restraints on food aid, beyond those already built into the program, make it difficult for the United States to pursue its national aims in a coherent, efficient, and expeditious way.

This is not to say that the humanitarian concern is ignored in Public Law 480. The law requires that *need exist.* Food aid cannot be given to a nation unless there is genuine need for it and it is clear that the nation cannot import it on a commercial basis. Citizens, then, can be gratified that the United States, while pursuing their ends as a national group, is also alleviating the misery of people all over the world. If they feel that this aid is inadequate (and it is), they are welcome, as individuals, to contribute to private or UN agencies to supplement the work of their government. They can pledge the 1 percent suggested by the United Nations or the more generous 10 percent recommended by Peter Singer.[127] The difference is that they will be acting as responsible moral individuals rather than compelling their government to act on their behalf as a fictional moral agent.

American Food Aid Should Be Inspired by Humanitarianism

Factual Background Before pondering the moral issue, we should look at some facts.

Most developing countries do not grow enough food for their own needs. In 1976, Latin America, Africa, and Asia had to import about sixty million tons of grain (the staple food of most peoples), and the figure continues to rise. This would not be so alarming if undeveloped countries had the money to meet their nutritional needs, but the fact is that there were in 1975 a total of sixty-one countries with per-capita GNP of less than $500 and thirty-six with per-capita figures of less than $250. In the same year, the per-capita GNP in the United States was $7,060. "The nations in difficulty are terribly poor, and generally speaking, income levels among the masses of rural people are well below the average in each of these countries."[128] The really desperate countries, constituting about a fourth of the world's population, have been called the Fourth World to distinguish them from such relatively prosperous states as China, the Koreas, Taiwan, Singapore, Japan, and the oil-exporting states. Even where the GNP has gone up significantly in states like Mexico and Brazil, the pattern of distribution is so one-sided (typical of Latin America) that the masses benefit very little or not at all.

"From 1950 to the early seventies, food production per person edged upward in a steady and rather predictable fashion. But average consumption levels have

[127]See Peter Singer, "Reconsidering the Famine Relief Argument," in Brown and Shue, p. 49.

[128]Sterling Wortman and Ralph W. Cummings, Jr., *To Feed This World* (Baltimore: Johns Hopkins University Press, 1978), p. 4.

fallen since 1972; and for those for whom consumption was just beginning to meet nutritional requirements, this reversal has been a crushing blow. Because food is primarily apportioned through purchasing power, a disproportionate share of the reduction has fallen on the world's poor."[129] In 1975, there were about four billion people in the world, and one billion of them suffered from malnutrition. The average American consumes about 3,300 calories a day; the average Southern Asian tries to survive on 1,900 calories a day.[130] The average American consumes five times as much grain per year as an Asian; the latter consumes it directly as cereal or bread, while the American consumes by far the greater portion of it in the form of meat (and alcohol).[131] "In the United States and Western Europe alone, more food is wasted by being fed to farm animals than the total world food shortfall. Through his high meat diet, which provides him with about twice as much meat as his body can use, the average American indirectly consumes enough grain to feed four Indians."[132] "The UN claims that one out of every eight people in the world is literally starving, and that almost half suffer from malnutrition of one kind or another."[133]

Although the United States has contributed more aid than any other country, its efforts fall far short of the 1 percent of the GNP recommended by the United Nations Conference on Trade and Development and less than those of some European nations that have come close to the target figure. This country uses a disproportionate share of the world's oil (essential for agricultural production) in its gas-guzzling cars, heating, and air conditioning.[134] "Professor David Pimentel and his colleagues at Cornell University have calculated that, if the entire world were to move toward the energy-intensive form of agriculture and the diet prevalent in the United States, known reserves of petroleum would be exhausted by agriculture alone within twenty-nine years."[135]

The ethical problem, then, is whether we have the duty not only to share our present surplus, but also, since our own productivity has limits, to cut down our consumption.

Singer's Humanitarian Argument Peter Singer argues that the people of the United States have a moral obligation to come to the aid of the starving people of the world. Thomas Nagel agrees, and argues that such action should not be considered an act of charity, since charity, however praiseworthy, is optional.

[129]Lester Brown, "Food Prospect," p. 76.
[130]See "How to Feed the Third World," *Economist,* March 22, 1975, p. 72.
[131]See Ziegler, *War, Peace, and International Politics,* pp. 417–418.
[132]Singer, p. 48.
[133]George, *How the Other Half Dies,* p. 11.
[134]"World Bank figures show that on average the one billion people in countries with per capita incomes below $200 consume only about 1 percent as much energy per capita as the citizens of the United States." Ibid., p. 33.
[135]Brown, *By Bread Alone,* p. 242.

Both hold that individuals, so far as they ignore the plight of much of humanity, are immoral.

Singer's approach is utilitarian, or consequentialist. His basic contention is that "if we can prevent something bad [starvation] happening without sacrificing anything of comparable moral importance, we ought to do it."[136] The implications of this proposition are tremendous. Even the implications of a much weaker version of the proposition would drastically change American aid policy: "If we can prevent something bad happening without sacrificing anything of moral significance, we ought to do so."

Singer considers the "nonconsequentialist" objection that people should be aided on the basis of merit or desert, not indiscriminately. Some suffer for failing to use their opportunities and therefore deserve no help. In answer, Singer says that "the individual Indian peasant in an overpopulated, drought-prone region had no opportunity to be anything other than he is."[137] In general terms: "Since famine, by its nature, affects a large number of people at a given time and place, there is always going to be some cause or combination of causes, whether climate, or overpopulation, or corrupt government, or outdated social customs, or even, to indulge in some Victorian fantasy, innate racial tendencies toward laziness, for which the individual starving person cannot be held accountable."[138]

Another nonconsequentialist objection is that people have greater obligations to those near them than to those remote from them. These obligations stem from concrete personal relations with members of the family, community, and nation and take precedence over supposed obligations to the abstract "other." Singer answers that "it is difficult to see any sound moral justification for the view that our obligations cease at the boundary of our own nation or kin."[139] When the needs of those nearest us are met, the needs of others exert a valid claim. When special obligations have been fulfilled, "the *needs* of strangers make a stronger moral claim upon us than the *wants* of those close to us."[140] Singer would defend the utility of meeting special obligations and does not hold that "we are all exactly equally responsible for the welfare of everyone in the world."[141] But the weak version of his principle would hardly affect special obligations, and the strong version would simply decrease catering to wants when "some people are starving and others have a surplus."

There are consequentialist or utilitarian objections to Singer's famine relief argument. It may be counterproductive. Aid may encourage the recipient country to do nothing about the political or social factors that place it in a position of need. It may be confirmed in its position of dependence. It may take no steps in trying

[136]Singer, p. 37.
[137]Ibid., p. 39.
[138]Ibid., p. 40.
[139]Ibid., p. 42.
[140]Ibid., p. 43. Emphasis added.
[141]Ibid., p. 44.

to control population. It may not try to improve its agricultural methods or system of distribution. Singer answers that we should take these and other factors into consideration. "The amount of aid available is always limited, hence the need to use it as effectively as possible."[142] We can make our aid conditional on specific actions by the recipient country. "I have argued that we have an obligation to prevent starvation if we can; but I have not argued that we have an obligation to make sacrifices that, to the best of our knowledge, will do nothing to prevent starvation."[143]

Another consequentialist objection is based upon the *advocacy* of the famine relief argument. If we emphasize the strong version of the principle, that is, that we should place the welfare of foreigners on the same level as that of ourselves, we would "turn off" a great many people who are unwilling to achieve this level of moral life and hence would do nothing. Singer's answer is that even if advocating a less demanding standard would be more effective in getting public support for moderate foreign aid, this fact would not alter the principle that we should do much more. "There is no inconsistency here, since in both our private and our public behavior we are trying to maximize the amount of benefit to the starving."[144] A moderate program would be better than the present one. Somewhere between the extremes of calling for *token aid* and calling for *maximum aid* is a kind of public appeal that "might make people realize that indulgence in an affluent life-style without making a serious effort to help those in need is morally wrong, without leading people to reject morality as hopelessly idealistic."[145]

Nagel's Humanitarian Argument Thomas Nagel comes to a similar conclusion, but with a different line of reasoning. A world system in which a condition of radical inequality prevails between the haves and the have-nots is manifestly unjust. We do not have to be committed to a particular theory of distributive justice to agree that the existence of such gross disparities between nations is an affront to justice, and we do not have to be equalitarians to realize that *this* degree of inequality among people is wrong. "We are not dealing with an abstract problem of inequality, but with something more specific and acute."[146] What we need to consider "is an extreme case, involving extreme needs."[147]

Individual states seek to carry out their own conceptions of distributive justice. Among and within these states there is great disagreement on what system should prevail. Is distributive justice best achieved by means of laissez-faire, a welfare state, or socialism? But this is not the issue here, for any approach would seek

[142]Ibid., p. 47.
[143]Ibid.
[144]Ibid., p. 48.
[145]Ibid., p. 49.
[146]Thomas Nagel, "Poverty and Food: Why Charity Is Not Enough," in Brown and Shue, p. 54.
[147]Ibid.

to protect all from grinding poverty. "Within the United States, for example, a system which permitted one-fourth of the population to starve while the rest were well off would be regarded as unacceptable even if this result arose without coercion or theft, by non-fraudulent economic transactions."[148] The system would not be legitimate. Individuals in such a state should be viewed not as objects of charity but as having been deprived of what is rightfully theirs. The wealth that fortunate individuals are asked to share with the unfortunate should not be regarded as something that they legitimately own and may (or may not) choose to share.

The same kind of approach is appropriate for the world system. It is true that there is no world government to carry out a formal theory of distributive justice, but there is enough intercourse between the nations and their people to justify, in some loose sense, viewing the world as a community. "Any system of property, national or international, is an institution of moral characteristics: claims of right or entitlement made under it, claims as to what is ours to use as we wish, carry only as much moral weight as the legitimacy of the institution will bear."[149] When radical economic inequalities persist over a period of time (not simply as results of isolated catastrophes), the system is seriously at fault. Even if the superiority of some countries is attributed to a "head start in technology, organization, and capital accumulation," and is not the result of colonialism or other wrongdoing, the system that makes it possible is faulty.

What can be done? There is no international power to check the economic power of the wealthy countries, to impose taxation, to redistribute property, to raise the bottom strata to a level of subsistence, to remedy the chronic malnutrition of the impoverished masses. What the rich have no right to, they are nonetheless able to retain. So Nagel must come to the same conclusion as Singer: "While foreign aid is not the best method of dealing with radical inequality—being comparable to private charity on the local scene—it is the only method now available. It does not require a strongly egalitarian moral position to feel that the U.S., with a gross national product of a trillion dollars and a defense budget which is 9 percent of that, should be spending more than its current two-fifths of 1 percent of GNP on nonmilitary foreign aid, given the world as it is."[150] For Singer, the wealthy should share the wealth; Nagel agrees, but holds that they should not be that wealthy to start with.

Nagel insists that this aid be "truly humanitarian." That is, it should be above political considerations. This would seem to follow from his belief that the differential in wealth is unjustified. Just as humanitarian concerns in time of war can dictate that a state forgo military advantages that result from certain acts (say, bombing hospitals), so too, in time of peace, the political advantages that certain

[148]Ibid., p. 58.
[149]Ibid., p. 57.
[150]Ibid., p. 61.

forms of food aid can provide should be forgone when basic and universal needs are involved.

The Statehood Objection Two general objections to humanitarian aid by states must be examined. One is that this should be left to private efforts, since the function of a government is to look after the interest of its own people. A state, by definition, is bound only to seek its own advantage. This is not a sound argument. A society can have national goals directed toward the welfare and/or justice of its own people, but it can also aspire to international goals directed toward the welfare and/or justice of other people. A government can do whatever its people demand: it can take the high road or the low road. A state may be judged good or bad by virtue of what it accomplishes for other states, as well as on the basis of what it accomplishes for itself. An individual in a democracy is bound to follow the majority in *whatever* it does, domestically or internationally, so long as the act or policy does not seriously outrage his or her moral sensibilities. It is difficult to imagine how humanitarian aid to others, when one's own community is not significantly deprived thereby, could be viewed as morally outrageous.

Individuals are members of several collectives, from the family, the community, and the nation to the human race itself. Their sense of loyalty to each is important and justified, but they constantly have to ask themselves how the narrower collective can better serve the wider one. No class membership is self-sufficient and insulated from wider memberships. While serving the family, individuals have to be sensitive to how the family may serve the wider goals of the community—to which they also feel some devotion. They may serve their economic class or professional group, but still be concerned with the role that that group can play in advancing the legitimate ends of the national group to which they belong and to which they accept responsibilities. Similarly, they cannot exclude from their thinking the concerns of the widest group of all: humanity. To cut off this series of wider responsibilities at the national level is arbitrary and rests upon a question-begging definition of the state. Why, if individuals can use their presence in a group to further the interests of wider groups, can they not also use their status as Americans to promote a national policy that seeks the welfare of humanity itself? The answer based on the distinction between voluntary membership, say, in charitable organizations, and involuntary membership in the state is inadequate. An individual's membership in a family is involuntary also, yet he or she may be required to make sacrifices on its behalf. Membership in labor unions is often not voluntary either, and the workers who object to what it does with their money may find it almost as difficult to resign as the spoiled child who would like to resign from a family that has decided not to buy him or her a new bike.

All this is not to derogate private charity. It is simply to defend the propriety of benevolence on a national scale through the auspices of an elected government. It is important to do this, because the potential of food aid on a national scale is greater than that which can be generated by private humanitarians. A government can marshall resources, awaken national consciousness, organize the necessary means, cut red tape, provide transport, and do a great many other things that private organizations cannot do.

The Population Objection The second general objection to humanitarian aid is based on the fact of increased population in the underdeveloped world. Statistics can be provided that are quite alarming. We may be told, for example:

> We estimate that it took until about the year 1600 before total population reached one billion: that is, thousands and thousands of years. Another billion people were added between 1600 and 1900, a period of 300 years. A third billion were added between 1900 and 1950, a period of 50 years. The four billion mark was passed about 1975, so that the time required to add a billion has been cut to 25 years. If the population of the earth continues to increase at this accelerating rate, we will indeed soon have a planet on which there is "standing room only."[151]

The birth rate in undeveloped countries is typically much higher than in developed countries. India alone added 12.8 million to the world population in 1972. "Although world food output has expanded impressively over the past generation, population growth so far has absorbed all but a fraction of the increase."[152]

The lesson is clear. Food aid will contribute to the survival of the poor, they will multiply, and the problem of overpopulation will be even worse. Growing population wipes out gains made in the GNP of the struggling nation. While the GNP goes up, the *per-capita* GNP goes down. Just as domestic productivity cannot keep pace with the growing population, foreign aid for underdeveloped nations cannot keep pace with their burgeoning populations.[153] Not only is it impossible to save the malnourished and starving of the world, but the very attempt is self-defeating. It is wiser and ultimately more humane to let the unfortunate perish. A grim expression of this point of view is that of the scientist Garrett Hardin, who compared the human situation to life on a lifeboat.[154] There is not enough space (or food) on the lifeboat to rescue everyone. There is a point at which the survival of all is jeopardized by bringing more people aboard. "The boat is swamped, and everyone drowns. Complete justice, complete catastrophe." If food aid is given to the poorest countries, many of their people will survive; but this is only temporary, for the birth rate, far exceeding the death rate, will in time create food needs that the world will find impossible to meet. In terms

[151]Ziegler, pp. 414–415. Ziegler himself is not arguing in this context against food aid.

[152]Brown, *By Bread Alone,* p. 250.

[153]"At the United Nations conference on population in Bucharest in 1973 spokesmen for the poor nations repeatedly said in effect: 'We poor people have the right to reproduce as much as we want to; you in the rich world have the responsibility of keeping us alive.' " Garrett Hardin, "Carrying Capacity as an Ethical Concept," in Lucas and Ogletree, p. 121.

[154]See Garrett Hardin, "Living on a Lifeboat," *Bioscience* 24 (October 1974): 561–568.

of suffering, this would be a greater catastrophe than the ones that unaided countries now would face.[155]

Hardin's arguments purport to be ethical—even humanitarian. He is concerned about human life: "Every life saved this year in a poor country diminishes the quality of life for subsequent generations."[156] And he believes that consequences (or utility) are the measure of morality. But one must examine the specific situation. He quotes Joseph Fletcher with approval: "We should give if it helps but not if it hurts."[157] When does food assistance hurt? When it goes to a country "already populated beyond the carrying capacity of its land."[158] This contributes to even greater population with attendant misery greater than would have been the case had nothing been done. The demands on the land are intensified. India is a good example. Indians in need of fuel and energy have denuded their forests and now burn natural fertilizer (cow dung) that should be enriching the impoverished soil. Food assistance not only increases the population (and demand for even more food), but also contributes to the destruction of the environment. Deforestation of the hills of Nepal resulted from food relief. This produced floods that killed tens of thousands of people in Bangladesh in 1974. The desire to keep everyone alive "regardless of the consequences for future human beings" is not humanitarianism but *amiability*.[159] This can be a weakness; it is detrimental to true charity. "Thou shalt not exceed the carrying capacity of any environment" is "a legitimate member of a new Decalogue."[160]

In answer to this argument, the following points can be made. (1) The productive capacity of the world today is more than adequate to meet the needs of all its starving and undernourished people. Much of the land is inefficiently cultivated. Much is devoted to nonfood crops or to luxury foods. Much of it is not cultivated at all. In Colombia in 1960 the largest farmers who controlled 70 percent of the tillable land cultivated only 6 percent of it; and in Ecuador only 14 percent of the tillable land is cultivated.[161] The productive potential of the United States has not yet been reached. (2) The cause of starvation today is not scarcity of food. The cause is politicoeconomic: The starving masses in the Third World lack the *means* to acquire food. If they had land, they would grow their own. If they had money, they would buy their food. Food production meets effective purchasing power. The well-to-do in both wealthy and poor countries

[155]Another form of this "humanitarian" argument is based on the notion of "triage": After a battle, medical personnel will tag the wounded as "hopeless," "badly wounded but not hopeless," and "injured." This is a kind of sorting. Efforts are first directed toward the second group, then the third, and finally the first. With respect to food aid, some would deny it to countries that are "hopeless," because the available amount of aid is not enough to do any good, and to the "injured," because their situation is not serious.

[156]Ibid., p. 566. Italicized in original.

[157]See Hardin, "Carrying Capacity as an Ethical Concept," p. 131.

[158]Ibid., p. 130.

[159]Ibid., p. 133.

[160]Ibid., p. 134.

[161]See Lappé and Collins, p. 15.

have no difficulty acquiring food. The eating habits in wealthy countries are well known, and even in the poor countries the elite dine well. An increase of the GNP in poor countries usually has little effect on the plight of the masses; this is so even when the increase is represented on a per-capita basis. (3) The contention that the rate of population growth would accelerate with the greater availability of food not only is false, but runs directly counter to all the evidence. It is precisely the well-fed countries that limit their growth, while the ill-fed countries seem out of control. As China has solved its food problem, its birth rate has gone down. In India the situation is just the opposite. The correlation between birth rate and starvation conditions is really quite remarkable. In view of this, it certainly does not follow that food relief (if it is of the right kind) will produce such overpopulation that all attempts to feed the hungry will be futile. Various explanations have been given for the fact that poor people tend to have more children than those who have moderate means and security. One is that poor parents want to ensure their own survival by producing children who will take care of them in their old age. The more offspring, the better are their prospects. And since child mortality is so high, many babies must be produced to increase the chance that some will grow to maturity.[162] A poor couple with few children at its side is poor indeed.

This is not to say that the increase of the human population on a planet with finite recourses is a matter of no concern. But it is not yet serious enough to warrant "humanitarian" acceptance of starvation for the poor. The affluent are a bit too smug in view of the fact that *their* number is increasing also and makes much heavier demands on the world's resources.[163] "Far more helpful than current populations statistics would be a system of 'weighted' population growth figures, adjusted for the average per capita consumption of the existing population in each country or region being analyzed. Such revised 'weighted population growth' statistics would clearly show the U.S. and other developed, affluent countries equal to or surpassing the population growth of such traditional 'culprits' as India and Mexico."[164] That we might not be able to save ten billion persons tomorrow is no reason why we should not try to save one billion today, while doing what we can to forestall excessive population growth and environmental deterioration. The Malthusian debacle is not here yet,[165] and while strug-

[162]In places where child mortality has been reduced by Western science, the old tradition still operates: "play safe" and have lots of children. But infant mortality is a reality in many countries. Figures for children who died in 1970–1976 per 1,000 population under one year of age in selected countries: Brazil, 94; India, 122; Indonesia, 125; Uganda, 160; Niger, 200. The figure for the United States in the same period was 15.

[163]The average North American, for example, consumes about five times as much grain as the average Bengali. The United States in 1975 had a per-capita consumption equivalent to 11,000 kilograms of energy; Uganda consumes 55 and Niger the equivalent of 35 kilograms per capita.

[164]George R. Lucas, Jr., "Political and Economic Dimensions of Hunger," in Lucas and Ogletree, pp. 21–22.

[165]Garrett Hardin exaggerates when he says, "We are only a few moments from the end of the orgy." Hardin, *Exploring New Ethics for Survival: The Voyage of the Spaceship Beagle* (Baltimore: Penguin Books, 1972), p. 175.

gling to avert it, we can find a more moral recourse for starvation than to let it run its course.

James Sellars tries to raise us to a higher level. Holding that Hardin and others "underestimate the limits of human productivity," and that technocrats "overestimate them,"[166] he stresses the ideal of interdependence and cooperation among the peoples of the world. Americans should not disregard the condition of everyone else in the world. Our wheat is *not* unconditionally ours, when others are starving; nor are the minerals of other states unconditionally theirs, when others require it. The United States is "almost entirely dependent on imports" for its manganese, cobalt, chromium, titanium, miobium, strontium, and sheet mica, as well as (to a somewhat lesser extent) its aluminum, platinum, tin, tantalium bismuth, fluorine, asbestos, and mercury.[167] "Ecologists like Hardin who keep talking about the organic nature of the environment should readily understand the organic nature of the human enterprise. For better or worse, we are firmly interlocked with all the others."[168] Sellars does not want to sound moralistic: he is looking for a new identity or metaphor for American aspiration. He decides on a sheaf of wheat, no strand of which "is wholly independent in its growth of its neighboring threads." The quotation is from Pierre Teilhard de Chardin. "Mankind," says Sellars hopefully, "is emerging from a recent past of separateness into a new organic whole. Mankind is being 'planetized' at last, and Teilhard was certain that this is for the good, for it moves man toward a new and fuller identity."[169]

When human beings adopt such a view, they have gone far beyond Hardin's denial of aid for India because of the "carrying capacity" of that particular environment. If the world's people cannot be brothers and sisters, they can at least be partners. The condition of the Indians is thus examined in the broader context of the world, rather than their own political borders.

Public Law 480 We must now turn to the question of what kind of food aid is most beneficial to those who need it. We may find that present policies are of little use and that entirely different approaches should be tried.

The first thing we should note is the decline of American food assistance beginning around 1973. "At a time of record international food prices, shrinking reserve stocks of grain, and increased rates of malnutrition among the world's poor—in short, the very time when the world need for food aid is at its highest —the quantities of food supplied by the United States under P.L. 480 have fallen sharply. . . ."[170] Under Title I, shipment of metric tons of wheat (in thousands) went from 13,705 in 1965 to 5,765 in 1970 to about 1,000 in 1974. Corn and

[166]James Sellars, "Famine and Interdependence," in Lucas and Ogletree, p. 105.
[167]Ibid., p. 112.
[168]Ibid., p. 113.
[169]Ibid., p. 117.
[170]Brown, *By Bread Alone,* p. 64.

sorghum dropped from 1,289 in 1973 to 454 in 1974.[171] Shipment under Title II, always less than under Title I, has also sharply dropped. Wheat, for example, dropped from 1,649 in 1973 to an estimated 718 in 1974, while dried milk dropped from 26 to zero in the same period. Rice dropped from 248 in 1972 to zero in 1974. There were good reasons for this, of course, but they were not humanitarian in nature: concern for inflated food prices in the United States, the opportunity for commercial sales, the need to serve political or military ends. In 1974, for example, about half of American food aid went to South Vietnam and Cambodia.[172] In mid-1973, Chile, with its foreign-exchange reserves exhausted and in need of bread, asked the United States for wheat on credit. We refused. The Allende government fell in September of the same year. American food assistance is not only declining in amount but is apportioned very selectively.

The sad fact is that it is doubtful that food aid under Title I would do very much for the starving people in any case, for the consumer usually has to pay for it. This works out very well for the upper classes in recipient nations, but what about the others? "As drought reports brought food aid to West Africa in the early seventies, most of the relief grains arriving in Upper Volta and the Ivory Coast were sold on credit to the peasants at usurious rates of interest. One observer familiar with the area contends that since the harvests would not be adequate to repay the depts, the peasants and their children would be forced to work for their creditors to pay back their debts. Thus food aid kept in motion the process of virtual enslavement of the rural people."[173] Persons who have no money or cannot get a local loan must rely on Title II food (if there is any available) or starve.

Even when the United States accepts local currency for its food loans, it expects to benefit. The preamble to PL 480 specifies this goal: "to develop and expand export markets for United States agricultural commodities." This can be achieved directly or indirectly. Developing countries, not having to use their dollars to buy food, could use them to buy capital goods for industry, thus sustaining a market for American exports of material and luxury foodstuffs. Until 1971, 25 percent of the American-owned local currency could be loaned at very low interest rates to American corporations investing in the recipient country. Under this provision, "419 subsidiaries of American firms in thirty-one countries established or expanded their operations at very low cost."[174] This sort of thing is called "development," but the question is, development for whom? The minority who are fortunate enough to work for the locally or internationally owned corporations have income with which to buy food, and the government personnel and bureaucrats through whose hands the PL 480 food shipments pass do also, but

[171] These are U.S. Department of Agriculture figures.

[172] "Between 1968 and 1973, South Vietnam alone received twenty times the value of food aid that the five African countries most seriously affected by drought received during the same period." Lappé and Collins, p. 337.

[173] Ibid., p. 329.

[174] Ibid., p. 331.

the masses do not benefit. In fact, if "development" means industrialization, they are worse off than before, because their nation, by design, is confirmed in its role as a food-importing state. American policy has been not to relieve hunger but to create permanent markets for its agricultural exports.

Food aid has had the effect of keeping food prices low in underdeveloped countries. This is fine for the people who have an income: employees of urban businesses and agricultural enterprises specializing in cash crops for exports. But it does little for those with little or no purchasing power or the land with which to grow their own food. The effect of PL 480 has been to discourage domestic production of food for domestic consumption. Local growers cannot compete with wheat from the United States, and turn increasingly to crops and products (food and nonfood) for export. Frances Moore Lappé and Joseph Collins discuss the cases of Taiwan and South Korea, where the people have been made dependent on wheat while exporting rice; Colombia, where land formerly used for wheat is employed for cattle grazing, flowers, and vegetables for export; and Bolivia, where wheat production has stagnated.[175] To create markets for its food, the United States must make nations *dependent* on it, and further impoverishment of the landless poor is the result.

The suffering was intensified, of course, when local currency became no longer acceptable after 1971. The stated American goal was to assist underdeveloped countries "graduate" from PL 480 status. One way to do this is to tie PL 480 food loans to commercial purchases. "In order to receive food aid, the potential recipient had to accept one condition: agreement to purchase in the future on commercial terms, American agricultural commodities in the future. In 1973, our government made food credit to the Dominican Republic conditional upon much larger commercial purchases. In 1975, P.L. 480 loans to Egypt for wheat and to South Korea for rice were tied to additional commercial purchases of these commodities."[176]

A new aid bill was passed by Congress late in 1975. Advertised as humanitarian, it contained this passage: "In furnishing food aid under this act, the President shall . . . assure that allocation of commodities or concessionary financing is based upon the potential for expanding markets for American abundance abroad." The "market," wherever possible, will be *commercial;* the "abundance" is *surplus.* The humanitarianism comes out in the passage requiring that 80 percent of PL commodities go to countries whose per-capita GNP is less than $250. This is a great step forward, although there is still no assurance that the food will find its way into the hands of those most in need *within* the recipient country.

The World Bank Two other forms of American aid must now briefly be examined: participation in the World Bank and the United States Agency for International Development (AID).[177]

[175]Ibid., pp. 332–335.

[176]Ibid., p. 335.

[177]For much of what follows, the author is deeply indebted to Lappé and Collins, chaps. 41 and 42.

After a period of time during which the World Bank concentrated on industry and large-scale agriculture, it seemed to enter a new era in the seventies in which small farmers and the rural poor would come into their own. Even if it keeps its word that almost half its rural credit will go to small farmers (less than twelve acres), more than half will go to *nonsmall* farmers, who constitute about 20 percent of landowners in the underdeveloped world. No provision is made for loaning money to the millions of people who have no land but would like to be farmers. The World Bank still believed (1974) that the hopes of raising production rested with the large farmers. So long as they continue to monopolize the land and technical apparatus, this is indisputably true! These large farmers are expected to produce a crop that is profitable—it need not be for home consumption, it need not be food. The bank itself stated: "Lending only to those with investment opportunities sufficient to produce a significant marketable surplus is perhaps the best way to reduce the level of default."[178] So a lot of loans go to big operators in such things as cotton, rubber, bananas, palm oil, tea, and livestock—which does much for the operators, a little for their underpaid workers, and practically nothing for the rest of the population. The bank does not want to upset anyone who is important, stating: "In many countries, avoiding opposition from powerful and influential sections of the rural community is essential if the program is not to be subverted from within."[179] Perhaps it is just as well that "three fourths of its loans do not go to agriculture at all but for commercial development."[180]

A.I.D. New legislation for AID (1975) strikes the right note, calling for land reform so that farmers work their own land and for progress toward self-sufficiency in food. Among the points that Lappé and Collins make to show that these aims are disregarded are: (1) AID spokesmen call for focus on "income-producing units rather than farm producers." One brochure states that the first goal of the "new aid" is to "promote profitable production."[181] (2) Two expensive irrigation projects in Morocco will benefit "only about 1000 families, or less than one tenth of 1 percent of the farm families in Morocco."[182] (3) In 1976, AID granted $700,000 and loaned $6 million to assist a great many coffee growers in Haiti, many of them small. What will this do for self-sufficiency? And how did the coffee growers fare when Brazilian, Colombian, and Guatemalan coffee reentered the world market and depressed the price? (4) Much AID money goes to pay the salaries of American technicians. Their advice may benefit the grower who can afford the right seeds, fertilizer, and machines, but will do little for the small farmer and nothing at all for the landless laborers. (5) AID has loaned money to the Latin American Development Corporation (LAAD)—$17 million by 1976.

[178]World Bank, *Assault on World Poverty* (Baltimore: Johns Hopkins University Press, 1975), p. 143.
[179]World Bank, "Rural Development," Sector Policy Paper, February 1975, p. 40.
[180]Lappé and Collins, p. 348.
[181]Ibid., p. 351.
[182]Ibid., p. 352.

LAAD is a holding company, among whose shareholders are the Bank of America, Borden, John Deere, Goodyear, and Ralston Purina. Some of its projects are "processing and marketing beef, growing and exporting fresh and frozen vegetables, cut flowers, ferns, and tropical plants, wood products, seafood."[183] Most of these things are destined for export or upper-class consumption in Latin America. This does not advance self-sufficiency—nor even local producers unless they are already well established. (6) Before Salvador Allende was elected president, Chile was the biggest recipient of American aid in Latin America. Allende soon carried out a massive land redistribution program. The United States drastically eliminated food aid (refusing even to accept cash) and blocked loans from the World Bank. After Allende's overthrow by a military junta, aid was resumed. "By 1975, Chile under the junta was receiving six times more aid than the rest of Latin America put together."[184] And that was the end of land reform. (7) Other underdeveloped countries have suffered as a result of American foreign policy. Since most aid is dispersed by the Executive Branch, it can be employed as a political weapon. Many underdeveloped countries have suffered because of "unrealistic" positions. "How can AID address itself to the fundamental issue of hunger—the re-ordering of social relationships—when, as an arm of the United States government, its effective constituency is not the hungry majority?"[185] (8) Far more money is spent on military assistance and military credit sales than for economic development in general, and much of the latter has very little to do with food.

Self-sufficiency in food is a worthy goal, but it is better attained by growing food for local consumption than by trying to profit on the international market with export crops. Undeveloped countries have the means (land, climate, labor) to succeed in the former; in the latter, they are bucking an international system and are bound to fail.

Neocolonialism There is, of course, no more colonialism in the world, but American aid programs in food and other things tend to achieve some of the same results. Cash crops are no longer grown under the threat of guns and whips[186] and foreign interests do not exclusively own the plantations, but that does not mean colonialism is dead.

The United States (and other advanced countries) seeks to create markets for its commodities. Developing countries supply us with cheap minerals, rubber, cotton, coffee, tea, meat, and strawberries, while we sell them manufactured goods and processed food. It may be more profitable for American companies to get their strawberries from Mexico than Texas, their pineapples from the Philippines than Hawaii, and their meat from Argentina than Nebraska. It is also often

[183]Ibid., p. 355.
[184]Ibid., p. 359.
[185]Ibid., p. 361.
[186]See Walter Rodney, *How Europe Underdeveloped Africa* (London: Bogle-L'Ouverture Publications, 1972), pp. 171–172.

cheaper to *process* these foods in the backward country. A drain takes place: real wealth in terms of labor power and material goods is siphoned from the poor to the rich. American money is invested in backward countries (along with local capital). Profits are made by American investors and the local elite, while a little trickles down to the local employees (most of whom work for subsistence wages). "This drain, significantly, results *not* from explicit imperialism and exploitation, but rather from the quiet operation of market laws seemingly beyond anyone's control, so-called objective world prices. Billions of dollars are taken from the poor and given to the rich through the impersonal mechanism of freely negotiated international trade pricing."[187] In most cases, the export earnings fail to cover the cost of imported foodstuffs. The trade balance is unfavorable, loans and grants must be made, and the developing country continues to be dependent on the American people. In a vain attempt to create credits, they are forced to continue to provide cheap labor, raw materials, and foodstuffs. The aid program is part of this general neocolonialism and in many ways perpetuates it.

The underdeveloped nations are in debt, their farmers are in debt—they must get money where they can. They are "hooked on exports."[188] The world's hungriest people are often the *real* food donors! "In 1974, the United States ranked third among the world's leading food importers, close behind Japan and West Germany. And over two thirds of our imports come from underdeveloped countries."[189] That the leaders of developing countries do not take the rather obvious actions that would relieve the distress of their populations can be attributed to the fact that the local political and economic aristocracy is content to remain in a neocolonial posture so long as its power, prestige, and profit are secured.

What Can We Do? If PL 480 (Title I) is misguided and the World Bank and AID are ineffective in dealing with world hunger, what do we turn to? Title II of PL 480 is an outright grant of free food and can serve as a humanitarian response to hunger. Although its dispersements are very low, it has a role to play in dealing directly with present human misery. But it obviously does not get at the root of the problem. Food aid must be enlightened. It must do more than ward off the evils of periodic catastrophes. It must somehow get at the causes of chronic food shortage. It must deal with other people in a way that will help them become increasingly self-reliant in their food production. Some of these ways are implicit in the criticism of present policy.

Among the things that could be done are the following. (1) Take advantage of local labor—the only thing that many nations have in abundance. Distribute food as wages for clearing fields, building irrigation facilities, and other tasks that will contribute toward the future growing of food in the recipient nation itself. (2) Encourage local businesses in the enterprise of processing food, so that profits are not drained from the country by the great foreign corporations. (3) Discourage

[187]Rosen and Jones, pp. 147–148.
[188]See Lappé and Collins, chap. 27 ("If It's So Bad, Why Does It Continue?").
[189]Ibid., p. 214.

the practice of growing cash crops for export, so that the land can be used for the growth of foodstuffs for local consumption. (4) Take land out of the hands of multinational corporations so that it can be cultivated for local use and profit instead of for the profit of foreign entrepeneurs. (5) Let the countries grow the crops that the people have traditionally eaten, rather than train them to be dependent on imported grain, meat, processed food, and Coca-Cola. (6) Encourage land redistribution so that landless laborers will have their own plots to tend and to live on. Farmers will work better and be more productive when they are working for their own families instead of for native plantation owners or United Brands or Del Monte. (7) Supply light equipment for small farmers, as well as advice on seeds and fertilizer, but do not insist that they use modern techniques appropriate to large estates at home and abroad. Chemical fertilizer, for example, with the rising cost of energy, may be a bad investment. So too may heavy equipment.[190] Labor-intensive agriculture should be the focus rather than energy-intensive enterprises.[191] (8) Make loans or grants available for small and landless farmers who will grow food for local consumption. (9) Do not dump food on urban centers when to do so ruins the market for local producers. (10) Make loans available for small-scale factories, dispersed through the countryside, which will make products for local consumption.

We must guard against oversimplification. Not all these injunctions may be applicable everywhere; they may not always be consistent with one another; situations may change. They do not exhaust the list of beneficial possibilities. The main goal must be kept in mind: Assist the developing nation to utilize its own natural and human resources to meet its own needs and to approach a state of nutritional self-sufficiency. "Food self-reliance means reuniting agriculture and nutrition." Only after this is achieved will trade become "an organic outgrowth of development, not the fragile hinge on which survival hangs."[192]

These suggested measures may not always be popular with ruling aristocracies in underdeveloped states, but these leaders cannot be *utterly* impervious to the needs of their people. Strings can and should be attached to foreign aid.[193] The donor has a right to require responsibility at the other end. "Responsibility would be a willingness on the receiver's part, expressed in an agreement and in subsequent practice, to turn the giver's largesse into the fullest effect with the quickest end-point possible."[194] But the strings should be for the purpose of easing the hunger of the masses rather than advancing the interests of the United States.

[190]Even the advanced agricultural system of the United States requires the equivalent of about nine calories of energy for every calorie of food produced. And this does not take into account the processing, transportation, and distribution of the food! See Lucas, in Lucas and Ogletree, p. 11.
[191]"We cannot look at technology in agriculture as freeing people from labor when productive work is what people need and want more than anything else." Lappé and Collins, p. 153.
[192]Ibid., pp. 378, 376.
[193]"Those who give food without any strings attached simply because people are starving and without first studying the consequences obviously do not care primarily about saving human lives; they choose to use human beings as pawns in some other game—power politics, 'relief rackets,' or image making." Fletcher, "Feeding the Hungry: An Ethical Appraisal," p. 67.
[194]Ibid., p. 63.

Where aid will create greater misery (a possible outcome, if Hardin and Fletcher are right) or where it does no good, it should be forgone. But where it does do good, we are bound to provide it: "I for one," says Fletcher, "would contend that a humane ethics calls for more than cheap grace; that when we share we ought to do it even if it hurts."[195]

The employment of food for the national self-interest has been called *prudential.* In light of the needs of millions of human beings and the failure of our "prudential" programs to meet those needs, a better term for the policy would be *ignoble.* One who has seen the starving children in the Sahel might even employ the term *monstrous.* Our motive should be the truly moral one of humanitarianism. But this worthy motive succeeds only if it is *enlightened* humanitarianism. American citizens must educate their representatives in Congress and Congress should write laws that reflect the enlightened humanitarianism of their constituencies. "Hunger is not a scourge but a scandal."[196]

Summary of the Issues

The two fundamental positions in this debate are based on the inimical notions of national self-interest and humanitarianism. The first side defines "statehood" in terms of self-interest and rejects all analogical arguments that conclude that the state is subject to the same kind of obligations that obtain for persons. The United States should openly proclaim its commitment to self-interest. When we can serve ourselves by serving others, we should do so. There are ways that a careful food aid program can do this: (1) *National prosperity* can sometimes be promoted by food on a cash, concessionary, or gratis basis. (2) *Political advantage* can sometimes be secured by helping friendly regimes, arousing support for democracy, achieving trade and cultural agreements, and so forth. (3) *Military and strategic advances* can be obtained in the form of allies and bases. (4) *The cause of peace* can be promoted by alleviating conditions in sensitive places that might contribute to war. Examination of Public Law 480 reveals that it has sometimes served these purposes and sometimes not.

Even if we suspended the principle of self-interest and appealed to that of merit, we would find that many needy countries do not deserve our help, for they (1) have made no attempt to control their growing populations, (2) spend excessive proportions of their GNP on military goods, (3) economically oppress their own people, (4) are riddled by political corruption, (5) emphasize agricultural products for export instead of for their own food needs, and (6) leave vast areas of arable land lie idle.

The other side emphasizes the great need in the world for food and the great difference between what Americans have and what people in Latin America, Africa, and Asia have. It rejects the statehood argument as question-begging and

[195]Ibid., p. 65.

[196]George, p. 357.

urges Americans to transcend self-interest (and "merit" also). What is at issue here is not prudence, but morality. Americans have a duty to be humanitarian in their food aid. Singer's humanitarian argument is consequentialistic. Nagel's humanitarian argument is based on a theory of distributive justice applied on a worldwide scale. The problem of food distribution is too great and too complex to be left to the kind of private philanthropy that the other side prefers.

Invoked at many points in the debate is the population problem. One side argues that food aid only postpones and increases catastrophe, for population will increase more rapidly as a result of food aid. Many parts of the world are already hopelessly overpopulated. In trying to save all today, we create misery for the next generation. The humanitarian side answers: (1) The productive capacity of the world today is more than adequate to meet the needs of its people. Much land in starving countries is inefficiently cultivated, used for nonfood or luxury food, or not cultivated at all. (2) The chief cause of starvation in the world is politico-economic, not scarcity in food and land. (3) Population growth tends to *decelerate* when food is in greater supply.

Present American policy is not serving humanitarian ends. PL 480 has been harmful more often than helpful to the people who need aid. The World Bank has been of little help to small farmers and none at all to landless farmers. AID has never addressed itself to the fundamental issue of hunger. The American performance in poor countries has been that of neocolonialism. Our actions toward them have been to further our own interests—often at their expense.

The second side calls for a program of *enlightened* humanitarianism. This would require getting at the *cause* of chronic food shortage and achieving self-reliance in the poor country by taking advantage of local labor and resources. Its regime has to be dealt with, but American aid should come with strings clearly attached. Concrete and specific suggestions are offered.

Discussion Questions

1. Would you be willing to give up meat for one day a week in order to save one life a year in India? Why?
2. Do you accept the idea that a state is an entity that exists solely to serve the interests of the people who make it up? Why?
3. Do you think that the majority of Americans really want to help the rest of the world on purely humanitarian grounds? Why?
4. Would you draw the line on food aid between catastrophic need and chronic need? Any problems?
5. What is to prevent do-gooders from aiding the poor of this world through private organizations? Why does it have to be paid for from public funds? And operated by the government? Discuss.
6. Do you think that the concept of "the deserving poor" provides an acceptable criterion for food aid? Why?
7. Do you think that failure on the part of a poor nation to promote birth control excuses other nations from providing it with food aid? Why? Does it *require* other nations to refuse aid?

8. Do you think that countries where the poor are oppressed by their own people should be given food aid? Why?
9. If you wanted to practice enlightened humanitarian food aid to a specific country, what kind of aid would you offer and under what conditions?
10. Explain and discuss this quotation: "Aid is like champagne: in success you deserve it, in failure you need it."
11. Senator Humphrey would use food grants to win the cold war (he calls the idea "terrific"). Do you agree with him? Why?
12. Find out what you can about food distributed last year through PL 480. What is your reaction?
13. What percentage of the American GNP do you think should be pledged to aid the poor in other parts of the world? Why?
14. Do you think that the United States has fairly treated its own poor? Does this have any implications for foreign food aid? Discuss.
15. Critically appraise Singer's argument.
16. Critically appraise Nagel's argument.
17. Would you want to be on a lifeboat with Garrett Hardin? Why?
18. Would you agree that food aid should be withheld from a country "already populated beyond the carrying capacity of its land"? Why?
19. Why is it true that an increase in GNP (or even GNP per capita) usually has little effect on the plight of the masses? What, if anything, do you think can be done about this?
20. Is it true that socialist or Communist countries in the Third World have come closer to solving their food problems than have other countries? If so, does it follow that humanitarianism must favor socialism or Communism? Why?
21. What is meant by "weighted population growth"? Why, on such an approach, are Americans greater culprits than Indians?
22. Does Sellers's concept of *partnership* offer a more realistic approach than *brotherhood*? Explain.
23. Do you agree that PL 480 has, on balance, not served humanitarian goals? Explain. Is there any hope for the future?
24. Do you agree that the World Bank has not done much to relieve the food problem? What about AID? Explain.
25. Do you believe that the charges of neocolonialism leveled against wealthy Western nations are fair? Explain.
26. What, if anything, does the problem of food aid have to do with "war and peace"?
27. Do you agree with President Reagan's view that it should not be illegal to sell American baby formula to underdeveloped countries? Why?

For Further Reading

Philip H. Abelson, ed. *Food: Politics, Economics, Nutrition and Research.* Washington: American Association for the Advancement of Science, 1975.

William Aiken and Hugh LaFollett, eds. *World Hunger and Moral Obligation.* Englewood Cliffs, N.J.: Prentice-Hall, 1977.

P. T. Bauer and John O'Sullivan. "Foreign Aid for What?" *Commentary* 66 (December 1978):41–48.

Lester R. Brown. *By Bread Alone.* New York: Praeger Publishers, 1974.

Lester R. Brown. "Food Prospect." *Diogenes,* no. 103 (Fall 1978):51–77.

Lester R. Brown. *The Twenty-ninth Day.* New York: W. W. Norton, 1978.

Peter G. Brown and Henry Shue, eds. *Food Policy: The Responsibility of the United States in the Life and Death Choices.* New York: Free Press, 1977.

D. S. Burgess. "Answer to Life-Boat Ethics." *Theology Today* 35 (October 1978):265–272.

Daniel Callahan. *The Tyranny of Survival.* New York: Macmillan Publishing Co., 1973.

Erick P. Eckholm. *Losing Ground: Environmental Stress and World Food Prospects.* New York: W. W. Norton, 1976.

Susan George. *How the Other Half Dies.* Montclair, N.J.: Allenheld, Osmun & Co., 1977.

Herman Kahn et al. *The Next 200 Years.* New York: Morrow, 1976.

Frances Moore Lappé and Joseph Collins. *Food First: Beyond the Myth of Scarcity.* Boston: Houghton Mifflin Co., 1977.

George R. Lucas, Jr., and Thomas W. Ogletree, eds. *Lifeboat Ethics: The Moral Dilemma of World Hunger.* New York: Harper & Row, 1976.

Martin McLaughlin et al. *The United States and World Development: Agenda 1979.* New York: Praeger Publishers, 1979.

Clyde Lee Miller. "World Hunger, Poverty and Ethics." *Cross Currents* 27 (Fall 1977): 308–320.

Heather Johnston Nicholson and Ralph L. Nicholson. *Distant Hunger.* West Lafayette, Ind.: Purdue University, 1979.

T. Peters. "Messianic Banquet and World Hunger." *Religion in Life* 47 (Winter 1978): 497–508.

Arthur Simon and Paul Simon. *The Politics of World Hunger.* New York: Harper's Magazine Press, 1973.

James R. Simpson. "Humanism and Hunger." *Humanist* 40 (March–April 1980): 41–42+.

Lester A. Sobel, ed. *World Food Crisis.* New York: Facts on File, 1975.

Ross B. Talbot, ed. *The World Food Problem and U.S. Food Politics and Policies: 1972–1976.* Ames: Iowa State University Press, 1977.

Chapter 9

EPISTEMOLOGY, PSYCHOLOGY, AND METAPHYSICS

Having begun with ethical theory, we will conclude with ethical theory. Here, however, rather than *expound* ethical theories, as was done in the first chapter, we will make a theoretical examination of ethical theory itself. Instead of arguing that x is good or that y is right, we will discuss the philosophical context in which such argumentation takes place.

Ethical theory employs concepts and judgments. Propositions are asserted that are assumed to be true or false. What do they *mean*? What are they asserting about reality? How can we distinguish true propositions from false ones? How does ethical knowledge differ from factual knowledge? Is ethical knowledge possible at all? The discipline that raises such questions and tried to answer them is called *meta-ethics.* Since meta-ethics is concerned with meaning, method, and the nature of truth (in the sphere of ethics), it is a part of *epistemology:* that branch of philosophy which studies the nature, criteria, and validity of knowledge. The first section of this chapter is thus in the field of epistemology, for it is an essay in meta-ethics.

Ethical theory sets forth principles for moral behavior, criteria that distinguish ethical conduct from unethical conduct, norms to guide human action. While psychology *describes* human action, ethics *prescribes* it. Although the two disciplines have different ends, they are not irrelevant to one another. Suppose that a psychologist holds that all human actions are self-serving. If this were true, would it make any sense for the ethicist to argue that people have a duty to others? Or suppose that the psychologist holds that we not only necessarily serve ourselves, but do so in a specific way. If this were true, would it make any sense for the ethicist to require us to serve ourselves in some other way? The view that concern for the self is at the root of all human action is called *egoism. Psychological egoism* holds that this in fact is the case; *ethical egoism* holds that this ought to be the case. The second section of this chapter examines the claims of psychological and ethical egoism. Is it true that human beings are or ought to be egoists? What bearing, if any, does psychological truth have on ethical truth?

Another important ethical issue is raised in the context of the science of psychology: Are all human actions (whether egoistic or nonegoistic) determined by exceptionless natural law? If it is the case that human behavior is determined by given circumstances, can we be said to be free? If we are not free, does it make sense to prescribe what we ought to do? In the broader context, determinism is a position in *metaphysics:* ultimate reality is such that human actions are necessarily what they in fact are. The third section of this chapter examines various kinds of determinism, appraises their truth, and indicates the bearing they have on ethical theory.

META-ETHICS

Fact and Value

Factual Propositions Judgments about facts express what is the case—in the past, present, or future. The judgment that Caesar crossed the Rubicon is true if and only if Caesar did in fact cross that river. The judgment that there is snow on Pike's Peak is true if and only if snow is present on that mountain. The judgment that the Republicans will win control of Congress in 1998 is true if and only if this indeed is the outcome in that year. Reality has certain characteristics, and we truly describe it when we state what those characteristics are. Whether or not we know that a descriptive proposition does indeed correspond to reality, we do believe that it is either true or false. Factual judgments and propositions are true when they express *what is what,* and false when they do not.[1]

How do we know whether factual propositions are true or false? A great many of them are validated by experience. Directly or indirectly, they are established on the basis of sense data.[2] We may be quite sure that Caesar crossed the Rubicon, although we did not see him do it, because ancient records and letters that we can examine constitute grounds for the judgment. We have good evidence for believing that it is very probable that Caesar took this momentous step. The proposition is a hypothesis like the law of gravity or the theory of evolution, each of which has a strong empirical basis. That there is snow on Pike's Peak can be directly verified: we travel to the mountain and perceive the snow. That the Republicans will control Congress in 1998 cannot be known for sure until the 1998 elections, but there could be empirical evidence now and in future years that

[1]We are using *judgment* and *proposition* almost synonymously. Strictly speaking, however, a proposition is what is expressed or asserted in a judgment, while a judgment is a claim that the proposition is true.

[2]The term *sense data* is intended in a broad sense, so that it includes data of feelings and other internal states as well as the data provided by the five senses.

make the outcome more or less likely. Factual judgments in natural science and much of ordinary thinking rest, directly or indirectly, on what can be experienced.

There is another way of validating judgments about reality that does not depend upon experience. When judgments can be validated in this way, they are said to be *a priori.* There is much disagreement among philosophers on the role of a priori judgments. Some philosophers (rationalists) hold that the human mind has the capacity to go beyond experience and apprehend necessary relations in reality, nature, or experience. They talk about "clear and distinct ideas" and appeal to the truths of mathematics as examples of what the mind can discover independently of experience. That a straight line is the shortest distance between two points can be known without drawing lines and measuring them, and that two plus three equals five can be known with certainty apart from counting two groups of objects. Some rationalists also believe that fundamental truths about the universe and God can be grasped by pure reason. While recognizing the usefulness of empiricism and the scientific method, the rationalist believes that such an approach does not carry us far enough and would supplement it with the a priori approach.

At the other extreme are the philosophers who hold that the a priori approach has very limited use. For them, it functions only as a principle of consistency. A proposition can be known to be true a priori only when it is a tautology:

> All purple cows are purple.
> No bachelor is married.
> If p implies q and p is the case, then q is the case.

These statements are known to be true simply on the basis of the meanings of their terms. They do not represent any insight into reality but are true simply by definition. A proposition can be known to be false a priori only when it is a self-contradiction:

> Some purple cows are not purple.
> Many bachelors are married.
> p implies q, but p is the case and q is not.

These statements are false, not because the world is a certain way, but because they are inconsistent with the meanings of their own terms. Tautologies and self-contradictions are *analytic*—that is, their truth or falsity depends upon the rules of language rather than the state of affairs in the world.

What about sentences that do purport to say something about the world? These we can call *synthetic.* If they can be confirmed or disconfirmed, directly or indirectly, they are empirical. If they cannot, they are cognitively meaningless. Those philosophers who take a limited view of a priori thought thus deny the possibility of a synthetic a priori judgment. If a proposition is synthetic, it must be *empirical;* if it is a priori, it must be analytic. Synthetic a priori truth is impossible. Positive knowledge rests on sense data alone.

Deductive logic and mathematics are very useful, but they are not systems of knowledge. Deductive logic is simply a consistent system of meanings. All its propositions are true by definition—of such terms as *all, no, some, if . . . then, or,* and the like. A valid argument is one in which such terms are employed consistently. A conclusion follows necessarily from the premises because it is tacitly contained within the premises. Deduction does not yield new knowledge. Mathematics has the same kind of necessity. Theorems and corollaries follow from the axioms and postulates. If the latter are true, so are the former. *Are* these ultimate premises true? This depends upon the interpretation given to the primitive terms they employ. One interpretation (say, from logic) may make them tautologies. Another interpretation (say, from physics) may make them synthetic, in which case they could serve as the basis of a system of positive knowledge, testable, directly or indirectly, by sense observation. A consistent deductive mathematical system may be purely a priori (in which case it says nothing about the world) or it may say something about the world (in which case it is empirical rather than a priori).

Ethical Propositions An ethical proposition, unlike a factual proposition, asserts not what was, is, or will be the case, but what *ought* to be the case. It is prescriptive rather than descriptive. The following are factual propositions:

All bachelors are unhappy.
If you keep your promises, you will be believed.
The draft law has been reactivated.

The following are ethical propositions:

Bachelors should get married.
You ought to keep your promises.
It is the duty of qualified young people to serve in the armed forces.

Ethical propositions also purport to recognize intrinsic goods and evils, while factual judgments restrict themselves to conditional goods and evils. The following are factual propositions:

Jogging is a good way to strengthen your body.
Smoking is bad for your health.
People seek pleasure.

The following are ethical propositions:

Physical health is good.
Physical infirmity is bad.
Pleasure is good.

As we saw in the preceding chapters, arguments on concrete moral issues contain a mixture of factual and ethical propositions. The final decision on whether nonmarital sex, for example, is moral is best made in the light of certain factual considerations as well as ethical considerations. We need to know the consequences of nonmarital sex for the agent's health, mental well-being, and relationships with family members. We need to know its effect on the institution of marriage and the stability of society. At the same time we ponder certain ethical propositions such as "pleasure is good" and "you ought to keep your promises" and try to decide whether they are true and in what way they apply to the problem of nonmarital sex. We may, in view of the different factual circumstances people find themselves in, make a distinction between acceptable nonmarital sex and unacceptable nonmarital sex. A moral decision on this issue and most others is not very responsible if the factual dimension is ignored. Psychology, sociology, anthropology, biology, physics, and economics all have contributions to make. But in the end, a judgment must be made that is ethical in nature: Nonmarital sex (under certain circumstances) is wrong (or right).

We need to know the effects of public sector strikes (a factual concern) in order to declare whether they ought to be tolerated, but we also have to rely on certain ethical concepts such as the value of individual freedom, the nature of justice, and the importance of the greatest happiness of the greatest number. We need to know something about the history and economics of racial discrimination in order to ascertain the moral propriety of affirmative action and forced busing. But, again, an appeal to ethical convictions on justice and freedom will eventually have to be made.

A conclusion about what ought to be the case requires a great deal of knowledge about what *is* the case. Ethical theory by itself seldom points to conclusions about specific problems of human action. Neither the Mosaic laws nor Kant's imperatives cover all the situations in which decisions must be made, and they cannot be used in any perfect, conclusive, and consistent way without an examination of the facts of the matter. At the same time, a complete account (assuming that such a thing is possible) of a problematic situation will not contain in itself a solution or logically imply one. The crucial step from *is* to *ought* requires an ethical judgment.

When people are engaged in ethical disputation, what are they really arguing about? Some philosophers (e.g., G. E. Moore) maintain that they often are arguing about the truth of ethical judgments. Is pleasure really good? Is knowledge a greater good? Is justice a matter of equality or should it be based on need or merit? Is it always one's duty to tell the truth? We argue not only about efficacious means but about proper or *justified* ones; we argue not only about probable consequences, but about suitable or *worthwhile* ones. Expedience and profitability are discussed in the light of the moral values involved in both means and ends. Other philosophers (e.g., A. J. Ayer) hold that such dispute is fruitless and that most people argue about questions of fact. They point out certain facts that their opponents may have overlooked; they point out consequences; they supply cases and statistics. If, when the full array of facts is before both disputants, disagreement still exists, there is not much more that can be done—except, perhaps, to question the validity of the other side's argument or the logical consistency of its position. Each disputant may complain about the moral insensitivity of his or her opponent, but they will have to agree to disagree.

It is the contention here that ethical disputation involves both ethical principles and factual circumstances. Enough, perhaps, has been said about the latter. Let us now turn our attention to the former and ask whether ethical judgments are empirical, a priori, or something else.

The Descriptive Approach: Naturalism

Whether ethical judgments are empirical or not depends on the meaning of basic ethical terms. If *good* is defined as "pleasure," then "pleasure is good" is a tautology. More important, the relative goodness of various states of experience can empirically be ascertained on the basis of the amounts of pleasure contained in them. If *right* means "productive of the greatest good," then, again, it is an empirical matter to determine which act is likely to produce the most good (pleasure). If Bentham and Mill really intended these meanings for *good* and *right* (which is doubtful), their theories are wholly empirical. Factual knowledge of acts and consequences is all that is required for ethical judgment. Ethical propositions take their place with other factual propositions describing the problematic situation.

Aristotle identifies goodness with a certain form of human development. If one has a clear conception of essential human nature, then actions and attitudes can be judged empirically on the basis of how they contribute to this ideal of humanity. How is the ideal of humanity discovered? Presumably, by observing actual persons and noting what the best of them are. Plato's theory is empirical in one sense, for actions and attitudes can be empirically compared with an ideal conception of humanity also, but in another sense it is a priori, for this conception is based on knowledge of transcendent reality in the realm of Forms. It could be argued that Aristotle's knowledge of essential humanity is based on a priori thought also, but his ethical theory is derived from a view of what nature is and is therefore naturalistic. It purports to derive what *ought* to be the case from what *is* the case.

A religious ethics may be regarded as naturalistic if it holds that "morality" and "obedience to God's will" are synonymous.[3] Knowledge of God's will may

[3]A supernaturalistic approach may thus be naturalistic! This is not as paradoxical as it sounds. G. E. Moore charges that all ethical theories that derive evaluative propositions from descriptive propositions have committed the "naturalistic fallacy," whether these descriptive propositions are naturalistic (in the narrow sense) or *metaphysical.* The key point is the transition from the *is* (however derived) to the *ought.* Many naturalistic theories are based on empirical conceptions of what is the case, but some of them are not. It is for this reason that this section is entitled "The Descriptive Approach: Naturalism" instead of "The Empirical Approach: Naturalism."

be derived from a priori conceptions or from empirical examination of engraved tablets, but no special a priori thought of an *ethical* sort is required to determine whether an act is moral. The passage from what is the case (God's will) to what ought to be the case (human actions) is smooth and automatic. If, however, the theory raises questions about the goodness of God and the validity of his injunctions, it is clearly outside the field of naturalistic ethics. Most religious theories do rely on a priori conceptions of goodness and rightness rather than simply identifying morality with obedience to a powerful being.

Other naturalistic approaches to ethics are not so puzzling as those of Aristotle, Plato, and religion. David Hume, who in 1739 pointed out the deceptive tactics of writers who slip from *is* to *ought,*[4] sought to be consistently empirical in his discussion of the sentiments of approbation or disapprobation actually experienced by people when they confront human behavior. Those actions that indicate character traits that tend to produce pleasure for the agent or others are approved; those that indicate traits that produce pain are disapproved. The criteria of morality, as well as their application, are matters for empirical investigation. All qualities that are virtues are found, inductively, to be those that are useful or immediately agreeable to ourselves or to others. Hume has indeed moved from the *is* to the *ought,* but not deceptively. He starts out with a definition: Virtue is a quality of character that arouses a sentiment of approbation in those who consider it. He then finds, empirically, that all such virtues fall into certain categories. No special a priori insight into the nature of the good is required.

Various subjectivist theories are similar. One may hold that to call an action right or a thing good is simply to say that it is *generally approved of.* Or one may hold that the person who calls an action right or a thing good is simply saying that *he or she* approves it. In both cases, the ethical judgment is derived from sentiments that can in principle be empirically detected. Propositions containing words like *good* and *right* can be translated into statements in which these words have disappeared. The resulting proposition is a factual statement. Once again, value has been derived from empirical fact.

The same sort of approach is made in relativistic theories that define *right* or *good* as that which is held in high esteem by a particular society and *wrong* or *bad* as that which is repugnant to a particular society. The fact of disagreement is no problem, for there is nothing absurd about a world containing societies with

[4]"In every system of morality, which I have hitherto met with, I have always remark'd, that the author proceeds for some time in the ordinary way of reasoning, and establishes the being of a God, or makes observations concerning human affairs; when of a sudden I am surpriz'd to find, that instead of the usual copulations of propositions, *is,* and *is not,* I meet with no proposition that is not connected with an *ought,* or an *ought not.* This change is imperceptible; but is, however, of the last consequence. For as this *ought,* or *ought not,* expresses some new relation or affirmation, 'tis necessary that it shou'd be observ'd and explain'd; and at the same time that a reason should be given, for what seems altogether inconceivable, how this new relation can be a deduction from others, which are entirely different from it." David Hume, *A Treatise of Human Nature* (Oxford: Clarendon Press, 1949), book 3, part 1, sec. 1, p. 469.

different standards. Just as the anthropologist is helpful in establishing the basis for the naturalism of Aristotle and Plato, and the psychologist in establishing the basis for the naturalism of Hume and the subjectivists, the sociologist provides the empirical data for the relativist. In all cases, passage is made from fact to value without calling in the aid of a priori judgment.

The ethical theory of John Dewey is based upon the *desires* of human beings. Whatever is desired is a potential value and is thus worthy of striving for. But not everything desired is, for Dewey, *desirable.* The function of thought is to identify those desired objectives that override others and merit special effort. This may be accomplished by a factual examination of causes and effects, means and ends, connections within experience itself. Dewey does not say we should have aims that transcend our desires, but only that we achieve a clear conception of what our desires really are and how some must be subjected to others. We are to satisfy our desires, but in an enlightened, creative, and experimental way. This is a naturalistic theory, for the fundamental principle is that of success in action, and success depends upon thinking seriously about the relation between what we want and what we do. The passage from the *is* to the *ought* consists merely of a more scientific grasp of the problematic situation and our own concerns than would be the case if we acted sheerly from habit or impulse.

These theories are all naturalistic in this sense: Knowledge of what is the case is all we need in order to have knowledge of what ought to be the case. Value judgments are a special class of factual judgment. When what *is* the case is known empirically, the ethical theory is purely empirical (Hume, Dewey); when it is known by other means (Plato, some religious theories), it is only partly empirical, but naturalistic nonetheless.

The Normative Approach: Nonnaturalism

Refutation of Naturalism Naturalistic ethical theories are criticized by two groups of philosophers. One group (most notably, G. E. Moore) holds that genuine ethical judgments are a priori; the other (most notably, A. J. Ayer) holds that ethical utterances are neither empirical nor a priori. Both groups object to empirical interpretation of sentences containing ethical terms.

Moore argues that the good is not identical with anything in nature or experience. Goodness is an objective but indefinable quality that is discerned a priori by the mind. "Pleasure is good" is not a tautology, but expresses a judgment that pleasurable experience possesses a particulár attribute. This statement, as well as such statements as "ignorance is bad," has a truth value that mere analysis of language cannot establish. To ignore the fact that people make a priori synthetic judgments is to miss the essential aspect of ethical thought. Some of these judgments are true, some of them are false. The statement "One ought to promote the good" is also not true by definition, but is based on a priori knowledge of the connection between goodness and oughtness. Suppose we view the proposition as an implicit definition of *ought.* So long as the implied definition employs an ethical term (in this case, *good*), we are clear of naturalism. Moore's basic point is that ethical terms cannot be defined by (reduced to) *nonethical* terms. To define *bad* in terms of *good* is permissible, but not in terms of *painful, repugnant,* or *unpopular.* Ethical concepts are not reducible to nonethical concepts—empirical metaphysical, or religious. To do so is to commit the "naturalistic fallacy."

Nor can we, according to Moore, infer statements containing ethical terms from premises containing only descriptive terms. Consider the argument "Sex is good because it is pleasurable, and pleasure is good." If *good* means the same thing in the premise and the conclusion, the argument is not fallacious. If, however, *good* means "pleasure" in the premise and "morally desirable" in the conclusion, a fallacy has been committed. It would perhaps be better to call the fallacy one of equivocation rather than the naturalistic fallacy. If the fallacy is that of trying to define the undefinable, as is done when the second premise is construed as a definition of *good,* the fallacy is better regarded as an instance of the "definist fallacy."[5]

Utilitarianism may be said to fall in the category of a priori, nonnaturalistic ethical theory.[6] Theories of self-realization, instrumentalism, subjectivism, and relativism, however, do not. A condition of human development may be *denoted* by the word *good,* but it is not *designated* by it, for the attribute conveyed by the word is unique.[7] "Success in action" means one thing; "moral action" means something else. Societies may esteem certain things, but the goodness of these things is not contained in the proposition that they are esteemed. Whether these things are good or bad must be judged by a priori reason.

The deontological ethical theories also hold that ethical judgment about duty and prima facie duty is an a priori matter. There is nothing in the facts themselves that proclaim obligation. All that the facts can indicate is what indeed is the case —past, present, or future. Societies may condemn murder, but its wrongness is a matter of a priori reason, not a simple deduction from the fact that it has been condemned. One's obligation to tell the truth is not entirely based on the known consequences of lying. Whatever naturalistic criterion someone might attempt to give to an ethical term, we are justified in asking whether an action that falls under the criterion is *in addition* right. Knowledge of ethical imperatives rests on practical reason, intuition, the conscience, or some such faculty. The views of Kant and Ross thus fall in the category of a priori, nonnaturalistic ethical theory.

[5]For a valuable analysis of the logic of naturalism, see William K. Frankena, "The Naturalistic Fallacy," *Mind* 48 (1939).

[6]While Moore would accept this statement for some of its adherents (e.g., Henry Sidgwick), he does not accept it for Bentham and Mill. According to Moore, Mill identified *pleasure* and *good, desired* and *desirable.*

[7]*Black* denotes coal but does not *mean* "coal." Coal is just one of the things that the term applies to. Even if it were the *only* thing the word applied to, *coal* would not be synonymous with *black.* If, in a small town, Harry Fletcher is both mayor and postmaster, we would not say that "mayor of Podunk" and "postmaster of Podunk" *mean* the same thing, although it is indisputable that they both *denote* the same person.

Ayer versus Naturalism and Nonnaturalism Ayer's views in ethics are based upon a criterion of cognitive meaning that not only demolishes naturalistic ethics but nonnaturalistic ethics as well.

Against naturalism, he argues that psychological and sociological interpretations of ethical utterances fail to capture what people really mean when they make them. On this point, Ayer and Moore stand on common ground. Among those who would join them is A. C. Ewing: "All I can say is that when I try to see what I mean when I use ethical terms I find that I have present to my consciousness an idea generically different from any empirical psychological concepts, and that I am as clearly aware of this as I am of what I mean in almost any other case of meaning."[8]

Subjectivism in all its forms, says Ayer, is an incorrect analysis. To say that an act is right or good is *not* to say that it is generally approved of, simply because it would not be self-contradictory for someone to say, "*X* is generally approved of, but it is wrong." One may be mistaken if one says that parents raising their own children is generally approved of but is wrong, but the view is not self-contradictory. People who say that an act is right or good are not necessarily saying that they approve it, for it is not self-contradictory for them to say that they sometimes approve of something that is bad or wrong. They may, for example, approve of cheating in a golf match, while believing that it is wrong. Utilitarianism, if interpreted naturalistically, also represents a poor analysis of how people use ethical language. It is not self-contradictory to hold that x is pleasant but not good (e.g., a feeling of glee when one's rival fails). And it is not self-contradictory to hold that y does not promote the greatest good but nonetheless is right (e.g., paying creditors). Relativism also is a poor analysis of language. It is not self-contradictory to hold that society prizes something that is wrong (e.g., patriotism) or to hold that society condemns something that is right (e.g., nonmarital sex).

Does Ayer's discussion imply that only a priori judgments capture the essence of ethical judgment? No. A priori truth is limited to analytic propositions. Synthetic a priori propositions are impossible. Only synthetic statements that are empirical have cognitive significance. We can conceive of empirical evidence that would count for and against such a proposition as "The first Europeans to set foot in the New World were twelfth-century Vikings." But we cannot conceive of empirical evidence that would strengthen or weaken the contention that knowledge is good or that truth-telling is right. Such utterances are not testable. Intuition or some other mysterious intellectual operation is a "worthless test of a proposition's validity." Disagreement in ethical "judgments" is rife simply because they employ pseudoconcepts and are thus not judgments at all. Ethical utterances, being neither analytic nor empirical, are neither true nor false. They are cognitively meaningless. One may say, "He stole the money." This is descriptive and may be adjudged true or false. Truth is served in no way by the addition of "that action was wrong."

[8]A. C. Ewing, quoted in Hospers, *Human Conduct,* p. 537.

The Case for Nonnaturalism Since the nonnaturalists have rejected the notion that ethical judgments are empirical, they must somehow establish the possibility of genuine synthetic a priori propositions. They must show that Ayer and other logical empiricists are mistaken. To do so, they appeal to the convictions of the plain person, the morally sensitive individual, the objective and disinterested spectator. They admit that "first principles" cannot be proved (if they could, they wouldn't be "first" principles), but claim that their truth can be discerned a priori. *Unprovable* and *unknowable* are not synonymous. They point out the arbitrariness of a criterion of meaning that excludes all but the analytic and empirical.

They argue that subjectivist and relativist theories based on what in fact is valued overlook an important consideration: Individuals and collectivities not only direct their moral approval to certain things and actions, but believe that these things and actions are worthy of approval and that other people and groups should approve them as well. "I approve *x*" is often uttered with the conviction that *x* is *entitled* to approval by me and everyone else. One would not claim that one's approval is *moral* approval unless this were the case. Nonnaturalists point out the general agreement in the human race that there are real differences between alternative actions. Surely Saint Francis was a better human being than Adolf Hitler!

They also point out that much disagreement in particular cases dissolves when all the facts of the situation are known. When this is so, the disputing parties can make their a priori pronouncements on a common basis. Individuals in our society, for example, regard the killing of parents as the depth of moral degradation, while individuals in another culture regard such an act as one of exalted duty. If the former believed as the latter do that the parents' lot in the next life would be greatly enhanced if they passed away at age forty-five instead of at age seventy, they too might recognize their duty to be that of dispatching their parents before it was too late. When two people share the same conception of what is the case, they very often will agree on what ought to be the case. Factual knowledge is the preliminary for ethical knowledge. And when the former is achieved, disagreement in the latter may still occur, but it is not as "notorious" as charged.

If Ayer is correct, all the ethical viewpoints relied upon in the preceding chapters are worse than false: They are based upon either faulty language analysis (naturalism) or cognitively meaningless sentences (nonnaturalism). It is at this point that we might note an attempt on the part of the nonnaturalists to exploit some of the insights of the naturalists against the common enemy.

As we have seen, the nonnaturalists will welcome facts: they will try to perceive the ethical situation in as broad and deep a factual perspective as possible. The facts will not themselves contain the ethical answer, but will provide a context in which a priori ethical judgment can most effectively operate. Concrete ethical dilemmas can better be solved in full knowledge of history, causal connections, and mitigating factors. Facts, while not sufficient, are necessary conditions for responsible ethical decisions.

Moreover, the nonnaturalists will point out that many naturalistic theories possess the plausibility they have because of a priori aspects that have been overlooked. The humanism of Aristotle and Plato is not really derived from observing what people in general do, but from an a priori concept of what human nature can be. There is nothing self-contradictory in saying that most humans do *x* or *y*, but that *x* and *y* are wrong. Aristotle and Plato have high conceptions of humanity that are based upon a priori distinctions between better and worse expressions of humanity. This idealizing tendency is present in all theories of self-realization. We are enjoined to realize not just *any* self or one that is typical for the species, but one conceived to be worthy and admirable. Mill's utilitarianism, ideal utilitarianism, and rule utilitarianism all, in obvious ways, may be viewed as theories basically a priori. Unlike Ayer (and Moore), we place them squarely in the nonnaturalistic camp.[9] Religious ethical theories for the most part are a priori, not only in their theology, but in their ethical conceptions. If we believe that God should be obeyed, we do so not because of his power, but because of his goodness. We do not believe that *goodness* and *power* are synonymous, that "might makes right." The good and the right must be ascertained independently of the fact of sheer power.

One naturalistic theory relies upon the concept of "the ideal observer." The ideal observer is strictly *impartial.* He either has no stake in the matter to be evaluated or is able completely to suspend his bias. He is *fully informed* on all the relevant facts of the situation—circumstances and consequences. He has a powerful *imagination* that enables him to assess the feelings and interests of all the beings involved. He is calm and dispassionate and possesses no psychological "hangups" that would distort his *objectivity.* The good or the right, by definition, would be that which such a hypothetical being would morally approve. This naturalistic theory is suggested in the writings of David Hume. Hume was reluctant to call "virtue" whatever *X, Y,* or *Z* happened to approve on this or that occasion. He talked about qualified spectators (people who were informed, disinterested, and sympathetic) and the need to "correct our sentiments."[10]

That this theory is hypothetical does not, of course, mean that it is a priori rather than empirical. And this is so even if no ideal observer can be found—although Hume believed that it was not difficult in most cases to determine what an ideal observer would say. But the popularity of the theory does indicate that some naturalists who want to appeal to empirical expressions of moral approval

[9]It has convincingly been argued that Mill was quite aware that he was not *proving* his fundamental principle that pleasure is good and the only good in that famous chapter of *Utilitarianism* (IV), but only showing that it had widespread support in the ethical judgments of humanity. It would be absurd to propose something as a value that no one in fact desired! See Edward W. Hall, "The 'Proof' of Utility in Bentham and Mill," *Ethics* 60 (October 1949); Mary Warnock, *Ethics since 1900* (London: Oxford University Press, 1960); Hardy Jones, "Mill's Argument for the Principle of Utility," *Philosophy and Phenomenological Research* 38 (March 1978).

[10]For an excellent exposition of this aspect of Hume's ethics and its relation to his subjectivism and utilitarianism, see Ronald J. Glossop, "The Nature of Hume's Ethics," *Philosophy and Phenomenological Research* 27 (June 1967): 527ff.

are reluctant to define the ethical terms on the dispositions of individuals or even that of *most* individuals. They want to be able to say: "So-and-so says that *x* is right, but it is wrong." "Society says that *y* is wrong, but it is right." Or even: "Everyone (else) says that *z* is good, but it is bad." As has often been pointed out, the theory can be used to make one's own belief in ethics true almost by definition ("It is what the ideal observer would say!"), but more important, it offers a definition that is very difficult to apply on empirical grounds. If one cannot empirically determine what the ideal observer would say, one is tempted to speculate a priori on what that observer would say. In doing so, one comes very close to the nonnaturalist approach of Moore, Ross, Ewing, Blanshard, Pritchard, Sidgwick, and others: a priori ethical judgments can be made by a sensitive and objective and intelligent mind.[11]

Dewey's theory would seem to be simply calling for intelligent action that would be in the end and the process gratifying for the individual. But individuals do not always behave in this way. Dewey tells us that they *should.* Dewey holds that an *effective* life is better than an *ineffective* one. But how does he know this? That evolution creates beings with instruments for solving practical problems does not itself mean that these beings ought to employ these instruments. Dewey will use intelligence not for the *survival* of the life of the individual or the species, but to *enrich the quality of life.* This suggests an a priori ethical conviction.

Beyond Truth

The Emotive Theory of Ethics If, as some philosophers believe, normative sentences have no cognitive significance, what function do they perform? One answer is that they perform an *expressive* function. Terms like *good, bad, right,* and *wrong,* while not designating any real conception, do carry emotive force. Sentences that contain them, therefore, express feelings rather than conveying information. If people say that stealing money is wrong, they are evincing a negative emotion toward stealing. It is as if they said, "Stealing money—ugh!" And if they say that telling the truth is right, they are evincing a positive feeling about truth-telling. It is as if they said, "Truth-telling—hurrah!" Not all adjectives are names of properties or qualities.

There is no real conflict between two people who react emotionally in different ways to the same things. When two people have different feelings about strawberry ice cream, we do not believe that one of them is correct or "true" while the other is incorrect or "false." To use the language of Charles Stevenson, this kind of disagreement is not one of *belief,* but one of *attitude.* The two people are not saying different and incompatible things about the world; they are merely evincing different feelings. We cannot even say that expressive sentences of this kind are true if and only if the emotion is actually felt. It is quite possible for a person

[11]Or, in Rashdall's words, "a well-bred Englishman."

to evince a feeling without actually having it. People may say that lying is wrong without actually having negative feelings about it, just as it is possible for them to say that strawberry ice cream is delicious while loathing it. This is thus quite different from the subjective naturalist approach that Ayer criticized above. "*X* is good" is not a statement that the speaker approves of *x* (which could be true or false), but is an utterance that evinces a feeling that the speaker is not claiming actually to have. The utterance is no statement at all; it is thus neither true nor false.

Normative sentences may also be made in order to evoke or arouse feelings in others. Parents may wish to evoke negative feelings in their child toward lying and say in tones of obvious disapproval, "Lying is *wrong*!" Perhaps they wish to influence the child's future actions. Such sentences may, then, sometimes perform the *directive* function. "You ought to tell the truth" is a way of commanding others to tell the truth. But directive sentences are no more true or false than expressive sentences.

We may argue about the facts of a particular situation or about the consequences of certain types of action, but not about the attitudes toward them. It is quite possible that a disagreement in belief is the basis for a disagreement in attitude, but there is no assurance that agreement in belief, once it has been achieved, will be followed by agreement in attitude. Two people may be in perfect accord on the consequences of telling a lie in a particular situation (or of lying in general), but still disagree on whether the action is wrong. Their emotional reactions are different, and the only recourse at this point would be to mount an emotional appeal that would somehow alter their feelings.

Nonnaturalists are correct in saying that something important is overlooked in naturalistic theories. But what is overlooked is not some a priori property. It is instead the emotional reaction expressed in noncognitive utterances. The nonnaturalists will not, of course, accept this approach either. They will admit that emotions are often present in ethical discourse, but will argue that one reacts emotionally to good things and bad things because they are seen to *be* good and bad. One does not *mean* by one's judgments that *x* warms one's heart and *y* curdles one's souls. Emotions are ways of reacting to what is believed to be the case—on both the factual and normative levels.

The Existentialism of Sartre The emotive theory of ethics is not the only approach that denies the cognitive element in ethical "judgment." Existentialism also views ethics as an enterprise unrelated to considerations of truth and falsity. In the writings of Jean-Paul Sartre we find ethical value to be grounded in action, free and creative.

One of the slogans of existentialism is that existence precedes essence. What this means is that we were not created with implicit human potentialities that we are to realize or express during our lifetime. We do not exemplify a human essence that is to unfold in time. We simply exist. As individuals we are unique; we cannot be reduced to a set of concepts. Our essence, what we are to be, is not given us by God or nature: it is made by us through the actions we choose to perform. If we do brave deeds, we are brave; if we think philosophical thoughts, we are philosophical. "To be ambitious, cowardly, or irritable is simply to conduct oneself in this or that manner in this or that circumstance."[12] "To be is to act, and to cease to act is to cease to be."[13] Through these actions, the self takes on attributes. The "project toward self" (which is what constitutes selfness) in never finished. The free being has a "constantly renewed obligation to remake the Self."[14]

Are there any guideposts? We have seen that there is no Aristotelian or Thomistic essence that the human being is to realize. For Sartre, there is no God and thus there are no divine commandments. There are no philosophical imperatives, principles, or models. There is nothing at all that will condemn or justify the choices that an individual must make. Man is compelled at every moment to "invent man." "*Nothing,* absolutely nothing, justifies me in adopting this or that value, this or that particular set of values. . . . In this world where I engage myself, my acts cause values to spring up like partridges."[15] The human task is to impose reason on an absurd universe, fashion a self, and give significance to human action. "Nothing can ensure me against myself, cut off from the world and from my essence by this nothingness which I *am.* I have to realize the meaning of the world and of my essence; I make my decision concerning them—without justification and without excuse."[16]

Certain feelings arise in us that remind us of our human condition as solitary centers of consciousness ("being-for-itself") hovering over an all but intractable physical world ("being-in-itself"). *Anguish* is experienced when we realize that the one thing we cannot do is to will that we may not be free. Freedom is a burden that we cannot lay down. We may try to conceal from ourselves that we freely choose our actions by appealing to some form of psychological or physical determinism: I did the deed because, in view of my personality, training, and the external factors at work, I was compelled to. Or we may appeal to some ethical or religious creed to which we habitually give lip service: I did the deed because Christian ethics, moral law, or social standards required it. Or we may find justification in the fact that we are engrossed in a career or profession: I only did what any person would have done to succeed in a life-long project. These escapes are instances of "bad faith": the attempt to find the causes of action outside the free consciousness. We are *condemned* to be free. Although we are free to attempt to conceal our freedom from ourselves, our success can only be temporary. Anguish will break through. "I flee in order not to know, but I can not avoid knowing that I am fleeing; and the flight from anguish is only a mode of becoming

[12]Sartre, *Being and Nothingness,* p. 476.
[13]Ibid.
[14]Ibid., p. 35.
[15]Ibid., p. 38.
[16]Ibid., p. 39.

conscious of anguish. Thus anguish, properly understood, can be neither hidden nor avoided."[17]

Anguish must be distinguished from fear. When we think of what others (or nature) may do to us, we experience fear; when we think of what we have the power to do to ourselves, we experience anguish. We may fear artillery fire, but feel anguish when we realize that how we act under fire is our own choice. We may be fearful in traversing a mountain path, but feel anguish when we realize that, despite our prudence and conviction that suicide is wrong, we may decide to leap into the chasm. Anguish reminds us that we must chart our own course through an unmapped wasteland, guided only by a self that is always in the making.

If we are existentialists we also experience *forlornness,* for we are alone and must take the responsibility for our own actions. There is no God to reassure us or forgive us or die for us, no institution to support us, and no people with whom to share the blame. We experience *despair,* for we cannot depend upon the cooperation of other people (for they, too, are free) or the tractableness of the physical world (for it is insensitive to our concerns and fundamentally absurd). We experience *dread,* for we can never be sure that we have acted wisely. Every act is fraught with consequences and no act can be undone. We experience *nausea* when we are confronted with the senseless being-in-itself that is physical reality. When the veneer of meanings that we have imposed on it slides away and sheer existence unveils itself in its unintelligible and alien plenitude, we recoil in disgust. It is too much *(de trop).*[8]

There would seem to be an objective ethical standard in all of this: Act authentically, without excuse and without apology; affirm your freedom, engage yourself, and hope for the best. It must be remembered, however, that all individuals *do* act freely, however hesitant they may be and whatever elements of bad faith they exhibit. Each individual creates his or her own self, no matter how he or she seems to shrink from the task. Since there are no standards except those that as individuals we impose on ourselves, authentic existence cannot be a *morally superior* mode of being. Although the existentialists may respect "authenticity," they cannot set it forth as an ethical model—simply because there *are* no ethical models. Values are created by free individuals, and all individuals are free. "I emerge alone and in dread in the face of the unique and first project which constitutes my being; all barriers, all the railings, collapse, annihilated by the consciousness of my liberty; I have not, nor can I have, recourse to any value against the fact that it is I who maintain values in being. . . ."[19]

In any case, existentialist ethics takes its place beside emotive ethics as a theory that dispenses with ethical judgments. These theories are not concerned to set forth true principles for moral behavior—empirical or a priori. The former sees

[17] Ibid., p. 43.

[18] See Sartre, *Nausea,* tr. Lloyd Alexander (New York: New Directions, 1964), pp. 126–129.

[19] Sartre, *Being and Nothingness,* p. 39.

the significance of moral choice or preference in the creative act; the latter sees the significance of moral choice or preference in the emotional reaction. They are "beyond truth and falsity."

For Further Reading

A. J. Ayer. *Language, Truth and Logic.* rev. ed. London: Victor Gollancz, 1946.

Simone de Beauvoir. *The Ethics of Ambiguity.* New York: Citadel Press, 1964.

Ronald J. Glossop. "Hume, Stevenson, and Hare on Moral Language." In Donald W. Livingston and James T. King, eds. *Hume: A Re-evaluation.* New York: Fordham University Press, 1976.

John Hospers. *Human Conduct: An Introduction to the Problems of Ethics.* New York: Harcourt, Brace & World, 1961. Chapter 11.

G. E. Moore. *Principia Ethica.* Cambridge: At the University Press, 1903.

Jean-Paul Sartre. *Being and Nothingness: An Essay in Phenomenological Ontology.* Translated by Hazel E. Barnes. New York: Philosophical Library, 1956.

Jean-Paul Sartre. *Existentialism.* Translated by Bernard Frechtman. New York: Philosophical Library, 1947.

Moritz Schlick. *Problems of Ethics.* Translated by David Rynin. New York: Prentice-Hall, 1939.

Wilfrid Sellars and John Hospers, eds. *Readings in Ethical Theory.* 2nd ed. New York: Appleton-Century-Crofts, 1970. Part 2.

Charles L. Stevenson. *Ethics and Language.* New Haven, Conn.: Yale University Press, 1946.

Edvard Westermarck. *Ethical Relativity.* New York: Harcourt, Brace, 1932.

EGOISM

Psychological Egoism

Psychology and Ethics The theory of psychological egoism, in its most general form, holds that every conscious act that one does is motivated by what one believes serves one's own best interest. All actions are intended to be self-serving.

> A beggar in Madrid was asking alms; a passer-by said to him, "Aren't you ashamed to beg like this, when you can work?" "Sir," replied the mendicant, "I ask you for money, not advice," and turned his back with true Castilian dignity. The beggar was haughty; his vanity was easily wounded; he asked alms out of self-love, and would not suffer reprimand out of ever greater self-love.
>
> A missionary in India saw a fakir loaded with chains, naked as an ape, lying on his belly and lashing himself for the sins of his fellows, who gave him coins. "What self-renouncement!" said a spectator. "Self-renouncement!" repeated the fakir scornfully, "I lash myself in this world only to serve you the same in the next, when you will be the horse and I the rider."

> Whoever said that self-love is the basis of all our emotions and actions was right; it isn't necessary to prove that men have faces, nor that they possess self-love. It is the instrument of our preservation; it is like a provision for perpetuating mankind; it is essential, it is dear to us, it is delightful, and it should be hidden.[20]

Psychological egoism purports to be a description, however unflattering, of human nature.

What is its relation to ethics? Ethics is concerned with how people ought to act rather than how they do *in fact* act. Yet, if psychological egoism is true, much of ethical theory becomes absurd or pointless. Those ethical theories that require individuals to sacrifice their interest in those cases where their duty lies elsewhere are demanding the impossible. Utilitarianism and religious and deontological ethics require the agent to act counter to human nature. If all people are egoists, it is absurd to tell them to promote the general welfare, love others, or discharge their social obligations. Those ethical theories that require individuals to serve themselves are pointless if the individual is psychologically determined to do this anyway.[21] The truth of psychological egoism thus tends to negate the significance of both universalistic and egoistic ethics.

If, however, psychological egoism is false, ethical theory is not affected. Universalistic theories can plausibly require individuals to serve others, and egoistic ethical theories can plausibly require individuals to serve themselves. Although psychological egoism has at times (especially in the eighteenth and nineteenth centuries) been regarded as true by most philosophers and psychologists, it enjoys very little professional support today. Let us see why.

Various Arguments for Psychological Egoism One argument for psychological egoism is this: "All acts are done by a self. The self can have no motives but that which appeals to its own interests. The actions it chooses will therefore be selfish." This is an obviously poor argument. The words *selfish* and *unselfish* mark a difference in human action. We would ordinarily call the action of a person who shared a lunch with a luckless co-worker "unselfish" and the action of one who consumed it under the nose of the hungry friend "selfish." These words play a useful role in ordinary language. To call all actions "selfish" simply because they have been undertaken by selves is to give the word a new meaning for purpose of winning an argument—which is an instance of the fallacy of question-begging definition. Moreover, the manuever serves no theoretical purpose, for users of the language would have to coin another set of terms to mark the distinction that *selfish/unselfish* previously marked.

[20]Voltaire, "Self-Love," *Satirical Dictionary,* trans. Paul McPharlin (Mount Vernon, N.Y.: The Peter Pauper Press, 1945), p. 91.

[21]Egoistic ethical theories (which will be discussed in the next section) do not agree on what the individual's true interest is, and versions of what psychological egoism means also vary. So it is possible that a particular theory of ethical egoism is rendered absurd by a particular version of psychological egoism rather than simply pointless.

Another argument, this one put forth by hedonists, is: "Individuals are concerned solely with their own pleasure. They always choose to do the act that will produce immediate pleasure." This is false on empirical grounds. People may drink bitter medicine. They may suffer the pain of torture. They may force themselves to read a boring textbook. The argument may be amended in such a way as to take into account pleasure in the long run. We may be told that sick people, prisoners, and students are really pursuing pleasure in a rational and prudent way. The sick people wish to banish the pain of illness and regain the pleasure of health. The prisoners are thinking of the greater pain that will befall them if their colleagues find out that they have revealed their secrets. The students may be anticipating the pain of poor grades or the pleasure of graduation. But this view of human motivation is also false, because it is easy to think of cases in which individuals do *not* subordinate the immediate future to pleasurable consequences in the remote future. *X* does not lay down his cigarette after reading about the pains of lung cancer. *Y* does not save her money for a joyous trip to Europe. *Z* does not decline the party invitation in order to review for an exam.

Perhaps it is true that individuals always respond to the prospect of their own pleasure—immediate *or* remote. Somewhere along the line, it is said, one may find a package of pleasure that motivates every action. The person who gets up early and works hard all morning in order to play golf that afternoon is motivated by the pleasure of the golf game. The person who sleeps till midmorning is motivated by the pleasure of the warm bed. The critic may devise complex hypothetical cases to show that the prospect of pleasure, near or remote, is not the motive: *X* gives money anonymously to charity that she could have spent to remodel her home. *Y* volunteers to perform a hazardous mission that will probably cost him his life. *Z* labors long and hard to complete an important scientific study that will bring neither renown nor a bigger bank account. The adherents of egoism will try to get around all our stipulations in order to find that hope for pleasure that motivated *X, Y,* and *Z.*

At this point we have to ask them two questions: (1) How do you *know* that there is pleasure somewhere along the line? (2) How can you be sure that the amount of anticipated pleasure exceeds that of the anticipated pain? Their answer to the first question may be that *any* action that it pleases us to do generates pleasure. This is undoubtedly true. *X, Y,* and *Z* all derive pleasure from the sheer fact that they are doing what they have chosen to do. Even the person who decides to work in a leper colony will derive pleasure—if for no other reason than simply that it is his or her desire to do the work. This suggests that the egoist has put the cart before the horse. People have desires—centered in external objects and enterprises. It is only because they *have* these desires that it is pleasurable to gratify them. The desire comes first; the pleasure is derivative. The golfer wants to play golf, and gets pleasure from it only because of the desire. Rabbit hunters are not hunting pleasure—they are hunting *rabbits.* The egoist has confused the pleasure that accompanies a chosen activity with the motive for performing it.

This is not to deny that desire for pleasure may occasionally be the motive. One may abstract the feeling of savoring a fine wine or sinking into a hot tub from the activity and deliberately seek it. But a great many actions are motivated by desires in which the thought of pleasure is not present. *A* gives to charity because she wants to help diabetes victims. *B* studies hard because he wants to increase his knowledge. *C* does brave deeds because she wants to be honored. *D* does moral acts because he wants to be moral. That there is satisfaction in doing these things does not mean that this pleasurable feeling is the motive; for if *A, B, C,* and *D* did not have their respective desires, they would not experience the pleasurable "reward." Looking now at the second question, we find that the egoists cannot supply an acceptable answer. We have granted that they will find some pleasure, but surely they cannot convince us that the pleasure of saints, martyrs, war heros, or dedicated researchers exceeds the pleasure, in either the long run or the short, of other courses of action open to them.

Let us, then, forget pleasure and consider another formulation of the egoistic argument: "Whatever one decides to do, it is one's *own* wish that finally prevails. Since all people act on the basis of what they want, their conduct is egoistic. They necessarily indulge their own desires." This argument ignores the difference between desires that are centered in things outside the agent and those that are centered in the agent. One may indeed act with the motive to enhance one's own wealth or power. This is surely egoistic. But one may also act to benefit others or to obey the moral law. This is not egoistic. One may have two desires at the same time: to get rich and to be honest. If one decides to do the latter, one is doing what one wants to do in a sense, but is also refraining from doing something else that one wants to do. One wants the money, but the desire to be moral prevails. Much of life consists in declining to satisfy certain genuinely felt wants in preference to others that are thought to be more important. When one indulges a desire that is objectified in benefit for others or in moral laws, one is following one's own desires, but they are of an entirely different order from those that advance the condition of one's own life. The only thing to be gained by calling all desires or wants egoistic is to make egoism true by definition. What is lost are convenient terms that distinguish self-centered, selfish, egoistic desires on the one hand from other-centered, benevolent, or moral desires on the other. All motives are linked with desires. Why lump these desires together as one type when they exhibit such variety?

The most pernicious egoistic claim is that the desire to be moral is egoistic. As we have seen, pleasure or satisfaction is sometimes held up by the hedonist as the motive—although there would be no pleasure if the desire to be moral for its own sake did not already exist. But hedonism aside, it is sometimes claimed that the desire to be moral is egoistic because it expresses the obsession to exhibit one's own selfishly conceived moral goodness! We may grant that it is egoistic to be moral for the sake of the praise of our neighbors, but to accuse the person dedicated to morality of egoism because *it is he or she who has adopted this object of action* is surely to do violence to ordinary word usage.

Suppose you are faced with a choice between two actions, one in which you profit at the expense of someone else and the other in which you sacrifice something on behalf of others. Whichever you choose, you will be branded as an egoist. If you do the first, you have chosen your advantage over that of the other. If you do the second, you have indulged your own (benevolent or moral) desire!

Hume and Butler Another version of this interest-desire argument looks like an empirical argument but turns out to be as question-begging as the one we have just looked at. Its exponent says that beneath every so-called unselfish action there lurks a selfish motive. The moral person really wants to be respected, the saint really wants to be loved, the martyr really wants to go to heaven, the honest person really wants to stay in business. If we adduce cases where no selfish motives can be exposed, we are told to keep looking, for one is there. If we still can't find one, we are told that we haven't looked deeply enough. How can the egoist be sure? As a counter to this argument, John Hospers writes:

> If the psychological egoist is permitted to argue in this way, an opponent could argue as follows: "All desires are really *un*selfish. Sometimes it doesn't look that way, and sometimes people do seem to desire selfish ends, but look a little deeper and you'll find lurking behind every selfish desire an unselfish one. True, you may not actually find it, but that only shows that you haven't looked hard enough." Probably no one would accept such an argument; yet logically it is exactly parallel to the argument of the psychological egoist.[22]

That desires and motivations do represent *interests* does not mean that they are all the same. In the broad sense, they are all "interested"; but in another sense of "interested," some are and some are not. It is not self-contradictory to talk about *disinterested* interests (or desires or motives). As Hume pointed out, it is sometimes easier to establish the possibility of disinterested desires for the *harm* of others than disinterested desires for the *welfare* of others. Vengeance provides an example. The villain in *High Noon* was determined to shoot down Gary Cooper ("He made a vow while in state's prison, vowed it'd be my life or his'n. . . ."). To accomplish this he was willing to risk his life or at least another term in prison. If we can regard certain acts of vengeance as "disinterested" in the sense that concern for the self is all but obliterated, why can we not regard certain acts of altruism as disinterested also? To agree that all motives are "interested" in one sense is not to agree that they are "interested" in another sense.

Joseph Butler, who along with Hume was one of the very few people who questioned the reigning egoism of their day, distinguished the "cool" principles of self-love, benevolence, and conscience from "hot" phenomena like desires, inclinations, and impulses. Actions done from the latter are neither egoistic nor nonegoistic, for questions of the advantage of self or others or morality have not

[22]Hospers, *Human Conduct,* p. 155.

come up. But reflection would have shown that these actions are indeed relevant to these questions. For some do serve the self, hurt the self, benefit others, and harm others. Some impulses will be found to serve (or conflict with) one interest, some with another. An impulse might be checked, Butler suggested, if it were found to conflict with the principle of self-love. The trouble with many people, he said, is that they do not have *enough* self-love![23] Similarly, generous impulses might be checked if on reflection they did not indeed serve the interest of the other. Butler's concern was to bring actions under the control of rational principles rather than to indulge desires heedlessly. Rational concern for self, others, and morality is better than blind attachment to casually experienced objects of desire.

	SELF	*OTHERS*	*CONSCIENCE*
Actions done on behalf of	1 Egoism	2 Altruism	3 Morality
Actions done against	4 Masochism	5 Malice	6 Immorality

The implication of Butler's essay is that conscious acts fall into several categories, of which egoism is only one—and not the worse one. The first three tendencies are acceptable (rational). The conscience may condone or even require egoism and altruism in some cases, while ordering one to give way to the other in other cases. The last three are unacceptable (counter to rational principles), and may in addition be condemned by conscience. If it is true that egoism is only one of the six possible kinds of conscious action, then the theory of psychological egoism is false. The possibility of masochism, malice, and deliberate immorality is just as destructive to the truth of egoism as is the possibility of altruism and morality.

Ethical Egoism

Duty Toward Oneself Even though psychological egoism may be false as a description of human action, ethical egoism could be true as a prescription for human action. Although people do not in fact always seek to pursue their own best interest, they *ought* to do so. One's basic obligation is to oneself, and any obligation one may owe to others must be derived from the basic concern that one owes to oneself. If two knights want the same damsel or two politicians want

[23]"I have looked upon the world for four times seven years; and since I could distinguish betwixt a benefit and an injury, I never found man that knew how to love himself." William Shakespeare, *Othello,* act 1, sc. 3.

the same office, each is justified in doing whatever is necessary to foil the rival, even if it involves killing. "Maintain holy thy highest hope," says Nietzsche. "Cast not away the hero from thy soul." "Do what thou wilt" was the only rule in Gargantua's abbey as described in Rabelais. Machiavelli praised the "inhuman cruelty" of Hannibal and took Caesar Borgia as his model for *The Prince.*

There is no self-contradiction in the view that each person ought to get what he can for himself or herself, with no concern for others. It is sometimes argued that ethical egoism is inconsistent because it tells both knights and both politicians that they should dispatch their respective rivals, that each should overcome the other. Since the directive cannot be carried out, egoism is supposed to be self-contradictory. But the theory cannot be refuted so easily. It does not say that *X* should defeat *Y* and *Y* should defeat *X* but that each must choose what he or she most wants and should employ the most effective means available for this end. *X* may decide that he or she is overmatched and retire from the field. *X* may decide that he or she has a good chance and engage in combat. Each may or may not be mistaken. Ethical egoism is not mindless or fanatical. Even Machiavelli had praise for certain rulers who were "astute." One is deserving of moral praise when one seeks to serve oneself; one deserves even more praise when one's acts are indeed productive of that end. As is the case in universalistic theories, both the motive and the effectiveness of the agent may be scrutinized. What ethical egoism says is: "Seek to get the best deal for yourself in all situations."

Even so, such a conception seems to be the antithesis of true morality. Still, since important philosophers have held it, the theory merits our attention. Plato, Aristotle, and self-realizationists in general have set forth ideals for human nature that require actions that are self-serving in the most enlightened way. Thomas Hobbes, who provides a naturalistic theory of ethics *after* the state is created, holds to a normative theory of egoism for the state of nature and argues that the individual retains certain rights even in civil society.[24] Even John Locke, who opposed Hobbes in many important ways, held that one is obliged to obey law because of the rewards and punishments attached. There are three kinds of law: (1) *Divine law* is made by God and is promulgated to humanity "by the light of nature, or the voice of revelation." "This is the only true touchstone of moral rectitude; and by comparing them to this law, it is that men can judge of the most considerable moral good of their actions. . . ."[25] (2) *Civil law* is made by common-

[24]"The *right of nature,* which writers common call *jus naturale,* is the liberty which each man hath, to use his own power, as he will himself, for the preservation of his own nature; that is to say, of his own life, and consequently, of doing any thing, which in his own judgment, and reason, he shall conceive to be the aptest means thereunto. . . . A covenant not to defend myself from force, by force, is always void. For, as I have showed before, no man can transfer, or lay down his right to save himself from death, wounds, and imprisonment, the avoiding whereof is the only end of laying down any right; and therefore the promise of not resisting force, in no covenant transferreth any right; nor is obliging." Thomas Hobbes, *Leviathan* (New York: Collier Books, 1962), chap. 14, pp. 103, 110.

[25]John Locke, *An Essay concerning Human Understanding,* ed. A. C. Fraser (Oxford: Oxford University Press, 1894), II, 28, vol. 1, p. 475.

wealths and is enforced by stated punishments and rewards in this life. (3) *The law of opinion or reputation* is made by the likes or dislikes of particular societies. No one can escape the commendation and discredit of others in the community. Moral law seems to be involved at all levels, for a moral law is a command of a being who has the power to reward and punish "by some good or evil, that is not the natural product and consequence of the action itself."[26] Morality consists in obeying rules for egoistic reasons: "Moral good and evil, then, is only the conformity or disagreement of our voluntary actions to some law, whereby good or evil is drawn on us, from the will and power of the lawmaker. . . ."[27] Our highest moral obligation is to divine law, for it is enforced "by rewards and punishments of infinite weight and duration in another life. . . ."[28]

The famous rights of life, liberty, and property are rational aspects of divine law. It was the assumption of Locke and his legion of eighteenth-century followers that God is a wise and benevolent being and that observation of his law would not only promote the general welfare but the happiness of individuals, and this would be the case *in this life.* Natural law is not arbitrary. Alexander Pope expressed the situation:

> Thus God and Nature link'd the gen'ral frame,
> And bade Self-love and Social be the same.[29]

This idea was expressed in numerous religious tracts, as well as in Adam Smith's *Wealth of Nations.* It is the "enlightenment" view that self-expression along rational lines would benefit both the individual and society, and that God intended both. And there were two levels of "enforcement": this life and the next.

Bentham did not have much to say about the next life, but he did believe that many reforms had to take place in society before egoism would truly serve the general interest. That is why he was so concerned to revise the system of law and jurisprudence. He also would seek to train and educate people to pursue the general good by finding personal satisfaction in unselfish action (the "internal sanction"). Bentham was thus in the strange position of holding a nonegoistic ethics while at the same time believing in psychological egoism. Not having God to rely on, he could not encourage egoistic actions indiscriminately until all the sanctions were in place in this world!

Those who argue for individualistic action because it is thought to produce the greatest general welfare are not, of course, ethical egoists. Self-serving motives receive their blessing because they tend to be in their consequences beneficial to all. Is there anything that can be said on behalf of ethical egoism when a system

[26]Ibid., p. 474.
[27]Ibid.
[28]Ibid., p. 476.
[29]Alexander Pope, *An Essay on Man,* Epistle III.

of sanctions (divine, social, and/or internal) is *not* in place? One could argue that the essence of ethics is virtue and that the achievement of a certain virtuous disposition is the greatest good for the individual. One's highest interest is to cultivate a particular kind of person. The individual should not merely seek his or her interests in general, but his or her ultimate interest—which is to be virtuous. This is something which the individual must do, for no one else can.

This is certainly a more attractive theory than the one that holds that the moral individual is one who most successfully avoids punishments and secures rewards from other persons, society, and God, but it has fatal defects. (1) What is virtue? If it is defined in terms of obedience to moral law, we have abandoned egoism for a universalistic position. We have appealed to ethical values beyond sheer self-interest. If *virtue* simply means an arbitrarily prescribed condition of humanity, then the argument is circular. Egoism is right because it leads to virtue; virtue is right because it is the culmination of successful egoism. (2) If virtue is an objective and intrinsic good, then it is something that is good *for everyone.* One should then be as concerned to contribute to the virtue of others as to one's own. Egoism is transcended. The universe is better off in having virtuous individuals. I will do what I can—in my own person and that of others. Perhaps this is the ethical goal of theories of self-realization.

Why Be Moral? Finally, we will look at a version of ethical egoism that is more plausible than the ones we have just considered. The problem is, however, that this "version" may not be a version of ethical egoism at all! Some have expressed the position this way: "There is no reason why I should not do what I want to do. You may talk about my 'obligation' to others, but I don't recognize such an obligation. In the absence of compelling moral law, I will do whatever I like, intelligently, to be sure, but my own desires, whether self-serving or benevolent, shall be the basis of my conduct." This view is perhaps one of moral skepticism rather than ethical egoism, but it does represent the resolve to dispense with external standards and to rely on those projected by an unfettered self. It is in spirit quite compatible with the ethics of John Dewey.

Suppose the skeptic asks the question "Why be moral?" Within the context of skepticism, no compelling answer can be given, for morality does not exist and everyone is free to do as he or she pleases. The best we could do is to indicate a normative code of some kind and try to show that a person's own desires would be better served by following it than by ignoring it. We would be telling the person to "assume a virtue" for prudential reasons. It is doubtful that we could make a plausible case.

Can the question "Why be moral?" be answered within the context of naturalistic ethics? Since there is no reason to act in accordance with principles that are true by definition, no compelling answer can be given in this context either. Society may approve *x,* but why should the agent seek to promote *x*? To be popular or respected? To stay out of jail? To get ahead in business? But these considerations do not always apply. Clever scoundrels can often do very well for themselves. Aristotle may define "good man" along certain lines, but the agent may prefer to be a different kind of person for reasons of his or her own. The claim made by the self-realizationists that the "good" person is happier is just not so. And what about the person who is not interested in happiness? Dewey may define morality as acting intelligently and with foresight, but the agent may find this dull.

Perhaps the question we have been considering cannot even be meaningfully *raised* in the contexts of skepticism and naturalism. It seems to be asking for an answer based on normative standards—which manifestly cannot be given if the existence of such standards is denied. Can the question be meaningfully raised in the context of nonnaturalistic ethics?

One conceivably could grant that there are objective normative principles, but still ask why one should obey moral law when one's inclination is to do otherwise. The answer to the question may consist in offering personal inducements. Just as the skeptic and the naturalist may accept reasons for being "moral" that are based on social acceptance or the desire to be esteemed by their neighbors, the nonnaturalist may occasionally be impressed by such considerations also. But such an answer really misses the mark, for it offers rewards for doing what morality sets forth as a matter of *duty* rather than prudence. Moreover, many cases can be imagined in which the rewards from others fail to compensate individuals who find that moral law requires them to do something that is very painful, dangerous, or unprofitable. Similarly, an answer based on the satisfaction of having known they have done their duty is unsatisfactory. A good conscience is an important and gratifying thing to have, but if it is thought of as a pleasant feeling, the objective that moral action is to produce, the meaning of moral law is again distorted. One achieves a comfortable conscience only when one acts in awareness that the moral law requires certain actions because they are *right*—not because the agent feels good in having done his or her duty. Indeed, one will not feel this satisfaction unless one is devoted to the moral law to start with. Moreover, again, many cases can be imagined in which the rewards of a good conscience may be outweighed by the sacrifices to one's own interests that an act of principle would require.

Perhaps the only answer that can be given to the question is in terms of consistency. If we really believe that nonnaturalistic ethics requires action that conforms to duty, we are admitting that it has its own claims beyond what may or may not please us. We admit that what we *want* to do may on occasion differ from what we *ought* to do. If we believe that there are moral rules, then we can hardly deny that they apply to us as well as to other people, and that they apply to us today when it is burdensome to obey them just as they applied to us yesterday when it was not. But why should we obey? We know that the rules should be obeyed because that is what morality *means.* The question "Why should I be moral?," then, is really rather ridiculous. If *nonmoral* reasons are given for being moral, they are ulterior to the enterprise of ethics, and the essence of morality itself is surrendered. What about *moral* reasons? These are superfluous, for morality provides its own reasons. Asking "Why should I be moral?" is like asking "Why should I do what I should do?" or "What does the morality of morality consist of?"

Individuals who accept the validity of nonnaturalistic ethics have embraced a doctrine that presents principles that take precedence over their desires. They have accepted the proposition that there is one overriding interest to which their other interests are subordinate. They may on occasion find that they are not strong enough to do what they ought to do, but their acceptance of morality in the first place will assure them that they have failed on these occasions. If they recognize nonnaturalistic goods, they must in consistency value them. If they recognize nonnatural duties, they must in consistency discharge them. They may admit failures in their own lives and in others', but these *are* failures—that is, the agent did not do what he or she ought to have done. "I was right or justified in not being moral" is a self-contradiction," just as "I was right or justified in being moral" is a tautology. "Morality for morality's sake" is the only legitimate stance for anyone who espouses nonnaturalistic ethics.

For Further Reading

Joseph Butler. *Sermons.* New York: Robert Carter and Bros., 1873.

John Hospers. *Human Conduct: An Introduction to the Problems of Ethics.* New York: Harcourt, Brace and World, 1961. Chapter 4.

David Hume. *An Enquiry Concerning the Principles of Morals.* Many editions. Appendix 2 ("Of Self-Love").

Wilfrid Sellars and John Hospers, eds. *Readings in Ethical Theory.* 2nd ed. New York: Appleton-Century-Crofts, 1970. Part 5.

FREEDOM AND DETERMINISM

Determinism

Determinism and Ethics It is often argued that human actions must be free if ethics is to have any significance. If the individual is not free to obey (or disobey) moral law, there can be neither obligation nor responsibility. We cannot praise or blame actions unless they were freely undertaken; we cannot praise or blame human qualities unless they were freely cultivated; we cannot praise or blame people unless they were authors of their own conduct. If actions, qualities, and people necessarily are what they are, we must accept them for what they are instead of saying what they ought to have been. We do not say that ice should not be cold, because it is not within the power of ice to be anything else. We do not say that iron filings should not have moved toward the magnet, for they were not free to have done otherwise. While there are limits to what a person can be (e.g., ten feet tall) and what a person can do (e.g., outrace a speeding bullet), the advocate of free will holds that people have free choice in a great many situations (e.g., to cheat on an examination or refrain from cheating). Unless we are capable of choosing from among alternative courses of action, in accordance with our own desires and purposes, it is idle to hold ourselves to, or measure ourselves by, ethical standards. Such standards might be applicable to a God ("unmoved mover"), but assuredly not to human beings.

Fatalism and Predestination There are many views of the world that are supposed to imply a denial of freedom. One is *fatalism.* Everything that people do, as well as what happens to them, is predetermined from the beginning of time. "Fate," "fortune," or "kismet" rules; no one can escape his or her preordained destiny.

> DEATH SPEAKS: There was a merchant in Bagdad who sent his servant to market to buy provisions and in a little while the servant came back, white and trembling, and said, "Master, just now when I was in the marketplace I was jostled by a woman in the crowd and when I turned I saw it was Death that jostled me. She looked at me and made a threatening gesture; now, lend me your horse, and I will ride away from this city and avoid my fate. I will go to Samarra and there Death will not find me." The merchant lent him his horse, and the servant mounted it, and he dug his spurs in its flanks and as fast as the horse could gallop he went. Then the merchant went down to the marketplace and he saw me standing in the crowd and he came to me and said, "Why did you make a threatening gesture to my servant when you saw him this morning?" "That was not a threatening gesture," I said, "it was only a start of surprise. I was astonished to see him in Bagdad, for I had an appointment with him tonight in Samarra."[30]

This is fatalism, the belief that what will be, will be. We are not told why or how the events occur; it is all quite mysterious. The soldier says that he will die—"if the bullet has my name on it." Cicero says he will not consult a doctor, for if he is going to die, he will die. Fatalism is really more an emotional attitude that it is a philosophical doctrine. "What will be, will be" is, of course, a tautology. The questions are *why* and *how* will it be, and what does human choice have to do with it?

Another theory that seems to imply a denial of freedom is *predestination.* The omnipotence of God means that his will is sovereign. What happens in the world, as well as the nature of the world, is part of God's plan, and God's will shall be done. Although one's salvation rests upon what one does and what one is, one's condition and conduct, like everything else in the universe, is determined by the will of God. Most Christian theologians have espoused a theory of predestination.

[30]W. Somerset Maugham, *Sheppey* (New York: Doubleday and Co., 1934).

Paul wrote: "We know that in everything God works for good with those who love him, who are called according to his purpose. For those whom he foreknew he also predestined to be conformed to the image of his Son. . . . And those whom he predestined he also called; and those whom he called he also justified; and those whom he justified he also glorified."[31]

Augustine, who condemned the Pelagians as heretics for teaching that human beings contribute something to their salvation, wrote: "God does even concerning the wills themselves of men what He will, when He will. . . . He has the wills of men more in His power than they themselves have."[32] Although Augustine sometimes argues that divine *foreknowledge* does not negate human freedom, he holds that human actions are the *result* of grace (or punishment) rather than the cause: "What else but His gifts does God crown when He crowns our merits?"[33] Thomas Aquinas, who stressed God's reason rather than his will, wrote: "Let us then consider the whole of the human race as we consider the whole universe. God has willed to manifest His goodness in men: in respect to those whom He predestines, by means of His mercy, in sparing them; and in respect of others, whom He reprobates, by means of His justice in punishing them. This is the reason why God elects some and rejects others."[34] Martin Luther, an Augustinian and follower of Paul, believed in justification through faith and taught that faith itself is a gift of God.[35] Although he subscribed to the doctrine of predestination, he did not like to talk about it—for practical reasons. Ignatius Loyola, founder of the Society of Jesus, believed in justification by works (as well as faith), yet subscribed to the doctrine of predestination—while emphasizing human freedom. He too would not publicize predestination.

> It must . . . be borne in mind, that although it be most true, that no one is saved but he that is predestinated, yet we must speak with circumspection concerning this matter, lest perchance, stressing too much the grace or predestination of God, we should seem to wish to shut out the force of free will and the merits of good works. . . . For the like reason we should not speak on the subject of predestination frequently; if by chance we do so speak, we ought to temper what we say as to give the people

[31]Romans 8:28–30. See also Romans 9:14–18: "What shall we say then? Is there injustice on God's part? By no means! For he says to Moses, 'I will have mercy on whom I have mercy, and I will have compassion on whom I have compassion.' So it depends not upon man's will or exertion, but upon God's mercy. For the scripture says to Pharaoh, 'I have raised you up for the very purpose of showing my power in you, so that my name may be proclaimed in all earth.' So then he has mercy upon whomever he wills, and he hardens the heart of whomever he wills."

[32]Augustine, quoted in Herbert A. Deane, *The Political and Social Ideas of St. Augustine* (New York: Columbia University Press, 1963), p. 70.

[33]Ibid., p. 21.

[34]Thomas Aquinas, *Summa Theologica,* Part 1, Question 23. Anton C. Pegis, ed., *Basic Writings of Saint Thomas Aquinas* (New York: Random House, 1945), vol. 1, p. 247. See also Prima Secundae of *Summa Theologica,* Question 112 ("On the Cause of Grace"), Pegis, vol. 2, p. 1012ff.

[35]See Martin Luther, *A Treatise on Christian Liberty.*

> who hear no occasion of erring and saying, "If my salvation or damnation is already decreed, my good or evil actions are predetermined"; whence many are wont to neglect good works and the means of salvation.[36]

The most uncompromising view of predestination is stated by John Calvin:

> They [the Schoolmen] say it is not stated in so many words that God decreed that Adam should perish for his rebellion. As if, indeed, that very God, who, Scripture proclaims, "does whatsoever he pleases" (Ps. 115:3), would have created the noblest of his creatures to an uncertain end. They say that he had free choice that he might shape his own fortune, and that God ordained nothing except to treat man according to his own deserts. If such a barren invention is accepted where will that omnipotence of God be whereby he regulates all things according to his secret plan, which depends solely upon itself?[37]

Calvin refused to soften his doctrine by making a distinction between God's will and God's permission, or between predestination and foreknowledge.

Rationalism and Scientific Determinism A third theory that seems to negate human freedom is *determinism.* Determinism, rather than talking about fate or God's will, holds that all events, human and otherwise, are caused by antecedent factors in the world itself according to exceptionless law. Every event is indeed in principle predictable—if we but know the laws. *Rationalistic determinism* stresses the rationality of reality, its unity, order, and the necessity of the connections of its parts. Spinoza is a good example of a rational determinist. Taking geometry as his model, he believed that reason could grasp the nature of the logical system and, proceeding deductively, banish accident, spontaneity, chance, and "final causes." *Scientific determinism* also holds that the world is lawful, but this is a methodological assumption rather than a priori concept: If we seek laws, we must assume that there *are* laws; if we want to predict the future on the basis of what we have found in the past, we must assume that nature is uniform. "Chance" is simply a name for "undiscovered cause." If the results are different, there must be a difference among the antecedents. While no necessary connections are claimed, the scientific approach has discovered many general laws that are exceptionless and make possible the successful prediction of future events. The scientific approach, unlike the rational approach, is based on experience and induction. Tentative generalizations, causal laws, and hypotheses are all tested and confirmed by experience. Human sciences (psychology, sociology, history, politics, etc.) are in principle no different from the physical sciences (physics,

[36]Ignatius Loyola, *Spiritual Exercises,* 14, 15. See Henry Bettenson, ed., *Documents of the Christian Church* (New York: Oxford University Press, 1947), p. 365.

[37]John Calvin, *Institutes of the Christian Religion,* ed. John T. McNeill, trans. Ford Lewis Battles (Philadelphia: Westminster Press, 1960), III, 23, vol. 2, p. 955.

chemistry, biology, etc.). Both versions of determinism stress law and aspire to successful prediction.

Let us now look more closely at the implications for ethics if determinism is true.

Four Kinds of "Freedom" Is it true that individuals lack *freedom of action*? Sometimes, of course, they do. If I am chained and thrown into a pit, my action of dropping into the hole is not free. And if the pit is full of water, I am not free to refrain from inhaling the water and drowning. Physical law has constrained my actions. But in a great many other cases I may be said to have freedom of action in the sense that I have freedom of choice. Whether I wear a brown suit or a blue suit tomorrow is a choice that I may make. Whether to support disarmament or not is a choice that I must make. Whether to share my food with a starving neighbor represents another choice. In any ordinary sense of "freedom," the agent possesses it in many situations. But, it might be argued, even here the agent is not *really* free, since the selection that the agent makes from the alternatives is itself determined by psychological law.

Is it true that individuals lack *freedom of choice*? Sometimes, of course, they do. They may be compelled to a course of action in a situation in which there is no reasonable alternative. We may be compelled by *external circumstances* to take certain courses of action that we do not really want to adopt. A ship's captain in a storm may be compelled to jettison its cargo (Aristotle's example). A poverty-stricken parent may be compelled to go on welfare in order to get food for the children. An employee may be compelled to endure the insults of the boss in order to keep a job for another year until retirement. Although these unfortunate people may have freedom of action, they really do not have freedom of choice. They are constrained by external circumstances. We may also be compelled to act as we do by *other people.* I give up my money to the mugger in order not to be shot. I drive at the speed limit in order not to be arrested. I come home for dinner on time in order to avoid the complaints of my family. All these actions are cases of doing what I might not otherwise do. Although it is difficult to draw the line between compulsion and noncompulsion, there are cases that clearly fall into each category. The examples above are clearly cases of compulsion. A clear case of noncompulsion would be that of someone giving me a sound logical argument for doing something (e.g., voting for Henry Kissinger). Where advertising campaigns fall is not so clear.

A second kind of constraint where the agent cannot be said to have freedom of choice is *internal compulsion.* If a person with a serious psychotic affliction is driven to commit murder or even steal (as in kleptomania), we would not say that he or she has freedom of choice. That person is compelled to do what on calme occasions he or she would deplore—"catch me before I do it again!" The literature of psychiatry is full of bizarre cases of afflicted people having no control ovei themselves in certain situations. Even people who are more or less "normal" may be placed in a certain situation that in conjunction with their personal histories produce actions that can in no sense of the world be called "chosen." We might also add the effect on conduct of drugs, alcohol, and deprivation of food or sex. Some impulses indeed *are* "irresistible."

When individuals are compelled to do an action, they are not held responsible. They are rendered about as helpless by lack of freedom of choice as by freedom of action. In both cases, we would excuse the action and refrain from calling it immoral. We would simply say that these people could not help doing what they did.[38] We would remand them to a hospital rather than a prison.

Still, there are a lot of cases in which people perform actions with genuine freedom of choice. The person who chooses to wear a purple shirt to a cocktail party is not compelled to do so. The student who selects a major in elementary education is not compelled to do so. Nor is the person who decides to have an extramarital affair, the person who cheats on his or her income-tax report, the woman who decides to abort a healthy fetus, and the man who refuses to serve in the military forces. These people have selected particular desires to advance their aims, perhaps, of attracting attention, engaging in a particular profession, securing sexual excitement, achieving wealth, avoiding bringing an unwanted life into the world, taking a stand for pacifism. Presumably the desire to be moral is involved in their choices or at least is taken into account in their deliberations. The actions are in accordance with actually experienced desires.

It is at this point that it may be argued that the desires themselves are determined, and given the agent's nature and situation they could not have been other than what they were. This is the deception of freedom: because we do what we *want* to do, we are free.

Is it true that individuals lack *freedom of desires*? Conceivably, in some cases they do. The strict and careful training of an individual, isolated from society, could produce a being whose desires are not really his or her own. Brainwashing may also engender or foster desires that are in some sense alien to the subject's nature. An oppressive political system might control the media and other conditions of life in such a way as to produce a selected set of desires among its people. But, again, most human actions do not fall into this category. The desires on which most people act are their own. People weigh one desire against another. They examine means and ends, causes and consequences. One would hope that the desire to be moral is one of their desires. People can control their desires and they can work to strengthen some while eradicating others. People can *think*—morally and factually—and their conception of what is the case and what ought to be the case will have some bearing on which desires they respond to as well as which desires are actually experienced. Surely, reflective people who in the light of their conception of the facts and the moral law decide that it is *this* desire of theirs that they will satisfy (rather than *that* desire) may be said to be free—even if it is admitted that psychology will someday be a science and provide us

[38]A previous act, however, which led to the compelled action—such as beginning to take drugs—could be blamed on the agent.

with the laws that describe these processes. We may admit that the action is caused, but insist that an important component in the causal whole is the individual's own desires and thoughts. If one's own desires and judgments have an important say in what one does, one may be said to be free and held accountable for one's actions. We are more ready to hold a person accountable for an act of premeditated murder than for murder done in the heat of passion, because we believe that the former was done in greater freedom than the latter. It is not causality that destroys freedom and responsibility, but the *kind* of cause that is operating.[39]

People who fail to exercise thought are also free, because it is their own thoughtless nature that is operating. They are responsible for not being more reflective. "Ignorance is no excuse" is true. It is only when people are ignorant of something that they could not reasonably have been expected to know that they can be excused. The person who begins taking drugs is responsible for becoming a drug addict. The mariner who does not check the charts is responsible for the ship's going aground. But the nurse who gives the patient medicine from a mislabled bottle is not, nor is someone who goes out with a cunning and deceitful married person. What about people whose ignorance is of moral law? They did not do their duty because they did not know what it was. Such people are seldom excused, for they are expected to "know right from wrong." But if, as a result of training and upbringing in a completely foreign culture, they have acquired erroneous views, we might tend to excuse their actions. We hesitate to impose on them our own standards, which are utterly foreign to *them.* We may hold them responsible for their actions, but not responsible for having done wrong.[40]

The individual who wants to eliminate freedom and responsibility on the basis of determinism is still not satisfied. Is not the person's tendency to experience a certain range of desires, to weigh them a certain way, to be reflective—are not all these a function of the sort of person he or she is? Since everything is affected by one's temperament, nature, or character, and since character is formed from genetic endowment, early training, and subsequent experience—over which the individual has no control—one cannot be said to be free and responsible.

Is it true that individuals lack *freedom of character*? It is conceivable that some of them do. It is perhaps possible to create a specific kind of personality in the fashion of Pygmalion. Selective breeding or cloning could produce an intended set of biological qualities, and careful conditioning at all times could produce and retain an intended character. But for most people this is not the case. Most people

[39]The word *determine* often has the connotation of "compulsion," but while all compulsive acts are caused (or determined), not all caused (or determined) acts are compulsive. Hume in his classical essay "Of Liberty and Necessity" does not ascribe that "unintelligible sense of necessity" to the causal relation but understands it simply in terms of the uniformity of nature.

[40]It is sometimes useful to resort to the distinction between actions that are *subjectively* right or wrong and those that are *objectively* right or wrong. The conscientious act of an individual from an exotic culture could be called "objectively wrong" but "subjectively right."

will oppose having their character made for them and will eventually rebel against those who try to do it—as Eliza Doolittle did and her countryman John Stuart Mill. Character does change. What causes it to change? External factors and historical circumstances all play a role, but so also does the self itself. The old self has a say in what the new self will be. The old self does not preside over the creation of a new self *ex nihilo,* but it may deliberately take steps to refashion itself. Arthur may realize that his quick temper has gotten him into trouble in the past and may seek devices that will enable him to control it and finally produce a more tolerant and placid temperament. Cheryl may take stock of her moral values, be disgusted, and embark on a project of moral reform. Bertrand may realize that he has been used as a doormat and sign up for a course in assertiveness. Often the recognition of a handicap inspires excellence in the very area that is deficient. Glenn Cunningham, whose legs were horribly burned in childhood, became a great miler. Demosthenes, who stuttered, became a great orater. Helen Keller, blind and deaf, became a renowned author and lecturer. In the moral area, Augustine, a libertine and hedonist, became a Christian saint. Biographies and autobiographies abound in accounts of character transformations, often quite startling, brought about simply because the person was dissatisfied with what he or she was. If it is true that people do have some freedom in what character they exhibit, they can be held accountable for what they are. We are reluctant to accept as an excuse from a person who is always late, "Sorry, but I've never been able to get to places on time." Or from a murderer, "I've always had a violent nature." Or from a procrastinator, "I always put off things; that's just the way I am." The "grand error" of the fatalist, says Mill, is to assume that one's character has been formed *for* him, and not *by* him. "We are exactly as capable of making our own character, *if we will,* as others are of making it for us." The will may, through painful experience or admiration of someone else, be caused to aspire to an improvement of character. "If we have the desire, we should know that the work is not so irrevocably done as to be incapable of being altered."[41] If we do *not* have the desire to change, we have no right to complain about "necessity"! There are limits to this kind of freedom, as is the case with the other kinds. There's not much a person can do who does not have a sense of humor. But there are a great many character traits that can be altered.

We have tried to show that in the areas of action, choice, desire, and character people have substantial freedom—even if the thesis of determinism is accepted. Although our actions may take place according to law, we are responsible for them. In one sense, they "could not have been otherwise"—given the laws and realities. But in another sense, they *could* have been otherwise. A pilot *could* have turned back when storm clouds appeared—if he or she had not been thinking of a date in Kansas City or had correctly appraised the turbulence of the air or had

[41]John Stuart Mill, *A System of Logic* (New York: Longmans, Green and Co., 1959), book 6, chap. 2 ("Liberty and Necessity"), p. 550.

had a more acute sense of duty to the passengers or had been of a more cautious disposition. But these are all internal factors stemming from the pilot's own desires, knowledge, and character. He or she was at least partially responsible for the accident.

Praise and Blame Is it appropriate to *praise* or *blame* people in a deterministic universe? We do have the tendency to praise people who do good things and exhibit good qualities—even when their actions are not "free" in the sense described above. We are pleased to praise an aspect of the universe that is good, whether or not that parcel of goodness is necessitated or not. We praise the goodness of the mother who chooses to work in order to provide food for her children, and we praise the effort of the alcoholic who has managed to stay "dry" for five years. But we also praise the musician and artist who were born with genius, and the strength and grace of an Earl Campbell and an O. J. Anderson who were also very favorably endowed.

Blame, however, seems to be apportioned more selectively. Most people would blame an agent only for actions that were "freely" done or for qualities that are "freely" exhibited. If we are not consistent utilitarians, we are quite willing to blame agents who do wrong actions or display bad qualities whether the blame will do any good or not. We blame the Iranian militants for seizing the American hostages, although our judgment cannot improve matters. And we blame people in the past (e.g., Hitler) who are necessarily beyond our control. But we excuse agents who had no real choice or who acted compulsively. Some people, however, do blame agents for being or doing that over which they have no control. Psychotic killers, for example, are blamed for being what they necessarily are. They represent a *bad* area of the universe and are heartily condemned. Indeed, a few people would prefer to rid the world of their presence rather than lock them up in a prison hospital.

The fact that actions can often be predicted seems to have little effect on whether they are praised or blamed. Knowing what I do about Edith's character and circumstances, I predict that she will respond to a worthwhile charity drive, but do not withhold my praise when she comes through as expected. I expect Fred to work hard when given a marketing assignment, but am prepared to praise him when he does. I predict that Gertrude will forget our luncheon date, but nevertheless blame her for doing so. Such cases would indicate that determinism (which makes prediction possible) does not destroy the tendency to praise and blame.

It might also be noted that individuals themselves do not feel that their freedom is in jeopardy if others can predict their actions in many cases. Everyone knows that a certain person will pay his debts promptly. He is aware of this but believes that his actions are free. A woman does not experience a sense of dwindling freedom when her husband accurately predicts that she will accept a job offer. A teacher does not lament his loss of freedom because his students expect him to appear in class. Others may know how agents will use their freedom!

Some have argued that we should tone down our tendency to praise and blame. Although there are important senses of "freedom" recognized in common thought and speech, the fact is that human actions, *given* all the factors of self and circumstance, could not have been otherwise. While we can be pleased when good things occur and distressed when they do not, we should not be so quick to condemn others when they are immoral or to praise ourselves when we are moral. While not dispensing with moral judgment, we should recognize the handicaps of others and the advantages of ourselves. *Tout comprendre, c'est tout pardonner*—to understand everything is to forgive everything. There is no place in a deterministic universe for vindictiveness or overweening pride.[42]

One thing, at least, is clear. Praise and blame as *actions,* and ultimately reward and punishment, have useful roles to play in social life. The *act* of praising others may provide important encouragement—and not just for small children. The *act* of blaming others may alter their future actions. It may be important to them to avoid disapproval. Reward is related to praise in the same way that punishment is related to blame. Praise may be a form of reward, punishment a form of blame. When reward and punishment are well advised, they have the beneficial result of bettering conduct and improving human qualities. Reward and punishment need not be matters of retribution but may be instances of contributing to worthwhile consequences. Psychologists and sociologists have not yet told us all we need to know in order to use rewards and punishments efficaciously, but, if determinism is true, there are laws to distinguish ways that work from those that do not. There are, in principle, other laws that state how human behavior can be altered. Anyone who works in therapy or rehabilitation relies on them. If determinism is false, the work of clinical psychologists, social workers, and penologists would seem to be without theoretical foundation.

Human Subjects We may approve of the efforts of people who seek to improve behavior and character without subscribing to the ideal of total domination expressed in such books as Orwell's *1984,* Huxley's *Brave New World,* Karp's *One,* Skinner's *Walden II,* or Arendt's *Origins of Totalitarianism.* The purpose of dealing with human beings in a scientific way is not to produce a specific human type or even to engender a conscience inspired by high moral ideals. The purpose of such efforts should rather be to increase the possibilities for the four kinds of freedom discussed above. A human organism trained and programed always and immediately to do what is "right" would have lost its humanity, and with it the

[42]It would appear, however, that Elizabeth L. Beardsley goes too far when she writes: "It is all very well, then, to judge that Jones performed a morally worthy act under great odds; but such a judgment is superficial and unstable. For, if determinism is true, these vaunted 'odds' disappear upon examination; and Jones is seen to have done only what the causal factors in his situation, unknown as well known, brought forth. So did Smith, and so do we all." "Determinism and Moral Perspectives," *Philosophy and Phenomenological Research* 21 (September 1960): 11. In seeing a prisoner taken away for execution, one should say, "There but for the grace of God go I."

possibility of genuine moral action, as surely as one that is trained to do "wrong." A person must have the possibility not only of obeying moral law but also of disobeying. There is indeed a sense in which morality requires freedom, if it is only the limited kind described above. Freedom can exist in the lap of determinism, but it can also, when scientific technology is applied in a systematic way to human subjects, be destroyed by it.

Freedom and Predestination What about fatalism and predestination? We need not expend any more space on fatalism, but the doctrine of predestination merits some attention. Is human freedom possible in a universe that is controlled from beginning to end by an omnipotent God?

> Oh Thou, who didst with pitfall and with gin
> Beset the world I was to wander in,
>   Thou wilt not with Predestined Evil round
> Enmesh, and then impute my Fall to Sin!
>
> Oh Thou, who Man of baser Earth didst make
> And ev'n with Paradise devise the Snake:
>   For all the Sin wherewith the Face of Man
> Is blackened—Man's Forgiveness give—and take![43]

Without claiming to provide a complete answer to this question, we can note that many of the points made in the discussion of determinism can be applied to the doctrine of predestination. (1) Individuals do not have freedom of action when God has contrived (through the workings of natural law or by special miracle) to place them in a physical condition in which there are no alternatives to a particular action. Daniel was not free to leave the fiery furnace. Jonah was not free not to be tossed in the sea or swallowed by the whale. But usually God provides us with freedom of choice. The Pharaoh of Egypt could choose whether or not to let Moses and his people depart in peace. Eve could choose whether to eat or reject the forbidden fruit. (2) Individuals do not have freedom of choice when God has contrived (through the workings of natural law or by special miracle) to place them in a dilemma where both alternatives are counter to their desires. Leah had no real choice in obeying her father, Laban, and becoming the wife of Jacob. Moses was not free to enter the promised land, and Adam was not free to remain in Eden. The unfortunate people who were "possessed" by evil spirits had no real freedom. But God permits us to act in situations in which we are not compelled by circumstances, others, or ourselves; we follow our desires. The brothers of Joseph carried out their own desires when they sold him into slavery. Pontius Pilate was free to "wash his hands" of concern for the accused Jesus. Jezebel was free to do unjust acts against Naboth and others. (3) Individuals do not have freedom in their desires when God places them in a situation

[43]Edward FitzGerald, *Rubáiyát of Omar Khayyám.*

where their desires are inculcated in them by an outside agency. Paul, after his experience on the road to Damascus, was no longer free to persecute the followers of Jesus. But usually people are permitted to experience their own desires and act upon them. Examples: Adam in the Garden, Jesus when exposed to diabolical temptation, Samson when he lay down with Delilah. (4) Individuals do not have freedom of character when God has specifically decreed that it be of a certain kind. Jesus, perhaps, was not free to alter his blessed nature, nor Satan his evil nature. But the Bible is full of stories of individuals who aspire to greater character and through their own efforts achieve it. Moses at the start of his career was an unprepossessing leader. Jacob was originally a "con artist." David, after succumbing to the beauty of Bathsheba and repenting, led a blameless sexual life.

Sometimes, in the Judeo-Christian tradition, God intervenes in history in a specific and irresistible way. In these cases, individuals are not free. But most of the time God achieves his ends through the working of natural law. He utilizes human nature and the actions that flow from it. Saul was ambitious but irresolute. Samson was courageous but weak. Judas was greedy and faithless. The prophets thought deeply and spoke eloquently. Since what they did was a function of what they were, how they felt, and how they thought, they may be said to be free.

> Free choice is the cause of its own movement, because by his free choice man moves himself to act. But it does not of necessity belong to liberty that what is free should be the first cause of itself, as neither for one thing to be cause of another need it be the first cause. God, therefore, is the first cause, Who moves causes both natural and voluntary. And just as by moving natural causes He does not prevent their actions from being natural, so by moving voluntary causes He does not deprive their actions of being voluntary; but rather is He the cause of this very thing in them, for He operates in each thing according to its own nature.[44]

The burning bush and the parting of the Red Sea were miracles, but the conduct of the Jewish people was not. The problems set for Abraham and Job were ordained by God, but the reaction of these men to the situations that were contrived for them was according to their respective natures.

We must remember, of course, that the *whole* is predestined, just as for determinism the whole is determined by natural law. But within the whole, the parts make a difference. God has desired to work through human "freedom" to achieve his ends; he has not imposed it by fiat. That God knows in advance how Esther and Peter will *use* their freedom does not mean that they are not free—any more than I feel that when some of my acts are predicted in advance by my friends they cease being free.

The Puritans, who of all Christians believed most deeply in divine providence or predestination, had a vivid sense of their own freedom. Their will and con-

[44]Thomas Aquinas, *Summa Theologica,* Part 1, Question 83; Pegis, vol. 1, p. 787.

science made a difference. They held themselves and others responsible for their own action, and when they were not talking about the pilgrim's progress, they were storming the heavens.

Indeterminism

The Argument for Indeterminism Perhaps, after all, determinism, is not true. It is not easy to establish the doctrine through speculative reason, and it is impossible to establish it empirically (or even show that its truth is probable). It certainly is not immediately obvious that the universe is orderly, that its parts are linked by necessary connections or that the sequence of events is regular and uniform. Psychology is far from being a rigorous science, and the social "sciences" lag far behind the natural sciences in the dependability of their laws. The formulation of laws governing human behavior is damnably difficult. While predictions sometimes are somewhat better than a guess, the most that can be claimed for them is that they are based on tendencies and statistical probabilities. We do not have to rely on relative frequency when we predict the speed and arc of a projectile, but we do when we try to predict the behavior of a person. Seventy percent of children who commit felonies come from broken homes. Sixty-four percent of marriages will end in divorce. Eighty percent of homosexual males hate (or is it love?) their mothers.[45] The art of psychological therapy shows about as many failures as successes. Some studies show that the chances of recovering from a mental or emotional illness are about as good for those who do not see a psychiatrist as for those who do.

Even in the physical sciences there are events that so far defy submission to natural law. The Heisenberg principle, which is widely accepted by scientists, states that it is impossible in principle to predict both the velocity and the position of tiny particles. While statistical predictions for groups of particles is possible, predictions for single micro-events are not. It is quite possible that microscopic particles have a life of their own and that no matter how sophisticated our instruments become, no patterns for their behavior will be revealed. "Chance," then, would not be simply a name for undiscovered cause, but the very essence of matter. The visible universe seems to be orderly only because of the *statistical* dependability of the particles that make it up. It is as if a major league shortstop may confidently be expected to have a fielding average of around .945, although whether he will make an error on a given play is a case of sheer chance. Or as if a pair of dice were not subject to natural law but had been shown to come up with a seven or eleven about 25 percent of the time. We are pretty sure about the course of a projectile because the statistical probabilities of the groups of particles involved approach certainty, but at any time an aberrant event can occur. Beneath

[45]These relative-frequency statements are fabricated for purposes of example.

the apparent regularity of macroscopic events, there is some free play or randomness by the microscopic particles themselves. So goes the argument.

Most of us are not in position to say with any confidence whether the universe is completely orderly and thus deterministic or whether it has aspects that are free and thus indeterministic. The former assumption seems to have worked better in the past, so far as the development of knowledge and ability to control events are concerned. But to say that to continue to assume it is the wise or practical thing to do would be to beg the question. And to say, on the other side, that we are free because we have a *consciousness* of freedom, is also not conclusive. "Practically, our consciousness of the moral law, which, without a moral liberty in man, would be a mendacious imperative, gives a decisive preponderance to the doctrine of freedom over the doctrine of fate."[46] Our consciousness may be an illusion.

James: Practical Consequences What would be the consequences in our life of *believing* that determinism (or indeterminism) is true? William James argued that the psychological consequences of believing in indeterminism are much more beneficial or rewarding than those that would follow from a belief in determinism. To believe in determinism is to believe, on occasion, that what ought to be is impossible, that the universe is "afflicted with an incurable taint, an irremediable flaw."[47] Regret is pointless—every evil thing had to occur. James prefers to believe that there is chance in the world—real possibilities rather than inexorable necessities.

> What interest, zest, or excitement can there be in achieving the right way, unless we are enabled to feel that the wrong way is also a possible and a natural way,—nay, more, a menacing and an imminent way? And what sense can there be in condemning ourselves for taking the wrong way, unless we need have done nothing of the sort, unless the right way was open to us as well? I cannot understand the willingness to act, no matter how we feel, without the belief that acts are really good and bad. I cannot understand the belief that an act is bad, without regret at its happening. I cannot understand regret without the admission of real, genuine possibilities in the world. Only *then* is it other than a mockery to feel, after we have failed to do our best, that an irreparable opportunity is gone from the universe, the loss of which it must forever after mourn.[48]

In order to strive, we must feel that something really is at stake. The human being's vital aim is to improve the conditions of life. If we were convinced that

[46]William Hamilton, quoted in Mill, *An Examination of Sir William Hamilton's Philosophy,* vol. 2, p. 275.

[47]James, "The Dilemma of Determinism," in *Essays on Faith and Morals,* p. 162.

[48]Ibid., p. 175–176.

the past and present were "purely good," we could wish that the future would resemble them. We could say with T. H. Huxley: "Let me be wound up every day like a watch, to go right fatally, and I ask no better freedom."[49] But things are not all that good. There are problems to be solved, victories over evil to be won.

What splendid opportunities would be lost if we withdrew our efforts because of an unproven conviction that we are determined! James would call the kind of "freedom" described in the previous section ("soft determinism") a "quagmire of evasion."[50] Although admitting that "evidence of an external kind to decide between determinism and indeterminism is . . . strictly impossible to find," James would affirm as his first act of freedom that he is free.[51]

Other Consequences of the Belief in Indeterminism Although it may be difficult for many of us to conceive of human freedom in this indeterministic sense, James sees only good consequences for those who can affirm the idea and then act on it. But there is another side to the story. One unfortunate consequence of the belief in indeterminism is that we could not count on certain human actions taking place. Friends may have kept their promises before, but there is no reason to believe that they will keep *this* one. The minister may rise in the pulpit and begin reading from *Hustler* magazine instead of from the Scripture. The motorist coming around the curve may suddenly decide to take the left lane instead of the right. The stranger might slap us in the face instead of supplying the time of day we have requested. These capricious acts may supply some excitement but would make the conduct of life very difficult. Not only would we have no reasonable expectation for the behavior of others, but we could not even trust our own. We might be seized with the impulse to do the most unspeakable things at any moment. We would be afraid to go out of the house.

Indeterministic human nature would be one in which there is no basis in the self for its actions. There would be no ground in a more or less permanent character to serve as a causal component for the acts that people perform. It is doubtful that we could even use the terms *human nature* and *character* in a meaningful way. The whole area of human behavior would be chaotic; chance and randomness would reign. It is true that human reality does not appear to be this way, but there are many human acts not yet subsumed under law. The point is that there *is* no law. Our rough descriptions and generalizations of human nature conceal a basic unlawfulness that at any time can erupt. The kind of freedom based on desire, reflection, and personality operating lawfully in situations where choice is possible seems preferable to the kind of freedom in which *anything* can happen.

[49]See William James, *Pragmatism: A New Name for Some Old Ways of Thinking* (New York: Longmans, Green and Co., 1946), p. 120.
[50]James, *Essays on Faith and Morals,* p. 149.
[51]Ibid., p. 150, 146.

The notions of training and education would have no point, for there is no effect in personality or action that can possibly be produced. Therapy and rehabilitation would be based on the mistaken belief that certain regimens or conditioning programs can make a real difference on the subject. These consequences of indeterminism apply not only when we try to alter the nature and behavior of others but also when we engage in projects to reform or improve our own selves. The success of clinical psychology and social rehabilitation is already questioned by many people. If indeterminism is true, their failure is assured; attempts to achieve for human behavior the kind of control enjoyed by scientists over physical events are a waste of time. Praise and blame, punishment and reward are totally inefficacious, and the only practical function they serve is to enable spectators to express their own feelings toward the objects of their wrath (or esteem).[52]

What about the important ethical concept of *responsibility*? Can we hold agents responsible when what they are and what they feel and think are not important components of the cause of what they do? It would seem not. If there is no permanent self from which the actions flow, what is it that we can hold responsible? It is almost as if one's action were something that happened *to* one instead of something done *by* one. We tend to excuse the accidental or capricious act that is done when a person is "not himself." If indeterminism is true, all actions would fall in this category, because, being not connected with character, they are uncharacteristic. Not only are praising and blaming futile, but there is nothing in the situation that is praise*worthy* or blame*worthy.*[53]

What about the ethical concept of *duty*? Can it be meaningful if indeterminism is true? Can I be obligated to do an action if sheer chance operates? It would seem not. If my concept of moral law, my Kantian "good will," my estimate of the situation, the good habits I have tried to inculcate, and my control over inclinations cannot be expected to determine my actions, what does? Nothing. One cannot be said to have a duty when one has no resources in one's own nature for responding to it. It would make more sense to call iron filings rushing to a magnet dutiful than to call filings flying in all directions dutiful. The former, at least, are responding to a law based on what they are; the latter are not responding to *anything.*

The Indeterminism of Sartre There is, however, no reason to believe that what we might *prefer* to be true (determinism) is what in fact is the case. Indeterminism *is* a repugnant theory, but it may be true. We might prefer to have the freedom

[52]"If punishment had no power of acting on the will, it would be illegitimate, however natural might be the inclination to inflict it." Mill, *An Examination of Sir William Hamilton's Philosophy,* vol. 2, p. 291.

[53]There is the possibility of ambiguity here. *Blameworthy* for consistent utilitarians might mean "an act or quality for which blame would be efficacious." For them, an act could be wrong, but, if blaming it had no good consequences, the act would not be *blameworthy.* We are using *blameworthy* in a less technical sense to refer to acts or qualities that are wrong or bad. It is thus possible to say an act is blameworthy, while admitting that there is no point in actually dispensing the blame.

possible in dcterminism than that which indeterminism inflicts upon us. It does seem to be, in the phrase of existentialists, "dreadful freedom." The existentialists on the basis of their phenomenological analysis of the human situation do believe that indeterminism is true. While their account of freedom may not convince us, it does what few other indeterministic theories do: It makes the idea of human freedom *conceivable.*

Sartre calls the human individual "being-for-itself" *(être-pour-soi).* Physical reality is "being-in-itself" *(être-en-soi).* The first is conscious subject; the latter is object. Being-in-itself is plenitude (and basically absurd); it becomes meaningful only in consciousness. The phenomenon is the in-itself as it appears to the for-itself.

> Consciousness considered apart is only an abstraction; but the in-itself has no need of the for-itself in order to be; the "passion" of the for-itself only causes *there to be* in-itself. The *phenomenon* of in-itself is an abstraction without consciousness but its *being* is not an abstraction.[54]

The world that we ordinarily live in (the "real" world) is composed of the phenomenal objects of experience.

Being-for-itself knows the being-in-itself by negating it. The plenitude must be cut down in order that it may take on specific qualities. Meanings must be excluded in order that meanings may be present to consciousness. Poised before the plentitude of the being-in-itself is the nothingness of the being-for-itself. Consciousness must "nihilate" being in order to make it determinate. Consciousness is not the object (or anything else), but it must invest its nothingness in the object in order to know it. The nothingness that is consciousness must be made to "haunt" being-in-itself.

> The irreducible quality of the *not* comes to add itself to that undifferentiated mass of being in order to release it.[55]

> Man is the being through whom nothingness comes to the world. . . . This *nothing* is human reality itself as the radical negation by means of which the world is revealed.[56]

> "There is" being because I am the negative of being, and worldliness, spatiality, quantity, instrumentality, temporality—all come into being only because I am the negation of being. These add nothing to being but the pure, nihilated conditions of the "there is"; they only cause the "there is" to be realized.[57]

[54]Sartre, *Being and Nothingness,* p. 622.
[55]Ibid., p. 15.
[56]Ibid., pp. 24, 181.
[57]Ibid., p. 217.

An inhabitable universe is created by hollowing out objects from the opaque and baffling given. The "real" or phenomenal world is simply the in-itself plus nothing!

Being-for-itself not only must create the world in which it lives, but also necessarily creates itself. While the for-itself seems to have a passion "to lose itself in order that the affirmative 'world' might come to the In-itself," the for-itself can establish itself only *in terms of the* in-itself![58] Both projects are freely carried out, however one may try to conceal this fact from oneself. In the act of knowing, as in all our acts, we produce an act that no prior state of ourselves or the world can determine. We achieve a "break with being." "Every nihilating process must derive its source only from itself. . . . Every psychic process of nihilation implies, then, a cleavage between the immediate psychic past and the present. This cleavage is precisely nothingness."[59]

All human actions are free. In the strict sense they are uncaused, for they are produced by the nothingness that is human consciousness. Even ends and objectives are constituted by *acts* of consciousness. "Causes and motives have meaning only inside a projected ensemble of non-existents. And this ensemble is ultimately myself as transcendence; it is Me in so far as I have to be myself outside of myself."[60]

But has not Sartre shown us that a person's essence is created by his or her acts, that one makes one's own characteristics through the acts one chooses to perform? As we saw at the end of the first section of this chapter, cowardly people are people who do cowardly deeds, and honest people are people who do honest deeds. A particular kind of self is created and undergoes changes in nature through the lifetime of the subject. Does not the self as constituted on Monday have any input into how the self will be constituted on Tuesday? It is important here to note that Sartre did *not* say that cowardly deeds are deeds that are done by cowards. The deed comes first. Between the old self and the new self there is a break, a rupture. In engaging ourselves in a certain line of action, we at the same time *disengage* ourselves from what we were and what we sought before. Consciousness always seeks to surpass the present reality of the world and the self. The self always acts *beyond* the self. "The essence that was made in the past never explains the act performed in the future. One's actions are not even determined by what he has made himself to be."[61] This explains why we experience anguish: Anguish "is constituted when consciousness sees itself cut from its essence by nothingness or separated from the future by its very freedom."[62]

Anguish, of course, is only one of the penalties we have to pay for our freedom. Some of the others have been discussed above. In addition, we might note the

[58]Ibid.
[59]Ibid., p. 27. See also pp. 78–79.
[60]Ibid., p. 437.
[61]Runkle, *Anarchism: Old and New,* p. 279.
[62]Sartre, *Being and Nothingness,* p. 35.

acute problems of love, community, and politics that necessarily beset a society of subjects each possessing transcendent freedom.[63] Each of us must see the other as an object for our own use, yet we occasionally realize that we ourselves are "being-for-others" and feel our selfhood threatened and our being contaminated.

Now this may not be the kind of universe that we would have created (or that Sartre would have created). It is surely not the kind of universe that a wise and benevolent God would have created. But it is, for Sartre, the kind of universe we must dwell in. There is nothing better we can do than to accept our freedom and take up the burden of our complete responsibility. We will create values and legislate our own duties, just as we invest the world with our chosen meanings and engage ourselves in our selected projects. That we must do all these things —without standards in nature or from beyond nature, without stable and dependable characters, and in the context of an irrational world that limits the range of our freedom but never cancels it—is a fact of life beyond our control. With all our freedom, we humans are both more and less than "a useless passion." We are more, for our consciousness sustains the structured world. We are less, for we are ultimately the nothingness of our consciousness.

For Further Reading

Thomas Aquinas. *Summa Theologica.* Many editions. Part 1, Question 23; Prima Secundae, Question 112.

Richard B. Brandt. *Ethical Theory.* Englewood Cliffs, N.J.: Prentice-Hall, 1959. Chapter 20.

Gerald Dworkin, ed. *Determinism, Free Will, and Moral Responsibility.* Englewood Cliffs, N.J.: Prentice-Hall, 1970.

John Hospers. *Human Conduct: An Introduction to the Problems of Ethics.* New York: Harcourt, Brace & World, 1961. Chapter 10.

David Hume. *An Enquiry concerning Human Understanding.* Many editions. Section 7 ("Of Liberty and Necessity").

William James. "The Dilemma of Determinism." In William James, *Essays on Faith and Morals.* Cleveland: World Publishing Company, 1962.

John Stuart Mill. *An Examination of Sir William Hamilton's Philosophy.* Boston: William V. Spencer, 1868. Chapter 16 ("Of the Freedom of the Will").

John Stuart Mill. *A System of Logic.* New York: Longmans, Green and Co., 1959. Book 6, chapter 2 ("Liberty and Necessity").

Gerald Runkle. *Anarchism: Old and New.* New York: Dell Publishing Co., 1972. Chapter 10.

B. F. Skinner. *Walden II.* New York: Macmillan Co., 1948.

David Elton Trueblood. *Philosophy of Religion.* New York: Harper & Bros., 1957. Chapter 19.

[63] See Runkle, pp. 283–298.

INDEX